Praeger Handbook of Black American Health

Praeger Handbook of Black American Health

2nd Edition

*Policies and Issues Behind Disparities
in Health, Volume II*

Edited by IVOR LENSWORTH LIVINGSTON

Foreword by David Satcher

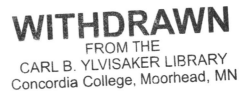

PRAEGER

Westport, Connecticut
London

Library of Congress Cataloging-in-Publication Data

Praeger handbook of Black American health : policies and issues behind disparities in health / edited
  by Ivor Lensworth Livingston ; foreword by David Satcher.—2nd ed.
      p. cm.
    First ed. published under : Handbook of Black American health.
    Includes bibliographical references and index.
    ISBN 0–313–32477–8 (set: alk. paper)—ISBN 0–313–33220–7 (vol. 1: alk. paper)—ISBN 0–313–33221–5
  (vol. 2: alk. paper)
    1. African Americans—Health and hygiene—Handbooks, manuals, etc. 2. African
  Americans—Medical care—Handbooks, manuals, etc. I. Title: Handbook of Black
  American health. II. Livingston, Ivor Lensworth.
  RA448.5.N4H364 2004
  362.1'089'96073—dc22   2003069010

British Library Cataloguing in Publication Data is available.

Library of Congress Catalog Card Number: 2003069010
ISBN: 0–313–32477–8 (set)
        0–313–33220–7 (vol. 1)
        0–313–33221–5 (vol. 2)

First published in 2004

Praeger Publishers, 88 Post Road West, Westport, CT 06881
An imprint of Greenwood Publishing Group, Inc.
www.praeger.com

Printed in the United States of America

The paper used in this book complies with the
Permanent Paper Standard issued by the National
Information Standards Organization (Z39.48–1984).

10 9 8 7 6 5 4 3 2 1

To my parents, who gave me the opportunity to have "conscious" unlimited dreams and, by their actions, to better understand the importance of resiliency, tolerance, tenacity, introspection, self-awareness, and courage in the pursuit of these dreams.

To my wife, Shaffarian ("Toy"), who has been my coworker, confidante, "objective" critic, and principal supporter of my ideas and "audience to the world;" my daughter, Litonya Selima, and son, Stefan Lensworth, who, for all of my professional life, have always been very helpful, supportive, and tolerant of my evolutionary insights, as well as my atypical, and other, pursuits.

To the millions of African Americans and other people of color, who by virtue of the color of their skin, continue to disproportionately experience the ill-effects of a morally unjust and unequal society but who will, in the near future, have an abundance of opportunity and the increased quality and quantity of life that they truly deserve.

Contents

VOLUME II

PART IV: SOCIOPOLITICAL, ENVIRONMENTAL, AND STRUCTURAL
          CHALLENGES

Illustrations

TABLES

FIGURES

Abbreviations

AA	African Americans
AA	Alcoholics Anonymous
AAASPS	African American Antiplatelet Stroke Prevention Study
AACN	American Association of Colleges of Nursing
AACTG	Adult Aids Clinical Trials Group
AADM	African American diabetes mellitus
AAHPC	African American hereditary prostate cancer
AAP	American Academy of Pediatrics
AAP	American Academy of Periodontology
AASK	African American Study of Kidney Diseases and Hypertension
ACAS	Asymptomatic Carotid Atherosclerosis Study
ACCESS	A Case Control Etiologic Study of Sarcoidosis
ACE	Angiotensin converting enzyme
ACEHSA	Accrediting Commission on Education for Health Services Administration
ACEI	Angiotensin converting enzymes inhibitors
ACIP	Advisory Committee on Immunization Practices
ACOG	American College of Obstetricians and Gynecologists
ACS	American Cancer Society
ACT	American Council on Testing
AD	Alzheimer's disease
ADA	American Diabetes Association
ADC	Aid to Dependent Children
ADN	Associated degree in nursing
ADPKD	Autosomal dominant polycystic kidney disease
ADR	Annual Data Report

AF	Atrial fibrillation
AFCAPS/TexCAPS	Air Force/Texas Coronary Artery Prevention Study
AFDC	Aid to Families with Dependent Children
AHA	The American Heart Association
AIDS	Acquired immunodeficiency syndrome
ALL	Acute lymphoblastic leukemia
ALLHAT	Antihypertensive and Lipid-Lowering Trial to Prevent Heart Attacks
AMFRREHD	Action Model for Reducing Racial and Ethnic Health Disparities
AMI	Acute myocardial infarction
ARBs	Angiotensin receptor blockers
ARC-PA	Accreditation Review Commission on Education for Physician Assistant
ARIC	Atherosclerosis Risk in Communities Study
ASI	Addiction Severity Index
AUPHA	Association of University Programs in Health Administration
AVEG	AIDS vaccines evaluation group
AZT	Zidovudine
BB	Beta blocker
BBA	Balanced Budget Act
BF	Black female
BM	Black male
BMI	Body mass index
BRFSS	Behavioral Risk Factor Surveillance System
BSN	Science degree in nursing
CABG	Coronary artery bypass graft
CAD	Coronary artery disease
CALGB	Cancer and Leukemia Group B
CAM	Complementary and alternative medicine
CAPD	Chronic ambulatory peritoneal dialysis
CARDIA	Coronary Artery Risk Development in Young Adults
CAS	Chronic antigenic stimulation
CASI	Computer-assisted self-interviewing
CASS	Coronary artery surgery study
CBOs	Community-based organization
CBRR	Consumer Bill of Rights and Responsibilities
CCB	Calcium channel blocker
CCE	Chiropractic education
CCPD	Continuous cycling peritoneal dialysis
CD	Cadaver donor
CDC	Centers for Disease Control and Prevention
CEN	Certified emergency nurse
CEPH	Council of Education for Public Health
CHC	Community Health Center

CHD	Coronary heart disease
CHIP	Children's Health Insurance Program
CKD	Chronic kidney disease
CMS	Center for Medicare and Medicaid Services
CMV	Cytomegalovirus
CNS	Clinical nurse specialist
COHS	Cherishing Our Hearts and Souls
COPD	Chronic obstructive pulmonary disease
CORN	Council of Regional Networks for Genetic Services
CPCRA	Community Programs for Clinical Research on AIDS
CPR	Cardiopulmonary resuscitation
CPSC	Consumer Product Safety Commission
CRESPAR	Center for Research on Education of Students Placed at Risk
CRH	Corticotropin-releasing hormone
CRJ	Commission for Racial Justice
CRNA	Certified Registered Nurse Anesthetist
CSFII	Continuing Survey of Food Intake of Individuals
CT	Computed tomography
CTM	Community Transformation Model
CVA	Cerebrovascular accidents
CVD	Cardiovascular disease
CYP450	Cytochrome P450
DAPRO	Disadvantaged Area Support PRO
DAT	Dementia of Alzheimer's type
DAT	Dental Admission Test
DATRI	Division of AIDS Treatment Research Initiative
DAWN	Drug Abuse Warning Network
DC	Doctor of chiropractor
DDS	Doctor of dental survey
DFS	Disease-free survival
DHHS	Department of Health and Human Services
DIS	Diagnostic Interview Schedule
DMD	Doctor of dental medicine
DNA	Deoxyribonucleic acid
DO	Osteopathic physician
DOA	Dead on arrival
DOE	Department of Energy
DPP	Diabetes Prevention Program
DRE	Digital rectal exam
DSM III	Diagnostics and Statistical Manual of Mental Disorders (3rd Edition)
DSM-IV	Diagnostic and Statistical Manual (4th Edition)
EAF	European American females

EAM	European American males
EC	Enterprise communities
ECA	Epidemiologic Catchment Area Study
ECC	Early childhood caries
ECFMG	Educational Commission for Foreign Medical Graduates
ECG	Electrocardiogram
ED	Emergency Department
EF	Etiological fraction
E-I-I	Environment-institutions-individuals
ELSI	Ethical, legal, and social issues
EMTALA	Emergency Medical Treatment and Labor Act
EPA	Environment Protection Agency
EPO	Erythro-poietin
EPSDT	Early periodic screening detection and treatment
ER	Emergency room
ESLD	End-stage liver disease
ESRD	End-stage renal disease
EZ	Empowerment zones
FDA	Food and Drug Administration
FEV_1	Forced expiratory volume in one second
FLP	Front-Line providers
FMPV	Female-to-male partner violence
FPL	Federal poverty level
FRC	Family Resource Center
FRCS	Filter Resource Capability System
FSGS	Focal and segmental glomerulosclerosis
GAO	General Accounting Office
GBC	Group B streptococcal infection
GDM	Gestational diabetes mellitus
GIS	Geographic Information System
GME	U.S. Graduate Medical Education
GRAD	Genomic Research in African Diaspora
GSS	General social survey
H. pylori	Helicobacter pylori
HAART	Highly active antiretroviral therapy
HAD	HIV-associated dementia complex
HAV	Hepatitis A virus
HBCU	Historically Black college or university
HBM	Health belief model
HBV	Hepatitis B virus
HCC	Hepatocellula carcinoma
HCFA	Health Care Financing Administration

HCV	Hepatitis C virus
HDL	High-Density Lipoprotein
HDV	Hepatitis D virus
HEI	Healthy Eating Index
HER	Health education-risk reduction
HEV	Hepatitis E virus
HFC	Health field concept
Hgb F	Fetal hemoglobin
HGP	Human Genome Project
HIV	Human immunodeficiency virus
HIVD	Human immunodeficiency virus-dementia
HLA	Human leukocyte antigens
HPA	Hypothalamic-pituitary-adrenocortical
HPA-axis	Hypothalalamic pituitary adrenal axis
HPC	Heredity prostate cancer
HPEA	Health Profession Educational Assistance
HPTN	HIV Prevention Trials Network
HR	Hazard ratio
HRSA	Health Resources and Service Administration
HRT	Hormone replacement therapy
HTN	Hypertension
HU	Hydroxyurea
HVTN	HIV vaccine trials network
IARC	International Agency for Research on Cancer
ICD-9	Ninth Revision of the International Classification of Diseases
ICH	Intragency Counsel of the Homeless
IDDM	Insulin-dependent diabetes mellitus
IDU	Injecting drug user
IFG	Impaired fasting glucose
IgE	Immunoglobulin E
IGT	Impaired glucose tolerance
IHD	Ischemic heart disease
IMG	International medical graduates
IMR	Infant mortality rate
IOM	Institute of Medicine
IPV	Intimate partner violence
IR	Institutionalized racism
IUD	Injection drug use
JNC	Joint National Committee
K/DOQI	Kidney Disease Outcomes Quality Initiative
LBW	Low birth weight
LDL-C	Low density lipoprotein cholesterol

LE	Life expectancy
LIP	Licensed independent practitioners
LPN	Licensed practical nurse
LRD	Living related donor
LURD	Living unrelated donor
LVH	Left ventricular hypertrophy
LVN	Licensed vocational nurse
MAC	Mycobacterium avium complex
MAST	Michigan Alcoholism Screening Test
M.B.A.	Master of business administration
MCHC	Mattapan Community Health Center
MD	Allopathic physician
MDIUS	Midlife development in the United States
METs	Metabolic equivalence
MHA	Master of health administration
MHC	Major histocompatibility complex
MHSA	Master of health services administration
MI	Myocardial ischemia
MICRO-HOPE	Microalbuminuria, cardiovascular and renal outcomes—Heart Outcome Prevention Evaluation
MID	Multiple infarct dementia
MM	Multiple myloma
MMF	Mycophenalate Mofetil
MMWR	Morbidity and Mortality Weekly Report
MODOPP-C	Medicine, osteopathy, dentistry, optometry, pharmacy, podiatry, and chiropractic
MOTTEP	Minority Organ Tissue Transplantation Education Program
M.P.A.	Master of public administration
M.P.H.	Master of public health
MSM	Men who have sex with men
MST	Multisystemic therapy
NAACP	National Association for the Advancement of Colored People
NAEP	National Assessment of Educational Progress
NASCET	North American Symptomatic Carotid Endarterectomy Trial
NCCAM	National Center on Complementary and Alternative Medicine
NCEP	National Cholesterol Education Program
NCHS	National Center for Health Statistics
NCI	National Cancer Institute
NCIPC	National Center for Injury Prevention and Control
NCLEX-RN	National Council Licensure Examination for RN
NCMHD	National Center for Minority Health Disparities
NCS	National Comorbidity Study
NEISS	National Electronic Injury Surveillance System

NHAMCS	National Hospital Ambulatory Medicare Care Survey
NHANES	National Health and Nutrition Examination Survey
NHANES II	Second National Health and Nutrition Examination Survey
NHANES III	Third National Health and Nutrition Examination Survey
NHBPEP	National High Blood Pressure Education Program
NHDS	National Hospital Discharge Survey
NHGC	National Human Genome Center
NHGRI	National Human Genome Research Institute
NHIS	National Health Interview Survey
NHSC	National Health Service Corps
NHSDA	National Household Survey on Drug Abuse
NIAAA	National Institute of Alcohol Abuse and Alcohol
NIAID	National Institute of Allergy and Infectious Diseases
NICHD	National Institute of Child Health and Development
NIDA	National Institute of Drug Abuse
NIDCD	National Institute on Deafness and Other Communication Disorders
NIDCR	National Institute of Dental and Craniofacial Research
NIDDK	National Institute of Diabetes and Digestive and Kidney Diseases
NIDDM	Non-insulin-dependent diabetes mellitus
NIH	National Institutes of Health
NIHSS	National Institutes of Health Stroke Scale
NINDS	National Institute of Neurological Disorders and Stroke
NKDEP	National Kidney Disease Education Program
NMR	Neonatal mortality rate
NMW	Nurse midwife
NP	Nurse practitioner
NRC	Nuclear Regulatory Commission
NSAL	National Survey of American Life
NSBA	National Survey of Black Americans
NSDUH	National Survey of Drug Use and Health
NSHAPC	National Survey of Homeless Assistance Providers and Clients
NUL	National Urban League
OAS	Office of Applied Studies
OC	Oral contraceptives
O.D.	Optometry degree
ODM	Organ donors per million
OEO	Office of Economic Opportunity
OGTT	Oral glucose tolerance test
OMB	Office of Management and Budget
OPTN	Organ Procurement and Transplantation Network
OR	Odds ratio
ORMH	Office of Research and Minority Health

ORWH	Office of Research on Women's Health
PA	Physician assistant
PACTG	Pediatrics AIDS Clinical Trials Group
PCP	Pneumocystis carinii pneumonia
P.C.P.	Primary care providers
PDR	Proliferative diabetic retinopathy
PEHD	Program to Eliminate Health Disparity
PIR	Poverty income ratio
PNMR	Postneonatal mortality rate
PRAISE	Partnership to Reach African Americans to Increase Smart Eating
PRO	Peer review organization
PSA	Prostate specific antigen
PSR	Proliferative sickle-cell retinopathy
PSS	Progressive systemic sclerosis
PTCA	Percutaneous transluminal coronary angioplasty
PTDM	Posttransplant diabetes mellitus
RBC	Red blood cells
RCT	Randomized clinical trial
REACH	Racial and Ethnic Approaches to Community Health
RFA	Request for applications
R.N.	Registered nurse
RRT	Renal replacement therapy
RSV	Respiratory syncytial virus
RTOG	Radiation Therapy Oncology Group
SA	Sympatho-adrenomedullary
SADR	Social and Demographic Research Institute
SADS-RDC	Schedule for Affective Disorders and Schizophrenia Research Diagnostic Criteria
SAMHSA	Substance and Mental Health Services Administration
SAPAC	Self-administered Physical Activity Check
SBE	Service-based enumeration
SCD	Sickle-cell disease
SCD	Sudden cardiac death
SCOR	Specialized Centers for Research
SEER	Surveillance Epidemiology and End Results
SES	Socioeconomic status
SFU	Size of a small family unit
SI	Special intervention
SIDS	Sudden infant death syndrome
SPPM	Sociopsychophysiological model
SRC	Sociopsychophysiological Resource Center
SSI	Supplemental Security Income
STDs	Sexually transmitted diseases

TBI	Traumatic brain injury
TC	Total cholesterol
TCA	Trycyclic antidepressant
TNFa	Tissue necrosis factor alpha
TPA	Tissue plasminogen activator
TSDF	Treatment, storage, and disposal facilities
UAP	Unlicensed Assistive Personnel
UC	Usual care
UGT	Glucuronosvitransferase
UNOS	United Network for Organ Sharing
USCM	United States Conference of Mayors
USDHHS	U.S. Department of Health and Human Services
USM	U.S. medical schools
USPHS	U.S. Public Health Service
USRDS	U.S. Renal Data System
VAST	Veterans Administration Symptomatic Trial
VCV	Varicella-Zoster viral encephalitis
VFC	Vaccines for children
VISIONS	Vigorous Interventions in Ongoing Natural Settings
VLBW	Very low birth weight
VPS	Vaccine Preparedness Study
WF	White female
WHO	World Health Organization
WM	White male
YE	Yersinia enterocolitica
YLL	Years of life lost
YMC	Youth Mediation Corps
YPLL-75	Years of potential life lost before the age of 75
YRBSS	Youth Risk Behavior Surveillance System

Sociopolitical, Environmental, and Structural Challenges

CHAPTER 27

The Role of the Family in African American Health

HECTOR F. MYERS, ANGELA T. ECHIVERRI, AND BRANDI N. ODOM

INTRODUCTION

Current epidemiological evidence indicates a persistent disparity in health status, morbidity, and mortality among racial/ethnic minorities relative to non-Hispanic Whites, with African Americans, especially those who are poor, evidencing the greatest health disadvantage of all groups in the United States, regardless of the health status indicator used (Health United States, 2001). Therefore, one of the major social challenges we face today is to understand these health disparities by identifying those factors that contribute to, or maintain, these persistent differences and to design innovative interventions to close the gap.

In this chapter, we focus attention on the contributors to chronic diseases where the disparities are most striking. We argue that the disproportionate burden of chronic diseases and early mortality among African Americans is attributable to socioeconomic, cultural, environmental, and personal risk factors and that these influences are ultimately mediated through the risks and resources of the African American family over time. We also argue for the need to develop and test interventions that target the reduction of family risk factors and the enhancement of family resistance resources as an important public health priority. In making this case, first we offer an integrative biopsychosocial adversity model as a heuristic for organizing our review and discussion of how the biological, psychosocial, and behavioral characteristics and history of the family influence the health trajectory of its members over time. Second, we use this framework for organizing a selective review of the literature on the contributions of the African American family to functional health status by focusing attention on the family's biological attributes and history, the family's burden of psychosocial and behavioral adversities, and the role that the family's psychosocial advantages play in moderating these risks. We also note that family risks and resources impact individual health mediated through stress-responsive biological control mechanisms (e.g., HPA axis, SAS, serotonergic, and immune systems function) whose responses to chronic stress exposure confer risk for the development of chronic illnesses. Finally, we summarize the findings, draw several conclusions, and offer suggestions for directions for future research, especially the development and testing of interventions that can enhance the health and psychological resilience of African American families and their members.

HEALTH STATUS OF AFRICAN AMERICANS

Current evidence indicates that African Americans fare poorly in health status, such that the average life expectancy for African Americans is seven years less than for Whites, and they have the highest rates of hypertension and related sequelae of all groups and the highest rate of cardio-vascular disease and stroke-related mortality than all other groups (American Heart Association, 1998). They also have rates of diabetes that are only slightly lower than those of American Indians and Hispanics (Health United States, 2001) but experience the worst disease-related impairment, and African American diabetics are 6.6 times more likely to suffer from end-stage renal disease, are significantly more likely to have amputations secondary to diabetes, and are at higher risk for mortality from this disease than White diabetics (Carter et al., 1996).

African American men have the highest incidence rates of all types of cancers, especially prostate, lung, and oral cavity cancers, and African American women have the highest incidence rates of lung and colorectal cancers and the highest mortality rates from breast and cervical cancer of any group of women in the United States (American Cancer Society, 1997).

African American women also experience significantly more adverse birth outcomes than all other groups, including higher rates of low birth weight (LBW = <2,500gm), and have three times the rate of very low birth-weight (VLBW = <1,500gm) babies than White women (Schoendorf et al., 1992). African American infants are also three times more likely to die of causes attributable to perinatal events and are twice as likely to die in the first month of life as White infants (Schoendorf et al., 1992). This Black–White differential is even more troubling when we consider the paradoxical finding that the mortality rate is lower among infants born to African American teens compared to their White counterparts and to older African American women. Geronimus (1992) speculates that this may indicate faster physiologic aging or a "weathering" phenomenon in African American women. There is also some counterintuitive evidence that while LBW and infant mortality rates are higher in less educated and poorer women of all ethnic groups, the Black–White differential in LBW and infant mortality is smaller among the less educated and larger among the most educated (Shiono et al., 1997). This suggests that African American women derive less reproductive benefit from upward mobility than White women.

We have seen a marked decline in the incidence and mortality from HIV/AIDS in the United States. However, African Americans are disproportionately overrepresented in the current wave of the disease, especially among women and youth (CDC, 2002). In 2000, African Americans accounted for 47 percent of all new AIDS cases, 63 percent of new cases among women, and 65 percent of new pediatric and adolescent AIDS cases (CDC, 2002).

This disproportionate burden of morbidity has been linked to a greater clustering of risk factors among African Americans that are directly or indirectly shaped by the attitudes, beliefs, and practices of the family, including unhealthy diets, obesity, sedentary lifestyle, smoking, abuse of alcohol and illicit drugs, unprotected sex, and exposure to chronic and debilitating stress. For example, 46 percent and 42 percent of African American men and women have high cholesterol, 23 percent smoke, 65.4 percent are at risk for health problems because they are overweight or obese, and 66.8 percent are at high risk because of lack of physical activity (CDC, 2002; Flegal et al., 2002; Health United States, 2001).

African Americans are also overrepresented among those affected by the abuse of alcohol and illicit drugs, as well as by violence and involvement in the criminal justice system. Jones-Webb (1998) reported that 53 percent of African American men report alcohol use, have higher rates of heavy drinking than their white counterparts (15 percent and 12 percent, respectively), and are more likely to die of alcohol-related illnesses and injuries, such as cirrhosis and automobile accidents (Jones-Webb, 1998). In addition, alcohol is an important contributor to the higher rate of intimate partner violence among African Americans (23 percent reported recent male-to-female violence, 30 percent reported recent female-to-male violence), with 30 to 40 percent of male and 27 to 34 percent of female perpetrators of partner violence reported drinking at the time of the incident (Caetano et al., 2001).

Rates of illicit drug use among African Americans are also comparatively high, with 7.4 percent reporting illicit drug use (SAMHSA, 2002), and drug offenses accounted for 27 percent of the total growth among Black prison inmates (U.S. Department of Justice, 2002).

African Americans are also at a disproportionate risk for injury or death due to violence, with homicide being the fifth leading cause of death for African American adults between the ages of 25 and 44. African Americans are also overrepresented among those incarcerated. In 2001, 10 percent of African American men between the ages of 25 and 29 were in prison; they accounted for 43 percent of all sentenced inmates, and most were incarcerated for drug or violent offenses (i.e., 52 percent of African American inmates are violent offenders). Similar results are evident for African American women, who are five times more likely than White females to be in prison (U.S. Department of Justice, 2002). The high rates of alcohol, drug abuse, violence, and incarceration are all contributors to the economic instability and chronic stress burden of African American families and are indirect contributors to the poorer overall health status of this population.

The long-term consequences of this disproportionate burden of morbidity and risk are also exacerbated by the comparatively lower rate of health insurance coverage (i.e., 10.5 percent of those < age 18 and 22.8 percent of those 18–64 years) (Ni & Cohen, 2002), which limits access to effective and timely treatment. Also, a recent review of the quality of health care received indicates that African Americans and other persons of color face both institutional and provider barriers on access to good quality health care, even when health insurance is available and differences in health-care utilization are controlled (Smedley et al., 2002). The latter increases the likelihood that these populations will experience a more severe disease course and greater disability and death.

CONCEPTUAL PERSPECTIVE

Many factors have been offered to account for the health disadvantages of African Americans, including poverty, exposure to chronic life stresses, such as racism and discrimination, inadequate health knowledge and cultural beliefs that affect symptom recognition and health-care seeking behaviors, excess burden of health behaviors that confer risk for disease, as well as inadequate access to quality medical care (Kington & Nickens, 2000; Myers et al., 2002; Williams, 1999). However, we argue that all of these factors exert their effects either directly or indirectly through the family.

The proposed family adversity model, depicted in Figure 27.1, is a modification of a multidimensional model of cumulative adversity and health proposed by Myers and Hwang (in press a), and integrates the perspectives from a number of models of stress and functional outcomes. These include the family stress model of economic hardship by Conger et al. (2002), biobehavioral models of stress and disease, including McEwen's (1998) work on "allostatic load," and Geronimus' (1992) work on the "weathering hypothesis," as well as Singer and Ryff's (1999) model of life histories and health risks as predictors of health trajectories.

In this model we make explicit that *(1) sociostructural risk factors*, such as the family's material resources and history, and exposure to community risks and access to community resources and *(2) biological risk factors*, such as genetic risks and the family's medical and psychiatric histories, interact over time to increase *(3) the family's burden of psychosocial adversities* and *(4) behavioral adversities*. The latter are hypothesized to be the primary family-level transmitters of risk. The psychosocial adversities include a heavy burden of life stresses (Clark et al., 1999; Myers et al., 2002); a hostile/coercive or neglectful parenting style (McLoyd, 1998; Repetti et al., 2002); an

Figure 27.1
Family contributions to health and illness

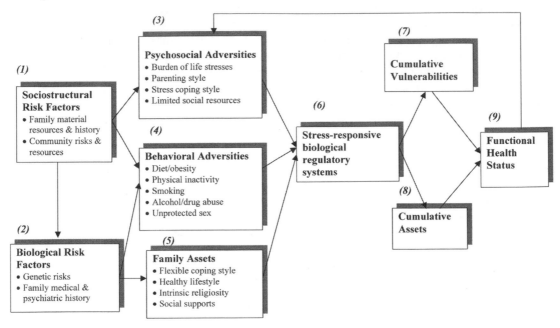

Source: Adapted from Myers & Hwang (2003).

avoidant, angry or effortful stress coping (James, 1994); and limited social resources for support (Taylor et al., 1997). The behavioral adversities include health-endangering behaviors such as inadequate diet, obesity, physical inactivity (Kumanyika, 1998), smoking, alcohol and drug abuse (Caetano et al., 2001; Frone et al., 1997; Myers et al., 1995), unprotected sex, especially with high-risk partners (Laumann & Youm, 1999; Wyatt et al., 1998), and lifetime history of traumatic experiences (Wyatt et al., 2002).

The model also acknowledges, however, that the adversities-biological processes-health status pathways are influenced by the family's strengths and resources for coping, which we label as the *(5) family's resources and assets.* These assets moderate risk and include psychological characteristics, such as flexible role functions and coping strategies (Bowman, 1992; McAdoo, 1998), healthy lifestyles (Myers et al., 1995), intrinsic religiosity (Levin et al., 1995; Mattis, 1997; Musgrave et al., 2002), supportive, but authoritative, parenting (Hill, 1995; Myers & Taylor, 1998), and the availability and use of adequate social support and caregiving resources (Burchinal et al., 1996; Hatchett & Jackson, 1999).

All of these family risks and assets are hypothesized as exerting their effects through *(6) biobehavioral mediators* through disruptions in the sympathoadrenomedullary, hypothalamic-pituitary-adrenocortical, serotonergic, and immunologic systems. Chronic, long-term exposure to stress results in the resetting of these physiological response mechanisms and physiologic "wear and tear" or "allostatic load" (McEwen, 1998), and this, in turn, is hypothesized to contribute over time to *(7) cumulative vulnerabilities* and ultimately to *(9) adverse health outcomes* (McEwen, 1998; Seeman et al., 1997).

Adverse health outcomes also contribute additional burdens of stress and adversities on individuals and families over time by generating new stressors (i.e., higher medical costs, loss of income, increased caretaker burden). This increases the demands on the family's coping and support resources and increases the likelihood of greater distress, depression, and functional impairment of both the affected family members and their caregivers (Minkler & Fuller-Thompson, 1999). Thus, family stresses and illnesses are reciprocally related, with greater stress exposure increasing risk for illnesses and the presence of illnesses and these in turn, increasing the likelihood of greater stress burden.

However, this stress–disease relationship is moderated by the family's assets and resources, which also accumulate over time. Therefore, we hypothesize, consistent with life-course developmental theory and life history research (Elder, 1998; Singer & Ryff, 1999) that it is the balance between the family's *(7) cumulative vulnerabilities* and *(8) cumulative advantages or assets* over the life course that should ultimately contribute to the functional status and health trajectories of family members.

We acknowledge that no empirical studies have tested this conceptual model. Therefore, the model is offered as an integrative and organizing framework for investigating the direct, indirect, and reciprocal effects that the risks and resources of the African American family might play in contributing to the greater burden of illness experienced by this population. A full review of the entire model is beyond the scope of this chapter; therefore, we provide a more detailed discussion of the evidence for sociostructural and biological risk factors, which set the stage for risk; for psychosocial and behavioral adversities, which exacerbate risk; for family assets that moderate risk; and for stress-responsive biological systems, which serve as the mechanism through which the effects of family risks and resources are expressed in disease and dysfunction.

SOCIOSTRUCTURAL RISK FACTORS

The disadvantaged health status of African Americans can be linked directly to their persistent social disadvantage. The African American population continues to grow, now accounting for 13 percent of the population of the United States, and more African Americans are upwardly mobile (i.e., 17 percent of men and 24 percent of women are employed in managerial and professional occupations, and 28 percent of families have incomes > $50,000/year) (McKinnon & Humes, 2000). However, on average, the African American family continues to lag far behind White families and is facing new and more complex social and economic challenges. Data from the U.S. Census Bureau (1999) (see Table 27.1) indicate that the African American population is relatively young, with 33 percent under age 18 and only 8 percent over age 65. On average, they are also less educated, with only 14 percent of African American men over the age of 25 and 16 percent of African American women over the age of 25 having a bachelor's degree or more.

The size and composition of African American families appear to be getting worse, with more than half (53 percent) of all families headed by a single parent, and slightly less than half of all families were headed by women (45 percent). Although a significant percentage of African Americans were employed (66 percent labor force participation) and only 9 percent were unemployed, this is significantly lower than for Whites (74 percent in the civilian labor force and 4 percent unemployed). Among those who were employed, most African American men (48 percent) were in service or laborer occupations, as were 36 percent of African American women. These positions generally have lower pay and are less stable than managerial or professional positions, in which African Americans continue to be underrepresented. It is not surprising, therefore, that African American families have lower average incomes and are overrepresented among the poor. For example, 21 percent of African American married couple families in 1999 reported incomes of less than $25,000 a year, compared to only 14 percent of White families. This economic deprivation is even greater in female-headed families, where 67 percent report incomes of less than $25,000 a year. As a consequence, three times as many African American families were poor (26 percent) compared to White families (8 percent). The discrepancy is even greater in female-headed families, where 41 percent of

Table 27.1
Demographic characteristics of the Black population in the United States

	Blacks	non-Hispanic Whites
% of population < age 18	33%	24%
% of population > age 65	8%	14%
Family Structure		
% of married couple families	47%	82%
% of single-parent families	53%	18%
% married couple families with two members	34%	45%
% of married couple families with five or more members	20%	12%
% female-headed families with two members	37%	57%
% female-headed families with five or more members	14%	5%
Employment		
% of the civilian labor force	12%	74%
% unemployed	9%	4%
% of men employed in service or laborer occupations	48%	25%
% of women employed in service or laborer occupations	36%	21%
% of men employed in sales, administrative support	20%	20%
% of women employed in sales, administrative support	38%	41%

female-headed African American families were poor compared to 21 percent of White female-headed families.

African American families are also typically larger than their White counterparts; fewer African American married couples had only two members (34 percent vs. 45 percent) and more had five or more members (20 percent vs. 12 percent, respectively) than White families. Among female-headed

Table 27.1 (continued)

Education

% of men over age 25 with bachelors degree or more	14%	31%
% of women over age 25 with bachelors degree of more	16%	25%

Income

% of married couples reporting incomes <$25,000	21%	14%
% of female-headed families reporting incomes < $25,000	67%	46%
% poverty rate	26%	8%
% poverty rate of female-headed families	41%	21%

Source: McKinnon & Humes (2000).

families, fewer of the African American families consisted of two members (37 percent vs. 57 percent), and more consisted of five or more members (14 percent vs. 5 percent) than their White counterparts.

In their review of the demographic trends in African American families, Taylor, Tucker, Chatters, and Jayakody (1997) noted that a high percentage of unmarried African American youth (81 percent of males and 59 percent of females) reported having had intercourse, were less likely than White teens to use contraceptives (54 percent vs. 69 percent), were more likely to have unplanned pregnancies (i.e., pregnancy rate = 357 vs. 61) and have birthrates that were twice that of Whites, and those that become mothers were significantly less likely to finish high school or to be employed and had higher rates of poverty and receive welfare. These trends are repeated among adults and are likely to become institutionalized across family generations.

Therefore, compared to White families, African American families are generally larger, have their children younger, are less well educated, more likely to be single-parent families and to be unemployed and on welfare or employed in lower-pay and less stable occupations, and consequently are more likely to have lower incomes and to be poor. In addition, a large percentage of these families are impacted by alcohol and drug abuse, and a disproportionate number of African American men are incarcerated or involved with the criminal justice system and are at substantially greater risk of premature death from violent crime. This disadvantaged socioeconomic and sociocultural position exposes a larger percentage of African Americans to adverse environmental contributors to health risks, including poorer nutrition, weaker schools, greater exposure to environmental pollutants (e.g., lead-based paints, recycling plants, heavy industry jobs, etc.), greater exposure to illicit drugs and community violence, and continued susceptibility to discrimination in employment, housing, and access to quality health care. These factors account substantially for the health and functional disparities between African Americans and Whites (see Kington & Nickens, 2000; Smedley et al., 2002;

Williams, 2000 for reviews of these issues). Unfortunately, the current national economic and political climate is likely to extend this disadvantage to several future generations of African American families.

BIOLOGICAL RISK FACTORS

In addition to the sociostructural disadvantages noted above, the health of African American families is also affected in part by biological predispositions that increase their risk for certain disorders. There is substantial evidence implicating differences in biological predispositions as likely contributors to the greater burden of disease experienced by African Americans, especially for essential hypertension, diabetes, and poor birth outcomes. While there continues to be some debate about whether all of these differences are genetically mediated (e.g., sodium metabolism in hypertension), there is growing consensus that these diseases are the products of dysregulated biological mechanisms and that the group differences in vulnerability reflect both differences in the exposure to stress and other factors that serve as triggers for the dysregulation (Myers et al., 1996) and possibly a lower threshold for biological reactivity to these risk factors (see Saab et al., 2000 for a review of this evidence). In the case of essential hypertension, there is substantial evidence that a family history of hypertension is associated with enhanced risk for developing this disease and for earlier onset of the disease, as well as for greater cardiovascular stress reactivity. This tendency toward physiologic hyperreactivity has been found in normotensive children and adults with a positive family history, and this enhanced family-mediated risk appears to be transmitted through a genetically mediated tendency toward sodium retention (Grim et al., 1995), greater stress exposure and cardiovascular stress reactivity (Myers et al., 1996), and the ineffective management of negative affect, especially anger-hostility (Johnson & Gant, 1996; Myers & McClure, 1993).

There is also substantial evidence that a number of biological, psychosocial, and behavioral factors are implicated in the risk for adverse birth outcomes and that ethnic groups differ in the clustering of these factors (Dunkel-Schetter & Lobel, 1998). Risk factors include family history of poor birth outcomes, maternal stress and HPA reactivity (Sandman et al., 1997), lifestyle (Shiono et al., 1997), exposure to family or community violence (Collins et al., 1998), and inadequate family support (Feldman et al., 2000). Geronimus (1992) argues that the evidence of disproportionate adverse birth outcomes among African American women, especially the clustering of problem births in younger women relative to their White counterparts, is suggestive of a "weathering" or premature physiologic aging phenomenon. This biological vulnerability appears to be the cumulative effect of early exposure to chronic social stresses (i.e., high demands and low resources), the clustering of health-damaging behaviors (e.g., obesity, poor nutrition, physical inactivity), concurrent chronic illnesses (e.g., hypertension, diabetes), and inadequate social support.

PSYCHOSOCIAL ADVERSITIES

There is a growing body of evidence suggesting that ethnic differences in physical health may be due to a substantial degree to differential exposure to chronic and acute life stressors (Williams et al., 1997). African Americans, especially those from lower social classes, often report more negative life events and greater and more frequent exposure to "generic life stressors" (i.e., stressors that are a usual part of modern life—financial, occupational, relationships, parental, etc.), and report more psychological distress from these stressful life experiences than do their White counterparts (Myers et al., 2002). Therefore, they are more likely to be vulnerable to the long-term effects of high chronic stress burden and presumably higher allostatic load. Chronic stressors due to financial strain, inadequate housing, crowding, and violence may also contribute to more frequent activation of stress-response systems and prolonged exposure to stress hormones (McEwen, 1998).

However, such a simple explanation of differential stress burden underestimates the true complexity of the minority stress–health relationships. For example, race conditions social class such that not only is exposure to life stressors greater among the poor, but racial/ethnic minorities also experience greater stress burden and poorer health outcomes at all equivalent levels of socioeconomic status (Williams, 1999). This race–SES relationship can have direct effects on health through additional stress burden and higher allostatic load, as well as indirect effects through structural barriers of access to health care and other social resources (i.e., housing, employment, safety), acceptance of societal stigma of inferiority (i.e., acceptance of inferiority status), high risk and unhealthy lifestyles, and ineffective coping and negative affective states (e.g., depression and hostility) (Clark et al., 1999; Williams, 1999).

In the case of African American families, greater burden of life stresses, especially economic hardships, adversely affect the functional adjustment of low-income African American children mediated through emotional distress in caregivers, disruptions in the caregiver relationships, and punitive, nonsupportive parenting (Conger et al., 2002; McLoyd, 1997). Unfortunately, such complex generic family stress models have not yet been tested in predicting physical health status, either overall or in accounting for ethnic differences in health status.

An important source of additional stress for African Americans is a by-product of family structure. There is a substantial body of evidence linking intimate relationship stresses and conflict to parenting behavior, parental distress, and the functional adjustment of children (Repetti et al., 2002), as well as risk for physical illnesses, such as hypertension and CVD (Jonas & Lando, 2000). As noted above, a larger percentage of African American families are single-parent families or augmented families that typically include an unmarried mother and children who are coresident with grandparents. Although adaptive, these families typically experience more financial stresses, more disruptions, parenting strains, and potential role conflicts than their more stable two-parent counterparts (Conger et al., 2002; Taylor et al., 1997).

In addition to greater burden of these generic life stresses, African Americans and other persons of color experience additional stresses from racism and discrimination that add to their overall stress burden. In their recent review of the extant literature on racism and its effects on African Americans, Clark et al. (1999) discussed the empirical evidence of the effects racism has on mental and physical health. They acknowledge that both intergroup and intragroup racism, as well as attitudinal (i.e., prejudice) and behavioral (i.e., overt discrimination) racism are significant stressors and propose that racism exerts its effects on biopsychosocial processes in a model that is similar to the model proposed here.

For African American families, racism and discrimination have both direct and indirect effects on the health and well-being of the family. Racism exerts direct effects by constraining life opportunities by limiting social mobility and condemning entire generations of these families to chronic poverty (i.e., restricted access to quality education and meaningful employment, undermining the economic health of the family, and limiting access to quality housing). It also exerts its effects indirectly through multiple pathways. To the extent that racism and discrimination contribute to the persistent poverty of African American families, they contribute indirectly to the instability of the family structure, to the greater burden of adversities faced by these families, to greater parental distress and poorer parenting practices, to the likelihood of exposure to family and community violence (Burton & Jayakody, 2001; McLoyd, 1997), and to greater burden of adverse health behaviors and health outcomes (Clark et al., 1999).

The extended African American family, while an important resource for survival, may also bring additional stresses. For example, African American elderly are disproportionately burdened by custodial and caretaking responsibilities of grandchildren. The increase in the number of grandparents who are raising grandchildren is one of the unanticipated and underrecognized fallouts of the cocaine/

crack abuse, HIV/AIDS, and teen pregnancy epidemics of the 1980s and 1990s (Minkler & Fuller-Thompson, 1999). Data from the U.S. census reported by Minkler & Fuller-Thompson (1999) indicated that in 1997, 13.5 percent of African American children were living with grandparents. This is a 44 percent increase from 1980 (Lugaila, 1998), with the greatest increase evident in skipped generation families in which the birth parents were not coresidents (Casper & Bryson, 1998). Szinovacz (1998) noted that census data underestimate the true prevalence of grandchildren living with grandparents, with custodial grandparenting rates in the National Survey of Families and Household (NSFH) as high as 26.0 percent in African American grandmothers.

There is also substantial evidence that caregiving grandparents are especially vulnerable to a host of problems, including depression, social isolation, poverty, and reduced quality of life (Minkler & Fuller-Thompson, 1999). In their secondary analysis of the NSFH data, Minkler and Fuller-Thompson found that caregiving grandparents were 50 percent more likely to have functional limitations and lower self-reported satisfaction with health and were almost twice as likely as noncaregiving grandparents to report clinically significant levels of depressive symptoms, even after controlling for precaregiving depression and demographic characteristics (Minkler et al., 1997). Grandparents who had to step in to care for their grandchildren due to parental incarceration because of drug addiction, incapacitation, or death due to AIDS or violent crime report feeling more anger, shame, and perceptions of entrapment in this "time-disordered role" (Minkler et al., 1997).

However, while the additional stress burden associated with assuming caregiving responsibilities for grandchildren increases risk for psychological distress and depression in all groups, several studies indicate that African American grandmothers reported less distress and less negative impact from their caretaking responsibilities on their mental health and social lives than White grandmothers (Pruchno, 1999). The lower impact of child-care burden on African American grandmothers may be explained by the fact that African American grandmothers traditionally play key roles as support for the African American family during times of crisis and are often embedded in large supportive social networks (e.g., other parenting grandmothers and other sources) that provide emotional and other tangible assistance. The same was not true for White grandmothers.

BEHAVIORAL ADVERSITIES

The greater burden of adversities exerts its effects on health directly through a host of health risk behaviors, including diet, obesity, physical inactivity, the use of abusable substances, and high-risk sexual behaviors (Myers et al., 1995).

Diet and Obesity

There is substantial evidence linking diet, especially a high-fat, high-calorie, high-sodium, low-calcium, and low-potassium diet, and obesity to a host of chronic medical conditions, including hypertension, heart disease, stroke, diabetes, hypercholesterolemia, breast and colon cancer, as well as poorer overall health (American Heart Association, 1998; American Cancer Society, 1997). Unfortunately and because of both cultural and socioeconomic reasons, the African American diet is typically poor (Airhihenbuwa et al., 1996; Kumanyika, 1998). In addition and as a direct consequence of a poor diet and a more sedentary lifestyle, obesity is pandemic, especially among African American women. In a recent report in JAMA by Flegal et al. (2002), more than half of African American women age 40 or older were obese (BMI $\geq$ 30), and 80 percent were overweight (BMI $\geq$ 25). This trend is evident in childhood and adolescence and may be linked to cultural beliefs (e.g., "a fat baby is a healthy baby") and traditions (e.g., family gatherings, church functions), to psychological compensation for, and adaptation to, socioeconomic deprivation, as well as cultural notions of beauty (i.e., preferences for a larger body size) and greater tolerance for moderate obesity among African Americans (Allan, 1998; Cachelin et al., 2002; Kumanyika, 1998). The latter serves as a social reinforcer for heavier body mass and may undermine efforts to manage and/or to lose weight. For example, in a sample of 500 African American women, Kumanyika (1998) notes that while awareness of the health risks of obesity was high, the perceived social costs of being overweight were more limited. They reported that 40 percent of those who were moderately and severely overweight considered themselves to be attractive or very attractive.

Dietary habits and parental body mass are the direct by-products of family attitudes, beliefs, and eating practices and shape the behaviors and tastes of all family members. Therefore, it is not surprising that food preference and body mass cluster within families (Wickrama et al., 1999), and this burden of risk is carried over the life span into old age and contributes to greater impairment and earlier mortality (Harris et al., 1997).

Physical Inactivity

A sedentary lifestyle, which is a direct contributor to obesity and risk for CVD, is also more prevalent among African American children and women. As a group, African American children spend a disproportionate amount of time watching TV (Durant et al., 1994), and adolescent and adult African American women are significantly less likely to exercise than White women (Crespo et al., 2000; Health United States, 2001). This is especially true for the poor and is related at least in part to concerns about issues of safety, lack of adequate recreational resources, child care, and family caretaking responsibilities, as well as lack of social support. These obstacles become more significant with increasing age (Wilcox et al., 2000). The combination of poor dietary habits, physical inactivity, and obesity constitutes a major health risk complex for African Americans and deserves special attention in all risk reduction interventions for these families.

Smoking and Substance Abuse

Smoking, alcohol, and drug abuse have all been linked as risk factors for a variety of chronic illnesses, including CVD, diabetes, liver disease, and cancer. In addition, alcohol and illicit drug use and abuse have also been linked to enhanced risk for injury and death from accidents, violence, and cardiac events (American Heart Association, 1998). These risk behaviors exacerbate the effects of the other psychosocial and behavioral risk factors. The epidemiological evidence indicates that while African Americans initiate smoking later than Whites, more men smoke than women, and those who smoke, smoke more cigarettes, evidence a preference for higher tar and menthol cigarettes, and have high rates of smoking-related illnesses (Health United States, 2001; Kabat et al., 1991). On the other hand, African American women are less likely to smoke than White women and have lower rates of smoking-related problems (Health United States, 2001).

Alcohol and illicit drug abuse are major risk factors for both African American men and women, especially among the poor. The high rates of alcoholism and drug abuse in inner-city communities have been devastating to African American families. They undermine the integrity and stability of the family by draining its financial resources and contribute to family disruption through unemployment, spousal and child abuse, teen maladjustment, substance abuse and delinquency, and parental incarceration (Hastings & Hamberger, 1997; Wallace et al., 1995). They also contribute to risk for adverse birth outcomes and developmental deficits through prenatal exposure to alcohol (Richardson et al., 2002), and cocaine and other drugs (Morrow et al., 2001), which adds to the overall burden of family stress and places children on negative functional and health trajectories.

High-Risk Sexual Behavior

The high teen pregnancy rates and high STD and HIV infection rates in African Americans are also attributable, at least in part, to family processes. Poverty, single-parent families, inadequate parental or other adult supervision, and weak parent–child relationships are all risk factors for early sexual debut, more frequent sexual activity, inconsistent or inadequate use of contraceptives, and greater risk for STDs and unintended pregnancy (Moore & Chase-Landsdale, 2001). This risk is even greater in those who are sexually abused, which increases the likelihood of revictimization, poor sexual decision making, riskier sexual behavior, and STD and HIV risk (Parillo et al., 2001; Wingood & DiClemente, 1997; Wyatt et al., 2002). Living in a two-family household with employed adults and stronger parent–child relationships substantially reduces these risks (Moore & Chase-Landsdale, 2001).

Health-Care Behaviors

Symptoms and disease management also influence the development of chronic illnesses, disability, and dysfunction. There is a substantial body of evidence indicating that African Americans, especially men, are significantly more likely to underrate the significance of clinical signs and symptoms, to seek informal kinship sources of care for early symptoms, and to delay seeking appropriate professional care (Harden et al., 1997; Snowden, 1998). Noncompliance with medical recommendations with respect to taking medications and making recommended lifestyle changes, especially in diseases like hypertension and diabetes, also contribute to more severe disease progression, greater burden of disability, and earlier mortality. This reticence to seeking professional help and following medical advice has been attributed to a variety of factors, including health-care socialization, health beliefs, and inadequate knowledge, especially with respect to symptom recognition (Ofili, 2001). In addition, there is growing evidence that economic barriers to access to care and perceived racism from the health-care system are important contributors to delays in help-seeking (Lillie-Blanton et al., 2000; Smedley et al., 2002). In their recent study, Lillie-Blanton et al. (2000) found that more than half of the African Americans surveyed believed that race affects the health care they receive and that they receive lower-quality care and were concerned about being treated fairly. However, concern about the affordability of health coverage was greater than perceived racial barriers to care. These health-care attitudes, beliefs, and behaviors are established and maintained within families and transmitted across generations. Thus, an important target for intervention is health education, including attention to compliance with health-care recommendations and coping with institutional racism.

Taken as a whole, it is hypothesized that it is the combination of long-term exposure to sociostructural adversities and burden of psychosocial adversities faced by African Americans that contribute to their overall greater vulnerability to disease and dysfunction. This vulnerability is further enhanced by high-risk behaviors and by preexisting biological attributes. Special attention needs to be focused on the clustering of these risk factors within the African American family and the development of cumulative vulnerabilities over the life course.

FAMILY ASSETS AND RESOURCES—FROM RISK TO RESILIENCE

The African American family has historically faced more than its share of sociostructural and psychosocial burdens. However, these families have also demonstrated considerable resilience and adaptability to their social circumstances. In fact, it has been argued that the diversity of African American family arrangements, including extended and augmented families, reliance on kinship networks of support, flexibility in role functions, and the strong connections to the church and other community resources are all evidence of the strength and resilience of these families (Bowman, 1992; McAdoo, 1998). All of these attributes have been shown to moderate the stress–health and functional status relationships in African American adults and the elderly.

Stress Appraisal

The impact that exposure to chronic stress has on health is moderated by how one interprets or appraises and responds to the stressful experience (Lazarus & Folkman, 1984). Stress appraisal involves the weighing of one's resources against the demands of the stressor in order to determine how large a threat the stressor is to well-being. For African American families, stress appraisal is likely to involve not only the subjective examination of resources versus demands but also the filtering of stressful experiences through one's unique cultural lens. For example, African American women typically serve as the traditional center of families and are often responsible for the emotional, physical, and spiritual well-being of its members, and in many cases, they also must share or carry a major responsibility for the economic viability of the family. They must cope with their own burden of life stresses, as well as manage the impact stresses have on other members of the family (McAdoo, 1998; Reid & Bing, 2000). This is illustrated in the acceptance of the responsibility for the care of other relatives, especially grandchildren, in response to major family crises (Minkler et al., 1997). Accepting this "strong woman" image is an additional burden of stress, and cultural expectations dictate that they should be able to handle life challenges, which may hinder some women from seeking timely assistance in meeting their personal needs from professional and/or formal assistance programs. On the other hand, many gain considerable psychological satisfaction from fulfilling these strong traditional roles, which contributes to their resilience, resourcefulness, and flexibility in dealing with stressful situations (Reid & Bing, 2000).

Coping

Another important moderator of risk is the family's resources for coping and the use of flexible, adaptive coping strategies, including anticipation, sublimation, humor, altruism, and spirituality in coping with life challenges (Bowman, 1992; Diehl et al., 1996). In his review of coping with role demands by African American men, Bowman (1992) notes that there is greater marital satisfaction, greater feelings of perceived control, and greater satisfaction with their role function in those families where men assume flexible roles. Given the often precarious socioeconomic conditions of many African American men, failure to make such adjustments both increases personal stress and under mines family stability. Unfortunately, there is a dearth of studies that investigate what specific strategies African American families use in coping with stresses that are specifically associated with more positive health outcomes. It can be inferred from the positive outcomes reported in risk reduction interventions that target African Americans for a variety of adverse outcomes that identifying risk factors and acting proactively to address them is an important coping strategy.

Also, in a theoretical discussion of issues surrounding coping in women, Banyard and Graham-Bermann (1993) argued that coping as it is traditionally measured is largely influenced by education and income, such that those with more resources typically cope "better." In this respect, individuals' social position and their environments can either constrain or enhance their resources and choice of coping strategies (Taylor, Roberts, & Jacobson, 1997). Members of marginalized groups, either because of ethnicity, social class, gender, and/or age, may face special challenges to active coping. Limitations in finances, knowledge, access to requisite technical expertise or other resources, and cultural, social, or psychological barriers may discourage active coping. In the case of African American men and women, assertiveness is often misperceived as aggressiveness or arrogance and responded to with fear or punitive action. Additional research is still needed to investigate this hypothesis and to determine under what conditions assertive versus emotion-focused coping yields more positive health outcomes for African Americans.

Studies by James (1994) on John Henryism investigated the efficacy of active, effortful coping in predicting health outcomes in African American adults, especially when SES is considered. For example, research on effortful coping with adversity indicated that when compared to higher-SES African Americans and Whites from all SES groups, young African American men high in John Henryism but with low socioeconomic resources (James, 1994) have higher blood pressure and greater risk for hypertension. Thus, John Henryism appears to be relatively benign for higher SES African Americans and Whites. However, for African American men with limited resources, the benefits of effortful coping (i.e., economic survival) appear to be tempered by increased health risks.

Given that African Americans are often confronted with chronic stressors that are not easily ameliorated, it is not surprising that effortful, active coping strategies might yield mixed results. Such coping strategies may not produce the desired changes in status and opportunity and may in fact produce high levels of anger and frustration, which might account for the higher levels of blood pressure seen in these individuals. Unfortunately, we do not know how prevalent this coping strategy is among African American families or what effect long-term use has on their health and well-being.

There has also been limited attention given to identifying the range of coping strategies that are most adaptive for African American families at different stages along the socioeconomic continuum. It is very likely that healthy functioning in the face of chronic stress exposure requires the development of a different array of active and passive coping strategies in families that differ in structure and access to resources.

Parenting Strategies

The quality of the parent–child relationship is a primary predictor of psychological and behavioral adjustment of children (see Repetti et al., 2002 for a discussion of this literature). This literature consistently identifies warm, supportive parenting and a close parent–child relationship as protective against a variety of adverse child outcomes. On the other hand, coercive, aggressive, punitive, cold, neglectful parenting confers significant risk for psychological and behavioral maladjustment. These results appear to hold regardless of ethnicity but appear to be especially damaging to children facing significant socioeconomic disadvantage (McLoyd, 1997, 1998). However, in the case of African American children in these high-stress, high-risk families, several studies have suggested that the parenting style that is most protective is one that combines parental nurturance, along with clarity of expectations and demandingness or authoritativeness (Conger et al., 2002; McCabe et al., 1999; Myers & Taylor, 1998). These authors argue that greater attention to rules and guidelines, enforced with warmth and nurturance, may be essential for these families in order to moderate the host of risk factors that can impinge on their lives. Similar requirements may not be as necessary in more affluent families, although some have argued that this may still be true for affluent African American families.

It is still unclear, however, whether such a parenting style has the same protective effect on physical health as it has on psychosocial adjustment. It is reasonable to suspect that the health benefits of authoritative parenting would be contingent on the extent to which African American parents hold health-enhancing beliefs and enforce healthy eating, exercise, timely health-care seeking and other similar behaviors. It would be useful for future prevention interventions with high-risk African American children and families to integrate effective parenting strategies into their health-promotion, disease-prevention curricula.

Religiosity

Substantial literature indicates the salience and benefits of religion and religious participation in the lives of African American families (Mattis, 1997; Taylor, 1993). In addition, both cross-sectional and longitudinal studies indicate that there are aging-related changes in the pattern of predominant religious behaviors, with participation in organized religious activities remaining high until late old age. However, religious attitudes and private religious behaviors (i.e., prayer, reading religious materials, watching or listening to religious programs) actually increase with age (Koenig et al., 1988).

This literature also suggests that there are important Black–White differences in religiosity. Historically, African Americans have relied on religion and on the church as important sources of spiritual, emotional, and material support in coping with life stresses and report greater satisfaction with the results of their religious coping efforts (Levin et al., 1995; Wade-Gayles, 1995). The Black church has also served as a powerful political force for social change and an opportunity for social status (Ellison, 1995).

However, the evidence on the effect of religiosity on well-being, both overall and as a function of ethnicity, is mixed, suggesting the need for more rigorous studies and more critical analysis (Ellison, 1995). Many studies suggest that religious beliefs and practices are associated with enhanced health and life satisfaction (Levin et al., 1995), greater perceived control (Koenig et al., 1988), less depression, and greater social integration, especially in the elderly (Idler, 1987). A number of other studies have suggested, however, that the relationship between religiosity and psychological well-being is more complex than is generally believed. For example, Nelson (1989) found that African American elderly who were more active in church attendance and engaged in more private religious practices were more depressed than White elderly. On the other hand, in his sample of adult and elderly southerners, Ellison (1995) found that religious coping was associated with lower depression in White respondents but was unrelated to depression in African Americans. He argued that this unexpected finding suggests that other factors might temper the effectiveness of religious experiences and practices in moderating risk for depression in this sample of elderly southern African Americans. Unfortunately, we cannot determine from the data in either study whether religious coping was ineffective in preventing depression or whether those who were depressed were simply more likely to engage in more religious coping in an effort to deal with their distress.

Additional evidence in support of the complex relationships between religiosity and health is provided by Strawbridge et al. (1998). They contrasted nonorganizational religiosity (i.e., prayer, importance of religious and spiritual beliefs) versus organizational religiosity (i.e., attendance at services and other religious activities) as moderators on stress and depression in the Alameda County survey of adults. Their results indicated that while religiosity is protective for mortality and morbidity, it buffers some stressors but appears to exacerbate others. They found that nonorganizational religiosity was unrelated to depression, while organizational religiosity had a weak, negative association with depression. However, while both forms of religiosity buffered the effect of nonfamily stressors (i.e., financial, health), nonorganizational religiosity exacerbated the effects of child problems, and organizational religiosity exacerbated the effects of marital problems, child and/or spousal abuse, and caregiving. Thus, religiosity may benefit those facing nonfamilial stressors but may make coping with family crises worse.

Recent studies of African American women suffering from chronic illness also found that religious coping was associated with less depression and anxiety but did not find a similar association with physical health outcomes (Woods et al., 1999). In this respect, religious coping may be effective in reducing the psychological distress associated with chronic stressors but may not be effective in ameliorating the negative effects of chronic stressors on health outcomes.

Taken as a whole, the evidence suggests that religion is an important spiritual and social resource for African American adults and the elderly, who report greater religious involvement and use of religious coping than Whites. However, the evidence also indicates that religion does not yield uniformly positive effects, especially as a buffer for psychological well-being. Less evidence is available testing the utility of religion as a buffer for physical health and health behavior.

Social Support Resources

A substantial body of evidence examines the importance of social relationships and availability of adequate instrumental and emotional support on health. The evidence indicates that social supports can serve as both a protector against adverse health outcomes as well as a moderator of stress in reducing its impact on health (Cohen et al., 2000), including improved functional status and quality of life (Seeman et al., 1996; Unger et al., 1999). Similarly, social isolation, inadequate social support, and problematic interpersonal relationships can have adverse effects on health and well-being, especially for women and the elderly (Burg & Seeman, 1994; Newsom & Schulz, 1996), as well as for those with debilitating physical illnesses, depression, or cognitive decline (Unger et al., 1999). In fact, there appears to be a reciprocal relationship between physical impairment and social support, especially among the elderly, such that the availability of social support reduces functional impairment in those with significant chronic illnesses, and in turn, functional impairment is associated with an attenuation of support or reduction in access to supports (i.e., fewer friendship contacts, inability to attend church or other social functions, reduction in perceived self-efficacy, etc.) (Newsom & Schulz, 1996).

Evidence of the positive effects of social support have been obtained with White and ethnic minority populations, and many studies have reported that African American adults and elderly tend to rely heavily on larger family and other informal social networks for support (Antonucci & Jackson, 1987; Pruchno, 1999). It is unclear, however, whether there are differences in the reliance on informal social networks as a function of social class and family composition among African American families and what aspects of social network support enhance health.

It is also important to note that reliance on informal social networks may also exacerbate the stress burden, especially for women and the elderly. In some cases, such support may also contribute to health risk behaviors (e.g., reinforce poor dietary habits and tolerance of excess body mass) and indirectly encourage delaying professional help-seeking (Harden et al., 1997; Snowden, 1998).

STRESS-RESPONSIVE REGULATORY MECHANISMS AS BIOBEHAVIORAL MEDIATORS OF RISK

The burden of psychosocial adversities contributes to disease and dysfunction mediated through a number of biological regulatory mechanisms that are responsive to stress. Modern theories of stress all define disease and dysfunctions as the products of dysregulations in the sympathoadrenomedullary (SAM), hypothalamic-pituitary-adrenocortical (HPA), serotonergic, cardiovascular, immunologic, and other systems. McEwen (1998) argued that disease results when normal allostatic responses to stress become dysregulated, which subsequently overtaxes the system and results in physiologic wear and tear, which he defined as "allostatic load." A good example of this model is essential hypertension, which is conceptualized as a disease that results from the dysregulation of blood pressure control mechanisms due to persistent and pathological autonomic hyperreactivity to stress (Anderson et al., 1992).

Recent studies by McEwen and Seeman (1999) and Singer and Ryff (1999) provide compelling empirical support for this argument. In their review, McEwen and Seeman (1999) argued for a more comprehensive model of the effects of stress on disease that includes genetic load, life experiences, individual health habits, and physiological reactivity, all of which interact over time to produce gradients of risk for disease. Specific attention is given to increasing mortality and morbidity rates as one descends the socioeconomic gradient, which reflects the cumulative burden of coping with life demands with inadequate resources for coping.

Singer and Ryff (1999) tested this hypothesis using data from the Wisconsin Longitudinal Study (WLS). Using social relationships (i.e., parental bonding in childhood and relationship intimacy as adults) and household income in childhood and adulthood as their measures of adversity and advantage and a rating system that characterized distinct life histories based on positive and negative ratings on these two dimensions, they demonstrated that there was a strong direct association between the extent of lifetime adversity relative to advantages in ordering life histories. Those with higher relative disadvantages (i.e., negative economic and social relationships at each measurement point), especially those with persistent negative social relationships, evidenced higher allostatic loads (i.e., impaired immune function, elevated blood pressure, and later-life illness and chronic disease propensity) compared to those with balanced or more advantaged histories. Their analyses also confirmed that downward social mobility was more adverse than upward mobility, which provides a more sensitive analysis of the effect of SES on health than is possible when only the current socioeconomic status of individuals is assessed. It is also very likely that tracking SES changes of families over time would be even more instructive in understanding group differences in health trajectories.

Singer and Ryff (1999) also identified a group of resilient elderly who evidenced lower allostatic loads despite relatively disadvantaged histories, which they attributed to the presence of compensatory social relationship histories. This is an understudied group, especially resilient minority adults and elders, that could yield valuable information for programs designed to foster healthy aging and that might help to close the health disparities gap.

These intriguing ideas and methodologies have not yet been directly applied to investigating the greater burden of adverse health outcomes in African Americans over the life course. The one exception to this is the work by Geronimus (1992) on the "weathering hypothesis," which is hypothesized to account for some of the persistent African American versus White differences in birth outcomes. This work demonstrates the utility of investigating health differentials at different developmental stages. Using national infant mortality data comparing African American and White mothers by age cohorts, Geronimus found that these groups differed in patterns of neonatal mortality rates over the predominant first childbearing ages. Her results indicated that compared to White infants, African American infants of teen mothers experienced a survival advantage relative to infants whose mothers were older and in their prime childbearing years (i.e., 20s and 30s). She argued that this evidence indicates that there may be population differences in prime childbearing years and suggested that African American women appear to experience an earlier aging or weathering process and speculated that this difference was probably a consequence of prolonged, effortful coping with socioeconomic inequality, racial discrimination, and greater risk of exposure to environmental hazards. This burden of risk is likely to be exacerbated as these women get older by the development and untreated progression of chronic illnesses (e.g., hypertension, diabetes), by the clustering of behavior patterns that are adversarial to health (e.g., obesity, alcohol, and drug use, etc.), and by increasing stress burden.

SUMMARY AND FUTURE DIRECTIONS

In this chapter, we provide a selected review of the extant evidence of the role the African American family plays in accounting for some of the excess health burden and early mortality of African Americans. The evidence strongly implicates the family, indicating that factors such as family poverty, single-parent structure, and a disproportionate burden of chronic stress, as well as unhealthy diets, pandemic obesity, and other risk behaviors all contribute to excess morbidity. However, the availability of additional resources for support through extended or augmented family structure, flexibility in role function, nurturant, but demanding, parenting style, and religiosity are also protective resources. We offer an integrative, biopsychosocial perspective as a heuristic for organizing and understanding how factors in several domains of family experiences and functioning might contribute to risk for chronic illness or serve as protective factors that contribute to better functional health status. We argue that racial/ethnic differences in health status reflect differences in health trajectories over the life course of each group. It is important to note that many of the ideas in this model have not been formally tested, but we suggest that there would be substantial benefits to the field if comprehensive conceptual risk-resource models such as this were used to guide future studies.

There continues to be considerable interest in the African American family. However, this attention continues to be unbalanced with more attention given to identifying family characteristics that confer risk for dysfunction and relatively less attention to what attributes contribute to resilience. There is a substantial need for future studies to focus attention on studying resilience resources and documenting how and under what circumstances factors such as social support and religiosity exert their protective effects. Such information would inform the development and testing of more effective health promotion—disease prevention interventions.

The research on African American families is also rather fragmented and is often not guided by well-articulated theoretical perspectives. This is especially true in studies of family contributions to physical illnesses, where attention is focused separately on the effects of external forces or on biological factors and/or on health behaviors, without any systematic effort to integrate these effects. There can be little doubt that risk factors for chronic illnesses operate simultaneously and are likely to exert their effects synergistically on the family, such that the effects of external stressors are likely to be more damaging if the family is also impacted by family conflict, poor health habits, and limited social support resources than if these additional risk factors were not present. Such integrative analyses would enhance our understanding of family influences on health.

Although attention was not given to intervention studies in this chapter, a number of interventions have been developed specifically to address CVD, cancer, diabetes and other chronic illnesses in African Americans. Several of these interventions have yielded positive results, especially short-term changes, such as Project Joy (Yanek et al., 2001), Wisewoman (Rosamond et al., 2000), and the Heart Smart Program (Johnson et al., 1991). There also appears to be substantial need for creating new family life centers that combine both direct health-care delivery and health promotion education that focus on the family as the primary mediator of health for its members. Such an approach recognizes that the most successful programs utilize existing community resources such as the church, barbershops, health clinics, and other community-based organizations (CBOs) and provide integrated, one-stop shopping in the delivery of services. These studies appear to be even more successful if they also integrate cultural considerations into their service delivery and health promotion curricula (Myers & Hwang, 2003).

However, with a few exceptions (e.g., the Heart Smart Program) (Johnson et al., 1991), even the best programs target individual children, youth, or adults, but not entire families. While family-based interventions pose many new challenges to intervention agents, the yield from such interventions in terms of long-term stability of behavior change by changing the family system is likely to exceed the costs and difficulties of designing such interventions.

It is time that family researchers and health researchers join forces and collaborate in the development of interventions that maximize family resources and minimize family risks in an effort to close the health status gap for African American families.

REFERENCES

Airhihenbuwa, C.O., Kumanyika, S., Agurs, T.D., Lowe, A., Saunders, D., & Morssink, C.B. (1996). Cultural aspects of African American eating patterns. *Ethnicity & Health, 1(3)*, 245–260.

Allan, J.D. (1998). Explanatory models of overweight among African American, Euro-American, and Mexican American women. *Western Journal of Nursing Research, 20(1)*, 45–66.

American Cancer Society. (1997). Cancer facts & figures. *Surveillance research report.*

American Heart Association. (1998). *Cardiovascular diseases biostatistical fact sheet.*

Anderson, N.B., McNeilly, M., & Myers, H.F. (1992). Toward understanding race differences in autonomic reactivity: A proposed contextual model. In J.R. Turner, A. Sherwood, & K.C. Light (Eds.), *Individual differences in cardiovascular response to stress* (pp. 125–145). New York: Plenum Press.

Antonucci, T.C., & Jackson, J.S. (1987). Social support, interpersonal efficacy, and health: A life course perspective. In L.L. Carstensen & B.A. Edelstein (Eds.), *Handbook of clinical gerontology* (pp. 21–31). New York: Pergamon Press.

Banyard, V.L., & Graham-Bermann, S.A. (1993). Can women cope? A gender analysis of theories of coping with stress. *Psychology of Women Quarterly, 17*, 303–318.

Bowman, P.J. (1992). Coping with provider role strain: Adaptive cultural resources among Black husband-fathers. In A.K.H. Burlew, W.C. Banks, & H.P. McAdoo (Eds.), *African American psychology: Theory, research, and practice* (pp. 135–154). Thousand Oaks, CA: Sage.

Burchinal, M.R., Follmer, A., & Bryant, D.M. (1996). The relations of maternal social support and family structure with maternal responsiveness and child outcomes among African American families. *Developmental Psychology, 32(6)*, 1073–1083.

Burg, M.M., & Seeman, T.E. (1994). Families and health: The negative side of social ties. *Annals of Behavioral Medicine, 16(2)*, 109–115.

Burton, L.M., & Jayakody, R. (2001). Rethinking family structure and single parenthood: Implications for future studies of African-American families and children. In A. Thornton (Ed.), *The well being of children and families: Research and data needs* (pp. 127–153). Ann Arbor: University of Michigan Press.

Cachelin, F.M., Rebeck, R.M., Chung, G.H., & Pelayo, E. (2002). Does ethnicity influence body-size preference? A comparison of body image and body size. *Obesity Research, 10*, 158–166.

Caetano, R., Schafer, J., & Cunradi, C.B. (2001). Alcohol-related intimate partner violence among White, Black, and Hispanic couples in the United States. *Alcohol Research & Health, 25(1)*, 58–64.

Carter, J.S., Pugh, J.A., & Monterrosa, A. (1996). Non-insulin dependent diabetes mellitus in minorities in the United States. *Annals of Internal Medicine, 125*, 221–232.

Casper, L.M., & Bryson, K.R. (1998). Coresident grandparents and their grandchildren: Grandparent-maintained families. *Population Division Working Paper.* Washington, DC, No. 26, U.S. Bureau of the Census.

Centers for Disease Control (CDC). Behavioral Risk Factor Surveillance System, Prevalence Data, Nationwide–2000. Available at http://apps.nccd.cdc.gov/brfss/race. Accessed October 2002.

Clark, R., Anderson, N.B., Clark, V.R., & Williams, D.R. (1999). Racism as a stressor for African Americans: A biopsychosocial model. *American Psychologist, 54(10)*, 805–816.

Cohen, S., Underwood, L.G., & Gottlieb, B.H. (2000). *Social support measurement and intervention: A guide for health and social scientists.* New York: Oxford University Press.

Collins, J.W., David, R.J., Symons, R., Handler, A., Wall, S., & Andes, S. (1998). African-American mothers' perceptions of their residential environment, stressful life events, and very low birthweight. *Epidemiology, 9(3)*, 286–289.

Conger, R.D., Wallace, L.E., Sun, Y., Simons, R.L., McLoyd, V.C., & Brody, G.H. (2002). Economic pressure in African American families: A replication and extension of the family stress model. *Developmental Psychology, 38(2)*, 179–193.

Crespo, C.J., Smit, E., Andersen, R.E., Carter-Pokras, O., & Ainsworth, B.E. (2000). Race/ethnicity, social class and their relation to physical inactivity during leisure time: Results from the Third National Health and Nutrition Examination Survey, 1988–1994. *American Journal of Preventive Medicine, 18(1)*, 46–53.

Diehl, M., Coyle, N., & Labouvie-Vief, G. (1996). Age and sex differences in strategies of coping and defense across the life span. *Psychology and Aging, 11*, 127–139.

Dunkel-Schetter, C., & Lobel, M. (1998). Pregnancy and childbirth. In E. Blechman & K. Brownell (Eds.), *Behavioral medicine and women: A comprehensive handbook.* New York: Guilford Publications.

Durant, R.H., Baranowski, T., Johnson, M., & Thompson, W.O. (1994). The relationship among television watching, physical activity, and body composition of young children. *Pediatrics, 94,* 449–455.

Elder, G.H. (1998). The life course as developmental theory. *Child Development, 69(1),* 1–12.

Ellison, C.G. (1995). Race, religious involvement and depressive symptomatology in a southeastern U.S. community. *Social Science & Medicine, 40(11),* 1561–1572.

Feldman, P.J., Dunkle-Schetter, C., Sandman, C.A., & Wadhwa, P.D. (2000). Maternal social support predicts birth weight and fetal growth in human pregnancy. *Psychosomatic Medicine, 62(5),* 715–725.

Flegal, K.M., Carroll, M.D., Ogden, C.L., & Johnson, C.L. (2002). Prevalence and trends in obesity among U.S. adults, 1999–2000. *Journal of the American Medical Association, 288(14),* 1723–1727.

Frone, M.R., Russell, M., & Cooper, M.L. (1997). Relation of work-family conflict to health outcomes: A four-year longitudinal study of employed parents. *Journal of Occupational & Organizational Psychology, 70(4),* 325–335.

Geronimus, A.T. (1992). The weathering hypothesis and the health of African-American women and infants: Evidence and speculations. *Ethnicity & Disease, 2,* 207–221.

Grim, C.E., Henry, J., & Myers, H.F. (1995). High blood pressure in Blacks: Salt, slavery, survival, stress & racism. In J.A. Laragh & B.A. Brenner (Eds.), *Hypertension* (pp. 171–207). New York: Raven Press.

Harden, A.W., Clark, R., & Maguire, K. (1997). *Informal and formal kinship care.* Report for the Office of the Assistant Secretary for Planning and Evaluation. Task Order HHS-100-95-0021. Washington, DC: U.S. Department of Health & Human Services.

Harris, T.B., Savage, P.J., Tell, G.S., Haan, M., Kumanyika, S., & Lynch, J.C. (1997). Carrying the burden of cardiovascular risk in old age: Associations of weight and weight change with prevalent cardiovascular disease, risk factors, and health status in the Cardiovascular Health Study. *American Journal of Clinical Nutrition, 66(4),* 837–844.

Hastings, J.E., & Hamberger, L.K. (1997). Sociodemographic predictors of violence. *The Psychiatric Clinics of North America, 20(2),* 323–335.

Hatchett, S.J., & Jackson, J.S. (1999). African American extended kin systems: An empirical assessment in the National Survey of Black Americans. In H.P. McAdoo (Ed.), *Family ethnicity: Strength in diversity* (pp. 171–190). Thousand Oaks, CA: Sage.

Health United States. (2001). National Center for Health Statistics. Hyattsville, MD.

Hill, N.E. (1995). The relationship between family environment and parenting style: A preliminary study of African American families. *Journal of Black Psychology, 21(4),* 408–423.

Idler, E.L. (1987). Religious involvement and the health of the elderly: Some hypotheses and an initial test. *Social Forces, 66(1),* 226–238.

James, S.A. (1994). John Henryism and the health of African Americans. *Culture, Medicine & Psychiatry,* 163–182.

Johnson, C.C., Nicklas, T.A., Arbeit, M.L., Harsha, D.W., Mott, D.S., Hunter, S.M., Wattigney, W., & Berenson, G.S. (1991). Cardiovascular intervention for high-risk families: The Heart Smart Program. *Southern Medical Journal, 84(11),* 1305–1312.

Johnson, E.H., & Gant, L.M. (1996). The association between anger-hostility & hypertension. In H.W. Neighbors & J.S. Jackson (Eds.), *Mental health in Black America* (pp. 95–116). Thousand Oaks, CA: Sage.

Jonas, B.S., & Lando, J.F. (2000). Negative affect as a prospective risk factor for hypertension. *Psychosomatic Medicine, 62(2),* 188–196.

Jones-Webb, R. (1998). Drinking patterns and problems among African-Americans: Recent findings. *Alcohol Health & Research World, 22(4),* 260–264.

Kabat, G.C., Morabia, A., & Wynder, E.L. (1991). Comparison of smoking habits of Black and Whites in a case-control study. *American Journal of Public Health, 81,* 1483–1486.

Kingston, R.S., & Nickens, H.W. (2000). Racial and ethnic differences in health: Recent trends, current patterns, future directions. In *America Becoming: Racial Trends & Their Consequences, Vol. 2* (pp. 253–310). Washington, DC: National Academy of Sciences.

Koenig, H., Smiley, M., & Gonzalez, J.A.P. (1988). *Religion, health & aging.* Westport, CT: Greenwood Press.

Kumanyika, S.K. (1998). Obesity in African Americans: Biobehavioral consequences of culture. *Ethnicity & Disease, 8(1)*, 93–96.

Laumann, E.O., & Youm, Y. (1999). Racial/ethnic group differences in the prevalence of sexually transmitted diseases in the United States: A network explanation. *Sexually Transmitted Diseases, 26*, 250–261.

Lazarus, R.S., & Folkman, S. (1984). *Stress, appraisal & coping.* New York: Springer.

Levin, J.S., Chatters, L.M., & Taylor, R.J. (1995). Religious effects on health status and life satisfaction among Black Americans. *Journals of Gerontology: Series B: Psychological Science & Social Sciences, 50(3)*, S1545–S1563.

Lillie-Blanton, M., Brodie, M., Rowland, D., Altman, D., & McIntosh, M. (2000). Race, ethnicity, and the health care system: Public perceptions and experiences. *Medical Care Research & Review, 57(Supplement 1)*, 218–235.

Lugaila, T. (1998). Marital status and living arrangements: March, 1997. *Current Population Reports.* Washington, DC: U.S. Bureau of the Census, pp. 20–514.

Mattis, J. (1997). Spirituality and religiosity in the lives of Black women. *African American Research Perspectives, 3*, 56–60.

McAdoo, H.P. (1998). African-American families: Strengths and realities. In H.I. McCubbin, E.A. Thompson, A.I. Thompson, & J.A. Futrell (Eds.), *Resiliency in African-American families* (pp. 17–30). Thousand Oaks, CA: Sage.

McCabe, K.M., Clark, R., & Barnett, D. (1999). Family protective factors among urban African American youth. *Journal of Clinical Child Psychology, 28(2)*, 137–150.

McEwen, B.S. (1998). Stress, adaptation, and disease: Allostasis and allostatic load. In S.M. et al. (Eds.), *Annals of the New York Academy of Sciences. Vol. 840: Neuroimmunomodulation: Molecular aspects, integrative systems, and clinical advances* (pp. 33–44). New York: New York Academy of Sciences.

McEwen, B.S., & Seeman, T. (1999). Protective and damaging effects of mediators of stress: Elaborating and testing the concepts of allostasis and allostatic load. In N.E. Adler, M. Marmot, B.S. McEwen, & J. Stewart (Eds.), *Socioeconomic status and health in industrial nations: Social, psychological, and biological pathways* (pp. 30–47). New York: New York Academy of Sciences.

McKinnon, J., & Humes, K. (2000). The Black Population in the United States: Population characteristics. *Current Population Reports, No. P20 530.* U.S. Census Bureau. Washington, DC: U.S. Department of Commerce.

McLoyd, V. (1997). The impact of poverty and low socioeconomic status on the socioemotional functioning of African-American children and adolescents: Mediating effects. In R.D. Taylor & M.C. Wang (Eds.), *Social and emotional adjustment and family relations in ethnic minority families* (pp. 7–34). Mahwah, NJ: Lawrence Erlbaum Associates.

McLoyd, V. (1998). Socioeconomic disadvantage and child development. *American Psychologist, 53(2)*, 185–204.

Minkler, M., & Fuller-Thompson, E. (1999). The health of grandparents raising grandchildren: Results of a national study. *American Journal of Public Health, 89(9)*, 1384–1389.

Minkler, M., Fuller-Thompson, E., Miller, D., & Driver, D. (1997). Depression in grandparents raising grandchildren: Results of a national longitudinal study. *Archives of Family Medicine, 6*, 445–452.

Moore, M.R., & Chase-Landsdale, P.L. (2001). Sexual intercourse and pregnancy among African American girls in high-poverty neighborhoods: The role of family and perceived community environment. *Journal of Marriage & the Family, 63(4)*, 1146–1157.

Morrow, C.E., Bandstra, E.S., Anthony, J.D., Ofir, A.Y., Yue, L., & Reyes, M.L. (2001). Influence of prenatal cocaine exposure on full-term infant neurobehavioral functioning. *Neurotoxicology & Teratology, 23(6)*, 533–544.

Musgrave, C.F., Allen, C.E., & Allen, G.J. (2002). Spirituality and health for women of color. *American Journal of Public Health, 92(4)*, 557–560.

Myers, H.F., Anderson, N.B., & Strickland, T. (1996). Biobehavioral perspective for research on stress and hypertension in Black adults: Theoretical and empirical issues. In R. Jones (Ed.), *African American mental health* (pp. 1–36). Hampton, VA: Cobb & Henry.

Myers, H.F., & Hwang, W-C. (in press). Cumulative psychosocial risks & resilience: A conceptual perspective on ethnic health disparities in late life. In *Ethnic disparities in aging health*. Washington, DC: National Research Council.

Myers, H.F., & Hwang, W-C. (2003). Ethnocultural issues in behavioral medicine. In L.M. Cohen, D.E. McChargue, & F.L. Collins (Eds.), *The Health psychology handbook: Practical issues for the behavioral medicine specialist* (pp. 456–468). Thousand Oaks, CA: Sage.

Myers, H.F., Kagawa-Singer, M., Kumanyika, S.K., Lex, B.W., & Markides, K.S. (1995). Panel III: Behavioral risk factors related to chronic diseases in ethnic minorities. *Health Psychology, 14(7)*, 613–621.

Myers, H.F., Lewis, T.T., & Parker-Dominguez, T. (2002). Stress, coping & minority health: Biopsychosocial perspective on ethnic health disparities. In G. Bernal, J. Trimble, K. Burlew, & F. Leong (Eds.), *Handbook of racial and ethnic minority psychology*. Thousand Oaks, CA: Sage.

Myers, H.F., & McClure, F. (1993). Psychosocial factors in hypertension in Blacks: The case for an interactional perspective. In J.C.S. Fray & J.G. Douglass (Eds.), *Pathophysiology of hypertension in Blacks* (pp. 90–106). New York: Oxford University Press.

Myers, H.F., & Taylor, S. (1998). Family contributions to risk and resilience in African American children. *Journal of Comparative Family Studies, 29(1)*, 215–229.

Nelson, P.B. (1989). Ethnic differences in intrinsic/extrinsic religious orientation and depression in the elderly. *Archives of Psychiatric Nursing, 3(4)*, 199–204.

Newsom, J.T., & Schulz, R. (1996). Social support as a mediator in the relation between functional status and quality of life in older adults. *Psychology of Aging, 11(1)*, 34–44.

Ni, H., & Cohen, R. (2002). *Trends in health insurance coverage by race/ethnicity among persons under age 65 years of age: United States, 1997–2001*. National Center for Health Statistics. Hyattsville, MD: U.S. Department of Health & Human Services, 2002.

Ofili, E. (2001). Ethnic disparities in cardiovascular health. *Ethnicity & Disease, 11(4)*, 838–840.

Parillo, K.M., Freeman, R.C., Collier, K., & Young, P. (2001). Association between early sexual abuse and adult HIV-risky behaviors among community-recruited women. *Child Abuse & Neglect, 25*, 335–346.

Pruchno, R. (1999). Raising grandchildren: The experiences of Black and White grandmothers. *The Gerontologist, 39(2)*, 209–221.

Reid, P.T., & Bing, V.M. (2000). Sexual role of girls and women: An ethnocultural lifespan perspective. In C.B. Travis et al. (Eds.), *Sexuality, society, and feminism* (pp. 141–166). Washington, DC: American Psychological Association.

Repetti, R.L., Taylor, S.E., & Seeman, T.E. (2002). Risky families: Family social environments and the mental and physical health of offspring. *Psychological Bulletin, 128(2)*, 330–366.

Richardson, G.A., Ryan, C., Willford, J., Day, N.L., & Goldschmidt, L. (2002). Prenatal alcohol and marijuana exposure: Effects on neuropsychological outcomes at 10 years. *Neurotoxicology & Teratology, 24(3)*, 311–320.

Rosamond, W.D., Ammerman, A.S., Holliday, J.L., Tawney, K.W., Hunt, K.J., Keyseling, T.C., Will, J.C., & Mokdad, A.H. (2000). Cardiovascular disease risk factor intervention in low-income women: The Nortch Carolina WISEWOMAN project. *Preventive Medicine, 31(4)*, 370–379.

Saab, P.G., Llabre, M.M., Fernander-Scott, A., Copen, R., Ma, M., DiLillo, V., McCalla, J.R., Davalos, M., & Gallaher, C. (2000). Ethnic differences in blood pressure regulation. In P.M. McCabe et al. (Eds.), *Stress, coping & cardiovascular disease* (pp. 145–180). Mahwah, NJ: Lawrence Erlbaum Associates.

Sandman, C.A., Wadhwa, P.D., Chicz-DeMet, A., Dunkel-Schetter, C., & Porto, M. (1997). Maternal stress, HPA activity, and fetal/infant outcomes. *Annals of the New York Academy of Sciences, 814*, 266–275.

Schoendorf, K.C., Hogue, C.J.R., Kleinman, J.C., & Rowley, D. (1992). Mortality among infants of Black as compared with White college-educated parents. *New England Journal of Medicine, 326*, 1522–1526.

Seeman, T.E., Bruce, M.L., & McAvay, G.J. (1996). Social network characteristics and onset of ADL disability: MacArthur studies of successful aging. *Journals of Gerontology, Series B: Psychological Sciences & Social Sciences, 51(4)*, S191–S200.

Seeman, T.E., Singer, B.H., Rowe, J.W., Horwitz, R.I., & McEwen, B.S. (1997). Price of adaptation—allostatic load and its health consequences: MacArthur studies of successful aging. *Archives of Internal Medicine, 157*, 2259–2268.

Shiono, P.H., Rauh, V.A., Park, M., Lederman, S.A., & Suskar, D. (1997). Ethnic differences in birthweight: Lifestyle and other factors. *American Journal of Public Health, 87(5),* 787–793.

Singer, B., & Ryff, C.D. (1999). Hierarchies of life histories and associated health risks. In N.E. Adler, M. Marmot, B.S. McEwen, & J. Stewart (Eds.), *Socioeconomic status and health in industrial nations: Social, psychological, and biological Pathways* (pp. 96–115). New York: New York Academy of Sciences.

Smedley, B.D., Stith, A.Y., & Nelson, A.R. (2002). *Unequal treatment: Confronting racial & ethnic disparities in health care.* Washington, DC: National Academies Press.

Snowden, L.R. (1998). Racial differences in informal help-seeking for mental health problems. *Journal of Community Psychology, 26(5),* 429–438.

Strawbridge, W.J., Shema, S.J., Cohen, R.D., Roberts, R.E., & Kaplan, G.A. (1998). Religiosity buffers effects of some stressors on depression but exacerbates others. *Journal of Gerontology, Behavior, Psychology, and Social Sciences, 53(3),* S118–126.

Substance Abuse & Mental Health Services Administration (SAMHSA). (2002). *Illicit drug Use. 2001 National Household Survey of Applied Studies.* Office of Applied Studies.

Szinovacz, M.E. (1998). Grandparents today: A demographic profile. *The Gerontologist,* 38, 37–52.

Taylor, R.J. (1993). Religion and religious observances. In J.S. Jackson, L.M. Chatters, & R.J. Taylor (Eds.), *Aging in Black America* (pp. 101–123). Thousand Oaks, CA: Sage.

Taylor, R.D., Roberts, D., & Jacobson, L. (1997). Stressful life events, psychological well being and parenting in African American mothers. *Journal of Family Psychology, 11(4),* 436–446.

Taylor, R.J., Tucker, M.B., Chatters, L.M., & Jayakody, R. (1997). Recent demographic trends in African American family structure. In R.J. Taylor, J.S. Jackson, & L.M. Chatters (Eds.), *Family life in Black America* (pp. 14–62). Thousand Oaks, CA: Sage.

Unger, J.G., McAvay, G., Bruce, M.L., Berkman, L., & Seeman, T. (1999). Variation in the impact of social network characteristics on physical functioning in elderly persons: MacArthur studies of successful aging. *Journal of Gerontology, Series B: Psychological Sciences & Social Sciences, 54(5),* S245–S251.

U.S. Census Bureau. (March 1999). *The Black population in the United States: March 1999 (update).* Washington, DC: The U.S. Census Bureau, U.S. Department of Commerce, PPL-130, December.

U.S. Department of Justice. (2002). Corrections Statistics. Washington, DC: Office of Justice Programs, Bureau of Justice Statistics Bulletin, U.S. Department of Justice.

Wade-Gayles, G. (Ed.). (1995). *My soul is a witness: African-American women's spirituality.* Boston: Beacon Press.

Wallace, J.M., Bachman, J.G., O'Malley, P.M., & Johnston, L.D. (1995). Racial/ethnic differences in adolescent drug use. In G.J. Botvin, S. Schinke, & M.O. Orlandi (Eds.), *Drug abuse prevention with multiethnic youth* (pp. 59–80). Thousand Oaks, CA: Sage.

Wickrama, K.A.S., Conger, R.D., Wallace, L.E., & Elder, J. (1999). The intergenerational transmission of health-risk behaviors: Adolescent lifestyles and gender moderating effects. *Journal of Health & Social Behavior, 40(3),* 258–272.

Wilcox, S., Castro, C., King, A.C., Houseman, R., & Brownson, R.C. (2000). Determinants of leisure time physical activity in rural compared with urban older and ethnically diverse women in the United States. *Journal of Epidemiology & Community Health, 54(9),* 667–672.

Williams, D.R. (1999). Race, socioeconomic status, and health: The added effects of racism and discrimination. In N.E. Adler et al. (Eds.), *Socioeconomic status and health in industrial nations: Social, psychological, and biological pathways* (pp. 173–188). New York: New York Academy of Sciences.

Williams, D.R. (2000). Racial variations in adult health status: Patterns, paradoxes, and prospects. *America becoming: Racial trends and their consequences, Vol. 2.* (pp. 371–410). Washington, DC: National Academy of Sciences.

Williams, D.R., Yu, Y., Jackson, J.S., & Anderson, N.B. (1997). Racial differences in physical and mental health: Socio-economic status, stress and discrimination. *Journal of Health Psychology, 2(3),* 335–351.

Wingood, G.M., & DiClemente, R.J. (1997). The effects of an abusive primary partner on the condom use and sexual negotiation practices of African American women. *American Journal of Public Health, 87,* 1016–1018.

Woods, T.E., Antoni, M.H., Ironson, G.H., & Kling, D.W. (1999). Religiosity is associated with affective status in symptomatic HIV-infected African-American women. *Journal of Health Psychology, 4(3)*, 317–326.

Wyatt, G.E., Forge, N.G., & Guthrie, D. (1998). Family constellation and ethnicity: Current and lifetime HIV-related risk taking. *Journal of Family Psychology, 121*, 93–101.

Wyatt, G.E., Myers, H.F., Williams, J.K., Kitchen, C.R., Loeb, T., Carmona, J.V., Wyatt, L.E., Chin, D., & Presley, N. (2002). Does a history of trauma contribute to HIV risk for women of color? Implications for prevention and policy. *American Journal of Public Health, 92(4)*, 660–665.

Yanek, L.R., Becker, D.M., Moy, T.F., Gittlesohn, J., & Koffman, D.M. (2001). Project Joy: Faith based cardiovascular health promotion for African American women. *Public Health Reports, 116 Suppl. 1*, 68–81.

CHAPTER 28

Disparities in Medication Use, Action, and Prescribing for African Americans

AKIMA R. HOWARD, CAROLYN FORD, AND
HUGH M. MCLEAN

INTRODUCTION

A growing body of medical evidence suggests that significant treatment-related disparities exist between Black Americans and other racial groups (Agency for Healthcare Research and Quality [AHRQ], 2001). In general, not only do Blacks differ genetically in their response to certain medications, but also cultural and social differences concerning medication use and prescribing widen the health gap further (Matthews & Johnson, 2000). It is for these and other reasons that pharmaceutical issues have to be discussed in any comprehensive attempt to address racial health disparities. This chapter focuses on important global medication-related issues. More specifically, genetic variations in drug response, important medication-related treatment barriers that affect the health status of Black Americans, and measures to reduce modifiable disparities are discussed.

FACTORS AFFECTING MEDICATION USE

According to the National Pharmaceutical Council, cultural beliefs have a profound impact on patients' attitude and behavior regarding their own health and treatment (Levy & Hawks, 1999). Cultural beliefs regarding drug effects are perhaps the most significant factors in determining medication compliance or adherence (Levy & Hawks, 1999). For example, African Americans often believe that medications are too strong or that addiction to chronically prescribed medications will occur (Snow, 1993). This belief often leads to premature discontinuation of drug therapy or to self-regulation of medication. Immigrants from different countries with different medical cultures may also have different expectations regarding prescribed medicines, drug side-effect profile, dosage form preference, or other aspects of drug therapy. This clash between patient and provider expectations may result in medication noncompliance or nonadherence. Unfortunately, it has been shown that patients labeled as noncompliant or nonadherent are sometimes considered "undesirable" and do not receive the best care from providers (Smedley et al., 2002).

This problem is magnified by the fact that the majority of health-care providers are not of ethnically diverse backgrounds. According to a 1998 report from the U.S. Department of Health and Human Services (DHHS) Health Resources and Services Administration (HRSA), minorities made up less than 10 percent of the health professions workforce. Important differences in how major ethnic groups interact with providers and view disease and prescription medications have serious health status implications. All health professionals, especially pharmacists, regardless of ethnic or racial background, must be trained to provide culturally competent care to culturally diverse clients.

PROBLEMS WITH MEDICATION ADHERENCE

Adherence versus Compliance

The term "medication compliance" has become outdated and replaced by "medication adherence" for several reasons. According to *Merriam-Webster's Collegiate Dictionary* (1998), compliance is defined as yielding to the wishes of others. Consequently, with medication compliance, patients are expected to follow the health-care provider's orders and comply with their instructions. This way of thinking implies that there is no place for the patient in the drug therapy decision-making process. The term "compliance" also gives the connotation that the recommended advice is always correct and in the patient's best interest. This is assuming that the condition being treated has been properly diagnosed, that the treatment is appropriate and effective, that drug therapy does more good than harm, and that the prescribed regimen is understandable and achievable (i.e., directions are simple, dosing is convenient, cost and side effects are acceptable). The reality is, however, that patients often recover without having rigidly complied with their health-care provider's directions. In some instances, patients do not recover, and some even get worse. There are instances when medications should be discontinued, such as when unpleasant or dangerous adverse effects develop. There are even times when drugs are prescribed unnecessarily in an effort to placate the patient. The aforementioned facts further challenge the premise on which compliance is based.

Causes of Medication Nonadherence

Nevertheless, medication adherence is a very significant issue. Nonadherence has been designated by the National Council on Patient Information and Education as "America's other drug problem" (Bond & Hussar, 1991). In 1990, DHHS reported that 48 percent of the U.S. population and 55 percent of the elderly fail to comply in some way with their medication regimen (Kessler, 1992). Although all cases of medication nonadherence are not serious enough to impair health, studies have documented that 25 percent of patients use medication in a way that poses some threat to their health (Sackett & Snow, 1979; Weigman & Cohen, 1999).

Several studies have identified multiple factors that contribute to medication nonadherence (Rantucci, 1997). The main contributors are patient's health beliefs, nature of communication between the patient and the health professional, and psychological factors. Health beliefs that contribute to medication nonadherence include the perceived lack of seriousness of the disease, ignorance regarding implications of nontreatment, perceived ineffectiveness of the recommended treatment, lack of social support, complex medication regimens, lengthy therapies, and the presence of adverse effects.

Beliefs regarding drug properties and effects are of central importance in determining medication adherence. Attitudes toward medicines tend to be driven by national characteristics, culture, and philosophy (Levy & Hawks, 1999). Some African Americans complain that some medicines are too strong, "too chemical," and that they do not want to get hooked (Snow, 1993). Many prefer their own home remedies to those that doctors might prescribe. These patients usually go to the doctor for diagnoses, not for treatment. Others go to make sure that their treatments are doing the job or that their condition is under control.

Barriers in communication also contribute to nonadherence. Lack of direct contact with the doctor, lack of explicit, appropriate, clear, and adequate treatment instructions, and lack of feedback also contribute to medication nonadherence. Other factors include perceived lack of strategies by health professionals to modify cultural attitudes and beliefs, perceived unfriendliness and lack of concern for patient, low patient satisfaction with the patient–provider encounter, and failure to involve the patient in the decision-making process about his or her own health.

Psychological barriers that tend to promote medication nonadherence include a history of negative experience or no experience with a particular medication. From time to time, patients have a psychological desire to exert control over the disease or condition that appears to be beyond control, which may lead to nonadherence. In 2002, the Commonwealth Fund released a significant report that suggests significant problems still exist in health-care processes that influence a patient's decision to adhere to medical treatment (Betancourt et al., 2002). The study reported that communication problems between patients and physicians are very common. Patients in this study reported that their doctor did not listen to everything they had to say, they did not fully understand their doctor, or they had questions during the visit but did not ask them. A large percentage (25 percent) of respondents reported that they did not follow their doctor's advice. Many who did so reported disagreement with the doctor. Patients also cited medication cost as a barrier to complying with physician's advice. In an attempt to save money, some patients may "ration" their medications (take less than prescribed) in an attempt to make it last over a longer period of time. Finally, difficulty understanding health information, including instructions for taking prescriptions, prevented compliance as well.

TRUST AND CULTURAL COMPATIBILITY BETWEEN PATIENT AND PRESCRIBER

Understanding and respect for the culture of minority patients are essential to building a trusting relationship. It is believed that trust is perhaps the most significant determinant of treatment adherence and may be more important to therapeutic outcome than any medical procedure or drug. If patients perceive that the health-care provider is judging them negatively, trust will not develop and willingness to accept treatment recommendations may be adversely influenced.

According to Betancourt et al. (2002), minority patients still feel that they are being treated with disrespect during health-care visits. Reasons for feeling this way often were related to aspects of communication—the patient thought he or she was spoken to rudely, talked down to, or ignored. Seventeen percent of these patients attributed the perceived disrespectful treatment to the fact that they lacked or had little medical insurance (Collins et al., 2002).

The distrust that African Americans have for the medical system is also often linked to the infamous Tuskegee Syphilis Study funded by the Centers for Disease Control (Edgar, 1992). Black male participants in the Tuskegee Study, which began in 1932, were told that they were being treated, when in reality they received very little or no treatment (Edgar, 1992). This practice continued even after it was discovered that syphilis could be treated effectively with penicillin.

Many minority patients place great value on nonverbal communication of health-care providers. Minority patients are very sensitive to eye contact, body posture, tone of voice, facial expression, and head nods, especially of nonminority providers (McDonagh, 2000). Moreover, if a language barrier exists, even greater importance is placed on body language. Some patients may also feel slighted if the doctor does not physically examine them. Adequacy of the aforementioned gestures serves to foster a trusting relationship between patient and provider. Lack of trust often directly results in nonadherence to medical advice (King, 2002).

Some pharmacies have responded to the call to eliminate the physical barriers that separate the patient from the pharmacist in an attempt to reduce the perception of desired isolation from patients. To accomplish this, many drugstores have converted the traditional pharmacy layout of high counters and glass walls that separate the pharmacist from the patient to a more open, accessible layout.

Cultural stereotyping has also contributed to the respect issue, and, in some instances, it has adversely affected patient health outcomes. The most recent findings by the Institute of Medicine suggest that some providers assume that minority patients are less able to participate in therapeutic programs (Smedley et al., 2002). Therefore, these providers may not involve minority patients in health education or preventive medicine or may even delay referral to specialists such as diabetes educators. The providers believe that the minority patients either lack the required skills or will not benefit from participation.

COST OF PHARMACEUTICALS AND ACCESS TO HEALTH INSURANCE

Prescription Drug Spending

The high cost of prescription medication is a nationwide concern. In 1980, health-care expenditures were 8.9 percent of the gross national product; by 2008, they are expected to reach 16.2 percent (Posey, 2000). The cost of prescription drugs in 1998 accounted for 20 percent of the total increase in health-care costs. It is the fastest growing segment within health care and is widely perceived as driving the jump in payers' costs, employers' premiums, and employees' copayments. A Blue Cross Blue Shield report predicts that drug prices will continue to rise by 15 percent to 18 percent for at least the next five years (Posey, 2000).

Prescription drug use is increasing, more people are on prescription drugs as the population ages, and medicines that are more expensive are being used. Moreover, increases in drug spending can be attributed to the fact that prescription drugs are being used for conditions that were once pharmacologically untreatable or once treated with medical or surgical procedures.

Unfortunately, elderly people, especially minorities, are affected the most by rising prescription costs. Although advances are being made regarding prescription drug benefits for seniors and a Medicare drug benefit will be implemented on January 1, 2006, historically, Medicare has not covered prescription drugs. Annual prescription costs last year rose 18 percent for women 70–79 and 20 percent for women 80 and older. A person on a fixed income such as Social Security will get an annual increase of only about 3.5 percent. Thus, high drug prices are forcing many seniors and people with chronic diseases to choose between essential medication and the necessities of life. Senior citizens are forced to make a choice between food and medicine, between paying their rent and having medicine, between having heat and other utilities and having medicine.

Many minority patients, regardless of their age, also reported that they cannot afford prescription medicines (Betancourt et al., 2002). African Americans and Hispanics were more likely than Whites and Asians to report that following physician's medical advice is too costly (30 percent and 41 percent versus 24 percent and 27 percent, respectively).

Inability to afford prescriptions can adversely affect health outcomes and increase overall health-care costs. Some patients who decide to do without the drugs will either suffer, get sicker and end up in the emergency room or hospital at very high costs to Medicare and the health-care system in general, or even die.

Access to Health Insurance

Disparities in health care are often attributed to differences in income and insurance status. In 2000, the Census Bureau determined that 38.7 million Americans had no health insurance (Mills, 2000). Of the Americans who did not have insurance in 2000, 18.5 percent were Black (Mills, 2000).

More recent data show that in the first half of the year 2001, approximately 20.2 percent of noninstitutionalized Blacks under the age of 65 years were without health insurance (Rhoades, 2001).

The lack of insurance in some ethnic groups is even more dramatic (for instance, among Hispanic men, 37 percent have no health insurance). Nonetheless, declines in insurance coverage explained only one-fifth of the change in access to a usual source of care.

The literature suggests that although income and insurance status are important, they are by no means the only factors. Uninsured patients may be any of the following (Campbell, 1999; Kronick & Gilmer, 1999):

• Less likely to have a regular source of care and a recent physician visit;
• More likely to delay seeking medical care;
• Less likely to use preventive services;
• Experience a generally higher mortality and a specifically higher in-hospital mortality rate;
• Three times more likely than privately insured individuals to experience adverse health outcomes; and
• Four times more likely than insured patients to be hospitalized and to seek emergency medical care.

It is important to note that recent findings of the Institute of Medicine report revealed that even minority patients with private health insurance still receive lower-quality care than Whites (Smedley et al., 2002). This report indicated that the pattern was so widespread and severe that it contributed to the higher death rates and shorter life spans. Factors such as language barriers, inadequate insurance coverage, bias among doctors and nurses, and a significant lack of minority physicians were reported to be confounding variables as to why minority patients received inferior treatment.

FACTORS AFFECTING DRUG ACTION IN THE BODY

Genetic Variations That Affect Drug Response

It has been axiomatically established that individual patients, particularly from different races, may respond differently to medications. The underlying reasons for the interindividual and interracial variability in drug response have not been fully elucidated. Several plausible rationalizations have been presented in an attempt to clarify this conundrum. Among them are environmental factors, diet, culture, and genetics. The lack of a thorough understanding of the numerous factors that influence this variability in drug response has been rather vexing to both physicians and patients. It is now becoming increasingly obvious that pharmacogenetics play a significant role in the interracial variability in drug response. In fact, racial and ethnic differences in drug responses have been reported for a variety of drugs (Matthews & Johnson, 2000; Poolsup et al., 2000; Wood, 2001). One factor that has posed an impediment to the elucidation of racial differences in therapeutic response, from an African American perspective, is the fact that Black Americans are quite often underrepresented in clinical trials (Exner et al., 2001; King, 2002).

Although there are several interconnected reasons for the interracial and intraracial variability in drug actions, ostensibly the most important aspects are genetic variability between individuals in their ability to biotransform (metabolize) drugs, due to expression of polymorphic enzymes, and variability in pharmacodynamic processes, due to receptor polymorphisms (Poolsup et al., 2000; Wood, 2001). Several studies exist that fully explain the role of polymorphisms on the biotransformation of drugs (Goldstein, 2001; Ingleman-Sundberg, 2001; Lee et al., 2002). For an elaborate treatise on this topic, the reader is referred to the aforementioned references. This chapter, however, focuses on pharmacogenetics as it relates to the more common polymorphisms that are germane to the differences between African Americans and Caucasians, in terms of their response to drug therapy.

Role of the Cytochrome P450 Enzyme System

A vast majority of drugs are biotransformed by the cytochrome P450 enzyme system (CYP450). This system consists of numerous families, of which CYP1, CYP2, and CYP3 are primarily responsible for the elimination of several commonly used drugs. Within each family, there are subfamilies, which are denoted by letters such as CYP2A, CYP2B, and CYP2C. The members of these subfamilies are referred to as isoenzymes. These isoenzymes are intimately involved in the biotransformation of a variety of xenobiotics. The activities of these isoenzymes vary between persons and populations. This variation has been ascribed to environmental, physiologic, and genetic factors. Many of these isoenzymes exhibit significant polymorphisms that divide the population into essentially two phenotypes (Wennerholm et al., 2002), extensive metabolizers and poor metabolizers. The clinical significance of these polymorphisms is that patients whose genes encode drug-metabolizing enzymes that exhibit less than normal activity would have impaired biotransformation of the drugs that are normally substrates for these enzymes. Such a person would be classified as a poor metabolizer of these specific drugs, whereas patients whose genes encode drug-metabolizing enzymes that exhibit normal activity would be referred to as extensive metabolizers. The frequencies of these polymorphisms are distributed differently among different racial and ethnic groups. Therefore, the proportion of people with impaired metabolism of a particular drug differs among these racial and ethnic groups (Bertilsson, 1995; Wood, 2001; Xie et al., 2001).

Debrisoquin hydroxylase (CYP2D6) is involved in the biotransformation of more than 30 commonly prescribed medications (Evans et al., 1993). These include analgesics such as codeine, beta receptor antagonists such as propranolol, antidepressants such as imipramine, and antipsychotics such as haloperidol and thioridazine. Previous studies have established that approximately 7–10 percent of U.S. and European Caucasians are deficient in CYP2D6 activity, whereas only approximately 1.9 percent of American Blacks exhibit a CYP2D6 deficient trait (Evans et al., 1993). The clinical significance of this difference is that American Blacks, who are classified as extensive metabolizers, would be less likely than Caucasians to experience exaggerated effects of drugs that are primarily inactivated by CYP2D6. The remainder of this section focuses on the effects that select CYP450 isoenzymes (e.g., CYP2D6) have on select drugs that are used to treat diseases that disproportionately affect Blacks.

Cardiovascular Agents.   Edeki et al. (1995) reported that the beta adrenergic receptor antagonism occasioned by timolol is more pronounced in individuals who have diminished CYP2D6 activity (poor metabolizers), than in extensive metabolizers. This intimates that African Americans may not exhibit the same response to beta blockers as Caucasians (Matthews & Johnson, 2000).

There are other plausible rationalizations for the differences between African Americans and Caucasians, in terms of their response to beta adrenergic blockers. It has been suggested that differences in plasma renin activity may be the underlying reason. This notion is supported by the fact that a significantly higher percentage of Caucasians have higher plasma renin activity than Black Americans. In addition to blocking beta adrenergic receptors, beta blockers are also thought to elicit their therapeutic response by lowering plasma renin activity, thus rendering them less effective in African Americans (Matthews & Johnson, 2000). In addition, several reports have suggested that another genetically determined variable that may account for the interracial difference in response to beta blockers may be polymorphisms of the beta adrenergic receptors (Johnson, 1993; Matthews & Johnson, 2000; Wood, 2001). It has been postulated that the distribution of adrenergic receptor polymorphisms differs significantly among populations of different racial backgrounds, including Whites, Blacks, and Asians (Wood, 2001).

Another class of cardiovascular drugs that has exhibited different therapeutic efficacy in African Americans and Caucasians is angiotensin converting enzyme (ACE) inhibitors. The consensus is that there is diminished response to ACE inhibitors in African Americans, compared to Caucasians (Exner et al., 2001; Matthews & Johnson, 2000). The prevailing rationalization for this disparity is the fact that African Americans have lower renin levels than Caucasians, and thus it is not surprising that ACE inhibitors are generally not as efficacious, when administered alone, in African Americans as in Caucasians. For instance, in a recent study, it was shown that enalapril (an ACE inhibitor) was associated with a significant reduction in the risk of hospitalization for heart failure among White patients with left ventricular dysfunction, but not among similar Black American patients (Exner et al., 2001).

Several lines of evidence now seem to indicate that other genetically determined variables may be involved. It has been suggested that the long-term benefits of ACE inhibition may be related to factors other than a reduction in circulating angiotensin (Baruch et al., 1999; Exner et al., 2001). According to Baruch et al., ACE inhibition results in increased kinin activity, which may exert favorable long-term effects on the heart, through the release of endogenous nitric oxide, which is a known vasodilator. The bioactivity of endogenous nitric oxide is reportedly lower in Blacks than in Whites, perhaps related to polymorphisms of the endothelial nitric oxide synthase receptors (Wood, 2001).

Anticoagulants.   Another CYP450 isoenzyme that exhibits clinically significant polymorphism is CYP2C9, which plays a pivotal role in the inactivation of the isomer of warfarin that is primarily responsible for the drug's anticoagulant effects. Reportedly, two CYP2C9 alleles that produce a phenotype of poor metabolism occur in 11 percent and 8 percent of Caucasians, but only 3 percent and 0.8 percent of African Americans (Wood, 2001; Xie et al., 2001). The clinical import of this polymorphism is that it is likely that African Americans would require a different dose of warfarin than Caucasians to achieve similar anticoagulant effects.

Central Nervous System Agents.   Although it is generally accepted that African Americans respond differently to psychopharmacologic agents than Caucasians, there is still a distinct paucity of well-defined studies designed to ascertain the underlying reasons for this obvious disparity. Nevertheless, an abundance of empirical evidence seems to suggest that there are genetically determined differences between Blacks and Whites, in terms of their biotransformation of psychopharmacologic agents. Several studies have indicated that Black American patients exhibit higher plasma tricyclic antidepressant (TCA) levels, tend to respond better and faster to TCAs, but manifest more deleterious effects than Caucasians (Strickland et al., 1991). The higher plasma TCA levels in Blacks have been ascribed to diminished activity of the enzymes, particularly CYP2C19, that are responsible for their metabolism, compared to Caucasians. This notion is consistent with the fact that Mephenytoin hydroxylase (CYP2C19) has been shown to exhibit interracial differences in polymorphisms. Matthews and Johnson (2000) have reported that in older adults there is a higher incidence of slow metabolizers (18.5 percent) among African Americans than among Caucasians (4.1 percent). The clinical significance of this interracial difference is that CYP2C19 is involved in the biotransformation of a variety of psychopharmacologic agents, including imipramine (TCA), diazepam, mephobarbital, and hexobarbital (Matthews & Johnson, 2000).

Lithium is generally considered the drug of choice for the treatment and prevention of manic episodes. Several lines of evidence now buttress the notion that African Americans have less efficient cell membrane sodium-lithium countertransport than Caucasians, which causes higher red blood cell (RBC)/plasma lithium ratios in African Americans. It has been postulated that intra-RBC lithium concentrations mirror intraneuronal lithium concentrations. Therefore, it seems intuitively obvious that the existence of higher RBC/plasma lithium ratios in Black patients means that the dosage of lithium should be lower for Blacks than Caucasians, in order to achieve similar therapeutic effects and also to minimize the possibility of lithium-induced deleterious effects (Strickland et al., 1991). Other psychopharmacologic agents such as carbamazepine and benzodiazepines appear to exhibit different pharmacokinetic profiles in Black and White patients, perhaps related to the previously mentioned CP2C19 polymorphisms.

Gastrointestinal Agents.   CYP2C19 is also involved in the biotransformation of omeprazole (prilosec), a proton pump inhibitor that is frequently used in combination with amoxicillin to treat *Helicobacter pylori (H. pylori)* infection associated with peptic ulcers. Furuta et al. (1998) reported that the rate of response to the dual therapy of omeprazole and amoxicillin is dependent on the CYP2C19 genotype, ranging from 28 percent in patients who are extensive metabolizers, to 100 percent in those who are poor metabolizers. As mentioned previously, the phenotype of poor metabolizers is fairly rare in Caucasians (2–5 percent), while in older African Americans, the prevalence of slow metabolizers is approximately 18.5 percent. Thus, it is quite likely that dual therapy of omeprazole/amoxicillin might be more efficacious in older African Americans than in Caucasians of all age groups.

Nonsteroidal Anti-inflammatory Agents.   Celecoxib (Celebrex®), a COX-2 inhibitor that is used primarily to treat a variety of inflammatory diseases such as arthritis, has a different pharmacokinetic profile in Black Americans than in Caucasians. Limited data have indicated that plasma concentration of celecoxib is apparently 40 percent higher in African Americans than in Caucasians (Celecoxib, 2000). Although the cause of this disparity is not known, it has been postulated that celecoxib is primarily metabolized by CYP450, which suggests that genetically determined polymorphisms may be involved. The clinical significance of this disparity is also not immediately obvious, but it certainly warrants further investigation.

Nicotine and Related Agents.   Ethnic differences in the biotransformation of nicotine and its metabolite, cotinine, have also been reported. According to Benowitz et al. (1999), the metabolism of nicotine and cotinine is slower in Blacks than in Whites. This disparity is presumably related to polymorphisms in CYP2A6 and UDP glucuronosyltransferase (UGT) enzymes. More research is needed to ascertain if these polymorphisms have significant clinical importance.

SUMMARY/RECOMMENDATIONS

It is immediately obvious that race is an important determinant of drug effectiveness. Clearly, more research needs to be devoted to the underlying causes of these racial differences, with a view to the identification of the genetic determinants, rather than focusing solely on the obvious phenotypic manifestations of race (Wood, 2001). The following recommendations are presented as potential means by which most of the disparities in medication actions can be remedied.

- More research needs to be conducted to ascertain specific polymorphisms in African Americans.
- More research needs to be conducted to ascertain the peculiarities in the pathogenesis of diseases that are prevalent in African Americans.
- Significantly more Blacks should be included in clinical trials of drugs. Attempts should be made to include and study drug effects in different ethnic variations of Blacks especially since the population is not heterogeneous (i.e., Caribbean, African, South American, etc.).
- Prescribers need to be made aware of polymorphisms in metabolizing enzymes and receptors and their clinical import.
- Dosing recommendations should be adjusted to account for pharmacogenetic differences between races.
- Prescribers need to be aware of the fact that phenotyping may yield erroneous results, as there is significant intraracial variability, in terms of drug response.

A thorough understanding of the scope of the interracial differences in drug response would allow for optimal therapy for patients of different racial backgrounds.

SOCIAL FACTORS THAT AFFECT DRUG ACTION IN THE BODY

Many societal, patient-specific variables affect drug action in the body. Diet, smoking status, and alcohol consumption should all be considered when evaluating drug response. Each of these factors has a profound impact on medication activity (Rowland & Tozer, 1995).

Nutrition and Body Weight

Nutritional status and diet can affect drug activity in numerous ways. Kumanyika and Odoms (2001) discuss in detail the implications of nutrition on the health status of Blacks. This section, however, looks at the interconnectedness of nutrition, body weight, and the action of medications in the body.

Obesity is twice as prevalent in Black women as compared to White women (Kumanyika & Odoms, 2001). This obesity may be a result of greater consumption of calories than those expended, which can result in overweight or obesity. The significance of obesity as it relates to drug action in the body is the fact that some drugs are highly lipid-soluble and, therefore, tend to accumulate in patients with excess body weight. The clinical importance is that consumption of highly lipid-soluble drugs in obese or overweight patients may cause the drug to linger in the body longer until it is metabolized to a more polar and excretable compound. Some opioid analgesics and anesthetics are examples of highly lipid soluble drugs.

The manufacturer's recommended dose of most drugs is derived from the results of clinical testing in patients with approximately normal body weight (70kg). Although doses can usually be adjusted on a milligram per kilogram basis, this is an inaccurate method for dosage adjustment in patients who are morbidly obese (Ritschel & Kearns, 1999). Additionally, large variations in normal body weight affect drug concentrations. Patients with higher body weight may experience low drug concentrations, and those with lower body weights may experience higher drug concentrations depending on the distributive properties of the medication.

Conversely, undernourishment may lead to inadequate protein synthesis and protein stores. The resultant effect is hypoalbuminemia or low protein stores in the blood. Many drugs are highly bound to plasma proteins. The degree of protein binding is a significant factor in determining a drug's normal dose since only the unbound (free) drug is pharmacologically active (Ross & Rosenberg, 2000). Patients with low protein stores are more susceptible to toxicity resulting from an increase in free circulating drugs. Additionally, severe protein deficiency can also affect drug metabolism (Rowland & Tozer, 1995).

The sixth report of the Joint National Committee on detection, evaluation, and treatment of high blood pressure (JNC VI) reports that the prevalence of high blood pressure in African Americans is the highest in the world. Black patients receiving medications for hypertension should be counseled regarding the numerous interactions that exist between antihypertensive medications and nutrients. For example, a patient's attempt to reduce salt intake per medical advice may result in a patient's buying salt substitutes. Unfortunately, salt substitutes are high in potassium. Significant drug interactions exist between many antihypertensive medications and potassium. Excessive potassium intake may put patients at risk for cardiac abnormalities and muscle weakness; further complicating and worsening their health status.

Diet can affect drug therapy in various ways and should be considered a part of any drug therapy regimen. Ross and Rosenberg (2000) appropriately encourage us to consider drug–nutrient interactions especially when a medication is over- or underperforming.

Alcohol and Tobacco

Alcohol consumption and cigarette smoking can produce significant interactions with various medicines. The effect of alcohol and tobacco on the action of medications is important, especially since Blacks are associated with a higher incidence of drinking-related complications, and more than 45,000 die annually from tobacco-related diseases (Headen & Robinson, 2001). Both alcohol and tobacco induce liver enzymes (cytochrome P-450) that are responsible for metabolizing drugs in the body. The clinical consequence is diminished drug effects if the drug is being eliminated from the system too rapidly (Ritschel & Kearns, 1999). Alcohol intake and smoking status must be taken into account when designing a drug therapy regime regardless of race or ethnicity.

FACTORS AFFECTING MEDICATION PRESCRIBING

Both patient- and prescriber-related factors contribute to disparate medication prescribing in Black patients. These factors may include unawareness of differences in drug action in minority patients, internal prescriber biases that prevent adequate assessment and communication, influence of the patient's perceived ability to pay for prescribed medicines, and drug therapy decision making based on clinical trials where Black patients were inadequately represented (Krishnan et al., 2001; Schneider et al., 2001; Cleeland et al., 1997). In addition, recent media attention has even focused on pharmacies that are struggling with issues like reimbursement for high-cost medicines from third-party payers (i.e., Medicaid) and fear of theft of controlled substances in certain neighborhoods (Morrison et al., 2000).

MINORITY UNDERREPRESENTATION IN DRUG LITERATURE AND CLINICAL TRIALS

The literature regarding differences in physiologic drug activity in African Americans was discussed previously. Health-care providers must consider these racial variations in drug response and consult the *health disparities literature* when making drug-therapy decisions about minority patients. Although the health disparities literature is growing, there is still a need for more definitive data with exact recommendations regarding drug therapy for Black patients. In the meantime, health professionals need to be aware of the limitations of the current drug literature from which nationally accepted treatment guidelines and health policy are derived (Elnicki et al., 1999).

Since Blacks are disproportionately underrepresented in clinical trials, data from studies conducted in other races may not be applicable (Gifford et al., 2002; Shavers et al., 2002). It is critical that Blacks are fairly and adequately represented in clinical trials, especially those investigating new medicines for diseases that disproportionately affect Blacks (e.g., heart disease, cancer).

Limited participation of Black Americans in clinical trials may be a result of the mistrust in the medical establishment that predates the Tuskegee Syphilis Study, which intentionally withheld treatment from African American men with syphilis in an attempt to study the long-term effects of the disease (Edgar, 1992; cited in Gifford et al., 2002; Harris et al., 1996; cited in Shavers et al., 2002).

Examples from the Literature

HIV Trials.   Gifford et al. (2002) conducted a study sponsored by the Agency for Health Care Research Quality to determine the characteristics of participants in clinical trials for HIV medications and whether or not HIV patients had access to research trials and experimental medication. The investigators found that Blacks and Hispanics were less likely to be participants in clinical trials and to have received medications than Whites. Gifford et al. reported in 1996 that although 49 percent of all patients receiving care for HIV infection were White, they made up 62 percent of HIV-infected adults participating in clinical trials, whereas 33 percent of all patients being treated for HIV infection were Black but made up only 23 percent of HIV-infected adults participating in clinical trials (Gifford et al.).

Gifford et al. (2002) reported that in 1996, 32 percent of HIV-infected adults receiving care attempted to get experimental medications; 24 percent received experimental therapy at some point during their illness, but the other 8 percent were unsuccessful in their attempts to obtain experimental medications. The investigators suggested that the significant difference between limited attempts of Black and Hispanic patients to obtain experimental medication may be due to an unawareness of clinical trials and available drug therapy and negative attitudes regarding clinical research in the Black community (Gifford et al., 2002).

Cancer Trials.   Similar findings were noted in two other studies published in the *Journal of the National Medical Association* that investigated the lack of participation by Blacks in cancer drug research (Mouton et al., 1997; Harris et al., 1996). Lack of awareness of clinical trials and mistrust in the medical system were again cited as barriers to participation. Other factors noted include lack of transportation to the research site and ineffective communication between the researcher and patient (Harris et al., 1996). Since cancer is the second leading cause of death in Blacks, it is imperative that they are appropriately represented in clinical drug trials exploring effective treatments (Brookes, 1997).

Strategies for Inclusion of Blacks in Clinical Trials

In 1987, the National Institutes of Health (NIH) implemented a policy *encouraging* the inclusion of women and minorities in clinical trials in an attempt to address the issue of underrepresentation (NIH, 2001). Despite this policy, data from a review conducted by the U.S. General Accounting Office showed that full implementation and investigator's compliance with the policy could not be assured. Consequently, Congress converted this policy into public law through a section in the NIH Revitalization Act of 1993. This Inclusion Policy was revised in 1994, mandating that women and minorities must be included in all of its clinical research studies. The significance of this revision is that the NIH would not fund any research that did not demonstrate compliance with this policy (NIH, 2001).

Despite the NIH's attempt to reduce disparities in minority participation in clinical research, a significant number of drug trials are funded by other organizations where no such inclusion policy is mandated. The Food and Drug Administration (FDA) is responsible for assuring that medications are safe and effective before they go to market. Often times, however, claims of safety and efficacy are based on information gathered from clinical testing in predominantly non-Black patients. As health-care professionals, providers should deem it their personal duty to stay abreast of opportunities for their patients to become involved in clinical trials.

Useful Web Sites for Information on Clinical Drug Trials

The CenterWatch Clinical Trials Listing Services on the Internet at http://www.centerwatch.com is an excellent source of clinical trial information. The Web site is designed for both patients and health-care professionals. At the CenterWatch Web site, clinical trials are listed by medical area. A patient with a particular disease can identify what clinical trials are being conducted in that disease area, including the geographical location of the study and information about the investigators.

Another useful program is the HopeLink® Clinical Trial Service located on the Internet at http://

www.hopelink.com. It is another free program designed to increase awareness and participation in cancer clinical trials. HopeLink® is a comprehensive database of over 1,800 trials under way for development of new cancer drug therapies. The database provides enrollment and eligibility requirements and accelerates enrollment into clinical trials.

The major factor limiting the effectiveness of these Web-based services is the fact that information dissemination to patients requires computer and Internet access, technology literacy, or an up-to-date health-care provider.

PERCEIVED ABILITY TO PAY FOR MEDICINES AFFECTING PRESCRIBING

The impact that expensive medicines and lack of insurance have on pharmaceutical health disparities was discussed previously. Another factor that further influences this picture is the prescriber's perception of the patient's ability to pay for the medicine or intervention prescribed. As of this writing, much media attention has been given to the actions of some states' attempts to reduce health-care costs. Medicaid patients in some states have been, and others will be, denied access to some of the newest, state-of-the-art medications.

A newspaper article published by the Associated Press describes the process of pharmacy reimbursement from Medicaid and the implications of the newly proposed legislation (Cook, 2002). When a Medicaid patient fills a prescription, the state pays the pharmacy for the cost of the drug plus a flat fee. Several states are considering reducing Medicaid reimbursement to pharmacies. This will result in either a financial loss for the pharmacy filling the prescription, or a loss to the patient who is turned away from the pharmacy because of having Medicaid insurance. This may ultimately influence the medicine that is prescribed if the physician thinks that the patient will have difficulty filling the prescription. Some states are even urging doctors to prescribe less expensive generics in an attempt to explore other cost-cutting options.

In an attempt to halt the restrictions of medicines to poor Medicaid patients, the Pharmaceutical Manufacturers of America has filed a suit in the U.S. District Court for the District of Columbia (Pharmaceutical Manufacturers of America, 2002). The suit requests that the federal court issue a "preliminary injunction invalidating a program approved by the Secretary of Health and Human Services and implemented by the state if Michigan that would restrict Medicaid beneficiaries' access to prescription drugs unless the manufacturer pays the state additional rebates far beyond the significant rebates required by federal law."

As of this writing, the following 12 states have passed legislation or announced administrative plans to restrict access to medicines for Medicaid patients: Florida, Hawaii, Illinois, Louisianna, Michigan, Minnesota, Mississippi, New Mexico, North Carolina, Ohio, Vermont, and West Virginia. Although supporters of the legislation contend that the "prior authorization" mechanism allows doctors to prescribe drugs not covered on the plan, PhRMA insists that the likely effect will be doctors prescribing less expensive medications rather than going through the hassle of obtaining prior authorization (Pharmaceutical Manufacturers of America, 2002). States are actually urging pharmacies to obtain better drug pricing from manufacturers as a means to reduce health-care costs.

PRESCRIBING PAIN MEDICATION IN THE BLACK COMMUNITY

"Oligoanalgesia" is a common finding in the Black community. Oligoanalgesia is a term that was coined to describe the inadequate treatment of pain (Todd et al., 1993; Bonham, 2001; Todd et al., 2000). Many researchers have tried to establish a link between ethnicity and physicians' pain medication prescribing patterns. Bonham (2001) provides a comprehensive review of the health disparities pain literature entitled, "Race, Ethnicity, and Pain Treatment: Striving to Understand the Causes and

Solutions to the Disparities in Pain Treatment." This paper addresses the biological and cultural disparities in pain treatment thoroughly and summarizes the literature from 1985 through 1999. Most of the studies reviewed by Bonham showed that Blacks and Hispanics were more likely to be undertreated for pain as a result of problems with pain assessment, including language and cultural barriers, and prescriber stereotyping that limits appropriate pain treatment (Bonham, 2001).

The issue of improper pain assessment and treatment is even further complicated by the fact that some pharmacies refuse to stock certain narcotics depending on their neighborhood or locale. This may be a result of fear of robbery or drug diversion.

The *New England Journal of Medicine* published an article in the April 2000 issue entitled, "We Don't Carry That"—Failure of Pharmacies in Predominantly NonWhite Neighborhoods to Stock Opioid Analgesics. The impetus for study was the observed difficulty by the investigators' Black and Hispanic patients to obtain commonly prescribed narcotic analgesics from their neighborhood pharmacies (Morrison et al., 2000). The objective of the study was to determine the availability of commonly prescribed opioids in New York City pharmacies. Of the 347 pharmacies surveyed, 51 percent had insufficient pain medications to adequately treat a patient with severe pain. Sixteen percent had no opioids in stock. Of these, 66 percent were in predominantly non-White neighborhoods.

This poses a serious problem for Black patients with legitimate pain control needs. It is not uncommon for pharmacists to question the legitimacy of a prescription solely based on the appearance and mannerisms of the person presenting the prescription. Fear of being party to illicit drug use coupled with sound professional judgment may cause a pharmacist to tell a person that the requested narcotic medication is not in stock and to offer to order it. This usually buys the pharmacist time to verify the legitimacy of the prescription. The fact is, drug diversion is real, and it is irrespective of ethnicity or race. Pharmacists are trained to look out for it. Pharmacy training coupled with one's own preconceived notions about the narcotic-seeking behavior of certain types or classes of patients further contribute to the health disparities picture.

WORKABLE SOLUTIONS

Cultural Competence Training for Health Professionals

Health-care providers should receive cultural competence training in order to establish various methods of effective communication with the patient (Zweber, 2002). Cultural competence is being able to respect and honor the beliefs, interpersonal styles, attitudes, and behaviors of another culture (Zweber, 2002; McDonagh, 2000; Levy & Hawks, 1999). Culture has been determined to have a major impact on patients' health beliefs and participation in the health-care system. Pharmacists, especially, should receive cultural competence training since it is their primary responsibility to provide information about medications and their use. Strategies that pharmacists can use to provide culturally competence pharmaceutical care are listed in Table 28.1.

Drug Company–Sponsored Free or Low-Cost Prescription Programs

The inability of many patients to obtain prescribed medications is a serious obstacle to keeping patients well and keeping health-care costs low. Pharmaceutical companies have developed programs that provide free medication to the uninsured and the working poor. The Pharmaceutical Research and Manufacturers of America has created a directory of the growing number of programs available for needy patients. The directory lists the name of the 31 companies sponsoring the programs in 2002. Copies of the directory can be downloaded from the PhRMA Web site at http://www.phrma.

Table 28.1
Tips on how to provide culturally competent pharmaceutical care

How to Provide Culturally Competent Pharmaceutical Care
Examine how your own cultural background affects your view of health care
Identify the cultures represented in your geographic area or the cultures you serve
Explore the beliefs, experiences, status of cultures that you serve; demonstrate sincere interest and ask open-ended questions; a patient relationship must be established
Acknowledge and respect cultural differences
Do not generalize or stereotype. Within a particular culture, determine individual perceptions, beliefs, preferences, and needs
Enhance the pharmacy environment with welcoming and attractive culturally relevant materials such as pamphlets about their medications and disease process
Develop therapeutic plans that are compatible with cultural beliefs; negotiate and educate other health care providers to accomplish this goal
Use culturally sensitive educational approaches and materials; (i.e., provide audiovisual education for ethnic populations in the waiting area, provide bilingual leaflets on pharmacy procedures: How to get prescriptions filled or what to do if problems arise)
Learn some phrases of the non-English speaking ethnic groups in your community; Create a card file of commonly used pharmacy phrases in the most often used languages
Become familiar with culturally based resources in your community; Have materials available for referral as needed;
Use a trained interpreter for language barriers, if possible. Become familiar with interpreting services; If services are not available, a family may be helpful; In-service pharmacy staff on use of interpreters
Have available prescription labels and auxiliary languages in other languages; pictograms may help to convey some messages
In-service pharmacy staff on cultural sensitivity and competence

Source: McDonagh (2000).

org/searchcures/dpdpap/pa99.pdf. The directory also includes information about how to make a request for assistance, which prescription medicines are covered, and basic eligibility criteria. Table 28.2 lists the companies participating in 2002 and their toll-free telephone numbers.

The task of obtaining medication and information from 31 different pharmaceutical companies can be daunting. In an effort to reduce some of the workload required to obtain medications for patients, several medication assistance programs have been developed. Medicare offers its own computer-based drug assistance program. RxHope® is a privately owned, PhRMA-supported Web portal for physicians to submit applications for patient assistance over the Internet. The Pharmacy Connection is another Internet-based program that helps providers to access free medications for their patients as well. The Pharmacy Connection is presently sponsored by the Virginia Health Care Foundation. Finally, RxAssist is a national program supported by the Robert Wood Johnson Foundation. RxAssist is a user-friendly Web-based tool that assists health-care professionals to easily access these patient assistance programs. Visit their Web site at http://www.rxassist.org.

Prescription Drug Discount Cards for Seniors

Selected pharmaceutical manufacturers offer Discount Drug Card programs to Medicare recipients who have no other prescription coverage. A list of these programs can be retrieved from the RxAssist

Table 28.2
PhRMA drug manufacturers sponsoring drug assistance programs

Pharmaceutical Company	Toll Free Number	Pharmaceutical Company	Toll Free Number
Abbott Laboratories	(800) 222-6885	Merck & Co., Inc.	(800) 994-2111
Agouron Pharmaceuticals, Inc.	(888) 777-6637	Novartis Pharmaceuticals	(800) 257-3273
ALZA Pharmaceuticals	(800) 577-3788	Ortho Biotech, Inc.	(800) 553-3851
Amgen, Inc.	(800) 272-9376	Ortho Dermatological	(800) 797-7737
AstraZeneca	(800) 355-6044	Ortho-McNeil Pharmaceutical, Inc.	(800) 797-7737
Aventis Pasteur	(800) 822-2763	Otsuka America Pharmaceutical, Inc.	(800) 242-7014
Aventis Pharmaceuticals	(800) 221-4025	Parke-Davis	(800) 646-4455
Bayer Corporation Pharmaceutical Division	(800) 468-0894	Pfizer, Inc.	(800) 646-4455
Biogen, Inc.	(800) 456-2255	Pharmacia Corporation	(800) 242-7014
Boehringer Ingelheim Pharmaceuticals, Inc.	(800) 556-8317	Procter & Gamble Pharmaceuticals, Inc.	(800) 830-9049
Bristol-Myers Squibb Company	(800) 332-2056	Rhone-Poulenc Rorer, Inc	(800) 221-4025
Centocor, Inc.	(800) 964-8345	Roche Laboratories, Inc.	(800) 772-5790
DuPont Pharmaceuticals Company	(800) 474-2762	Roxane Laboratories, Inc.	(800) 556-8317
Eisai, Inc.	(800) 226-2072	Sandoz Pharmaceutical Corporation	(800) 257-3273
Fujisawa Healthcare, Inc.	(800) 477-6472	Sankyo Pharma	(800) 268-7327
Genentech, Inc.	(800) 879-4747	Sanofi-Synthelabo, Inc.	(800) 446-6267
Genetics Institute, Inc.	(800) 999-2349	Schering Laboratories/Key Pharmaceuticals	(800) 521-7157
Genzyme Corporation	(800) 745-4447 x17808	Searle	(800) 242-7014
Gilead Sciences, Inc	(800) 226-2056	Serono Laboratories, Inc.	(800) 582-7989
GlaxoSmithKline	(800) 722-9294	Sigma Tau Pharmaceuticals, Inc.	(800) 999-NORD
Hoechst Marion Roussel,Inc.	(800) 221-4025	SmithKline Beecham Pharmaceuticals	(800) 722-9294
Immunex Corporation	(800) 321-4669	Solvay Pharmaceuticals, Inc	(800) 256-8918
Janssen Pharmaceuticals	(800) 652-0227	3M Pharmaceuticals	(800) 328-0255
Knoll Pharmaceutical Company	(800) 240-3820	Takeda Pharmaceuticals America	(877) 825-3327
Lederle Laboratories	(704) 706-5933	Uimed Pharmaceuticals, Inc.	(800) 256-8918
Eli Lilly and Company	(800) 545-6362	Wyeth-Ayerst Laboratories	(704) 706-5933
The Liposome Company, Inc.	(800) 335-5476	Zeneca Pharmaceuticals	(800) 355-6044

Source: Pharmaceutical Manufacturers of America (July 2002).

Web site at http://www.rxassist.org/pdfs/Comparative_Chart_of_Drug_Discount_Cards.pdf. Although information on these programs for seniors is also contained in the 2002 Directory of Patient Assistance Programs on PhRMA's Web site, the RxAssist link extracts information that is relative only to seniors.

There are no enrollment or annual fees for any of these drug card programs. Medications manufactured by each company are covered under the program. Patients who qualify, based on their annual household income, either pay a copay for prescriptions or receive a percentage off the drug cost. Patients enrolled in programs that charge a percentage of the drug cost should be encouraged to shop around until they have identified a pharmacy with the lowest price. Greater savings to the patient will be realized using this method. For programs that charge a flat fee per prescription, shopping around for low prices would be superfluous (from the patient's perspective). The following drug discount cards are available: GlaxoSmithKline Orange Card, LillyAnswers, Novartis Care Card, Pfizer for Living Share Card, and Together Rx Card. The company that sponsors each card is obvious except for the Together Rx Card. This single card may be used for medicines manufactured by several drug companies, including Abbott Laboratories, AstraZeneca, Aventis Pharmaceuticals, Bristol-Myers Squibb Company, GlaxoSmithKline, Johnson & Johnson, and Novartis.

CONCLUSION

Several attempts are being made to address health disparities in the African American community. In 2000, the National Institutes of Health developed the National Center for Minority Health and Health Disparities (NCMHD). This organization serves as "the focal point for coordinating and focusing on minority health disparities research with a focus on basic and clinical research, training, and the dissemination of health information" (http://ncmhd.nih.gov). The institute is providing funding to institutions to develop a robust minority health research environment capable of performing health disparities research and discovering new data that may positively impact the health status of Black Americans. Recently, NCMHD awarded grants to several institutions that successfully responded to an Excellence in Partnerships for Community Outreach, Research on Disparities in Health and Training (Project Export) request for applications (RFA). This looks promising.

The Pharmaceutical Manufacturers of America published a survey of pharmaceutical companies that have drugs in the pipeline to treat diseases that predominantly affect African Americans. This document is entitled the "2002 Survey of New Medicines in Development for Major Diseases Affecting African Americans" and can be accessed from the Pharmaceutical Manufacturers of America Web site (http://www.phrma.org). Of the 249 medicines listed in this document, 90 are for the treatment of cancer, a disease that disproportionately affects Blacks more than Whites.

In addition to increasing health disparities research and advances in pharmaceutical technology and medicines targeted at minorities, much can be accomplished by paying special attention to developing trusting and caring relationships with our patients. Health professionals should attempt to nurture positive relationships as opposed to projecting an impartial, objective, standoffish image.

Pharmacists are well positioned to positively impact the modifiable pharmaceutical disparities discussed throughout this chapter. Staying abreast of the health disparities literature and opportunities for patient participation and prescription assistance programs and clinical trials, and keeping an open mind about cultures and backgrounds that are not similar to our own may help to reduce some of the disparities seen with medication use, action, and prescribing.

REFERENCES

Agency for Healthcare Research and Quality (AHRQ). (2001). Addressing Racial and Ethnic Disparities in Healthcare: Fact Sheet. Retrieved March 31, 2002, from http://www.ahrq.gov/research/disparit.htm

Baruch, L., Anand, I., Cohen, I.S., Ziesche, S., Judd, D., & Cohn, J.N. (1999). Augmented short- and long-term hemodynamic and hormonal effects of an angiotensin receptor blocker added to angiotensin converting enzyme inhibitor therapy in patients with heart failure. *Circulation, 99*, 2658–2664.

Benowitz, N.L., Perez-Stable, E.J., Fong, I., Modin, G., Herrera, B., & Jacob, P. (1999). Ethnic differences in N-glucuronidation of nicotine and cotinine. *The Journal of Pharmacology and Experimental Therapeutics, 291*, 1196–1203.

Bertilsson, L. (1995). Geographical/interracial differences in polymorphic drug oxidation: Current state of knowledge of cytochrome P450 (CYP)2D6 and 2C19. *Clinical Pharmacokinetics, 29*, 192–209.

Betancourt, J., Green, A., & Carrillo, J. (2002). Cultural competence in health care: Emerging frameworks and practical approaches. Retrieved from the Commonwealth Fund Web site at http://www.cmwf.org/ programs/minority/betancourt_culturalcompetence_576.pdf

Bond, W., & Hussar, D. (1991). Detection methods and strategies for improving medication compliance. *American Journal of Hospital Pharmacy, 48*(9), 1978–1988.

Bonham, V.L. (2001). Race, ethnicity, and pain treatment: Striving to understand the causes and solutions to the disparities in pain treatment. *Journal of Law, Medicine, & Ethics, 29*, 52–68.

Brookes, J. (1997, December). Cancer clinical trials: barriers to African American participation. *Closing the Gap*, Retrieved from The Office of Minority Health Resource Center Web site at http://www.omhrc.gov/ctg/ct-07.htm

Campbell, J.A. (1999). Current Population Reports: Health Insurance Coverage 1998. U.S. Department of Commerce, Economics & Statistics Administration. U.S. Census Bureau. October.

Cleeland, C.S., Gonnin, R., Baez, L., Loehrer, P., & Pandya, K.J. (1997). Pain and treatment of pain in minority patients with cancer: The eastern cooperative oncology group minority outpatient study. *Annals of Internal Medicine, 127*, 813–816.

Collins, K.S., Hughes, D.L., Doty, M.M., Ives, B.L., Edwards, J.N., & Tenney K. (March 2002). Diverse communities, common concerns: Assessing health care quality for minority Americans. Retrieved from the Common Wealth Fund Web site: http://www.cmwf.org/programs/minority/collins_diverse communities_523.pdf

Cook, R. (2002, March 11). Pharmacies threaten to drop Medicaid as states consider cutting payments. *Nando Times*. Retrieved March 12, 2002, from http://nandotimes.com/healthscience/story/297560p-2613844c. html

Edeki, T.I., He, H., & Wood, A.J.J. (1995). Pharmacogenetic explanation for excessive beta-blockade following timolol eye drops: Potential for oral-ophthalmic drug interaction. *Journal of the American Medical Association, 274(20)*, 1611–1613.

Edgar, H. (1992). Outside the community. *Hastings Center Report, 22(6)*, 32–35.

Elnicki, D.M., Halperin, A.K., Shockcor, W.T., & Arnoff, S.C. (1999). Multidisciplinary evidence-based medicine journal clubs: Curriculum design and participants' reactions. *American Journal of Medical Science, 317(4)*, 243–246.

Evans, W.E., Relling, M.V., Rahman, A., McLeod, H.L., Scott, E.P., & Lin, J.S. (1993). Genetic basis for a lower prevalence of deficient CYP2D6 oxidative drug metabolism phenotypes in Black Americans. *The Journal of Clinical Investigation, 91*, 2150–2154.

Exner, D.V., Dries, D.L., Domanski, M.J., & Cohn, J.N. (2001). Lesser response to angiotensin-converting enzyme inhibitor therapy in Black as compared with White patients with left ventricular dysfunction. *New England Journal of Medicine, 344(18)*, 1351–1357.

Furuta, T., et al. (1998). Effect of genetic differences in omeprazole metabolism on cure rates for *Helicobacter pylori* infection and peptic ulcer. *Internal Medicine, 129*, 1027–1030.

Gifford, A.L., et al. (2002). Participation in research and access to experimental treatments by HIV-infected patients. *New England Journal of Medicine, 346*, 1373–1382.

Goldstein, J.A. (2001). Clinical relevance of genetic polymorphisms in the human CYP2C subfamily. *British Journal of Clinical Pharmacology, 52*, 349–355.

Harris, Y., Gorelick, P.B., Samuels, P., & Bempong, I. (1996). Why African Americans may not be participating in clinical trials. *Journal of the National Medical Association, 88(10)*, 630–634. Abstract retrieved May 31, 2002, from PubMed database.

Headen, S.W., & Robinson, R.G. (2001). In R.L. Braithwaite & S.E. Taylor (Eds.), *Health issues in the Black community* (pp. 347–383). San Francisco: Jossey-Bass.

Ingelman-Sundberg, M. (2001). Pharmacogenetics: An opportunity for a safer and more efficient pharmacotherapy. *Journal of Internal Medicine, 250*, 186–200.

Johnson, J.A. (1993). Racial differences in lymphocyte beta-receptor sensitivity to propranolol. *Life Sciences, 53*, 297–304.

Joint National Committee on Detection, Evaluation, and Treatment of High Blood Pressure. The sixth report of the Joint National Committee on detection, evaluation, and treatment of high blood pressure (JNC VI). *Archives of Internal Medicine, 157*, 2413–2446.

Kessler, D. (1992). A challenge for American pharmacists. *American Pharmacist, NS32(1)*, 33–36.

King, T.E., Jr. (2002). Racial disparities in clinical trials. *New England Journal of Medicine, 346*, 1400–1402.

Krishnan, J.A., Diette, G.B., & Rand, C.S. (2001). Disparities in outcomes from chronic diseases: Impaired patient–physician partnerships may be an important cause in minorities. *British Medical Journal, 323*, 950.

Kronick, R., & Gilmer, T. (1999). Explaining the decline in health insurance coverage, 1979–1995. *Health Affairs, 18*, 30–47.

Kumanyika, S.K., & Odoms, A. (2001). Nutrition. In R.L. Braithwaite & S.E. Taylor (Eds.), *Health issues in the Black community* (pp. 419–447). San Francisco: Jossey-Bass.

Lee, C.R., Goldstein, J.A., & Pieper, J.A. (2002). Cytochrome P450 2C9 polymorphisms: A comprehensive review of the in-vitro and human data. *Pharmacogentics, 12*, 251–263.

Levy, R., & Hawks, J. (1999). Cultural diversity and pharmaceutical care. Retrieved May 31, 2002, from the National Pharmaceutical Council Web site: http://www.npcnow.org/issues_productlist/PDF/culturaldiversity.pdf

Matthews, H.W., & Johnson, J. (2000). Racial, ethnic, and gender differences in response to drugs. In E.T. Herfindal & D.R. Gourley (Eds.), *Textbook of therapeutics: Drug and disease management* (7th ed., pp. 93–103). Philadelphia: Lippincott, Williams, & Wilkins.

McDonagh, M.S. (2000). Cross-cultural communication and pharmaceutical care. *Drug Topics, 18*, 94–104.

McEvoy, G.K. (Ed.). (2000). American Hospital Formulary Service Drug Information. Bethesda, MD: *American Society of Health-Systems Pharmacists.*

Merriam-Webster's collegiate dictionary (10th ed.). (1998). Springfield, MA: Merriam-Webster.

Mills, R. (2000, September). Health insurance coverage: Current population reports. Retrieved on May 31, 2002, from the U.S. Census Bureau Web site: http://www.census.gov/prod/2001pubs/p60-215.pdf

Morrison, R.S., Wallenstein, S., Natale, D.K., Senzel, R.S., & Huang, L. (2000). "We don't carry that": Failure of pharmacies in predominantly nonWhite neighborhoods to stock opioid analgesics. *New England Journal of Medicine, 342*, 1023–1026.

Mouton, C.P., Harris, S.R., Solorzano, P., & Johnson, M.S. (1997). Barriers to Black women's participation in cancer clinical trials. *Journal of the National Medical Association, 89(11)*, 721–727. Abstract retrieved May 31, 2002, from PubMed database.

National Institutes of Health (NIH). (2001, November). Monitoring adherence to the NIH policy on the inclusion of women and minorities as subjects in clinical research: Comprehensive report fiscal year 1998 & 1999 tracking data. Retrieved May 31, 2002, from http://www4.od.nih.gov/orwh/salmonrpt.pdf

Pharmaceutical Manufacturers of America. (2002, July). *2002 directory of prescription drug patient assistance programs.* Retrieved July 5, 2002 from http://www.phrma.org/pap/pa99.pdf

Pharmaceutical Manufacturers of America for the Press. (2002, July 1). *PhRMA, physicians, patients call on states to halt plans to deny access to medicines for nation's most vulnerable.* Retrieved July 5, 2002, from http://www.phrma.org/mediaroom/press/releases/01.07.2002.446.cfm

Poolsup, N., Li, W.P.A., & Knight, T.L. (2000). Pharmacogenetics and psychopharmacotherapy. *Journal of Clinical Pharmacology and Therapeutics, 25(3)*, 197–220.

Posey, L.M. (2000). Drug pricing: A hot issue for pharmacists, patients. *Pharmacy Today, 6(11)*, 1 & 13.

Rantucci, M. (1997). *Pharmacists talking with patients: A guide to patient counseling.* Philadelphia: Lippincott, Williams, & Wilkins.

Rhoades, J. (2001). *The uninsured in America—2001.* Retrieved October 31, 2002, from http://meps.ahrq.gov/papers/st4/stat04.pdf.

Ritschel, W.A., & Kearns, G.L. (1999). Physiological and pathological factors influencing drug response. In J.I. Graubart (Ed.), *Handbook of basic pharmacokinetics* (pp. 377–386). Washington, DC: American Pharmaceutical Association.

Ross, E.M., & Rosenberg, I.H. (2000). Nutrition. In S.G. Carruthers, B.B. Hoffman, K.L. Melmon, & D.W. Nierenberg (Eds.), *Clinical pharmacology: Basic principles in therapeutics* (pp. 341–362). New York: McGraw-Hill.

Rowland, M., & Tozer, T.N. (1995). Individualization: Genetics. In D. Balado (Ed.), *Clinical pharmacokinetics: Concepts and applications* (pp. 203–229). Media, PA: Williams & Wilkins.

Sackett, D., & Snow, J. (1979). The magnitude of compliance and noncompliance. In R. Haynes, D. Taylor, & D. Sackett (Eds.), *Compliance in health care* (pp. 11–22). Baltimore: John Hopkins University Press.

Schneider, E.C., Cleary, P.D., Zaslavsky, A.M., & Epstein, A.M. (2001). Racial disparity in influenza vaccination: Does managed care narrow the gap between African Americans and Whites? *Journal of the American Medical Association, 286,* 1455–1460.

Shavers, V.L., Lynch, C.F., & Burmeister, L.F. (2002). Racial differences in factors that influence the willingness to participate in medical research studies. *Annals of Epidemiology, 12,* 248–256.

Smedley, B.D., Stith, A.Y., & Nelson, A.R. (Eds.). (2002). Unequal treatment: Confronting racial and ethnic disparities in health care. Washington, DC: Institute of Medicine.

Snow, L. (1993). *Walkin over medicine.* Boulder, CO: Westview Press.

Strickland, T.L., Ranganath, V., Lin, K.M., Poland, R.E., Mendoza, R., & Smith, M.W. (1991). Psychopharmacologic considerations in the treatment of Black American populations. *Psychopharmacology Bulletin, 27(4),* 441–448.

Todd, K.H., Samaroo, N., & Hoffman, J.R. (1993). Ethnicity as a risk factor for inadequate Emergency Department analgesia. *Journal of the American Medical Association, 269,* 1537–1539.

Todd, K.H., Deaton, C., D'Adamo, A.P., & Goe, L. (2000). Ethnicity and analgesic practice. *Annals of Emergency Medicine, 35,* 11–16.

Weigman, S., & Cohen, M. (1999). The patient's role in preventing medication errors. In M. Cohen (Ed.), *Medication Errors* (p 14.6). Washington, DC: American Pharmaceutical Association.

Wennerholm, A., et al. (2002). The African-specific CYP2D6*17 allele encodes an enzyme with changed substrate specificity. *Clinical Pharmacology and Therapeutics, 71(1),* 77–88.

Wood, A.J.J. (2001). Racial differences in response to drugs: Pointers to genetic differences. *New England Journal of Medicine, 344(18),* 1393–1396.

Xie, H.G., Kim, R.B., Wood, A.J., & Stein, C.M. (2001). Molecular basis of ethnic differences in drug disposition and response. *Annual Review of Pharmacology and Toxicology, 41,* 815–850.

Zweber, A. (2002). Cultural competence in pharmacy practice. *American Journal of Pharmaceutical Education, 66(2),* 172–176.

CHAPTER 29

24–7 on the Front Line: African Americans and the Emergency Department Experience

REYNOLD LEWIS TROWERS

INTRODUCTION

The all-too familiar ambulance blazes down the street, lights flashing and warbling siren at full blast. Outside, wary motorists open a path while the emergency driver swerves safely past the less considerate daring to court a collision. Inside, paramedics aggressively attend to the stricken patient, providing oxygen, starting intravenous lines, and giving medications. En route to the hospital, the driver contacts the Emergency Department (ED) staff, alerting them to the afflicted patient's pending arrival and the nature of the medical emergency. The Emergency Department staff assembles in the treatment room donning gowns and gloves. They set up the resuscitation and treatment equipment, knowing that, for several hours, this brief respite might be their last.

The ambulance screams into the driveway. The automated doors of the Emergency Department fly open. The paramedics rush the gurney into the treatment area while simultaneously conveying to the ED staff information about the patient's condition and his responses to field treatment. The ED team takes over. Its head physician barks out orders. The clock ticks. The team works in precision, with every member of the resuscitation team well versed in his or her responsibilities. The medical team's actions are purposeful, practiced, dedicated, quick-witted, and skilled—directed to saving the life of the patient. Everyone's actions are directed to preserve life and stabilize the patient.

The ED staff performs dozens of procedures, administers tests, and provides life-preserving medications. Finally, the patient's vital signs begin to improve, and their efforts are rewarded. The patient's condition is now stabilized. The team decides to admit the patient to the inpatient services. The appropriate medical team responds. They escort the patient to the medical wards, operating room, or intensive care unit. The ED staff preps, because in the distance can be heard yet another series of wailing and warbling sirens.

The above-mentioned scenarios and others like them play themselves out every minute of every hour of every day somewhere in America. With the popularity of television dramas like *ER* as well as a barrage of reality hospital shows, the public is very familiar with Hollywood's version of emergency medicine, and, it's a rare individual who hasn't either required ED services or known someone who has. Nevertheless, the reality of what happens in an ED is neither available through the click of a television remote nor comprehensible during the stress-filled moments of one's own personal crisis. Indeed, even many in the medical profession are unversed in this arena.

Yet both the medical community and the public at large must commit to an understanding of the ED if the two main goals of Healthy People 2010 are to be realized: (a) increase quality and years of healthy life and (b) eliminate health disparities (USDHHS, 2000). These two very ambitious goals require a broad understanding of the dynamics and complexities surrounding the issues of healthy living and the reduction of disparities between various ethnic and racial groups in the United States. In essence, the ED is at the forefront, especially in minority and disfranchised communities, in attempting to address the health-care needs of these communities.

This chapter delves into just how the ED deals with this frontal assault and what changes can be made to improve the ED's chances of success in this highly critical endeavor. In addition to exploring some of the features of the Emergency Department experience, other areas to be discussed will include The Emergency Department's role as a medical safety net; inappropriate use of the Emergency Department; appropriate uses and conditions evaluated in the Emergency Department; guidelines for evaluating true emergencies; and recommendations for improving the services of the Emergency Department.

EMERGENCY DEPARTMENT AS SAFETY NET

Emergency Departments play a very important role in the health care of all communities. From 1997 through 2000, ED utilization increased by 14 percent, from 94.9 million to 108.0 million visits annually, while the number of hospital EDs in the United States decreased from 4,005 to 3,934.

The reason for this, as demonstrated through the experience at Harlem Hospital Center (which serves as a focal point for this chapter), as well as research results, is that the ED has become a safety net for patients who lack access to primary medical care (McCraig & Ly, 2002). Failures of the medical care system, which led to EDs being the safety net, are primary reasons that the largest per capita users of hospital emergency services are African Americans. Data from the 1999 National Health Interview Survey indicated that approximately 17 percent of the noninstitutional civilian population reported making at least one visit to the ED, and 5 percent made two visits or more (NCHS, 2001). As illustrated in Figure 29.1, African Americans utilize emergency medical services at a much higher rate than Caucasians in the United States. The utilization rate of the ED for African Americans was 67 percent higher than for Whites (McCraig & Ly, 2002). Further examination of Figure 29.1 shows significant differences by race in all age groups except for persons 75 years of age and older.

The immediacy with which patients must be seen varies a great deal. The level of immediacy is assigned on arrival at the ED by the triage staff. The NHAMCS item categorized immediacy into four groups: emergent (less than 15 minutes), urgent (15–60 minutes), semiurgent (1–2 hours), and nonurgent (2–24 hours). For 25.6 percent of ED visits, the hospital staff recorded this visit as "unknown or no triage." As can be seen in Figure 29.2, 15.7 percent of ED visits were classified as emergent, 31.2 percent as urgent, 16.9 percent as semi-urgent, and 10.7 percent as nonurgent.

Table 29.1 shows the percent distribution of ED visits by immediacy with which the patient should be seen according to age and race. As seen under emergent care, Blacks exceeded Whites only in the 65 and above age groups. Other noteworthy differences existed first in the semiurgent category for all age groups 15 years and above. In the category nonurgent, African Americans exceeded Whites in all age categories. The greater use by African Americans of the ED for nonurgent matters underscores the fact that, as a group, African Americans tend to use the ED as the source for their medical care.

Figure 29.1
**Annual rate of emergency department visits by patient's age and race,
United States, 2000**

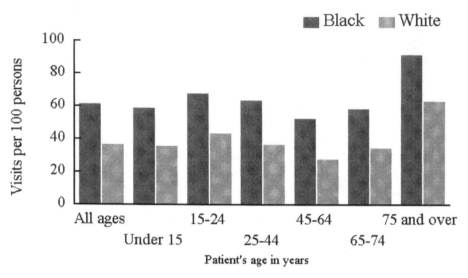

Source: McCraig & Burt (2001a). National Hospital Ambulatory Medical Care Survey, 2000.

Figure 29.2
**Percent distribution of emergency department visits by
immediacy with which the patient should be seen, United
States, 2000**

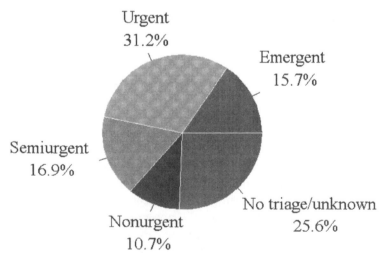

Source: McCraig & Burt (2001a). National Hospital Ambulatory Medical Care Survey, 2000

Table 29.1
Percent distribution of emergency department visits by immediacy with which the patient should be seen according to patient's age and race, United States, 2000

Patient's age and race	Emergent	Urgent	Semiurgent	Nonurgent	Unknown /no triage
Race and age					
White	16.5	32.3	16.2	10.0	25.0
Under 15 years	10.4	29.1	22.0	13.7	25.0
15-24 years	14.2	33.1	16.4	11.1	25.3
25-44 years	13.4	33.5	16.1	10.3	26.6
45-64 years	19.9	32.5	15.1	8.5	24.1
65-74 years	26.9	34.6	10.5	5.6	22.4
75 years+	29.3	32.4	10.1	5.2	23.0
Black	12.2	27.7	19.5	13.3	27.3
Under 15 years	7.9	25.7	21.8	15.1	29.5
15-24 years	8.4	27.1	19.9	13.1	31.5
25-44 years	10.7	29.4	19.2	14.6	26.1
45-64 years	17.9	26.7	20.1	12.0	23.3
65-74 years	19.9	32.7	13.6	-	26.3
75 years+	33.7	28.9	-	-	21.3

Source: McCraig & Burt (2001b). National Hospital Ambulatory Medical Care Survey, 2000. (Advance Data No. 326, Table 4—Selected portions extracted).

Emergency medicine has advanced greatly over the last two decades. Twenty years ago, doctors working in EDs were usually trained in one of the traditional medical disciplines of internal medicine, surgery, pediatrics, or family practice. These doctors frequently took on shifts in the ED for moonlighting opportunities and worked their "real jobs" during the day.

Emergency staffs are largely educated specifically in the specialty field of emergency medicine. Physicians are often residency-trained and board-certified in this specific branch of medicine. Nurses undertake additional education in the specialty and many pursue certification as a CEN (certified emergency nurse). Physician's assistants, nurse practitioners, and other physicians "extenders" utilized as providers in Emergency Departments must obtain additional training, orientation, and continuing education in order to qualify for a position in the ED. Emergency equipment for resuscitating and monitoring patients is highly sophisticated. Medical procedures previously performed only in operating rooms or intensive care units are now routinely conducted in the ED.

Despite these advances in emergency care, ED staffers are the most overworked professionals in the field of medicine for the simple reason that too many citizens frequent emergency services. This disproportionately high number of patients often reflects a failure of the medical system, individual culpability, lack of knowledge on the part of the patient, or a combination of all three.

INAPPROPRIATE USE OF THE EMERGENCY DEPARTMENT

Anywhere from 30 percent to 70 percent of patients who utilize Emergency Departments have medical conditions that could be more appropriately managed in another medical setting. A significant number of patients arrive in the ED with nonemergency conditions (see Figure 29.2). One of the reasons for this is that many patients simply do not recognize that their medical issues are not emergencies. Individuals in pain, for example, are generally focused on prompt relief or assurances that their problems are not serious in nature. They don't often stop to think that their primary care providers (PCP) may be the appropriate medical experts to consult regarding their current concern. Patients may also have a real or perceived notion that their PCPs may not be available to evaluate them. To make matters worse, a significant number of persons either cannot remember their primary care provider or claim that they do not have one.

The problem of patients forgetting the names of their PCP is particularly prevalent among African Americans. This issue is one that I rapidly became acquainted with only in the 1980s. I obtained my medical school training in the late 1970s at the Program in Medicine at Brown University and its affiliated hospitals in Providence, Rhode Island. As a medical student attempting to perfect the art of acquiring a patient's medical history, I learned that an essential part of that history included knowledge of primary care and identifying the primary care provider. In this environment, the vast majority of patients (greater than 90 percent) could list a physician who they considered to be their PCP in this environment.

In the early 1980s, while completing residency training in hospitals based in east and central Harlem, I sadly encountered almost the reverse situation. Here, patient after patient could not provide the name of a primary care provider. Many patients freely admitted that Emergency Departments were their sole source of medical care. These patients included a large number of persons with chronic medical conditions such as diabetes and hypertension.

Twenty-years later, having bridged the new millennium divide, one would hope that the primary care issue would have improved. The reasons that it hasn't are cloudy. It is true that a greater number of African Americans can now identify and align themselves with a PCP than in years past. The influences of managed care, including mandatory managed care for Medicaid recipients, have had a positive impact.

When patients are interviewed directly, there are clearly issues that potentially compromise the delivery of good primary care. Although greater numbers of people are being assigned to health maintenance organizations and primary care providers, a significantly high number of individuals do not schedule appropriate appointments for preventive exams and health maintenance. Anecdotal experience from my practice and that of other practitioners who service large numbers of African Americans reveal some significant challenges in incorporating primary care objectives.

In an interview conducted for this article minutes before his Martin Luther King Day, 2003, address at Cedar Sinai Hospital in Los Angeles, Dr. Louis W. Sullivan, former secretary of the U.S. Department of Health and Human Services, focused on the increasing percentage of minorities and poor people who lack insurance as one of the primary causes for frequent and inappropriate use of emergency departments:

Emergency departments are under a great deal of stress, particularly in the inner cities. Fourteen percent of the population, [are uninsured]. An equal number have insurance that underserves their needs. Thirty percent live in medically underserved areas. Emergency rooms are obligated to help whoever walks through the door." (Interview with Dr. Louis W. Sullivan, February, 2003)

If It Ain't Broke . . .

"Why should I sit for hours waiting to see a doctor if I feel fine?" "If I miss work to visit the doctor, I won't get paid." Those are sentiments commonly expressed by many ED visitors, people whose health-care philosophy revolves around an 'if it ain't broke, don't fix it" mentality. Despite attempts by a variety of agencies and public education programs, many individuals do not seek medical care until they feel ill.

The result is that many patients come to EDs for nonemergency issues. However, EDs simply do not provide good primary care. First, the Emergency Department practitioners generally have no prior relationship with patients presenting for care, and access to previous medical records is difficult or impossible.

Second, the nature of emergency medicine forces the practitioner to focus on the patient's chief complaint (the problem as stated by the patient) or any evident life-threatening problems. A male patient coming to the ED for a cold, for example, will not get potentially important cancer-screening exams. Unless the patient complains of suggestive symptoms in his "chief complaint," he probably will not have a prostate digital exam or have a prostate specific antigen serum performed. Women presenting to the emergency department with viral illnesses will likewise generally not receive potentially important cancer-screening exams like a breast exam, unless she directs the practitioner to the breast in her "chief complaint."

Third, it is not the mission of emergency departments, nor do they have the time or resources, to provide primary care for their clients. For children, appropriate immunization protection is a very important primary care objective. Therefore, when a child is brought to the emergency department for care, an immunization history is generally obtained, but it is not routine practice to administer vaccines (except for tetanus) in emergency departments.

A True Emergent Condition

A true emergent condition, for people of all ages, generally falls into the life- or limb-threatening category. In other words, emergent conditions will result in death or serious disability if not treated immediately or in a relatively short period of time. The episodic care that emergency departments are so often forced to render flies in the face of primary care objectives.

To eliminate such unnecessary visits and improve the health of patients, nearly all EDs, upon discharging patients, will give them specific instructions to make follow-up appointments with primary care providers. Historically, patient compliance with these appointments is extremely low. Recent data compiled during a six-month period in early 2002 revealed that only 7 percent of patients referred to community clinics from the Harlem Hospital Emergency Department actually showed up on the date and time assigned.

In addition, many minorities have had negative past experiences with the health-care system, resulting in avoidance behavior. A historical incident within a prior generation of my own family reflects the mentality of many even in the new millennium. My paternal grandmother grew up and raised a family of nine children in Panama. Her contact with the health-care systems in Panama was minimal. She delivered all of her children at home (with midwives) and used a variety of herbs, plants, and other home remedies to treat the variety of family illnesses and injuries over the years.

The one child whom she did bring to the hospital for seizures ultimately died from a brain tumor. For years afterward, my grandmother's impression of the "hospital" was that it was the place that people went to die, a place to be avoided at all costs.

Others avoid a system where they feel powerless, disrespected, and genuinely afraid. Unfortunately, it isn't unusual to hear citizens report stories of horrific experiences in hospitals or clinics. A woman recently diagnosed with systemic lupus erythematosis began to seek medical attention for her symptoms several years prior to the determination of her ultimate diagnosis. She felt that many of the physicians did not take her symptoms of joint pain, skin changes, and hair loss seriously. She stated that several providers thought that she was suffering from stress or "boyfriend problems." One physician even insisted that she see a psychiatrist because her condition was not physical.

A practitioner who finally spent a greater amount of time discussing her condition with her and performed the appropriate tests to diagnose lupus finally correctly diagnosed her condition. As you might expect, this woman's overall impression of the health-care system is not highly favorable, and the negative manner in which she was treated does not stay with just her. In communities in which word of mouth is often a most credible source of information, her experience may generate grave concerns about primary care providers among large groups of people and their descendants.

APPROPRIATE USE OF THE EMERGENCY DEPARTMENT

While the ED is not to be used as a primary health-care facility, there are a variety of legitimate conditions why patients should visit the ED for services. The kind of treatment provided in the ED is, to a large extent, a result of existing legislation. For example, several laws passed by the U.S. Congress impact the burden on EDs. More specifically, the 1986 Emergency Medical Treatment and Labor Act (or EMTALA) requires EDs to conduct a screening examination. Additionally, if the patient requires emergency treatment and the hospital is ill equipped to handle the problem, the ED must treat and stabilize the patient to the best of its ability, before transferring the patient to another facility. The Balanced Budget Act (BBA) of 1997 requires Medicaid and Medicare programs to reimburse hospitals for emergency care that a reasonable person would consider necessary.

A landmark article published in 1990 in the *New England Journal of Medicine* described rather shocking statistics establishing that African Americans in inner-city environments similar to central Harlem have extremely high mortality rates. The two authors, Dr. Colin McCord and Dr. Harold Freeman, both then based at Harlem Hospital, presented further evidence that "Black men in Harlem were less likely to reach the age of 65 than men in Bangladesh" (McCord & Freeman, 1990, p. 173). Excess mortality rates (mortality rates that exceeded those expected) were determined and ranked. These conditions constitute legitimate reasons to visit the ED at Harlem Hospital, or any other ED for that matter.

The top ten causes of excess mortality found in Harlem were:

1. Cardiovascular Disease
2. Cirrhosis
3. Homicide
4. Neoplasm
5. Drug Dependency
6. Diabetes
7. Alcohol Use
8. Pneumonia and Influenza

9. Disorder of Newborns

10. Infection

Although these statistics are related to mortality data, they correspond closely to the typical presentations that are seen daily in EDs even if the patient does not die. The aforementioned conditions all may result in serious life-threatening conditions that are typical and legitimate reasons to come to the ED for medical care. However, the development of these conditions or their life-threatening complications is largely preventable and, if treated with preventive measures in advance, would reduce the necessity for ED visits. Statistics consistently reveal that African Americans are more likely to be hospitalized for preventable conditions than Caucasians (Gaskin & Hoffman, 2000).

Cardiovascular Disease

Cardiovascular diseases encompass a wide variety of presentations that primarily affect the heart. The most common related symptoms are chest pain, breathlessness, irregular heartbeat, nausea, lightheadedness, and development of a cold sweat. There is no doubt that a patient who presents with these complaints could potentially have a real life-threatening emergency, which requires immediate evaluation and care.

Nevertheless, if we examine the established risk factors for cardiovascular disease, it is clear that many of them are modifiable by lifestyle changes and/or good primary care. Strong risk factors for cardiovascular disease, such as hypercholesterolemia, hypertension, diabetes, cigarette smoking, physical inactivity, obesity, and postmenopause, are potentially modifiable by lifestyle, diet, and/or medicinal interventions (Bakris et al., 2002).

High Cholesterol Levels

Low-density lipoprotein component of cholesterol contributes significantly to the development of cardiovascular disease. African Americans, especially those living in inner cities, tend to consume diets that are calorie and fat-dense. Although only one-third of the body's cholesterol comes from dietary intake, significant reductions in saturated fat intake, increase in fiber ingestion, and exercise can greatly lower cardiovascular risk (American Heart Association, 2002). If these modifications do not adequately lower the risk, a variety of "statin" drugs are now available that have been quite effective in many individuals.

Hypertension

This is a major risk factor for cardiovascular disease, that disproportionately affects African Americans (Collins & Winkleby, 2002). The American Heart Association (AHA) reports that 36.7 percent of African American men and 36.6 percent of African American women have high blood pressure (American Heart Association, 2002). These percentages are among the highest found in any racial or ethnic group. The AHA also reports that 30 and 20 percent of all deaths of African American men and women, respectively, are attributable to hypertension.

Although there may be a major genetic predilection for the development of hypertension in African Americans, this condition can generally be controlled well with a combination of dietary changes and medications if necessary (Bakris et al., 2002; JNC, 1997).

I frequently encounter patients in the ED who claim that they know when their blood pressure is elevated because they develop a headache or other nonspecific symptoms. This tendency to self-diagnose hypertension by symptoms is extremely dangerous. Hypertension has been dubbed the "silent killer" for good reason. Many people still do not realize that they may have markedly high blood pressures without any symptoms at all. It is all too often a catastrophic event, such as a myocardial infarction, stroke, or the onset of renal failure that uncovers years of uncontrolled hypertension (Sicca & Douglas, 2001).

Cigarette Smoking

Cigarette smoking plays a major role in increasing morbidity and mortality in all persons. However, it has particularly detrimental affects on African Americans. Data compiled by the National Health Interview Survey (NHIS) in 1999 indicate that 28.7 percent and 20.8 percent of African American men and women, respectively, smoke cigarettes (AHA Heart Facts, 2002). The use of cigarettes accelerates the development of atheromatous disease (clogging of the blood vessels) via a variety of mechanisms. Cigarette smoke also contains carbon monoxide that constricts blood vessel and nicotine that raises the blood pressure and further constricts arteries. Cigarette smoke certainly enhances the detrimental effects of hypertension and high cholesterol on the blood vessels and heart (AHA Heart Facts, 2002). Although simply forsaking cigarettes is a "no-brainer" in terms of reducing risk for cardiovascular disease, the intensely addictive qualities of nicotine make the cessation of smoking one of the most difficult habits to break.

Physical Inactivity and Obesity

Both of these conditions are often linked to each other. I have already mentioned the salutatory effects of reducing weight and increasing exercise on a number of risk factors. Obesity is often a multifactorial problem, with some individuals suffering from an endocrine disease or genetic predilection. Many persons, however, have developed such poor eating habits that obesity has become an epidemic in the African American community.

The National Centers for Disease Control (CDC) reports that 58.4 percent of African American men are overweight, using the 95th percentile of body mass index (BMI). The BMI is determined by dividing the person's weight by the square of his or her height. The statistics for African American women are even more disturbing. Close to 68 percent of these women in the 20–74 age range are obese (AHA Heart Facts, 2002). Morbid obesity (body mass index greater than 40) is a major health risk for any number of medical conditions. Low-income and otherwise disadvantaged individuals tend to consume diets that are calorie- and fat-dense. Until recently, it was quite difficult to get a fresh salad in the food establishments in central Harlem or find a gym to do the needed exercise and workout.

Despite the fact that healthy food alternatives are more available in Harlem and other African American communities post-1990s, the obesity problem continues to worsen. The American Heart Association reports that physical inactivity is more prevalent among women than men, among African Americans than Caucasians, and among the less affluent than the more affluent (AHA Heart Facts, 2002).

An extremely disturbing trend involves the fact that children in the African American and other communities are significantly more obese on average than prior generations. Twelve percent of African American boys and 16.4 percent of African American girls are obese (CDC/NCHS, 1994). These trends have been getting only worse over the last several years. We can clearly expect more diabetes and cardiovascular disease and their complications than were seen in prior generations.

Cardiovascular Disease in Women.   The most common cause of death in postmenopausal women is cardiovascular disease. In fact, cardiovascular disease kills elderly women more than cancer and the next four most frequent causes of death combined. Premenopausal women do suffer from cardiovascular disease; however, it is a rare phenomenon. For years, it was generally felt that the administration of HRT (hormone replacement therapy) significantly reduced the risk of developing cardiovascular disease. Within the last year, studies have seriously questioned the effectiveness of these drugs (Waiting Group for the Women's Health Initiative, 2002). There have even been some reports that some of the hormone combinations actually increase the risk of cardiovascular disease (including stroke) and certain cancers. Further studies are needed to clarify these issues.

Cirrhosis and Alcohol Abuse

Liver disease is extremely prevalent in African American communities, with cirrhosis implicated as the number two cause of excess mortality (McCord & Freeman, 1990). The etiology for much of the liver disease seen in African American communities is alcohol abuse, however, other causes have emerged and continue to be major contributors to the problem. Alcohol and some infectious etiologies will be discussed.

It was an unusually slow night in the Harlem Hospital emergency department until approximately 10:15 P.M., when an EMS crew called to say that they were transporting a critically ill patient to the hospital. The patient was well known to the emergency department staff. He was one of our "frequent flyers," a man who would generally visit the ED once or twice a week. Alcohol was this man's demon, an addiction so strong that he was unable to stop drinking despite multiple attempts at detoxification.

Alcohol is toxic to the liver when it is imbibed frequently and in large quantities. It is important to recognize that the progression from a normal to cirrhotic liver usually takes many years. The liver undergoes a slow metamorphosis of enlargement and fatty change and eventually deteriorates into a shrunken and scarred organ. If a person stops drinking alcohol before the late stages of liver damage occurs, the organ will often regenerate and return to normal functioning.

A number of hepatitis viruses adversely affect the liver. Hepatitis "B" and "C" are notorious in causing liver cirrhosis (CDC Hepatitis Fact Sheet, 2003, p. 1). These infections are contracted via body fluid exposure, such as blood exposure through needlesticks or sexual contact. Hepatitis "B" is usually associated with an acute illness characterized by jaundice, malaise, nausea, vomiting, and fever. Most of these patients recover after a rather protracted illness, without permanent liver damage. A few will develop chronic hepatitis that may progress to cirrhosis.

Hepatitis "C" was previously known as non-A, non-B hepatitis until the virus was definitively identified several years ago. Hepatitis "C" tends to be a more subtle infection. Many millions are infected without their knowledge. Unfortunately, significant numbers of people with this disease eventually develop liver cirrhosis. Early diagnosis and treatment with antiviral drugs may modify the disease and ward off the development of this devastating complication. Conditions leading to liver cirrhosis are largely preventable. Alcohol abuse is prevalent in many African American communities. If this behavior were abated, probably more than 90 percent of the cases of cirrhosis would be prevented.

Homicide and Interpersonal Violence

Interpersonal violence, including homicide, ravages the African American community. According to a 1994 report from the Centers for Disease Control between 1985 to 1991 the homicide and nonnegligent manslaughter rates for males between the ages of 15 and 19 increased by 127 percent (Morbidity and Mortality Weekly Report, 1994). By 1991 males of these ages were more likely to be arrested for murder than were males in any other five-year age group. African American males are disproportionately represented among homicide victims. Supplemental Homicide Reports suggest that African Americans constituted nearly 61 percent of all adolescents (10–20 years of age) known to have committed murder in 1990.

Firearm death rates for Black males aged 15–19 in the United States in 1989 ranged from 15.5 per 100,000 for those residing in nonmetropolitan areas to 143.9 per 100,000 for those residing in the central cities. Comparable rates for white males were 3.0 and 21.5, respectively. Nonfirearm rates for males showed a similar geographic and racial pattern, as did rates for females of both races (Hawkins, 1996).

The etiology for this is varied. At the first National Conference on Domestic Violence sponsored by the Office of Community Services in 1993, a group of five scholars and practitioners met to discuss domestic violence as it relates to the African American community in the area of domestic violence. One clear problem that they pinpointed was that the approach of work being done in the field(s) of domestic violence was formulated from a "one-size-fits-all" analytical viewpoint (excerpt National Conference on Domestic Violence 1993, Institute on Domestic Violence in the African American Community).

Conventional wisdom is that domestic violence means the same thing to all people; therefore, policies and intervention strategies have typically been designed from a singular mainstream perspective. Many in the field also note the lack of information concerning strategies to address this problem among African Americans.

There is also a lack of scholars and practitioners in the field who are able to provide guidance in this area. The group believed that such mainstream perspectives and beliefs explain why approaches and responses that have been successful with Whites have failed to address the needs of African Americans. To be more responsive to the community, academics and practitioners in the field require accurate information, guidance, and support.

In the 1980s and 1990s in Harlem, drug-related violence was rampant. Homicide was determined to be the number three cause of excess mortality in Harlem (McCord & Freeman, 1990). Many of the victims whom I treated for penetrating injuries (bullet and stab injuries) during that time had suffered wounds that they openly admitted resulted from neighborhood drug activity. Other victims were unable or unwilling to give any explanation for the violent act. Most emergency physicians are familiar with the "code of silence," where victims refuse to disclose information about circumstances of the act perpetrated against them.

Interpersonal violence including homicide is not exclusively a "disease" of African American men. Women, the elderly, and children are also victims at an unacceptably high rate (National Coalition against Domestic Violence, 2004). Serious assaults on women are usually perpetrated by a known male acquaintance (husband, boyfriend, etc.). Pregnant women are also assaulted frequently, resulting in harm to the women and sometimes the developing child (Gazmararian, 2000).

The 1980s and early 1990s were remarkable and yet tragic years. I was a young attending physician working in the emergency department at Harlem Hospital. During those years, I experienced firsthand the devastation of homicide on individuals, families, and the society as a whole. The hospital was inundated with victims of interpersonal violence. Every evening and night, patients were brought to the hospital with gunshot wounds and stabbing injuries. The situation was so dire that Harlem Hospital was dubbed the "knife and gun club," with some club members being rolled in on what seemed like a revolving-door basis. These victims require aggressive care, from the prehospital care rendered by the Emergency Medical Services, through the entire hospital stay. In light of the high acuity level of many of these victims, teams of medical and support personnel are required to stabilize and treat these patients.

Harlem Hospital, like other level one trauma centers, must maintain a comprehensive emergency department and trauma surgery team. Trauma centers must have operating rooms and staff, including anesthesiologists, available at all times. Some victims of trauma must literally be in the operating suite and under the surgeon's knife within minutes of arrival in order to save their lives. Recovery rooms and intensive care units must be set up to receive these patients postsurgery. Radiology, pathology, and blood bank support must also be readily available at all times. Trauma victims often require prolonged hospitalizations, rehabilitation, and psychological support.

Those who assault the elderly are more often family or acquaintances than strangers. Additionally, abuse, neglect, and overt assaults by caregivers (including family members) are prevalent but generally underreported, crimes. Aquaintances and friends, versus strangers, more frequently assault the elderly (Ahmad & Lachs, 2002). We have discovered a disturbing trend of elder abuse perpetrated by drug-abusing adult children and grandchildren who reside with the parent. These children will attempt to obtain money from the elder relative and abuse the elder relative in the process. Elder relatives have been emotionally and physically hurt and even killed as the child attempts to steal checks and other funds to support his or her drug habit.

Neoplasm

Cancer, malignancy, or neoplasms are words that send shivers through laypersons and medical professionals alike. Many persons consider cancer to be a diagnosis that is essentially a death sentence. However, some of the greatest achievements in medicine over the last couple of decades have occurred in the diagnosis, treatment, and prevention of cancer. Nevertheless, African American communities are disproportionately affected by cancer. Late-stage disease at diagnosis is unfortunately all too common and adversely affects morbidity and mortality statistics (Li et al., 2003).

The American Cancer Society consistently reports that African Americans have higher rates of most malignancies than Caucasians (Miller et al., 1993). African American men have the highest rate of prostate cancer in the world (NCI, 2002; ACS, 2003). In addition, at the time of diagnosis, the stage of these malignancies tends to be more advanced in African Americans. Thus, African Americans die from a potentially survivable disease (NCI, 2002).

Patients should be screened for a variety of cancer and precancerous conditions in the primary care setting. Unfortunately, many individuals are unwilling or unable to have these examinations done. It is distressing for emergency department staff to diagnose a malignancy in persons who should have had the diagnosis made far sooner in the primary care setting.

Drug Dependency

Emergency departments evaluate and treat persons frequently with "drug-related problems." Some of these problems are directly related to the drugs and their physiologic effect on the body, while other problems relate to the broad scope of consequences that drug use and dependency tend to foster.

In the late 1970s and early 1980s, I treated numerous patients who were chronic users of intravenous drugs like heroin. Many patients overdosed on drugs presented daily to our ED. Our ED staff was diagnosing bacterial endocarditis, septic embolization, cellulitis, osteomyelitis, stroke, and renal failure related to intravenous drug use on a daily basis. AIDS-related complications were also seen frequently.

Use of the smokable forms of cocaine had a major negative impact on health of those individuals who engaged in that activity. During that time of prevalent cocaine use, the Drug Awareness Warning Network (DAWN) reported an approximate 600 percent increase in emergency department visits in inner-city communities like Harlem. (DAWN is an organization that collects data relating to the trends and medical complications of drug-using behavior. Data related to the impact of illicit drug use in the emergency setting is one of the areas of analysis [DHHS, 2002].) Cocaine-related chest pain, myocardial ischemia/infarction, arrhythmias, seizures, stroke, hypertensive emergencies, and pulmonary complications are presentations with which all emergency medical staff is familiar.

Several years ago, I treated a desperately ill man who was brought into our ED comatose with a core body temperature of 110 degrees, rhabdomyolysis, and a massive hemorrhagic stroke. Reportedly, he had been smoking crack cocaine for many hours before his presentation to our emergency department. The patient was aggressively treated, stabilized, and admitted to the intensive care unit. Even before the patient left the unit, we received a notification from the emergency medical services that two gunshot wound victims were being brought to our hospital. We soon found out that these two victims were involved in cocaine trafficking and their injuries were a result of that activity. Within two hours, we witnessed a graphic demonstration of direct and indirect consequences of drug use on three individuals, two of whom later died.

Diabetes

Diabetes has become an increasingly challenging problem among African Americans. Persons with diabetes are on the increase in the United States, and African Americans are disproportionately affected. The National Health Interview Surveys (NHIS) show that African Americans have a rising prevalence of diabetes. The same studies also indicated that African Americans have significantly higher rates of diabetes than Caucasians (Ni et al., 2003).

Type II (maturity onset) diabetes affects African Americans much more frequently than Type I (juvenile onset) disease. It is very clear that diabetes can be controlled in the vast majority of individuals by diet, exercise, and medications. More and more evidence indicates that obesity may contribute to insulin resistance and the development of maturity-onset diabetes (Kuzmarski et al., 1994). Obese individuals and African Americans (whether obese or not) tend to have higher than normal levels of insulin when fasting. Most researchers feel that these "hyperinsulinemia" levels reflect a predilection for the development of Type II diabetes, (NIH, 2002). Aggressive diet and weight control measures may certainly prevent the development of diabetes or result in adequate control of the disease without medications (American Diabetes Association, 1997; El-Kebbi et al., 2003).

Pneumonia, Influenza, and Other Infections

As is typical with most Emergency Departments, patient presentations to the ED and the hospital census increase significantly with the onset of late fall/winter and the influenza season. Influenza is a serious and potentially deadly disease. Elderly persons or those persons with chronic diseases such diabetes, asthma, COPD, cardiovascular disease, sickle-cell disease or immunodeficiency disorders are particularly at high risk for complications and death related to the "flu." Although viral in etiology, patients who contract influenza sometime develop bacterial pneumonia, meningitis, and/or sepsis. Severe influenza pandemics in the United States over the last one hundred years in the United States have resulted in over 120,000 deaths (Fauci et al., 1998).

The appropriate administration of the influenza vaccine can often prevent influenza completely or ameliorate symptoms, reducing or eliminating the morbidity and mortality from this potentially devastating disease. A number of antiviral agents are now available that are highly effective in reducing the severity of symptoms and complications of influenza. The most common cause of bacterial pneumonia in adults is the pneumococcus bacteria. A pneumococcal vaccine effective against the 23 most common serotypes of pneumococcus has been available for several years. Individuals at risk for influenza should also obtain vaccination for pneumococcus approximately every three years (USDHHS, 1997).

Newborn Disorders

A detailed discussion of newborn disorders is beyond the scope of this chapter. There is an abundance of evidence, however, that good prenatal care, with particular emphasis on the health of the mother, can greatly reduce and sometimes eliminate many newborn disorders and result in fewer birthing complications. More African Americans must access comprehensive prenatal care resources shortly after the confirmation of the pregnancy.

GUIDELINES FOR EVALUATING TRUE EMERGENCIES

It is frequently difficult for the public to distinguish true emergencies from those conditions that do not require emergency care. The problem really relates to the fact that the public often must self-evaluate their signs and symptoms and self-triage the level of severity. Although this is extremely difficult to do, there are effective guidelines. The following typical symptoms and presentations are designated with a red, yellow or green flag, depending on potential severity.

Red flag conditions are generally acute emergencies that require immediate access to emergency care, usually via EMS. These conditions require rapid assessment, diagnosis, and treatment. The potential for deterioration and possible permanent disability or death is high.

Yellow flag conditions generally require an ED visit and treatment; however, these conditions are not likely to rapidly deteriorate. Patients with these conditions should generally come to the emergency department for care via means other than EMS.

Green flag conditions are generally of a benign or chronic nature. Emergency care is rarely required for these conditions, and primary care is probably the most appropriate vehicle for evaluation and treatment.

Red Flag Conditions

Chest Pain.   Chest pain can indicate serious pathology, ranging from myocardial ischemia/infarction, to pulmonary emboli, to vascular disruptions such as aortic dissections. Many other conditions result in chest pain of a benign nature; however, it may be difficult for the lay public to make those distinctions. Pain that is severe, pressurelike, smothering, or associated with other symptoms such as shortness of breath, palpitations, sweating, syncope, nausea, vomiting, or radiation to the arms, back, jaw, or abdomen should be taken very seriously, and immediate access to emergency care is necessary.

Shortness of Breath.   Difficulty or inability to catch ones' breath can indicate severe life-threatening pathology. It may be a result of the exacerbation of a chronic condition like asthma or COPD. It may also herald a de novo serious problem such as a pulmonary embolism or myocardial infarction. Rapid treatment of many of these conditions can result in full recovery without residual problems.

Neurological Problems.   A great emphasis in emergency medicine over the last few years has been placed on rapid assessment and treatment of patients with neurological signs and symptoms. In light of the prevalence of hypertension and diabetes (known risk factors for stroke) in the African American community, it is essential that these communities are educated about available treatments for stroke. The use of "clot-busting drugs" (thrombolytics) has had a beneficial effect in reducing mortality and residual neurological deficits. These treatments are extremely time-sensitive and generally must be administered within three hours of the onset of symptoms. Clearly, these patients must access emergency care as quickly as possible. In addition, patients with seizures of any type must be stabilized and evaluated promptly.

Altered Mental Status.   Literally hundreds of conditions can result in some sort of brain dysfunction and alteration of consciousness. These presentations may result in depressed mentation (lethargy, stupor, coma) or, conversely, agitation, confusion, or psychotic-like states. The etiology could be related to metabolic or toxic problems such as hypoglycemia, hypoxia, and drugs or could be related to trauma or structural problem such as a stroke. These patients need rapid and aggressive evaluation and treatment.

Trauma.   Significant trauma nearly always requires "red flag" priority care. Airway, breathing, and circulation assessments including hemorrhage control require medical expertise and equipment. Emergency services personnel are specifically trained in these skills. They are also experts in the extrication, immobilization, and transport procedures, which are critically important in order to prevent the exacerbation of an injury of the head, neck, or spine.

Pregnancy-Related Conditions.   Early-, middle-, and late-stage pregnant patients might present with signs and symptoms that warrant rapid-access emergency medical care. Abdominal pain accompanied by irregular or missed menstrual periods may indicate an ectopic pregnancy. Many women with an ectopic may not have realized that they were pregnant at the time of evaluation (Carson & Buster, 1993, p. 1174). Women with second-trimester pain and bleeding must be evaluated promptly for the possibility of an impending miscarriage. Third-trimester bleeding, with or without pain, is generally an obstetrical emergency, which requires emergency evaluation, stabilization, and often an emergency cesarean.

Yellow Flag Conditions

Fever.   Fever is generally the body's response to various infectious insults. An extremely high fever (104 degrees plus) may result in various degrees of brain dysfunction and may alter the mental status. These patients need upgrading into the red flag category. Most others with milder fever and absent other red flag symptomatology generally require medical care without need for emergency medical services assistance.

Pain.   Pain is a symptom, not a diagnosis. Severe pain involving the chest, abdomen, head, or extremities may be indicative of dangerous pathology and should be given red flag priority. Most other pain presentations in the absence of other significant symptoms can be evaluated and treated with yellow flag priority.

Moderate and Minor Trauma.   Patients who present with moderate or minor trauma can generally be evaluated and treated in the yellow flag priority scheme. Contusions, abrasions, and lacerations where the bleeding can be controlled with commonly employed first-aid techniques fall in this category. It is important to keep in mind that head trauma may appear to be relatively innocuous at first and develop worsening problems over time. Persons who lose consciousness or have other neurological signs such as seeing stars or experiencing amnesia after head trauma need more urgent evaluation.

Skin Rashes and Allergic Reactions.   The majority of patients who present with skin rashes can be evaluated with yellow flag priority. However, there are certain rashes associated with high fever, diffuse peeling of the skin, blisters, or bulla require more urgent care. Of note, allergic reactions associated with hives, particularly swelling of the skin (angioedema) and deeper tissues in the body, are an emergent problem requiring red flag priority. Most other rashes are not associated with life threats (even though they may be contagious). These generally have yellow or green flag priority.

Green Flag Conditions

Most chronic and minor medical problems should be evaluated and treated in settings other than the emergency department. Arthritic pain, colds and other minor viral syndromes, minor rashes, minor muscle or back pain, and chronic conditions without new symptomatology are appropriately managed in the primary care setting. Many managed care organizations and emergency departments provide telephone information lines where the public may address questions to a medical professional regarding the most appropriate level of care required for their medical complaints.

Expectations upon Arrival to the Emergency Department

Whether patients arrive in the ED via their own devices or via EMS, there are certain procedures that are fairly standard in most hospitals. Patients should expect to be triaged, which is the department's way of determining which patients are the most urgently ill or injured.

Patients are not necessarily evaluated and treated based on time of arrival. Those patients with urgent or immediate life- or limb-threatening conditions will always be treated before patients with less emergent problems.

Patients should be prepared to articulate the reasons why they are seeking care. It is also very important to determine the past medical history (prior medical problems, surgery, etc.) and any medication that the person is taking. It is very difficult for some people to remember all the medications and dosages. Therefore, it is advisable keep a card, in a wallet or purse, that lists that information. Patients are also be asked about drug and nondrug allergies, habits such as smoking, alcohol, and illicit drug use, and menstrual, contraceptive, and obstetrical history in women.

Many EDs are also asking questions related to domestic violence, child abuse, or elder abuse depending on the circumstances. It is tremendously important for patients to be open and honest with the health-care providers so that appropriate care can be rendered. Depending on the urgency assessment, patients may be brought back directly for care or asked to remain in the waiting area until a practitioner is available.

Patients should remember that they have a right to:

a. A medical screening exam with appropriate diagnostic tests as indicated (regardless of ability to pay).

b. Know the name of any medical practitioner, nurse, aid or technician involved in their care.

c. Have all procedures explained in layperson terms before consent is requested.

d. Refuse specific procedures.

e. Request translation services if language is a barrier to complete comprehension.

f. Request and obtain pain medication.

g. Request and obtain assistance in formulating advanced care directives and choosing a health-care proxy.

h. Refuse admission to the hospital and request transfer to another facility if arrangements can be made.

RECOMMENDATIONS FOR IMPROVING THE SERVICES OF THE EMERGENCY DEPARTMENT

Access to Improved Technology

As previously discussed, a patient's lack of knowledge concerning his or her personal managed care provider is a frequent obstacle to ascertaining important information when entering the emergency department. However, the increasing use of computerized medical information systems utilized during the registration process upon entry into emergency departments can often identify the particular primary and managed care providers with whom patients are affiliated even if the patient cannot recall that information. Clerks logging in patients can also check for prior visits to the hospital, identify emergency contact individuals, and obtain medical insurance information.

Advancements in medical information systems are also expanding the capabilities of retrieving medical information from prior ED visits and hospitalizations. Laboratory, radiology, and other diagnostic modalities have been increasingly computerized and networked among regional hospitals. In addition, pharmacies are increasingly being networked with other pharmacies in the region and state allowing the retrieval of patients' medication and prescription histories.

The same technology also allows medical professionals to obtain rapid references regarding diagnostic and therapeutic criteria. Access to the Internet and downloaded information on computers and handheld palm devices allow the medical team to access quick and accurate medical information. A number of diagnostic tools that can greatly assist the clinicians in working through difficult diagnostic clinical scenarios have been incorporated in several hospitals' EDs.

Patients who present to the ED with chest pain may have a potentially life-threatening problem. As mentioned previously, this warrants a high triage designation (red flag), resulting in a rapid assessment in a monitored section of the unit. Despite these precautions, a significant proportion of these patients will not have cardiac-related pain (Pope, 2000). The etiology of their pain may be quite benign, requiring neither hospitalization nor prolonged observation in the ED. While the patient's history and physical exam are essential in distinguishing cardiac from less serious noncardiac pain, other modalities have and are being developed that enhance diagnostic accuracy (Selker et al., 1998). These modalities include computerized risk assessment of severity based on symptoms, electrocardiogram analysis, and cardiac enzyme determinations. This technology is being refined to help determine the severity of other presentations, such as abdominal pain, headache, extremity injuries, and the like.

Disparities in Care: What Can Be Done?

Due to the fact that African Americans utilize emergency services for appropriate and inappropriate reasons at a much higher rate than the majority population, a multifaceted approach is required to redirect care for nonemergency conditions, improve primary care objectives, and educate the public about the appropriate use of the ED.

Many inner-city communities largely populated by African Americans have morbidity and mortality statistics that exceed those found in places that the U.S. government had designated as natural disaster areas (Jenkins et al., 1977; McCord & Freeman, 1990). Designated disaster areas receive special considerations, including significant political and financial commitments.

The same level of resources must be put forth in inner-city communities. These commitments must include major efforts to eradicate root causes of poverty, lack of insurance, and limited access to primary care. Hospitals have to aggressively embrace new technologies in addition to hiring and utilizing staff that are specifically trained and committed to the practice of emergency medicine.

Every opportunity should be taken to educate emergency patients. Educational modalities may include written materials, videostapes, and one-on-one teaching. Verbal and written instructions must be given to patients prior to discharge. Many hospitals now telephone patients the day following the ED visit to assure that they understand their diagnosis and follow-up instructions. Such outreach should be required in every ED setting. African American men and women commit to healthy life choices and instill the same in children. Exercise, dietary discretion, and positive thinking must become fundamentals in their lives.

Citizens must educate themselves about prevention and model appropriate behavior for children and others. Also, persons with known medical conditions such as diabetes or hypertension must become thoroughly familiar with their diagnosis, treatments, and medications. These individuals should also carry identification with them at all times that indicates their medical condition and medications.

CONCLUSION

As mentioned in the introduction, the major goals of Healthy People 2010 are to increase quality and years of healthy life and to eliminate disparities (USDHHS, 2000). As shown, those major disparities occur most frequently when dealing with inner-city minority communities.

The emergency department has become the front-line health-care provider for a disproportionately high and ever increasing number of African Americans. Disparities in health care are graphically demonstrated daily in emergency departments that service significant African American populations. It is critical that the EDs in these areas as well as the surrounding communities at large arm themselves with the appropriate knowledge, medical staff, technology, and mentality required to attempt to achieve those major goals.

The negative trends generating and sustaining disparities in health care are often systematic of a more widespread malaise (one dealing with disparities in education, workfare, social economic status). However, resolving disparities in health care need not await the resolution of such national social epidemics that ride political roller coasters, depending on the politics of the day and the political administration of the moment.

Many of the solutions are accessible here. They are accessible now. It takes due diligence with education, personal discipline, financial commitment, and compassion. Such due diligence lies at our fingertips.

REFERENCES

Ahmad, M., & Lachs, M. (2002). Elder abuse and neglect: What physicians can and should do. *Cleveland Clinic Journal of Medicine, 69(10)*, 801.

American Cancer Society (ACS). (2003). Statistics for 2003. Available at http://www.cancer.org/docroot/STT/stt_0_2003.ASP?siteasea=STT&Level=1. Accessed on December 17, 2003.

American Diabetes Association. (1997). Report of the Expert Committee on the Diagnosis and Classification of Diabetes Mellitus. *Diabetes Care, 20*, 118.

American Heart Association, Heart Facts. (2002). All Americans, CDC/NCHS and the American Heart Association, 4–7.

Bakris, G.L., Ferdinand, K.C., Douglas, J.G., & Sowers, J.R. (2002). Optimal treatment of hypertension in African Americans. *Postgraduate Medicine, 12(4)*, 2–7.

Carson, S.A., & Buster, J.L. (1993). Ectopic pregnancy. *New England Journal of Medicine, 329*, 1174–1181.

Centers for Disease Control. (CDC). (2003). Hepatitis B Fact Sheet. Atlanta, GA; Division of Vival Hepatitis, Centers for Disease Control and Prevention, National Center for Infectious Diseases.

Centers for Disease Control (CDC). (2003). Hepatitis C Fact Sheet. Atlanta, GA; Division of Vival Hepatitis, Centers for Disease Control and Prevention, National Center for Infectious Diseases.

Centers for Disease Control and Prevention (CDC)/National Center for Health Statistics (NCHS) (1994).

Collins, R., Hyattsville, MD. & Winkleby, M.A. (2002). African American women and men at high and low risk for hypertension: A signal detection analysis of NHANES III, 1988–1994. *Preventive Medicine, 35(4)*, 303–312.

Department of Health and Human Services (DHHS). (2002). Emergency Department trends from the Drug Abuse Warning Network (DAWN): preliminary estimates. Substance Abuse and Mental Health Services Administration (January–June).

El-Kebbi, I.M., Cook, C.B., Ziemer, D.C., Miller, C.D., Gallina, D.L., & Phillips, L.S. (2003). Association of younger age with poor glycemic control and obesity in urban African Americans with type 2 diabetes. *Archives of Internal Medicine, 163*, 69.

Fauci, A.S., et al. (1998). *Harrison's principles of internal medicine* (14th ed.). New York: McGraw-Hill.

Gaskin, D.J, & Hoffman, C. (2000). Racial and ethnic differences in preventable hospitalizations across 10 states. *Medical Care Research Review, 57(Supple 1)*, 85–107.

Gazmararian, J.A. (2000). Violence and reproductive health, knowledge and future research directions. *Maternal and Child Health Journal* (special issue) *4(2)*.

Hawkins, D.F. (1996). Ethnicity race class and adolescent violence (CSPV-006). Center for the Study and Prevention of Violence, Institute of Behavioral Science, University of Colorado.

Jenkins, C.D., Tuthill, R.W., Tannenbaum, S.I., & Kirby, C.R. (1997). Zones of excess mortality in Massachusetts. *New England Journal of Medicine, 296*, 1354–1356.

Joint National Committee (JNC) on Prevention, Detection, Evaluation, and Treatment of High Blood Pressure (1997). *Archives Internal Medicine, 157(21)*, 2719–2728.

Kuzmarski, M.J., Fiegal, K.M., Campbell, S.M., & Johnson, C.L. (1994). Increasing prevalence of overweight among U.S. adults: The National Health and Nutrition Examination Surveys, 1960 to 1991. *Journal of the American Medical Association, 272*, 295, 211.

Li, C., Malone, K.E., & Daling, J.R. (2003). Differences in breast cancer stage, treatment, and survival by race and ethnicity. *Archives Internal Medicine, 163*, 23.

McCord, C., & Freeman, H. (1990). Excess mortality in Harlem. *New England Journal of Medicine, 322*, 173–177.

McCraig, L.F. & Burt, C.W. (2001a). National Hospital Ambulatory Medical Care Survey: 2000. Hyattsville, MD: National Center for Health Statistics.

McCraig, L.F. & Burt, C.W. (2001b). National Hospital Ambulatory Medical Care Survey: 2000. Advance Data from Vital and Health Statistics No. 326. Hyattsville, MD: National Center for Health Statistics.

McCraig, L.F., & Ly, N. (2002). National Hospital Ambulatory Medical Care Survey: 2000 emergency department summary. Advance Data, 326 (April 22nd).

Miller, B.A., Reis, L.A., & Hankey, B F. (1993). Cancer statistics review 1973–1990, National Cancer Institute, NIH Pub. 93-2789, 1.

Morbidity and Mortality Weekly Report (1994). Current trends in homicides among 15–19-year-old males—United States, 1963–1991. *Morbidity and Mortality Weekly Report 43(40)*, 725–727.

National Cancer Institute (NCI). (2002). Cancer Control & Population Sciences: SEER Cancer Statistics Review, 1973–1999.

National Center for Health Statistics (NCHS). Health, United States, 2001 with Urban and Rural Health Chartbook. Hysttsville, MD, 2001.

National Coalition Against Domestic Violence (NCADV) (2004). Poll Finds Domestic Violence is Women's Main Concern. Available at http://www.ncadv.org/press_release.html. Accessed on January 17, 2004.

National Diabetes Informational Clearinghouse. (2002, April). National diabetes statistics. NIH publication 02-3892, Fact sheet.

Ni, H., Coriaty-Nelson, Z., Schiller, J., Hao, C., Cohen, R.A., & Barnes, P. (2003). Early release of selected estimates based on data from the January–June 2003 National Health Interview Survey. National Center for Health Statistics. Available at http://www.cdc.gov/nchs/nhis.htm. Accessed in December 2003.

Pope, J.H. (2000). Missed diagnoses of acute cardiac ischemia in the emergency department. *New England Journal of Medicine, 342*, 1163–1170.

Selker H.P., et al. (1998). Use of the acute cardiac ischemia time-insensitive predictive instrument (ACI-TIPI) to assist with triage of patients with chest pain or other symptoms suggestive of acute cardiac ischemia. *Annals of Internal Medicine, 129*, 845–855.

Sicca, D.A., & Douglas, J.G. (2001). The African American Study of Kidney Disease and Hypertension (AASK); new findings. *Journal Clinical Hypertension, 3(4)*, 244–51.

U.S. Department of Health and Human Services Centers for Disease Control and Prevention. (1997, July). C.D.C. Vaccine Informational Statement.

U.S. Department of Health and Human Services (USDHHS). Healthy People 2010. (2nd ed.). (2000). With understanding and improving health and objectives for improving health. 2 vols. Washington, DC: U.S. Government Printing Office.

Waiting Group for the Women's Health Initiative. (2002). Risks and benefits of combined estrogen and progestin in healthy postmenopausal women: Principal results from the Women's Health Initiative, randomized controlled trial. *AMA Express*.

CHAPTER 30

Homelessness and Health Problems among African Americans

RICHARD A. ENGLISH,
FARIYAL ROSS-SHERIFF, AND ALTAF HUSAIN

INTRODUCTION

Homelessness among African Americans is not well understood or explored. While most studies have documented the large presence of African Americans among the homeless, in few studies have they been the principal object of analysis. There is some evidence that homelessness has been on the rise among African Americans, especially since the 1980s and the 1990s. Clearly, major policy changes over the past two decades in the availability of affordable housing (Midgley et al., 2000, pp. 243–245), racial discrimination in housing (Millennial Housing Commission Report, 2002), long-term joblessness (Wilson, 1987, 1996), health problems (Geronimus, 1992, 1998; LaPlante & Carlson, 1996; McNeil, 1993), and affordable health care (Geiger, 1996) have exposed many African Americans to the risk of poor and inadequate housing, low-wage jobs and unemployment, and poor health outcomes and care.

In this chapter we address specifically the plight of African Americans who are homeless. What is the disproportionality among the homeless? It is well documented that African Americans are uncommonly burdened by untreated illnesses, lack of access to quality health care, and lack of treatment for long-term and chronic diseases (USDHHS, 2000). What is the status of health care for the African American homeless population? What health-care services do African Americans use for their health-care needs?

The purpose of this chapter is to explore homelessness among African Americans and to compare it with that of other Americans and to examine health issues in the lives of homeless adult African Americans. We first examine key demographic components of homelessness in the United States and compare them with those of homeless adult African Americans. Next, we present data on the health problems of African Americans. Using data from the National Survey of Homeless Assistance Providers and Clients (NSHAPC),[1] we examine the health status of homeless adult African Americans (U.S. Census Bureau, 2000b). We explore the interaction of health and homelessness among African Americans. What happens to homeless African Americans with serious health challenges? Do they just get sick and die? The answers to these two latter questions are beyond the scope of this chapter. They are being raised due to their importance for public policy and social intervention. What can be done? In conclusion, we offer some recommendations for behavioral interventions and research.

STATE OF HOMELESSNESS IN THE UNITED STATES: AN OVERVIEW

A description of the state of the homeless in America is presented in this section. It is based on a comprehensive analysis of national and regional data on demographic and other characteristics of homeless people. In these data information is provided on the numbers of homeless and proportion of homeless people nationally and in selected regions, on the numbers and proportions of African American homeless populations, their geographic dispersion, and some of the critical dynamics of homelessness.

Fundamental to the question of homelessness in America is, Why are so many people homeless in America? Elliot Liebow (1993) addressed this question at the end of his book on homelessness. Liebow wrote that "there are many homeless people in America and that is a shame. Shame on you, shame on me, shame on America. Shame because it is the result of choices we have made; shame because it does not have to be" (Liebow, 1993, p. 223). Liebow's point was simply this: people are not homeless because of their condition of physical disability, unemployment, grave illness, mental health, drugs or alcohol abuse, and other misfortunes of life. For Liebow, homelessness is not an individual matter; rather, "homeless people are homeless because they do not have a place to live" (Liebow, 1993, p. 224). Additionally, Liebow argued that homelessness is deeply rooted in poverty. From our perspective, poverty and personal misfortunes place people at risk for homelessness. However, homelessness is also a result of failed public policies and too often the lack of comprehensive policies that address the multifaceted aspects of homeless people's lives. Among these policies are those dealing with affordable housing, employment, health, and mental health. The challenge for policymakers is to ensure that these policies address the needs of poor people and minorities of color. In the case of health and mental health, there is an additional concern that future policies address issues of prevention and early intervention.

Definition of Homelessness, and How Large is America's Homeless Population?

There is no universally agreed upon definition of the population experiencing homelessness. Some researchers have taken practical and literal definitions of homelessness. Burt in her 1987 survey of a representative sample of large cities (100,000 or more residents) "defined people as homeless if they met any of three tests:

- They said they had no home or permanent place to live.
- They said their home was a shelter, a hotel paid for with vouchers for the homeless, or a place not intended for sleeping.
- They said they lived in someone else's home but did not have a regular arrangement allowing them to stay there at least five days a week" (Burt, 1992, listed in Jencks, 1994, p. 10).

Rossi (1989, pp. 10–13) defined homelessness literally as not having customary and regular access to a conventional dwelling. Similarly, Jencks (1994, p. 7) took a narrow perspective and defined homeless as those people who slept in a public place or a shelter during a given week. Sosin et al., (1988) defined homelessness as residential instability. Some researchers have combined the practical/ literal perspective of defining homelessness and added a sociological dimension. In addition to the residential dimension of homelessness, Snow and Anderson (1993) added a familial support dimension and a role-based dignity and moral worth dimension. Beyond conceptualizing homelessness as the absence of a dwelling place or conventional permanent housing, homelessness is viewed as (1) a familial-support system and (2) a role based on dignity and moral worth.

Homelessness as the presence or absence of familial support emphasizes social bonds and relationships. Dignity and moral worth are associated with the role of homeless. When the homeless are stigmatized, they have are prone to have low levels of dignity. Many researchers, policymakers, and homeless providers utilize the definition of homeless found in the Stewart B. McKinney Homeless Assistance Act enacted in July 1987 (U.S. Congress, 1987), which was renamed the McKinney-Vento Homeless Assistance Act.

Because of difficulties in counting the homeless, many researchers restrict their inquiry to localities and geographic regions and focus upon certain aspects of service delivery systems for the homeless. Given the varied conditions under which the homeless live, including shelters, on the streets, in cars and parks, under bridges, on sidewalks, and at other unconventional locations as well as temporary domicile with families and friends, it is difficult to obtain a reliable count of the entire population of homeless persons. It has been documented in countless studies that homeless persons are highly mobile and transitory, moving from place to place, not static. For many homeless people, homelessness is an intermittent and short-term experience, rather than long-term and permanent (Sosin et al., 1988).

Most of the studies reported in this chapter use the definition of homeless found in the Stewart B. McKinney Homeless Assistance Act (P.L. No. 100-77). According to this act a homeless person (U.S. Congress, 1987) is:

(1) an individual who lacks a fixed, regular, and adequate nighttime residence;

[or]

(2) an individual who has a primary nighttime residence that is:
    (A) a supervised publicly or privately operated shelter, designed to provide temporary living accommodations (including welfare hotels, congregate shelters, and transitional housing for the mentally ill);
    (B) an institution that provides a temporary residence for individuals intended to be institutionalized; or
    (C) a public or private place not designed for, or ordinarily used as, a regular sleeping accommodation for human beings.

This definition is applied to homeless families as well. Thus, it is broad and inclusive of a wide range of persons experiencing homelessness in varied, unconventional locations.

Historically, there has been a disagreement about defining and counting the homeless (Culhane & Hornburg, 1997). This debate gained momentum in the 1980s. During the 1980s, there was considerable disagreement among government agencies, citizen groups, advocates, and scholars about the numbers of homeless individuals in the U.S. population. However, there was no disagreement that homelessness had become a major national problem (English & Ross-Sheriff, 1998). The U.S. Department of Housing and Urban Development (USHUD, 1984) estimates were on the low side, 250,000 to 350,000. Bassuk (1984) indicated that the National Coalition for the Homeless in 1983 reported that there were 2.5 million homeless persons in the United States. Further, she indicated this number probably increased to 3 million in 1984. In 1983, Mitch Snyder, a leading advocate for the homeless, estimated there were 2 million to 3 million homeless persons in America (Hombs & Snyder, 1983). The debate continues in the twenty-first century.

In two recent national counts of homeless in 1996 and in 2000, estimates of the homeless ranged from 280,527 to 800,000. The first count was reported by the U.S. Census Bureau (2000a). They reported that nationally 280,527 people were counted in emergency and transitional shelters for the homeless, at soup kitchens, on the streets, and at targeted nonsheltered outdoor locations identified by local governments. The bureau decided not to release its count on targeted nonsheltered outdoor locations realizing that this was not an accurate, full, and complete count of persons or families designated as homeless. The bureau emphasized the limitations of these data and warned that both counts should not be used as measures of the population experiencing homelessness (U.S. Census Bureau, 2001).

The second count of 800,000 homeless people on given day was reported in the National Survey of Homeless Assistance Providers and Clients (Burt et al., 1999). Extrapolating based on these two counts, these researchers estimated that between 2.3 and 3.5 million persons experienced homelessness at least once over the course of the year.

The U.S. Census Bureau (2000b) count of 280,527 homeless persons in shelters and at targeted nonsheltered locations is not intended to be a national comprehensive enumeration of the homeless. It is a snapshot of shelter users on a particular night and two nights at selected outdoor locations where the homeless congregate. It is an undercount of the homeless since it excludes large numbers of persons experiencing homelessness who are not found at these locations on these particular nights.

Although the 1996 national survey, NSHAPC, was conducted over a two-month period throughout the United States, it is also an undercount of persons experiencing homelessness. It was restricted to homeless persons using services provided for the homeless and excluded those who did not use the service. These service providers offered an extensive range of services, and therefore, the survey is likely to have included a large number of persons experiencing homelessness in local communities. While both the NSHAPC study and the census figures are undercounts, the NSHAPC study is more comprehensive than the 2000 census (U.S. Census Bureau, 2000a).

The discussion of counting the homeless and attempts to achieve an estimate of a national count of homelessness at a particular time are flawed by methodological and conceptual problems, the fluidity and diversity of the homeless population, and local and national politics. Given the reality that homeless services and programs are funded by federal, state, and local governments, the debate among advocates, service providers, policymakers, and politicians about how many persons are homeless in the United States and what services they need continues to be a highly contested matter.

Cordray and Pion (1997) suggest that achieving estimates of the number of homeless persons would be helpful if underlying conceptual definitions of homelessness are clarified (i.e., what is meant by homeless) and that a broad definition of homelessness is advised in order to serve multiple constituencies. Further, these researchers suggest that segmenting the total homeless population into "policy-relevant components" would address the issue of the highly diverse and complex composition of the homeless. Perhaps most importantly and instructively for our purpose is Cordray and Pion's advise to those seeking estimates of the homeless population. At the outset of the research they suggest that investigators identify the intended uses of the estimates. Is the goal of the estimate to assess the magnitude of the problem, to improve services, and/or to plan for short- or long-term service delivery for the population? These are examples of critical questions they raise (Cordray & Pion, 1997, pp. 84–85). For purposes of this chapter, our goal is to establish a reasonable national estimate of persons experiencing homelessness in order to gauge the magnitude of the problem nationally, particularly among African Americans.

In summary, the national estimates of homeless persons from 1983 to 2000 have ranged from 2 million to 3.5 million during any given year. In their 2003 annual report on hunger and homelessness, the U.S. Conference of Mayors reported that the demand for emergency shelter had increased on the average by 13 percent across its 25 survey cities (USCM, 2003, p. 35). The percentage of increase ranged from a low of 1 percent in Kansas City and Philadelphia to a high of 226 percent in Louisville, Kentucky. In Washington, D.C. there was an 12 percent increase in demand for emergency shelter (USCM, 2003, p. 78). The clear implication is that the number of homeless persons in these major cities of America had also increased. Regardless of the count, the number of persons experiencing homelessness has not diminished.

Why were these studies selected? Criteria for selecting research studies for this chapter included (1) current national data on homelessness; (2) data that covered information about African American homeless; (3) data that provided demographic information for comparing African American homeless with other racial and ethnic groups; and (4) regional studies on homeless families with a range of circumstances, including experiences of African American homeless families.

METHODOLOGY OF SELECTED STUDIES

For a discussion of the status of homelessness in America, we draw from three national data sources to develop a profile of homeless people and three regional sources of data to develop a profile of homeless families. The national sources include (1) the U.S. Conference of Mayors (USCM) 2003 annual national survey of hunger and homelessness in 25 cities, (2) the National Survey of Homeless Assistance Providers and Clients (NSHAPC) study conducted by the U.S. Bureau of Census in 1996 (Burt et al., 1999), and (3) the U.S. Census Bureau 2000(b) data on emergency and transitional shelter populations. The regional sources of data on homeless families include (1) the Stanford Studies of Homeless Children and Youth (1991), (2) Homeless Families Today (Institute for Children and Poverty, 1998), and (3) a study of Homeless Families Seeking Shelter in Washington, D.C. (English & Ross-Sheriff, 1998). A brief description of each of these data sources along with their methodologies is presented below.

National Data Sources

1. The USCM annual survey of hunger and homelessness in America 2003   The 2003 United States Conference of Mayors' (USCM, 2003) Status Report on Hunger and Homelessness in America's Cities is an annual survey that has been conducted since 1987. In the survey, homeless persons are defined as "those who reside in shelters, on the streets, in cars, or in other locations not intended as residences" (USCM, 2003, p. 109). A questionnaire is mailed to the members of the task force (i.e., the mayors of the 25 cities as the respondents for the questionnaire). The 2002 status report covers the period starting from November 1, 2002, to October 31, 2003. The purpose of the survey is to develop a demographic profile of the hungry and the homeless as well as the causes of hunger and homelessness. Respondents are asked to assess the demand for emergency food assistance and emergency shelter in their cities as well as the capacity of local agencies to meet that demand. In the survey information is also elicited about exemplary programs or best practices being implemented in response to hunger and homelessness. Finally, the survey focuses on the availability of affordable housing for low-income people and requests respondents to gauge the impact of the economy on hunger and homelessness.

2. NSHAPC Survey, 1996   The 1996 National Survey of Homeless Assistance Providers and Clients (NSHAPC) was a study conducted by the Interagency Council of the Homeless (ICH) "to provide information about the providers of homeless assistance services and the characteristics of homeless clients who use services" (Burt et al., 1999, p. 1). The data were collected between October and November 1996, based on a "statistical sample of 76 metropolitan and non-metropolitan areas, including small cities and rural areas (Burt et al., 1999, p. xvii).[2] The ICH is a working group of the White House Domestic Policy Council. Under the auspices of the ICH, the survey was designed and funded by 12 federal agencies. The U.S. Bureau of Census collected the data and the Urban Institute of Washington, D.C., conducted the analysis (Burt et al., 1999, xvii).

The 4,207 clients in the NSHAPC survey were clients of homeless assistance programs, emergency shelters, housing and food services, health services, soup kitchens, and street outreach programs. Because the NSHAPC survey sample was from programs providing an extensive range of services for the homeless, it is likely to have included the vast majority of homeless persons in the communities with services for the homeless. The sample also included service users who were previously homeless and nonhomeless. However, it did not include homeless who do not use services or those in communities that have few or no homeless assistance services. For this chapter only those clients who were homeless are included in our analysis (N = 2,643).

The researchers in the NSAHPC survey adopted the definition of homelessness used in the Stewart B. McKinney Homeless Assistance Act of 1987 (U.S. Congress, House, 1987). Clients were interviewed in face-to-face interviews. A wide array of topics were covered. For the analysis used in this chapter only the following topics are included:

- Current living condition
- Demographic characteristics
- Employment
- Income
- Physical health and medical history in past year

3. The U.S. Census Bureau 2000, Census 2000 Special Reports, Emergency and Transitional Shelter Populations: 2000   In census 2000, the U.S. Census Bureau enumerated homeless people living in emergency and transitional shelters on March 27, 2000. In addition, "the Census Bureau developed a specialized operation to enumerate people at selected service locations serving people without conventional housing" (U.S. Census Bureau, 2000a, p. 2). This specialized operation was called the Service-Based Enumeration (SBE). It was conducted March 27–29, 2000, "at shelters, soup kitchens, regularly scheduled vans and targeted non-sheltered outdoor locations" (p. 2). The bureau issued disclaimers that its enumeration of "people without conventional housing" had limitations and was not to be considered a count of the homeless. The Census Bureau defined people without conventional housing "as the population who may be missed in the traditional enumeration of housing units and group quarters" (p. 1). Persons living in shelters for abused women or for domestic violence were not included in these data.

Regional Data Sources

4. The Stanford Studies of Homeless Families, Children and Youth, 1991   During 1990 and 1991 the Stanford University Center for the Study of Families, Children and Youth conducted nine interconnected studies on homeless families with children and youth under 18 years of age, in two northern California counties, Santa Clara and San Mateo. The studies focused on processes that lead families in and out of homelessness. Emphasis was given to internal experiences of families as they were influenced by external societal and economic factors. Three ethnic groups were included in the study: African Americans, Hispanics of Mexican descent, and non-Hispanic Whites. Respondents in the study were families contacted through agencies and shelters. Homeless families that never used services were not included, nor were homeless families in shelters for battered women.

The purpose of these studies was not to conduct a census of homeless families and individuals in the two counties. For example, homeless parents and children living in the streets, in cars, parks, and empty buildings were not included. Rather, these studies of homeless families with children that sought services or shelter attempted to determine why some families are more successful than others in finding a home. These studies of the homeless, formerly homeless, and at-risk families had a combined total of 809 families with 1,021 adults and 1,720 children (N = 2,741).

5. Homeless Families Study, Our Challenge Tomorrow: A regional perspective (1997)   The Institute for Children and Poverty collaborated with the Graduate School of International & Public Affairs at Columbia University and conducted a survey on the demography of families throughout New York City and northern New Jersey during the spring of 1997. Using an interview schedule,

Table 30.1
Demographic characteristics of homeless people in America from selected national studies, 1996, 2000, and 2002 (in percentages)

Demographic Information	U.S. Census[1] (2000) N= 163,028	Mayors Conference[2] (2002) N=25 cities	NSHAPC[3] (1996) N=2643 clients
Race[4]			
African American	40	50	43
White	41	35	40
Hispanic	20	12	12
Other	10	3	5
Gender			
Male	62		67
Female	38	NA	33
Age			
<18			1
18-24	NA	NA	10
25-44			61
45-64			21
65+			2
Employment			
Employed		22	43
Unemployed	NA	78	56
Education			
<high school			39
High school or higher	NA	NA	61

[1] *Sources*: U.S. Census Bureau (2000a). Current Population Survey, March 2000, Racial Statistics Branch, Population Division. Available at: http://www.census.gov/population/socdemo/race/black/ppl-142/tab21.txt

[2] U.S. Conference of Mayors (USCM). (2002). The Status of Hunger and Homelessness in America's Major Cities. Washington, D.C.: Author. Available at: http://www.usmayors.org/uscm/home.asp The data collected by the Mayors Conference are related to each city, rather than aggregated across all cities. However, data reported for race and employment are aggregated based on the total number of individuals in the survey of all the cities.

[3] *Source*: U.S. Census Bureau (2000b). *National Survey of Homeless Assistance Providers and Clients (NSHAPC)*. Available at: http://www.census.gov/prod/www/nshapc/NSHAPC4.html

[4] On the race categories, the percentage adds up to over 100 percent because of overlap between Whites and Hispanics. Whites include Hispanic Whites.

data were collected from 743 homeless heads of households living in 14 emergency and transitional family shelters.

6. Homeless families seeking shelter in Washington, D.C., 1998   This study of 550 families seeking emergency shelter during 1997 was based on the agency intake records of the Family Resource Center (FRC) of the Community Partnership for the Prevention of Homelessness, an agency providing emergency and transitional shelter services through a Continuum of Care approach to individuals and families in Washington, D.C. The subjects were largely females and African American (95 percent) heads of households with children.

The purpose of this study of homeless families seeking emergency shelter was twofold: (1) to document the profiles of families seeking emergency shelter and (2) to determine and document the conditions of these families and where they were living while waiting for emergency shelter. Families

Table 30.2

A comparison of demographic characteristics of nonhomeless and homeless African American populations, 1999 and 1996

Characteristics	African American Non-homeless Population[1] (N=35,509 in thousands)			African American Homeless Sample (1136)		
	Category	N	%	Category	N	%
Age group	<19	12,710	36%	<18	12	1%
	20-24	2,762	7%	18-24	96	9%
	24-44	10,862	31%	25-44	779	69%
	45-64	6,419	18%	45-64	227	20%
	65+	2,755	8%	65+	13	1%
Gender	Males	8,879	44%	Males	769	68%
	Females	11,157	56%	Females	367	32%
Income	<2499	109	1%	0	166	15%
	2500-9,999	547	5%	<1200	186	16%
	10,000-24,999	4611	40%	1200-8,399	616	54%
	25,000-49,999	4704	41%	8401-11,999	92	8%
	50,000-74999	1,124	10%	12000-14,400	69	6%
	75,000 +	445	4%			
Level of Education	Less than high school	4,316	22%	Less than high school	377	37%
	High school Diploma/GED	7,030	35%	High school diploma/GED	399	35%
	More than a high school	8,669	43%	More than High school	319	28%
Employment	NA			Yes	512	45%
				No	623	55%

[1] *Source*: U.S. Census Bureau (2000a).

with children seeking emergency shelter must do so at the FRC, a centralized intake service for families in the District of Columbia. The data for this study were collected and analyzed in 1998.

The data from the above six studies were extracted to obtain a demographic profile of the homeless in the United States at the national and regional levels (see Tables 30.1 and 2). The national profile (Table 30.2) is representative of homeless persons, while the regional profile (Table 30.3) presents demographic information on homeless families.

DEMOGRAPHIC PROFILE

Key questions in this section are: What are the demographic characteristics of homeless adults in the nation? How do they compare with African Americans? How do African American homeless compare with nonhomeless African American adults?

Table 30.3
Demographic characteristics of homeless families in America from selected regional studies: California, New York, Washington D.C., 1991, 1997, 1998

Demographic Information	Stanford Study (1991)	New York Study (1997) N=743 Heads of Households	Washington D.C. (1998) N=550 Heads of Households
Race[1]			
African American	25%	59%	97%
White	29%	3%	1%
Hispanic	36%	32%	1%
Other	10%	6%	2%
Gender			
Male		11%	5%
Female	NA	89%	95%
Age	NA	< 18 4% 19-25 38% 26-33 18% >34 40%	20-29 45% 30-39 35% 40-49 15% 50-59 2%
Employment			
Employed		9%	7%
Unemployed	NA	91%	93%
Education			
<high school		59%	52%
High school or higher	NA	41%	45%
Marital Status of Parents			
Married		24%	9%
Single		81%	80%
Never married		60%	-
Other	NA	16%	9%
Number of children per family	NA	0-1 30% 2 26% 3-4 27% 5 or more 23%	1 43% 2 31% 3 16% 4 or more 8%
Age of children in Shelter			
Under 1 year old			5%
Under 5		47%	48%
5-18	NA	53%	47%
Median Annual Household Income		$11,440	$3,684

[1] On the race categories, the percentage adds up to over 100 percent because of overlap between Whites and Hispanics. Whites include Hispanic Whites.

A majority of the homeless persons in the United States are men. In both the U.S. Census 2000 report (2000b) and NSHAPC Survey over 60 percent of the homeless are men (see Table 30.1). In these data slightly more African Americans are homeless than either Whites or Hispanics. In the Mayors' Status Report on Hunger and Homelessness (USCM, 2003) 50 percent of the homeless persons are African Americans.

Depending on what data are available, these three national data sets reveal that homeless persons are predominantly African American (40 percent, 50 percent, 43 percent), male (62 percent and 67 percent), between the age range of 25 to 44 (61 percent), with high levels of unemployment (56 percent and 78 percent), and high school education and higher (61 percent). As seen in Table 30.1, not all these data are present in all three data sets all the time.

What percent of the 2 million to 3.5 million homeless are African American? What reasonable estimates can be derived? Few researchers have estimated the numbers of homeless African Americans in the United States. Based on a review of a number of research studies, Jencks (1994) reported that 45 percent of homeless adults in the United States in 1987 were African American (Jencks, 1994, p. 22). From the proportions of the national studies cited in this chapter (see Table 30.1) we have extrapolated a conservative estimate of African American homeless persons. Based on the percentages of 40, 50 and 43 percent African Americans in the three national data sets, respectively, we estimate that there are between 320,000 (40 percent of 800,000) and 400,000 (50 percent of 800,000). This estimate is disproportionately higher than the population of any other racial or ethnic group in America.

For a comparison of homeless African Americans and the nonhomeless African American population, we selected demographic characteristics of each group from the U.S. Census Bureau, Current Population Survey March 2000 and from the NSHAPC sample (U.S. Census Bureau, 2000b) (see Table 30.2). In the U.S. African American population (2000), slightly more than a third of the population is under age 18 (36 percent) while about 1 percent of the African Americans in the NSHAPC sample reported being under age 18. This proportion, in the latter sample, does not indicate the number of homeless children who are African American. Regional studies of African American homeless families reveal significant numbers of families with minor children (English & Ross-Sheriff, 1998).

The largest proportion of homeless people in the NSHAPC Survey are between the ages of 25 and 44 (69 percent), while only 31 percent of 25- to 44-year-olds are in the nonhomeless African American population. About an equal number of those who are 45 to 64 years old are in the nonhomeless population in the U.S. Census 2000(b) (18 percent) and homeless population in the NSHAPC survey (20 percent). Very few older African American adults (those 65 years old and older) are homeless (1 percent in the NSHAPC survey) compared with 8 percent nonhomeless African American in the U.S. Census 2000(a) data. Homelessness is prevalent among African Americans who are in their mid-20s to mid-40s (age 25 to 44). There are low to modest numbers of homeless African Americans who are younger (under age 24) and older (over 65 years of age). Thus, there are fewer homeless persons at both ends of the age spectrum among African Americans. There is an imbalance in the gender ratio in the nonhomeless African American population (44 percent are men). There is a more pronounced imbalance in the gender ratio in the homeless sample (68 percent male and 32 percent female).

Homeless African Americans are significantly undereducated compared to those in the nonhomeless African American population. Almost one-half (43 percent) of African American nonhomeless have more than a high school education. Only 28 percent of the African American homeless in the survey sample have gone beyond high school.

Clearly, the homeless are poor people. Yet, in the NSHAPC Survey African American homeless report higher levels of income than other studies. In these data 54 percent of the homeless respondents had monthly incomes of $100 to $699, which is approximately in the annual income range of $1,200 to $8,399. Six percent had monthly incomes of $1,000 to $1,200, that is, an annual income of $12,000 to $14,000. In the nonhomeless U.S. African American population a majority are above the poverty level (76 percent). In the White population 92 percent are above the poverty level (U.S. Census Bureau, 2000a). More than two-thirds of the nonhomeless African American population in 2000 was in the labor force (67 percent). Among the homeless in the NSHAPC Survey less than one-half were in the labor force (45 percent).

In describing the status of homelessness among African American families in regional studies, we draw upon the Stanford Studies of Homeless Families, Children and Youth (1991) in two northern California counties, Santa Clara and San Mateo, the New York and Northern New Jersey Study of Homeless Families, and the English and Ross-Sheriff study of Homeless Families Seeking Emergency Shelter in Washington, D.C. Demographic data from these three studies are presented in Table 30.3.

In the Stanford Studies (1991) African Americans constituted about 4 percent of the population in both counties and 25 percent of the homeless families. Non-Hispanic Whites are 70 percent of the counties' population and 29 percent of the homeless families. Hispanics constituted 20 percent of the population in the two counties and have 25 percent of homeless families. Thus, while African Americans had the smallest proportion of homeless families in the two counties, they were the most overrepresented of the three groups. The African American families in the Stanford Studies were more likely to be "single parents, to have never married, to have received government aid, and to be long-term residents of the area" (Stanford Center, 1991, p. 18). These researchers concluded that homelessness among African Americans was "associated with long-term poverty, participation in the welfare system, and the problems of single parenthood" (Stanford Center, 1991, p. 18). In the Stanford Studies as well as in other studies, social support from families and friends made a powerful difference between being housed and homeless. The Stanford investigators replicated Rossi's (1989) Chicago study of homeless individuals. Rossi found that homeless persons had fewer kin or friends living in the Chicago area. The Stanford researchers reported that their homeless families had lower levels of social support than other poor, nonhomeless families. Even though homeless families had almost as many relatives living in the Bay Area as did poor, at-risk families, homeless families had less reliable family support. These researchers reported that families who were poor and at risk for homelessness were able to stay with their relatives for longer periods of time than homeless families. These researchers were careful to point out that low levels of social support alone do not cause homelessness. Rather, they, in combination with low income and housing costs or other crises, can push a family into homelessness (Stanford Center, 1991, pp. 15–16).

Choi and Snyder (1999) conducted a study of 80 homeless families (70 percent African American and 80 percent headed by women) living in shelters in Buffalo and Syracuse, New York. Both cities have large racially segregated inner cities. The median age of these parents was 31 years of age (age range 17 years to 49 years). Most of them (60 percent) were single and not married and had less than a high school education (Choi & Snyder, 1999, p. 52). Choi and Snyder reported that as a group these families were cut off from both informal and formal systems of care and social supports. Forty-one percent indicated that they did not have any informal support from family, kin, or friends. Those with family ties reported that their relatives were only a little better off economically than themselves; thus, doubling up with relatives or friends was of short-term duration.

The heads of the household in the New York region study (Institute for Children and Poverty, 1998) are predominantly female (89 percent). A majority are African American (59 percent), single (60 percent), with less than high school education (59 percent), and between the ages of 19 and 30 (56 percent). These are young, unmarried mothers with two to three children "who grew up in poverty." Describing the childhood of these homeless families, the Institute for Children and Poverty (1998) notes further that a majority of the "parents who are homeless today lived in poverty as children; more than half (53%) grew up in families that received some type of family assistance-most frequently Aid to Families with Dependent Children (AFDC, now Temporary Assistance to Needy Families) and/or food stamps." The other half of homeless parents came from different backgrounds. They did not grow up in poverty but rather in working-class families who were self-sufficient and did not use public welfare. Now they are homeless and losing ground from more stable situations.

In their study of homeless families seeking emergency shelter in Washington, D.C., English and Ross-Sheriff (1998) analyzed the administrative records of 550 families seeking emergency shelter in 1998. The heads of households are predominantly female (95 percent), African American (97 percent), 20 to 39 years of age (80 percent), and single (80 percent), and a little over half had less than high school education (52 percent). Few of the subjects in the study (9 percent) are married, and close to half (45 percent) had high school and post–high school education (Table 30.3). Most of these African Americans are unemployed (93 percent). For the women in this study, public welfare, TANF is the principal source of their monthly income. At the time they completed their application/interview for emergency shelter, the majority of these homeless families were living with either relatives or friends. Only a few were living on the street, a finding that is replicated in other studies. Contrary to general viewpoints, the heads of households in the study had small families. About three-quarters of them had only two children, who accompanied them while seeking emergency shelter.

This review of regional studies of homeless families reveals a profile of young women with two to three under school age children. They have low educational attainment, few, if any, job skills, and poor employment outcomes. Most of these young women are African Americans and in the Stanford Studies overrepresented among the homeless. Those with these attributes who are not homeless are at risk for homelessness.

Homelessness among African Americans is largely a problem of adults between the ages of 25 and 44. A majority of them are men. Homeless families are largely headed by women who are unmarried. African Americans are disproportionately represented among homeless men and female-headed families.

HEALTH PROBLEMS AND AFRICAN AMERICANS

African Americans in general have poorer health and are worse off in regard to access and quality of health care compared to White Americans. While the health status of African Americans has improved over the past several decades, the persistence of poor health outcomes has gone unabated (Smedley et al., 2002). Aggravated by living in the streets, lack of access to health care, and lack of stable living environments to take care of one's self and others, the health outlook of homeless African Americans is expected therefore to be worse.

In this chapter we first present selected literature on health care and homelessness. Next, we examine some health issues related to nonhomeless African Americans followed by comparative analyses of selected diseases of homeless African Americans and nonhomeless population of African Americans. Data from NSHAPC survey (Burt et al., 1999) and *Healthy People 2010* (USDHHS, 2000, vol. 1) are used for these analyses.

Selected Literature on Health Care and Homeless

Health problems and diseases associated with homelessness are well documented in the literature. Furthermore, it is commonly agreed that homelessness increases the risk of developing health problems (Institute of Medicine, 1988; Zuk, 1995; Hudson, 1998). The Committee on Health Care Services for Homeless People noted, "Homeless people are at high risk for a broad range of acute and chronic illnesses" (Institute of Medicine, 1988, p. 39). They also noted that recent data from individual published reports in the medical literature indicate that homelessness is associated with a number of physical and mental health problems. They observed three types of interaction between health and homelessness. First, "some health problems precede and causally contribute to homelessness"; second, health problems arise from homeless conditions, that is, health problems as a consequence of homelessness; and third, "homelessness complicates the treatment of many diseases" (Institute of Medicine, 1988, p. 39).

Research studies on homeless populations indicate that homeless people have high rates of illnesses and disabilities (Breakey et al., 1989; Kushel et al., 2001), and they get neither the level nor the quality of health-care services they need. In a secondary analysis of the NSHAPC data (ICH, 1999), Kushel et al. (2001) found that 63 percent of the homeless had one or more ambulatory care visits. Thirty-two percent had visited an Emergency Department, and 23 percent had been hospitalized. These research reports document high rates of illnesses and health-care problems of the homeless. Further research is required to document the case of African Americans.

Some Health Issues Related to Nonhomeless African Americans

In a report of the surgeon general, African Americans are said to have a disproportionate burden of health problems. The report further indicates that "mortality rates until age 85 are higher for Blacks than for Whites" (USDHHS, 2001, p. 56). Disparities in morbidity are also pronounced. In selected diseases, the following rates are provided for African Americans:

- diabetes is more than three times that of Whites;
- heart disease is more than 40 percent higher than that of Whites;
- prostate cancer is more than double that of Whites;
- HIV/AIDS is more than seven times that of Whites. HIV/AIDS is one of the top five causes of death for African Americans;
- breast cancer is higher than it is for Whites, even though African American women are more likely to receive mammography screening than are White women;
- infant mortality is twice that of Whites (USDHHS, 2001, p. 56).

Smedley et al. (2002) in *Unequal Treatment: Confronting Racial and Ethnic Disparities in Health Care* attribute poor health outcomes for racial and ethnic minorities as compared with Whites to low-quality health services and lack of access to routine medical procedures (pp. 2–3). Based on their review of a large body of published research, they identify the following barriers to quality health services and routine medical procedures: (1) lack of access to appropriate cardiac medication, (2) lack of access to coronary artery bypass surgery, (3) lack of access to peritoneal dialysis and kidney transplantation, and (4) lack of access to basic clinical services such as intensive care. These authors concluded that "even when variations in such factors as insurance status, income age, co-morbid conditions, and symptom expression are taken into account" (p. 3), these disparities prevailed. Finally, these authors observed that the differences in health-care services and access to certain routine medical procedures "are associated with greater mortality among African American patients" (p. 3).

Comparative Analyses of Selected Diseases of Homeless and Nonhomeless African American Populations

Homeless African Americans have major health problems with liver (4 percent), arthritis, rheumatism, and joint problems (22 percent), chest infection, colds, coughs, and bronchitis (21 percent), and problems walking, lost limb, and other handicaps (13 percent). The incidence of these diseases among the nonhomeless African American population is much lower (see Table 30.4). In the nonhomeless African American population, the incidence of the following diseases is much higher than in the homeless African survey sample: diabetes (8 percent), high blood pressure (25 percent compared to 18 percent for the homeless), heart disease/stroke (10 percent), and cancer (3 percent).

A critical difference in health problems between homeless African nonhomeless African Americans may lie in their access to health care. In Table 30.5 data are provided in terms of utilization of

Table 30.4
Prevalence of selected diseases among the nonhomeless adult population of African Americans and the homeless African Americans (in percents)

Type of health problem	African American General Population[1]	African American Homeless Population[2]
Diabetes	1671 7.7%	72 6%
High Blood Pressure	5463 24.8%	208 18%
Heart disease/stroke	2105 9.5%	70 6%
Problems with your liver	215 1.0%	47 4%
Arthritis, rheumatism, joint problems	3710 16.9%	256 22%
Chest infection, cold, cough, bronchitis	800 3.6%	244 21%
Cancer	683 3.1%	15 1%
Problem walking, lost limb, other handicap	2007 9.1%	151 13%

[1] *Source*: Pleis (2002).
[2] *Source*: U.S. Census Bureau (2000b).

medical hospital, hospital emergency room/hospital outpatient clinic, community health clinic, and a private doctor's office. Nonhomeless African Americans are four and one-half times (70 percent) more likely to use a private doctor's office for health care than homeless persons (15 percent). The predominant method of care for homeless African Americans is a hospital emergency room/hospital outpatient clinic.

The homeless data are self-reports on health problems. Since the homeless underutilize private doctors, it is likely that they are not aware of their health condition; they have not been diagnosed. Nor are they likely to have health insurance and preventive care (Tessler & Dennis, 1989). Usually, when patients, especially the poor, seek help through the hospital emergency room, a health problem has already been expressed.

CONCLUSION

In a 1997 editorial in the *American Journal of Public Health*, the following appeared: "The relationship between homelessness and health has been clearly demonstrated in numerous studies

Table 30.5
Comparison of health-care utilization between the nonhomeless adult population of African Americans and African Americans homeless (in percents)

Health care	African American General Population[1]		African American Homeless Population[2]	
	N	%	N	%
Last time treated for health problem				
6 months ago or less	13,889	64.3%	326	28%
Bet 6 to12 months	4,194	19.4%	150	13%
A hospital emergency room/ hospital outpatient clinic	1638	8.8%	728	62%
A community health clinic	3759	20.1%	286	25%
A private doctor's office	13,091	70.1%	179	15%
Other sources	181	1.0%	325	25%

[1] *Source*: Pleis (2002).
[2] *Source*: U.S. Census Bureau (2000b).

over the past decade. Homelessness is injurious to people's health and the situation in which homeless people are often compelled to live may be as hazardous to their health as the streets themselves" (Breakey, 1997, p. 153). Research studies reviewed in this chapter provide further support for the finding of the strong relationship between homelessness and poor health.

Data provided in this chapter support the idea and importance of not treating the homeless as a homogeneous population. For African Americans it is also the case. African American homeless are diverse in composition and differ from the nonhomeless African American population in terms of health status and health care. Therefore, differential interventions are indicated.

African American homeless constitute a substantial component of the U.S. homeless in the year 2000. It is largely composed of men. However, there are an increasing number of women who are heads of households with dependent children. The African American homeless are largely between the ages of 25 and 44 and are in the prime of their lives. This is the age range in which most Americans have already made critical life decisions: education, marriage, and employment. These homeless adults have not formed marital ties in any significant numbers, and when they have those relations, they do not appear to have lasted. They are undereducated and without jobs. Homelessness among young children and youth is not revealed in the several studies reviewed in this chapter.

Clearly, there is a research need to document childhood homelessness. Similarly, homelessness among the African American elderly is not documented in the studies reviewed in this chapter.

Access to health care beyond the emergency room would greatly benefit homeless African Americans. Preventive, early intervention, and comprehensive medical care would reduce the high incidence of their health problems. The chronic diseases such as diabetes, heart, hypertension, arthritis, respiratory illnesses, and muscular skeletal infections require ongoing care and social supports. Social supports provided by family and friends encourage proper health care. There is strong evidence that homeless persons have weak and tenuous social supports. Efforts to build and restore healthy family ties and other primary group supports through community groups, religious, and other affiliative ties are all positive interventions for helping the homeless.

There is a pressing need to conduct research of homeless African Americans and the unique factors associated with their becoming homeless. Research will provide understanding about the dynamics of the risk factors associated with their homelessness and effective, empirically based strategies of intervention and prevention.

NOTES

The authors thank their colleagues Jacqueline Marie Smith for her helpful comments on this chapter; Ms. Audrey M. Thompson for her bibliographic research; Soleman Abu-Bader and Ms. Gail Desmond for their technical assistance; and Mrs. Ponnomma David for her clerical and organizational support.

1. The NSHAPC was conducted in 1996, the findings were reported in Burt et. al (1999), and the data were made available to the public in 2000 (U.S. Census Bureau, 2000b). In this chapter, we make use of the findings (Burt et al., 1999) and the primary data for our analyses (U.S. Census Bureau, 2000b). We accessed the primary data through the Urban Institute, and the same data are available through the U.S. Census Bureau (U.S. Census Bureau, 2000b).

2. This survey was not intended to produce a national count of homeless people.

REFERENCES

Bassuk, E.L. (1984). The homelessness problem. *Scientific American, 251(1)*, 40–44.

Breakey, W. (1997). It's time for the public health community to declare war on homelessness. *American Journal of Public Health, 87(2)*, 153–155.

Breakey, W., Fischer, P., Kramer, M., Nestadt, G., Romanoski, A., Ross, A., Royall, R., & Shine, O. (1989). Health and mental health problems of homeless men and women in Baltimore. *Journal of the American Medical Association, 262*, 1352–1357.

Burt, M.R. (1992). *Over the edge: The growth of homelessness in the 1980s*. New York: Russell Sage.

Burt, M.R. (2001). *What will it take to end homelessness?* Washington DC: Urban Institute.

Burt, M.R., Aron, L.Y., Douglas, T., Valente, J., Lee, E., & Iwen, B. (1999). *Homelessness: Programs and the people they serve. Findings of the National Survey of Homeless Assistance Providers and Clients*. Available at http://www.urban.org/url.cfm?ID=310291.

Choi, N.G., & Snyder, L.J. (1999). *Homeless families with children: A subjective experience of homelessness*. New York: Springer.

Cordray, D.S., & Pion, G.M. (1997). What's behind the numbers? Definitional issues in counting the homeless. In *Understanding homelessness: New policy and research perspectives*. Washington, DC: Fannie Mae Foundation, pp. 69–100.

Culhane, D.P., & Hornburg, S.P. (Ed.). (1997). *Understanding homelessness: New policy and research perspectives*. Washington, DC: Fannie Mae Foundation.

English, R.A., & Ross-Sheriff, F. (1998). Study of homeless families seeking emergency shelter in Washington, D.C. A report submitted to Fannie Mac Foundation, Washington, DC.

Geiger J. (1996). Race and health care: An American dilemma? *New England Journal of Medicine, 335(11)*, 815–816.

Geronimus, A.T. (1998). Preliminary paper for discussion at the November 1998 research meeting of the Aspen

Institute's Roundtable on Comprehensive Community Initiatives project on race and community revitalization.

Geronimus, A.T. (1992). The weathering hypothesis and the health of African American women and infants. *Ethnicity and Disease 2(3)*, 222–231.

Hombs, M.E., & Snyder, M. (1983). *Homelessness in America: A forced march to nowhere.* 2d ed. Washington, DC: Community for Creative Non-violence.

Hudson, C.G. (1998). *An interdependency model of homelessness: The dynamics of social disintegration.* Lewiston, NY: Edwin Mellen Press.

Institute for Children and Poverty. (1998). *Homeless families today, our challenge tomorrow: Regional perspectives.* New York: Institute for Children and Poverty.

Institute of Medicine. (1988). *Homelessness, health and human needs.* Committee on Health Care for Homeless People, Washington DC: National Academy Press.

Interagency Council on the Homeless (ICH). (1999). *Homelessness: Programs and the people they serve.* Findings of the National Survey of Homeless Assistance Providers and Clients. Washington, DC: Prepared by the Urban Institute—Martha Burt, Laudan Y. Aron, Toby Douglas, Jesse Valente, Edgar Lee, & Britta Iwen.

Jencks, C. (1994). *The homeless.* Cambridge: Harvard University Press.

Kushel, M.B., Vittinghoff, E., & Haas, J.S. (2001). Factors associated with the health care utilization of homeless persons. *Journal of the American Medical Association, 285(2)*, 200–206.

LaPlante, M., & Carlson, D. (1996). Disability in the United States: Prevalence and causes, 1992. *Disability Statistics Report (7).* Washington, DC: National Institute on Disability and Rehabilitation Research, U.S. Department of Education.

Liebow, Elliot. (1993). *Tell them who I am: The lives of homeless women.* New York: Penguin Books USA.

McNeil, J.M. (1993). Americans with disabilities: 1991–1992. *Current population reports, Household Economic Studies P70–33.* Washington, DC: U.S. Bureau of the Census.

Midgley, J., Tracy, M.B., & Livermore, M. (Eds.). (2000). *The handbook of social policy.* Thousand Oaks, CA: Sage, pp. 243–245.

Millennial Housing Commission Report. (2002). *Meeting our nation's housing challenges.* Report of the Bipartisan Millennial Housing Commission. Washington, DC.

Pleis, C.R., Jr. (2002). *Summary health statistics for U.S. adults: National Health Interview Survey, 1998.* National Center for Health Statistics. *Vital Health Statistics, 10(209).*

Rossi, P.H. (1989). *Down and Out in America.* Chicago, IL: University of Chicago Press.

Smedley, B.D., Stith, A.Y. & Nelson, A.R. (Eds.). (2002) *Unequal treatment: Confronting racial and ethnic disparities in health care.* Washington, DC: National Academies Press.

Snow, D.A., & Anderson, L. (1993). *Down on their luck: A study of homeless street people.* Berkeley: University of California Press.

Sosin, M., Colson, P., & Grossman, S. (1988). *Homelessness in Chicago: Poverty and pathology, social institutions and social change.* Chicago: School of Social Service Administration, University of Chicago Press.

Stanford Center for the Study of Families, Children and Youth. (1991). *The Stanford studies of homeless families, children and youth: [preliminary report].* Stanford, CA: Author, 1991.

Tessler, R.C., & Dennis, D.L. (1989). A synthesis of NIMH funded research concerning persons who are homeless and mentally ill. Program for the homeless mentally ill. Division of Evaluation and Service Systems Liaison. Washington, DC: National Institute of Mental Health Press.

U.S. Census Bureau (2000a). Current Population Survey, March 2000, Racial Statistics Branch, Population Division. Available at: http://www.census.gov/population/socdemo/race/black/ppl-142/tab21.txt.

U.S. Census Bureau (2000b). *National Survey of Homeless Assistance Providers and Clients (NSHAPC).* Available at: http://www.census.gov/prod/www/nshapc/NSHAPC4.html

U.S. Census Bureau (2001). *Census Special Report Series, CENSR 01-2, Emergency and Shelter Population: 2000.* Washington, DC: U.S. Government Printing Office.

U.S. Conference of Mayors (USCM). (2003). The Status of Hunger and Homelessness in America's Major Cities. Washington, DC: Author. Available at http://www.usmayors.org/uscm/hungersurvey/2003/onlinereport/HungerAndHomelessnessReport2003.pdf

U.S. Congress, House. (1987). The Stewart B. McKinney Homeless Assistance Act (P.L. 100-77, Sec 103 (2) (1), 101 Stat. 485).

U.S. Department of Health and Human Services (USDHHS). (2000). *Healthy People 2010*, 2d ed. Vol. 1. Washington, DC: Author.

U.S. Department of Health and Human Services (USDHHS). (2001). *Mental health: Culture, race, and ethnicity—A supplement to mental health report: A report of the surgeon general*. Rockville. MD: U.S. Department of Health and Human Services, Public Health Services, Office of Surgeon General.

U.S. Department of Housing and Urban Development (USHUD). (1984). *A report to the secretary on the homeless and emergency shelters*. Washington, DC: Author.

Wilson, William J. (1987). *The truly disadvantaged: The inner city, the underclass, and public policy*. Chicago: University of Chicago Press.

Wilson, William J. (1996). *When work disappears: The world of the new urban poor*. New York: Alfred A. Knopf.

Zuk, I. (1995). Physical Health Issues. In Rich, D.W., Rich, T.A., and Mullins, L.C. (eds.). *Old and homeless— double jeopardy, An overview of current practice and policies*. Westport, CT: Auburn House.

CHAPTER 31

African Americans, Spirituality, and Health: The Impact on Beliefs, Attitudes, and Behaviors

MARTHA R. CROWTHER, B. LEE GREEN, AND
TONYA D. ARMSTRONG

INTRODUCTION

Increasingly, there is discussion in the literature regarding the relation between religion, spirituality, and health among African Americans and the role of the church in that association. The Black church has played a significant role in the lives of African Americans in a variety of ways, which include providing spiritual guidance, educational programs and services, emotional and psychological support, political advocacy, community development services, financial support, and other roles. The church has also been a significant contributor to the health and well-being of its members. This role, although thought to be innovative, has been a part of the church from the beginning. We are now witnessing local, state, and national agencies and organizations looking to partner with the church and its spiritual leaders to deal with the health issues of African Americans (e.g., Public Law 104–193, 1996).

The Classification of Two Important Issues

Before reviewing the literature on African Americans, health, and faith, we briefly discuss two issues that influence this topic: the ethnic diversity within the African American community and the importance of defining both spirituality and religiosity given that the constructs are broad and overlapping and that there is a considerable amount of discussion among researchers concerning how to distinctly define the terms. African Americans traditionally encompass persons of African descent that include individuals from Africa and the Caribbean and those born in America. There is no evidence to date to suggest that there would be differences in the relation between spirituality and health among these different groups, primarily because the studies conducted and reviewed thus far have ignored the ethnic diversity within the African American population and focused on Christianity, ignoring other religious groups. While the majority of African Americans are Christian, we want to acknowledge that there are African Americans of other religious and faith traditions and that their belief systems and practices may impact their health differently. However, since the majority of African Americans are Christian and the literature has focused on Christian churches, belief systems, and practices, this chapter focuses on Christianity.

There is a considerable amount of discussion in the literature regarding spirituality and religion. They are often regarded as indistinguishable constructs, although some scholars argue that religion and spirituality are uniquely different, with religion referring to a group activity that involves specific behavioral, social, doctrinal, and denominational characteristics (e.g., Fetzer Institute, 1999) and spirituality referring to a personal quest for meaning and a relationship with a transcendent force (Armstrong & Crowther, 2002). Religion and spirituality have also been conceptualized to foster the development of the other. For example, religious practices encourage spiritual growth, while spiritual practices are often a salient aspect of religious participation. Many scholars argue that it is possible to adopt the outward form of religious behavior without developing a relationship with God, sometimes referred to as an extrinsic orientation to religion (e.g., Allport & Ross, 1967). It is argued that among African Americans the constructs work in concert with each other. The religious context, which provides the background for the lives of most African Americans, has served only to enrich the spiritual experiences of this population. Thus, religion and spirituality must both be considered in examining health outcomes among African Americans.

As previously mentioned, historically, the African American church has played a central role in the lives of African Americans. Additionally, the health status of the African American community has been tied to the importance the church has placed on health and well-being issues. The Black church has been a leader in the movement to incorporate organized religion in health promotion and disease prevention efforts (Crowther et al., 2002). The Black church has built strong relations with health professionals, universities, and other institutions and organizations to promote health prevention. Thus, it is important to consider the African American church in a chapter focused on health disparities. In this chapter, we review the literature on health, spirituality, and religion among African Americans, the role the Black church and clergy play in prevention and intervention programs, and collaborations between the Black church and other organizations and institutions.

THE ROLE OF RELIGION AND SPIRITUALITY IN THE LIVES OF AFRICAN AMERICANS

Religion and Spirituality are Important Aspects of Life for Many African Americans

Religion and spirituality shape individual, family, and communal relations across the life course. Sanders (2002) suggests that a primary source of support for many African Americans is spirituality. This spirituality is often tied into some form of organized religion.

There is some evidence to suggest that there are ethnic differences in spiritual beliefs and practices (e.g., Armstrong, 1999; Cavendish et al., 1998); thus, we might expect some differences in the content and transmission of spirituality between ethnic groups. Characteristic of African American families is the significant interplay between spirituality and religiosity. The impact of the Black church as an institution on African American families is difficult to overestimate. The Black church has long served as a type of extended family (Boyd-Franklin, 1989; Lincoln & Mamiya, 1990) and even today continues to provide initial training in leadership for many African American youth that is not systematically offered in most mainstream educational settings. Moreover, the church helps to address systemic problems in the culture (Richardson, 1991). A spiritual approach must encompass history, racism, discrimination, economic loss, and the like, if it is to be relevant to most African American families (Smith, 1997). Unfortunately, as Smith (1997) noted, spirituality is often marginalized in the service of economic values.

In addition to the Black church, Black families exert significant influence on the spiritual development of children. In a qualitative study of African American parents, Hurd et al. (1995) reported that the cultivation of spirituality through belief in, and respect for, God was a common theme across the interviews. Because of the oral tradition that has been highly developed in African cultures, the role and impact of storytelling are a primary means of such cultivation (Boyd-Franklin, 1989). More research is needed to understand the specific mechanisms by which African American families transmit distinctly spiritual values to their children.

In turn, the transmission of spiritual values in Black families is best fostered in the context of a supportive community. Haight (1998) conducted a four-year ethnographic study of an African American community, which revealed that spirituality played an active part in how children were socialized and resulted in a sense of support. Haight suggested that this support contributed to coping with racism, discrimination, and inadequate educational and occupational opportunities. Moreover, Brody et al. (1996) demonstrated in a sample of African American youth ages 9–12 that formal religiosity was positively associated with family cohesion and negatively associated with family conflict, internalizing, and externalizing problems. It is important to keep in mind that, although there is a positive correlation between a child's attributions of God and those of his or her own parents, a child's relationship with God can be significantly more complex than the parent–child relationship (Maurer, 1967).

In examining studies on African American elders, there appears to be a high level of religious involvement and spirituality among elderly African Americans (e.g., Hill, 1972; Jackson et al., 1990; Taylor, 1993; Levin et al., 1994). For many older African Americans, spirituality is informed by Christian principles, which come to life in the practice of "Monday through Saturday spirituality." That is, spiritual individuals have often moved beyond sole reliance on the formalized structures of religious settings (Edwards, 1987) to discover liberating truths for themselves, their families, and their communities.

AFRICAN AMERICANS AND HEALTH DISPARITIES

Since the Report of the Secretary's Task Force on Black and Minority Health was released (USDHHS, 1985), researchers have continued to document the disparities that exist between the health of the majority population and populations of color, particularly African Americans. African Americans had the highest total age-adjusted death rate during the period 1990–1998 (Keppel et al., 2002). African Americans are also twice as likely to develop hypertension as other ethnic groups (Kumanyika et al., 1989) and have higher incidence rates and death rates for most cancers.

"In 1996, life expectancy at birth for Black males increased for the third consecutive year to a record high of 66.1 years, following a period of year-to-year declines in life expectancy from 1984–1993" (Eberhardt et al., 2001). Although Black men are living longer, their life expectancies are 7 years less than that for all men. Black women born in 1996 can expect to live to the age of 74, which is five years less than the life expectancy figure for all women (Eberhardt et al., 2001).

The leading causes of death for African Americans in 1996 included heart disease, lung cancer, stroke, HIV/AIDS, unintentional injuries, prostate cancer, homicide, diabetic complications, breast cancer, pneumonia, influenza, chronic obstructive pulmonary disease, and perinatal conditions. African Americans died from several of these diseases at dramatically greater rates than the overall population. For example, in 1996 African Americans died at twice the rate from prostate cancer and diabetic complications than the overall population, and the age-adjusted mortality rate for stroke for the Black population was two-thirds higher than that for the overall population (Eberhardt et al., 2001).

To improve access to health care, however, both nonfinancial and financial barriers must be overcome. The capacity to deliver health-care services to underserved populations should include strategies to enable minority groups to use the health-care system effectively (Eberhardt et al., 2001). The church and its spiritual leaders can be a vital component in this effort.

It is important to understand the factors that put African Americans at risk for adverse health outcomes. Behavioral factors include, but are not limited to, smoking, poor nutrition, and having sedentary lifestyles. Environmental factors entail exposure to toxins and access to health care. Psychological factors include attitudes and beliefs toward health and health behaviors, as well as strategies employed to cope with stressful life events.

Spirituality, Religion, and Health Promotion

Despite efforts to eliminate the health disparities among African Americans and the majority culture, health disparities continue to exist (Thomas, 1992). Numerous health promotion programs have been conducted in African American churches and in the community to reduce health problems that affect African Americans (Caspersen et al., 1986; Ford et al., 1991). Yet African Americans continue to report low exercise rates, to smoke, and to eat an inadequate amount of fruits and vegetables (Caspersen et al., 1986; Ford et al., 1991; Baranowski, 1986). For example, several health promotion programs have been implemented in churches to lower the risks associated with adverse health outcomes, such as eating more fruits and vegetables (Kumanyika & Adams-Campbell, 1991). Other studies have assessed the barriers to participating in various health promotion programs (Airhihembuwa et al., 1995), while other investigators have focused on the attitudes and beliefs of African Americans to determine what impact attitudes and beliefs have on health behaviors and subsequent health outcomes (Airhihembuwa et al., 1995; Lewis & Green, 2000).

Reducing the prevalence of these and other behaviors that endanger the health of African Americans demands strategies such as public and provider education, prevention research, and policy and environmental changes that facilitate healthy living. To be effective, however, these strategies must be supported and endorsed by the church and its spiritual leaders.

The Importance of Health Beliefs.   Health beliefs also play a role in health behaviors, thus contributing to health outcomes or status. Weitzel suggested that perceptual variables such as health beliefs, knowledge, and health values directly influence health behaviors (Weitzel & Waller, 1990). Several models have been developed to help explain individual health behavior. For example, the Health Belief Model (HBM) is one of the most widely used models in explaining health-related behaviors. The model was developed by researchers from the Public Health Service because of concern for a lack of participation in its health-promoting programs. The model states that persons take preventive action if they believe (1) they are susceptible to the disease, (2) the disease would be severe, (3) taking an action would be beneficial by reducing the susceptibility of the disease, and (4) barriers are not difficult to overcome. Research is needed to adapt this model specifically to African Americans. Specifically, investigators should gather qualitative data to understand what beliefs African Americans have concerning their health and to assist in developing programs that will decrease and eventually eliminate disparities in health status (Rosenstock, 1974; Strecher & Rosenstock, 1997).

Fate and destiny are yet other factors that researchers are exploring in order to understand the complex relationship between health attitudes, behaviors, and outcomes of African Americans. A few researchers have associated a belief in fate and destiny to specific behaviors such as seat belt usage. For example, Colon (1992) found that there was a significant difference in seat belt usage between African Americans and Caucasians because of the increased belief in destiny by African Americans. African Americans who believed in fate and destiny were less likely than Caucasians to wear a seat belt, a proven safety device. Others have also looked at the link between pessimistic and fatalistic attitudes toward health. The literature has shown, for example, that some African American men and women have these pessimistic and fatalistic attitudes regarding cancer (Bloom et al., 1987; Denniston, 1981; Freeman, 1989) and that they are more terrified of cancer in greater magnitude or more so than the general population (Underwood, 1991). In light of these studies, there continues to be a dearth in the literature concerning what role a belief in fate and destiny has on taking preventive health-care measures to reduce health problems.

While African Americans understand the severity of diseases such as cancer, they often fail to acknowledge their relationship with carcinogenic agents associated with the disease. This also seems to be the case when African Americans seek medical advice for chronic diseases such as cancer and cardiovascular disease. In combination, these negative perceptions and health beliefs may cause African Americans to have later detection and poorer prognosis of their disease. Health beliefs may also have a positive or negative impact on an individual's decision to participate in health promotion activities. With this in mind, it becomes necessary to understand the health beliefs that presently exist within the African American community.

Health Beliefs in the African American Community. Many of the beliefs and perceptions regarding health may stem from the religious beliefs among African Americans. For example, many have the belief that God is in control of their health and that only through prayer and their belief in God will their condition be healed. The church in the African American community can play an active role in changing the present health perceptions and beliefs of this segment of the population. Spirituality plays a major role in African American culture (Jones, 1991; Roberson, 1985). The outward expression of spirituality is often seen in religious activities such as church attendance among Christians (Jennings, 1996). It has been identified as a potential indicator for health behaviors and illness among African Americans (Roberson, 1985; Gilroy, 1987; Jemmott & Jemmott, 1991; Mbiti, 1970). According to Clark-Tasker, African Americans believe that illness may be due to failure to live according to God's will and an acceptance of fate and destiny (Clark-Tasker, 1993).

A study conducted among African American women found that they were less likely than White women to practice preventive health behaviors, which are defined as behaviors by which individuals actively improve or maintain their health status. Duelberg's explanation for these differences was attributed to lower levels of personal control among African American women (Duelberg, 1992), which was defined as an individual's belief that he or she can bring about good events and avoid bad events (Peterson & Stunkard, 1989).

According to Jennings (1996), if individuals relate spirituality to personal control, cancer health behaviors would be useless in the face of God's will. The belief that "God will take care of me" summarizes the perspective of many in this community that no matter what they do, a greater force has more control. Researchers need to focus on these beliefs when designing culturally appropriate health promotion programs targeting subgroups within this population.

Jennings explained that personal factors might provide insight into the way African Americans respond to cancer (Jennings, 1996). Researchers have identified psychosocial responses such as fear, underestimation, fatalism, and pessimism as personal factors that might inhibit Blacks from participating in cancer health promotion behaviors (Cardwell & Collier, 1981; Long, 1993). Price et al. (1993) attempted to determine Black adult males' knowledge and perceptions of prostate cancer by using the Health Belief Model. The results showed the men to be fatalistic in their views of cancer and lacking knowledge of the disease. Almost 60 percent were unaware that Black men were more susceptible to prostate cancer than White men. Forty-five percent believed that if they developed prostate cancer, it would kill them, and another 28 percent were uncertain. Approximately 10 to 20 percent of the respondents were unsure or did not agree with the benefits of a prostate examination.

Health education can play an important role in bridging the gap between negative belief systems and preventive health practices. Health professionals can incorporate spiritual and religious beliefs and practices into their prevention and intervention strategies to increase adherence and gain credibility. For example, several psychologists spoke at a religious summit sponsored by the Black Church Initiative promoting healthy behaviors. They discussed the importance for women of taking care of their own health needs and sexual wellness. The psychologists highlighted strategies African American women can employ to "reorganize their priorities to put themselves first, prevent crises, manage stress and address their physical, emotional, and spiritual health" (Smith, 2002, p. 19).

CHURCH-BASED PREVENTION, INTERVENTION, AND RELATED PROGRAMS

Church-based mental and physical health programs are gaining in popularity among African Americans in different denominations such as Presbyterian, Methodist, Baptist, Lutheran, and so forth. Many church leaders are providing guidance that will enable their church members to take advantage of the wide range of health services and programs that are made available to them. Many are providing targeted health education and health promotion programs to fit the unique needs of their congregations.

Taylor and colleagues (Taylor et al., 2000) reviewed the literature in the area of mental health service delivery in faith communities and found that several factors impact the delivery of mental health services, among them size of the congregation, congregation age, socioeconomic status, and education background, as well as religious training of clergy and clergy orientation with respect to community activism. Their review also indicated that for many, the clergy is their first professional contact for help with personal problems. Generally, the clergy receive little preparation in recognizing mental illness and have an apparent lack of knowledge of standard referral services offered. The literature indicates that more educated clergy are more likely to refer the person to mental health services. Given that often the clergy are the first professional contact members have and given the pivotal role the clergy play in church-based programs, they represent important resources for needed collaboration.

Smith and Merit (1997) examined the impact of education and support provided by African American churches in encouraging health promotion activities for blood pressure management. In a related program, Kong (1997) described a community-based program, which included churches, and played a valuable role in increasing the number of African American hypertensives who received treatment. There is also evidence that supports the role of ministers in providing assistance for African Americans (Okwumabua & Martin, 1997; Neighbors et al., 1998).

HIV/AIDS

An example of the role clergy can play is addressing the HIV/AIDS prevention and intervention efforts in the African American community. According to Swartz (2002), AIDS is the leading cause of death among African Americans between the ages of 25 and 44. Approximately half of the new cases of HIV in the United States each year are African Americans. Additionally, approximately 60 percent of children who are HIV positive are African American. Despite the increase in HIV among African Americans, there still remains a significant amount of resistance and denial. However, there are clergy throughout the country taking the lead in discussing HIV and AIDS among African Americans. This past March marked the twelfth anniversary of the Black Church Week of Prayer for the Healing of AIDS, a week of education and AIDS awareness that highlighted the role that churches are playing in addressing the AIDS crisis (Swartz, 2002). The Black Church Week of Prayer is the largest AIDS awareness program in the United States that targets the African American community. Activities during the week include focus of HIV/AIDS education in worship, educational programs, and providing AIDS education to members and the community.

Partnerships between Universities and the Black Church

Institutions such as universities are developing and implementing successful collaborations with faith-based organizations throughout the country to meet the needs of religious communities. One such example is the Carter Center at Emory University, which has established an Interfaith Health Program that helps congregations to implement mental health, substance abuse, violence prevention, HIV/AIDS, and other health programs and services.

Success has been demonstrated in a number of church-based health education and health promotion programs. An African American church-based nutrition and exercise program developed by researchers at Johns Hopkins found that women were adopting healthier lifestyles as a result of the program. The program was in partnership with 16 churches in the Baltimore area and included over 500 individuals who were asked to lose weight and choose more healthful foods. Women in the study who were a part of the church-based program did much better on changing exercise habits compared to women who were part of a self-help group. In this study, researchers worked with community members, leaders, and pastors to design strategies to encourage better lifestyle choices. The effect of utilizing the church was also found in a study to help smokers quit. Again, researchers at Johns Hopkins found that smokers had a much better success rate when they received support from their pastors, as well as support from fellow church members. It is suggested by the researchers that the best smoking-cessation programs are those that are tailored to the individual and spiritually based (Yanek et al., 2001).

The University of North Carolina has developed a project called the Partnership to Reach African Americans to Increase Smart Eating (PRAISE; Ammerman, 2002). This project is designed to partner with Black churches in order to (1) identify barriers and motivators for dietary change, (2) develop different intervention strategies that are culturally and spiritually sensitive, (3) evaluate the effectiveness of the interventions related to dietary changes, and (4) examine the effect of dietary change on selected biochemical parameters. Sixty churches were recruited to participate in the program, and the churches were divided into different intervention groups. The program is designed to reach whole congregations and to build on the unique strengths and abilities of the church. Pastors and other church leaders play a significant role in the development and implementation of the program.

In their 20-year review of lay health adviser programs among African Americans, Jackson and Parks (1997) reviewed the growing lay health adviser movement. Among their findings was the recommendation that professional educators should rely on the collective wisdom of the community to identify, recruit, select, and train lay health advisers. They cite a number of studies that confirm the value of seeking the collective wisdom of the African American religious community in health promotional outreach programs.

Jackson and Reddick (1999) describe the Health Wise Church Project, a community outreach initiative between a diverse group of African American churches and a university health education program developed for early detection and illness prevention networks among older church members. Their four-stage model illustrates how organizations achieve collaborative partnerships that sustain community interest throughout the project. The findings suggest that it is important to involve community partners during the early phase of project planning.

Strategies for Church-Based Interventions

Many different strategies have been employed to partner with faith communities for improving the health of the African American community (Centers for Disease Control and Prevention, 1999). Several key strategies are essential for a successful partnership. Wimberly (2001) notes that there are critical steps in order for church-based programs and partnerships to be effective. The first step is to identify the appropriate individuals within the church who will assist in addressing the health needs of the congregation as well as being a point person for collaboration with outside agencies and organizations. The second step relates to becoming aware of the resources and services that are designed to specifically address the unique needs of the church. This might include local, state, and national resources that can aid and assist the church and its members in addressing the specific health needs. The third step is to connect the resources with the people who need them. This can be overlooked at times because individuals assume that the connection is made. A concerted effort must be made to ensure that the services and programs that are available are indeed made available and are utilized by those who are in dire need of the services and programs. The church's spiritual and cultural norms (e.g., emphases on mortality and stewardship) make it ideal for health promotion and disease prevention. The church and its spiritual leaders can make a significant contribution to addressing the health disparities that exist in our society. This can be done only in a collaborative spirit that fosters similar goals and objectives. It should be emphasized, however, that the church should not be expected to take total control of the health issues of its congregation because of its other ongoing responsibilities. This fact notwithstanding, the church can be the central organization that brings other organizations and services together in an effective way.

CONCLUSIONS AND RECOMMENDATIONS

Discussions regarding African Americans tend to focus on the social, economic, and health problems within the community. This focus overlooks a major strength and source of resources within the community—faith. During significant periods in African American history, organizations such as the National Association for the Advancement of Colored People (NAACP) were formed, and churches played a major role in social and political activities (Coke & Twaite, 1995). The church was not only an agent for social reform but also a place to engage in religious practices (Coke & Twaite, 1995). Partly as a result of the social and political injustices, group solidarity, racial identification, religion, and spirituality have been consistent themes in the life-course development of African Americans.

The Black church is still the centerpiece of the African American community. Thus, African American ministers are in a unique position to significantly impact attitudes, beliefs, knowledge, and behavior. Church members, as well as community persons who do not attend church regularly, often seek ministers first when they have mental or physical health concerns (Chatters, 2000; Swartz, 2002). Because of this, Black ministers can provide and direct persons in the direction of prevention and intervention strategies without the resistance often encountered by other health professionals. However, ministers need to be informed and willing to provide guidance and direct persons to the appropriate resources. Health professionals can play a larger role in assuring that clergy have access to health information and feel comfortable seeking assistance when it becomes necessary.

African Americans have relied on their faith to cope with adversity. Chatters (2002) asserts that religious coping has often been viewed by social and behavioral scientists as passive and used primarily to "deal with emotional consequences of stressful circumstances" (p. 351). This longstanding view is being challenged given the preponderance of individual accounts among African Americans and the meaning they ascribe to their efforts. As the religious coping literature grows, investigators are examining the multiple ways in which African Americans use religious and spiritual beliefs and practices to cope with daily hassles, strains, and racism (Chatters, 2000). Additionally, the relation between cognition and spirituality is being explored, for example, using cognitive content and strategies to derive meaning and address issues of control (Chatters, 2000).

Qualitative research that primarily involves probing and in-depth analysis is an important area for understanding the relation between religion, spirituality, and health among African Americans. Investigators often assume they know the meanings of religious terms such as faith, spirituality, salvation, healing, grace, and redemption among African Americans (Chatters, 2000). Not explicitly inquiring about the meanings of these terms within the community can lead to faulty assumptions and interfere with important and needed health promotion and prevention efforts. Therefore, quali-

tative research could focus on how various religious factors contribute to the development, maintenance, and modification of health beliefs, attitudes, and behaviors throughout the life course, with a
particular focus on the messages parents transmit to their children, adulthood, and older age. Additionally, qualitative research needs to be conducted on the impact of different faith traditions on
health. A first step in that direction is to understand how different religious and faith traditions
conceptualize health and the core religious terms described before.

The African American religious community has a history of collaboration with institutions and
organizations in the health promotion efforts using faith-based approaches (Crowther et al., 2002).
Faith and nonfaith-based organizations have worked across denominational boundaries in conjunction
with public and private health-care providers, academe, and research organizations to forge partnerships with African American churches. These partnerships have provided the impetus and resources
necessary for communities to organize conferences, programs, or workshops that promote mental
and physical health. These collaborations provide a unifying framework as the trend shifts toward a
greater role of incorporating spirituality, organized religion, nonfaith-based institutions, academe, and
a wide spectrum of health-care professionals in health promotion and prevention efforts.

Future research is encouraged to focus on other religious/spiritual belief systems within the African
American community to broaden understanding of health, disease, religion, spirituality, and their
interconnection. As this research looks for dynamic differences, it should pay particular attention to
cohort differences in the expression of religious and spiritual beliefs and practices. For example,
within a faith system, do the younger and older adults worship the same way? There may be trends
that are missed if different age groups are not assessed.

In the case of mental health and related behaviors, the church has traditionally been a protective
factor against suicide in the African American community (Neeleman et al., 1998). Unfortunately,
there has been an increase in the suicide rates among African American young people. Neeleman et
al. (1998) suggest that the increase in the suicide rate among African American young people may
be caused by increasing secularization. The Black church, along with mental health professionals,
needs to develop strategies to combat the increase in suicide rates among young African Americans.

In sum, the literature on spirituality, religion, and health is enjoying a resurgence of interest among
social, behavioral, and health scientists and practitioners. Scholars and practitioners who have worked
in the area of African American social and health issues are aware of the importance African Americans place on their spiritual and religious beliefs and practices. Faith and health have been linked
together within the African American community for quite some time. African Americans have used
their religious and spiritual beliefs and practices to cope with some of life's most challenging circumstances. It is time now to take the research and the coping strategies African Americans employ
to a new level in an attempt to understand the mechanisms that will lead to positive and sustaining
health practices within the African American community. It is hoped that these practices will, in
turn, contribute to the reduction in racial health disparities, while African Americans continue to trail
their White counterparts on most known indications of health.

REFERENCES

Airhihembuwa, C., Kumanyika, S., Agurs, T., & Lowe, A. (1995). Perceptions and beliefs about exercise, rest,
    and health among African Americans. *American Journal of Health Promotion, 9,* 426–429.

Allport, G., & Ross, J. (1967). Personal religious orientation and prejudice. *Journal of Personality and Social
    Psychology, 2,* 423–43.

Ammerman, A. (2002). Process evaluation of the church-based PRAISE project: Partnership to reach African
    Americans to increase smart eating. In A. Steckler & L. Linnan (Eds.), *Process evaluation for public
    health interventions and research* (pp. 96–111). San Francisco: Jossey-Bass.

Armstrong, T.D. (1999). The impact of spirituality on the coping process of families dealing with pediatric HIV or pediatric nephrotic syndrome (Doctoral dissertation, University of North Carolina at Chapel Hill, 1998). *Dissertation Abstracts International, 59*, (12-B), 6482.

Armstrong, T., & Crowther, M. (2002). Spirituality among older African Americans. *Journal of Adult Development, 9(1)*, 3–12.

Baranowski, T. (1986). Promoting exercise among minority group families. *Health Education Focal Points, 2*, 7–9.

Bloom, J., Spiegel, D., & Kang, S.H. (1987). Cancer awareness and secondary prevention practices in Black Americans: Implications for prevention. *Family and Community Health, 10(3)*, 19–30.

Boyd-Franklin, N. (1989). *Black families in therapy: A multisystems approach* (pp. 78–91). New York: Guilford Press.

Brody, G.H., Stoneman, Z., & Flor, D. (1996). Family wages, family processes, and youth competence in rural married African American families. In E.M. Hetherington & E.A. Blechman (Eds.), *Stress, coping, and resiliency in children and families* (pp. 173–188). Mahwah, NJ: Lawrence Erlbaum Associates.

Cardwell, J.J., & Collier, W.V. (1981). Racial differences in cancer awareness: What Black Americans know and need to know about cancer. *Urban Health, 12(3)*, 29–32.

Caspersen, C.J., Christenson, G.M., & Pollard, R.A. (1986). Status of the 1990 physical fitness and exercise objective-evidence from NHIS 1985. *Public Health Reports, 101*, 587–592.

Cavendish, J.C., Welch, M.R., & Leege, D.C. (1998). Social network theory and predictors of religiosity for Black and White Catholics: Evidence of a "Black sacred cosmos"? *Journal for the Scientific Study of Religion, 37*, 397–410.

Centers for Disease Control and Prevention. (1999). *Engaging faith communities as partners in improving community health*. U.S. Department of Health and Human Services, 1–16.

Chatters, L.M. (2000). Religion, spirituality and health: Public health research and practice. *Annual Review of Public Health, 21*, 335–367.

Chatters, L. (2002). Religion and health: Public health research and practice. *Annual Review of Public Health, 21*, 335–367.

Clark-Tasker, N. (1993). Cancer prevention and early detection in African Americans. In M. Frank-Stromber & S.J. Olson (Eds.), *Cancer prevention in minority populations: Cultural implications for health care professionals* (pp. 133–170). St. Louis: C.V. Mosby.

Coke, M.M., & Twaite, J.A. (1995). *The Black elderly: Satisfaction and quality of later life*. Binghamton, NY: Haworth Press.

Colon, I. (1992). Race, belief in destiny, and seat belt usage: A pilot study. *American Journal of Public Health, 82(6)*, 875–877.

Crowther, M., Parker, M., Larimore, W., Achenbaum, A., & Koenig, H. (2002). Rowe and Kahn's model of successful aging revisited: Spirituality the missing construct. *The Gerontologist, 42*, 613–620.

Denniston, R. (1981). Cancer knowledge, attitudes, and practices among Black Americans. *Progress in Clinical Biological Research, 83*, 225–235.

Duelberg, S. (1992). Preventive health behaviors among Black and White women in urban and rural areas. *Social Science and Medicine, 34(2)*, 191–198.

Eberhardt, M.S., Ingram, D.D., & Makuc, D.M. (2001). Urban and rural health chartbook. *Health, United States, 2001*. Hyattsville, MD: National Center for Health Statistics.

Edwards, K.L. (1987). Exploratory study of Black psychological health. *Journal of Religion and Health, 26*, 73–80.

Fetzer Institute, National Institute on Aging Working Group. (1999). *Multidimensional measure of religiousness/ spirituality for use in health research*. A Report of a National Working Group Supported by the Fetzer Institute in Collaboration with the National Institute on Aging (pp. 1–84). Kalamazoo, MI: Fetzer Institute.

Ford, E.S., et al. (1991). Physical activity behaviors in lower and higher socioeconomic status populations. *American Journal of Epidemiology, 133*, 1246–1256.

Freeman, H. (1989). Cancer in the socioeconomically disadvantaged. *Cancer, 39*, 266–288.

Gilroy, J. (1987). Ethnic perspectives on cancer nursing: The Black American. *Oncology Nursing Forum, 14(1)*, 66–69.

Haight, W.L. (1998). *Gathering the spirit at First Baptist Church: Spirituality as a protective factor in the lives of African American children. Social Work, 43 (3)*, 213–221.

Hill, R.B. (1972). *The strengths of Black families.* New York: Emerson Hall.

Hurd, E.P., Moore, C., & Rogers, R. (1995). Quiet success: Parenting strengths among African Americans. *Families in Society: The Journal of Contemporary Human Services, 76*, 434–443.

Jackson, J.S., Antonucci, T.C., & Gibson, R.C. (1990). Cultural, racial, and ethnic minority influences on aging. In J.E. Birren & K.W. Scahie (Eds.), *Handbook of the psychology of aging* (3d ed., pp. 103–123). San Diego: Academic Press.

Jackson, E.J., & Parks, C.P. (1997). Recruitment and training issues from selected lay health advisor programs among African Americans: A 20 year perspective. *Health Education & Behavior, 24(4)*, 418–432.

Jackson, R.S., & Reddick, B. (1999). The African American church and university partnerships: Establishing lasting collaborations. *Health Education & Behavior, 26(5)*, 663–675.

Jemmott, L.S., & Jemmott, J.B. (1991). Applying the theory of reasoned action to AIDS risk behavior: Condom use among Black women. *Nursing Research, 40(4)*, 228–234.

Jennings, K. (1996). Getting Black women to screen for cancer: Increasing health beliefs into practice. *Journal of the American Academy of Nurse Practitioners, 8(2)*, 52–59.

Jones, J.M. (1991). Racism: A cultural analysis of the problem. In R.L. Jones (Ed.), *Black psychology* (pp. 609–635). Berkeley, CA: Cobb & Henry.

Keppel, K.G., Pearcy, J.N., & Wagener, D.K. (2002). *Trends in racial and ethnic-specific rates for the health status indicators: United States, 1990–98.* Healthy People Statistical Notes, 23, Hyattsville, MD: National Center for Health Statistics, 1–16.

Kong, B.W. (1997). Community-based hypertension control programs that work. *Journal of Health Care for the Poor & Underserved, 8(4)*, 401–409.

Kumanyika, S., et al. (1989). Beliefs about high blood pressure prevention in a survey of Blacks and Hispanics. *American Journal of Preventive Medicine, 1*, 21–26.

Kumanyika, S., & Adams-Campbell, L.L. (1991). Obesity, diet, and psychosocial factors contributing to cardiovascular disease in Blacks. *Cardiovascular Clinics, 21 (3)*, 47–73.

Levin, J.S., Taylor, R.J., & Chatters, L.M. (1994). Race and gender differences in religiosity among older adults: Findings from four national surveys. *Journals of Gerontology: Social Sciences, 49*, S137–S145.

Lewis, R.K., & Green, B.L. (2000). Assessing the health attitudes, beliefs, and behaviors of African Americans attending church: A comparison from two communities. *Journal of Community Health, 25*, 211–224.

Lincoln, C.E., & Mamiya, L.H. (1990). *The Black church in the African American experience.* Durham, NC: Duke University Press.

Long, E. (1993). Breast cancers in African American women: Review of the literature. *Cancer Nursing, 16(1)*, 1–24.

Maurer, A.B. (1967). Children's conceptions of God. In J. Bugental (Ed.), *Challenges of humanistic psychology.* New York: McGraw-Hill.

Mbiti, J.S. (1970). *African religion and philosophies.* Garden City, New York: Anchor-Doubleday.

Neeleman, J. Wessely, S., & Lewis, G. (1998). Suicide acceptability in African and White Americans: The role of religion. *The Journal of Nervous and Mental Disease, 186(1)*, 12–16.

Neighbors, H.W., Musick, M.A., & Williams, D.R. (1998). The African American minister as a source of help for serious personal crises: Bridge or barrier to mental health care? *Health Education and Behavior, 25(6)*, 759–77.

Okwumabua, J.O., & Martin, B. (1997). Stroke belt initiative: The Tennessee experience. *Journal of Health Care for the Poor & Underserved, 8 (3)*, 292–300.

Peterson, C., & Stunkard, A.J. (1989). Personal control and health promotion. *Social Science and Medicine, 28*, 819–828.

Price, J.H., Colvin, T.L., & Smith, D. (1993). Prostate cancer: Perceptions of African American males. *Journal of the National Medical Association, 85*, 941–947.

Public Law 104–193 (1996). Personal responsibility and work opportunity reconciliation act. *Public Law No. 104–193*, 104, 110 Statute 2105.

Richardson, B.L. (1991). Utilizing the resources of the African American church: Strategies for counseling professionals. In C.C. Lee & B.L. Richardson (Eds.), *Multicultural issues in counseling: New approaches to diversity.* Alexandria, VA: American Counseling Association.

Roberson, M.M. (1985). The influence of religious beliefs on health choices of Afro-Americans. *Topics in Clinical Nursing, 7(30)*, 57–63.

Rosenstock, I.M. (1974). The health belief model and preventive health behavior. In M. Becker (Ed.), *The health belief model and personal health behavior* (pp. 470–473). Thorofare, NJ: Charles B. Slack.

Sanders, R.G.W. (2002). The Black church: Bridge over troubled water. In J.L. Sanders & C. Bradley (Eds.), *Counseling African American families* (pp. 73–84). The Family Psychology and Counseling Series. Alexandria, VA.

Smith, A. (1997). *Navigating the deep river: Spirituality in African American families.* Cleveland, OH: United Church Press.

Smith, D. (2002). Psychologists promote healthy behavior at religious summit. *APA Monitor, 33(9)*, 19.

Smith, E.D., & Merritt, S.L. (1997). Church-based education: An outreach program for African American churches. *Ethnicity & Health, 2(3)*, 243–255.

Strecher, V.J., & Rosenstock, I.M. (1997). The health belief model. In K. Glanz, F.M. Lewis, & B.K. RImer (Eds.), *Health behavior and health education: Theory, research and practice* (pp. 41–59). San Francisco: Jossey-Bass.

Swartz, A. (2002). Breaking the silence: The Black church addresses HIV. *HIV Impact* (pp. 1–2). Washington, DC: Department of Health and Human Services, Office of Minority Health Resource Center.

Taylor, R.J. (1993). Religion and religious observances. In J.S. Jackson & L.M. Chatters (Eds.), *Aging in Black America* (pp. 101–123). Newbury Park, CA: Sage.

Taylor, R.J., Ellison, C.G., Chatters, L.M., Levin, J.S., & Lincoln, K.D. (2000). Mental health services in faith communities: The role of clergy in Black churches. *Social Work, 45(1)*, 73–87.

Thomas, V. (1992). Explaining health disparities between African American and White populations: Where do we go from here? *Journal of the National Medical Association, 84*, 837–840.

Underwood, S. (1991). African American men: Perceptual determinants of early cancer detection and cancer risk reduction. *Cancer Nursing, 14(6)*, 281–288.

U.S. Department of Health and Human Services (USDHHS). (1985). *Report of the Secretary's Task Force on Black and Minority Health.* Washington, DC: U.S. Government Printing Office.

Weitzel, M.H., & Waller, P. (1990). Predictive factors for health promotive behaviors in White, Hispanic, and Black blue-collar workers. *Family and Community Health, 13*, 23–24.

Wimberly, A.S. (2001). The role of Black faith communities in fostering health. In R. Braithwaite & S. Taylor (Eds.), *Health issues in the Black community (2d ed.)* (pp. 129–150). San Francisco: Jossey-Bass.

Yanek, L.R., Becker, D.M., Moy, T.F., Gittelsohn, J., & Koffman, D.M. (2001). Project joy: Faith based cardiovascular health promotion for African American women. *Public Health Reports, 116*, 68–81.

CHAPTER 32

Health, Disparity, and the Older Population: Greater Disparity between Black and White, or within Black?

RON C. MANUEL AND
JACQUELINE MARIE SMITH

INTRODUCTION

The 2.9 million Black (African American) persons aged 65 years or older in the year 2000 constituted slightly over 8 percent of the nation's older (aged 65 years or over) population. In 2015, the time at which the initial birth cohorts of the baby boom generation begin to retire in sizable numbers, the 4.5 million Black older Americans expected at that time will constitute about 9 percent of the expected 45.9 million persons aged 65 years or older. While the older population in general will grow by about 30 percent between 2000 and 2015, the Black older population will increase by roughly 50 percent (U.S. Bureau of the Census, 2000, 2001).

T. Lynn Smith (1957), writing near the beginning of academic interest in the special conditions of aging among Black Americans, questioned whether the fast-paced growth in the Black older population (also observable in midcentury [1900s] data) meant an increasingly impoverished older Black population. Smith's question about the implication of population size and growth in the Black older population motivates additional thinking. Reasonably, increasing size in a population typically means increasing variation and greater diversity in the population. Greater diversity, of course, can mean greater disparity, contrasted to greater homogeneity, within the population. This chapter considers the significance of diversity for health disparities within today's Black older population. The objective in the chapter is to review data from a systematic testing of a historically recognized (Jackson, 1970) and increasingly assumed (Jackson & Sellers, 2001; Williams, 2002), but never systematically tested, observation in the literature: that the health disparity within the Black older population equals or exceeds the disparity between the Black and White older populations. Practically, finding distinctive disparity within the Black older population suggests that strategies at reducing racial disparities in the older population may reside less in targeting all Black older persons and more in targeting special at-risk subgroups within the Black aged and aging population.

HEALTH, RACE, AND AGE IN HISTORICAL AND CONCEPTUAL CONTEXT

Before examining the empirical evidence for the thesis, consider briefly the existing literature and theoretical context for which the arguments in this chapter have greatest cumulative relevance. First, a manageable focus for observing health must be delineated. Subsequently, extending this conceptualization to the knowledge base on age and race will lead, logically, to the guiding hypothesis that there is greater health diversity within the Black older population than between it and the typically contrasted population of White older persons.

Conceptualizing Health

The evaluation of the health of the Black aged depends on the definition of health. Lawton and Lawrence's (1994) conceptualization of health as a fuzzy-set, many-faceted phenomenon highlights the complexity surrounding the conceptualization and measurement of the concept. The fuzzy-set characterization of health suggests the possibility of overlooking critical aspects of health in any attempt to observe evidence for it. Of course, critically missing, unobserved, conceptual dimensions of health increase the errors in its measurement. To describe a person as optimally healthy when, with a more complete set of measurement indicators of health, the description would point to less than optimal health points to the importance attached to the decision making about what health is and how to observe it.

Contributors to the Institute of Medicine's (IOM) recent *Guidance for the National Healthcare Disparities Report* (Swift, 2002) introduce a useful matrix for fashioning indicators of health's complexity. The matrix is a cross-tabulation of patient needs (staying healthy, getting well, living with illness/disability, and coping with the end of life) with dimensions of health care (access, utilization, cost, and quality). The intersection, for example, of the patient need for staying healthy with the health-care dimension of access easily suggests the importance of indicators of the presence of health insurance for preventive care screenings.

The complexity of observing health, of course, has been recognized at least since the World Health Organization (WHO [1959]), nearly half a century ago, defined health not simply as the absence of disease but a state of total physical, psychological, and social well being. In this chapter, while the systematic study of health in line with the IOM's report is beyond our scope, we do examine multiple, nationally representative data sets to observe multiple facets of health.

Multiple Data Sources for Health Measures.   The well-known and methodologically respected National Health and Nutrition Examination Survey III (NHANES III) data for 1988–1994 (USDHHS, 1996) offers a rich collection of health and health-related data and serves as the primary data source. The NHANES III information is supplemented with data from the Midlife Development in the United States (MIDUS) Survey of Minority Groups (Chicago and New York City), 1995–1996 (see Hughes & Shweder, 2002) and the final (1992) wave of the National Survey of Black Americans (NSBA), Panel Data (see Jackson et al., 1996; Jackson & Gurin, 1997). Data from the 1992 Health and Retirement Survey are also analyzed (RAND, 1994).

Multiple Health Indicators.   Although not ideally representative of the entire spectrum of health, the study of multiple indicators, across varying conceptual dimensions of health, across multiple data sets, can help reduce potential measurement errors. This report on health is based on data from 11, conceptually varied indicators of health. In addition to the data on mortality and survival (Figure 32.1), figures 32.2 through 32.12 show data (from multiple data sets), respectively, for (1) diagnosis by a physician with one or more of the health conditions associated with the leading causes of death in the United States (heart disease, cancer, stroke, and diabetes [Figure 32.2]); (2) diagnosis of two or more such health conditions (Figure 32.3); (3) inability to do at least one of the daily personal care behaviors (dress, feed, stand, or walk independently [Figure 32.4]); (4) inability to do at least one of the daily instrumental behaviors (prepare meals, walk, climb steps, stoop, lift, do chores, or manage affairs [Figure 32.5]); (5) the perception of personal care behavior limitations (Figure 32.6); (6) the perception of instrumental behavior limitations (Figure 32.7); (7) difficulty hearing on the telephone (Figure 32.8); (8) difficulty seeing to read (Figure 32.9); (9) having one or more dental problems (Figure 32.10); (10) poorly self-evaluated health (Figure 32.11); (11) reports within the last week of one or more of the following depressive symptoms: everything is an effort, unable to get going, life is unenjoyable, depression, restless sleep, unhappy, lonely, sad (Figure 32.12). The indicators permit a broad assessment of health, one that is in line with the World Health Organization's (WHO, 1959) conceptualization that health refers to physical, psychological, and behavioral competence.

One exception to the WHO's definition of health is made, however. No attempt is made to conceptualize or observe indicators of social health. Indicators typically used for observing social health, such as social integration, were judged as more appropriately representing social structural circumstances that influence physical and psychological health. Providing for the clear distinction between the measures of health and their behavioral and social determinants is central to studying the central thesis in this chapter.

Conceptualizing Health with Race and Age

Racial group health disparities in the United States have, historically, shown a Black disadvantage (Du Bois, 1906; USDHHS, 1985; Schneider et al., 2002). Hypotheses exist (along with supportive and nonsupportive data) that these differences grow larger within the older population, with double (National Urban League [NUL] 1964; Ferraro & Farmer 1996) and multiple jeopardy (Lindsay, 1971) for the Black aged. Other hypotheses and data suggest that the differences diminish, converge, or level off (Dowd & Bengtson, 1978; Beckett, 2000), reverse (the crossover effect) (Manton et al., 1979; Manton & Stallard, 1997; Preston et al., 1996), or vary depending on age cohort within the older population (Gibson, 1994). A brief summary of each of these can prove instructive not simply for sketching the historical context for which this report has relevance but for pointing the way to the conceptual context that underlies the thesis in this chapter.

Double Jeopardy and Health Disparity of the Black Aged.   The NUL in 1964 was among the first to draw attention to the special circumstances of health, race, and aging. It declared the Black aged to be in a position of double jeopardy, first by "being Negro, and second, by being aged. Age merely compounded those hardships accrued to him as a result of being a Negro" (NUL, 1964, p. 1). Soon, similar concepts, including triple and multiple jeopardy, were used to extend the idea. Thus, to be Black, old, and female or poor suggested even direr circumstances within the Black older population (Lindsay, 1971).

The National Urban League's concept of double jeopardy was useful for drawing attention, politically, to the special plight of the Black aged. The concept was not systematically tested until years later, however. Dowd and Bengtson (1978), treating the concept as a theory about the interaction of race and age, found empirical support for their self-assessed health indicator but failed to find support for a measure of self-perceived life satisfaction. Age leveled race differences, when acting on life satisfaction, rather than increased them. Social Security, Medicare, and other legislation favorable to the older population, presumably, help to level race differences fueled earlier during the life course by health-care barriers such as race-related unemployment and irregular employment. More recent and more systematically researched studies, such as that by Ferraro and Farmer (1996), however, have not found support for the idea, although Ferraro and Farmer point to the faster-paced decline in health in their Black sample at all ages.

Crossover Effect and Health Disparity of the Black Aged.   Other concepts have had more fruitful outcomes for the development of the literature than the double jeopardy conceptualization. Data on mortality, available from national vital statistical reports, offered an early and, at the time, largely the only window for observing the health of the Black aged. Manton et al.'s (1979) analysis of mortality data, for example, pointed to a crossover effect in data on age, race, and mortality disparities. The crossover effect occurs when, after about age 75 to 85, the White death rate exceeds the Black death rate, whereas before about age 75, the Black rate exceeds the White rate. Now, aging not only was seen to exert a leveling effect on racial disparities in health, but also was capable of reversing race-related health differences (see Manton & Stallard, 1997).

Mortality selection is reasoned to operate producing the crossover effect. According to the mortality selection hypothesis, the least healthy in economically disadvantaged populations are selected out from the population through mortality, leaving the healthier behind (within their birth cohort). These survivors compare favorably to their nondisadvantaged counterpart at later life-course stages, when age-related disease processes begin to take their toll (Manton & Stallard, 1997). Preston et al.'s (1996) data suggest, however, that the convergence and crossover of mortality disparities may not be real but rather represent an artifact of the methodology for age determination. Age over-reporting, the tendency to report being older than is the case, occurs disproportionately among Black older respondents. This tendency may make the crossover more apparent than real. Manton and Stallard's (1997) analysis, however, suggests that even with adjustments made for age misreporting, evidence for the crossover hypothesis accrued for several disease-specific mortality rate comparisons.

Alternating Patterns of Healthy and Less Healthy Age Groups.   Gibson (1994) used the crossover and mortality selection hypotheses to make sense of neither reversing, leveling, or doubling patterns in the data she examined, but an alternating pattern of healthy and less healthy age groups, all within the Black older population. Not observing this pattern within the White older population, Gibson concluded that age and health are more strongly related in the White, than Black, older population.

As important as Gibson's work is for the insights it shows possible from the continuing study of interracial patterns in health, the findings most importantly bring this brief review of the major streams of theorizing about the Black aged full circle to the thesis of this chapter. Differences across age cohorts, among the Black aged, offer additional insights to pinpoint sources shaping the health of the Black aged.

Beyond Traditional Conceptualizations: Late Life within-Race (Black) Health Disparity

In addition to age and typically expected gender and social class influences (Smith & Kington, 1997), health (and health-care) differences among Black older adults have been found to vary, for example, with dietary intake (Kumanyika & Odoms, 2001) and other personal health behaviors (Berkman & Mullen, 1997), as well as with less often studied social structural influences such as race-related identity (Thompson et al., 2002) and discrimination (LaVeist et al., 2001). A literature increasingly unveiling the heterogeneity within the Black older population easily prompts the often expressed, but, as noted, never systematically tested, idea that the diversity and thus potential disparity within the Black older population equal or exceed those between this population and its White counterpart. Before looking at empirical evidence for this thesis, consider the theoretical significance attached to the idea, if true.

The Assumption of Black Aged Homogeneity.   Manuel's (1982b) summary of the pre-1980s gerontological literature on measuring race/ethnic effects provides a convenient starting point for a thesis emphasizing intragroup (Black) diversity. Manuel observes, as he does again in 2000 (Manuel, 2000) when characterizing the literature since 1980, that what is known about the Black aged is predominantly based on the assumption that knowing an individual's racial group label indicates his or her history, culture, and social experience. The assumption is that all persons of a specified label are the same.

Unfortunately, no consensus exists on what it is that is the same within races. No consensus exists on what the race effect in health, or health care, means. Is the effect simply an ethnic, that is, cultural difference? Or is the effect biologically or sociologically interpretable? Following Sowell (1994), racial differences mean cultural differences. Thus, reasoning from Haynes and Smedley's (1999) recent report on the unequal burden of cancer, race disparities in health-care referrals would reflect simply race-linked cultural preferences in the when, where, and how of seeking health care. Attendant practical implications for reductions in disparity, here, rest with changing attitudes, beliefs, and preferences.

The cultural interpretation contrasts with the "what can be done/do nothing" implication for those for whom race differences mean biogenetic differences. Krieger et al. (1999), on the other hand, attribute observed disparities in Black health and health care as most directly a result of racist and discriminatory social structures in American life, including health-care access.

Regardless of the interpretation, the implication for theory and practice is clear. To understand how to reduce racial disparities in health, indeed whether a reduction is possible, calls for more information than simply whether one is Black or not. Information is needed on the sociocultural and behavioral race-related experiences that mediate the effect of race on health.

An Individual Differences Perspective.   Gurin et al.'s (1980) early finding, using 1972 National Election Survey data, that a respondent of known race may not, given the choice, identify with that group anticipated more recent findings that identity is a matter of individual degree. Individual-level race/ethnic identity among Manuel's (1982a) Black older respondents varied with both the perception of currently experienced and lifelong, race/ethnic-linked social injustices (e.g., "I have/have not had the same chance as Whites to live where I want"), as well as perceived commonality with the experiences of the race/ethnic group (e.g., "I feel praised when other blacks are praised"). James Jackson and his colleagues, in several reports examining the National Survey of Black Americans, have conceptualized various continua of race/ethnic identity. Broman et al. (1988) write about variation in feelings of closeness to various categories of Black persons, including, for example, lower-class Blacks and elite Blacks. Allen et al. (1989), on the other hand, write about variation in the endorsement of Black separatism.

More recently, Thompson (1999), emphasizing racial identity salience differences, demonstrates a correlation between identity and reports of race-related discriminatory experiences, while Ren et al. (1999) show that increasing degrees of perceived discrimination correlate with perceptions of health.

The point is clear without an exhaustive review of this literature. First, Black older persons vary in their identification with the sense of peoplehood, history, and sociocultural experiences presumably marking their racial label. Second, different experiences have varying health outcomes. To the extent that this intragroup variation and its impact on health is left unobserved and untangled (whether in the absence or presence of a demonstrated interracial group difference), to a similar extent ambiguities will continue to arise in the interpretations and implications for reducing racial disparities in health.

Psychology of aging's *individual differences perspective* (see, e.g., Hertzog, 1985) offers one paradigm that motivates thinking anew about sources for intragroup differences and disparities in health. The individual differences perspective highlights, within the course of the aging process (intraindividual changes), the importance of identifying interindividual differences. Within the broad course of known and assumed age (and time)-related changes, the perspective focuses on identifying the individual-level experiences that slow or accelerate these changes. By extension, among the broad set of known and assumed cumulative life-course experiences defining Black aged identity, one may ask, What individual differences become highlighted by virtue of the significance they have for varying health consequences—all within the Black subgroup? The insights that come from observing inter-racial differences must be extended to allow insights that can come from observing intra-racial or within-group (Black) differences. Both individual biobehavioral (e.g., personal daily dietary intake, personality, genetic makeup) and contextual or social structural (e.g., institutionalized familial, class, cultural arrangements) differences provide likely sources for the understanding sought. Here sources can begin to be identified for understanding what produces distinctive Black aged health disadvantage. Here the social forces underlying the Black disadvantage appear, and here targeted efforts can likely be most efficiently fashioned for reducing the health disparity of the Black aged.

Erasing racial health disparities may have as much to do with identifying, and recognizing in

Figure 32.1
Life expectancy by age, by year, by race, by gender for the United States

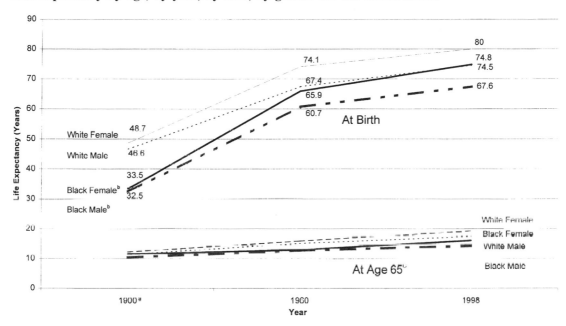

Source: Eberhardt et al. (2001).

[a] Data are for death registration states for the period 1900–1902 (10 states and the District of Columbia) and include deaths of nonresident persons.
[b] Data for 1900 and 1960 are for "all other races" (other than White). Black persons however, accounted for over 90 percent of all racial groups other then White.
[c] For readability, the exact life expectancy values were omitted for the population at age 65.

policies and social reform programs, the important sources for individual differences within the Black aged population as treating all Black aged as a homogeneous group. Williams et al. (1997) illustrate the point well. Race differences in their health measures result, in part, from hypothesized race-related discrimination experiences and other stressors, independent of social class influences. Thus, improving health in the Black older community, in part, would point, most directly, to targeting (say, for health promotion messages) persons who are victims of race discrimination or other stressors.

Data are not available to represent the conceptual ideas sketched here in a theoretically concise or efficient manner. Data exist, however, to permit testing the efficacy of a select and manageable number of the hypothetically likely social and behavioral sources shaping diversity within the Black older population. (See Figures 32.2 through 32.12 that display as many as 15 sources for variation in health within the Black older population.) These sources can be most efficiently discussed as the empirical findings associated with each are presented.

THE DIVERSITY OF HEALTH AMONG THE BLACK AGED: THE HYPOTHESIS AND EMPIRICAL FINDINGS

It is hypothesized that health disparities within the Black older population equal or exceed the disparities that distinguish the Black older population from the White older population. Further, both social structural and behavioral differences within the Black older population are expected to provide sources for understanding the hypothesized within-race disparity.

Figure 32.2
Ninety-five percent confidence intervals (CIs) for odds ratios for prevalence of a health condition, by race (N=6,596 [unweighted]), by social/behavioral differences within-race (Black [N=1,260]), among persons aged 60 years or older[a]

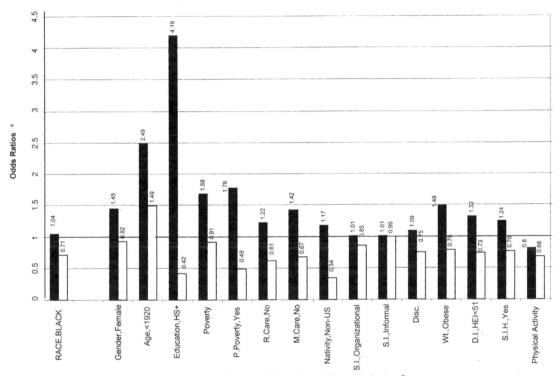

Race or within-race (Black) social/behavioral difference indicators [b]

[a] *Source*: Data based on weighted tabulations from the National Health and Nutrition Examination Survey III (UDHHS 1996), except for Disc., where the sources are Jackson and Gurin (1997) and Hughes and Shweder (2002).

[b] Labels attached to dichotomously distributed indicators (variables) refer to the higher scored value. Continuously distributed variables (without a label following the indicator) are named to reflect the highest scored value. Indicator abbreviations are defined as follows: Age=born 1920 or before, Education= high school or higher, Poverty= ratio of household income to poverty threshold, P. Poverty=perception of inadequate income for food, R. Care=regular source of care, M. Care=hospital and medical care, coverage under Medicare, S.I., Organizational=organizationally socially integrated, S.I., Informal=informally socially integrated, Disc.=perceived racial discrimination, Wt. Obese=Body Mass Index ⩾ 30, D.I., HEI <51=dietary intake (Healthy Eating Index <51), S.I.H.=smoker in household.

[c] Odds ratios are from variance adjusted (SUDAAN [Shah, Barnwell, & Bieler 1997]) logistic regression models with the health indicator regressed on race or, respectively, each of the within-race (Black) social/behavioral indicators. Odds ratios with confidence intervals including 1.0 are not statistically significant.

Figures 32.1 through 32.2 show the results of tests for this hypothesis from, as noted, multiple data sets (albeit primarily focusing on the NHANES III data, unless otherwise noted) and multiple indicators of health. Each of the health indicators (conditions, disabilities, and symptoms and subjectively evaluated health) is considered, in turn, below.

Life Expectancy

The analysis begins with a study of life expectancy (Figure 32.1), often seen as the most general indicator of the health and survival in a population. Life expectancy is a measure of the average number of years of life remaining at a given age, assuming a set of constant age-specific mortality rates. Figure 32.1 shows selected expectancies since 1900. Clearly, phenomenal gains in life expectancy occurred during the last century for each of the age-by-gender-by-race groups. Although life expectancy for Black males, at birth, increased from 61 years in 1960 (roughly taken to represent sociocultural conditions just before the Great Society legislation of the 1960s) to 68 years in 1998, it is also clear that the roughly 7-year White male advantage has remained. The 8-year White female advantage (relative to the Black female) decreased to a 5-year advantage during this same period.

As important as the racial comparison is for revealing disparity in health, there is much more to learn, even from these very broad data, about where the disparity particularly resides. The five-to seven-year racial difference in life expectancy stands alongside a gender difference within the Black population of seven years. Examining more specific health outcomes, including next the health conditions with which mortality is most often associated, can make the point more clear.

Selected Health Conditions

Figures 32.2 and 32.3 portray the significance of the thesis for selected health conditions. (The sections below are arranged such that the discussion under each health outcome [health condition, functional health, etc.] first considers racial contrasts [Black non-Hispanic relative to White non-Hispanic] followed by within race [Black] contrasts.) To maximize sample size during the analyses, the older population is defined as persons aged 60 years or older—a definition that is consistent with the age criterion for participation in programs associated with the Older Americans Act. The data show the 95 percent confidence intervals for the odds of a disadvantaged health status across the 11 separate indicators.

Differences between Black and White.   Figures 32.2 and 32.3 show data on the presence or absence of disease. No racial difference appears in these complexly sampled, variance-adjusted, and weighted NHANES III data in respondent reports of having had a physician's diagnosis of one of the conditions associated with the leading causes of death in the United States (heart disease, cancer, stroke, diabetes). Figure 32.2 shows that 95 percent of the time, the odds among the Black aged of having one or more of these long-term, often eventually disabling conditions was .71 to 1.04 as likely as in the White subgroup. That is, Black older persons are from .71 times as likely, to as much as 1.04 (4 percent) more likely, to report one or more conditions. Any confidence interval that includes 1.0 is not significant, indicating that the racial difference observed is simply a chance deviation from 1.0. The odds on the health outcome are the same in both the Black and White groups.

Figure 32.2 shows a measure of comorbidity, highlighting persons reporting two or more of the conditions. Again, no racial difference appears, with the odds ranging between .67 and 1.06 for having been diagnosed with two or more of the conditions.

Differences Within-Black.   Consider now differences within the Black subgroup on the health conditions. Two sources are searched for these differences: social structural differences and personal behavioral differences.

Social Structural Sources of Within-Black Differences.   The social structure refers to the relatively enduring social arrangements and groups established by humans as they interact. The group-creation and boundary-setting activities associated with this interaction include definitions for who can and cannot participate. Boundaries in U.S. society frequently are set on the basis of gender, age, and socioeconomic distinctions (in addition to racial distinctions). Experiences associated with membership in these subgroups, among the Black aged, often define the subgroups in distinctive ways, including health-related consequences.

Figure 32.3

Ninety-five percent confidence intervals (CIs) for odds ratios for prevalence of 2+ conditions, by race (N = 6,596 [unweighted]), by social/behavioral differences within-race (Black [N = 1,260]), among persons aged 60 years or older[a]

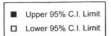

■ Upper 95% C.I. Limit
□ Lower 95% C.I. Limit

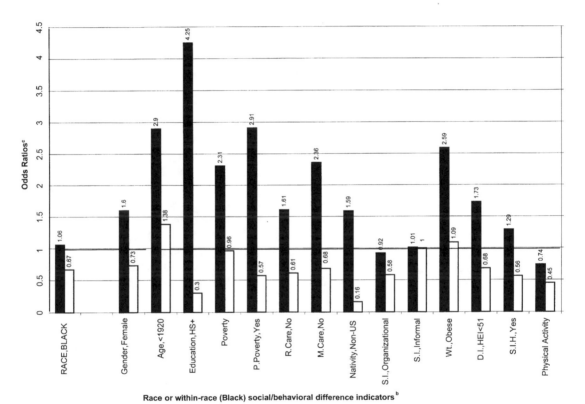

Race or within-race (Black) social/behavioral difference indicators[b]

[a] *Source*: Data based on weighted tabulations from the National Health and Nutrition Examination Survey III (USDHHS 1996).

[b] Labels attached to dichotomously distributed indicators (variables) refer to the higher scored value. Continuously distributed variables (without a label following the indicator) are named to reflect the highest scored value. Indicator abbreviations are defined as follows: Age=born 1920 or before, Education=high school or higher, Poverty=ratio of household income to poverty threshold, P. Poverty=perception of inadequate income for food, R. Care=regular source of care, M. Care=hospital and medical care coverage under Medicare, S.I., Organizational=organizationally socially integrated, S.I., Informal=informally socially integrated, Wt. Obese=Body Mass Index ⩾ 30, D.I., HEI <51=dietary intake (Healthy Eating Index <51), S.I.H.=smoker in household.

[c] Odds ratios are from variance adjusted (SUDAAN [Shah, Barnwell & Bieler, 1997]) logistic regression models with the health indicator regressed on race or, respectively, each of the within-race (Black) social/behavioral indicators. Odds ratios with confidence intervals including 1.0 are not statistically significant.

Figures 32.2 and 32.3 show that age (birth) cohort varies with both of the health condition measures. Persons born during or before 1920, aged 68 to 74 years or older at the time of the survey (1988–1994), are contrasted with persons born after 1920. Problems with health conditions are particularly highlighted among those born in 1920 or before. An individual differences perspective suggests the utility of the life-course conceptualization for making sense of these data. Persons in the older cohort experienced the Great Depression of 1929 as adults or during their late formative years. The conceptualization highlights the Great Depression's potential life-course impact on health.

It is unclear in these cross-sectional data, of course, that the legacy of the depression for health during late life outweighs the more plausible maturational effects—also shown in these data on age and health. Whether attributing age's influence on health to a generational or maturational effect, the individual differences perspective directs attention to see that Black persons differ in health conditions by their age cohort.

Neither gender nor social class differences influence the prevalence of health conditions among the Black older respondents. Of the remaining, less often studied, social structural indicators (health-care access [having a regular source of care and having hospital and medical care coverage under Medicare], nativity, social integration [organizational contacts, including club and church participation, and individual contacts, including frequency of talking with friend and family], and perceived racial discrimination), only differences in social integration, specifically organizational contacts, influence comorbidity. In agreement with the literature documenting the benefits of social support for health, persons more socially integrated, in club and church activities, are less likely report multiple health conditions. Again, with cross-sectional data on social support (NHANES III), it is unclear whether the primary direction of influence is from health to social integration or from social integration to health. The latter follows the idea that within-group differences in the development and use of organizational linkages (again, following a life-course perspective) can differentially contribute to health in late adulthood.

Behavioral Sources of Within-Black Differences.   The health of populations is most often attributed to personal behavioral, not social structural, sources. Healthy personal daily dietary intake, in particular, and, increasingly, physical activity (*Morbidity and Mortality Weekly Report* [MMWR], 2001) are promoted as the ways to avoid the health conditions that so often are the cause of death. Figures 32.2 and 32.3 show whether Black older persons whose health behaviors are optimal distinguish themselves by reporting fewer health conditions. Persons practicing optimal behaviors (Healthy Eating Index [HEI] score equal or greater than 51 out of 100 [Kumanyika & Odoms, 2001], living in a smoke-free environment, controlling weight [a BMI less than 30 (DHHS, 2001], and physically active), in fact, less likely report a health condition (Figure 32.2) or conditions (Figure 32.3). Of these relationships, however, only physical activity and weight control exert statistically significant effects.

Diet's failure to play a significant role in the distribution of health conditions is not altogether surprising. The controversy, or perhaps complexity, that surrounds dietary intake's health-related influence (see, e.g., Poppitt et al., 2002) is perceptively more than that surrounding the effect of exercise (MMWR, 2001) and weight control (USDHHS, 2001). The fact that dietary intake and also smoking were not related to the two health condition measures suggests that this group of Black older persons is an elite surviving population. Following the arguments of the mortality selection hypothesis, these may be persons for whom smoking and diet have not been risk factors for health over the life course. Greater clarity in the findings would call for longitudinal data to see the effect of these behavioral variables that take their toll on health over time.

Functional Disability

The study of health conditions, in short, shows that while race differences do not appear in the reports of physician-diagnosed health conditions associated with the leading causes of death, there are behavioral differences and often overlooked social structural differences within the Black older population. Diabetes, stroke, and other health conditions often lead to disabilities for functioning. Figures 32.4 through 32.9 show six indicators, respectively, of health-related disability.

Differences between Black and White.   Clark (1997) observed distinctively higher Black disability in the National Long Term Care Survey. The data in Figure 32.4, for the index of having at least one of the daily personal care disabilities (inability, without help, either to dress or feed self or to stand or walk), are not consistent with this expected effect. Disability does not vary by race during late adulthood in the NHANES III data examined here. Race differences also did not appear for the disabilities associated with personal daily instrumental behavior (ability to prepare meals, walk, climb steps, stoop, lift, do chores, or manage affairs [Figure 32.5]).

The next two figures show, however, that Black older persons more likely perceive needing help with daily personal care (Figure 32.6) or help with daily instrumental behaviors (Figure 32.7). While the Black older population, no more often than their White counterpart, report difficulty in the ability to hear telephone conversations (Figure 32.8), they are more likely to report difficulty in the ability to see to read (Figure 32.9).

Differences Within-Black.   Differences within the Black older population appear across age, gender, and social class among the typically studied social structural indicators (Figures 32.4 and 32.5). Black older females report at least one daily personal care disability from 23 percent to over 2 times (2.24) more often than their Black male counterparts. Females are from 48 percent to 2.14 times more likely than males to report at least one of the daily instrumental activity limitations. Similar evidence appears for class and age differences. On the other hand, excepting organizational affiliation, none of the remaining social structural indicators (health-care access, nativity, perceived race discrimination) varied significantly within the Black population on the personal care and instrumental disability behaviors. Predicted behavioral differences again highlight the importance associated with individuals' personal control of their weight and physical activity, but not their dietary intake or whether they live in a household where a member smokes.

Differences among the Black aged in the perception of needing help with the daily personal care and instrumental behaviors (Figures 32.6 and 32.7) occur across age, gender, and social class (having less than a high school education and having an income below the poverty threshold), as well as vary with differences in social integration and physical activity. Slightly varying but similar within-race differences additionally appear in Figures 32.8 and 32.9 for the disabilities associated with sight and hearing.

Oral Health, Emotional Well-being, and the Overall Perception of Health

Differences between Black and White.   Black older persons relatively more often report symptoms of oral health problems (perceived need for fillings, extractions, pain relief, gum treatments, and general dental work) and depressive symptoms (perception of unhappiness, loneliness, sadness, restless sleep, depression, or that life is unenjoyable, everything is an effort, or you can't get going) are generally more likely to perceive their health as poor to fair (Figures 32.10 through 32.12).

The poorer self-assessed health in the Black subgroup agrees with perhaps one of the more established findings in the literature (Ferraro & Kelley-Moore, 2001). Little information exists on oral health in the older population and less in the Black older population. As a target for one of the Healthy People 2000 and 2010 objectives (USDHHS, 1992), dental health is an indicator to which more attention needs to be given.

Differences Within-Black.   Oral health problems within the Black sample are heightened among the impoverished, the native-born, the less socially integrated, the less active, and the oldest (Figure 32.11).

Figure 32.4
Ninety-five percent confidence intervals (CIs) for odds ratios for prevalence of a personal care disability, by race (N = 6,596 [unweighted]), by social/behavioral differences within-race [Black (N = 1,260]), among persons aged 60 years or older[a]

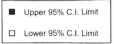

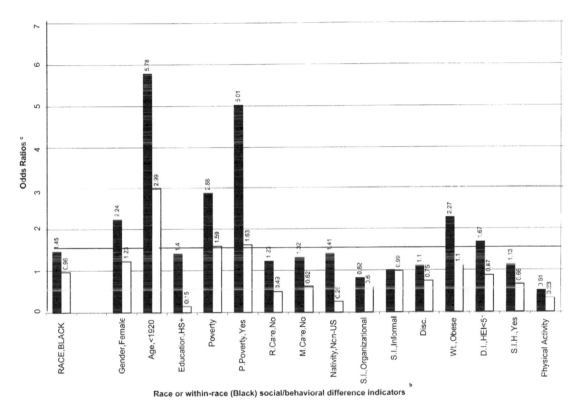

Race or within-race (Black) social/behavioral difference indicators[b]

[a] *Source*: Data based on weighted tabulations from the National Health and Nutrition Examination Survey III (USDHHS 1996), except for Disc., where the sources are: The National Survey of Black Americans, Panel Data (Jackson & Gurin, 1997) and the MIDUS Survey of Minority Groups (Hughes & Shweder, 2002).

[b] Labels attached to dichotomously distributed indicators (variables) refer to the higher scored value. Continuously distributed variables (without a label following the indicator) are named to reflect the highest scored value. Indicator abbreviations are defined as follows: Age=born 1920 or before, Education=high school or higher, Poverty=ratio of household income to poverty threshold, P. Poverty=perception of inadequate income for food, R. Care=regular source of care, M.Care=hospital and medical care coverage under Medicare, S.I., Organizational=organizationally socially integrated, S.I., Informal=informally socially integrated, Disc.=perceived racial discrimination, Wt. Obese=Body Mass Index eg 30, D.I., HEI<51=dietary intake (Healthy Eating Index <51), S.I.H.=smoker in household.

[c] Odds ratios are from variance adjusted (SUDAAN [Shah, Barnwell, & Bieler, 1997]) logistic regression models with the health indicator regressed on race or, respectively, each of the within-race (Black) social/behavioral indicators. Odds ratios with confidence intervals including 1.0 are not statistically significant.

Figure 32.5

Ninety-five percent confidence intervals (CIs) for odds ratios for prevalence of an instrumental activity disability, by race (N = 6,596 [unweighted]), by social/behavioral differences within-race (Black [N = 1,260]), among persons aged 60 years or older[a]

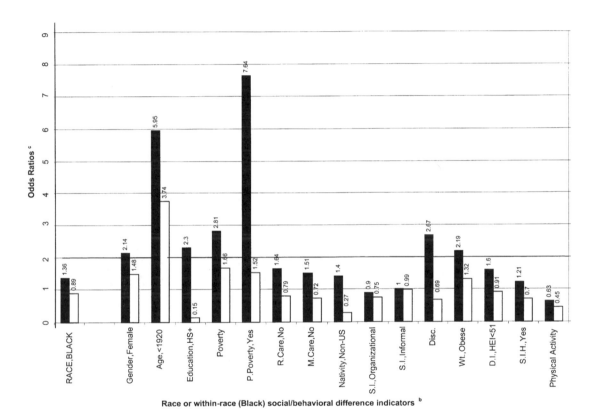

Odds Ratios[c]

Race or within-race (Black) social/behavioral difference indicators[b]

[a] *Source*: Data based on weighted tabulations from the National Health and Nutrition Examination Survey III (USDHHS 1996), except for Disc., where the sources are: The National Survey of Black Americans, Panel Data (Jackson & Gurin, 1997) and the MIDUS Survey of Minority Groups (Hughes & Shweder, 2002).

[b] Labels attached to dichotomously distributed indicators (variables) refer to the higher scored value. Continuously distributed variables (without a label following the indicator) are named to reflect the highest scored value. Indicator abbreviations are defined as follows: Age=born 1920 or before, Education=high school or higher, Poverty=ratio of household income to poverty threshold, P. Poverty=perception of inadequate income for food, R. Care=regular source of care, M. Care=hospital and medical care coverage under Medicare, S.I., Organizational=organizationally socially integrated, S.I., Informal=informally socially integrated, Disc.=perceived racial discrimination, Wt. Obese=Body Mass Index ≥ 30, D.I., HEI<51=dietary intake (Healthy Eating Index <51), S.I.H.=smoker in household.

[c] Odds ratios are from variance adjusted (SUDAAN [Shah, Barnwell, & Bieler, 1997]) logistic regression models with the health indicator regressed on race or, respectively, each of the within-race (Black) social/behavioral indicators. Odds ratios with confidence intervals including 1.0 are not statistically significant.

Figure 32.6

Ninety-five percent confidence intervals (CIs) for odds ratios for prevalence of perceived personal care behavior limitations, by race (N = 6,596 [unweighted]), by social/behavioral differences within-race (Black [N = 1,260]), among persons aged 60 years or older[a]

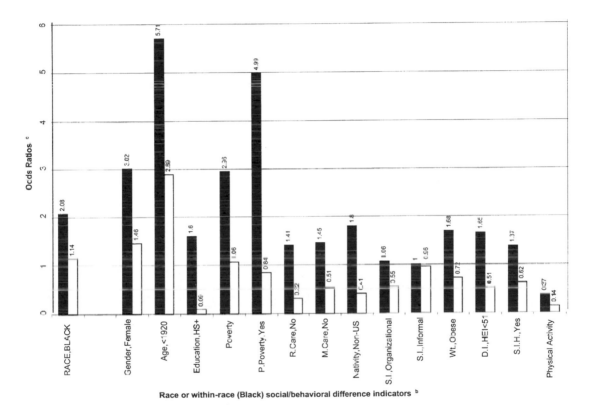

[a] *Source*: Data based on weighted tabulations from the National Health and Nutrition Examination Survey III (USDHHS, 1996).

[b] Labels attached to dichotomously distributed indicators (variables) refer to the higher scored value. Continuously distributed variables (without a label following the indicator) are named to reflect the highest scored value. Indicator abbreviations are defined as follows: Age=born 1920 or before, Education=high school or higher, Poverty=ratio of household income to poverty threshold, P. Poverty=perception of inadequate income for food, R. Care=regular source of care, M. Care=hospital and medical care coverage under Medicare, S.I., Organizational=organizationally socially integrated, S.I., Informal=informally socially integrated, Wt. Obese=Body Mass Index $\geq$ 30, D.I., HEI <51=dietary intake (Healthy Eating Index < 51), S.I.H.=smoker in household.

[c] Odds ratios are from variance adjusted (SUDAAN [Shah, Barnwell, & Bieler, 1997]) logistic regression models with the health indicator regressed on race or, respectively, each of the within-race (Black) social/behavioral indicators. Odds ratios with confidence intervals including 1.0 are not statistically significant.

Figure 32.7

Ninety-five percent confidence intervals (CIs) for odds ratios for prevalence of perceived instrumental behavior limitations, by race (N = 6,596 [unweighted]), by social/behavioral differences within-race (Black [N = 1,260]), among persons aged 60 years or older[a]

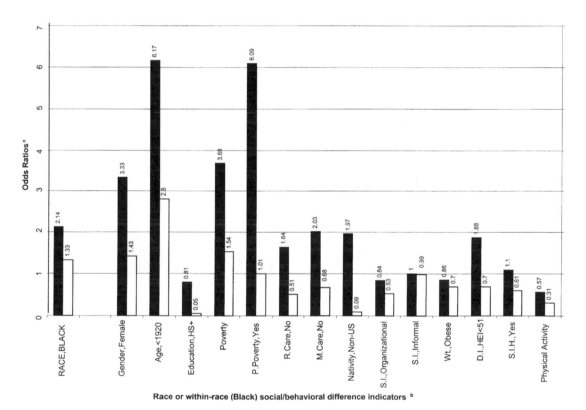

[a] *Source*: Data based on weighted tabulations from the National Health and Nutrition Examination Survey III (USDHHS, 1996).

[b] Labels attached to dichotomously distributed indicators (variables) refer to the higher scored value. Continuously distributed variables (without a label following the indicator) are named to reflect the highest scored value. Indicator abbreviations are defined as follows: Age=born 1920 or before, Education= high school or higher, Poverty=ratio of household income to poverty threshold, P. Poverty=perception of inadequate income for food, R. Care=regular source of care, M. Care=hospital and medical care coverage under Medicare, S.I., Organizational=organizationally socially integrated, S.I., Informal=informally socially integrated, Wt. Obese=Body Mass Index≥30, D.I., HEI<51=dietary intake (Healthy Eating Index < 51), S.I.H.=smoker in household.

[c] Odds ratios are from variance adjusted (SUDAAN [Shah, Barnwell, & Bieler, 1997]) logistic regression models with the health indicator regressed on race or, respectively, each of the within-race (Black) social/behavioral indicators. Odds ratios with confidence intervals including 1.0 are not statistically significant.

Figure 32.8

Ninety-five percent confidence intervals (CIs) for odds ratios for prevalence of difficulty hearing on telephone, by race (N = 6,596 [unweighted]), by social/behavioral differences within-race (Black [N = 1,260]), among persons aged 60 years or older[a]

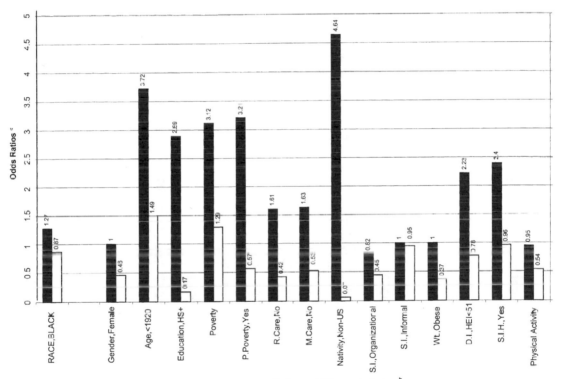

[a] *Source*: Data based on weighted tabulations from the National Health and Nutrition Examination Survey III (USDHHS, 1996).

[b] Labels attached to dichotomously distributed indicators (variables) refer to the higher scored value. Continuously distributed variables (without a label following the indicator) are named to reflect the highest scored value. Indicator abbreviations are defined as follows: Age=born 1920 or before, Education= high school or higher, Poverty= ratio of household income to poverty threshold, P. Poverty=perception of inadequate income for food, R. Care=regular source of care, M. Care=hospital and medical care coverage under Medicare, S.I., Organizational=organizationally socially integrated, S.I., Informal=informally socially integrated, Wt. Obese=Body Mass Index; eg30, D.I., HEI<51=dietary intake (Healthy Eating Index < 51), S.I.H.=smoker in household.

[c] Odds ratios are from variance adjusted (SUDAAN [Shah, Barnwell, & Bieler, 1997]) logistic regression models with the health indicator regressed on race or, respectively, each of the within-race (Black) social/behavioral indicators. Odds ratios with confidence intervals including 1.0 are not statistically significant.

Figure 32.9

Ninety-five percent confidence intervals (CIs) for odds ratios for prevalence of difficulty seeing to read, by race (N = 6,596 [unweighted]), by social/behavioral differences within-race (Black [N = 1,260]), among persons aged 60 years or older[a]

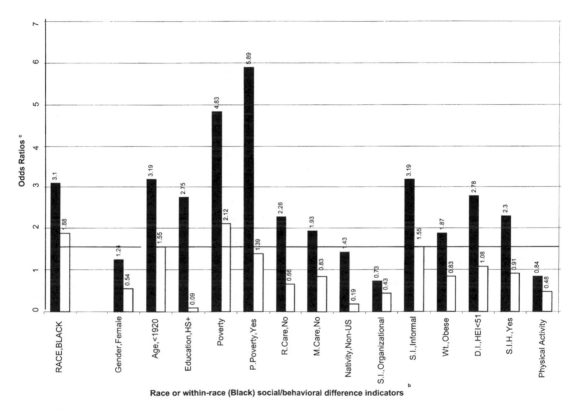

[b] Labels attached to dichotomously distributed indicators (variables) refer to the higher scored value. Continuously distributed variables (without a label following the indicator) are named to reflect the highest scored value. Indicator abbreviations are defined as follows: Age=born 1920 or before, Education= high school or higher, Poverty= ratio of household income to poverty threshold, P. Poverty=perception of inadequate income for food, R. Care=regular source of care, M. Care=hospital and medical care coverage under Medicare, S.I., Organizational=organizationally socially integrated, S.I., Informal=informally socially integrated, Wt. Obese=Body Mass Index; eg30, D.I., HEI<51=dietary intake (Healthy Eating Index < 51), S.I.H.=smoker in household.

[c] Odds ratios are from variance adjusted (SUDAAN [Shah, Barnwell, & Bieler, 1997]) logistic regression models with the health indicator regressed on race or, respectively, each of the within-race (Black) social/behavioral indicators. Odds ratios with confidence intervals including 1.0 are not statistically significant.

Figure 32.10

Ninety-five percent confidence intervals (CIs) for odds ratios for prevalence of dental problems, by race (N = 6,596 [unweighted]), by social/behavioral differences within-race (Black [N = 1,260]), among persons aged 60 years or older[a]

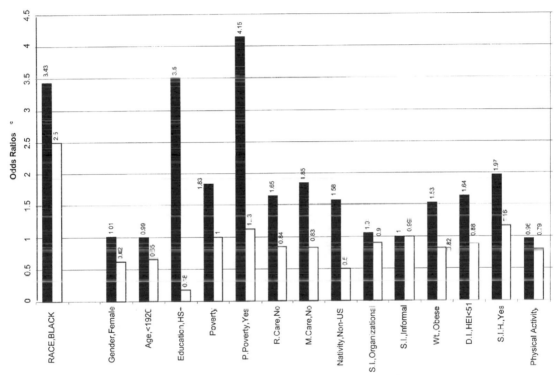

Race or within-race (Black) social/behavioral difference indicators [b]

[a] *Source*: Data based on weighted tabulations from the National Health and Nutrition Examination Survey III (USDHHS, 1996).

[b] Labels attached to dichotomously distributed indicators (variables) refer to the higher scored value. Continuously distributed variables (without a label following the indicator) are named to reflect the highest scored value. Indicator abbreviations are defined as follows: Age=born 1920 or before, Education= high school or higher, Poverty= ratio of household income to poverty threshold, P. Poverty=perception of inadequate income for food, R. Care=regular source of care, M. Care=hospital and medical care coverage under Medicare, S.I., Organizational=organizationally socially integrated, S.I., Informal=informally socially integrated, Wt. Obese=Body Mass Index; eg30, D.I., HEI<51=dietary intake (Healthy Eating Index < 51), S.I.H.=smoker in household.

[c] Odds ratios are from variance adjusted (SUDAAN [Shah, Barnwell, & Bieler, 1997]) logistic regression models with the health indicator regressed on race or, respectively, each of the within-race (Black) social/behavioral indicators. Odds ratios with confidence intervals including 1.0 are not statistically significant.

Figure 32.11

Ninety-five percent confidence intervals (CIs) for odds ratios for prevalence of poor/fair self-assessed health, by race (N = 6,596 [unweighted]), by social/behavioral differences within-race (Black [N = 1,260]), among persons aged 60 years or older[a]

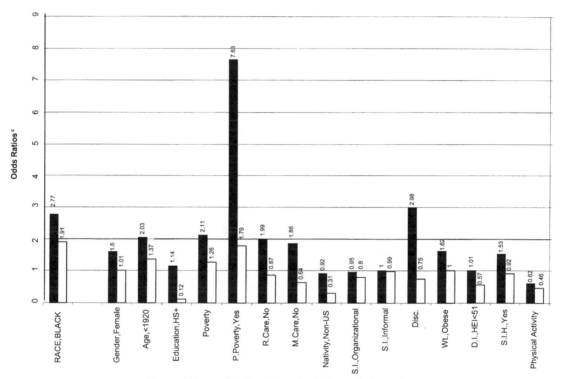

Race or within-race (Black) social/behavioral difference indicators [b]

[a] *Source*: Data based on tabulations from the National Health and Nutrition Examination Survey III (USDHHS, 1996), except for Disc., where the sources are: The National Survey of Black Americans, Panel Data (Jackson & Gurin, 1997) and the MIDUS Survey of Minority Groups (Hughes & Shweder, 2002).

[b] Labels attached to dichotomously distributed indicators (variables) refer to the higher scored value. Continuously distributed variables (without a label following the indicator) are named to reflect the highest scored value. Indicator abbreviations are defined as follows: Age=born 1920 or before, Education= high school or higher, Poverty= ratio of household income to poverty threshold, P. Poverty=perception of inadequate income for food, R. Care=regular source of care, M. Care=hospital and medical care coverage under Medicare, S.I., Organizational=organizationally socially integrated, S.I., Informal=informally socially integrated, Disc.=perceived racial discrimination, Wt. Obese=Body Mass Index≥30, D.I., HEI<51=dietary intake (Healthy Eating Index < 51), S.I.H.=smoker in household.

[c] Odds ratios are from variance adjusted (SUDAAN [Shah, Barnwell, & Bieler, 1997]) logistic regression models with the health indicator regressed on race or, respectively, each of the within-race (Black) social/behavioral indicators. Odds ratios with confidence intervals including 1.0 are not statistically significant.

Figure 32.12

Ninety-five percent confidence intervals (CIs) for odds ratios for prevalence of depression symptoms, by race (N = 6,596 [unweighted]), by social/behavioral differences within-race (Black [N = 1,260]), among persons aged 60 years or older[a]

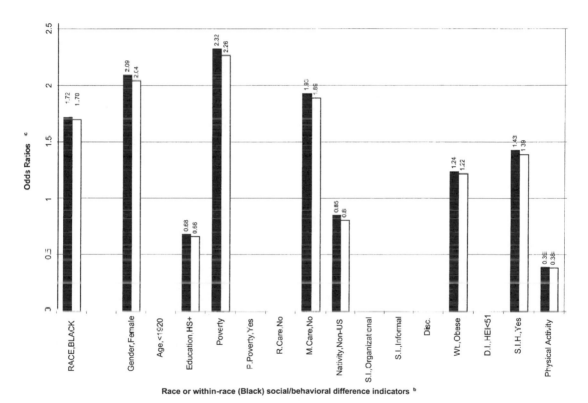

[a] *Source*: Data based on weighted tabulations from the National Health and Retirement Survey, Wave 2 (RAND, 1994).

[b] Labels attached to dichotomously distributed indicators (variables) refer to the higher scored value. Continuously distributed variables (without a label following the indicator) are named to reflect the highest scored value. Indicator abbreviations are defined as follows: Age=born 1920 or before, Education= high school or higher, Poverty= ratio of household income to poverty threshold, P. Poverty=perception of inadequate income for food, R. Care=regular source of care, M. Care=hospital and medical care coverage under Medicare, S.I., Organizational=organizationally socially integrated, S.I., Informal=informally socially integrated, Disc.=perceived racial discrimination, Wt. Obese=Body Mass Index≥30, D.I., HEI<51=dietary intake (Healthy Eating Index < 51), S.I.H.=respondent smokes, Physical activity=vigorous activity during the last week. Data are not available for missing frequency bars.

[c] Odds ratios are from logistic regression models with the health indicator regressed on race or, respectively, each of the within-race (Black) social/behavioral indicators. Odds ratios with confidence intervals including 1.0 are not statistically significant.

585

Likewise, the racial differences noted, respectively, for depression and the global health measure join differences identifiable within the Black subgroup. Differences within the Black group on depressive symptoms and the global health measure appear for gender, age, class, social integration, and nativity, among the structural variables, and physical activity, smoking, and obesity, among the behavioral variables. Generally, the results reinforce the thesis of the importance of conceptualizing and observing within-group differences.

CONCLUSION

Black older persons in the United States are not a homogeneous group. This is not a new observation (see Jackson, 1970), and it is an observation implicit in the questions and hypotheses (about double, triple and multiple jeopardy) that initially motivated the study of the Black aged as special aging population. The data reviewed here help to re-establish that often overlooked point. The question examined in this chapter expands previous work by framing the idea from a different perspective. In particular, the chapter addressed the increasingly asked, but never systematically tested, question of whether health differences within the Black older population rival those frequently emphasized as distinguishing Black from White older persons. The process of responding to this analytic question provided the opportunity to summarize recent, nationally representative data (from a variety of sources) on the relative and absolute state of health in the Black older population. Data from multiple indicators of health, chosen to model not simply the absence of disease but a broad picture of physical and psychological health, add to the evidence found for the thesis.

Typically, four to six sources for difference within the Black older population appeared on each of the health outcome measures. Physical activity, consistently, and weight control, to a lesser extent, but not dietary intake or living in a smoke-free household stand out as important behavioral differences within the Black older population that have health consequences. Differences in age or birth cohort, gender, social class, and social integration often constituted social structural sources for differences among the 11 health indicators. Generally, the same sources for within-race health outcomes appear both among the 5 indicators where no racial effect was found (the relatively more objective measures of health [daily personal care and instrumental activity disabilities] and physician-diagnosed health conditions) and the remaining relatively more subjective health indicators where racial contrasts appeared.

Implications for Future Work

Patterns in the data not consistent with the thesis are also intriguing for the insights they provide for future work. Neither health care, racial discrimination, nor, for the most part, nativity, among the social structural indicators, nor dietary intake nor exposure to tobacco smoke, among the behavioral measures, constituted sources for observing variation within the Black sample. Yet a substantial literature suggests that health outcomes and/or race vary with dietary intake (Erlinger et al., 2000) nativity (Angel et al., 2000), health-care access (Lille-Blanton et al., 2000), and race discrimination (Williams, 1999).

Consider health-care access, for example. It is reasonable that the concept has not been measured as thoroughly as it should. It may be that access differences and their impact on health outcomes refer less to Medicare coverage differences (as measured in this research) and more to differences, in, say, race-related hospital segregation among Medicare beneficiaries, as Smith (1998) confirms. In addition to information about health insurance, information on quality-of-care, and perceived quality-of-care, may be needed to give a more complete understanding of the role of health-care access in race-related health disparities.

Ensuring a representative set of indicators of the sources for disparity joins with the need to ensure a representative set of indicators of health and health-care outcomes. Because of the relatively greater availability of data from noninstitutionalized populations, for example, data on institutionalized care have not been factored into the conclusions of this report. While at any time only 2 percent of the Black older population (aged 65 years or older) is institutionalized, it is unclear that the traditionally available informal and familial caregiving social systems for this fast-growing (potentially more dependent) population can be sustained.

The cross-linkage of the components of health-care quality (timeliness, patient centeredness, safety, and effectiveness) with type of health-care need (preventive, curative, management, or end-of-life coping) provides one example of the conceptual focus needed to generate a representative set of indicators for systematically monitoring racial disparities in health, in both institutionalized and noninstitutionalized settings (see Swift, 2002). Cross-linking safety with managing disability, for example, readily reveals the need for an indicator of nursing home safety, or in-home safety, as one among other indicators in coming to a definitive conclusion about race-related disparities and whether such disparities as exist are being reduced over time.

In short, much work remains before a definitive conclusion can be brought to the thesis in this chapter. Nevertheless, strong support is found for the thesis that equal or greater variation in health exists within the Black older population than between it and the White older population. It is shown that global racial category labels, interpreted variably and haphazardly as proxies for defining a racial group sociocultural and biological commonalities, subsume many health-related, within-race sub-group differences. The assumption that all persons within a racial group are the same is not true. Failure to model this within-subgroup (race) and individual variation contributes to errors, not simply in the measurement of what race indicates but in what can be inferred to reduce the presumed effect of race on health outcomes. Gerontologists long ago understood that aging and the aged are not homogeneous phenomena. The same understanding needs to be brought to the study of aging and aged Black persons. The Black older population is as diverse as any other population, and the study of this population needs to model these differences.

Recommendation

Practically, the ideas discussed in this chapter suggest that the most efficient approach to reducing racial disparities in the older population's health may reside less in targeting the health behaviors (or the structural conditions of living) of all Black older persons and more in targeting the special subgroups within the Black older population where disparities cluster. The finding, for example, that Black older persons are two times more likely than their White counterparts to perceive limitations in their activities because of personal care and instrumental activity disabilities, must be joined with the finding, for example, that three times more female Black older persons report this perception than their male counterparts (Figures 32.6 and 32.7). No race difference exists in physician-diagnosed health conditions. Nevertheless, over two times more obese Black older persons than nonobese Black older persons report these conditions (Figures 32.2 and 32.3). Just as special attention is warranted for the Black older female, in reducing disabilities, being responsive to weight control messages targeted to the population at large becomes especially important for the Black aged who are obese. The efficient use of limited health promotional or other resources would call for targeting not all Black older persons but those within this population shown to experience the brunt of disadvantage: the impoverished, the inactive, the obese, the less socially integrated, the older cohorts, and females.

Nelson Mandela's familiar observation that "none of us are free until all of are free" seems most appropriate in concluding the points made in this chapter. While the nation's health has improved and is improving, there continues to be striking subgroup disadvantage within the country—serving to lower overall national rates on health indicators. Raising the country's global rankings on health and survival indicators, such as life expectancy (ranked 20th among males and 18th among females) and infant mortality (ranked 27th [Eberhardt et al., 2001]), depends on ensuring the same chances for good health for the least advantaged among us as that enjoyed by most of us.

REFERENCES

Allen, R.L., Dawson, M.C., & Brown, R.E. (1989). A schematic-based approach to modeling an African American social belief system. *American Political Science Review, 83*, 421–441.

Angel, J.L., Buckley, C.J., & Sakamoto, A. (2000). Duration or disadvantage? Exploring nativity, ethnicity and health in midlife. *Journal of Gerontology, Series B: Psychological Science and Social Sciences, 56*, S275–S284).

Beckett, M. (2000). Converging health inequalities in later life—an artifact of mortality selection? *Journal of Health and Social Behavior, 41*, 106–119.

Berkman, L.F., & Mullen, J.M. (1997). How health behaviors and the social environment contribute to health differences between Black and White older Americans. In L.G. Martin & B.J. Soldo (Eds.), *Racial and ethnic differences in the health of older Americans* (pp. 163–182). Washington, DC: National Academy Press.

Broman, C., Neighbors, H.W., & Jackson, J.S. (1988). Racial group identification and Black adults. *Social Forces, 67*, 146–158.

Clark, D.O. (1997). U.S. trends in disability and institutionalization among older Blacks and Whites. *American Journal of Public Health, 87*, 438–440.

Dowd, J.J., & Bengtson, V.L. (1978). Aging in minority populations: An examination of the double jeopardy hypothesis. *Journal of Gerontology, 33*, 427–436.

Du Bois, W.E.B. (1906). *The health and physique of the Negro American.* Atlanta, GA: Atlanta University Press.

Eberhardt, M.S., et al. (2001). *Health, United States 2001 with urban and rural health chartbook.* Hyattsville, MD: National Center for Health Statistics.

Erlinger, T.P., Pollack, M.P.P., & Appel, L.J. (2000). Nutrition-related cardiovascular risk factors in older people: Results from the Third National Health and Nutrition Examination Survey. *Journal of the American Geriatrics Society, 48*, 1486–1489.

Federal Interagency Forum on Aging-Related Statistics. (2000). *Older Americans 2000: Key indicators of well being.* Washington, DC: U.S. Government Printing Office.

Ferraro, K.F., & Farmer, M.M. (1996). Double jeopardy to health hypothesis for African Americans: Analysis and critique. *Journal of Health and Social Behavior, 37*, 27–43.

Ferraro, K.F., & Kelly-Moore, J.A. (2001). Self-rated health and mortality among Black and White adults: Examining the dynamic evaluation thesis. *Journal of Gerontology: Social Sciences, 56B*, S195–S205.

Gibson, R.C. (1994). The age-by-race gap in health and mortality in the older population: A social science research agenda. *The Gerontologist, 34*, 454–462.

Gurin, P., Miller, A., & Gurin, G. (1980). Stratum identification and consciousness. *Social Psychology Quarterly, 43*, 30–47.

Haynes, M.A., & Smeldy, B.D. (1999). (Eds.). *The unequal burden of cancer: An assessment of NIH research programs for ethnic minorities and medically underserved.* Washington, DC: National Academy Press.

Hertzog, C. (1985). An individual differences perspective: Implications for cognitive research in gerontology. *Research on Aging, 7*, 7–45.

Hughes, D.L., & Shweder, R.A. (2002). Midlife development in the United States (MIDUS): Survey of minority groups (Chicago and New York City), 1995–1996 (computer file). Chicago: Metro Chicago Information Center (producer). Ann Arbor, MI: Inter-university Consortium for Political and Social Research (distributor).

Jackson, J.J. (1970). Aged Negroes: Their cultural departures from statistical stereotypes and rural–urban differences. *The Gerontologist, 10*, 140–145.

Jackson, J.S., Brown, T.N., Williams, D.R., Torres, M., Sellers, S.L., & Brown, K. (1996). Racism and the physical and mental health status of African Americans: A thirteen-year national panel study. *Ethnicity & Disease, 6*, 132–147.

Jackson, J.S., & Gurin, G. (1997). National Survey of Black Americans, Waves 1–4, 1979–1980, 1987–1988, 1988–1989, 1992 (computer file), ICPSR version. Ann Arbor, MI: Inter-university Consortium for Political and Social Research (producer and distributor).

Jackson, J.S., & Sellers, S.L. (2001). Health and the elderly. In R.L. Braithwaite & S.E. Taylor (Eds.), *Health issues in the Black community* (pp. 419–447). San Francisco: Jossey-Bass.

Krieger, N., Williams, D., & Zierler, S. (1999). "Whiting out" White privilege will not advance the study of how racism harms health. *American Journal of Public Health, 89*, 782–783.

Kumanyika, S.K., & Odoms, Angela. (2001). Nutrition. In R.L. Braithwaite & S.E. Taylor (Eds.), *Health issues in the Black community* (pp. 419–447). San Francisco: Jossey-Bass.

LaVeist, T.A., Sellers, R., & Neighbors, H.W. (2001). Perceived racism and self and system blame attribution: Consequences for longevity. *Ethnicity & Disease, 11*, 711–721.

Lawton, M.P., & Lawrence, R.H. (1994). Assessing health. In M.P. Lawton & J. Teresi (Ed.), *Annual review of gerontology and geriatrics: Focus on assessment techniques* (pp. 23–56). New York: Springer.

Lille-Blanton, M., Brodie, M., Rowland, D., Altman, D., & McIntosh, M. (2000). Race, ethnicity, and the health care system: Public perceptions and experiences. *Medical Care Research Review, 57*, S218–S235.

Lindsay, I.B. (1971). *Multiple hazards of age and race: The situation of aged Blacks in the United States.* Special Committee on Aging, U.S. Senate. Washington, DC: U.S. Government Printing Office.

Manton, K., Poss, S.S., & Wing, S. (1979). The Black/White mortality crossover: Investigation from the perspective of the components of aging. *The Gerontologist, 19*, 291–390.

Manton, K.G., & Stallard, E. (1997). Health and disability differences among racial and ethnic groups. In L.G. Martin & B.J. Soldo (Eds.), *Racial and ethnic differences in the health of older Americans* (pp. 43–105). Washington, DC: National Academy Press.

Manuel, R.C. (1982a). The dimensions of ethnic minority identification: An exploratory analysis among elderly Black Americans. In R.C. Manuel (Ed.), *Minority aging: Sociological and social psychological issues* (pp. 231–247). Westport, CT: Greenwood Press.

Manuel, R.C. (1982b). Ethnic group identification. In D.J. Mangen & W.A. Peterson (Eds.), *Research instruments in social gerontology: Clinical and social psychology* (pp. 415–435). Minneapolis: University of Minnesota Press.

Manuel, R.C. (2000). The conceptualization and measurement of race: Confusion and beyond. *African American Research Perspectives, 6*, 7–17.

Morbidity and Mortality Weekly Report (MMWR). (2001). Increasing physical activity. Retrieved April 16, 2002 from http://www.cdc.gov/mmwr

National Urban League (NUL). (1964). *Double jeopardy: The older Negro in America today.* New York: National Urban League.

Poppitt, S.D., et al. (2002). Long-term effects of ad libitum low-fat, high carbohydrate diets on body weight and serum lipids in overweight subjects with metabolic syndrome. *American Journal of Clinical Nutrition, 75*, 11–20.

Preston, S.H., Elo, L.T., Rosenwaike, I., & Hill, M. (1996). African-American mortality at older ages: Results of a matching study. *Demography, 33*, 193–209.

RAND Corporation. (1994). RAND HRS Data File, 1994 [computer file, based on the Health and Retirement Survey (HRS), 1994. Washington DC: National Institute on Aging (producer)]. Santa Monica, CA: RAND Corporation.

Ren, X.S., Amick, B.C., & Williams, D.R. (1999). Racial/ethnic disparities in health: The interplay between discrimination and socioeconomic status. *Ethnicity & Disease, 9*, 151–165.

Schneider, E.C.A., Zaslavsky, A.M., & Epstein, A.M. (2002). Racial disparities in the quality of care for enrollees in Medicare managed care. *Journal of the American Medical Association, 10*, 1506–1509.

Shah, B.V., Barnwell, B.G., & Bieler, G.S. (1997). *SUDAAN Users Manual, Release 7.5.* Research Triangle Park, NC: Research Triangle Institute.

Smith, D.B. (1998). The racial segregation of hospital care revisited: Medicare discharge patterns and their implications. *American Journal of Public Health, 88*, 461–463.

Smith, P., & Kington, R.S. (1997). Race, socioeconomic status and health in later life. In L.G. Martin & B.J.

Soldo (Eds.), *Racial and ethnic differences in the health of older Americans* (pp. 106–162). Washington, DC: National Academy Press.

Smith, T.L. (1957). The changing number and distribution of the aged Negro population of the United States. *Phylon, 18,* 339–354.

Sowell T. (1994). *Race and culture: A world view.* New York: Basic Books.

Swift, E.K. (2002). *Guidance for the National Healthcare Disparities Report.* Washington, DC: National Academies Press.

Thompson, H.S., Kamarck, T.W., & Manuck, S.B. (2002). The association between racial identity and hypertension in African-American adults: Elevated resting and ambulatory blood pressure as outcomes. *Ethnicity & Disease, 12,* 20–28.

Thompson, V.L.S. (1999). Variables affecting racial-identity salience among African Americans. *Journal of Social Psychology, 139,* 748–761.

U.S. Bureau of the Census. (2000). Projections of the total resident population by 5-year age groups, race and Hispanic origin with separate age categories, middle series, 2011 to 2015. Retrieved June 4, 2002, from http://www.census.gov/prod/cen2000.

U.S. Bureau of the Census. (2001). Population by age, sex, race and Hispanic or Latino origin for the U.S. Retrieved June 4, 2002, from http://www.census.gov/prod/cen2000.

U.S. Department of Health and Human Services (USDHHS). (1985). *Report of the Secretary's Task Force on Black and Minority Health. (Vol. 1, Executive summary).* Washington, DC: U.S. Government Printing Office.

U.S. Department of Health and Human Services (USDHHS). (1992). *Healthy people 2000: National health promotion and disease prevention objectives, summary report.* Boston: Jones & Bartlett.

U.S. Department of Health and Human Services (USDHHS). (1996). National Center for Health Statistics. *Third National Health and Nutrition Examination Survey, 1988–94, Reference Manuals and Reports* (CD-ROM). Hyattsville, MD: Centers for Disease Control and Prevention.

U.S. Department of Health and Human Services (USDHHS). (2001). *The surgeon general's call to action to prevent and decrease overweight and obesity.* Rockville, MD: U.S. Department of Health and Human Services, Public Health Service, Office of the Surgeon General. Washington, DC: U.S. Government Printing Office.

Williams, D.R. (1999). Race, socioeconomic status and health: The added effects of racism and discrimination. *Annals of the New York Academy of Sciences. Socioeconomic status and health in Industrialized Nations: Social, Psychological and Biological Pathways, 896,* 173–187.

Williams, D.R. (2002). *Racial/ethnic variations in women's health: The social embeddedness of health.* American Journal of Public Health, 92, 588–597.

Williams, D.R., Yu, Y., Jackson, J.S., & Anderson, N.B. (1997). Racial differences in physical and mental health: Socio-economic status, stress and discrimination. *Journal of Health Psychology, 2,* 335–351.

World Health Organization (WHO). (1959). The public health aspects of aging of the population. Copenhagen: World Health Organization (Regional Office for Europe).

CHAPTER 33

Rural Health of Black America: A Complex Frontier

CAPTAIN MARK S. EBERHARDT

INTRODUCTION

One of the overarching goals of Healthy People 2010 is the elimination of health disparities (USDHHS, 2000). This chapter addresses the important and much neglected topic of the health status of rural Black American health. "Urban health" has become synonymous with Black American health; since the great majority (86 percent) of Black Americans live in metropolitan areas, the five million Black Americans living in rural areas and small towns have remained practically invisible (McKinnon & Humes, 2000). This subpopulation may be at increased risk as it would be subject to the health-care access problems of rural populations, in general, as well as the poorer health status of Black Americans.

This chapter explores the evidence that Black Americans in "rural" areas are at increased risk of having adverse health outcomes relative to urban Black Americans, rural White Americans, and urban White Americans. Several indicators are considered, including health risk factors, morbidity, health-care access and use, functional status, and mortality. Before discussing these indicators, it is prudent to consider several barriers that limit our understanding of rural Black American health: (1) the availability of rural health data, (2) the definition of "rural," and (3) the distribution of the rural Black American population.

Barriers to Understanding the Health of Rural Black Americans

The first barrier to understanding the health of rural Black Americans is the general limited availability of rural health information (Schur et al., 1998). For example, rural health survey research is often faced with (1) few rural study participants in national surveys producing statistically unreliable measures; (2) the high costs of special surveys due to the reduced efficiency of studying smaller, isolated communities; and (3) confidentiality concerns that prohibit releasing national survey data from residents in less populated areas.

The second barrier is the definition of "rural." Standard rural definitions have been proposed (Ricketts et al., 1998); however, the continued use of different rural definitions can lead to inconsistent study findings (Jonas & Wilson, 1997). Rural definitions have been based on (1) population

Figure 33.1
Percent of population who are Black American by county, United States, 2000

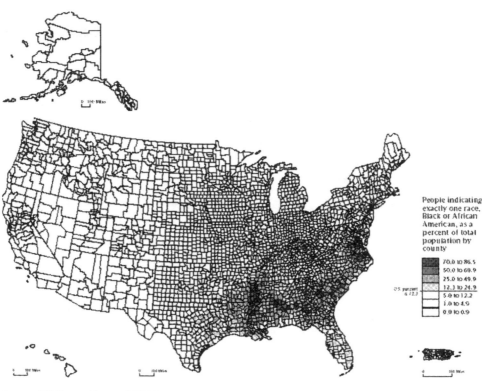

Source: US Census Bureau (2000a).

size (Howard-Pitney & Winkleby, 2002; Levin et al., 2001); (2) population density (Stoddard et al., 1994); and (3) socioeconomic measures and geographic proximity to an urban area (Jonas & Wilson, 1997). Rural area boundaries have also been defined based on (1) geopolitical borders (e.g., census tract or county), (2) residential characteristics (i.e., farm/nonfarm), and (3) statistical/social/historical criteria, such as metropolitan statistical areas, regional planning areas (Sharma et al., 2000), and economically disadvantaged areas (Barnett et al., 2000). Classifying urbanization in national health data systems can also be limited by available geographic detail. County-level data, when available, have proven useful (NCHS, 2001); however, Ricketts et al. (1998) assert that smaller areas, such as census tracts, are needed to adequately evaluate rural health. Thus, a review of the rural health survey research comes with the caveat that different urbanization classifications may produce conflicting findings.

The third barrier is the geographic distribution of rural Black Americans (Figure 33.1) that limits the use of national survey data for understanding the health of rural Black Americans. Nearly 9 percent of the rural U.S. population is Black American (Ricketts, 1999); however this group constitutes less than 2 percent of the rural populations in every U.S. region except the South. Approximately 90 percent of rural Black Americans live in the southern United States (NCHS, 2001). National surveys collect samples from all U.S. regions, a fact that reduces the number of rural Black American respondents included unless the survey sample sizes are very large or oversampling is done in the southern region.

Despite these difficulties, some research has examined health disparities of rural Black Americans

Table 33.1

Comparison of studies that have examined the status of rural African Americans

Study	Categories of people (or events) used in studies and definition of urbanization	Data source (n)	Data year
	Rural Black, urban Black, rural White, urban White		
Stokley et al., 2001	Non-metro, Metro	Natl. Immunization Survey (22,521 children)	1999
Barnett et al., 2000	Non-metro, Metro	Mortality and census data for Appalachia (n, ??? adults)	1980-97
Fingerhut et al., 1998	Non-metro, Metro	Natl. mortality and census data (n=399 counties, all ages	1987-95
Levin et al., 2001	"Rural*", "Urban**"(*50% of cities or towns with popn. <= 25,000; **all others)	South Carolina Behavioral Risk Factor Surveillance System (5,796 adults)	1995-97
Sharma et al., 2000	"Rural*", "Metro*" (*state planning commission code)	Missouri birth cohort (70,043 infants)	1995
Slifkin et al., 2000	Non-metro, Metro	Natl. Health Interview Survey (82,929 adults)	1994
House et al., 2000	Non-large metro, Large metro	University of Michigan national survey and Natl. Death Index (3,617 adults)	1986-94
Sarvela et al., 1997	Non-metro, Metro	Natl. Monitoring the Future Survey (128,791 teens)	1976-92
Jonas et al., 1997	Non-metro, Metro	Natl. Health Interview Survey (43,723 adults)	1991
Bell et al., 2000	Non metro, Metro	Natl. Health Interview Survey (43,723 adults)	1991
McMurry et al., 1999	Non-metro, Metro	North Carolina Cardiovascular Health in Children Study (2,113 children)	1990's
Hays et al., 1995	Low popn. areas, Higher popn. areas	North Carolina Established Popns. for Epidemiologic Studies of the Elderly (4,126 elders)	1986-90
Barnett et al., 2001	Size of largest locale in labor market area	Regional mortality and census data (n, ??? adults)	1985-95
Cowie et al., 1995	Non-metro, Metro	Natl. Health Interview Survey (84,572 adults)	1989

(Table 33.1) This chapter reviews these findings and focuses primarily on data from the Centers from Disease Control and Prevention's National Center for Health Statistics representative population based studies that have clear rural definitions. The findings of smaller studies are considered, when appropriate. Given the geographic location of rural Black Americans, most findings apply largely to the southern United States.

EVIDENCE OF HEALTH DISPARITIES BETWEEN RURAL BLACK AMERICANS AND OTHER GROUPS

Risk Factors

Disease risk factors are an important component of health disparities. Tobacco use is a general rural health concern and varies by race and type of tobacco. A study of rural women found that Black Americans smoked less than White Americans (Duelberg, 1992). Sarvela et al. (1997) found that smoking rates among rural Black American male adolescents (20 percent) were higher than among their urban counterparts (10 percent). They also noted that rural Black American smoked less (9 percent and 20 percent, female and male, respectively) than rural White American adolescents (33 percent and 34 percent, females and males, respectively). Smokeless tobacco use is less common among Black Americans than White Americans, and more common in rural areas, regardless of race (Bell et al., 2000). National data also indicate that the prevalence of chewing tobacco use is similar among rural low-income Black or White American men (Howard-Pitney & Winkelby, 2002).

Table 33.1 (continued)

White-Means, 2000	"Rural*", "City**" (* "live in a rural area or small city"; ** "small city with 50K-250K popn.")	Natl. Long Term Care Survey (4,534 elders)	1989
Miller et al., 1996	Non-metro, Metro	Natl. Maternal and Infant Health Survey (18,594 mothers)	1988
VanNostrand, 1993	Non-metro, Metro	Natl. Health Interview Survey (n, ??? elders)	1985-87
Reis et al, 1990	Non-metro, Metro	Natl. Health Interview Survey (276,442 adults)	1985-87
Farmer et al., 1993	Non-metro, Metro	Natl. mortality and census data (n, ??? infants)	1987
Duncan et al., 1995	Non-metro, Metro	Natl.Medical Expenditure Survey (32,276 adults)	1987
Gillum et al., 1996	Non-metro, Metro	NHANES I Epidemiologic Followup Study (7,260 adults)	1971-87
Kahn et al., 1994	"Rural*", "Urban**" (*not adjacent to metro. county or <20,000 popn. if adjacent; **all others)	Medicare data (9,932 elders)	1981-82 1985-86
Smith et al., 1995	Non-metro, Metro	Natl. Longitudinal Mortality Study (130,634 adults)	1979-85
Duelberg, 1992	Non-metro, Metro	Natl. Health Interview Survey (19,027 adults)	1985
	Other race/urban comparisons		
Mueller et al., 1998	Non-metro Black, metro Black, non-metro non-Hispanic White, metro non-Hispanic White	Natl. Health Interview Survey (112,246 person < 65 years old)	1992
Howard-Pitney et al., 2002	Non-large metro lower income Black or White, U.S average	NHANES III (3,013 men)	1988-94
Thomas et al, 1995	Non-metro non-White, Metro non-White, Non-metro White, Metro White	North Carolina health dept. case reports (12,275)	1985-93
Mansfield et al., 1999	"Metropolitan*", "urban*", or "rural"* Black or White (*USDA rural-urban Continuum Codes)	Area resource file (n, ??? All ages)	1990-92

Findings on the prevalence of chronic disease risk factors are mixed. In a South Carolina study of coronary heart disease (CHD) risk factors, Levin et al. (2001) found a higher prevalence of hypertension (35 percent and 26 percent) and overweight (71 percent and 54 percent) for rural Black Americans compared to rural White Americans. Daily consumption of fewer than 5 fruits or vegetables was more common among rural Black Americans (83 percent) than rural White Americans (72 percent), but physical inactivity rates were similar. Duelberg (1992) reported that Black American women exercise less than White American women, regardless of urbanization, after controlling for age, marital status, education, or income. A study in North Carolina determined that rural children had a higher prevalence of cardiovascular disease risk factors than urban children, such as obesity, higher blood pressure, and reduced physical fitness (McMurray et al., 1999). However, the prevalence of these risk factors was similar in rural Black American children and rural White American children. For example, obesity prevalence among rural children was 58 percent for Black Americans and 63 percent for White Americans; furthermore, logistic regression confirmed that rural residence, not race, was associated with obesity.

Morbidity

Prevalence.   Data are inadequate to determine whether rural Black Americans have excess chronic disease morbidity when compared to rural White, urban Black, or urban White Americans. Mueller et al. (1999) stated that "rural minorities experience disproportionately high rates of certain kinds of illnesses," (p. 239); however, this review provided few estimates for rural Black Americans.

Table 33.1 (continued)

Pathman et al., 2001	Area with low Black American population proportion Areas with high Black American population proportion	Regional census data (796 counties)	1990
Calle et al., 1993	Non-metro Black, Metro Black	Natl. Health Interview Survey (12,252 women)	1987
	Separate comparisons of race or urbanization		
CMS, 2002	Non-Hispanic. Black, Non-Hispanic White, Non-metro, Metro	Medicare data (39.6 million beneficaries)	1997
Adams et al. 1999	Black, White, Non-metro, Metro	Natl. Health Interview Survey (63,402 adults)	1996
Steinberg, et al., 2000	Black, White, Non-metro, metro	Natl. AIDS case reports (all ages)	1996
Casper et al., 2000	Black, White comparison only	Natl. mortality and census data (n, ??? women)	1991-95
Coward et al, 1997	Black, White, Non-metro, Metro	Local Florida survey (1,220 elders)	1994
Lannin et al., 1998	Black, White comparison only	Local survey in North Carolina (540 women)	1988-92
Lowery et al., 1998	Black, White, Non-metro and Metro	Natl. Maternal and Infant Health Survey (8,252 children)	1991
Singh et al., 2000	Non-Hispanic Black adults, non-Hispanic White, "rural*", "urban*" (*not specified)	Natl. Longitudinal Mortality Study (173,605 adults)	1979-89
Stoddard et al., 1994	Black, White, "Rural*", "urban*" (*popn. density)	Natl. Medical Expenditure Survey (7,578 children)	1987
Lannin et al., 1998	Black, White comparison only	Local survey in North Carolina (540 women)	1988-92

Hays et al. (1995) noted small differences in the self-reported prevalence of chronic conditions among North Carolina elders (65+ years): rural Black Americans (86 percent), urban Black Americans (84 percent), and rural White Americans (81 percent). Levin et al. (2001) did not find differences between rural White and rural Black Americans for self-reported heart disease prevalence in the South. Similarly, analyses of data from the National Health Interview Survey do not indicate significant differences between rural and urban Black Americans for self-reported heart disease, cancer, chronic bronchitis, or diabetes (Figure 33.2). In this analysis, counties were categorized into one of three metropolitan categories (large metro central, large metro fringe, or other metro counties) or one of two nonmetropolitan categories (with or without a city that has a population greater than 10,000). These results require confirmation because of the limited sample of Black Americans in rural areas, the possible underreporting of conditions due to reduced health-care access, and confounding by gender and region.

Diabetes prevalence appears similar for rural and urban Black Americans. While data from 1994 suggest that diabetes prevalence was higher in rural than urban Black Americans (Slifkin et al., 2000), more recent age-adjusted prevalence estimates from the National Health Interview Survey did not indicate a significant excess among rural African Americans (Figure 33.2). Other studies (Cowie & Eberhardt, 1995; Adams et al., 1999) also suggest that rural Black Americans do not have a higher diabetes prevalence.

Some preventable infectious diseases are a concern for rural Black Americans. Steinberg and Fleming (2000) noted that reporting of AIDS cases has increased more rapidly in rural areas relative to urban areas. Thomas et al. (1995) found that syphilis prevalence in rural North Carolina exceeded prevalence in urban areas and "rose substantially among (rural) non-White women of all ages while remaining relatively stable among their urban counter-parts" (p. 1120).

Limited research is published on rural Black American mental health. Jonas and Wilson (1997) found that the prevalence of negative mood among rural Black Americans tended to be higher (14 percent) compared with the prevalence among rural White Americans (8 percent); estimates of neg-

Figure 33.2
**Average annual age-adjusted prevalence (and 95 percent confidence interval)
of self-reported doctor-diagnosed chronic conditions by urbanization and race,
United States, 1997–1998**

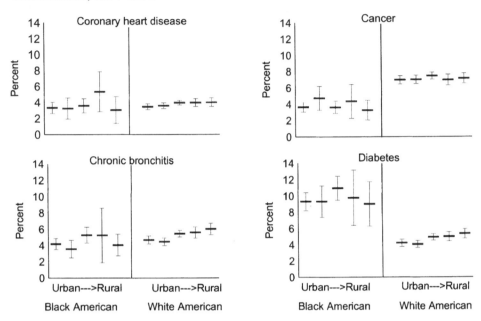

Note: 1) Urban → Rural refers to urbanization categories ranging from a central city of a large metro area
to a non-metro area without a city >10,000 popn. Ref. (NCHS, 2001)
2) Direct age adjustment to 2000 national standard.

Source: 1997–1998 National Health Interview Survey.

ative mood among rural and urban Black Americans were not significantly different. In this study, the highest prevalence of negative mood was in the least educated rural Black American women (26 percent), and the lowest prevalence was in more educated suburban White American men (4 percent).

Incidence.   Incidence data are more likely than prevalence data to provide unbiased estimates for comparisons of population subgroups. Unfortunately, few incidence data are available. Gillum and Ingram (1996) found that rural Black Americans had a higher stroke incidence (hospitalization or death) compared with urban Black Americans, and this excess varied between regions. They reported, for example, that in the southern United States, rural Black Americans had a 66 percent higher stroke incidence than urban Black Americans; in the other regions of the country, the rural-to-urban excess for Black Americans increased to 120 percent.

Cancer incidence among rural Black Americans is difficult to assess. Monroe et al. (1992) reported that rural areas have lower cancer rates overall, but few data were available for rural Black Americans, in particular. The Surveillance, Epidemiology, and End Results (SEER) program, which is a major source of cancer statistics, has difficulty producing rural Black American estimates because 90 percent of the registry population is urban (National Cancer Institute, 2002). For example, a lymphoma study with seven years of SEER data identified fewer than 8 annual incident cases, on average, in rural Black Americans (Devesa & Fears, 1992). Similarly, a report on state-based cancer registry data concluded that "too few states (n = 18) had sufficient numbers of (Black American)

Figure 33.3
Average annual percent of White and Black Americans with
limitation of activity due to chronic conditions by age and
urbanization, National Health Interview Survey, United States, 1985–
1987

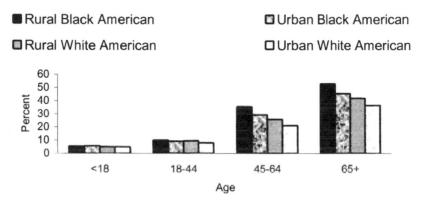

Source: Ries (1990).

cases to make meaningful comparisons between urbanization strata" (Fulton et al., 1997, p. IV–1).
Thus, cancer mortality, which is discussed shortly, is more informative for this topic.

Functional or Self-Assessed Health Status

Evidence exists that rural Black Americans are more likely to have reduced functional or self-assessed health status than either rural White or urban Black Americans. For example, of these groups, Ries (1990) found the highest prevalence of activity limitations due to chronic health conditions among rural Black Americans (Figure 33.3). Van Nostrand (1993) noted that, on average, rural Black American elders (≥ 65 years old) had more restricted activity days per year than urban Black American elders (approximately 45 and 40 days, respectively); rural and urban White American elders, however, had similar numbers of restricted activity days per year (approximately 30 days in both groups). In addition, this elder study found that fair or poor health was more common among rural Black Americans (55 percent) compared with urban Black Americans (42 percent), rural White Americans (35 percent), and urban White Americans (28 percent). On the other hand, rural residence was not significantly associated with functional status for Black Americans in North Carolina (Hays et al., 1995) or Black Americans (65+ years) living in Florida (Coward et al., 1997); however, this latter study, which controlled for age, gender, education, marital status, and poverty, found that self-assessed health status was lower for elders who were Black Americans or who lived in rural areas compared with elders who were White Americans or who lived in urban areas.

Mortality

All-cause death rates of rural Black Americans tend to be similar to those of urban Black Americans and rural White Americans, but higher than rates of urban White Americans. National mortality data indicate that the age-adjusted death rates in 1999 were similar for rural and urban Black Americans (Figure 33.4) and that death rates had decreased from the previous year for both groups (NCHS,

Figure 33.4
Average annual age-adjusted all-cause death rates by race and urbanization, United States, 1996–1998

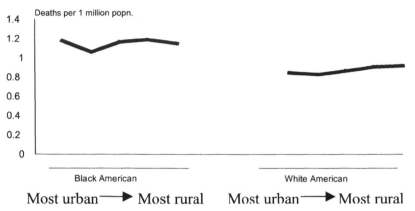

Note: 1) * Most urban → Most rural refers to categories of urbanization which range from central area of large metro area to non-metro area without a city > 10,000 popn.

Source: NCHS (2001).

Figure 33.5
Average annual age-adjusted cause-specific mortality by urbanization and selected race groups, United States, 1991–1995

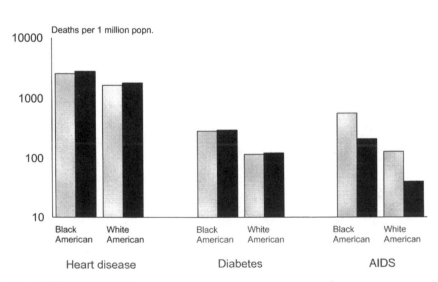

Source: Slifkin et al. (2000).

Table 33.2

Average annual percent change in coronary heart disease mortality rates for metropolitan and nonmetropolitan counties in Appalachia* by age and race, 1980–1997

| | | Percent Change | |
		Metropolitan	Nonmetropolitan
Ages 35-64	Black American men	-3.3	-2.2
	Black American women	-2.7	-1.9
	White American men	-3.6	-3.1
	White American women	-3.1	-2.3
Ages ≥65	Black American men	-2.7	-1.7
	Black American women	-2.7	-2.5
	White American men	-3.3	-2.9
	White American women	-3.2	-2.7

*Appalachia is composed of 399 counties and includes all of West Virginia and parts of 12 other states (AL, GA, KY, MD, MS, NY, NC, OH, PA, SC, TN, VA).

Source: Barnett et al. (2000).

2001). Mansfield et al. (1999) found that one of the strongest predictors of years of potential life lost was the percent of a county's population who were Black American, but this relationship was similar in rural and urban counties. A mortality follow-up study, which controlled for education, income, marital status, and health, suggested that mortality risk varied by sex, race, and urbanization (House et al., 2000). For example, the all-cause mortality hazard ratio among adults more than 64 years old was significantly higher for Black, compared to "non-Black," American men regardless of urbanization level; however, the mortality hazard ratio did not differ by race among rural women and for the most urban Black American women when compared with "non-Black" rural women (House et al., 2000, p. 1899). In a larger national study among adults more than 55 years of age, Smith et al. (1995) found that mortality risk was not significantly different between rural Black Americans and other rural residents, after controlling for age and gender.

Cause-specific mortality differences exist between rural Black Americans and those within other race and urbanization categories. Heart disease mortality among rural Black Americans is higher compared to urban Black Americans and White Americans (Figure 33.5). Barnett et al. (2000) noted that heart disease mortality in Appalachia, between 1980 and 1997, decreased for both White and Black Americans and in both urban and rural areas; however, the largest decrease was among younger, urban White American men, and the smallest decrease was among older, rural Black American men (Table 33.2). During 1991–1995, the highest heart disease mortality among Black American women (Figure 33.6) was in predominately rural areas of the southern United States (Casper et al., 2000). Stroke mortality among Black Americans is higher than among White Americans and has declined more slowly over the last three decades for rural areas compared with urban areas (Gillum, 1997). Some causes of mortality, however, are similar or lower for rural compared to urban Black Americans, for example, chronic liver disease (Singh & Hoyert, 2000), AIDS (Slifkin et al., 2000), and firearm homicide (Fingerhut et al., 1998).

Infant mortality studies that discuss urbanization present a complex pattern. In the United States in 1991–1995, infant mortality was twice as high for Black Americans compared with White Americans (Slifkin et al., 2000), and it was slightly higher for rural Black Americans compared with their urban counterparts (Figure 33.7). On the other hand, a more detailed study by Farmer et al. (1993) found excess infant mortality among Black Americans in urban compared with rural areas. The excess

Figure 33.6
Age-adjusted, average annual heart disease death rates (per 100,000) among Black American women ≥ 35 years old by county, United States, 1991–1995

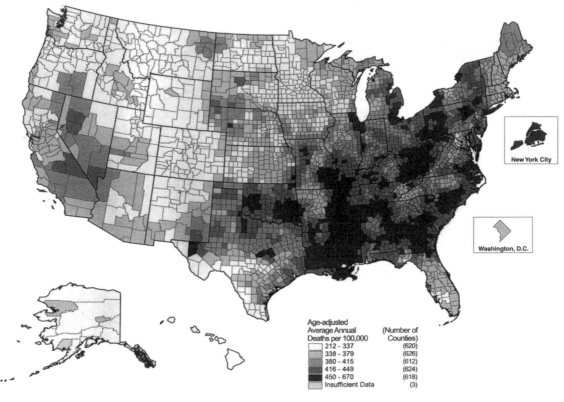

Source: Casper et al. (2000).

varied by geographic region. The urban-to-rural ratio for Black American infant mortality was 1.65 in the north-central United States and 1.03 in the southern United States.

Health-Care Utilization

Disparities in health-care utilization among rural Black Americans have produced conflicting findings. Ricketts (1999) reported that 94 percent of rural Black Americans had a usual source of health care compared with 87 percent of their urban counterparts. Mueller et al. (1998) found no significant differences in doctor visit rates for urban White and rural Black Americans. In contrast, when the process of care was reviewed, Mueller et al. (1999) noted that in rural North Carolina, hypertensive Black American men with less intense contact with the health-care system were more likely to discontinue antihypertensive medication than other rural men.

Studies on women's health have considered disparities in health-care utilization. Duelberg (1992) and Mueller et al. (1999) found evidence that rural Black American women had cervical cancer screening less frequently than other women. Slifkin et al. (2000) suggested that rural women in the United States were less likely to have a clinical breast exam than urban women, but whether or not rural minority women had lower exam rates than rural White American women could not be determined. An analysis of Medicare data (Slifkin et al., 2000) found that mammography use was higher

Figure 33.7
Infant deaths per 1,000 live births, United States, 1991–1995

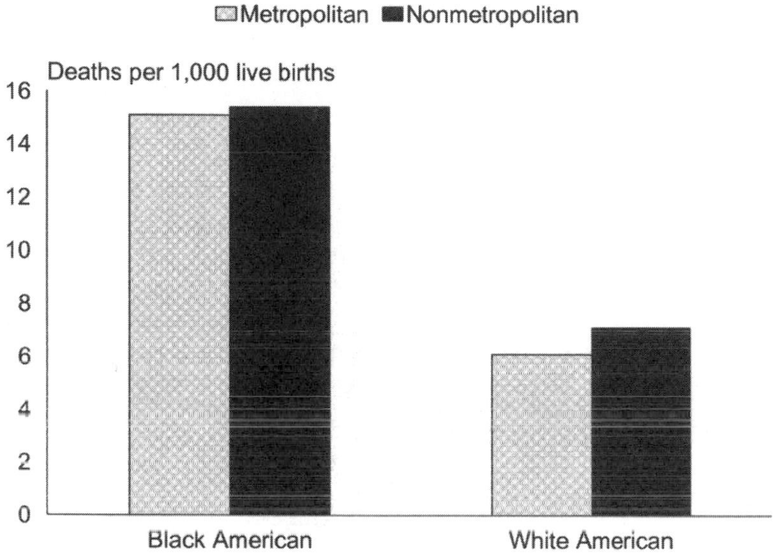

▨Metropolitan ■Nonmetropolitan

Source: Slifkin et al. (2000).

among White, compared with "non-White," American women living in rural areas; however, mammography usage did not vary between these race categories in urban women. Contemporary national survey data indicated that Black American and White American women did not vary significantly for mammography use (Breen et al., 2001); however, this study did not specifically examine racial disparities by rural and urban residence. Data from 1988 indicated that use of prenatal care did not vary significantly by urbanization for Black American mothers; overall, however, Black American mothers with low to medium maternal risk profiles received less adequate prenatal care compared to White American mothers with similar profiles (Miller et al., 1996).

Recent efforts may be addressing previous disparities in childhood immunization coverage. Data from the early 1990s (Lowery et al., 1998) suggested that rural American 2-year-old children were underimmunized compared with rural White American children. However, a 1999 national survey indicated higher immunization coverage (81 percent) among rural Black American children (19 to 35 months of age) compared with urban Black American children (72 percent) (Stokley et al., 2001); in this study, 80 percent of White American children had up-to-date vaccine coverage at all urbanization levels. These studies suggest greater improvement in immunization coverage during the 1990s for rural than for urban Black American children.

Among adults, Medicare data demonstrate that immunization rates differed by race but not urbanization status; "non-White" urban and rural adults were similarly underimmunized for influenza (~35 percent) and pneumonia (~12 percent) compared with their White American counterparts (~52 percent and ~23 percent, respectively) (Slifkin et al., 2000).

Using Medicare data, Kahn et al. (1994) reported that people who were Black Americans or poor received less quality hospital care compared with other hospitalized Medicare recipients: reduced quality of hospital care was also more pronounced in rural hospital settings compared with urban hospital settings. Using national data, White-Means (2000) noted a difference in health-care use by disabled elderly patients. Overall, Black Americans were less likely to use community medical services than other groups, particularly prescription drugs and physician services. Puzzling to the author was the significant observation that Black Americans in rural areas, small cities, and western states were more likely to use these services than both their urban counterparts and White Americans, regardless of urbanization.

While Medicare eligibility should avoid disparities in health-care utilization for Americans with similar health-care needs, differences exist in utilization and may reflect, in part, lower rates of supplemental health insurance coverage among rural and Black Americans. Medicare beneficiary data indicate that private supplemental health insurance coverage was reported by 4 percent of Black Americans, 91 percent of White Americans, 72 percent of more urban residents, and 28 percent of less urban residents (Centers for Medicare and Medicaid Services, 2002).

Inconsistencies in the findings between studies of health-care use and access may reflect inadequate identification of population subgroups with different care patterns. For example, Calle et al. (1993) reported that a subgroup with one of the lowest mammography screening rates was "near poor" rural Black American women. Therefore, more detailed analysis may be necessary to adequately estimate the magnitude of health-care utilization disparities among rural Black Americans.

DETERMINANTS OF HEALTH DISPARITY IN RURAL BLACK AMERICANS

Socioeconomic Status (SES)

SES is a major contributor to health disparities between population subgroups. Rural Black Americans have less income and education than urban Black Americans (U.S. Census Bureau, 2000a), and both SES measures are known risk factors for poor health and access to care (Pamuk et al., 1998; Strickland & Strickland, 1996). More rural Black American adults (34 percent) lack a high school degree compared with urban Black Americans (21 percent), rural White Americans (17 percent), or urban White Americans (11 percent). In 2000, nearly 38 percent of rural Black Americans with work experience earned less than $10,000 annually compared with 29 percent of rural White Americans, 28 percent of urban Black Americans, and 23 percent of urban White Americans (U.S. Census Bureau, 2000b).

Rural Isolation

Rural isolation creates distance barriers to urban resources (Ricketts, 1999), such as employment and health care, but its contribution to rural population subgroups disparities needs further study. Pathman et al. (2001) noted that town areas with a high proportion of Black Americans were less populated, poorer, and younger and had higher unemployment; however, no "meaningful differences" (p. 6) existed between low and high Black American composition areas for rural isolation.

Cultural and Societal Determinants

Cultural or societal factors may contribute to rural health disparities. Cultural norms for some rural areas have been described (Pathman et al., 2001) and include (1) seeking health care only when serious activity limitations exist; (2) avoiding preventive screening because of privacy concerns, distrust of outsiders, or a preference for informal social networks; and (3) use of traditional healing in lieu of unavailable health services. Strickland and Strickland (1996) reported that rural values and norms can limit the seeking of preventive health care, but it remains unclear if values vary by race.

In a largely rural North Carolina area, Lannin et al. (1998) noted that health belief variables explained 75 percent of the elevated odds ratio of Black, compared with White American, women for late-stage presentation of breast cancer (unadjusted odds ratio = 1.8, adjusted odds ratio = 1.2 after considering health beliefs). LaVeist et al. (2000) found that Black Americans were four times more likely to believe that racial discrimination is common in doctors' offices. The Institute of Medicine stated, "Bias, stereotyping, prejudice, and clinical uncertainty on the part of healthcare providers may contribute to racial and ethnic disparities in health care" (Smedley et al., 2002, p. 140), but no conclusion was stated regarding the contribution of rural residence for Black Americans.

The tendency for rural Black Americans to live in the southern United States may contribute to health status described by national surveys because of the regional health patterns. For example, the northeastern United States is associated with higher risk of Lyme disease (CDC, 2002); the upper U.S. latitudes are related to higher indoor radon exposure (Environmental Protection Agency, 2002); and the southern United States is associated with more years of potential life lost (Mansfield et al., 1999), higher motor vehicle injury mortality (Pickle et al., 1996), and higher rates of syphilis (CDC, 1998). Incidence of CHD is higher in the East (including the Southeast) than the West (Figure 33.7), and stroke incidence is higher in the Southeast than in other regions (Casper et al., 2000; Gillum & Ingram, 1996; Pickle et al., 1996). Barnett and Halverson (2001) stated, "Of the 23 labor markets in which African American men experienced increased CHD mortality . . . only one was located outside the South" (p. 1501). Thus, assessments of race/ethnic rural health disparities should include comparisons within regions.

Access to Health Care

A community's ability to respond to health disparities depends on local economic resources. Data from the 1990 U.S. census (Casper et al., 2000) confirmed the disproportionate geographic distribution of local economic resources; using income, unemployment rates, and the proportion of workers in white-collar jobs, researchers identified clusters of counties with unfavorable local economic profiles that they describe as "Appalachia, the Mississippi Delta, the Texas border counties, and the Cotton Belt counties of the South" (p. 52). Most rural Black Americans in the United States live in these clusters of rural, underdeveloped areas.

Potential barriers to health care for rural Black Americans include lack of health insurance, lack of health care providers or services, and racial bias in the health-care system (Pathman et al., 2001). Lacking health insurance may be the strongest predictor of reduced access to health care. Duncan et al. (1995) found that a higher percentage of rural Black Americans less than 65 years old were uninsured compared with urban Black Americans, rural White Americans, and urban White Americans. Mueller et al. (1998) stated that health insurance was the most salient determinant of utilization of health-care services; they found that, after controlling for demographic characteristics, health, and region, uninsured rural Black Americans, like all uninsured groups regardless of urbanization, were less likely to have physician visits compared with insured urban White Americans (Figure 33.8).

A regression analysis by Sharma et al. (2000) indicated that nonurgent emergency department (ED) visits were 1.6 more likely for Black American infants compared with White American infants; rural infants were 1.5 times more likely to have a nonurgent ED visit than urban infants. However, they found similar high levels of nonurgent ED use among Medicaid infants regardless of race or urbanization. Urban White American infants with private health insurance had the lowest nonurgent ED utilization. Sharma et al. concluded, "Poverty is more prevalent in rural areas and among blacks, and this increased (non-urgent ED) utilization by self-pay rural and black patients" (p. 1038). Stoddard et al. (1994) reported race and urbanization were not associated with having a doctor visit after considering insurance coverage.

Limited health-care providers and facilities and the need to travel farther for care are a burden for rural Americans (Ricketts, 1999). Doctors and dentists are less common in rural areas (NCHS, 2001). Health facilities are also less common. For example, few certified trauma centers exist in rural areas,

Figure 33.8
Adjusted odds ratio for a physician visit in the previous year
by race, urbanization, and health insurance coverage, United
States, 1992

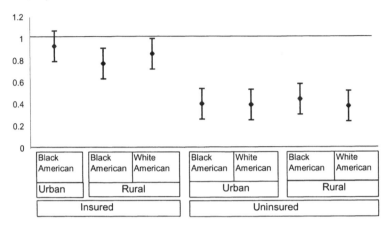

Note: Odds ratios are adjusted for age, education, sex, family income and size, health conditions and self-assessed health status, and region. Insured urban White American was the reference group.

Source: Mueller et al. (1998).

where rural Black Americans live (North Carolina Rural Health Research and Policy Analysis Center, 2002). Pathman et al. (2001) noted in a study of selected southern towns that the percentage of Black Americans in the population was not associated with the likelihood of being without a local physician; however, the distance to other health-care providers was greater in towns with a high percentage of Black Americans than in towns with a lower percentage. Residents in communities which were less than 60 percent Black American were 25–35 percent farther from subspecialty health services compared with primarily White American communities. Smedley et al. (2002) echoed a general concern that minority physicians, who are often in a solo practice and who often care for minority patients, were less able to obtain specialty referrals and hospital admissions for their patients.

NEED FOR RESEARCH AND PROGRAMS

Healthy People 2010 calls for the elimination of health disparities (USDHHS, 2000). To reduce the burden of race/ethnic health disparities in rural Americans, researchers and public health professionals have promoted numerous strategies. For example, Taylor et al. (2002) suggested (1) broad prevention efforts to identify and treat the causes of cardiovascular disease (CVD), (2) policy changes to remove the barrier of being uninsured, (3) outreach initiatives to improve contact with the rural community and provide health education, and (4) further research to investigate the relationship of environmental, social, and cultural factors on CVD. To reduce excess infant mortality, Farmer et al. (1993) suggested that rural health policies on infant health consider urbanization, geographic region, and state differences. To reduce excess adult mortality, Gillum (1997) suggested improvements in health education, hypertension detection, and aspirin use to reduce stroke mortality. Pathman et al. (2001) proposed that transportation services by hospitals and other health-care providers be expanded to address the distances that rural residents travel for health care. They also stated that it be clearly defined "whether the federal Health Professional Shortage Areas and Medically Underserved Areas designations for targeted federal assistance programs capture the distance challenges faced by some rural minorities" (p. 13). The Institute of Medicine (Smedley et al., 2002) recently stated that patient referrals should be studied to evaluate the practice arrangements of minority physicians by ethnicity, age, and urbanization. The National Rural Health Association (1999) has established a national agenda for minority health with proposals to improve (1) health data, (2) health policy and practices, and (3) health delivery systems. Though established for all rural race/ethnic minorities, these proposals have relevance to rural Black American health.

This chapter has explored the literature on rural Black Americans health (Table 33.1). Efforts to improve health will involve translating proven strategies into the daily management of health and identifying new approaches through continued research. Improved monitoring of the health of rural Black Americans is crucial to help to guide these efforts to success.

CONCLUSIONS

The evidence for health disparities between rural Black Americans and other race or urbanization subgroups is inconclusive. Studies discussed in the chapter encompass a long time span and many health outcomes and range from local to national in scope. In addition, the objectives of some studies were racial comparisons among rural populations; in other studies, examining urbanization among Black Americans was foremost. Although for many studies, rural Black Americans were at higher risk than other groups of having poorer health outcomes, some studies reported relatively positive findings for this population, such as White-Means (2000) and Stokley et al. (2001). Inconsistencies in the literature may be due to (1) methodologic differences, (2) complex interactions of the associated factors, or (3) geographic variability of these factors. It must be noted that some potential reasons for health disparity (e.g., environmental hazards) were not discussed and deserve consideration.

REFERENCES

Adams, P., Hendershot, G., & Marano, M. (1999). Current estimates from the National Health Interview Survey, 1996. National Center for Health Statistics. *Vital Health Statistics, 10*, 200.

Barnett, E., & Halverson, J. (2001). Local increases in coronary heart disease mortality among Blacks and Whites in the U.S. 1985–1995. *American Journal of Public Health, 91*, 1499–1506.

Barnett, E., Halverson, J.A., Elmes, G.A., & Braham, V.E. (2000). Metropolitan and non-metropolitan trends in coronary heart disease mortality within Appalachia, 1980–1997. *Annals of Epidemiology, 10*, 370–379.

Bell, R., Spangler, J., & Quandt, S. (2000). Smokeless tobacco use among adults in the Southeast. *Southern Medical Journal, 93*, 456–462.

Breen, N., Wagener, D., Brown, M., Davis, W., & Ballard-Barbash, R. (2001). Progress in cancer screening over a decade: Results of cancer screening from the 1987, 1992, and 1998 National Health Interview Surveys. *Journal of the National Cancer Institute, 93*, 1676–1677.

Calle, E., Flanders, W., Thun, M., & Martin, L. (1993). Demographic predictors of mammography and Pap smear screening in U.S. women. *American Journal of Public Health, 83*, 53–60.

Casper, M., et al. (2000). Women and heart disease: An atlas of racial and ethnic disparities in mortality, Office for Social Environment and Health Research. West Virginia University, Morgantown.

Centers for Disease Control and Prevention (CDC). (1998). Primary and Secondary Syphilis—United States, 1997, *Morbidity and Mortality Weekly Report, 47*, 493–496.

Centers for Disease Control and Prevention (CDC). (2002). Reported cases of Lyme disease, United States, 1999. (http://www.cdc.gov/ncidod/dvbid/lyme/distribution_density.htm).

Centers for Medicare and Medicaid Services. (2002). Medicare Current Beneficiary Survey, Table 8.4, 181–182. (http://cms.hhs.gov/mcbs/)

Coward, R., Peek, C., Henretta, J., Duncan, R., Dougherty, M., & Gilbert, G. (1997). Race differences in the health of elders who live alone. *Journal of Aging and Health, 9*, 147–170.

Cowie, C., & Eberhardt, M. (1995). Sociodemographic characteristics of persons with diabetes. In *Diabetes in America*, 2d edition, National Institute of Diabetes and Digestive and Kidney Diseases, NIH No. 95-1468, Bethesda, MD.

Devesa, S., & Fears, T. (1992). Non-Hodgkin's lymphoma time trends: United States and international data. Cancer Research (supplement), 52, 5432s–5440s.

Duelberg, S. (1992). Preventive health behavior among Black and White women in urban and rural areas. *Social Science and Medicine, 34*, 191–198.

Duncan, R., Seccombe, K., & Amey, C. (1995). Changes in health insurance coverage within rural and urban environments—1977 to 1987. *Journal of Rural Health, 11*, 169–176.

Environmental Protection Agency. (2002). Radon (http://www.epa.gov/iaq/radon/zonemap.html).

Farmer, F., Clarke, L., & Miller, M. (1993). Consequences of differential residence designations for rural health policy research: The case of infant mortality. *Journal of Rural Health, 9*, 17–26.

Fingerhut, L., Ingram, D., & Feldman, J. (1998). Homicide rates among U.S. teenagers and young adults. *Journal of the American Medical Association, 280*, 423–427.

Fulton, J., et al. (1997). Urbanization and cancer incidence, United States, 1988–1992. In H.L. Howe (Ed.), *Cancer in North America, 1989–1993*: North American Association of Central Cancer Registries, Volume 1, VI-1-9. Sacramento, CA.

Gillum R. (1997). Secular trends in stroke mortality in Black Americans: The role of urbanization, diabetes and obesity. *Neuroepidemiology, 16*, 180–184.

Gillum, R., & Ingram, D. (1996). Relation between residence in the southeast region of the United States and stroke. *American Journal of Epidemiology, 144*, 665–673.

Hays, J., Fillenbaum, G., Gold, D., Shanley, M., & Blazer, D. (1995). Black-white and urban-rural differences in stability of household composition among elderly persons. *Journal of Gerontology, 50B*, S301–S311.

House, J., et al. (2000). Excess mortality among urban residents. *American Journal of Public Health, 90*, 1898–1904.

Howard-Pitney, B., & Winkleby, M. (2002). Chewing tobacco: Who uses and who quits? Findings from NHANES III, 1998–1994. *American Journal of Public Health, 92*, 50–256.

Jonas, B., & Wilson, R. (1997). Negative mood and urban versus rural residence. Advance data from vital and health statistics; no 281. National Center for Health Statistics. Hyattsville, MD.

Kahn, K., et al. (1994). Health care for Black and poor hospitalized Medicare patients. *Journal of the American Medical Association, 271*, 1169–1174.

Lannin, D., Matthews, H., Mitchell, J., Swanson, M., Swanson, F., & Edwards, M. (1998). Influence of socioeconomic and cultural factors on racial differences in late-stage presentation of breast cancer. *Journal of the American Medical Association, 279*, 1801–1807.

LaVeist, T., Nicherson, K., & Bowie, J. (2000). Attitudes about racism, medical mistrust, and satisfaction with care among Black American and White cardiac patients. *Medical Care Research and Review, 57(Supplement 1)*, 146–161.

Levin S., Mayer-Davis, E., Ainsworth, B., Addy, C., & Wheeler, F. (2001). Racial/ethnic health disparities in South Carolina and the role of rural locality and educational attainment. *Southern Medical Journal, 94*, 711–718.

Lowery, N., Belansky, E., Siegel, C., Goodspeed, J., Harman, C., & Steiner, J. (1998). Rural childhood immunization rates and demographic characteristics. *Journal of Family Practice, 47*, 221–225.

Mansfield, C., Wilson, J., Kobrinski, E., & Mitchell, J. (1999). Premature mortality in the United States: The roles of geographic area, socioeconomic status, household type, and availability of medical care. *American Journal of Public Health, 89*, 893–898.

McKinnon, J., & Humes, K. (2000). The Black population in the United States: March 1999. U.S. Census Bureau. Current Population Reports. Series P20-530. Washington, DC: U.S. Government Printing Office.

McMurray, R., Harrell, J., Bangdiwala, S., & Deng, S. (1999). Cardiovascular disease risk factors and obesity of rural and urban elementary school children. *Journal of Rural Health, 15*, 365–374.

Miller, M., Clarke, L., Albrect, S., & Farmer, F. (1996). The interactive effects of race, ethnicity and mother's residence on the adequacy of prenatal care. *Journal of Rural Health, 12,* 6–17.

Monroe, A., Ricketts, T., & Savitz, L. (1992). Cancer in rural versus urban populations: A review. *Journal of Rural Health, 8,* 212–220.

Mueller, K., Ortega, S., Parker, K., Patil, K., & Askenazi, A. (1999). Health status and access to care among rural minorities. *Journal of Health Care for the Poor and Underserved, 10,* 230–249.

Mueller, K., Patil, K., & Boilesen, E. (1998). The role of uninsurance and race in healthcare utilization by rural minorities. *Health Services Research, 33,* 597–610.

National Cancer Institute. (2002). SEER, http://seer.cancer.gov/registries/characteristics.html).

National Center for Health Statistics (NCHS). (2001). Health, United States, 2001 with urban and rural health chartbook. Hyattsville, MD.

National Rural Health Association. (1999). A National Agenda for Rural Minority Health. http://www.nrharural.org/dc/issuepapers/ipaper16.html).

North Carolina Rural Health Research and Policy Analysis Center. (2002). Cecil G. Sheps Center for Health Services Research, University of North Carolina at Chapel Hill (http://www.shepscenter.unc.edu/research_programs/Rural_Program/maps/certtrauma.html)

Pamuk, E., Makuc, D., Heck, K., Reuben, C., & Lochner, K. (1998). Socioeconomic Status and Health Chartbook. Health United States, 1998. National Center for Health Statistics, Hyattsville, MD.

Pathman, D., Konrad, T., & Schwartz, R. (2001). The proximity of rural Black American and Hispanic/Latino communities to physicians and hospital services. North Carolina. This working paper is available at: http://www.shepscenter.unc.edu/research_programs/rural_program/wp72.pdf.

Pickle, L.W., Mungiole, M., Jones, G.K., & White, A. (1996). Atlas of United States Mortality. DHHS Pub. No. (PHS) 97-1015, National Center for Health Statistics, Hyattsville, MD.

Ricketts, T. (Ed.). (1999). *Rural health in the United States.* New York: Oxford University Press.

Ricketts, T., Johnson-Webb, K., & Taylor, P. (1998). Definitions of rural: A handbook for health policy makers and researchers. Office of Rural Health Policy, HRSA, Rockville, MD.

Reis, P. (1990). Health of Black and White Americans, 1985–87. National Center for Health Statistics. Vital Health Statistics, 10(171).

Rural Health Research and Policy Center. Report 72, University of North Carolina, Chapel Hill.

Sarvela, P., Cronk, C., & Isberner, F. (1997). A secondary analysis of smoking among rural and urban youth using the MTF data set. *Journal of School Health, 67,* 372–375.

Schur, C., Good, C., & Berk, M. (1998). Barriers to using national surveys for understanding rural health policy issues; Office of Rural Health Policy, Project Hope Walsh Center for Rural Health Analysis.

Sharma, V., Simon, S., Bakewell, J., Ellerbeck, E., Fox, M., & Wallace, D. (2000). Factors influencing infant visits to emergency departments. *Pediatrics, 106,* 1031–1039.

Singh, G., & Hoyert, D. (2000). Social epidemiology of chronic liver disease and cirrhosis mortality in the United States, 1935–1997. *Human Biology, 72,* 801–820.

Slifkin, R., Goldsmith, L., & Ricketts, T. (2000). Race and place: Urban–rural differences in health for racial and ethnic minorities. North Carolina Rural Health Research Program, Working paper series No. 66, University of North Carolina, Chapel Hill, NC.

Smedley, B., Stith, A., & Nelson, A. (Eds.). (2002). Institute of Medicine Committee on Understanding and Eliminating Racial and Ethnic Disparities in Health Care. *Unequal treatment: Confronting racial and ethnic disparities in health care.* Washington, DC: National Academy Press.

Smith, M., Anderson, R., Bradham, D., & Longino, C. (1995). Rural and urban differences in mortality among Americans 55 years and older: Analysis of the National Longitudinal Mortality Study. *Journal of Rural Health, 11,* 274–285.

Steinberg, S., & Fleming, P. (2000). The geographic distribution of AIDS in the United States: Is there a rural epidemic? *Journal of Rural Health, 16,* 11–19.

Stoddard, J., St. Peter, R., & Newacheck, P. (1994). Health insurance status and ambulatory care for children. *New England Journal of Medicine, 330,* 1421–1425.

Stokley, S., Smith, P., Klevans, M., & Battaglia, M. (2001). Vaccination status of children in rural areas of the United States: Are they protected? *American Journal of Preventive Medicine, 20,* 55–60.

Strickland, J., & Strickland, D. (1996). Barriers to preventive health services for minority households in the rural South. *Journal of Rural Health, 12,* 206–217.

Taylor, H., Hughes, G., & Garrison, R. (2002). Cardiovascular disease among women residing in rural America. *American Journal of Public Health, 92,* 548–551.

Thomas, J., Kulik, A., & Schoenbach, V. (1995). Syphilis in the South: Rural rates surpass urban rates in North Carolina. *American Journal of Public Health, 85,* 1119–1122.

U.S. Census Bureau. (2000a). Educational Attainment in the United States, March 2000. (http://www.census. gov/population/www/socdemo/education/p20-536.html).

U.S. Census Bureau. (2000b). Selected characteristics of people 15 years and over by total money income in 2000. (http://ferret.bls.census.gov/macro/032001/perinc/new01_003.htm).

U.S. Department of Health and Human Services (USDHHS). (2000). Healthy People 2010. 2d ed. With Understanding and Improving Health and Objectives for Improving Health. 2 vols. Washington, DC: U.S. Government Printing Office.

Van Nostrand, J. (1993). Common beliefs about the rural elderly: What do national data tell us? National Center for Health Statistics. *Vital Health Statistics, 3(28).*

White-Means S. (2000). Racial patterns in disabled elderly persons' use of medical services. *Journal of Gerontology, 55B,* S76–S89.

CHAPTER 34

School Reform Meets Prevention Science: Toward Ensuring More Hopeful Futures for African American Children

A. WADE BOYKIN AND ROBERT J. JAGERS

INTRODUCTION

Recent data indicate that, despite improvements in the overall health of the U.S. population, African Americans (people of color, in general) are significantly more likely than their White counterparts to be in poor physical and mental health and to die prematurely. The elimination of these racial and ethnic health disparities is an explicit objective of Healthy People 2010, which outlines the federal government's health agenda for the twenty-first century. The emerging field of prevention science is relevant to ameliorating such disparities and promoting physical and mental health within the African American community. More specifically, we are persuaded that developmental epidemiologically based prevention science (Kellam et al., 1999) holds significant promise for wellness promotion in the African American community.

Developmental Epidemiological-Based Prevention Science

Developmental epidemiologically based prevention science reflects a public health approach that integrates epidemiology, life-course development, and intervention trials technology (Kellam et al., 1999). Epidemiological studies have revealed that poverty and associated risk factors can compromise the physical health of infants and children (Cohall & Bannister, 2001) and support a negative developmental trajectory featuring, for example, early academic underachievement, affiliation with a deviant peer group, aggression and violence, substance abuse, and risky sexual behaviors. The ensuing school dropout, teen pregnancy, and health-compromising and antisocial behaviors dramatically increase the probability of adult unemployment, involvement in the criminal justice system, and poor physical and mental health.

Focus of the Chapter

In this chapter, we describe some of our efforts in the area of comprehensive elementary school reform, which represent an essential element of a wellness promotion initiative for the African American community. Our efforts assume that education is a primary means to achieve upward mobility in the United States. In this respect, we support the current thrust toward greater accountability in the education process. In addition, historical and contemporary circumstances dictate that academic success for African American children be linked with personal and collective well-being and liberation. As such, we advance an educational reform agenda that incorporates the social and emotional competence development of African American children.

This approach to education is intended to move beyond simply preparing children to find their prescribed place in the existing social order. We aspire to help children realize their potential and responsibility to struggle for cultural, sociopolitical, and economic self-determination and empowerment within the American democratic system. As such then, our conception of healthy development for African American children certainly includes actualizing academic competence, but it also includes social, emotional, community, and life transformational competences as well. In this chapter we situate the academic strivings of Black children in the context of the quest to reform public schooling. We justify and then outline our approach to school reform. Then we elaborate more fully on our school reform component that aims squarely at the promotion of social, emotional, and "transformative" competence.

ACADEMIC ACHIEVEMENT

For the last several decades there has been preponderant attention given to the educational experiences and academic attainment of African American students. This has certainly been fueled by the consistent perceptions that the schooling and achievement of all too many Black students have been woefully insufficient. Whether the issue has been basic literacy, access to public education, adequate schooling resources, busing and school integration, or poor academic achievement, the academic travails of African American students has been a long-standing preoccupation in African American communities and in American society at large (Watkins, 2001; Spring, 2001). In recent decades, dealing with the academic affairs of Black students has been variously captured through such efforts as the War on Poverty, the pursuit of equal educational opportunities, Educational Goals 2000, and most recently the No Child Left Behind Act (James et al., 2001). These recent initiatives presume that elevating their academic outcomes can raise the social and economic status of African American people.

The Achievement Gap

The focus on elevating the academic outcomes of Black students often is currently discussed in terms of an achievement gap between Black and White students. A major source of information on this gap is provided through data from the National Assessment of Educational Progress (NAEP). This periodic barometer has documented Black–White test score differences that have persisted over a 30 year span and that show up in math, reading and writing and at the three testing ages of 9, 13, and 17 years (see Figures 34.1 and 34.2 as examples).

According to one source, the trends in these scores suggest that the gap in reading will not close for another 30 years, and the one in math not for another 75 years (Hedges & Nowell, 1999). The achievement gap has been obtained in other test score data as well. It has shown up on college admission tests. As examples, Garibaldi (1997) reports that in the 1997 administration of the Scholastic Achievement Test, the average White score was 1052, while for Black students the average was only 857. Similar findings were obtained in the 1997 administration of the American Council on Testing's (ACT) instrument, with the average White ACT score standing at 21.7, and for Black students the average score was 17.1. The gap is present even in very young children. It exists among 3- and 4-year-olds in their scores on the Peabody Picture Vocabulary Test (Jencks & Phillips, 1998). While high school graduation rates have relatively equalized between Black and White students,

Figure 34.1
Average NAEP reading scores of 9-year-old students by race/ethnicity, 1975–1996

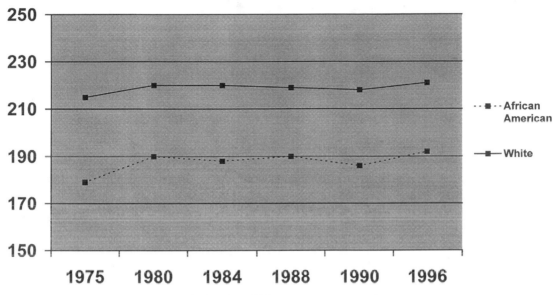

Source: Adapted from U.S. Department of Education (2001).

Figure 34.2
Average NAEP reading scores of 17-year-old students by race/ethnicity, 1975–1996

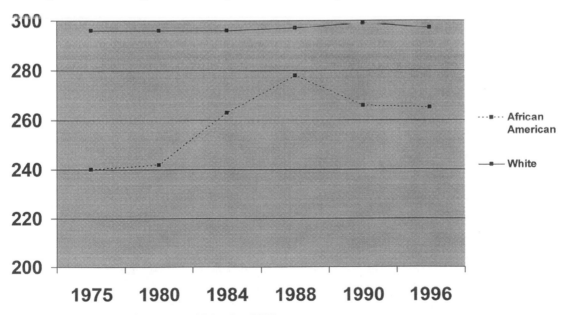

Source: Adapted from U.S. Department of Education (2001).

college-going rates remain disproportionately in favor of White students, as do the number of bachelor's degrees awarded (James et al., 2001). A gap exists in other markers of school success as well. Patton (1998) reports that there is an overrepresentation of Black students who have received special education placement. Black students in 1991 represented 16 percent of students attending public schools but 35 percent of those in special education.

Explanations for the Gap.   While several explanations for the gap have been offered over the years, current wisdom is that a substantial portion of the explanation rests with the nature and quality of the schooling experience (Hedges & Nowell, 1999; Ramey, 2000). Indeed, while a gap does exist at the inception of formal schooling, evidence points to this gap widening across students' years in school, in patterns that cannot be explained away by family background or socioeconomic status. This has led some to assert that in part the disparities may result from differential quality in instructional delivery, in educational structures and procedures, in available academic support programs, and in differential responses of Black and White students to their classroom experiences, especially as this latter concern entails interpersonal and cultural considerations (Jencks & Phillips, 1998; Lewis, 2001).

Attention certainly has been paid to how to close this problematic attainment disparity. Indeed, trends did seem to point to a gap narrowing, for example, on the NAEP up to the late 1980s. However, this gap has begun to widen again in more recent years (James et al., 2001). This pattern has, however, escaped a clear explanation. Perhaps before reasonable tactics can be offered, a discussion of the pattern of gap closing is in order. Indeed, such a discussion necessitates drawing a distinction between raising achievement levels per se and closing the achievement gap. This discussion also requires mention of whether closing the achievement gap, in and of itself, sufficiently captures the problem and its solution for extant African American students.

Possible Options.   Five possible options can be considered. Option one is to close the gap by reducing the performance of White students down to the average level for Black students. Certainly, this would seem nonsensical. It surely is not politically or socially defensible. However, this pattern is what is conjured up in the mind's eye of some who fear that a focus on the achievement of Black students would dilute the quality of education for White students, with the implicit assumption that substantially increasing the achievement levels for Black students is not realistically attainable.

Option two is to close the achievement gap by raising the achievement levels for Black students, while holding constant the achievement levels for White students. This is more palatable than the first option but would still be viewed as problematic by many, since no educational benefit is forthcoming for White students. As such, it may be difficult to marshal widespread support for interventions that fit this outcome profile. However, this pattern is essentially what is obtained in the NAEP data that figure so prominently in discussions on closing the Black–White achievement gap. Across the roughly 30 years of data gathering, for example, the performance levels for White 17-year-olds have remained roughly the same in reading, while there have been trends toward improvement over certain years for Black students. Still another option is to raise achievement levels for Black and White students alike; however, the increment slope would be steeper for Black than for White students. In this way all students benefit; however, relatively more benefit accrues for Black students. This conceivably would gather greater range of support than the previous two options.

Two other options are worth mentioning. A fourth is for both Black and White students to improve, with the increments roughly equivalent for the groups, and with now all students achieving beyond some preset criterion performance level. In this case, all students achieve beyond some absolute standard of performance, but the achievement gap remains, and presumably, to the extent that social or educational benefits accrue based on achievement level, these benefits would continue to be disproportionately allocated to White students. Moreover, this pattern would satisfy as raising achievement levels, but doing so without closing the performance gap between the two groups. Hence these two concerns are not one and the same. It should be noted that this pattern is what was advocated and sought in the effective schools movement of the 1980s (Edmonds, 1986).

A fifth option should be mentioned. Here the gap between White and Black students would reverse after the introduction of the educational intervention. That is, whereas initially White performance is higher than Black, after the intervention Black performance now crosses over and is higher than that for White students. This obviously does not close the achievement gap; it just replaces one for another. This outcome may not be defensible as well. However, such a pattern has been obtained in several studies conducted by the first author, by introducing learning contexts drawn from the extant cultural experiences of low-income African American students (Boykin & Bailey, 2000).

Of all the options presented, the third one perhaps is most optimal. Moreover, the fact that the achievement levels of Black and White students can be totally reversed under differing learning and performance conditions at least suggests that obtaining the third option is not beyond the realm of possibility, if the proper attention and energy are devoted to its manifestation.

CHALLENGES THAT REQUIRE INNOVATION AND SENSITIVITY

It is worth mentioning that the academic plight of African American students may not be fully addressed by an exclusive focus on "properly" closing the Black-White achievement gap. Just by equalizing the achievement test levels or other traditional academic outcomes for these two groups may not address all the educational challenges faced by a preponderance of Black students in this society. As members of a socially marginalized minority group, other adaptive skills should likely be sought that are not necessarily required of majority group children. This is addressed more fully below. Still further, by an excessive preoccupation with closing achievement gaps, we may obscure the growing reality that the range of skills required for gainful participation in twenty-first century American society may require competences not currently anticipated by current approaches to formal schooling. Indeed, it is possible that children from all walks of life may now be placed at risk for not being properly prepared for such future challenges. Our society at large may be placed at risk if our current students cannot adequately prepare for their future. This latter point deserves further comment.

Needed Transformation

The transformation of our public schools may be called for when we consider several developments that are co-occurring in our society that may be worthy of our attention. American society is graying as the baby boom generation advances in age. In the next decade, the median age for the U.S. population will be in the mid- to upper 50s. Life expectancies are increasing, and so people will be older for a longer time. There will thus be a smaller proportion of the American population who will be in their economically productive years, and consequently a smaller proportion of our society will be the effective economic producers, providing the goods, services, and revenues for society at large. Thus, the future workforce must be relatively more productive than workforces of the present or the past. Moreover, the future workforce must not only be more productive but work in positions requiring increasingly more demanding and technically more sophisticated competences.

Demographic Trends and Realities

Yet, given differential birthrates and immigration patterns among various subpopulations, this smaller, more productive, more highly trained future workforce will increasingly comprise people not of European descent, and indeed be drawn especially from groups that historically have had the most problematic schooling experiences in America (Datnow, 2000; Balfantz, 2000). Even now, in the one hundred largest school districts, the majority of enrolled students are Black and Latino (Young, 2002). Certainly it is no understatement that unless or until we are able to get more diverse children (especially African American and Latino) successfully through the formal educational process, then these children's communities in particular, yet American society at large, will simply fail to cultivate the reservoir of human talent that will be required if we are to meet the challenges and uncertainties in the years ahead.

These challenges are all happening while the very targets and objectives of formal schooling require changing as well. Indeed, changes are required in what it means to be literate and numerate in today and tomorrow's world. To prepare our children for the twenty-first century, indeed to enable our children to prepare the twenty-first century, there needs to be movement away from an exclusive focus on merely acquiring basic literacy and numeracy skills (i.e. getting students to read, write, and calculate per se). Instead, there should be movement toward getting them to think, read, and numerate in critical and constructive ways; to express themselves clearly and persuasively; and to raise and solve complex problems. Such is required if they are to be gainfully employed in the workplaces of the twenty-first century and able to manifest adaptive social participation in twenty-first century America, indeed in the global society. Certainly, transformation in the way we do schooling in America is called for.

School Transformation Modalities

When it comes to matters of school transformation, important distinctions should be made between school *change*, school *improvement*, and school *reform*.

School Change.   The overwhelming majority of school transformations are in the form of school change. School officials endeavor to do something different from what is presently going on. The rationale for the new activity could be hearsay or a good hunch or be done via political fiat. No database is typically consulted to support its adoption. Attention is insufficiently given to how to successfully implement the new activity. No data are collected to discern whether the change has been for the better. Yet all too often the change may be heralded by its promoters as something better than what had been done before, apparently simply because it is new. It could be a new textbook adoption, a reconstituted school with a new staff, a new principal, school uniforms, and the like.

School Improvement.   Less often implemented is school improvement. The school improvement approach is one that is data-driven, both in terms of implementing practices that have a track record of working in schools similar to the one it is now to be attempted in as well as in terms of efforts to gather data on-site to discern implementation effectiveness and whether enhanced outcomes result from the interventions. School improvement initiatives can run the gamut from evidence-based after-school programs, to standards-based curriculum modules, to ongoing professional development, classroom management strategies, leadership development activities, to exercises in building a sense of community and the like. Such efforts can likely lead to improved schooling outcomes and enhanced test scores for students, but such would not constitute school reform.

School Reform.   School reform implies all that is conveyed in school improvement, but beyond this, it also connotes comprehensiveness; that is, the changes reach into all aspects of the schooling enterprise and involve all categories of a school's stakeholders. School reform implies that the effort is sustained over time and that it is systemic, so that the various interventions are coordinated and interpenetrated, and that they coalesce around some common vision or set of principles. *School reform implies that a school has been reformulated.* It implies that the school has transformed its organizational and operational culture. School reform implies that there are not just changed activities but changed attitudes and roles and a changed atmosphere as well. Achieving authentic school reform has been accomplished in cases that are few and far between.

Many purported school reform models currently being advanced are really constituted of a limited set of often disconnected school improvement strategies. Such can certainly lead to enhanced outcomes. But authentic school reform has to be a targeted goal if we are to reach and sustain the high standards that will be expected of our nation's children, and especially for those from groups that traditionally have been placed at risk for educational failure. School reform means changing the educational core, as Elmore (1996) has said; or changing the grammar of schooling, as Tyack and Tobin (1994) have said; or changing the deep structure of schooling, as Tye (1998) has said; or expanding the definitional boundaries of the culture of power in schools, as Delpit (1995) would say; or loosening the hegemonic grip of traditional practices to ensure that schooling is a proactive extension of children's families and communities, as Hilliard (2001) would say.

School reform requires, therefore, changing the paradigm of schooling. It has been argued that the traditional schooling paradigm has been one of sorting children (Boykin, 2000). Schools have typically functioned to array children along a vertical pecking order from the best to the worst, and the corresponding quality of educational delivery, resources, and benefits is allocated accordingly. All too often this sorting gets done along the lines of race, class, and culture. From a sorting paradigm, the achievement gap then becomes a necessary and fully expected byproduct. The gap becomes evidence that the sorting function has been successfully executed. To ensure that all students achieve at high levels, and especially for this to be the case for African Americans and other educationally disfranchised groups, Howard University researchers and practitioners at the Center for Research on the Education of Students Placed at Risk (CRESPAR) have advocated a talent development model of school reform.

CRESPAR is a collaborative effort between Johns Hopkins University and Howard University with funding from the Office of Educational Research and Improvement, U.S. Department of Education. The stated mission of Howard University CRESPAR is to research, develop, evaluate, and disseminate school and community programs and practices that will ensure that each child achieves his or her full potential. Five projects at Howard have been initiated in pursuit of this mission. Two large-scale projects focus on developing and testing comprehensive models for elementary and secondary school reform. Three smaller projects allow for more concentrated research and development in the areas of professional development of classroom teachers, classroom assessment and evaluation strategies and practices, and the children's social and emotional competence promotion.

ADVOCATION OF A TALENT DEVELOPMENT PERSPECTIVE

From a talent development perspective, it is asserted that virtually all students can learn and perform at acceptably high levels, and this can be accomplished if we put in place, across the full spectrum of the schooling enterprise, multiple activities, programs, practices, and structures that yield multiple pathways for success for them, so that the possibility of children falling through the cracks of failure is substantially reduced (Boykin, 2000).

Figure 34.3 depicts the multiple components of our talent development paradigm of schooling at the elementary level. As can be seen, bracketing the core programs are several support activities. These support activities include an in-school tutorial program, which is particularly aimed at students in the first two grades and is designed to ensure that they have acquired the basic skills in reading and mathematics. We implement an after-school program for students in the upper elementary grades. This component serves to reinforce students' basic numeracy and literacy skills, bolster their critical thinking skills, problem-solving skills, and test-taking skills, and provide social and cultural enrichment opportunities for them. The school-family-community partnership element serves to cement

Figure 34.3

Components of the talent development elementary school project model of school reform developed by the Center of Research on the Education of Students Placed at Risk CRESPAR/ Howard University

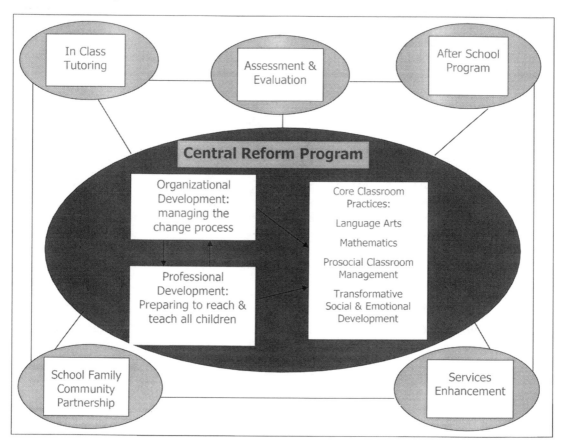

two-way functional relationships between schools and their staffs, on the one hand, and families and community volunteers and organizations, on the other. Examples here include parent education workshops that provided parents with strategies to support their children's academic and socioemotional development and a family resource center at a school, which among other things provides developmental opportunities for parents themselves.

Our student services component provides ongoing therapeutic support for students who need support in adjusting to the classroom community, and it also affords opportunities for these students' parents/caregivers and teachers to work constructively in support of positive outcomes for the children they share. We also implement assessment and evaluation services and technical assistance to discern the effectiveness of our various interventions and to help teachers and our tutors more accurately align their instructional activities with the students' academic needs.

As Figure 34.3 further illustrates, there are several activities more directly germane to core classroom functioning. We provide leadership support to school administrators so that they can more greatly exercise instructional, human relations as well as administrative leadership. We provide ongoing professional development interventions for teachers to bolster their content and pedagogical knowledge bases and to more greatly ensure that they possess both conceptual and procedural understanding of the strategies that we encourage them to deploy. In terms of the classroom activities per se, we concentrate in four areas. Teachers are to deploy our signature talent development reading and math frameworks that we call *Pathways to Reading* and *Step by Step Math*, respectively. They are also to deploy our prosocial classroom management system. They are also prepared to implement our social, emotional, and transformative curriculum modules and related activities. Our various school reform components are in varying stages of development. Each can be labor-intensive in its preparation and implementation. As such, no one school where the talent development model is in place currently manifests all of these components at the present time. But every component in some combination with others can be found among all of our school sites. We currently are working in ten schools in the Washington, D.C., metropolitan area.

Implementing a Talent Development Perspective

To accomplish this lofty educational objective requires that the various coordinated activities and practices implemented are ones based on the best available evidence that they will lead to enhanced outcomes for the students in question. This requires that an evidence based framework be self-consciously deployed in support of the school reform initiative.

This scenario calls for a decidedly evidence-based approach to program and practice implementation. The notion here is to pick interventions that are backed up by the best available evidence, not understood as solely scores on some arbitrary standardized test, suggesting that they are likely to yield the expected or desired outcomes. Accordingly, it would be necessary to have a reasonably clear idea of the underlying processes or mechanisms that likely account for the results. It is likewise crucial to discern the methods, resources, conditions, and preparation required to achieve the intervention successfully. Then, it is crucial to provide enabling conditions and resources required for successful implementation. The next step is to assess rigorously the quality of the implementation as it occurs, making the necessary adjustments in due course, presuming that there have been sufficient preparation, resources, and operational support. Then, the relevant outcomes are determined and assessed. These outcomes are linked to implementation practices, the quality of enabling conditions, and the proposed processes that underlie the corresponding practices and conditions. Necessary changes are then made to guide subsequent interventions at this site. Moreover, transcendent principles would be extracted and lessons learned that can travel to other sites to inform conceptually similar practices under even disparate schooling conditions (NAE, 1999).

This approach to education requires that teachers and administrators embrace the belief that virtually all students can acquire the school's valued outcomes provided that they are given sufficient time, appropriate instruction, and support. This belief, in turn, requires new and improved schooling and instructional knowledge and skills. This form of schooling, in turn, implies, for example, the need for results-driven staff development, whereas staff development success is judged primarily by whether it alters instructional practices in ways that benefit students. The goal is to improve the performance of students, predicated on school staff members increasing the performance of their craft as educators (Elmore, 2000).

The Importance of Psychosocial Integrity

The evidence base that seems most appropriate for pursuing a talent development approach to schooling that conforms with the requirements of an option three approach to the gap closing challenge seems to cohere around the principle of *psychosocial integrity* (Boykin & Allen, 2004). Integrity, by definition, means that there are complexity, coherence, and texture contained in people's life experiences. Such integrity exists in the experiences of people from diverse backgrounds, even among those whose experiences diverge from a mainstream middle-class standard. This integrity, in its variety of forms, produces social and intellectual assets that can be built upon in school settings. It is advanced that when knowledge of such assets is used to guide schooling practices, it can lead to enhanced outcomes. This line of argument emerges from the wealth of research findings pointing to effective practices that lead to higher learning outcomes for all students while simultaneously closing the achievement gap between majority and minority-group populations. Indeed, a substantial portion of such practices coheres around the concept of integrity.

Schooling practices, therefore, that acknowledge and build upon or draw out the existing or potential assets that people bring with them to schooling settings would more greatly ensure the development of academic talent. Integrity-based schooling activities fall roughly into five interrelated, yet distinct, categories. These are (1) promoting meaning making, (2) utilizing cultural resources of students, families, and their communities, (3) building a learning community, (4) providing a supportive, yet demanding, learning environment, and (5) directly imparting thinking and learning strategies and fostering critical engagement processes (Langer; 2001; Boykin & Bailey, 2000; Tharp et al., 2000; Lee, 2001; Greenleaf et al., 2001).

Meaning making conveys strategies that make connections among different topics, connections to students' own personal experiences and future endeavors, connections to their prior knowledge, and connections to the larger world in which they live, as examples. Cultural resources refer to family, community, and peer-based socialization experiences that give rise to funds of knowledge and to rituals, traditions, and practices that can be of educational value in school settings. Cultural resources refer as well to issues of popular culture and to diverse fundamental core values. In the present context, a learning community is one where learning becomes an interdependent exercise, so that a premium is placed on collaboration, and where student democratic participation in, and sense of ownership of, the learning process are fostered. An environment that is supportive, yet demanding, is one where encouragingly high expectations are set and where a focus on effort and improvement is promoted, along with a focus on sustained excellence.

To directly impart learning and thinking strategies entails providing students with tools that deepen and sharpen their understanding of subject matter and allow them to work independently as well. Moreover, from a talent development standpoint, learners are not viewed as passive, with learning construed as a pouring-in and pouring-out process. Instead, under the talent development model, there is a strong emphasis on strategies that foster critical thinking skills and therefore support a nonsuperficial engagement with the subject matter at hand (Waxman et al., 2001; Pressley & Woloshyn, 1995; Ferguson, 1998; Tucker et al., 2002; Kaplan & Maehr, 1999; Bell & Clark, 1998; Wasik & Bond, 2001; Langer, 2001; Lee, 2001; Marzano et al., 2001).

Integrity-based principles lie at the operational heart of all talent development activities. As such, then, they inform professional development workshops, the after-school program, and working with principals and parents and inhere in curriculum and classroom instructional activities. Consequently, these principles serve as common denominators to ensure coherence across the various school reform components such that whichever of our components are present at a given school, there will be a sense of commonality and organic connection among them.

The Importance of Seeking Multiple Outcomes

Another cornerstone principle of the talent development model is that multiple outcomes are sought. While it is crucial to secure higher achievement test scores, this cannot exhaust what should be expected, even required of students, especially from marginalized or educationally disfranchised groups. Their education process must be geared toward preparing children to help their families, schools, and communities to thrive in an increasingly complex global economy. In this connection we include a focus on children's social and emotional competence development in our school reform efforts.

Social and emotional competence encompasses an array of personal, interpersonal, decision-making, and relational characteristics (Zins et al., 2000). While such competences are valuable indicators of psychological health and well-being, they also can contribute to improved academic outcomes. For example, children with greater knowledge of situational cues for emotions are better liked by classmates than are other children (e.g., Garner et al., 1994). Prosocial interactions with peers has been linked to academic time on task (Elliot et al., 1988) as well as grades and achievement test scores (Wentzel, 1993).

Findings such as these have contributed to the growth of social and emotional learning programs. As expected, such programs have been shown to reduce risk behaviors and promote desirable academic and mental health outcomes (e.g., Catalano et al., 1999; Weissberg & Greenberg, 1997). Most programs are multicomponent, addressing school personnel, children, and families. It is clear that African American children and youth could benefit from participation in social and emotional learning programs. Unfortunately, the schools attended by African American children, especially those from low-income communities, lack the capacity to institute universal interventions needed to address both prevention and promotion needs for these children (National Research Council, 2002). Therefore, most African American children do not get access to competence enhancement programs until they are placed in social service or juvenile systems (USPHS, 2001). As a consequence, African American children are placed at serious social and emotional risk. For example, the structural violence associated with poverty and disfranchisement contributes to these children being exposed to high rates of community violence (e.g., Jenkins & Bell, 1997; Shakoor & Chalmers, 1991).

Such exposure to community violence has been associated with both internalizing and externalizing problem behaviors (e.g., Osofsky, 1995), to include violence. Within the school context, teachers tend to rate African American children and youth as lower in social skills (e.g., Feng & Cartledge, 1996) and more likely to display symptoms of conduct disorder (Costello et al., 1988) than students from other cultural groups. It follows that these children and youth receive harsher discipline and tend to be suspended and expelled more readily than their European American counterparts (Skiba et al., 2000).

These students who experience school-related "problems" also represent over 26 percent of the students identified by school personnel as being emotionally and/or behaviorally disturbed (U.S. Department of Education, 2000). In turn, evidence suggests that such negative school experiences contribute to a developmental trajectory that includes academic underachievement and other health-compromising behaviors like substance abuse, aggression, and delinquency (e.g., Dryfoos, 1997). This drastically increases the likelihood of school dropout and subsequent entry into the juvenile and/or adult justice system and virtually ensures under- and/or unemployment (Osher et al., 2002).

Beyond those children who are vulnerable to this troubling (dire) life trajectory, the majority of African American children simply deserve and need support to pursue healthy social and emotional development and to realize their potential. We are just on the threshold of knowing how systematically to provide such support through institutions such as public schools.

The Pursuit of Social and Emotional Competence

Our ongoing work in this regard is aimed at developing culturally grounded theory, research, and practice in the area of African American elementary school children's social and emotional competence development. In the present work, the focus is on cultivating the relational skills in teachers and students needed to create safe, supportive learning environments. A related aim is to prepare children to become agents of progressive change in family and community contexts.

Toward this end, we have used previous basic research to guide the development of a culturally grounded model of elementary school children's social and emotional competences (e.g., Humphries et al., 2000; Jagers, 1997; Jagers & Mock, 1993; Mock et al., submitted). Current research and development activities document and capitalize on the relationships among cultural orientations, moral emotions of empathy and guilt, social efficacy, and social skills in children in an effort to promote positive family and school relationships. We labor to create continuity in the ways in which children and key socializing agents (family members, teachers, and interested community residents) understand and support children's social and emotional competence development.

TEACHER PROFESSIONAL DEVELOPMENT TO SUPPORT STUDENTS' SOCIAL AND EMOTIONAL COMPETENCE

Within the school contexts, classroom teachers play a central role in children's academic, social, and emotional growth and development. This is especially true for children from low-income backgrounds (Waxman et al., 1997). Classroom teachers as implementers of school-based programs allow for sustained infusion of the program into the normal school day. While teachers are relied on to actively teach the program, it is perhaps more important to us that they demonstrate the self- and relational knowledge, attitudes, and behaviors that children are encouraged to acquire.

Yet, regardless of racial background, many teachers have internalized negative assumptions about the African American experience in general and the intellectual and social competences of low-income African American children in particular. Diminished teacher expectations can trigger a variety of feelings in them, including pity, frustration, anger, and/ or cynicism. This, in turn, can translate into either excessive permissiveness or harsh, punitive treatment of children. Such interactions likely contribute substantially to the poor school adjustment and discipline problems mentioned earlier in this chapter.

As such, our professional development sessions first seek to stimulate in teachers a certain level of critical cultural and sociopolitical consciousness. We encourage teachers to reflect on their professional goals and to consider that the education process for African American children must prepare them to assume responsible and transforming roles in their families, communities, and the broader society.

Teachers are asked to consider the developmental strengths and challenges of their students and to employ relational strategies with their students that are consistent with this understanding. One way of doing this is through regular class meetings. These meetings provide opportunities for building and maintaining mutually supportive teacher–student and student–student relationships and can be used for collective planning, updating, or consciousness-raising (Developmental Studies Center, 1998). We advocate an emphasis on positive recognition for successes and encouragement for effort. When inappropriate behavior does occur, the focus should be on brainstorming, selecting, and enacting a solution, rather than on blaming and punishing students (e.g., Nelsen et al., 2000). Strategies for establishing and maintaining constructive relationships with families are then discussed. The need for persistent, proactive, nonjudgmental, two-way communication is highlighted. Following this, teachers are introduced to a series of social and emotional curriculum modules for their students.

Social and Emotional Curriculum Modules

At CRESPAR, our social and emotional curriculum modules attempt to extend on, and deepen, existing evidenced-based programs through a critical treatment of self–other relationships in cultural and racial contexts. It seemed appropriate to align our modules with prescribed content standards in social studies in order to make it relevant to everyday classroom practice. Culturally appropriate books and films are recommended that can accent and bring additional substance to each module. These materials are intended to enhance core literacy and language arts skills among African American children. In addition, collaborative learning and hands-on activities are woven throughout the modules to appeal to, and accommodate, diverse learning approaches.

Modules first guide students through an exploration of who they are from a cultural history perspective so that they can appreciate various aspects of their personal and communal identities. This provides an initial framework for them to begin to recognize themselves as valuable and unique but deeply connected individuals. It also prepares them to learn to identify and understand the antecedents and consequences of their emotions, with special attention to self-awareness, anger and stress management, self-reward, persistence, and goal-setting.

Attention is then turned to various types of self–other relations. The critical need to respect others and a have a sense of social responsibility is supported by the discussion of interpersonal and situational cues and the importance of prosocial verbal and nonverbal communication processes. Research findings regarding victimization dictate that the causes of disagreements, social goals, decision making, and problem solving accompany a critical examination of familial, school, and community relations. The connection is made between school success and family and community well-being. Issues of poverty and oppression, including internalized oppression, are entertained in this context. Making transitions successfully from context to context and the importance of community service are highlighted. Only after these discussions is multiculturalism introduced. Even then, an emphasis is placed on adaptive ethnic solidarity, cultural sensitivity, and the participatory democratic process.

STUDENT SOCIAL-EMOTIONAL DEVELOPMENT VIA FAMILY STRENGTHENING

Despite the importance of school, families are the primary context for children's social and emotional growth and development. Indeed, research has shown that many of the more powerful risk and protective factors for child and youth problems have their origins in the family (Spoth et al., 2002).

Consistent with the talent development approach, a culturally grounded approach to family strengthening implies that African American family life is assumed to have integrity and relevance. Through a variety of workshops, we seek to utilize existing personal and collective assets to further support optimal outcomes for caregivers and their children. These workshops reflect best practices in the area and are designed to meet the specific concerns of low-income African American families. For example, the stress, anger, and frustration associated with personal financial strain and living in an underresourced community can undermine effective parenting (e.g., Elder et al., 1995). Thus, parents' social and emotional health and well-being, to include outlets and supports for coping, are addressed prior to entering into discussions of family roles and responsibilities. Attention is then turned to the historical context of Black child development. Notions of identity, oppression, empowerment, and liberation are discussed in their connection to parenting philosophies, goals, and developmental imperatives for children.

Separate workshop sessions are used to describe milestones for children's intellectual, social, and emotional competence development. Associated child-raising strategies and practices are discussed in this context. For example, discipline strategies are highlighted as excessive parental anger, and coercive and/or inconsistent parenting practices are associated with onset and persistence of children's problem behaviors (e.g., CPPRG, 1999). The role of sibling, peer, and teacher relations in conflict resolution and the contributions of household work in fostering responsibility are also entertained. In addition, the need for careful attention to media exposure is discussed.

Finally, the need for consistent proactive parental advocacy for children in school and community contexts is highlighted. Strategies for cultivating meaningful relationships with school personnel, especially classroom teachers, are provided. An effort is made to identify and develop partnerships with community members and organizations that can assist in supporting the healthy development of children.

CONCLUSION AND RECOMMENDATIONS

Education continues to play a pivotal role in the health and well-being of African American children and youth. Early school success requires academic preparation and social adjustment. Subsequent achievement is linked to the risk or protective functions of relationships within and outside the school. These relationships determine the nature and degree of access and support provided. The school reform efforts we presented can be construed as a multicomponent, universal program to foster and support academic and psychological health and well-being.

There are several implications for the work we outlined above. For example, continually increasing academic outcome levels for all students certainly should be the primary goal of a formal academic institution. This is strongly advocated for our talent development schools. Indeed, we have obtained highly promising results from our sites thus far in terms of boosting measured achievement levels. However, focusing exclusively on academic performance may be necessary but not sufficient as a schooling goal for many African American children, particularly those from marginalized backgrounds. More is needed to more greatly ensure their life success and their gainful participation in the fabric of American life and to protect them against possible threats to their social and emotional well-being. So we further advocate a full-bodied intervention focusing on students' social and emotional development, one that is fully integrated into the ongoing academic mission of a school.

Furthermore, we appreciate more than ever the importance of *ongoing* professional development for instructional staff persons. This means that professional development does not end but only begins with a particular workshop offering. The more crucial work is embodied in follow-up activities to include observations, planning support, classroom demonstrations, coaching, and feedback. Given this approach, it certainly complexifies the challenges faced by school reformers who pursue a multicomponent intervention strategy. In particular, it becomes crucial to coordinate or somehow coagulate the professional development work required across the various intervention areas. For example, it would be cumbersome and even time-prohibitive to put teachers through separate, parallel training and follow-up sessions for social and emotional development modules, language arts, classroom management, and mathematics, not to mention the problematics of having teachers ferret out what distinctly is required of them in these different domains. This is a challenge we are still attempting to successfully meet.

As one should now be aware, doing authentic school reform is difficult, daunting work. It is crucial to discern how to properly sequence the introduction of various reform components. Furthermore, given the labor and time intensity of the work, it is apparent that a proper balance must be struck between providing a school with direct service and providing only technical support in the various intervention domains. This again is a challenge that we are attempting to address in our work.

Still further, we cannot overemphasize the importance of tying in-school programs to interventions that are geared toward working with the surrounding community. This is particularly crucial with regard to matters of social and emotional development. In a recent national survey, nearly 50 percent of schools, especially those in low-income communities of color, indicated that a lack of staff training in working with families was a significant barrier to parent involvement (NCES, 1998). As such, we are interested in providing school–family partnership training to assist teachers in planning and executing proactive, persistent, and positive communication with families about the school and their children (e.g., Patrikakou et al., in press). The focus is on appreciating family strengths and challenges, conducting productive parent–teacher conferences, generating written and telephone communications that highlight student successes, and providing families with practical ways to support and extend what is being done in the classroom.

Our current focus on social and emotional competences speaks primarily to preventing interpersonal violence and fostering harmonious social relationships in family and school contexts. In our view this provides a foundation for community uplift. However, the social decision-making model that is central to our program is applicable to other health concerns as well. In this connection, we anticipate addressing unsafe sex, including HIV/AIDS, and substance use and abuse. This makes sense as epidemiological research suggests that a common set of risk and protective factors are associated with these problem behaviors. It is also the case that, at a minimum, achieving and maintaining a healthy lifestyle requires successfully negotiating each of these issues.

Strategies for implementing comprehensive wellness promotion programs also warrant attention. For example, Dryfoos (1995) has argued persuasively for full service schools. She takes the position that school and community agencies should collaborate to provide a comprehensive set of services, including quality education and social, emotional, and health promotion instruction and services as well as family programs. Our experiences support the need for, and challenges associated with, such a collaborative network for low-income African American children.

Finally, we are committed to collaborative community action research (Weissberg & Greenberg, 1997). This approach is rooted in an ecological perspective and emphasizes the close and meaningful collaboration among all stakeholders in the initiative. In this regard, collaborative community action research is concerned with outcomes but also highlights the underlying processes, which support the collaboration. As such, this research strategy closely corresponds with the overarching talent development philosophy, which guides our programmatic efforts.

NOTE

The work reported herein was supported by a grant (No. R-117-D40005) from the Office of Educational Research and Improvement, U.S. Department of Education. The findings and opinions expressed in this report do not reflect the position or policies of the National Institute on At-Risk Students, the Office of Educational Research and Improvement, or the U.S. Department of Education.

REFERENCES

Balfantz, R. (2000). Why do so many urban public school students demonstrate so little academic achievement? In M. Sanders (Ed.), *Schooling students placed at risk*. Mahwah, NJ: LEA, pp. 37–62.

Bell, Y., & Clark, T. (1998). Culturally relevant reading material as related to comprehension and recall in African American children. *Journal of Black Psychology, 24*, 455–475.

Boykin, A.W. (2000). The talent development model of schooling: Placing students at promise for academic success. *Journal of Education for Students Placed at Risk, 5, (1&2)*, 3–25.

Boykin, A.W., & Allen, B. (2000). Beyond deficits and difference: Psychological integrity in developmental research. In C. Yeakey (Ed.), *Edmund W. Gordon: Producing knowledge, pursuing understanding* (pp. 15–34). Raleigh, NC: JAI Press.

Boykin, A.W., & Allen, B. (2004). Cultural integrity and schooling outcomes of African American schoolchildren from low-income backgrounds. In P. Pufall & R. Unsworth (Eds.), *How American children lead their lives* (pp. 104–120). New Brunswick, NJ: Rutgers University Press.

Boykin, A.W., & Bailey, C. (2000, April). The role of cultural factors in school-relevant cognitive functioning: Synthesis of findings on cultural contexts, cultural orientations and individual differences. (Tech. Rep. No. 42). Baltimore and Washington, DC: Johns Hopkins University & Howard University, Center for Research on the Education of Students Placed at Risk.

Catalano, R.F., Berglund, M., Ryan, J.A.M., Lonczak, H.S., & Hawkins, D. (1999). Positive youth development in the United States: Research findings on evaluations of positive youth development programs. Washington, DC: U.S. Department of Health and Human Services.

Cohall, A.T., & Bannister, H.E. (2001). The health status of children and adolescents. In R.L. Braithewaite & S. Taylor (Eds.), Health issues in the Black community (2d ed., pp. 13–43). San Francisco: Jossey-Bass.

Conduct Problems Prevention Research Group (CPPRG). (1999). Initial impact of the FAST Track prevention trial for conduct problems: I. The high-risk sample. *Journal of Consulting and Clinical Psychology, 67*, 631–647.

Costello, E.J., Costello, A.J., Edelborck, C. Burns, B.J., Dulcan, M.K., Brent, D., & Janiszewski, S. (1988). Psychiatric disorders in primay care: Prevalence and risk. *Archives of General Psychiatry, 45*, 1107–1116.

Datnow, A. (2000). Power and politics in the adoption of school reform models. *Educational Evaluation and Policy Analysis, 22*, 357–374.

Delpit, L. (1995). *Other people's children: Cultural conflict in the classroom.* New York: New Press.

Developmental Studies Center. (1998). The ways we want our class to be: Class meetings that build commitment to kindness and learning. Oakland, CA: Developmental Studies Center.

Dryfoos, J.G. (1995). Full-service schools: revolution or fad? *Journal of Research on Adolescence, 5*, 147–172.

Dryfoos, J.G. (1997). The prevalence of problem behaviors: Implications for programs. In R.P. Weissberg, T.P. Gullota, R.L. Hampton, B.A. Ryan, & G.R. Adams (Eds.), *Healthy children 2010: Enhancing children's wellness* (pp. 17–46). Thousand Oaks, CA: Sage.

Edmonds, R. (1986). Characteristics of effective schools. In U. Neisser (Ed.), *The school achievement of minority children* (pp. 93–104). Hillsdale, NJ: Lawrence Erlbaum.

Elder, G.H., Eccles, J.S., Ardelt, M., & Lord, S. (1995). Inner-city parents under economic pressure: Perspectives on the strategies of parenting. *Journal of Marriage and the Family, 57*, 771–784.

Elliot, S.N., Gresham, F.M., Freeman, T., & McCloskey, G. (1988). Teachers' and observers' ratings of children's social skills: Validation of the Social Skills Rating Scales. *Journal of Psychoeducational Assessment, 6*, 152–161.

Elmore, R. (1996). Getting to scale with good educational practice. *Harvard Educational Review, 66*, 1–26.

Elmore, R. (2000). *Building a new structure for school leadership.* Washington, DC: Albert Shanker Institute.

Feng, H., & Cartledge, G. (1996). Social skills assessment of inner-city Asian, African, and European American students. *School Psychology Review, 25*, 228–239.

Ferguson, R.F. (1998). Teachers' perceptions and expectations and the Black–White test score gap. In C. Jencks & M. Phillips (Eds.), *The Black–White test score gap* (pp. 273–317). Washington, DC: Brookings Institution.

Garibaldi, A. (1997). Four decades of progress . . . and decline: An assessment of African American educational attainment. *Journal of Negro Education, 66*, 105–120.

Garner, P.W., Jones, D.C., & Miner, J.L. (1994). Social competence among low-income preschoolers: Emotions, socialization practices and social cognitive correlates. *Child Development, 65*, 622–637.

Greenleaf, C., Schoenbach, R., Cziko, C., & Mueller, F. (2001). Apprenticing adolescent readers to academic literacy. *Harvard Educational Review, 71*, 79–129.

Hedges, L., & Nowell, A. (1999). Changes in the Black–White achievement gap in achievement scores. *Sociology of Education, 72*, 111–135.

Hilliard, A. (2001). Race, identity, hegemony, and education: What do we need to know? In W. Watkins, J. Lewis, & V. Choe (Eds.), *Race and education: The roles of history and society in educating African American students* (pp. 7–33). Boston: Allyn & Bacon.

Humphries, M., Parker, B., & Jagers, R.J. (2000). Predictors of moral maturity among African American children. *Journal of Black Psychology, 26*, 51–64.

Jagers, R.J. (1997). Afrocultural integrity and the social development of African American children: Some conceptual, empirical, and practical considerations. *Journal of Prevention and Intervention in the Community, 16*, 7–34.

Jagers, R.J., & Mock, L.O. (1993). Culture and social outcomes among inner-city African American children: An Afrographic exploration. *Journal of Black Psychology, 19*, 391–405.

James, D., Jurich, S., & Estes, S. (2001). Raising minority academic achievement: A compendium of education programs and practices. Washington, DC: American Youth Policy Forum.

Jencks, C., & Philips, M. (1998). The Black–White test score gap: An introduction. In C. Jencks & M. Phillips (Eds.), *The Black–White test score gap* (pp. 1–51). Washington, DC: Brookings Institution.

Jenkins, E., & Bell, C.C. (1997). Exposure and response to community violence among children and adolescents. In J. Osofsky (Ed.), *Children in a violent society* (pp. 9–31). New York: Guilford Press.

Kaplan, A., & Maehr, M. (1999). Enhancing the motivation of African American students: An achievement goal theory perspective. *Journal of Negro Education, 68*, 23–41.

Kellam, S.G., Koretz, D., & Mosciki, E.K. (1999). Core elements of developmental epidemiologically based prevention research. *American Journal of Community Psychology, 27*, 463–482.

Kumpfer, K.L., & Alvarado, R. (1998). Effective family strengthening interventions. Juvenile Justice Bulletin. Washington, DC: U.S. Department of Justice, Office of Juvenile Justice and Delinquency Prevention.

Langer, J. (2001). Beating the odds: Teaching middle and high school students to read and write well. *American Educational Research Journal, 38*, 837–880.

Lee, C. (2001). Is October Brown Chinese? A cultural modeling activity system for underachieving students. *American Educational Research Journal, 38*, 97–141.

Lewis, J. (2001). Introduction: The search for new answers. In W. Watkins, J. Lewis, & V. Chou (Eds.), *Race and education: The roles of history and society in educating African American students* (pp. 1–6). Boston: Allyn & Bacon.

Marzano, R., Pickering, D., & Pollock, J. (2001). Classroom instruction that works: Research-based strategies for increasing student achievement. Alexandria, VA: ASCD.

Mock, L.O., Jagers, R.J., & Smith, P. (submitted). *Cultural and race-related factors associated with youth violence.* Manuscript submitted for publication.

National Academy of Education (NAE) Report. (1999). Recommendations regarding research priorities. Washington, DC: NAE.

National Center for Educational Statistics (NCES). (1998). *Parent involvement in children's education: Efforts by public elementary schools.* Washington, DC: U.S. Department of Education.

National Research Council. (2002). Minority students in special and gifted education. Washington, DC: National Academy Press.

Nelsen, J., Lott, L., & Glenn, H.S. (2000). Positive discipline in the classroom: Developing mutual respect, cooperation and responsibility in your classroom (3d ed.). Roseville, CA: Prima.

Osher, D., Woodruff, D., & Sims, A. (2002). Schools make a difference: The overrepresentation of African American youth in special education and the juvenile justice system. In D.J. Losen & G. Orfield (Eds.), *Racial inequality in special education* (pp. 93–116). Cambridge: Harvard Education Press.

Osofsky, J.D. (1995). The effects of exposure to violence on young children. *American Psychologist, 50*, 782–788.

Patrikakou, E.N., Weissberg, R.P., & Rubenstein, M.I. (in press). School–family partnerships. In A.J. Reynolds, H.J. Walberg, & R.P. Weissberg (Eds.), *Promoting positive outcomes in children and youth*. Washington, DC: Child Welfare League of America.

Patton, J. (1998). The disproportionate representation of African Americans in special education: Looking behind the curtain for understanding and solutions. *Journal of Special Education, 32*, 25–31.

Pressley, M., & Woloshyn, V. (1995). *Cognitive strategy instruction that really improves children's academic performance.* (2d ed.). Cambridge, MA: Brookline Books.

Ramey, M. (2000, April). Reducing the White–non-White achievement gap. Paper presented at the annual meeting of the American Educational Research Association, New Orleans.

Shakoor, B., & Chalmers, D. (1991). Co-victimization of African American children who witness violence and the theoretical implications of its effects on their cognitive, emotional and behavioral development. *Journal of the National Medical Association, 83*, 233–238.

Skiba, R.J., Michael, R.S., Nardo, A.C., & Peterson, R. (2000). The color of discipline: Sources of racial and gender disproportionality in school punishment. Bloomington: Indiana Education Policy Center Policy Research Report #SRS1.

Spoth, R.L., Kavanaugh, K.A., & Dishion, T.J. (2002). Family-centered preventive intervention science: Toward benefits to large populations of children, youth and families. *Prevention Science, 3,* 145–152.

Spring, J. (2001). *Deculturalization and the struggle for equality* (3d ed.). New York: McGraw-Hill.

Teacher and child variables as predictors of academic engagement among low-income African American children. *Psychology in the Schools, 39,* 477–488.

Tharp, R., Estrada, P., Dalton, S., & Yamauchi, L. (2000). *Teaching transformed: Achieving excellence, fairness, inclusion, and harmony.* Boulder, CO: Westview.

Tucker, C., Zayco, R., Herman, K., Reinke, W., Truillo, M., Carraway, C., & Ivery, P. (2002).

Tyack, D., & Tobin, W. (1994). The "grammar" of schooling: Why has it been so hard to change? *American Educational Research Journal, 31,* 453–479.

Tye, B., (1998). The deep structure of schooling: What it is and how it works. *Clearing House, 71,* 332–334.

U.S. Department of Education. (2001). 22nd annual report to Congress on the implementation of the Individuals with Disabilities Education Act. Washington, DC: Author.

U.S. Public Health Service (USPHS). (2001). *Mental health: Culture, race, ethnicity. A supplement to the surgeon general's report on mental health.* Washington, DC: Author.

Wasik, B., & Bond, M. (2001). Beyond the pages of a book: Interactive book reading and language development in preschool classrooms. *Journal of Educational Psychology, 93,* 243–250.

Watkins, W. (2001). Blacks and the curriculum: From accommodation to contestation and beyond. In W. Watkins, J. Lewis, & V. Chou (Eds.), *Race and education: The roles of history and society in educating African American students* (pp. 40–65). Boston: Allyn & Bacon.

Waxman, H.C., Huang, S.L. Anderson, L., & Weinstein, T. (1997). Classroom process differences in inner-city elementary schools. *Journal of Educational Research, 91,* 49–59.

Waxman, H., Padron, Y., & Arnold, K. (2001). Effective instructional practices for students placed at risk of academic failure. In G. Borman, S. Stringfield, & R. Slavin (Eds.), *Title I: Compensatory education at the crossroads.* Mahwah, NJ: LEA.

Weissberg, R.P., & Greenberg, M.T. (1997). School and community competence-enhancement and prevention programs. In W. Damon (Series Ed.) & I.E. Sigel & K.A. Renninger (Vol. Eds.), *Handbook of child psychology: Vol. 5. Child psychology in practice* (5th ed., pp. 877–954). New York: Wiley & Sons.

Wentzel, K.R. (1993). Does being good make the grade? Social behavior and academic competence in middle school. *Journal of Educational Psychology, 85,* 357–364.

Young, B. (2002). *Characteristics of the 100 largest public and elementary and secondary school districts in the United States: 2000–01,* NCES 2002–351. Washington, DC: U.S. Department of Education, National Center for Educational Statistics.

Zins, J.E., Elias, M.J. Greenberg, M.T., & Weissberg, R.P. (2000). Promoting social and emotional competence in children. In K.M. Minke & G.C. Bear (Eds.), *Preventing school problems-promoting school success: Strategies and programs that work* (pp. 71–100). Bethesda, MD: National Association of School Psychologists.

CHAPTER 35

Complementary and Alternative Health Practices in the Black Community: Existing and Emergent Trends

ERIC J. BAILEY AND
JACQUELINE A. WATSON

INTRODUCTION

Over the past decade, complementary and alternative medicine (CAM) has grown in popularity within the medical community and among people of various ages, racial/ethnic groups, socioeconomic levels, disciplines, and health status. During the past ten years, the number of published research articles on alternative medicine in medical journals has increased 10-fold. In the same period, the number of trade books published on this topic has increased 50-fold. In addition, Americans' hunger and interest in alternative medicine have influenced the U.S. health and medical systems to drastically change their approach to basic health and medical care for all Americans. With all the increased public interest in CAM therapies, products, and research, it is probable that this area of research will provide new information and strategies in reducing racial health disparities in the United States.

This chapter ties in with the overall theme of this book primarily because it examines complementary and alternative health practices from their current framework of orientation, their current use in treating chronic conditions as well as the sociopolitical, ethical, and funding issues related to their use and impact on the United States health-care system. In other words, with all of this attention on complementary and alternative medicine—*where do we go from here?*

Complementary and alternative medicine encompasses a wide range of therapies, treatments, and approaches. Acupuncture, homeopathy, chiropractic, herbal therapies, nutritional supplements, naturopathy, massage therapy, biofeedback, meditation, spiritual healing, Reiki, hypnosis, and yoga are just a few examples of complementary and alternative medicines.

According to the National Center on Complementary and Alternative Medicine (NCCAM) at the National Institutes of Health, CAM is defined as a group of diverse medical and health-care systems, practices, and products that are not presently considered to be part of conventional medicine. NCCAM categorizes complementary and alternative medicine into seven major categories:

- Mind-body medicine
- Alternative medical systems
- Lifestyle and disease prevention

- Biologically based therapies
- Manipulative and body-based systems
- Biofield
- Bioelectromagnetics (National Center on Complementary and Alternative Medicine, 2001)

Collectively, CAM is also often referred to as holistic or integrative medicine. However, there are differences between complementary, alternative, and integrative medicine.

The George Washington Center for Integrative Medicine in Washington, D.C., states that complementary and integrative medicine refers to the action of combining alternative modalities among themselves, as well as with conventional treatments, for maximum healing effect, whereas alternative therapies indicate a choice among equals (George Washington University Center for Integrative Medicine Web site 2002). Where one modality is an alternative to another treatment, it suggests that either might be safe and efficacious and therefore is considered a substitute for the conventional modality. One might be preferable to the other based on certain factors, but the outcomes are likely to be equal. Integrative medicine is considered as the ideal benchmark that health systems should strive for, that is, incorporating safe and efficacious complementary and alternative therapies, products and treatment modalities into conventional Western therapies, in an attempt to improve the overall health and well-being of individuals.

The Importance of Culture and Complementary and Alternative Medicine

Culture, ethnicity and environment all play a significant role in how one views health. Studies show that health behaviors are culturally determined, and therefore culture plays a central role in how, when and if people seek care, as well as in how they respond to treatments and recommendations prescribed (Blendon et al., 1989; Braithwaite & Lythcott, 1989; Collins, 1997; Forte, 1995; Martin & Panicucci, 1996).

In this chapter, we define culture as a system of shared beliefs, values, customs, and behaviors that are transmitted from generation to generation through learning (Bailey, 2000, p. 13). Culture is directly linked to Blacks' (African Americans') use of complementary and alternative medicine in six major ways. (We use the term "Blacks" and "African Americans" interchangeably.)

First, like culture, alternative medicine is a learned process. Alternative medical practices were already being passed down from generation to generation when the first enslaved Africans arrived in the Americas. Second, African Americans' continual use of alternative medicine is often a symbolic action by which the individual feels a need to have some control or gain a better understanding of the health problem that is occurring. Third, like culture, alternative medicine adds meaning to reality among those who stringently adhere to an alternative philosophy and treatment therapy and make it their way of life or a career and business opportunity. Fourth, alternative medicine, like culture, is integrated into the total fabric of the African American community. Alternative medicine provides a viable option for the individual African American primarily because of its easy accessibility within the African American community, its lower costs in comparison to mainstream medicine, and its historical connection with the older generation. Fifth, alternative medicine, like culture, is shared and viewed differently within the African American community. Different segments of the African American community tend to use alternative medicine more often than others, such as those who are older, southern, and rural. Sixth, alternative medicine, like culture, is adaptive. Complementary and alternative medicine is adaptive by the manner in which it fills an area of health-care need and understanding that mainstream conventional medicine cannot (Bailey, 2002).

Most of the CAM therapies used in the United States today were brought by the various racial/ethnic groups immigrating here. Much of the traditional healing therapies of Blacks (African American) people have their roots in slavery and traditional West African medicine. Africans and their descendants suffered from a wide range of illnesses, many of which, if they did not cause death, relied on their body's own defense mechanism or the resources within their own communities for healing. Many slaves believed that Western medicine was no more beneficial in treating common ailments than their own self-help practices. In fact, Western medicine was regarded as low-quality, and Africans turned to their own healers (general and specialists) for advice and treatment.

These unconventional practitioners, sometimes referred to as Negro doctors, Obeah people, slave healers, and witch doctors, played a central role in the health of Africans and their communities and continue to do so, though they were often misunderstood and generally dismissed by the Western world. Most of the early medicines were plant/herbal medicines, and uses were viewed from a spiritual perspective and within a religious context, rather than from a physical perspective. Plant leaves and roots were often boiled into teas or rubbed over the skin to successfully treat various ailments, and over time their use was recognized for the potential therapeutic benefits.

Today, many of these ancient African treatment modalities, though diluted since assimilated into Western culture, are being used by people of African descent and other ethnic groups in the United States. These therapies are playing an increasingly more important role in African American health and wellness and will continue to do so as the Western world continues to search for treatments and cures to diseases that commonly afflict our hemisphere.

CURRENT USES OF COMPLEMENTARY AND ALTERNATIVE MEDICINE IN AFRICAN AMERICAN POPULATIONS

Medical anthropology focuses on disease, illness, medical problems, theories of illness, and health-care systems in different cultural and ethnic groups from a biopsychosociocultural perspective. In other words, medical anthropologists investigate health care from a holistic perspective. An attempt is made to take a broader approach than other disciplines in order to ensure that all the possible factors are sufficiently investigated.

The biopsychosociocultural perspective means that one must recognize the biological, psychological, social, and cultural factors that are connected with each individual as they relate to health or illness. Therefore, the biopsychosociocultural model provides a blueprint for research, a framework for teaching, and a design for action in the real world of health care (Bailey, 2000).

Research Involving Alternative Medicine and African Americans

In order to uncover a detailed and in-depth analysis of African Americans' use of alternative medicine, Boyd et al. (2000) conducted the first national analysis of family and individual use of home remedies by African Americans. The major purpose of this study was to assess the relationship between sociodemographic characteristics and home remedy usage for African American families and individuals. The African American data originated from the National Survey of Black Americans (NSBA), a nationally representative cross-sectional sample of 2,107 adult (18 years old and older) African Americans living in the continental United States in 1979 and 1980.

In this analysis, "users" of home remedies were those respondents who indicated they used home remedies all the time or sometimes, whereas "nonusers" were those respondents who indicated that they never used home remedies. The data were analyzed from two perspectives: use of home remedies by the respondent's families and use of home remedies by the respondent (Boyd et al., 2000, p. 343).

Boyd et al.'s (2000) major findings were as follows:

- 69.6 percent of respondents reported that their families used home remedies;
- 35.4 percent of respondents reported that they used home remedies;

• Of the preparations used, 68.2 percent were home remedies or herbal preparations;

• 16.7 percent of preparations could not be placed into one of the aforementioned categories and were classified as "others."

The major sociocultural factors that were found to have a significant association with families' use of home remedies included family size, mother's education, father's education, importance of religion to the family, living with grandparent, and living in a rural area and southern geographic region of the country. For example, in the case of family size, families with 1 to 3 children were 35.4 percent less likely to use home remedies than were families with 7 to 20 children.

Additionally, bivariate analysis found the following significant associations:

• Males were 47.4 percent less likely to use home remedies than females;

• Individuals not living with a grandparent as a child were 26.3 percent less likely to use home remedies than individuals living with a grandparent as a child;

• Families in which the father had 11 years or less of education were 77 percent more likely to use home remedies than were families in which the father had some college or a college degree;

• Individuals who reported religion as being only fairly important or not too important to their families were 38.3 percent and 53.3 percent less likely to report that their families used home remedies than were individuals who reported that religion was very important to them;

• Individuals not living with a grandparent while growing up were 37.9 percent less likely to report that their families used home remedies than were individuals who lived with their grandparent while growing up; and

• Individuals who reported living in a nonrural area were 28.5 percent less likely to report that their families used home remedies than were individuals living in a rural area.

Although Boyd et al. (2000) stated that their study's findings among African Americans show some consistency with other studies, one major advantage was the richness of the data in addressing the study objectives.

In addition to Boyd et al.'s (2000) study, there is insightful cultural data from two other alternative medicine studies. Two different studies—one in New York City and the other in San Francisco—are indications that African Americans used alternative and complementary medicine similarly and differently than Caucasians. For example, Cushman et al. (1999) wanted to explore the use of complementary and alternative medicine among African American and Hispanic women residing in New York City. Focus groups were conducted with two groups of African American and two groups of Hispanic women (age 18–40 and 41–80; total sample: 39) as preparation for the development of a quantitative instrument to assess the prevalence and determinants of alternative and complementary medicine use among women of various ethnic backgrounds.

Cushman et al. (1999) found that herbs, usually taken in the form of infused teas, were used by all groups. Furthermore, these herbs and teas were the most common alternative and complementary treatment therapy mentioned across age and race/ethnic categories. Chamomile, cranberry, black chohosh, ginger, and mint, among others, were taken for a variety of conditions, including stomach discomfort, menstrual cramps, premenstrual syndrome (PMS), fibroid pain, and menstrual and menopausal symptoms. Other remedies mentioned in all groups, particularly for dealing with stress and preventing disease, were vitamins and nutritional supplements, prayer and spiritual healing, and meditation and relaxation techniques (Cushman et al., 1999).

Few race/ethnic differences emerged in the discussions of CAM remedies and treatment. Colonic cleansing and spiritual practices were mentioned more by African Americans than Hispanics. African American women also defined several terms for CAM such as pot likker (juice of green vegetables), tar and sugar (for colds), and red clay and turpentine or vinegar (to reduce swelling). Finally, all women in both race/ethnic groups mentioned learning about alternative remedies from older female relatives, particularly mothers and grandmothers.

In general, Cushman et al.'s (1999) study results suggested that African American and Hispanic women used a variety of treatments and practitioners, both to alleviate specific symptoms and for prevention. Generally, their knowledge of, and interest in, alternative and complementary medicine were high. Beyond health concerns that commonly vary by age (pregnancy, menopause), the women had similar health concerns and used similar modalities across age and race/ethnic categories (Cushman et al., 1999, p. 195).

In another alternative and complementary medicine study, Lee et al. (2000) researched the types and prevalence of conventional and alternative therapies used by women in four ethnic groups (Latino, Caucasian, Chinese, and African American) diagnosed with breast cancer from 1990 through 1992 in San Francisco and explored factors influencing the choices of their therapies. A total of 100 African Americans, 100 Latino, 82 Chinese, and 97 Caucasian women participated in the 30-minute telephone interview.

Lee et al. (2000) found that the most commonly reported alternative therapies were dietary therapies (26.6 percent), megavitamins (8.2 percent), other specialized diets (19.8 percent), spiritual healing (23.7 percent), herbal remedies (12.9 percent), physical methods (14.2 percent), and psychological methods (9.2 percent). Prevalence of use of these therapies varied by ethnicity. African Americans most often used spiritual healing (36 percent), Chinese most often used herbal remedies (22 percent), and Latino women most often used dietary therapies (30 percent) and spiritual healing (26 percent). Among whites, 35 percent used dietary methods, and 23 percent used physical methods, such as massage and acupuncture (Lee et al., 2000, p. 43).

In general, African American women were less likely than women of the other three ethnicities to use dietary and physical therapies, while Latino women were more likely to use mental, physical, and herbal therapies. Chinese women were less likely to use dietary and mental therapies, but they were two times more likely to use herbal therapies (Lee et al., 2000, p. 43). In addition to ethnicity, other demographic factors, including younger age and high school or higher education, were consistently associated with using alternative therapies.

SELECTED APPLICATION OF COMPLEMENTARY AND ALTERNATIVE MEDICINE IN AFRICAN AMERICAN POPULATIONS: CANCER AND DIABETES

Cancer

In order for clinical testing of an alternative medical treatment therapy for cancer to be truly effective in both the short and long term, there needs to be an alternative treatment program designed specifically for the African American population. One such study, entitled, "Fruit and Vegetable Consumption and Prevention of Cancer: The Black Churches United for Better Health Project," not only examined the protective effect from fruits and vegetables on cancer outcome among African Americans but also attempted to increase their consumption of fruits and vegetables.

Campbell et al. (1999) conducted this study, which encompassed members of 50 Black churches in ten rural counties located in eastern North Carolina. Churches were randomly assigned to either immediate intervention or delayed intervention (no program until after the follow-up survey) conditions. Churches in the five intervention counties received the planned 5-a-Day intervention program, whereas churches in the delayed intervention counties did not receive any program activities until after completion of the two-year follow-up survey. The final sample for this study comprised 2,519 individuals who completed both the baseline and follow-up surveys. The response was 77.3 percent (Campbell et al., 1999, p. 1391).

To identify culturally sensitive ways to make the programs and messages more relevant and appropriate for an African American church audience, Campbell et al. (1999) drew upon information from six focus groups conducted early in the project, pastor interviews, and ongoing feedback from church members. Strategies used included working within social networks, recognizing and developing expertise within the church to conduct programs, and obtaining help from pastors to incorporate spiritual themes into tailored messages, sermons, and other communications. In each church, the pastor selected a coordinator and three to seven members to form the Nutrition Action Team, which was responsible for organizing and implementing many of the program activities. In addition, an African American review group composed of pastors, project staff, and community members reviewed and approved all project materials.

Campbell et al. (1999) found similar amounts of fruits and vegetables consumed among the intervention and delayed intervention group. At baseline, the intervention group consumed an average of 3.84 (SE = 0.10) daily servings of fruits and vegetables, and the delayed intervention group consumed 3.65 (SE = 0.10) servings (p = .21). Participants in both groups consumed more fruits than vegetables. A one-year follow-up survey of a random subsample of participants indicated greater consumption, by one serving, in the intervention group. In addition, stratification according to church size and inclusion of various denominations increased the generalizability of the study findings to other southern Black churches. The two-year follow-up period also was longer than in many intervention studies and suggests that behavior changes observed at one year were maintained (Campbell et al., 1999, p. 1394).

Although this study was not able to definitively show the protective effects of fruits and vegetables against cancer, this cultural intervention strategy to increase fruit and vegetable consumption among various segments of the African American community was successful.

Diabetes

What is the role of alternative and complementary medicine in diabetes? Surveys indicate that diabetic patients are significant users of alternative medicines. For example, Ryan et al. (2001) found in their sample of 502 diabetic subjects and 201 control subjects that 31 percent were taking alternative medication and 44 percent were taking over-the-counter supplements. Garlic, echinacea, herbal mixtures, and glucosamine were the most commonly used alternative medicines.

McGrady and Horner (1999) state that alternative and complementary therapies may be very useful adjuncts to insulin by enhancing the effect of injected insulin and lowering blood glucose levels. Furthermore, the noninsulin-dependent diabetes mellitus patient may seek alternative and complementary therapies to lower blood glucose levels, decrease dosage of oral hypoglycemics, and decrease insulin resistance. In addition to specific effects on blood glucose, some alternative and complementary therapies may assist patients in managing the complications of diabetes. Spencer and Jacobs (1999) state that overall the most common types of alternative and complementary therapies applicable to patients with diabetes are mind-body, herbal, and diet therapies.

According to the National Institute of Diabetes and Digestive and Kidney Disorders (NIDDK, 2001), there are at least five types of alternative therapies for diabetes:

- Acupuncture: a procedure in which a practitioner inserts needles into designated points on the skin.
- Biofeedback: a technique that helps a person become more aware of, and learn to deal with, the body's response to pain.
- Chromium: needed to make glucose tolerance factor, which helps insulin improve its action.
- Magnesium: a deficiency in magnesium may worsen the blood sugar control in Type II diabetes.

• Vanadium: a compound found in tiny amounts in plants and animals that helps to normalize blood glucose levels in animals with Type I and Type II diabetes.

In addition to some new alternative medications used to treat diabetes mellitus, there is brand-new, verifiable evidence that diet and exercise can prevent and control an individual's Type II diabetes. The results of the Diabetes Prevention Program (DPP) by the NIDDK at the National Institutes of Health (NIH) conclusively show that Type II diabetes can be prevented or significantly delayed at onset. The study demonstrated that two different approaches—diet and exercise therapy and the administration of a diabetes medication, metformin—were both effective with the lifestyle intervention (American Diabetes Association, 2001).

The findings came from a major clinical trial (27 centers nationwide) conducted by the DPP, comparing diet and exercise to treatment with metformin in 3,234 people with impaired glucose tolerance. Of the 3,234 participants enrolled in the DPP, 45 percent were from minority groups: African Americans, Hispanic Americans, Asian Americans and Pacific Islanders, and American Indians. The trial also recruited other groups known to be at higher risk for Type II diabetes, including individuals aged 60 and older, women with a history of gestational diabetes, and people with a first-degree relative with Type II diabetes (U.S. Department of Health and Human Services, 2001).

The findings from the Diabetes Prevention Program revealed that participants assigned to the intensive lifestyle intervention group reduced their risk of getting Type II diabetes by 58 percent. On the average, members of this group maintained their physical activity at 30 minutes per day, usually with walking or doing other moderate-intensity exercise, and lost 5 to 7 percent of their body weight. Participants randomized to treatment with metformin reduced their risk of getting Type II diabetes by 31 percent.

Particularly encouraging was the fact that both lifestyle and medication interventions worked for African Americans, Caucasians, Latinos, American Indians, and Asian Americans and Pacific Islanders. The Diabetes Prevention Program is the first study to demonstrate that prevention strategies can work across the broad spectrum of racial and ethnic diversity (American Diabetes Association, 2001).

HEALTH-CARE DISPARITIES: IS THERE A CASE FOR INCORPORATING COMPLEMENTARY AND ALTERNATIVE MEDICINE?

Blacks in the United States have, and continue to experience, disproportionate rates of morbidity and mortality, and frustratingly, many of the diseases disproportionately affecting Blacks are preventable. Blacks are generally at or above the national average for diagnoses of hypertension, diabetes, cancer, obesity, and asthma, to name a few. Lack of access to culturally competent care, low socioeconomic status, poverty, lack of insurance, and race are all contributing factors.

Listed are some of the statistics we've grown accustomed to living with; the Centers for Disease Control refers to diabetes and obesity as the "twin epidemics," and Blacks have the highest rates of both. Diabetically related complications occur at higher rates among Blacks. According to the National Center for Health Statistics, diabetic death rates are highest for Blacks. Blacks experience higher rates of mortality from cancer and cardiovascular disease; heart disease strikes nearly twice as many African American women as white women; prostate cancer incidence and mortality rates are highest among African Americans; African American men have the lowest life expectancy (66 years vs. 74 years for Whites); lung cancer rates are higher for Black men than for any other group. When lung, prostate, breast, and colorectal cancers were examined by race, except for female breast cancer, African Americans had higher incidence and death rates than any other racial and ethnic group (Healthy People 2010, 2000; National Vital Statistics Reports, 2002; Keppel et al., 2002).

The unhealthy statistics don't just stop there; unfortunately, they affect our children, too. For example, asthma is 26 percent more prevalent in African American children than in Whites, and Black children under age 13 make up two-thirds of all reported pediatric HIV cases in the United States (Morbidity and Mortality Weekly Report, 2001).

The statistics by themselves paint a depressing picture but do not tell the whole story. As we learned from the recent Institute of Medicine report, "Unequal Treatment: Confronting Racial and Ethnic Disparities in Health Care" (Smedley, Stith & Nelson, 2002), Blacks receive a lower quality of health care than Whites, even after adjustment for socioeconomic differences and other health-care access-related factors. The alarming statistics we are faced with in the African American community is proof that solutions to eliminating these disparities are complex and require the collective efforts of multidisciplinary teams of individuals. It is clear that new, improved, and comprehensive approaches and strategies to treating diseases in the Black community must be embraced.

Using Complementary and Alternative Therapies

CAM products and treatment modalities are frequently used by Blacks to treat many of the diseases mentioned, though many patients are hesitant to inform their providers of the alternative therapies they are using. Most commonly used CAM and integrative therapies in the Black community are herbs and nutritional supplements. Remedies such as ginger tea to treat nausea, garlic to lower high blood pressure, herbal teas to soothe the nerves, chromium supplements to treat diabetes, antioxidants and vitamins to prevent heart disease, and special diets to treat HIV/AIDS all play an integral role in health promotion and disease prevention in the Black community. Equally important, the Black community's belief in the role of faith-based healing, through the healing powers of prayer, cannot be ignored and must be respected for its value and further researched.

It can be assumed, then, that if many of these unconventional therapies being used by patients, many of which are much less expensive than current pharmaceutical options, are showing evidence of preventing onset of diseases and reducing incidence rates and duration of illnesses, then we as a community must do all within our power to ensure that an infrastructure is created to support further understanding of their advantages. Appreciating the benefits of CAM and integrative medicine in the African American population and how it can be incorporated to eliminate health-care disparities will require the cooperation and collaborative efforts of many: politicians, academic and research institutions, churches, health-care providers, community-based organizations, international organizations, pharmaceutical companies, and the ultimate end users—patients.

Needed Actions

Several actions, some of which have already begun, need to take place in order for the benefits of CAM to be realized:

- Research studies that include Blacks of various ethnic groups, both as participants and as researchers, need to be conducted. This will allow us to learn about the different types of therapies being used, better understand how they work, quantify their therapeutic effects, and determine their safety.
- Current providers must be educated and trained about CAM theories and uses, and medical schools, nursing schools, and other health professional institutions must incorporate CAM principles into the curriculum. This has already begun to occur at several institutions, and the trend will undoubtedly continue.
- Providers must develop the ability to communicate with diverse populations and acquire the basic knowledge to understand culturally influenced health behaviors. This skill set, we know, positively impacts compliance and therefore can lead to improved health outcomes. Improved health outcomes are realized as providers can bridge cultural gaps between themselves, their patients, and their community.

• Global, national, and local collaborations and partnerships need to forged. This will further enhance our ability to obtain CAM facts that can improve access to quality care, compliance, health outcomes, and patient satisfaction and ultimately eliminate health disparities in the African American population.

POLICY, FUNDING, RESEARCH, AND COLLABORATIONS: WHERE DO WE GO FROM HERE?

The increased interest in, and use of, alternative and complementary medicine in the United States have garnered the attention of the White House, the National Institutes of Health, research scholars, and the general public. Despite this increased attention and general acceptance of alternative and complementary medicine, there is still a lack of insightful, detailed, and comprehensive analyses of African American alternative and complementary medicine. Using a medical anthropology approach, we not only can answer a number of sociocultural questions associated with African American alternative and complementary treatment therapies but can also give African American alternative and complementary medicine its proper attention, understanding, analysis, and inclusiveness in comparison to the other major ethnic and mainstream alternative medical systems in the United States.

Issues Need Addressing

In order for African American alternative medicine to become culturally perceived and culturally accepted on an equal status with mainstream alternative and medical systems, four major issues need to be addressed and implemented:

• First, there needs to be an acknowledgment by a major research institution or federal agency that African American alternative medicine exists and that it is a legitimate area of research investigation and training.
• Second, there need to be constructive conversation, discussion, and networking among research scholars and policy administrators on how to research this topic.
• Third, new funding mechanisms need to be developed at the national, regional, and local levels that support those who are interested in African American alternative medicine, particularly African Americans.
• Fourth, the federal government and major funding institutions must create and support on a long-term basis new research centers at historically Black colleges/universities or at institutions serving predominantly African Americans, in addition to community-based organizations with substantial minority researchers to ensure greater cultural acceptance and cultural connection to the wide variety of biopsychosociocultural factors that influence the use of alternative medicine in the African American community.

CONCLUSION

Culture and its relationship with alternative and complementary medicine are a key factor to appreciating this growing field of medical care and understanding its place within the African American community. The cultural acceptance of mainstream CAM approaches should also open up opportunities for the cultural acceptance of complementary and alternative medical practices in African American communities throughout the United States and the Caribbean.

By focusing more of our attention on the cultural aspect of alternative medicine, we can begin to answer a number of broad-based questions related to complementary and alternative medicine and African Americans:

• Why is mainstream society finally "culturally accepting" complementary and alternative medicine?
• How do you define concisely African American alternative medicine?

- How is complementary and alternative medicine in the African American population similar to, and/or different from, mainstream complementary and alternative medicine?

- What is the effect of complementary and alternative medicine on the health care-seeking pattern of African Americans?

- Can complementary and alternative medicine improve the health status of African Americans and reduce the health disparity between minority populations and majority populations?

- How can African American complementary and alternative medical practices become "culturally perceived and accepted" on an equal status with other mainstream alternative medical systems?

By answering these questions, we can begin to give complementary and alternative medicine in African American communities its proper attention, understanding, analysis, and inclusiveness in comparison to the other major ethnic and mainstream complementary and alternative systems in the United States.

COPYRIGHT ACKNOWLEDGMENT

The author and publisher gratefully acknowledge permission for use of the following material:
Excerpts from Eric J. Bailey. (2002). *African American Alternative Medicine: Using Alternative Medicine to Prevent and Control Chronic Diseases*. Westport, CT: Bergin & Garvey.

REFERENCES

American Diabetes Association. (August 8, 2001). *Press conference.*

Bailey, E. (2002). *African American alternative medicine: Using alternative medicine to prevent and control chronic diseases*. Westport, CT: Bergin & Garvey.

Bailey, E. (2000). *Medical anthropology and African American health*. Westport, CT: Bergin & Garvey.

Blendon, R., Aiken, L., Freeman, H., & Correy, C. (1989). Access to medical care for Black and White Americans: A matter of continuing concern. *Journal of the American Medical Association, 261*, 278–281.

Boyd, E., Taylor, S., Shimp, L., & Semler C. (2000). An assessment of home remedy use by African Americans. *Journal of the National Medical Association, 92*, 341–353.

Braithwaite, R., & Lythcott, N. (1989). Community empowerment as a strategy for health promotion for Black and other minority populations. *Journal of the American Medical Association, 26*, 272–283.

Campbell, M., Denmark-Wahnefried, M., Symons, M., Kalasbeek, W., Doods, J. Cowan, A., Jackson, B., Motsinger, B., Hoben, K. Lashley, J., Demissie, S., & McClelland, J. (1999). Fruit and vegetable consumption and prevention of cancer: The Black Churches United for better health project. *American Journal of Public Health, 89*, 1390–1396.

Collins, M. (1997, January–February). Increasing prostate cancer awareness in African American men. *Oncology Nursing Forum, 24*, 91–95.

Cushman, L., Wade, C., Factor-Litvak, P., Kronenberg, F., & Firester, L. (1999). Use of complementary and alternative medicine among African American and Hispanic women in New York City: A pilot study. *Journal of the American Medical Women's Association, 54*, 193–195.

Forte, D. (1995). Community-based breast cancer intervention program for older African American women in beauty salons. *Public Health Reports, 110*, 179–183.

George Washington Center for Integrative Medicine. (2002). Washington DC: Web site: www.integrativemedicinedc.com.

Healthy People 2010. (2000). *Understanding and improving health (2d ed.)*. Washington, DC: Department of Health & Human Services.

Keppel, K., Pearcy, J., & Wagener, D. (2002). Trends in racial and ethnic-specific rates for the health status indicators: United States, 1990–98. *Statistical Notes, Number 23*, 1–16.

Lee, M., Scarelett, S., Wrensch, M., Adler, S., & Eisenberg, D. (2000). Alternative therapies used by women with breast cancer in four ethnic populations. *Journal of the National Cancer Institute, 92*, 42–47.

Martin, J., & Panicucci, C. (1996). Health-related practices and priorities: The health behaviors and beliefs of community-living Black older women. *Journal of Gerontological Nursing, 22*, 41–48.

McGrady, A., & Horner, J. (1999). Complementary/alternative therapies in general medicine: Diabetes medicine. In J. Spencer & J. Jacobs (Eds.), *Complementary/Alternative medicine: An evidence based approach* (pp. 107–122). St. Louis: Mosby.

Morbidity and Mortality Weekly Report. (2001). *HIV-AIDS—United States, 1981–2000. Morbidity and Mortality Weekly Report, 50*, 430–433.

National Center for Complementary and Alternative Medicine (NCCAM). (2001). Major Domains of Complementary and Alternative Medicine (pp. 1–4). NCCAM Clearinghouse Pub. No. X-42 (December).

National Institute of Diabetes and Digestive and Kidney Disorders (NIDDK). (2001). *Medicines for people with diabetes.* NIDDK Web site: www.niddk.nih.gov

National Vital Statistics Reports. (2002). *Deaths: Leading causes for 2000.* Vol. 50, No. 16 (pp. 1–41). National Center for Health Statistics. Department of Health and Human Services.

Ryan, E., Pick, M., & Marceau, C. (2001). Use of alternative medicines in diabetes mellitus. *Annuals of Pharmacotherapy, 34 (7)*, 878–895.

Smedley, B.D., Stith, A.Y., & Nelson, A.R. (2002). Unequal Treatment: Confronting racial and ethnic disparities in health care: Confronting Racial and health disparities in health care. Committee on understanding and eliminating racial and ethnic disparities in health care. Institute of Medicine of the National Academies. Washington, DC: The National Academies Press.

Spencer, J., & Jacobs, J. (1999). *Complementary/alternative medicine: An evidence based approach.* St. Louis: Mosby.

U.S. Department of Health and Human Services. (2001, August 8). *Diet and exercise dramatically delay Type 2 diabetes.* News conference.

CHAPTER 36

Behind Bars: An Examination of Race and Health Disparities in Prison

VERNETTA D. YOUNG, REBECCA REVIERE, AND
YAW ACKAH

INTRODUCTION

To say that the correctional population in the United States has increased tremendously over the last few decades is an understatement. In 1980 there were just over one-half million (503,586) people in federal and state custody. Ten years later the number in federal and state prisons had evidenced an incredible 128 percent increase to 1,148,792 inmates. The next ten years saw an even larger proportionate increase in the correctional population (see Figure 36.1). By 2000 there were nearly two million people in custody, a 284 percent increase over the 1980 numbers (Bureau of Justice Statistics [BJS], 1997). Six months later, June 2001, there were 1,965,495 people in custody in federal and state prisons and local jails (Beck et al., 2002).

State institutions hold the largest proportion, 60 percent, of the total correctional population; jails hold 32 percent, and federal prisons, 7 percent of those incarcerated. Since 1990 there has been a 71 percent increase in the total number of prisoners in federal and state prisons and local jails. Although state prisons have continuously accounted for the largest number of prisoners in custody, the 73 percent increase in the state prison population over the last decade was much smaller than the increase in the federal prison population. In the last ten years the federal prison population has increased 139 percent; the jail population has increased 56 percent. The specific focus in this chapter is the health of inmates in state and federal prisons since individuals are in jail for a relatively short time. Overall changes in the demographics of the prison population, reasons for changes in incarceration rates, and health of these populations prior to imprisonment are presented first, followed with discussions of the health of, and health care for, women and men in prison and recommendations for the future.

CHANGES IN THE INCARCERATED POPULATION

Demographic Changes in the Prison Population

Gender. Males have historically accounted for the bulk of the correctional population. Unsurprisingly, at midyear 2001 they accounted for just over 93 percent of the total federal and state

Figure 36.1
U.S. correctional population

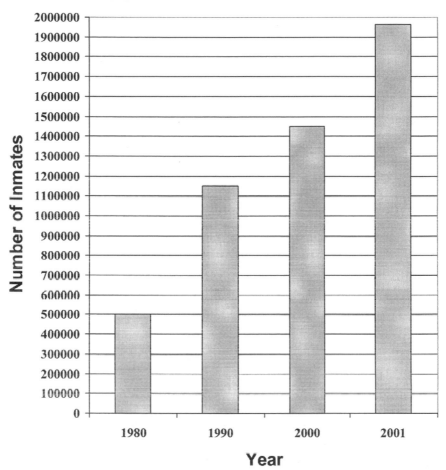

Sources: Correctional Populations in the United States (1980–1993); Beck et al. (2002).

prison population (1,311,195); females accounted for almost 7 percent of this population (94,336). However, the female inmate population has steadily increased from just over 4 percent of the total in 1985, to 5 percent in 1990, to almost 6 percent in 1995. Even though there continue to be more males in prison than females, the proportionate increases for females have been greater. Since 1990 there have been an 80 percent increase in the total number of male prisoners in federal and state correctional facilities and a 114 percent increase in the total number of female prisoners (Beck et al., 2002). Although males also accounted for a larger percentage of the local jail population (84 percent) than females (almost 12 percent), females make up a much larger percentage of the local jail population than of either the state or federal prison population.

   Race.   Minorities, especially African Americans, who account for an estimated 13 percent of the general population of the United States, are disproportionately represented in both federal and state correctional facilities. Langan (1991) noted that there was a steady increase in the proportion of Blacks entering prisons, from 22 percent in 1930 to almost one-half of the inmates admitted in 1996 (47 percent). At midyear 2001, Blacks accounted for almost 45 percent (872,900), Whites, 38

Table 36.1
Comparison of males by race for year 2000

RACE		
	WHITE	BLACK
Total Male Population 138,053,563	% White 75	% Black 12
Total Male Prison Population 1,237,469	% White 35	% Black 42
Number of Inmates per 100,000 Population 904	449	3457

Sources: Population figures from U.S. Census Bureau, Census 2000 Summary File 1. Prison population figures from Beck and Harrison (2001).

percent (752,500), and Hispanics, 15 percent (302,900) of the total federal and state prison and local jail population.

Gender and Race.   Interestingly, the proportions for males by race mirror the total distribution for all inmates, with Black males significantly outnumbering White males. Black males, who accounted for just 12 percent of the total male population, were incarcerated at a rate of 3,457 per 100,000 in 2000. Hence, Black males were 7.69 times as likely as White males (449 per 100,000) to be in prison (Beck & Harrison, 2001). The incarceration rate for Black males continued to increase, 3,535 per 100,000 in 2001 (Harrison & Beck, 2002) (Table 36.1).

Black (43 percent) and White (42 percent) females accounted for nearly equal proportions of the total female correctional population at midyear 2001, with Hispanic females accounting for 12 percent. Even so, there has been a significant change in the Black female prison population over the last two decades. Black females have experienced the largest increase of all groups. In 1980 there were 6,300 Black female prisoners. By 1990 the number of Black female prisoners had increased 219 percent to 20,100. Ten years later Black females, who make up roughly 13 percent of the total female population, made up 45 percent of the total female inmate population. Even more telling, Black females were incarcerated at a rate of 205 per 100,000 compared to a White female incarceration rate of of 34 per 100,000 (Beck & Harrison, 2001). This means that Black females were six times as likely as White females to be in prison. By midyear 2001 the number of Black females sentenced to correctional facilities had increased an incredible 1,003 percent to 69,500. The racial disparity is obvious (Table 36.2).

Age.   The age distribution of the correctional population has also changed over the last few decades. On the one hand, the number of inmates under age 18 held in state and federal prisons has declined. At year-end 1985 there were 2,300 persons under age 18 held in state prisons (Strom, 2000). This was about half of 1 percent of all state inmates. By June 2000 there were 3,915 state inmates under the age of 18; however, although the numbers had increased, the proportion has remained stable over the years. Furthermore, in 1990 there were 39 inmates under age 18 in federal prisons, but by 2000 there were no federal inmates in this age group (Beck et al., 2001). On the other hand, there has been a notable increase in the age of the prison population. In 1985 inmates between ages 35 and 44 accounted for 19 percent of all state prison inmates; those ages 45 to 54, 5 percent; and those ages 55 to 64, just under 2 percent. Recent statistics indicate that each of these age categories has increased significantly. There has been more than a 50 percent increase in the

Table 36.2
Comparison of females by race for year 2000

	RACE	
	WHITE	**BLACK**
Total Female Population 143,368,343	% White 75	% Black 13
Total Female Prison Population 83,668	% White 41	% Black 45
Number of Inmates per 100,000 Population 59	34	205

Sources: Population figures from U.S. Census Bureau, Census 2000 Summary File 1. Prison population figures from Beck and Harrison (2001).

number of inmates between 35 and 44, over 90 percent for those 45 to 54, and close to a 20 percent increase among the 55-to-64 age group.

Reasons for Disproportionate Incarceration of African Americans

Another major change in the correctional population is the type of offender admitted. Beatty et al. (2000) reported that over three-fourths of the increase in prison admissions from 1978 to 1996 resulted from the incarceration of drug offenders. The authors note, "The hammer of incarceration for drug offenses has by no means fallen equally across race or age categories, with young African American men suffering unprecedented rates of incarceration for drug offenses" (p. 3).

In the 1970s Blacks accounted for less than 25 percent of drug arrests in the United States. By the late 1980s this had increased to 42 percent (Provine, 1998). Between 1976 and 1980 the percentage increase in drug arrests for Whites was 70 percent compared to 450 percent for Blacks (Tonry, 1996). Currently, Black males incarcerated for drug offenses outnumber White males by a factor of between four and eight.

Consequently, the "literally incredible" explosion in the correctional population and the changing demographic profile of this population have been attributed to changes in sentencing policies at both the federal and state levels. The states began in the mid-1970s, when Maine adopted determinate sentencing, which required the setting of a specific sentence with no minimum and maximum term, and abolished its parole board. By 1985 all 50 states had moved toward determinate sentencing or sentencing guidelines. In 1984 Congress directed the U.S. Sentencing Commission to create sentencing guidelines and policies that would be "blind" to the offenders' race, sex, national origin, creed, and socioeconomic status and treat all offenders the same regardless of family, community, occupation, or education (Tonry, 1996). This resulted in mandatory sentencing that restricted parole and limited judicial discretion at the federal level. This new approach to sentencing included longer sentences for specific offenses and offenders, mandatory sentences for drug and weapons offenses, three-strike laws that imposed life sentences on repeat offenders, and more recently truth-in-sentencing laws that require offenders to serve at least 85 percent of their sentences. In addition, federal-level sentencing guidelines penalized the possession of crack cocaine, which is more likely to be used by African Americans (Steffensmeier & Demuth, 2000), more heavily than powdered cocaine in a 100:1 ratio.

Changes in the prison population mirror changes in the nation's population. The United States is becoming more racially and ethnically diverse; it is also becoming older. These demographic changes, coupled with sentencing policy changes, have contributed to a federal and state correctional population that is larger, older, more female, and importantly, Blacker than before. In this chapter the focus is on the health and health care of individuals incarcerated in state and federal prisons. The U.S. Department of Justice does not release statistics disaggregated by race, and most researchers follow suit; therefore, the discussion here primarily presents prisoners as a racially homogeneous group, rather than specifically representing the unique health profiles of African Americans in prison. However, because Black women and men are disproportionately represented in this population, their health and health care are of primary importance in any discussion of the health status of prison populations.

THE HEALTH OF INDIVIDUALS PRIOR TO INCARCERATION

As indicated above, the correctional population has changed demographically in the last few decades in terms of race, gender, and age. As in the general population, health profiles vary by demographic group. A brief overview of demographic differences in health in the general population follows to highlight the problems that may be present in the inmate population. If African Americans have poorer health in general, it follows that African Americans in prison will also have poorer health.

Health Disparities in the General Population

According to the Commonwealth Fund Health Care Quality Survey, 30 percent of African Americans between 18 and 64 were uninsured during 2001 compared with 20 percent of Whites; only 59 percent had job-based insurance compared with 70 percent of Whites; and 28 percent reported that they had no regular doctor compared with 19 percent of Whites (Collins et al., 2002). In addition, African Americans were more likely to report chronic diseases such as high blood pressure, heart disease, cancer, diabetes, asthma, anxiety/depression, and obesity than other adults (Collins et al., 2002). Further, African Americans have a higher incidence of, are more negatively affected by, and are more likely to die of end-stage renal disease and its related conditions (Cowie et al., 1994); they have more dialysis and transplant complications and greater problems relating to organ donation, compatibility, and availability (Livingston, 1993; Livingston & Ackah, 1992). Research indicates that minorities constitute 22 percent of all people with diabetes and that Black females are at a higher risk than their male counterparts (Pichert & Briscoe, 1997).

Blacks of all ages and all socioeconomic levels have more health problems than White Americans (Ferraro & Farmer, 1996). It was reported (SoRelle, 2000) that the racial gap is wider today than in 1950 for several leading causes of death, including heart disease, cancer, diabetes, and cirrhosis of the liver. The gap is smaller for the flu and pneumonia, and for homicide, while it remains unchanged for stroke and unintentional injuries.

Rich and Ro (2002) reported that there is an increased risk of death and disease for males, and this risk increases even further for African American males. They note that African American males have a higher prevalence of preventable diseases, as well as higher death rates from cardiovascular diseases, lung, colorectal, pancreatic, esophaseal, and stomach cancers, diabetes, and HIV/AIDS than other groups of men. In addition, Rich and Ro contend that posttraumatic stress, which occurs at a high level in urban communities, is a predisposing factor to drug use that in itself presents risk factors for other health problems such as hypertension, liver disease, cancer, violent injury, and HIV/AIDS, which disproportionately affect African Americans and other minorities. Scott and Mc-

Claughlyn (2001) reported that African American men have a much higher rate of prostate cancer than men in any other racial or ethnic group as well as a higher risk of fatality from stroke.

Heart disease is the number one killer of women followed by breast and colorectal cancer and stroke. Women as a group are also more likely to suffer from diabetes, osteoporosis, osteoarthritis, obesity, urinary incontinence, and Alzheimer's. Collins and Strumpf (2000) report that as age increases, the number of chronic conditions and disabilities also increases. Whereas 21 percent of women between 18 and 44 had at least one of the five chronic diseases of hypertension, diabetes, arthritis, heart disease, or cancer, 57 percent of the 45 to 64 and 80 percent of those over 65 had at least one of these serious diseases. The authors report that women over 65 receive less preventive care, and fewer breast exams, Pap tests, mammograms, hormone replacement therapy, and annual physical exams than their 45–64-year-old counterparts. However, they stress that lower income compounds the problems for poorer women, leading to higher rates of illness and greater problems getting needed care. HIV/AIDS is a leading cause of death for women between 25 and 44. Finally, there are significant differences by race, with minority women more likely than White women to suffer from cardiovascular diseases, diabetes, stroke, tuberculosis, hepatitis, and HIV/AIDS (Collins & Strumpf, 2000).

GENERAL HEALTH IN PRISON

Valid, reliable, and representative information on the health of state and federal prison inmates is not readily available. Many prisons lack comprehensive and accessible data on the health status of their inmates, and data on health conditions are usually self-reported by inmates or estimated from surveys of the health status of the noninstitutionalized civilian population (Maruschak & Beck, 2001). Data that are available from official sources are not disaggregated by race, although usually broken down by gender and age. The following discussion includes race-specific information when it is available. In the absence of hard race-specific health data in the prison population, it is logical to assume that the disproportionate incidence of morbidity and mortality in the general population is similarly reflected in the prison population.

According to the Bureau of Justice Statistics (Maruschak & Beck, 2001), 31 percent of state inmates and 23 percent of federal inmates reported having some physical impairment or mental condition, and 21 percent of state and 22 percent of federal inmates said they had a medical problem (excluding injury) after admission. Rates were higher for older and female inmates. An estimated 318,000 state and federal prisoners reported being injured since admission. Female inmates were more likely to be injured in an accident; male inmates, in a fight, and risks increased as time in prison increased. Further medical problems were more common among inmates who had been homeless or unemployed before their arrest.

The Bureau of Justice Statistics reported that there were 238,800 people with mental illnesses confined in U.S. jails and prisons in 1998 (Ditton, 1999), and in some states nearly 20 percent of inmates receive psychotropic medications (Beck & Maruschak, 2001). Ditton (1999) also reported that mentally ill prisoners were twice as likely as other inmates to have been homeless prior to incarceration, 40 percent were unemployed, and almost half were binge drinkers. In addition, estimates of the comorbidity rates of mental health disorders and substance abuse disorders range from 25 to 50 percent. Both groups are "considered hard to serve" and are "chronically underserved in most communities."

Counties are more likely to send mentally ill minority group members to prison rather than to state hospitals (Grekin et al., 1994). At the same time Black females and males in prison are less likely to receive mental health services (Steadman et al., 1991). Mental illness is clearly a particular problem for African Americans in prison.

Conklin et al. (2000) interviewed inmates about their preincarceration health status and behaviors. They found a high prevalence of chronic medical and mental health problems, high rates of infections and sexually transmitted diseases, and high rates of substance abuse. They reported that 53 percent of the newly admitted women inmates had mental health problems, 59 percent had drinking problems, and 39 percent had attempted suicide.

Race differences in prison health range from poorer oral health among Black prisoners (Mixson et al., 1990) to higher rates of circulatory system disease. This is the health backdrop for the older, Blacker, more female population that is now incarcerated. These are individuals who may have significant health problems upon entering prison and whose health-care needs have been ignored or given low priority because of a lack of medical insurance, family obligations, low socioeconomic status, and poor living conditions. It follows then that the largely African American population now entering prison likely has a host of medical problems and, in that sense, may be experiencing health problems more common among older individuals than among individuals their own age.

Because women are entering prison at an accelerated rate and because women and men have different health profiles, the health of incarcerated women and men is discussed separately.

THE HEALTH OF WOMEN IN PRISON

The rate of imprisonment for Black women is more than eight times the rate of imprisonment for White women (Amnesty International, 1999), and Black women typically have poorer health than White women. Further, women in prison have poorer physical and mental health than their counterparts outside prison. Consequently, African American women in prison are likely to be a fairly unhealthy group. Because the health-care system within prisons is largely based on a male model, these women have not only relatively poor health but also relatively poor health care. In this section, the discussion centers on the main health problems of women in prison and the resources available to meet these needs.

Physical Health Problems

Women enter prison with a multitude of physical health problems. They have higher morbidity and a higher number of medical encounters than male inmates (Acoca, 1998; Lindquist & Lindquist, 1999) and more health problems than their peers in the community. Most women who enter prison are poor; they have generally had poor health habits, a lack of quality health care, and exposure to traumatic events, including sexual and physical abuse.

The rates of chronic disease and conditions leading to chronic disease are high. For example, tuberculosis and hepatitis C are becoming increasingly common among female inmates. Obesity is a precondition for a number of health problems, and over half of incoming inmates in one study were overweight (Ingram-Fogel, 1991), particularly Black women. Health problems concentrated among African Americans such as diabetes, certain heart diseases, hypertension, and sickle-cell anemia are overrepresented in prisons.

Sexually transmitted diseases are particular problems facing women in prison. Estimates for HIV seroprevalence (the rate of positive test results) for women entering prison range from 2.7 percent to 14.7 percent, rates that are higher than for men (CDC, 1992; Dean-Gaitor & Fleming, 1999). Rates of other sexually transmitted diseases are also high; for example, according to the Centers for Disease Control and Prevention (CDC), female inmates have prevalence rates of 35 percent for syphilis, 27 percent for chlamydia, and 8 percent for gonorrhea (CDC, 1998). A survey by the California Department of Corrections revealed that 47.9 percent of the state's incoming female prison inmates were infected with hepatitis B, and 54.5 percent were infected with hepatitis C, and these rates are higher for rates for men with these diseases (Marble, 1996).

A larger than expected number report menstrual difficulties, headaches, back problems, fatigue, and abnormal Pap smears (Ingram-Fogel, 1991). Further, the likelihood of injuries reported since admission increased with length of time served in prison, with 60 percent of women who had served more than ten years reporting an injury due to an accident or a fight (Maruschak & Beck, 2001). As expected, more than half of women in prison report their physical health as being fair or poor (Brewer et al., 1998).

Substance Abuse

An increasing number of women are in prison for drug offenses (Lillis, 1994; Snell, 1994). Substance abuse straddles the dividing line between physical and mental health problems and signals a host of other physical and mental health problems. According to Henderson (1998), drug abuse is the primary reason women enter prison and the primary health problem of women in prison. The number of women who report regular drug use before incarceration has gone up over time (Acoca, 1998), as has the number with addictive disorders (Guyon et al., 1999). Survey data suggest that more than 80 percent of women inmates had used alcohol and/or other drugs regularly during their lifetimes and that 45 percent of women inmates (compared to 22 percent of men) required treatment for chronic substance abuse (Acoca, 1998).

Substance-abusing women differ from substance-abusing men and non-substance-abusing women who are in prison. For example, substance-abusing women have higher rates of liver disease and more physical health problems than men; they have higher rates of depression and eating disorders, lower self-esteem, and poor self-concepts; they have higher rates of past and present physical and sexual abuse; and they are more likely to be introduced to drug use by significant males in their lives but unlikely to receive support for recovery from these men (Kerr, 1998).

Langan and Pelissier (2001) examined 1,326 male and 318 female federal prisoners participating in a substance abuse treatment program. They reported that the women used drugs more frequently, used harder drugs, and used drugs for different reasons than the men. Moreover, the authors concluded that most substance abuse treatment programs in prisons were originally designed for male prisoners and may not address the special needs of female prisoners. Escalating rates of drug use and addictive disorders require specialized treatments and facilities, but at the same time that the numbers of women with these problems rise, inmate participation in treatment has declined from about 19 percent in 1991 to about 10 percent in 1997 (GAO, 1999).

Mental Health

It has been estimated that from 25 to 66 percent of all women in prison have some type of mental health problem, and African Americans have relatively high rates of mental health problems (Gupta, 1993). These rates are higher than for men in prison (Teplin, 1994) and for women in the community (Jordan et al., 1996; Lindquist & Lindquist, 1999). Besides substance abuse, common psychiatric problems are depression and personality disorders (Fazel & Denesh, 2002). Further, women who are substance abusers are likely to have a prior history of sexual and physical abuse and mental illness (GAO, 1999); they are separated from their children and their support systems as well as afraid of victimization, conditions that likely exacerbate existing problems (McCorkle, 1993). This population of women requires treatment that is sensitive to their conditions.

Issues of Motherhood

Women face a unique set of physical and mental health issues related to their childbearing and their children. According to the Bureau of Justice Statistics, the majority of women who are incarcerated have at least one child under age 18, and most of these lived with their children prior to being sent to prison (Mumola, 2000). In addition, it is estimated that 9 percent of these female inmates gave birth to their babies while incarcerated. Nearly half of all imprisoned parents were Black, and about a quarter were White (Mumola, 2000).

While roughly 90 percent of men report that the other parent is the current caregiver, only about 29 percent of women report the father as the current caregiver (Mumola, 2000). Mothers report that being separated from their children and the lack of involvement in their lives are the hardest things to bear about incarceration (Ingram-Fogel, 1993). This separation and the resultant stress and depression have serious implications for both the physical and mental health of these women.

Health Care for Women in Prison

The state of health care at women's prisons was the subject of a detailed report by Amnesty International (1999) on the medical ill treatment of female inmates in California, Florida, Virginia, and Washington, D.C. The American Civil Liberties Union of Washington state presented evidence of serious health-care deficiencies at the Washington Corrections Center for Women to the U.S. District Court in Tacoma. These challenges have called attention to a problem that had long been neglected.

Basic health-care services are offered to women in prison (Young & Reviere, 2001), although women generally describe their treatment as uncaring (Young, 2000). Substance abuse treatment was, until the late 1980s, "one program fits all," and issues specific to women's different psychological profiles were largely overlooked. More recently, programs designed for women have been more effective in helping women make positive lifestyle changes (Kerr, 1998). One success story in prison treatment seems to be in the introduction of hospice and palliative into American prisons. Developed in response to a sharp increase in inmate deaths, primarily from AIDS (Craig & Craig, 1999), these programs, when successful, integrate a multidisciplinary approach to the end-of-life treatment for inmates.

Because Black women are disproportionately represented in state and federal prisons, their unique health profiles should be an important consideration in planning and implementing health services. Black women have relatively high rates of chronic disease, mental health problems, and disabilities; further they have higher rates of specific disorders such as HIV, cervical and breast cancers, hypertension, diabetes, and sickle-cell anemia. Although most institutions do screen for these disorders, there are still some that fail to offer those services most important for Black women (Young & Reviere, 2001).

THE HEALTH OF MEN IN PRISON

Like women, men in prison have poorer health than their counterparts on the outside, and Black men have poorer health than White men. In addition, some health professionals contend that "men are left out in the cold" with regard to health screening and are less likely than women to seek medical advice or treatment (Trevelyan, 1989; Fareed, 1994). Consequently, many of their health needs before incarceration are neglected and receive attention only when the conditions become critical. The consequences of this neglect may be compounded for men in prison; roughly 21 percent of male state inmates reported medical problems, and 30 percent reported a physical impairment or mental condition (Maruschak & Beck, 2001).

Even though the health-care system within prisons is largely based on a male model, it is inadequate and not prepared to handle the range and severity of conditions presented by the exploding number of men in prison. Lindquist and Lindquist (1999) noted that the elevated levels of health conditions among inmates may be attributed to prior vulnerability, the institutional environment, and the impact of the interaction between these factors. Discussion of the main health problems of men in prison follows.

Physical Health Problems

The research literature on the health problems of incarcerated males is sparse. Forrest and Tambor (2000) compared a sample of 12- to 19-year-old incarcerated male youths with a sample of male adolescents in the community. They found that the incarcerated males had significantly poorer health in a number of areas; they evidenced more acute major disorders such as pneumonia, broken bones, and hepatitis and minor disorders such as tonsillitis, sprains, and colds.

At the other extreme, Fazel et al. (2001) reported that the most common illnesses among a sample of elderly male prisoners in English and Welsh prisons were cardiovascular, musculoskeletal, and respiratory. Over eight out of every ten prisoners in the sample had at least one chronic illness. Colsher et al. (1992) reported that the most common chronic illnesses of older male prisoners were arthritis, hypertension, ulcers, prostate problems, and myocardial infarction. The authors also reported increased rates of incontinence, sensory impairment, and flexibility impairment among the older inmates. A number of these health concerns mirror those for the general male population.

According to Maruschak (2001), in 1999 there were 22,581 male state and federal prison inmates known to be positive for the human immunodeficiency virus. They reported that while the number of male HIV-positive inmates has increased since 1995, the corresponding percentage of male HIV-positive inmates had remained relatively stable. Rates of HIV among African American males in prison are higher than for White males in prison (CDC, 1999). Villarino (2000) adds that the rate of active M. tuberculosis cases in correctional facilities is 50 times that of nonincarcerated individuals and that the factor that most increases the probability that the TB infection will progress is immune deficiency, such as HIV infection.

Another indication of the health problems of the incarcerated is the cause of death among inmates. Salive et al. (1990) examined death certificates for all male inmates in the Maryland state prisons between January 1979 and December 1987. They reported that for that time period, circulatory system disease was the leading cause of death, followed by suicide and homicide. However, in 1987 AIDS became the leading cause of death, and in 1981 drug overdose deaths peaked.

Lyons et al. (1994) looked at 2,313 inmate deaths in the New York state prisons from 1978 to 1992. They reported that over the study period accidental deaths, mainly from drug-related incidents and accidental injuries, increased as well as deaths from AIDS-related illnesses and natural causes. The increases in the latter were attributed to an increase in the drug offender and elderly inmate population.

Substance Abuse

Numerous reports chronicle the increase in the number of offenders incarcerated for drug possession and drug trafficking. As indicated earlier, Beatty et al. (2000) reported that since 1986 there has been monumental growth in the number of drug commitments to prisons. In 1986 there were 38,541 inmates admitted to prison on drug charges, but by the year 2000 this number had increased to 458,131. Beatty et al. (2000) note that this is "approximately the size of the entire U.S. prison and jail population of 1980." These inmates are also more likely than the general population to acquire chronic hepatitis C, which is spread primarily through sharing needles (Reindollar, 1999). Some estimate that as many as 30 percent of male prisoners have been infected with hepatitis C.

Another related concern is the presence of tuberculosis. Even though tuberculosis has long been present in prisons, the increase in drug abuse is leading to a corresponding increase in tuberculosis.

Maier (2002) presented the results of an investigative report on drug overdoses in state prisons. He reported that from 1990 to 2000 at least 188 men and women died of overdoses in state prisons and that the larger proportion of this total, 68 percent, overdosed between 1996 and 2000. Maier (2002) further reported that between 1998 and 2001 California, the state with the largest inmate population, reported 31 fatal overdoses followed by Maryland, with just over 20,000 reporting 15 fatal overdoses. Texas, with the second largest inmate population, had a reported 12 fatal overdoses.

Mental Health

American prisons and jails hold over a quarter of a million mentally ill inmates, with most housed in state prisons and local jails (Ditton, 1999). It is estimated that 9.6 percent of male state prisoners and 4.4 percent of male federal prisoners have some sort of mental condition (Maruschak & Beck, 2001). Among the males examined by Forrest and Tambor (2000), the incarcerated males had more psychosocial disorders, like speech problems, eating problems, and learning disability than the comparable community group. Fazel et al. (2001), in their study of elderly male inmates, found that one of the most common illnesses was psychiatric.

Health Care for Men in Prison

With the increased number of inmates who are suffering from mental health problems, institutions are faced with caring for those who are incapable of consenting to treatment. Failing and Sears (2001) reported that Pennsylvania correctional officials have been forced to consider alternatives. One approach has been to have inmates execute advance directives or living wills before they become incompetent. Another remedy is provided by Pennsylvania's guardianship law, the Incapacitated Persons Act. Under this approach the court appoints a "qualified individual" to provide consent for necessary treatment. Arizona, Colorado, Delaware, the District of Columbia, Indiana, Maryland, Missouri, Nevada, Ohio, Virginia, West Virginia, and Wyoming all treat individuals with mental health needs in separate housing units.

As indicated above, there has been an increase in the number of elderly inmates. According to the report, 16 of the 46 responding jurisdictions maintain separate housing for elderly inmates. In Ohio there is one small prison for males over 50 years of age, while Tennessee manages a geriatric unit at a boot camp (Corrections Compendium, 1997). In Oregon dormitory infirmary living quarters are provided with trained inmate assistants, whereas Rhode Island provides community acute care or long-term care hospitalization. Licensed hospice care and special care units are available in Colorado; Nebraska offers a boarding/nursing home-type living arrangement, chronic care clinics; Oklahoma offers single cells for elderly who may be open to exploitation; and Washington has 24-hour nursing staff and full-service infirmaries. Another approach, especially as it relates to elderly inmates, is the introduction of early release options (Corrections Compendium, 1997). For example, in Alaska inmates who are not physically able to repeat their crimes can be released early. In other states release may be dependent upon the type of crime committed, the degree of infirmity, the age of the offender, and the amount of time already served.

Another practice that aids in the control and maintenance of numerous health problems is diet. A number of institutions provide special diets for health purposes. These include therapeutic, diabetic, high-fiber, low-salt, low-fat, low-cholesterol, cardiac, liquid, and pureed (Corrections Compendium, 1997).

WHERE DO WE GO FROM HERE

Issues That Need Addressing

Correctional institutions have long been seen as reservoirs of physical and mental illness and of psychosocial problems, all of which flow back into the community as inmates are released. (Conklin et al., 2000, p. 1939)

Adequate Medical Care and Personnel.   The population housed in our correctional institutions is expanding. Prisons are providing health services to a diverse population, many of whom enter the institution deprived of the benefits of adequate health care. Not only is there a legal right, but there is also an ethical right to provide preventive treatment, medical care, and education to those in prison. As large numbers of African American women and men are incarcerated, improving health for those in prison could eventually have an impact on the wider Black community.

Inmates have a right to adequate medical care. This right was legally established in *Estelle v. Gamble* in 1976. The Supreme Court established that the test of cruel and unusual punishment in the area of adequate medical care turned upon whether there was evidence of *deliberate indifference* to serious medical need; in other words, an inmate should be provided with care that is comparable in quality and availability to that provided to the general public. Conklin et al. (2000) suggested the application of a public health approach to correctional health care to address this concern. Such an approach would include the early detection of diseases, early treatment of diseases, education and prevention, and steps to provide continuity of care once the individual has returned to the community.

McBride and Zahn (2000), in a three-part series on the Wisconsin prison system, identified a number of gaps still to be addressed. They reported that only one of three individuals diagnosed with asthma who entered the prison system survived. From 1994 to 2000 there were 146 inmate deaths in Wisconsin prisons. The largest proportion of these deaths were from cancer (25 percent), cardiovascular diseases (24 percent), suicide (14 percent), and AIDS (9 percent). However, prison health-care workers and prison security staff who provided the data contended that they were unable to give good medical care because they had little medical training, inadequate CPR instruction, and lack of information on inmate medical histories and were understaffed. The nurse-to-inmate ratio had gone from one nurse for every five inmates in 1992 to one nurse for every 140 inmates in 1999. In addition, the one doctor for every 1,143 inmates recommended by the National Commission on Correctional Health Care was exceeded by one doctor for every 2,484 inmates in Kettle Moraine Correctional Institution. McBride and Zahn (2000) also reported that a number of doctors and nurses hired by the Wisconsin State Department of Corrections had limits placed on their licenses to practice medicine or had their licenses suspended by the state Medical Examining Board. Clearly, one solution to poor health care in prison is the provision of adequate, well-qualified staff.

Charging for Medical Services.   Another issue facing prisoners is the increasing tendency in correctional institutions to charge inmates for medical services. In a recent study of prison authorities, 27 states reported charging for some forms of treatment (Corrections Compendium, 1998). Despite the low fee for service (usually between two dollars and five dollars), this may exacerbate health disparities that already exist; poorer Black inmates may be less likely to seek needed medical care as a result of the required payment.

Job Training.   Most women in prison eventually rejoin their children and their families, but job-training courses for women are still concentrated on homemaking or low-paid skills like beautician or launderer. Job-training for men in prison, on the other hand, often focuses on high-paying work such as welding and mechanics, but women have fewer opportunities (Gehring & Eggleston, 1996; Pollock, 1996). Job-training programs that provide skills and knowledge for a decent life after prison for inmates are a crucial part of improved health in a broad sense of the word for these individuals. Job skills may be even more important for African Americans coming out of prison as they are likely to have lower education levels than Whites coming out of prison.

SUMMARY

Recognizing the uniqueness and diversity of the correctional population with respect to race, gender, age, and prior health profile and addressing the myriad health concerns of these individuals will be a move toward improving the delivery of adequate medical care. African Americans are disproportionately imprisoned, and poor health and poor health care should not be added to the burden of incarceration. Problems of the prison system serve to maintain disparate health profiles of Blacks. Current staffing has not kept up with the explosion in the correctional population, nor has the provision of equipment and technology that would improve diagnosis and treatment. There are questions of space, training, and security and how these sometimes-conflicting concerns must mesh. A number of alternatives have been discussed before, but much more is needed to improve the health of African Americans in and ultimately out of prison. Most of those who enter prison eventually leave prison. It would serve those individuals, their families, and their communities to deliver them home with better health, better health education, and a commitment to maintaining their health and the health of their families. Health disparities can be reduced if prison officials, elected officials, and policymakers are willing to acknowledge and address the disproportionate burden of imprisonment on the African American community.

REFERENCES

Acoca, Leslie. (1998). Defusing the time bomb: Understanding and meeting the growing health care needs of incarcerated women in America. *Crime and Delinquency, 44(1)*, 49–70.

Amnesty International. (1999). Not part of my sentence: Violations of the human rights of women in custody. *United States of America, AI Index AMR.*

Beatty, P., Holman B., & Schiraldi, V. (2000). *Poor prescription: The costs of imprisoning drug offenders in the United States.* Washington, DC: Justice Policy Institute.

Beck, A., & Harrison, P. (2001). *Prisoners in 2000.* Washington, DC: Bureau of Justice Statistics, NCJ-188207.

Beck, A.J., Karberg, J., & Harrison, P. (2002). *Prison and jail inmates at midyear 2001.* Washington, DC: Bureau of Justice Statistics.

Beck, A.J., & Maruschak, L.M. (2001). Mental health treatment in state prisons, 2000. Bureau of Justice, *Special Report*, NCJ 188215.

Brewer, V., Marquart, J., Mullings, J., & Crouch, B. (1998). AIDS-related risk behavior among female prisoners with histories of mental impairment. *Prison Journal, 78(2)*, 101–119.

Bureau of Justice Statistics (BJS). (1997). Correctional populations in the United States, 1995. *U.S. Department of Justice*, NCJ-163916.

Center for Disease Control and Prevention (CDC) (1992). HIV prevention in the U.S. correctional system, 1991. *Journal of the American Medical Association. 268(1)*, 23.

Centers for Disease Control and Prevention (CDC). (1998). Assessment of sexually transmitted disease services in city and county jails—United States, 1997, *Morbidity and Mortality Weekly Report, 47(21)*, 429–431.

Centers for Disease Control and Prevention (CDC). (1999). AIDS rate in prison is six times national rate. *CDC News*, www.HIVdent.org/cdc.

Collins, K.S., & Strumpf, E. (2000). Living longer, staying well: Promoting good health for older women. *Commonwealth Fund.*

Collins, K.S., Tenney, K., & Hughes, D. (2002). Quality of health care for African Americans. *Findings from the Commonwealth Fund 2001 Health Care Quality Survey.*

Colsher P., Wallace, R., Loeffelholz, P., & Sales, M. (1992). Health status of older male prisoners: A comprehensive survey. *American Journal of Public Health, 82*, 881–884.

Conklin T., Lincoln T., & Tuthill, R. (2000). Self-reported health and prior health behaviors of newly admitted correctional inmates. *American Journal of Public Health, 90(12)*, 1939–1942.

Correctional Populations in the United States. (1980–1993). Bureau of Justice Statistics. U.S. Department of Justice.

Corrections Compendium. (November 1997). Inmate health care, Part II, *22(11)*.

Corrections Compendium. (October 1998). Inmate health care, Part I, *23(10)*.

Cowie, C., Port, F., Rust, K., & Harris, M. (1994). Differences in survival between Black and White patients with diabetic end-stage renal disease. *Diabetes Care, 17(7)*, 681–687.

Craig, E., & Craig, R. (1999). Prison hospice: An unlikely success. *American Journal of Hospice and Palliative Care, 16(6)*, 725–729.

Dean-Gaitor, H.D., & Fleming, P.L. (1999). Epidemiology of AIDS in incarcerated persons in the United States, 1994–1996. *AIDS, 13(17)*, 2429–2435.

Ditton, P.M. (1999). Mental health and treatment of inmates and probationers. Bureau of Justice Statistics. *Special Report, U.S. Department of Justice.*

Estelle V. Gamble, 97 S. Ct. 285 (1976).

Failing, L., & Sears, R. (2001). Medical treatment and mentally incompetent inmates. *Corrections Today, 63(4)*, 106–120.

Fareed, A. (1994). Equal rights for men. *Nursing Times, 90(5)*, 26–29.

Fazel, S., & Danesh, J. (2002). Serious mental disorder in 23,000 prisoners: A systematic review of 62 surveys. *Lancet 359(9306)*, 545–550.

Fazel, S., Hope T., O'Donnell, I., Piper, M., & Jacoby, R. (2001). Health of elderly male prisoners: Worse than the general population, worse than younger prisoners. *Age and Ageing, 30(5)*, 403–407.

Ferraro, K.F., & Farmer, M. (1996). Double jeopardy to health hypothesis for African Americans: Analysis and critique. *Journal of Health and Social Behavior, 37*, 27–43.

Forrest, C., & Tambor, E. (2000). The health profile of incarcerated male youths. *Pediatrics, 105(1)*, 286–292.

Gehring, T., & Eggleston, C. (1996). Vocational programs. In M. McShane & F. Willaims (Eds.), *Encyclopedia of American Prisons* (pp. 479–482). New York: Garland.

General Accounting Office (GAO). (1999). *Women in prison: Issues and challenges confronting U.S. correctional systems*. GAO/GGD-00-02, Washington, DC.

Grekin, P.M., Jemlka, R., & Trupin, E.W. (1994). Racial differences in the criminalization of the mentally ill. *Bulletin of the American Academy of Psychiatry and the Law, 22(3)*, 411–420.

Gupta, G. (1993). *The sociology of mental health*. Boston: Allyn-Bacon.

Guyon L., Brochu S., Parent I., & Desjardins, L. (1999). At-risk behaviors with regard to HIV and addiction among women in prison. *Women and Health, 29*, 49–66.

Harrison, Paige, & Beck, Allen. (2002). Prisoners in 2001. *Bureau of Justice Statistics Bulletin*, NCJ 195189.

Henderson, D.J. (1998). Drug abuse and incarcerated women. A research review. *Journal of Substance Abuse Treatment, 15*, 579–587.

Ingram-Fogel, C. (1991). Health problems and needs of incarcerated women. *Journal of Prison & Jail Health, 10*, 43–57.

Ingram-Fogel, C. (1993). Hard time: The stressful nature of incarceration for women. *Issues in Mental Health Nursing, 14*, 367–377.

Jones, C. (1992). Recent trends in corrections and prisoners' rights law. In C. Hartjen & E. Rhine (Eds.), *Correctional Theory and Practice* (pp. 119–138) Chicago: Nelson Hall.

Jordan, B.K., Schlenger, W.E., Fairbank, J.A., & Caddell, J.M. (1996). Prevalence of psychiatric disorders among incarcerated women. II. Convicted felons entering prison. *Archives of General Psychiatry, 53*, 513–519.

Kerr, D. (1998). Substance abuse among female offenders. *Corrections Today, 60(7)*, 114–119.

Langan, N., & Pelissier, B. (2001). Gender differences among prisoners in drug treatment. *Journal of Substance Abuse, 13(3)*, 291–301.

Langan, P. (1991). *Race of prisoners admitted to state and federal institutions 1966–1986*. Washington, DC: Bureau of Justice Statistics.

Lillis, J. (1994). Survey summary: Programs and services for female inmate. 1926–1986. Washington, DC: Bureau of Justice Statistics. *Corrections Compendium, 19*, 6–7.

Lindquist, C., & Lindquist, C. (1999). Health behind bars: Utilization and evaluation of medical care among jail inmates. *Journal of Community Health, 24(4)*, 285–303.

Livingston, I.L. (1993). Renal disease and Black Americans: Selected issues. *Social Science and Medicine, 37(5)*, 613–621.

Livingston, I.L., & Ackah, S. (1992). Hypertension, end-stage renal disease and rehabilitation: A look at Black Americans. *The Western Journal of Black Studies 16(2)*, 103–112.

Lyons, J., Greifinger R., & Flannery, T. (1994). Deaths of New York state inmates, 1978–1992. *New York State Department of Correctional Services.*

Maier, T. (2002, May 6). On dope row. *Insight on the News-National.*

Marble, M. (1996). Half of California's female prison inmates infected with hepatitis B. *Women's Health Weekly, 6.*

Maruschak, L.M. (2001). HIV in prisons and jails, 1999. *Bureau of Justice Statistics Bulletin*, NCJ 187456.

Maruschak, L.M., & Beck, A.J. (2001). Medical problem of inmates, 1997. Bureau of Justice Statistics, *Special Report*, NCJ-181644.

McBride, J., & Zahn, M. (2000). Wisconsin's death penalty. *JSOnline; Milwaukee Journal Sentinel.*

McCorkle, R. (1993). Fear of victimization and symptoms of psychopathology among prison inmates. *Journal of Offender Rehabilitation, 19*, 27–41.

Mixson, J.M., Eplee, H.C., Feil, P.H., Jones, J.J., & Rico, M. (1990). Oral health status of a federal prison population. *Journal of Public Health Dentistry, 50(4)*, 257–261.

Mumola, C. (2000). Incarcerated parents and their children. *Bureau of Justice Statistics Special Report*, NCJ-182335.

Pichert, J.W., & Briscoe, J. (1997). A questionnaire for assessing barriers to health care utilization: Part 1. *The Diabetes Educator, 23(2)*, 81–191.

Pollock, J. (1996). Women Inmates: Current Issues. In M. McShane & F. Williams (Eds.), *Encyclopedia of American Prisons* (pp. 501–508). New York: Garland.

Provine, Doris Marie. (1998). Too many Black men: The sentencing judge's dilemma. *Law and Social Inquiry, 23(4)*, 823–856.

Reindollar, R. (1999). HIV, inmates and corrections professionals. *American Jails*, 21–24.

Rich, J., & Ro, M. (2002). A poor man's plight: Uncovering the disparity in men's health. *A Series of Community Voices Publications.*

Salive, M., Smith G., & Brewer, T. (1990). Death in prison: Changing mortality patterns among male prisoners in Maryland, 1979–1987. *American Journal of Public Health, 80(12)*, 1479–1480.

Scott, B., & McClaughlyn, K. (2001). Men's health: Why you need to act now! *Closing the Gap. A Newsletter of the Office of Minority Health.* U.S. Department of Health and Human Services.

Snell, T. (1994). *Prison: Survey of State prison inmates, 1992. Special Report.* Washington, DC: Department of Justice: Bureau of Justice Statistics.

SoRelle, R. (2000). Gap between death rates for blacks and whites remains as large as in 1950. Circulation 101: e9026. http://circ.ahajournals.org/cgi/content/full/101/12/e9026. Accessed February 4, 2004.

Steadman, H.J., Holohean, E.J., & Dvoskin, J. (1991). Estimating mental health needs and service utilization among prison inmates. *Bulletin of the American Academy of Psychiatry and the Law, 19(3)*, 297–307.

Steffensmeier, D., & Demuth, S. (2000). Ethnicity and sentencing outcomes in U.S. federal courts: Who is punished more harshly? *American Sociological Review, 65*, 705–729.

Strom, K. (2000). Profile of state prisoners under age 18, 1985–97. *Bureau of Justice Statistics Bulletin.* NCJ 176989.

Teplin, L. (1994). Psychiatric and substance abuse disorders among male urban jail detainees. *American Journal of Public Health, 84(2)*, 290–294.

Tonry, Michael. (1996). *Sentencing matters.* New York: Oxford University Press.

Trevelyan, J. (1989). Well men. *Nursing Times, 85(12)*, 46–47.

Villarino, E. (2000). Screening and prevention of tuberculosis in correctional facilities. *HEEP (HIV Education Prison Project) News, 3(3)*, 1–4.

Young, D.S. (2000). Women's perceptions of health care in prison. *Health Care for Women International, 21(3)*, 219–234.

Young, V.D., & Reviere, R. (2001). Meeting the health care needs of the new female prisoner. *Journal of Offender Rehabilitation, 34(2)*, 31–48.

CHAPTER 37

Environmental Racism: Its Causes and Solutions

SHEILA A. FOSTER

INTRODUCTION

Minority, low-income populations disproportionately suffer from an array of environmental and health risks—including exposure to polluting facilities, congested roadways, lead paint, pesticides, and contaminated land (Cole & Foster, 2001). Increasing recognition is being given to these deplorable and at-risk conditions and African Americans are getting increasingly concerned about these living environments (Mohai, 2003; Bullard, 2002). Low-income populations are more likely than others to face severe hazards on the job, in the home, in the air they breathe, in the water they drink, and in the food they eat. Such risks are often accompanied by a lack of environmental amenities in their communities—including access to open space, parks, clean water, and waterfront resources (Swanson, 1999). The inequitable distribution of environmental hazards and environmental amenities has been appropriately termed "environmental racism."

This chapter describes the evidence, causes, and possible solutions to environmental racism. Although researchers continue to study the distribution of a variety of environmental hazards, most of the national studies, to date, have focused on racial disparities in the location of hazardous and toxic waste facilities. The focus on hazardous waste facilities, while not intended to diminish the importance of other environmental hazard exposures, is important because these facilities can pose great risks to human health and the environment and are the subject of much environmental activism in communities of color. However, regardless of the type of environmental hazard exposure, on a fundamental level, the issues are the same: determining the social and political forces that contribute to environmental injustice and creating policy reforms that address our most vulnerable communities.

In attempting to address the complex issues surrounding environmental racism, the chapter covers three main topical areas: (1) the unequal distribution of environmental hazards; (2) the complex web of causation: the role of race and space; and (3) the role of legal decisions and decision makers.

UNEQUAL DISTRIBUTION OF ENVIRONMENTAL HAZARDS

Since the 1960s, researchers have analyzed the distribution of numerous environmental hazards: garbage dumps, air pollution, lead poisoning, toxic waste production and disposal, pesticide poisoning, noise pollution, occupational hazards and rat bites (Cole & Foster, 2001; New York University School of Law, Environmental Law Center, 2002). Their overwhelming conclusion is that environmental hazards are inequitably distributed by income and/or race. In studies that looked at distribution by income *and* race, race was most often found to be the better predictor of exposure to environmental dangers (Mohai & Bryant, 1992). As discussed below, later studies have, in large part, confirmed these conclusions. The following sections illustrate some of the inequities in the United States regarding exposures to environmental hazards.

Evidence of Racial Disparities in Environmental Hazard Exposure

Toxic Waste Sites.   The United Church of Christ's Commission for Racial Justice (CRJ) authored the seminal study documenting the disproportionate distribution of toxic waste sites on a national level. The 1987 study, *Toxic Waste and Race in the United States*, measured the demographic patterns associated with commercial hazardous waste facilities and uncontrolled toxic sites (CRJ, 1987). The study found that race proved to be the most significant variable in determining the location of commercial hazardous waste facilities. Communities with the greatest number of commercial hazardous waste facilities had the highest percentage of non-White residents. The CRJ's study of *uncontrolled* waste sites produced similar findings. Three out of every five African American and Latino residents lived in communities with uncontrolled toxic waste sites. Furthermore, African Americans were heavily overrepresented in the populations of metropolitan areas with the largest number of such sites. These areas included Memphis, Tennessee (173 sites), St. Louis (160 sites), Houston (152 sites), Cleveland (106 sites), Chicago (103 sites), and Atlanta, Georgia (91 sites).

More recent national studies, with a handful of exceptions, continue to document the persistence of racial disparities in the location of waste facilities, some with varying results by ethnic group. For example, in 1994, the United Church of Christ's CRJ updated its 1987 study. This most recent study, based on an assessment of 530 commercial hazardous waste sites, found even greater racial disparities in the demographics of people living around such facilities. In particular, it found that from 1980 to 1993 the concentration of people of color (defined as the total population less non-Hispanic Whites) in all zip codes with a toxic waste site increased from 25 percent to 31 percent. Similarly, in 1993, as in 1980, the percentage of people of color in a community increases as commercial hazardous waste management activity increases (Goldman & Fitton, 1994).

Various researchers have sought to challenge the methodology and conclusions behind the CRJ studies. One of the most prominent challenges came from researchers at the Social and Demographic Research Institute (SADRI) of the University of Massachusetts, who challenged the findings of the earlier 1987 CRJ study (Anderson et al., 1994; Anderton et al., 1994; Anderton & Anderson, 1994). The SADRI researchers concluded that there is *not* a statistically significant pattern of racial or ethnic disparity in the distribution of commercial hazardous waste sites. Many factors explain the difference in outcomes between the CRJ and SADRI studies. First, SADRI researchers employed a significantly different methodology. The SADRI study used census tracts from 1980 and 1990, as opposed to zip codes, as the geographic unit of analysis. This may explain the difference in findings from the 1987 CRJ study, given that census tracts are smaller on average and tend to undercount "high pockets" of minority populations (U.S. Environmental Protection Agency, 1997). The SADRI researchers also used data from only metropolitan or rural counties, not from the entire United States, as their comparison group (nonhost tracts), possibly understating the relationship between race, ethnicity, and siting choices.

Notably, the most recent national study by Been and Gupta (1997) supports the conclusions of both the 1987 and 1994 CRJ studies, though using census tract data as in the SADRI study (Been & Gupta, 1997). These authors set out to analyze how the demographics of neighborhoods hosting toxic waste facilities changed over time. To do this, she used census data from the past three decades (1970, 1980, and 1990). Unlike the SADRI study, Been compared the demographics of host tracts to those of *all* nonhost tracts, versus the limited pool of nonhost tracts in the SADRI study. Been's study found that toxic waste sites are disproportionately located near African American and Hispanic populations. In particular, Been's analysis demonstrates that the percentage of African Americans or Hispanics in a census tract in 1990 is a significant predictor of whether or not that tract hosts a toxic waste facility. See Table 37.1 for treatment, storage, and disposal facilities (TSDF) in relation to census tract information.

Outdoor Pollutants.   In addition to exposure to toxic waste facilities, researchers have demonstrated other striking disparities in environmental hazard exposure. Minorities and low-income populations are disproportionately exposed to outdoor air pollution, especially fine particulate matter and the other pollutants regulated by the Clean Air Act (such as Nox, SO2, and lead) (Gelobter, 1989, 1992). See Table 37.2. African American and Native American populations have been shown to eat more fish laden with toxins than other populations (West, 1992; West et al., 1992).

Pesticides.   People of color reside in communities that disproportionately host pesticide production facilities or disposal sites and are more likely to be employed in occupations (such as migrant farmwork) that further expose them to dangerous pesticides (Perfecto, 1991; Perfecto & Velasquez, 1992). Similar studies document that minority and low-income workers are far more likely than the rest of the population to work in jobs with higher and more frequent exposure to toxic chemicals (Friedman-Jimenez, 1989).

Lead Poisoning.   African American children also have a greater risk of elevated blood lead levels than White children, for all income levels, and the disparity is greater for Black children who live in families with incomes below the poverty line (CDC Update, 1997). The effect of these existing inequalities on the health of impacted populations is further compounded by the fact that poor people of color also have the least access to health care and often cannot get it at all (U.S. GAO, 1992; Butts, 1992). See Table 37.3.

Taken together, the national studies conducted, to date, provide significant evidence that people of color bear a disproportionate burden of environmental hazards, particularly toxic waste sites in their neighborhoods. Numerous local studies, with some exceptions, have similarly concluded that racial disparities exist in the location of toxic waste facilities, based upon their assessment of particular cities, counties, or regions (Cole & Foster, 2001). No doubt, however, the scope and depth of the current research begs for further investigation of the relationship between race, class, and exposure to a variety of environmental hazards beyond toxic waste sites. Though researchers will continue to study the distribution of environmental hazards, including toxic waste sites, there is ample evidence that warrants concern for the health effects of these exposures on impacted communities and a closer look at the factors that might lead to the outcomes thus far documented.

THE COMPLEX WEB OF CAUSATION: THE ROLE OF RACE AND SPACE

Most statistical studies charting the disproportionate distribution of a variety of environmental hazards establish correlations, not causation. The question has thus arisen: what social, economic, and political forces have given rise to the unequal distribution of environmental hazards? The very terminology—environmental racism—that characterizes the problem suggests some degree of intentional discrimination on the part of polluters and policymakers. Indeed, the way in which "racism" has been conceptualized in society and in the law invites the demand for evidence of a "single bad actor"—an identifiable entity responsible for bringing about such exposure disparities (Foster, 1993). However, there is often no "smoking gun"—for instance, intentional targeting of communities of

Table 37.1

Proportions of certain racial and ethnic and lower-socioeconomic populations in census tracts surrounding waste treatment, storage, and disposal facilities (TSDF) compared with the proportions of these groups in other census tracts, 1994

Location of TSDFs	Demographic Breakdowns		
	African Americans	Hispanics	Persons Living Below the Poverty Line
	Percent		
Census tracts with either TSDFs or at least 50 percent of their area within 2.5 miles of a tract with TSDF	24.7	10.7	19.0
Census tracts without TSDFs	13.6	7.3	13.1

Source: Institute of Medicine (1999), *Toward Environmental Justice—Research, Education, and Health Policy Needs*. Washington, DC: National Academy Press.

Table 37.2

Proportions of African American, Hispanic, and White populations living in air-quality nonattainment areas, 1992

Pollutant	Demographic Breakdowns		
	African Americans	Hispanics	Whites
	Percent Living in Air-Quality Nonattainment Areas		
Particulates	16.5	34.0	14.7
Carbon monoxide	46.0	57.1	33.6
Ozone	62.2	71.2	52.5
Sulfur dioxide	12.1	5.7	7.0
Lead	9.2	18.5	6.0

Source: Institute of Medicine (1999), *Toward Environmental Justice—Research, Education, and Health Policy Needs*. Washington, DC: National Academy Press, Table 2-2, p. 15.

Note: Nonattainment areas refer to those areas that do not meet the National Ambient Air Quality Standards for various pollutants.

Table 37.3
Blood levels in children by race, ethnicity, and other selected factors

Children Aged 1 to 6 Years, 1991–94	Children With Blood Lead Levels Greater Than or Equal to 10 µg/dL			
	Residing in All Housing	Residing in Housing Built		
		Before 1946*	1946 to 1973*	After 1973*
	Percent			
TOTAL	4.4	8.6	4.6	1.6
Race and ethnicity				
American Indian or Alaska Native	DSU	DSU	DSU	DSU
Asian or Pacific Islander	DSU	DSU	DSU	DSU
Asian	DNC	DNC	DNC	DNC
Native Hawaiian and other Pacific Islander	DNC	DNC	DNC	DNC
Black or African American	11.5	22.7	13.2	3.3
White	2.6	6.6	1.9	1.4
Hispanic or Latino	DSU	DSU	DSU	DSU
Mexican American	4.0	13.0	2.3	1.6
Not Hispanic or Latino	4.2	DNA	DNA	DNA
Black or African American	11.2	21.9	13.7	3.4
White	2.3	5.6	1.4	1.5
Gender				
Female	3.3	7.1	2.8	1.5
Male	5.5	9.6	6.6	1.7
Family income level†				
Low	1.9	4.1	2.0	0.4
High	1.0	0.9	2.7	0
Geographic location				
Population ≥ 1 million	5.4	11.5	5.8	0.8
Population < 1 million	3.3	5.8	3.1	2.5

Source: U.S. Department of Health and Human Services (November 2000).

DNA=data have not been analyzed; DNC=Data are not collected; DSU=Data are statistically unreliable;
*Data for "all houses" are from a separate analysis on NHANES data; data for specific periods of time provided for information purposes
†Income categories defined using poverty-income ratio (PIR) (the ratio of total family income to the poverty threshold for the year). Low = PIR LE 1.300; middle = PIR 1.301–3.500; high = GE 3.501.

color by waste companies—that explains the phenomenon of environmental injustice. Instead, the disproportionate exposure of minorities to various environmental hazards results from a complex web of factors that can't be reduced to a simple causal explanation.

The Complexity of the Problem

The disproportionate accumulation of environmental hazards in low-income communities of color is attributable to a dynamic interaction of historical, social, political, and legal forces. Indeed, "environmental racism" is best viewed as a manifestation of larger structural inequalities in our society that produce other forms of social injustice, such as lack of adequate health care, jobs, and housing in low-income and minority communities. Given these structural inequalities, it is not surprising that low-income people of color are concentrated in the most dangerous sectors of our workforce, and in metropolitan areas that are exposed to some of the worst forms of pollution.

Residential Segregation.   One of the main contributing factors to environmental exposure disparities is the social location of low-income communities of color. Spatial segregation and isolation are key features of racial inequality in our society. This spatial inequality creates a vicious, self-perpetuating circle of causation, resulting in uniquely disadvantaged communities. In a 1992 report, the Environmental Protection Agency's Environmental Equity Workgroup concluded that racially disparate environmental hazard exposure results largely from the fact that "a large proportion of racial minorities reside in metropolitan areas," which attract toxic waste sites and are characterized by elevated exposure to various environmental hazards like air pollution and lead (U.S. EPA, 1992). The fact that many low-income people of color are relegated to polluted urban areas is not surprising given that their residential choices are limited by poverty and various forms of discrimination (Bullard, 2002).

Indeed, the inequitable distribution of environmental hazards in metropolitan urban areas has not come about by happenstance but can be historically traced to the patterns of residential segregation and its resulting structural inequalities. The influence of well-documented housing discrimination has shaped the demographics of urban and other disproportionately exposed communities. Scholars Douglas Massey and Nancy Denton have traced the historical roots of residential segregation to its nineteenth-century origins (Massey & Denton, 1993). They argue that over the course of several decades in the late nineteenth and early twentieth centuries, residential segregation was constructed and imposed through various public and private processes—discriminatory real estate practices, exclusionary and expulsive zoning, redlining, and White flight, among others—which both contained growing urban Black populations and limited the mobility of Blacks and other people of color. As Massey and Denton also document, the systematic segregation and isolation of racial groups continue to this day as a result of exclusionary real estate practices, racial and cultural bias, and pervasive discrimination. Empirical evidence, they show, demonstrates that real estate agents often limit the likelihood of Black entry into White neighborhoods through a series of exclusionary tactics and channel Black demand for housing into areas that are within or near existing ghettos. This discrimination by realtors is further enforced by the allocation of mortgages and home improvement loans, which systematically channel money away from integrated areas. In essence, race remains the "dominant organizing principle" for housing and residential patterns in spite of the Fair Housing Act and other civil rights reforms (Massey & Denton, 1993).

Such racial discrimination in the sale and rental of housing, as other scholars have recognized, "relegates people of color (especially African-Americans) to the least desirable neighborhoods, regardless of their income level" (Been, 1994, p. 1389). Inevitably, when a neighborhood becomes predominantly composed of people of color, once again racial discrimination in the promulgation and enforcement of zoning and environmental protection laws, the provision of municipal services, and the lending practices of banks often cause neighborhood quality to decline further, inducing those who can leave the neighborhood—the least poor and those least subject to discrimination—to do so (Been, 1994).

Applied to the problem of toxic waste facilities, Regina Austin and Michael Schill have demonstrated how, given the combination of poverty and racially discriminatory practices, there might be a number of scenarios involving some of these historical and social forces that would result in poor people of color either moving to, or being trapped in, neighborhoods with a disproportionate number of hazardous waste sites (Austin & Schill, 1991). For instance, in one scenario, communities where poor people of color now live may have originally been the homes of Whites who "worked in the facilities that generate toxic emissions." In those communities, Austin and Schill explain, the housing and industry may have "sprung up roughly simultaneously" and Whites may have "vacated the housing (but not necessarily the jobs) for better shelter as their socioeconomic status improved." In turn, poorer Latinos and African Americans "who enjoy much less residential mobility" may have taken their place. In another scenario, housing for African Americans and Latinos may have been built in the vicinity of existing industrial operations because "the land was cheap and the people were poor." In still another scenario, increasingly common these days, sources of toxic pollution may have been placed in existing minority communities (Austin & Schill, 1991, pp. 69–70).

Redlining and Discriminatory Real Estate Zoning.   In addition to discriminatory real estate and lending practices and "White flight," a variety of apparently neutral rules and decisions add to the creation and maintenance of racially identified and environmentally subordinate neighborhoods. For instance, Massachusetts Institute of Technology (MIT) economist Yale Rabin has demonstrated that, in communities across the country, many residential neighborhoods composed of people of color have been rezoned by White planning boards as industrial, a process Rabin calls "explosive zoning" (Rabin, 1990). While these zoning decisions were not made with reference to race, their impact, given racial segregation, has had profound racial implications. As Rabin explains, "[b]ecause it appears that [the rezoned] areas were mainly Black, and because whites who may have been similarly displaced were not subject to racially determined limitations in seeking alternative housing, the adverse impacts of explosive zoning on Blacks were far more severe and included, in addition to accelerated blight, increases in overcrowding and racial segregation" (pp. 101–102). These zoning practices permitted the intrusion of disruptive, incompatible uses and generally undermined the character, quality, and stability of Black residential areas. That is, "explosive zoning" permanently alters the character of a neighborhood, often depressing property values and causing community blight.

The Siting Process for Toxic Facilities.   This deterioration, in turn, allows heavy industry to locate in African American residential neighborhoods and also leads banks to stop loaning money for home improvement and maintenance because of improper zoning and residential blight. Because the proposed location of a hazardous facility, particularly near a White upper-socioeconomic neighborhood, often faces strong public opposition, there is a limited supply of land on which to site such facilities. Inevitably, private industry (and often public entities) focuses on industrial or rural communities, many of which are predominantly populated by people of color. Because land values are lower in heavily industrial and rural communities than in White suburbs, these areas are attractive to industries seeking to reduce the cost of doing business (Bernstein, 1991; Gerrard, 1994).

As one report has documented, waste facility developers affirmatively select sites in heavy industrial (urban) areas that have little or no commercial activity (Cerrell Associates, 1984). Furthermore, these communities are presumed to pose little threat of political resistance due to their subordinate socioeconomic and often racial status. Conventional industry wisdom also counsels private companies to target sites that are in neighborhoods "least likely to express opposition"—poorly educated and lower-socioeconomic neighborhoods. Since poor and minority communities often do not have the resources or government and industry contacts to initiate or sustain proactive political action found in more affluent communities, toxic facilities and other environmental hazards end up in their communities.

Sociologist Robert Bullard documented the way in which this underlying racial (and class) discrimination can operate to taint an otherwise facially "neutral" siting process. Bullard's documentation was recognized in a 1997 decision by the Nuclear Regulatory Commission's Atomic Safety and Licensing Board, which overturned a facility's permit. In an administrative appeal to block the siting of a uranium enrichment facility in a poor and African American area of Louisiana, Professor Bullard successfully argued that racism more than likely played a significant part in the selection process. Bullard demonstrated (through a statistical analysis) that at each progressively narrower stage of the company's site selection process, the level of poverty and African Americans in the local population rose dramatically until it culminated in the selection of a site with a local population that is extremely poor and 97 percent African American. The race-neutral siting criteria—including the criteria of low population and the need to site the facility five miles from institutions such as schools, hospitals, and nursing homes—operated in conjunction with the current racial segregation and the resulting inferior infrastructure (lack of adequate schools, road paving, water supply, etc.) in a manner that ensured that the final selection would be a poor community of color (NRC, 1997). Although a later administrative body reinstated the permit, Bullard's analysis illustrates the complex interaction of historical, social, and economic factors in producing environmental racism.

THE ROLE OF LEGAL DECISIONS AND DECISION MAKERS

Ultimately, it may be the "success" of environmental pollution control laws that is responsible for persistent racial disparities in environmental hazard distribution (Cole, 1992). Although environmental laws promise uniform protection from known environmental hazards, a host of regulatory tools and practices interact with structural inequalities to create distributional inequities in environmental protection. That is, although pollution control laws do not *produce* the structural inequalities discussed above (such as discriminatory housing, zoning, real estate practices, and lack of political power) they are, at worst, heavily dependent upon those inequalities and, at best, consciously blind to them.

The Narrow Focus of Pollution Control Laws

The distribution of environmental hazards is a result of a particular decision-making norm underlying pollution control laws. This norm, technocratic utilitarianism, aspires to produce the greatest good (environmental quality and health) for the largest number of people. It does so through the widespread use of scientific and technical decision-making techniques—that is, quantitative measurements of environmental risks and impacts—that distill environmental values to a common metric and that direct decision making to those options that minimize aggregated costs and maximize aggregated benefits (Foster, 2002). This model of technocratic utilitarianism and the complex methodology associated with quantifying and measuring the recognized variables presume that environmental and pollution control decision making "is a technical task and that our goals and objectives can be met through the application of experts' specialized tools" (Duane, 1997). Even with extensive public participation requirements embedded in environmental (and most administrative) processes, decision makers maintain substantial deference to the technocratic model by using public input to "check the math" rather than to question the structure of the underlying equations.

An Example of Legal Myopia.   In the context of siting hazardous waste (and other polluting) facilities, the technocratic model myopically focuses decision makers toward compliance with uniform environmental standards without regard to the distributional impacts of those standards. Although state siting regulations vary, some common themes illustrate the influence of this norm on the inequitable distribution of toxic waste facilities. The siting process begins with the prospective waste facility developer choosing an appropriate site and applying for a permit from the state environmental agency. The agency evaluates the application, then approves or rejects the permit application according to whether or not the applicant has met all the legal criteria for receiving a permit.

In assessing the suitability of a proposed waste facility site, such agencies rely primarily on technical criteria in assessing the facility. These agencies, in determining a proposed facility's suitability for a community, rarely look beyond the geological and environmental characteristics of the particular proposed site. Each permit is considered in a vacuum, requiring only that the individual facility at issue comply with applicable technical standards—such as compliance with uniform air pollution emission standards for a particular pollutant.

Agency officials generally do not consider the cumulative impact of preexisting facilities or land uses with the proposed facility, the potential for disproportionate location of facilities in the host community, or the demographics of the targeted community. Agency review tends to quantify the risks posed by one chemical or one polluting source and decide what an acceptable level of exposure is (based on uniform emissions limitations for that pollutant) without considering already existing exposures to other chemicals and/or nonsite pollution sources. Instead, most agencies would argue that current permitting laws do not allow them to look beyond these technical criteria. This is true. Permitting laws generally do not specify criteria allowing for a formal assessment of the demographics, health problems, quality of life and infrastructure of the surrounding community, or the cumulative and synergistic environmental or health effects of other facilities in the area.

Underestimating the Social and Health Costs Imposed on Minority Populations

The chemical synergy between multiple sources is likely to produce significant health impacts on our most vulnerable populations. Failure to take these cumulative and synergistic risks into account results in significantly underestimated harm suffered by low-income, minority communities. Moreover, there are often no formal criteria that take into account the siting processes' reliance on structural inequalities by waste facility developers—such as cheap land values, appropriate zoning, low population densities, and proximity to transportation routes—that steers such facilities into communities of color because of the interaction with historical and contemporary discrimination. This very myopia, however, allows permitting laws to perpetuate, and indeed exacerbate, distributional inequalities.

Reliance upon such myopic and technical decision-making techniques allows environmental decision makers to argue that difficult social and political questions are being resolved "scientifically." However, this model fails to account for distributional impacts and, instead, focuses on converting costs, benefits, and risks into a common metric so that they can be compared, traded off, and aggregated by analysts. As a result, current environmental laws are reliant upon uniform regulatory standards that impose social and economic costs on certain populations that may either be unnecessary, excessive, or disproportionate in relation to the benefits obtained by those populations. Although considering net benefits (or risks) in isolation of their *distribution* may satisfy the standard of efficiency, separating consideration of costs and benefits from their distribution surely violates most notions of equity and justice.

CONCLUSIONS AND RECOMMENDATIONS

Widening the Lens of Environmental Decision Making

Environmental laws have undergone, and are continuing to undergo, significant transformation to address their limited scope, particularly regarding the distribution of hazards by race and/or income.

However, these changes have proven to constitute only a few steps on a longer road to the type of policy and legal reform that will effectively address the problem of environmental racism.

The Impact of President Clinton's Executive Order

The problem of environmental racism or injustice in the United States has received increasing attention from policymakers and environmental decision makers. Most notably, Executive Order 12898, issued by President Clinton in 1994, was "promulgated to require federal agencies to make environmental equity part of their missions" with particular emphasis on environmental disparities received by minority populations and low-income populations (Executive Order, 1994). This order mandates, among other things, that each federal agency "identify and address" the "disproportionately high and adverse human health or environmental effects" of its programs, policies, and activities on people of color and on low-income communities. More recently, Environmental Protection Agency (EPA) administrator Christine Whitman, in a memo to top agency officials in 2001, reiterated the federal government's commitment to environmental justice, which she defines as the "fair treatment of people of all races, cultures, and incomes with respect to the development, implementation and enforcement of all environmental laws and policies and their meaningful involvement in the decision-making processes of the government" (U.S. EPA Press Release, 2001).

The executive order has transformed federal agencies and beyond, and it has affected laws and policies across a broad spectrum of environmental concerns. In some cases the impact was sudden and unexpected. The Nuclear Regulatory Commission, for example, cited the executive order as the basis for its denial of a permit for a uranium-enrichment facility in rural Lousiana, the first permit ever denied in NRC's history, because of the significant questions raised over the racial fairness of the siting of the plant in an African American community (NRC, 1997). Elsewhere, the transformation has been slower and deeper. However, nowhere has the policy transformation been more evident than at the Environmental Protection Agency itself, which has undergone a profound shift in perspective over the past decade (Gauna, 2001). The EPA has followed the dictates of the executive order by giving its regulators the discretionary authority under federal environmental statutes (e.g. the Clean Air Act, the Clean Water Act, the Resource Conservation and Recovery Act). With such authority, regulators can now determine whether a pollution permit proposed for a minority or low-income community will have a discriminatory impact, in part, by assessing whether the community has already been exposed to a disproportionate number of polluting facilities (as well as other adverse environmental exposures) and to take steps to either mitigate harmful exposures from the proposed facilities or to deny the permit altogether (Foster, 2000).

The EPA has also issued guidelines for communities of color wishing to file an administrative action pursuant to Title VI of the Civil Rights Law of 1964 to challenge state permit decisions that will have an adverse, disparate impact on their communities (U.S. EPA, 2000). As part of her commitment to keep environmental justice issues a "top priority," Whitman has promised to resolve the backlog of pending civil rights complaints under Title VI. These complaints charge state and local agencies with unjustly allowing new polluting land uses to be built in already-polluted minority neighborhoods (Kriz, 2001).

Limitations of Existing Reforms

Nevertheless, the executive order is limited in its scope and reach and, thus, ultimately, has failed to alter the structure of environmental decision making that has given rise to distributional inequities. The executive order does not change the substantive requirements and limitations for issuance of pollution permits under any of the federal environmental statutes. Rather, it simply grants permitting agencies the authority to implement its recommendations within the narrow confines of existing statutory and regulatory regimes. As previously discussed, much of our environmental regulatory regime is grounded in a technocratic model of decision making that excludes consideration of distributional and equity issues. It is thus no surprise that virtually every challenge to regulators' issuance of a pollution permit in an environmentally overburdened minority community on distributional grounds has failed (the decision of the NRC, referenced above, stands out as one of the few exceptions). This failure reveals a stark contrast between the increasing seriousness with which environmental justice challenges are treated at federal agencies (partly due to the favorable policies mentioned above) and the overwhelmingly negative outcomes of these challenges. In other words, while most regulators acknowledge environmental racism and the existence of distributional inequities on the basis of race (and often class), these regulators continue to allow polluting facilities in these overburdened communities (albeit sometimes with risk-reducing modifications to the permitted facility) (Foster, 2000).

Ultimately, environmental decision-making processes must undergo a fundamental restructuring to accommodate calls for equity and justice. This restructuring should involve the incorporation of a fuller impact of risk assessment for all environmental decisions, including meaningful participation by the risk-bearing communities and serious incorporation of distributional considerations in all environmental decisions.

Assessing Communities at Risk

Many federal and state agencies have resisted analyzing cumulative or synergistic risks and have interpreted their regulatory mandates quite narrowly to justify the failure to take such risks into account. Fortunately, there has been some movement, particularly at the EPA, to reflect concerns about cumulative risks in decisions about how much exposure to hazardous substances and facilities a particular community should bear (U.S. EPA, 1997–2). Environmental decision makers at all levels of government should continue to incorporate cumulative risk assessments in all of their decisions. Although less regulatory attention has been paid to synergistic environmental risks, regulators increasingly have good data available to them from scientific studies documenting the potent impacts of chemical combinations and synergies. As the science gets better and more voluminous, decision makers should take advantage of this knowledge to better understand the health and environmental impacts of populations exposed to a number of individual, technically "safe" polluting sources.

Beyond quantitative measurements of risk, environmental decision makers should take seriously the risk-bearing community's assessment of the environmental risks that they live with. Most decisions about exposure to additional environmental hazards do not reduce themselves to concrete, technical measurements and probabilities, particularly given the immense scientific uncertainty about synergistic interactions among various pollutants and sources of pollution. Therefore, it is important that regulators and other environmental decision makers receive and incorporate exposure and health information from risk-bearing, impacted communities. That is, "meaningful" participation of the public should become a standard feature of decisions about exposure to environmental risks.

It has proven exceedingly difficult to accommodate public input into processes emphasizing autonomous, technical decision making. Even though environmental decisions follow a tightly structured and open public process, consistent with most administrative agency processes, in practice, this requirement is frequently manipulated into "announce and defend" decision making in which meaningful outside input is effectively stillborn. Centralized bureaucrats, while promising meaningful participation, too often make decisions without full information about their true costs and benefits on the risk-bearing public. Even when good information from local impacted communities is requested and received, the regulatory and bureaucratic maze through which such information must pass to make a difference creates disincentives for gathering such information in the first place. "Meaningful" public (or community) participation requires an explicit recognition of the practical limitations of technical risk analysis and incorporation of multidimensional risk assessments and measurements, particularly those of the risk-bearing public. Meaningful participation of affected communities would assist in putting the technocratic decision-making model and its tools in their proper place and allow a fuller analysis of environmental impacts, one that affords a greater role to distributional and equity concerns.

Incorporating Equity and Distributional Justice in All Decision Making

Finally, the norms that govern our pollution control laws and policies must give way to greater concern for distributional fairness. Policymakers and regulators have not shied away from pushing along significant regulatory reforms to achieve "efficiency," most prominently in the form of market-based initiatives (e.g., emissions trading), which promise greater aggregate pollution reduction at lower costs (Gauna, 2001). The equitable distribution of the benefits and burdens of environmental protection must similarly become central to the implementation of existing laws and to proposed legal reforms. This means that regulators must explicitly take into account our prevailing social structure—for example, residential segregation, lack of access to health care, discriminatory land use processes, cumulative environmental exposures and health risks—and the ways in which that structure interacts with environmental norms to produce unequal environmental protection. When regulators are able to explicitly consider these structural realities, particularly as they affect vulnerable populations, only then will they be able to control and/or influence the distribution of hazardous facilities and land uses.

REFERENCES

Anderson, A.B., et al. (1994, July). Environmental equity: Evaluating TSDF siting over the past two decades. *Waste Age*, 83.

Anderton, D.L., et al. (1994). Environmental equity: The demographics of dumping. *Demography, 31*, 229.

Anderton, D.L., & Anderson, A.B. (1994). Environmental equity: Hazardous waste facilities: "Environmental equity" issues in metropolitan areas. *Evaluation Review, 18*, 123.

Austin, R., & Schill, M. (1991). Black, brown, poor & poisoned: Minority grassroots environmentalism and the quest for eco-justice. *Kansas Journal of Law & Public Policy, 1*, 69.

Been, V. (1994). Locally undesirable land uses in minority neighborhoods: Disproportionate siting or market dynamics. *Yale Law Review, 103*, 1383.

Been, V., & Gupta, F. (1997). Coming to the nuisance or going to the barrios? A longitudinal analysis of environmental justice claims. *Ecology Law Quarterly, 24*, 1.

Bernstein, J. (1991). The siting of commercial waste facilities: An evolution of community land use decisions. *Kansas Journal of Law & Public Policy, 1*, 83.

Bullard, R.D. (2000). Poverty, pollution and environmental racism: Strategies for building healthy and sustainable communities. Discussion paper prepared for the National Black Environmental Justice Network (NBEJN) Environmental Racism Forum World Summit on Sustainable Development (WSSD) Global Forum. Johannesburg, South Africa, July 2nd.

Butts, C.Q. (1992). The color of money: Barriers to access to private health care facilities for African-Americans. *Clearinghouse Rev. 26, 159, 160 n.5*, 161–62.

Centers for Disesase Control and Prevention (CDC), Update. (1997). Blood lead levels in the United States, 1991–1994. *Morbidity and Mortality Weekly Report, 46*, 143.

Cerrell Associates. (1984). *Political Difficulties Facing Waste-to-Energy Conversion Plant Siting, 29*, 43.

Cole, L. (1992). Empowerment as the means to environmental protection: The need for environmental poverty law. *Ecology Law Quarterly, 19*, 643.

Cole, L.W., & Foster, S.R. (2001). *From the ground up: Environmental racism and the rise of the environmental justice movement.* New York: New York University Press.

Commission for Racial Justice (CRJ), United Church of Christ. (1987). *Toxic wastes and race in the United States: A national report on the racial and socioeconomic characteristics of communities with hazardous waste sites.* New York: United Church of Christ.

Duane, T.P. (1997). Community participation in ecosystem management. *Ecology Law Quarterly, 24,* 772.

Executive Order No. 12, 898, 3 C.F.R. 389. (1994). *Federal actions to address environmental justice in minority populations and low-income populations.* Reprinted in 42 U.S.C. § 4321.

Foster, S.R. (1993). Race(ial) matters: The quest for environmental justice. *Ecology Law Quarterly, 20,* 739–741.

Foster, S.R. (2000). Meeting the environmental justice challenge: Evolving norms in environmental decision-making. *Environmental Law Reporter News and Analysis, 30,* 10992.

Foster, S.R. (2002). Environmental justice in an era of devolved collaboration. *Harvard Environmental Law Review, 26,* 2, 459.

Friedman-Jiménez, G. (1989). Occupational disease among minority workers: A common and preventable occupational health problem. *American Association of Occupational Health Nurses Journal, 37,* 64.

Gauna, E. (2001). EPA at 30: Fairness in environmental protection. *Environmental Law Reporter, 31;* 10,528.

Gelobter, M. (1989). The distribution of air pollution by income and race. Unpublished M.A. thesis, University of California at Berkeley, Energy and Resources Group.

Gelobter, M. (1992). Toward a model of environmental discrimination. In P. Mohai & B. Bryant (Eds.), *Race and the incidence of environmental hazards: A time for discourse* (pp. 64–81). Boulder, CO: Westview Press.

Gerrard, M.B. (1994). *Whose backyard, whose risk: Fear and fairness in toxic and nuclear waste siting.* Cambridge, MA: The MIT Press.

Goldman, B.A., & Fitton, L. (1994). *Toxic waste and race revisited: An update of the 1987 report on the racial and socioeconomic characteristics of communities with hazardous waste sites.* Center for Policy Alternatives, NAACP, United Church of Christ Commission for Racial Justice.

Kriz, M. (2001). Coloring justice green. *National Law Journal, 33,* 2419.

Massey, D.S., & Denton, N.A. (1993). *American apartheid: Segregation and the making of the underclass.* 1–16, 17–60, 83–114, 96–109. Cambridge, Massachusetts: Harvard University Press.

Mohai, P. (2003). Dispelling old myths: African American concerns for the environment. *Environment, 45(5),* 11–26.

Mohai, P., & Bryant, B. (1992). Environmental racism: Reviewing the evidence. In P. Mohai & B. Bryant (Eds.), *Race and the incidence of environmental hazards: A time for discourse* (pp. 163–176). Boulder, CO: Westview Press.

New York University School of Law, Environmental Law Center. (2002). *Reference table of environmental disparity studies.* Retrieved June 12, 2002, from http://www.nyu.edu/pages/elc/ej/studies.html.

Nuclear Regulatory Commission (NRC) Atomic Safety and Licensing Board. (1997, May 1). *In the matter of Louisiana energy services, L.P.,* 1997, LBP-97-8, 45 NRC 367, 390–392.

Nuclear Regulatory Commission (NRC). (1998, April 3). *In the matter of Louisiana energy services,* CLI-98-3.

Perfecto, I. (1991). Hazardous waste and pesticides: An international tragedy. In Mohai & Bryant (Eds.), *Environmental racism: Issues and dilemmas* (pp. 36–39). Ann Arbor: University of Michigan office of Minority Affairs.

Perfecto, I., & Velasquez, B. (1992, March/April). Farm workers: Among the least protected. *EPA Journal,* March/April, 13–14.

Rabin, Y. (1989). Expulsive zoning: The inequitable legacy of euclid. In C.M. Haar & J.S. Kayden (Eds.), *Zoning and the American Dream* (pp. 101–121). Chicago: Planners Press.

Swanson, S.F. (1999). Environmental justice and environmental quality benefits: The oldest, most pernicious struggle and hope for burdened communities. *Vt. L. Rev., 23,* 545.

U.S. Department of Health and Human Services. (2000, November). Healthy people 2010. 2d ed., vol. 1, *Objectives for improving health.* Washington, DC: U.S. Government Printing Office.

U.S. Environmental Protection Agency (EPA), Press Release. (2001). *Administrator Whitman reaffirms com-*

mitment to environmental justice. Retrieved August 21, 2002, from http://www.epa.gov/swerosps/ej/
html-doc/pr082101.htm.

U.S. Environmental Protection Agency (EPA). (2000). *Draft Revised Guidance for Investigating Title VI Administrative Complaints Challenging Permits, 65 Fed. Reg. 39649.* Retrieved Date from http://www.epa.gov/ocrpage1/docs/frn_t6_pub06272000.txt.

U.S. Environmental Protection Agency (EPA). (1992). Environmental equity: reducing risk for all communities, workgroup report to the administrator 1. *Environmental Equity Workgroup, EPA 230-R-92-008.*

U.S. Environmental Protection Agency (EPA). (1997). Interim final guidance for incorporating environmental justice concerns. *In EPAS NEPA Compliance Analysis, 2.1.1, 2.1.2, 3.2.1.*

U.S. Environmental Protection Agency (EPA). (1997–2). *Guidance on cumulative risk assessment part I planning and scoping.* Retrieved 12/2/02, from http://www.epa.gov/brownfields/html_doc/cumrisk2.htm.

U.S. General Accounting Office (GAO). (1992). Hispanic access to health care: Significant gaps exist 10. *GAO/PEMD-92-6.*

West, P.C. (1992). Invitation to poison? Detroit minorities and toxic fish consumption from the Detroit river. In Mohai & Bryant (Eds.), *Race and the incidence of environmental hazards: A time for discourse* (pp. 96–99). Boulder, Colorado: Westview Press.

West, P.C., et al. (1992). Minority anglers and toxic fish consumption: Evidence from a statewide survey of Michigan. In P. Mohai & B. Bryant (Eds.), *Race and the incidence of environmental hazards: A time for discourse* (pp. 100–113). Boulder, Colorado: Westview Press.

CHAPTER 38

Outreach to African American Communities: From Theory to Practice

BRIAN K. GIBBS AND
DEBORAH PROTHROW-STITH

BACKGROUND

There are many and varied indicators of poor health outcomes among minorities in America, with disparities measured in almost every disease category or outcome. Black infant mortality remains more than twice that of White infant mortality: 14 per 1,000 births versus 6 per 1,000 live births, respectively (NCHS, 2002). Life expectancy for Black men is 67.6 years—seven years less than that for White men (Braithwaite & Taylor, 2001). "Although a lack of health care coverage affects millions of Americans, ethnic and racial minorities are at greater risk of being uninsured" (Taylor & Braithwaite, 2001, p. 64).

While many factors affect the health of African Americans, this chapter argues that the greatest promise for the elimination of health disparities at the present time rests on our ability to change multiple and interrelated behaviors that have been shown to contribute to health disparities in minority populations. To date, research and intervention strategies designed to reduce the disparities in health outcomes have not translated into impressive results. The limited effectiveness of previous efforts may be due, at least in part, to the paucity of understanding of provider biases that influence the patient–provider interactions and the lack of tested interventions tailored to fit the needs of physicians and health-care organizations.

The intent of this chapter is to describe an inclusive, comprehensive, and multitiered model of intervention aimed at ultimately eliminating racial and ethnic disparities in health. The model is based on lessons learned from past efforts that, while not necessarily focusing on health, have been effective in improving health status and outcomes of disadvantaged groups. The model, called community transformation, emphasizes partnership and sustainability and focuses on building an effective, mutually beneficial working relationship between researchers and providers, community-based organizations, and the residents of the communities that are suffering from poor health outcomes.

Main Causes of Disparities

Jones (2001) has postulated three main causes for disparities in health status between minorities and nonminorities. In this chapter, we consider those three causes as well as three additional causes that highlight the historical experience of African Americans:

1. At the level of disease occurrence (with differentials attributable to differences in exposures to hazards, differences in resources for daily living, and the impact of racism on health, including its role in causing differences in socioeconomic status by "race").

2. At the level of access to health service. Barriers include distance, money, language, prejudice, time, and legal barriers.

3. At the level of treatment within the health-care system. Barriers include patient disrespect (as subtle as not giving the patient the full range of treatment options and as blatant as sterilization abuse), poor communication within the patient–provider encounter, differing resources depending on the site of care, differing levels of physician training with regard to protocol care, subtle biases with regard to treatment recommendations, and subtle biases with regard to assessing whether a patient will find a given treatment acceptable or will be able to afford a given treatment (Jones, 2001).

4. Health status of slaves. "The net effect of the tremendous mortality present in Africa before the slave trade, combined with the huge death toll secondary to the trade itself along with the Middle Passage, means that a 'slave health deficit' actually began with the Atlantic slave trade even before Blacks' arrival in the North American English colonies. . . . When not cast as lower animals, they were still not considered equals of the same caliber, or worthy of the same consideration, as their regular White European patients" (Byrd & Clayton, 2000, p. 184y).

5. Historical "second-class citizenship." Blacks were initially introduced into the health system as chattel, agricultural and commercial property such as cattle, pigs, and later as second-class citizens, without the benefit of adequate medical treatment (Byrd & Clayton, 2000).

6. Compromised commitment to wellness. This is not included to "blame the victim" but to acknowledge the impact of internalized racism on self-worth, self-advocacy, and entitlement to at least adequate services (Jones, 2000).

To our knowledge, there are no programs that look at health disparities on these six levels of causation simultaneously.

THE IMPORTANCE OF OUTREACH PROGRAMS AND ACTIVITIES IN REDUCING HEALTH DISPARITIES

The elimination of racial/ethnic disparities in health status and health care, major goals of *Healthy People 2010*, poses great challenges to the nation as a whole and to states in particular. The U.S. Department of Health and Human Services (USDHHS) has identified a set of leading health indicators that are being tracked to assess ongoing efforts at the federal, state, and local levels (Gibbs et al., 2002). Certain subsets of the population experience wide disparities in access to health services, outcomes of health care, and higher relative risk of poor health than the population as a whole. At the same time, demographic shifts are occurring in the United States that will result in these populations becoming the majority within the twenty-first century (Parangimalil, 2001).

Addressing factors that endanger the health of African Americans demands strategies such as public and provider education, prevention, research, policy, and environmental changes that facilitate healthy living. To be effective, however, "communities must be involved as partners in the design, implementation, and evaluation of interventions. The best intervention results have been achieved when people who benefit from interventions work closely with researchers and public health practitioners. This phenomenon emphasizes the fact that those in the health community have 'messages,' while individuals in target communities have 'lives.' A partnership between these two groups offers the best chance to bridge the divide" (Smedley & Syme, 2000, pp. 5–6).

The Role of Community-Based Organizations

An example of the role community-based organizations can play involves the Mattapan Community Health Center (MCHC) in Boston. In 1997, in response to high age-adjusted mortality rates, the MCHC began its Health Care Revival initiative to empower a Black community to engage in a dialogue about its health. A steering committee composed of community health advocates, academic and health department representatives, church leaders, and community leaders (including business owners) worked in tandem with the health center. The objective was to plan and implement this annual Health Care Revival meeting at which screening activities and the dissemination of health information are integrated with inspirational singing and Scripture readings. Results from participant evaluations showed a steady increase in the use of health center services, improved health outcomes, and an increase in the number of health improvement projects. As a result of these outcomes, this community-led initiative has successfully inspired and empowered a community to improve its health (Lawson & Young, 2002).

The Focus of the Chapter

This chapter (1) describes the theory and methods upon which the community transformation model is built, including the themes, obstacles, and strategies found in social transformation models that have preceded and influenced this model, (2) discusses community coalition building and the community transformation model itself, and (3) presents a working example of the community transformation model in the context of the Program to Eliminate Health Disparities, the field test being conducted at the Harvard School of Public Health's Division of Public Health Practice.

At the heart of health disparities is the fact that the United States is a racially divided nation where extreme racial inequalities continue to persist. Andrew Hacker's 1992 book *Two Nations: Black and White, Separate, Hostile, Unequal* documents the persistent disparities and is as stark in its contrasts as William Julius Wilson's more recent publication, *When Work Disappears*. Because racial segregation continues to be the dominant residential pattern, people of color are clustered in urban ghettos, barrios, reservations, and rural poverty areas. This pattern is created by de facto boundaries and restrictions set by a dominant White society. Racism creates and perpetuates separate and unequal communities where people of color live apart from Whites (Hacker, 1992; Wilson, 1996; Katz, 1989).

PEHD: THEORY AND METHODS

The Program to Eliminate Health Disparities (PEHD), housed in the Division of Public Health Practice at the Harvard School of Public Health, is designed to generate social transformation directed toward meeting human needs and enhancing quality of life, including economic equality, health care, shelter, human rights, and participation in democracy. A central principle of the program stresses equal access to adequate health care, affordable shelter, safe workplaces, and clean air and water. The failure to satisfy such basic needs is not the result of accident, but of institutional decisions, marketing practices, discrimination, and a quest for economic growth as the ultimate and only good.

In keeping with current literature, an array of socioeconomic factors impacts the health of subpopulations within the United States. Accordingly, our research into successful models and examples of social and economic transformation extends far beyond traditional public health. We take a multisector approach to examine the ways in which socioeconomic conditions have been uplifted. In identifying these models and examples, we extract tools and methods that can be used to produce an unconventional public health model for individual and social transformation that can be described, measured, and replicated for research purposes.

Specifically, the PEHD is creating a *Community Transformation Model (CTM)* to stimulate individual and community transformation and, thus, to increase health parity within the United States. The CTM draws upon several social movement experiences to develop tools and methods, including the Civil Rights Movement and the Environmental Justice Movement, using cultural activism as a key strategy.

SOCIAL TRANSFORMATION MODELS

"Since the first black landing in the United States in 1619, there has been a continual effort for justice in North America for people of African descent" (Bullard et al., 2001). The importance of social movements in generating "social problems" has received considerable attention from sociologists, and some have argued that the two are analytically inseparable. Our inventory of social transformation models is ongoing and represents the theoretical basis for our action. To date, we have discovered several models, both outside of, and within, public health, that serve as the foundation for our current work and the CTM. A few of these models are briefly described below.

Civil Rights Movement and Health Reform

The two-volume book by Drs. Michael Byrd and Linda Clayton, *An American Health Dilemma, Volume 1, A Medical History of African Americans and the Problem of Race: Beginnings to 1900* and *An American Health Dilemma, Volume 2, Race, Medicine, and Health Care in the United States: From 1900 to the Dawn of the New Millennium*, references two periods of health reform in U.S. history that have specifically addressed race-based health disparities. Both had dramatic and positive effects. The first period, which was linked to Freedman's Bureau legislation, lasted from 1865 to 1872. According to Byrd and Clayton, this "First Reconstruction in Black Health" led to the establishment of Black medical schools, hospitals, and clinics throughout the South, which helped to slow the Black death rates. "Although many of the Freedmen's Bureau hospital facilities were dirty, poorly maintained, and laced with corruption, they performed a yeomen service and probably blunted worst-case outcomes that would have occurred had they not been available" (Byrd & Clayton, 2000, p. 350).

The "Second Reconstruction in Black Health," as documented by Byrd and Clayton, lasted from 1965 to 1975 and was actually a result and part of the Black Civil Rights Movement. This transformation period brought about hospital desegregation rulings in the courts, the passage of the 1965 Civil Rights Act, the passage of Medicare/Medicaid legislation, a community and neighborhood health center movement, and the admission of Black physicians to White hospital staffs for the first time. During this period, dramatic improvement in virtually every measurable health status, utilization, and outcome parameter was observed; "By 1980, despite material and sometimes expensive health and programmatic interventions, new semantics, civil rights terminology, rules of racial etiquette, and token participation or gestures, it became clear that only small dents had been made in the edifice of the nation's centuries-old racial health dilemma" (Byrd & Clayton, 2000, p. 392). Table 38.1 illustrates the African American health experience in relationship to citizenship status from the year 1619 till 2001.

The Civil Rights Movement of the 1960s holds a wealth of ideas that can inform social transformation today and ultimately lead to decreasing health disparities. In addition to the aforementioned factors that contributed to closing the health gap, embedded in this movement was a much broader overtone of political factors. Most visibly, the passing of the Voting Rights Act made a marked difference in the quality of life of African Americans. This demonstrates that political empowerment is vital. In this vein, empowerment comes about through voter registration. This, however, should carry the caveat that in order to encourage voter registration in disadvantaged communities, these communities must be given an incentive to register. The implications of this are stark. In order to bring about parity in health, socioeconomically disadvantaged populations should be encouraged to vote. Politicians should be solicited to provide better social welfare programs in order to encourage voting.

Table 38.1
African American citizenship status and health experience, 1619–2001

TIME SPAN	CITIZENSHIP STATUS– YRS	% OF U.S. EXPERIENCE	CITIZENSHIP STATUS*	HEALTH & HEALTH SYSTEM EXPERIENCE
1619-1865	246	64.40%	Chattel slavery	Disparities/ inequitable treatment; poor health status & outcomes. "Slave health deficit" & "Slave health sub-system" in effect.
1865-1965	100	26.18%	Virtually no citizenship rights	Absent or inferior treatment and facilities. *De jure* segregation/ discrimination in South, *de facto* throughout most of health system. "Slave health deficit" uncorrected.
1965-2001	36	9.42%	Most citizenship rights	Southern medical school desegregation [1948], Imhotep Hospital Integration Conferences [1957-1964], hospital desegregation in federal courts [1964]. Disparate health status, outcomes, and services with apartheid, discrimination, institutional racism and bias in effect.
1619-2001	*382*	*100.00%*	*The struggle continues*	*HEALTH DISPARITIES/ INEQUITIES*

*According to Thomas Marshall's criteria, citizenship carries three distinct kinds of rights relative to the state: (1) civic rights, including legal equality, free speech, free movement, free assembly, and organizational and informational rights; (2) political rights, including the right to vote and run for office in free elections; (3) socioeconomic rights, including the right to have a job, collectively bargain, unionize, and access Social Security and welfare if necessary, (Byrd & Clayton, 2001).

Sources: Brinkley, A. *The Unfinished Nation: A Concise History of the American People* (New York: Alfred A. Knopf, 1993); Byrd & Clayton, (2000, 2001); Higginbotham, A.L. *In the Matter of Color: Race and the American Legal Process, The Colonial Period* (New York: Oxford University Press, 1978); Kluger, R., *Simple Justice: The History of Brown v Board of Education and Black America's Struggle for Equality* (New York: Alfred A. Knopf, 1976, paperback ed. New York: Vintage Books, 1977); Marable, M., *Race, Reform, and Rebellion: The Second Reconstruction in Black America, 1945–1990*, rev. 2d ed. (Jackson: University Press of Mississippi, 1991); Marshall, T.H. *Citizenship, Social Class, and Other Essays* (Cambridge, England: Cambridge University Press, 1950).

Environmental Justice

According to Bullard (1994), the Environmental Justice Movement attempts to address environmental enforcement, compliance, policy formulation, and decision making. It defines environment in very broad terms, as the places where people live, work, and play.

The struggle for environmental justice was not invented in the 1990s. People of color, individually and collectively, have waged a frontal assault against environmental injustices since before the first Earth Day in 1970. Many of these struggles, however, were not framed as "environmental" problems; rather, they were seen as addressing "social" problems. For example, the 1968 U.S. National Advisory Commission on Civil Disorders discovered that the systematic neglect of garbage collection and sanitation services in African American neighborhoods contributed to the urban disturbances in the 1960s. Inadequate services, unpaved streets, and lack of sewers and indoor plumbing were environmental problems in the 1960s and continue to be environmental problems today in many minority and poor neighborhoods (Bullard, 1990; Bullard et al., 2001).

Several successes have resulted from neighborhood campaigns to change sources of pollution by asserting new rights. Exercising the right to know, inspect, and negotiate encourages the prevention of chemical hazards before they occur. As activism takes hold in a community and leads to major or minor gains, it revitalizes the community, restoring its faith in the democratic process. In many instances, grassroots leaders have emerged from groups of concerned citizens (many of them women) who see their families, homes, and communities threatened by some type of polluting industry or governmental policy (Bullard, 1993). Those who have come through local environmental campaigns have subsequently received an education in law, science, politics, and human relations and emerge better equipped to assist their community in its future democratic development.

COMMON THEMES, OBSTACLES, AND STRATEGIES

Cultural Activism

Successful social transformation movements have used cultural activism as a strategy to transform communities around social issues. Cultural activism is a strategy for social change and liberation, challenging basic assumptions about society, transforming political power, and building political unity. It represents a way of giving voice to people in their own language and images, derived from historical memory and current experience. It offers a way for people to reflect on their relationship to daily life and to own and control their images and representations (Bullard, 1994; Bullard et al., 2001).

The term "culture," as used here, broadly refers to that complex whole that includes knowledge, beliefs, art, morals, law, customs, and other capabilities and habits acquired by people as members of society (Thomas & Quinn, 2001). Always in flux and filled with contradictions, it includes the writings, music, paintings, songs, stories, oral histories, street art, games, and dramas of a people that are significant to them. More than the sum of these manifestations, culture articulates human subjectivity, meaning, and a people's presence and identity in history. It represents the way a community of people reflects on, and represents, itself.

Cultural activism is a way of developing a community by connecting diverse people and making them feel they can act to build a movement, rather than function as spectators. The Civil Rights Movement, the struggles for woman's rights, and the fight against AIDS are strong examples of the use of cultural expression, particularly music and street theater. Cultural activism can also be a core feature of organizing for reducing health disparities, by developing artistic, organizing, cooperative, and leadership skills for social change. Its practices include expressing community identity, history, visions of the future, and aspirations of different people through their own symbols, language, and stories, in a socially conscious, public way rooted in social life.

Any social movement designed to achieve a reduction in racial and ethnic health disparities must be multicultural, multi-issue, and based on other successful international public health and social transformation models (Bullard et al., 2001). In order to build a movement for health parity, public health issues must be incorporated into a broader agenda for social justice, and public health must be infused with nontraditional strategies and methods. This means making common cause with the labor, civil rights, women's, peace, and environmental justice movements on an international basis and overcoming language and cultural differences. The crisis in health disparities is a potentially unifying phenomenon that can link seemingly separate issues and peoples. How will people imagine a society that transcends racism, sexism, and class? Social transformation means rethinking these relations.

Community Coalition Building

Application of Selected Strategies.   Community organizing, or coalition building, involves specific techniques and resources for identifying and engaging people, such as health center surveys, door-to-door surveys and interviews, establishing partnerships with existing organizations, and respectfully soliciting the support and involvement of community institutions (such as churches, mosques, or civic organizations) and city- or state-elected official(s). "Coalitions bring together members of various organizations to work together for a common purpose" (Brownson et al., 1999, p. 169).

Often a precipitating issue or event occurs at the local community level and serves as the impetus to mobilize individuals, private organizations, or federal and state agencies. The issue can involve the shutting down of a community health center, successive acts of violence in a community or across the city, or a story that grabs public attention. Community coalition building requires the initial support of an organization or group that seeks to advance efforts to develop community voice (Staples, 1984). The initial support or organizing body can originate in the local community, institutional settings, inside/outside bureaucracy, think tanks, and so on.

Successful community coalition building involves skillful, deliberate, and sincere application of strategies, such as listening to concerns and understanding self-interests. The organization providing the initial support must take into account cultural considerations that might involve race, class, religion, and gender preference (Stout, 1996). Taking self-interests and cultural factors into account will influence how the issue gets defined and who should be targeted for boycott or some other form of public embarrassment. It should also be pointed out that access to resources may significantly influence the leadership and decision-making format, which will also impact how strategic approaches or tactics are identified.

Establishing Issue-Oriented Campaigns. Community organizing and coalition building is expected to establish some type of campaign and explore the potential for collaborations with outside agencies and organizations, such as neighborhood health centers; national organizations, such as the American Heart Association; the city or state public health department; the news media; union organizers; and churches and mosques (e.g., stakeholders in a community, such as an academic research institution and a neighborhood health center, can join together to systematically improve the health status of the community). The focus of a community organizing effort can take the form of a specific short-term issue such as infant mortality, early intervention services, or school lunch programs. The focus of coalition building can also have implications for raising issues on a long-term basis such as Survivors of War Crimes, Survivors of Plane Crashes, or Americans with Disabilities.

Being Sensitive to the Culture and Cultural Needs of Communities. Facilitating a community's appreciation and use of its cultures can be a powerful tool for building community and empowering people. The creation and reaffirmation of community culture can advance grassroots organizing for reducing health disparities. Identifying shared history is a way of building community solidarity. Organizers search for autonomous spaces for action outside regular channels such as the mass media, elections, or other bureaucratic institutions that narrow the boundaries of legitimate political action. Some seek to present information in appealing and graphic ways. Others seek to create community. What may finally be most effective in shaping consciousness are those features of everyday life and popular culture that incorporate public health themes and images (Brownson et al., 1999).

THE COMMUNITY TRANSFORMATION MODEL (CTM)

"[T]he civil rights movement was essentially a political phenomenon in that blacks were engaging in struggles for power against Whites. In this context, movement centers, strategic planning, organizing, charisma, and preexisting institutions were central to the civil rights movement in that they enabled the Black community to effectively confront an entrenched opposition dedicated to keeping them subservient" (Morris, 1984, p. 277). The Division of Public Health Practice has gleaned several important concepts from the literature, from its inventory of successful models within other disciplines, its extensive experience working with its surrounding community, and its programmatic work with violence prevention. The CTM has its origins in social movement theory. According to social movement theory, "the term 'local movement center' refers to a dynamic form of social organization that varies in degree of organization and in its capacity to produce and sustain protest" (Morris, 1984, p. 284).

Local movement centers referred to the places where a dominated group assembled the required resources and strategically placed activists, and effective tactics and strategies for protest purposes were established. "A local movement center is thus a distinctive form of social organization specifically developed by members of the dominated group to produce, organize, coordinate, finance, and sustain social protest" (Morris, 1984, p. 284). While our focus is not to organize to protest, the CTM is introduced as a means to engage in planning and organizing to mobilize and focus preexisting resources involving community residents, community-based organizations, and community-focused institutions and agencies. The CTM will be continuously refined based on knowledge and experience gained from our public health practice interventions and researching other social transformation models.

Levels of Change

The Program to Eliminate Health Disparities will delineate models for social transformation in order to standardize the approach to program design and evaluation as an element of the transformation process. Currently, when public health professionals consider changes at any level, except the individual level, the approach taken is more narrow and haphazard. Efforts to change institutions often focus only on individual knowledge with little attention to organizational structure and institutional practices.

Whether working with communities, schools, hospitals, professional training institutions, professional associations, or government agencies, the intentional connection of strategies to change individuals (micro) with efforts to change institutions and society at large (macro) is critical. The CTM focuses on changes at several levels, using a variety of strategies. At the individual level, the CTM seeks to enhance knowledge, attitudes, and behaviors about health. Strategies employed at this level include traditional ones, such as health education and outreach, behavior modification, counseling, combating peer pressure, and other empowerment strategies. It also includes nontraditional strategies, such as voter registration, community organizing, protesting, and developing social and financial capital.

While understanding that the recipient of public health messages is crucial, we place equal, if not more, importance on the knowledge, skills, and behaviors of public health professionals. Providing professional training in cultural competence and bias, opportunities for practical experience, and incentive structures will be the means to elevate the aforementioned attributes of professionals. From these strategies, it is evident that the CTM seeks to intentionally connect efforts focused on individual change to a larger mission to change institutions and society (Williams & Rucker, 2000).

Violence Prevention

One example of the levels of change idea derives from the work of the Division of Public Health Practice in child and adolescent violence prevention. For those students who have many large and small unfair things happen to them (macro and micro insults) and are constantly faced with racism, sexism, and classism, teaching conflict resolution is not enough. Unless these teachings are directly connected to their leadership potential and the need to change the negative forces they face with the provision of strategies to do this, lessons, if learned, are diminished.

The CTM understands the need for synergy and building momentum. Thus, the strategies employed above are not compelled by the evaluation of a discrete program or intervention. For example, Rosa Parks was not the first person to refuse to give up her seat on the bus. At the other times, however, individuals may have evaluated the strategy of refusing to give up a seat and pronounced it a failure, with risk outweighing benefits.

In addition to having a synergistic basis, the CTM uses interventions to reinforce and enhance impact over time. Thus, the CTM is inherently based on longevity. The focus is on the long-term view of change.

Smoking Prevention

Reduction in smoking rates took 30 years of public health intervention to achieve. Many classroom education models were used, and of those, many were judged to be ineffective. Children still grew up to smoke, particularly in the early years just after the surgeon general's report. Those individuals who became the catalyst for change years after a classroom health education program on smoking prevention are never measured in the traditional evaluation because those changes don't occur within one or two years of the intervention. Also, classroom interventions were reinforced over time via other strategies in order to produce leaders and catalysts for change. The groundswell of force generated over a given period of time, not an individual intervention, eventually changed social norms and attitudes.

The above examples illustrate the benefits of studying past historical transformations and drawing lessons that inform future social change in an ultimate effort to eliminate health disparities.

Field-Testing the CTM

In response to the ever-increasing health disparities among minority populations, the Division of Public Health Practice has initiated several efforts under the Program to Eliminate Health Disparities (PEHD) to improve specific health disparities within the Roxbury community of Boston, where the division is housed. These efforts will constitute the demonstration projects through which the PEHD will field-test methodologies developed by its interdisciplinary team of investigators.

Project Description: Cherishing Our Hearts and Souls Coalition.   Strong community-based programs addressing cardiovascular diseases must draw on the lessons learned from the well-designed and rigorously examined programs of the 1970s and 1980s,[1] primarily the three U.S.-based community heart health programs: the Stanford Five-City Project,[2] the Minnesota Heart Health Program,[3] and the Pawtucket Heart Health Program.[4] These cardiovascular risk reduction community-based programs, perhaps more than any other group of community-based programs, set standards for effective community interventions.[5]

Cherishing Our Hearts and Souls (COHS) is a collaborative coalition-building effort established to improve the cardiovascular health of African Americans in the Roxbury neighborhood of Boston. This effort is achieved through a comprehensive, continuous, coordinated approach to the delivery of health services to the community (community-oriented primary care) combined with mobilization of the community to understand, identify, and address the impacts of racism on health.

The need to focus on racism and health was confirmed using data from the 1998 Roxbury Healthy Heart Survey. This survey was developed by the Healthy Heart Advisors, along with Dr. Camara Jones, a former faculty member. It was administered to 258 Roxbury households by the Healthy Heart Advisors. The survey asks a head of household about the health status of members of the household and asks the respondent questions about race, such as: "How often do you think about your race? Constantly? Once a day? Once a year? Never?" Forty-one percent of respondents said that they think about their race constantly, and 11 percent thought about their race once a day. Forty-two percent of respondents reported themselves as having hypertension, and 36 percent reported being overweight. Results from the data were discussed with the Healthy Heart Advisors and informed our understanding of community needs.

The coalition-building work began with a Racial and Ethnic Approaches to Community Health (REACH) 2010 Phase I grant from the Centers for Disease Control and Prevention. The coalition was funded for one year to develop its capacity and to produce a viable Community Action Plan inspired by community voices. The Central Coordinating Organization for COHS is the Program to Eliminate Health Disparities (PEHD). Original coalition members were Roxbury Comprehensive Community Health Center, Inc., Dimock Community Health Center, the Sisters Together Coalition, Vigorous InterventionS In Ongoing Natural Settings (VISIONS), Inc., and Paige Academy, as well as six community members who do outreach as Healthy Heart Advisors.

VISIONS, Inc., is an educational, nonprofit organization that conducts antiracism trainings in diverse settings. Paige Academy is a private school whose African-centered curriculum is based on the Nguzo Saba principles of Kwanzaa. Both are nontraditional partner organizations for a health coalition but prove invaluable to the coalition's mission because of their expertise around sociocultural issues that impact the community's ability to achieve health and wellness.

Each original partner organization had specific roles and objectives for coalition involvement and coalition building. Partners supported the coalition's growth while advancing aspects of the coalition's agenda to address cardiovascular disease and racism within the community. VISIONS, Inc., and Paige Academy focused on antiracism training and education, while the health centers received guidance from the PEHD in efforts to invite other health centers to join the coalition while developing a community-oriented primary care model for addressing the health needs of the community.

The Coalition-Building Process

Strategies Used to Achieve Functionality and Feedback.   The Cherishing Our Hearts and Souls project was launched in October 2000. During our first year, we engaged in a highly interactive process that strengthened and expanded the coalition and its community planning efforts. The PEHD met with individual coalition partners on a monthly basis throughout the planning year. These meetings assisted partners in monitoring progress and negotiating stumbling blocks, provided necessary administrative assistance, and facilitated cross-fertilization of ideas between coalition partners.

At bimonthly coalition-wide meetings, coalition partners provided a brief progress report of their work, and representatives of one partner organization gave a presentation on that organization's history and mission. Each partner was responsible for hosting the meeting on a rotating basis and planning and leading the agenda. Feedback from the first coalition meeting indicated that coalition members wanted time to get to know each other in a less formal way. In response to this feedback, the agenda of each coalition meeting thereafter included a "connecting exercise," which allows individuals in the coalition to discuss who they are, why they are present, and why this work is important to them personally. Coalition meetings have thus provided time and space for individuals from diverse personal and professional backgrounds to get to know each other and the significance of each other's work.

Within this context of mutual appreciation, the coalition was able to accomplish its main objectives for the Phase I planning year: to build the coalition's capacity and to develop a Community Action Plan incorporating broad community input. These two objectives were achieved simultaneously and with the help of all original coalition partners.

Workshops

A second, essential source of community input was a set of community-wide workshops dealing with heart disease and racism. These workshops assisted coalition members and community residents in identifying how racism affects the Roxbury community, identifying possible points of intervention, and developing strategies for dismantling or dealing with racism in Roxbury and Boston in general. The health component featured modules on the relationship between racism and health and on methods to work effectively with health-care providers.

VISIONS, Inc., led an antiracism workshop for coalition partners in January. The coalition then held its first large, community-wide workshop, Heart Disease and Racism I: Understanding the Relationship and Developing New Strategies, in April 2001, at the Twelfth Baptist Church in Roxbury. Sixty people came to this workshop, and forty of the attendees joined the coalition. The workshop provided an opportunity for the coalition to disseminate information, attract new members, and receive feedback. The day included an open microphone for community feedback on the topics of nutrition, cardiovascular disease risk factors, and racism as they relate to the Roxbury community. The six breakout groups submitted a total of 48 suggestions for improving cardiovascular health and reducing the impacts of racism. These suggestions formed the basis of the coalition's Community Action Plan.

Following the April community workshop, the coalition held eight strategy sessions to assist in the development of its Community Action Plan. The teams assembled varied from Harvard School of Public Health faculty and researchers to community members, community-based organizations including health center representatives, the American Heart Association, and Healthy Heart Advisors.

A second community workshop, Heart Disease and Racism II: Our Heart's Response to Racism, was held in May, also at the Twelfth Baptist Church. Fifty people attended, and the lively discussion indicated not only concern for their health but also the health of children and the impact of racism on them. The relationship between stress and racism was analyzed, and principles of stress management were discussed. Additional members joined the coalition as a result of their experience at this workshop.

Surveys. The coalition used several mechanisms to solicit and receive community feedback. COHS conducted a convenience sample survey during four events (two COHS community workshops, the premiere of the video *The Angry Heart*,[6] and a Roxbury men's health fair, 2001). Of the 235 respondents, 52 percent were women, 35 percent lived in Roxbury, and 46 percent worked in Roxbury. They reported high cholesterol (33 percent), heart disease (6 percent), a family member with heart disease (40 percent) and smoking (17 percent). Most, 71 percent, noted that heart disease was a very big or big problem in Roxbury, and 30 percent said that their knowledge of heart disease was fair to poor. Only 35 percent thought there was sufficient awareness of heart disease in Roxbury.

In addition to the community workshops and surveys, the PEHD received regular feedback from the Healthy Heart Advisors and their neighbors and from employees in the neighborhood health centers about the direction and implementation of Cherishing Our Hearts and Souls. Coalition partners used their own contacts to engage new coalition members, such as leaders of the faith communities and individuals from educational institutions.

Other accomplishments within the first year included completion of a community action plan that incorporated feedback solicited from the community; development of an antiracism after-school curriculum and teacher training manual for pilot testing; submission of an application to the Internal Review Board for pilot-testing the antiracism after-school curriculum; submission of a Phase II grant application; establishment of four working cluster areas within the coalition: Anti-Racism, Clinical Care and Research, Health Promotion, and Public Policy; and a first-year project evaluation.

Evaluation Activities and Results

The evaluation activities for the Phase I planning year include three forms of evaluation: process, summative, and formative evaluations.

The process evaluation assessed both the process of coalition development as well as a monitoring and feedback system. We collected process measures, including records of members attending meetings; assessment of partners' levels of knowledge and awareness of topics central to the Cherishing Our Hearts and Souls project; assessment of the effectiveness of meetings; and analysis of partner journal entries.

Toward the middle of the year, we initiated a more innovative means of monitoring our expected progress during our Phase I planning year. We engaged coalition partners to provide feedback and suggestions on three aspects of the project through a participatory evaluation of (1) strategies and activities, (2) skills and people, and (3) tools and resources. For each of these areas, coalition members worked in cluster groups to identify what the project had accomplished and what the project needed to do.

To obtain an overall summary of Phase I planning, we administered a 26-item questionnaire to all of our coalition members at the midyear point and at the end of the year to assess their satisfaction with the Cherishing Our Hearts and Souls coalition and project. We asked about leadership, planning, progress in completing products, and getting different segments of the community involved. We also assessed members' views on their personal and their organization's involvement in the Cherishing Our Hearts and Souls coalition.

The consistent feedback from our evaluation efforts assisted us with revisions of meeting and workshop training formats. Our coalition-building work over the first year was intensive and tremendously productive. We were particularly pleased with the large attendance and the richness of the racism and heart disease discussions during our community meetings. It is notable that State Senator Diane Wilkerson, Representative Gloria Fox, and City Councilor Mickey Roache were in attendance and that Black and Hispanic men made up 28 percent of the meeting participants. Our subsequent coalition partners' meetings have maintained excellent attendance and participation from state representatives, community health centers and organizations, and community residents.

Potential for Community Transformation

Cherishing Our Hearts and Souls coalition partners are working collaboratively to refine our objectives and strategies. The coalition has recently celebrated its second anniversary, and its membership continues to grow through active recruitment as well as by word of mouth in the community. The Health Promotion Cluster ensures that the coalition has a presence at community health fairs and events, inviting people to join the coalition and collecting survey data on residents' health-related attitudes, habits, and barriers to health-producing lifestyles. Survey results have indicated that over half of respondents (N = 254) consider themselves overweight, but approximately half do not exercise on a regular basis, due to lack of resources, time constraints, and lack of motivation. High blood pressure, high cholesterol, and diabetes are found at high rates. Over 80 percent of those who responded thought that heart disease is a big to very big problem in Roxbury, and 73 percent of those who responded thought that racism had an impact on heart disease. However, awareness of heart disease in Roxbury was perceived by most respondents as low.

Many of those who complete our surveys and read about the issues we are addressing sign up to join the coalition. Coalition partners express satisfaction from their involvement, feeling that the opportunity to discuss and strategize around racism and community priorities is both rare and valuable.

Based on the broad community input and the expanded capacity of the coalition, VISIONS, Inc., has collaborated with the PEHD to identify additional target audiences, venues for community-based antiracism workshops in Roxbury, and potential collaborators in the Boston area who do antiracism training. The PEHD and VISIONS, Inc. are developing antiracism training workshops specific to the relationship of racism to cardiovascular health status. The initial focus will be directed toward community residents, a second focus is on health-care providers, and a third area of focus involves training community residents to facilitate the antiracism training workshops themselves.

Training community residents to conduct antiracism workshops is an example of a sustainable investment in the community and a catalyst for cultural activism. As residents become involved in the transformation of their own community by building awareness and readiness for change, the potential for community transformation and eventual social transformation is cultivated.

Another CTM building block in this field-testing effort is the training of providers. Not merely a "cultural competence" course, antiracism training is designed to develop a critical consciousness in the trainees and tools for analyzing how racism, internalized racism, and other forms of systematic oppression impact health services.

The Anti-Racism Cluster also continues to identify additional educational settings in which to implement the antiracism after-school curriculum that was developed in Phase I. The curriculum aims to prevent racism from taking a toll on African American youth. By working with teachers and parents simultaneously with children, we plan to have a broad impact that could not be achieved through traditional public health methods alone.

As Thomas and Quinn (2001) also indicate, for Black people in the twenty-first century, health promotion and disease prevention can become a mass movement, on the scale of the Civil Rights Movement of the 1960s. Therefore, we continue to improve our outreach methods and our activity planning based on community input, and we continue to refine our process as a coalition based on the feedback of our continuously growing membership. The PEHD being at Harvard University proves challenging at times in our efforts to engage community residents, who can be skeptical of the intentions of the institution in working with the community. However, the investment of other stakeholders and experiences at coalition meetings build confidence in our effort. We continue to build the coalition as in the first year—through meaningful connections taking into account individual and organizational backgrounds, cultures, experiences, and priorities. Our work is thereby evolving with a long-term view of change making use of all the community's sectors and generations. With this broad involvement, a groundswell is forming that can be an unstoppable force for change, connecting individual with institutional, community, and societal changes.

CONCLUSION

Faced with ever increasing disparities in health among populations of color, especially African Americans, the Division of Public Health Practice at the Harvard School of Public Health is embarking on an exciting program to close the gap in these disparities by building social capital within a community. Although much has been written about the existence and causes of health disparities, very little progress has been made in devising and implementing programs that are actually able to reduce health disparities using public health approaches. The aim of the Program to Eliminate Health Disparities is to infuse public health practice and education with the knowledge, strategies and energy found in historically successful social movements, including the Civil Rights Movement, Union Organizing, the International Women's Movement, and Environmental Justice. In collaboration with community-based organizations, health centers, activists, educators, schools, and youth service programs, the Division and the Program to Eliminate Health Disparities are committed to transforming the health status of the residents of Roxbury and the nation.

NOTES

1. Shea, S., & Basch, C.E. (1990), A review of five major community based cardiovascular disease prevention programs, *American Journal of Health Promotion, 4(3)*, 203–287.

2. Farquhar et al. (1990), Effects of communitywide education on cardiovascular disease risk factors, *Journal of the American Medical Association, 264(3)*, 359–365.

3. Carlaw, R.W., Mittlemark, M.B., Bracht, N., & Luepker, R. (1984), Organization for a community cardiovascular health program: Experiences from the Minnesota Heart Health Program, *SOPHE, 11(3)*, 243–252.

4. Lasater, T.M., Lefebvre, R.C., & Carleton, R.A. (1988), The Pawtucket heart health program, *Rhode Island Medical Journal, 71*, 31–34.

5. U.S. Department of Health and Human Services (1990), Three community programs change heart health across the nation, Infomemo: Special Edition, Washington DC: NHLBI.

6. *The Angry Heart* is a video documentary that explores the impact of racism on heart disease among African Americans through the personal story of one man, Keith Hartgrove. Hartgrove, a 45-year-old resident of Roxbury, shares his experience as an African American living with heart disease. From symptoms to heart attack to quadruple bypass surgery to recovery, Keith chronicles his interactions with the medical staff he relies on for treatment and the African American community he depends on for support. Interwoven with his story are interviews with doctors, medical researchers, and members of Keith's family, church, and community. Their perspectives and relationship to Keith are very different, yet they all confirm that his experience is typical within the African American community. These interviews help place the relationship between race and heart disease in a broader context within the American medical community as well as the African American community and the American community as a whole.

REFERENCES

Abraham, M. (1995). Transforming marital violence from a "private problem" to a "public issue." South Asian Women's Organizations and Community Empowerment.

Braithwaite, R.L., & Taylor, S.E. (Eds.). (2001). *Health issues in the Black community*; 2d ed. (pp. 3–12; 62–80; 471–488; 543–559). San Francisco: Jossey-Bass.

Brownson, R.C., Baker, E.A., & Novick, L.F. (1999). *Community-based prevention: Programs that work.* Gaithersburg: Aspen, pp. 169–170, 183–198.

Bullard, R.D. (1990). *Dumping in Dixie: Race, class, and environmental quality.* Boulder, CO: Westview, pp. 33–35.

Bullard, R.D. (1993). *Confronting environmental racism: Voices from the grassroots.* Boston: South End, pp. 15–75.

Bullard, R.D. (1994). *Unequal protection: Environmental justice and communities of color.* San Francisco: Sierra Club, pp. 11–17, 234–243.

Bullard, R.D., Warren, R.C., & Johnson, G.S. (2001). The quest for environmental justice. In R.L. Braithwaite & S. Taylor (Eds.), *Health issues in the Black community*, 2d ed. San Francisco: Jossey-Bass.

Byrd, W.M., & Clayton, L.A. (2000, 2001). *An American health dilemma.* 2 vols. New York: Routledge.

Gibbs, B.K., Nsiah-Jefferson, L., & Prothrow-Stith, D. (2002). Invited white paper: Policy, systems, and programs to reduce racial and ethnic health disparities. Presented at the Commonwealth Fund: New York.

Hacker, A. (1992). *Two nations: Black, White, separate, hostile, unequal.* New York: Maxwell Macmillan.

Hamburg, M. (1998). Eliminating Racial and Ethnic Disparities in Health. *Public Health Reports, 113(4)*, 372–375.

Hofrichter, R. (1993). *Toxic struggles.* Philadelphia: New Society.

Hofrichter, R. (Ed.). (2003). *Health and social justice: Politics, ideology, and inequity in the distribution of disease*, (pp. 1–56). San Francisco: Jossey-Bass.

Jones, C.P. (1997). The racism in "race." Presented at the annual meeting of American Public Health Association.

Jones, C.P. (2000). Levels of racism. *American Journal of Public Health, 908*, 1212–1215.

Jones, C.P. (2001). Invited commentary: "Race," racism, and the practice of epidemiology. *American Journal of Epidemiology, 154*, 299–302.

Katz, M.B. (1989). *The undeserving poor: From the war on poverty to the war on welfare.* New York: Pantheon Books.

Kawachi, I., Kennedy, B.P., Lochner, K., & Prothrow-Stith, D. (1997). Social capital, income inequality, and mortality. *American Journal of Public Health, 87*, 1491–1498.

Kennedy, B.P., Kawachi, I., Glass, R., & Prothrow-Stith, D. (1998). Income distribution, socioeconomic status, and self-rated health: A U.S. multi-level analysis. *British Medical Journal, 317*, 917–921.

Kennedy, B.P., Kawachi, I., Lochner, K., Jones, C., & Prothrow-Stith, D. (1997). (Dis)Respect and Black mortality. *American Journal of Public Health, 87*, 1491–1498.

Kennedy, B.P., Kawachi, I., Prothrow-Stith, D., & Gupta, V. (1998). Income inequality, social capital and firearm-related violent crime. *Social Sciences and Medicine, 47*, 7–17.

Lawson, E., & Young, A. (2002). Health care revival renews, rekindles, and revives. *American Journal of Public Health, 92*, 177–179.

Morris, A.D. (1984). *The origins of the Civil Rights Movement: Black communities organizing for change.* New York: Free Press, pp. 277–290.

National Center for Health Statistics (NCHS). (2002). *Infant, neonatal, and postneonatal mortality rates by race and sex: United States, 1975–2000.* National Vital Statistics Report, vol. 50, no. 15.

Office of Research and Health Statistics. (1994). *Neighborhood health status report: The health of Roxbury.* Division of Public Health, Trustees of Health and Hospitals Incorporated, the City of Boston.

Parangimalil, G.J. (July–September 2001). Latino health in the new millennium: The need for a culture-centered approach. *Sociological Spectrum, 21, 3*, 423–429.

Prothrow-Stith, D., Gibbs, B.K., Allen, A. (2003). Reducing health disparities: From theory to practice. *Cancer Epidemiology, Biomarkers & Prevention, 12* (March), pp. 256s–260s.

Smedley, B.D., & Syme, S.L. (2000). Promoting health. Intervention strategies from social and behavioral research. Institute of Medicine. Washington, DC: National Academy Press.

Staples, Lee. (1984). Roots to power. Westport, CT: Praeger, pp. 15–30.

Stith, C.R. (1995). Political religion. A liberal answer the question, "should politics and religion mix?" Nashville: Abingdon.

Stout, L. (1996). *Bridging the class divide: And other lessons for grassroots organizing.* Boston, Beacon Press, pp. 117–140.

Taylor, S.E., & Braithwaite, R.L. (2001). African American health. In R.L. Braithwaite and S.E. Taylor (Eds.), *Health Issues in the Black Community*, 2d ed. San Francisco: Jossey-Bass.

Thomas, S.B., & Quinn, S.C. (2001). Eliminating health disparities. In R.L. Braithwaite and S.E. Taylor (Eds.), *Health issues in the Black community*, 2d ed. San Francisco: Jossey-Bass.

Williams, D.R., & Rucker, T.D. (2000). Understanding and addressing racial disparities in health care. *Health Care Financing Review, 21*, 75–90.

Wilson, W.J. (1987). *The truly disadvantaged.* Chicago and London: University of Chicago Press.

Wilson, W.J. (1996). *When Work Disappears: The world of the new urban poor.* NewYork: Knopf, Random House.

PART V

Ethics, Research, Technology, and Social Policy Issues

CHAPTER 39

Health Policy and the Politics of Health Care for African Americans

SAMUEL L. BROWN

THE NATURE OF THE AFRICAN AMERICAN HEALTH DISPARITY PROBLEM

Health-care policy analysis and politics play a central role in the health-care delivery system. They serve as the mechanism through which public resources are allocated, which in turn determines the priorities of medical research, the supply of health-care providers, and the distribution of medical care.

In the United States, the government plays an important role in planning, directing, and financing health-care services. According to the Centers of Medicare and Medicaid, public programs account for nearly 40 percent of the nation's personal health expenditures; over 50 percent of all health and research development funds are provided by the government; the government finances the training of most physicians and other health-care personnel; and most community-based and university hospitals rely on Medicare for a significant share of their revenues (Heffler, Levitt, Smith, Smith Cowan, Lazenby & Freeland, 2001).

The current cadre of health policies and programs of the U.S. government evolved incrementally in response to clearly defined market imperfections that resulted in unmet needs. The role of government in the health sector has historically been one of support to the private sector, rather than that of a direct provider of health-care services. This role presents an interesting puzzle, which has baffled health policy analysts over the years. As a result, the United States has not pursued a comprehensive resolution to the health-care cost crisis, disparities in access to care, or the issues surrounding health-care quality.

This chapter examines the health-care system in the United States and persistence of racial disparities in health status and access to, and quality of, health care. It begins with a descriptive review of the health status of African Americans as it compares to that of White Americans. This section is followed with a discussion of the dimension of policy development in health. The next section discusses more specific policies and programs either developed or expanded over the past ten years aimed at eliminating racial disparities in health. The fourth and final section offers suggestions for improving the gains made in eliminating racial disparities in health.

Table 39.1

Life expectancy at birth according to race and sex, United States, selected years, 1990–1999 (Data are based on the National Vital Statistics System)

Specified Age and Year	All Races			White			Black		
	Both Sexes	Male	Female	Both Sexes	Male	Female	Both Sexes	Male	Female
At Birth	Remaining Life Expectancy In Years								
1990	75.4	71.8	78.8	76.1	72.7	79.4	69.1	64.5	73.6
1991	75.5	72.0	78.9	76.3	72.9	79.6	69.3	64.6	73.8
1992	75.8	72.3	79.1	76.5	73.2	79.8	69.6	65.0	73.9
1993	75.5	72.2	78.8	76.3	73.1	79.5	69.2	64.6	73.7
1994	75.7	72.4	79.0	76.5	73.3	79.6	69.5	64.9	73.9
1995	75.8	72.5	78.9	76.5	73.4	79.6	69.6	65.2	73.9
1996	76.1	73.1	79.1	76.8	73.9	79.7	70.2	66.1	74.2
1997	76.5	73.6	79.4	77.1	74.3	79.9	71.1	67.2	74.7
1998	76.7	73.8	79.5	77.3	74.5	80.0	71.3	67.6	74.8
1999	76.7	73.9	79.4	77.3	74.6	79.9	71.4	67.8	74.7

[1]Death registration area only. The death registration area increased from 10 states and the District of Columbia in 1900 to the coterminous United States in 1993.

[2]Includes deaths of persons who were not residents of the 50 States and the District of Columbia.

Notes: Beginning in 1997 life table methodology was revised to construct complete life tables by single years of age that extend to age 100. (Anderson, R.N., Method for Constructing Complete Annual U.S. Life Tables. National Center for Health Statistics. Vital Health Stat 2(129). 1999.)

Previously abridged life tables were constructed for five-year age groups ending with the age group 85 years and over. Data for additional years are available.

Source: National Center for Health Statistics (2001).

AN OVERVIEW OF THE STATUS OF AFRICAN AMERICAN HEALTH

At the midpoint of the year 2002 American society reached a near-consensus on the recognition of racial health disparities as a serious issue deserving the attention of government. A longitudinal examination of data from the National Center for Health Statistics (2003) reveals the general health of all Americans has improved over the past five decades in the United States. Notwithstanding this fact, African Americans continue to experience higher rates of morbidity and mortality than White Americans on just about every indicator of mental and physical health.

Table 39.1 shows that from 1990 to 1999, life expectancy for African Americans increased by 2.3 years (from 69.1 to 71.4 years). This increase is 1.3 years greater than that for the population as a whole during the same period (i.e., from 75.4 years to 76.7 years). African American males in 1999 continued to have the shortest life expectancy at birth; data from Table 39.1 show that from 1990 to 1999 their life expectancy increased from 64.5 to 67.8 years. The disparity in life expectancy between Black males and White males declined by 1.4 years (i.e., from 8.2 to 6.8 years); while the corresponding change for Black females and White females was .6 years (from 5.8 to 5.2 years).

Infant mortality is another common measure of the general health of populations. Over the decade of the 1990s, the African American infant mortality rate declined by a modest 3 percent, which was more than twice the rate of decline for Whites (data shown in Table 39.2). In spite of this decline, the Black/White disparity in infant mortality has not changed. African American infants were 2.3 times more likely to die than were White infants in both 1990 and in 1999. It seems that while some health gains were achieved over the past ten years, the racial health disparity in infant mortality remains unchanged.

Although not shown in Tables 39.1–39.3, there are NCHS data, that show that when asked to report on their health status, fewer African Americans report their health status as excellent/good

Table 39.2

Infant mortality rates, according to race/origin of mother, United States, selected years, 1990–1998 (Data are based on National Linked Birth/Infant Death Data Sets)

Race and Hispanic Origin of Mother	1990[1]	1991	1995[2]	1996[2]	1997[2]	1998[2]	1989-91[1]	1996-98[2]
Infant[3] deaths per 1,000 live births								
All Mothers	8.9	8.6	7.6	7.3	7.2	7.2	9.0	7.2
White	7.3	7.1	6.3	6.1	6.0	6.0	7.4	6.0
Black	16.9	16.6	14.6	14.1	13.7	13.8	17.1	13.9

*The number of states reporting the item increased from 23 and the District of Columbia (DC) in 1983–1987, to: 30 and DC in 1988; 47 and DC in 1989; 48 and DC in 1990; 49 and DC in 1991; and 50 and DC starting in 1995.

[1]Rates based on unweighted birth cohort data.

[2]Rates based on a period file using weighted data (National Vital Statistics System).

[3]Infant (under 1 year of age), neonatal (under 28 days), and postneonatal (28 days—11 months).

Notes: The race groups White, Black, American Indian or Alaska Native, and Asian or Pacific Islander include persons of Hispanic and non-Hispanic origin. National linked files do not exist for 1992–1994. Data for additional years are available.

Source: National Center for Health Statistics (2001).

than White Americans (Chappell, 2002). Further examination of these data reveals that as African Americans age, the disparity in self-reported health status widens.

Perhaps the most striking statistics are presented in Table 39.3. When death rates per 100,000 of the population are reviewed, a disturbing picture is seen. Black males and females are more likely to die than White males and females when data are age-adjusted. This fact was true throughout the entire decade of the 1990s.

When other NCHS data are examined, for example, it can be seen that African Americans are disproportionately affected by almost every major disease category, but not shown here. African Americans are 2.5 times more likely than White Americans to die from asthma, 5.8 times more likely than White Americans to die from homicide, 2.2 times more likely than White Americans to die from diabetes, 6.7 times more likely than White Americans to die from HIV, and 3.5 times more likely to die from hypertensive heart disease (National Center for Health Statistics, 2003).

Potential Causes and Possible Explanations for Racial Disparities in Health

The previous section of this chapter detailed the fact that race is closely associated with the health status of populations in the United States. On almost every major health measure (mortality, morbidity, and disability), African Americans have poorer health than their White counterparts (National Center for Health Statistics, 2001) (Table 39.4).

The lack of health insurance coverage is often cited (e.g., Gornick, 2000; Williams & Rucker, 2000) as a reason for the racial disparity in access to care. Table 39.4 details the percentage of Americans who are uninsured in the United States. It shows that African Americans are more likely to be uninsured than White Americans.

A second potential explanation for disparities in utilization of health care is the type of insurance. Given the propensity of managed care to restrict access to care through utilization management techniques, some African American health-care advocates have been concerned. The concern is that as the nation moved toward the adoption of managed care as the solution to the health-care cost crisis, African American health consumers would be disproportionately harmed. Others have argued

Table 39.3

Death rates for all causes, according to sex, race, United States, selected years, 1990–1999 (Data are based on the National Vital Statistics System)

Sex, Race	1990	1991	1992	1993	1994	1995	1996	1997	1998	1999
All Persons										
ALL AGES, AGE ADJUSTED	938.7	925.5	910.9	931.5	920.2	918.5	902.4	887.3	875.8	881.9
ALL AGES, CRUDE	863.8	860.3	852.9	880.0	875.4	880.0	872.5	864.7	864.7	877.0
Male										
ALL AGES, AGE ADJUSTED	1,202.8	1,182.6	1,161.2	1,181.8	1,160.9	1,150.3	1,117.5	1,090.5	1,064.6	1,061.8
ALL AGES, CRUDE	918.4	912.1	901.6	923.5	915.0	914.1	896.4	880.8	876.4	882.0
FEMALE										
ALL AGES, AGE ADJUSTED	750.9	741.6	731.2	751.0	745.0	748.2	742.8	736.3	732.7	743.6
ALL AGES, CRUDE	812.0	811.0	806.5	838.6	837.6	847.3	849.7	849.2	853.5	872.2
White Male										
ALL AGES, AGE ADJUSTED	1,165.9	1,146.4	1,125.6	1,143.0	1,123.4	1,112.7	1,086.1	1,062.5	1,038.5	1,035.8
ALL AGES, CRUDE	930.9	926.2	917.2	938.8	931.6	932.1	918.1	906.3	904.4	911.2
BLACK MALE										
ALL AGES, AGE ADJUSTED	1,644.5	1,622.0	1,591.4	1,629.3	1,589.8	1,582.3	1,513.9	1,446.7	1,410.6	1,412.5
ALL AGES, CRUDE	1,008.0	998.7	977.5	1,006.3	987.8	980.7	939.9	893.9	877.7	880.0
White Female										
All Ages, Age Adjusted	728.8	719.8	709.5	728.9	723.5	726.6	723.3	718.3	715.1	725.7
ALL AGES, CRUDE	846.9	847.7	844.3	879.4	880.1	891.3	896.2	897.8	903.7	924.1
BLACK FEMALE										
ALL AGES, AGE ADJUSTED	975.1	968.3	954.4	977.7	965.0	970.1	956.3	940.7	938.2	955.0
ALL AGES, CRUDE	747.9	744.5	736.2	760.1	752.9	759.0	753.5	742.8	746.4	761.3

Notes: Age-adjusted rates for all years differ from those shown in previous editions of Health, United States. Age-adjusted rates are calculated using the year 2000 standard population starting with Health, United States, 2001. Bias in death rates results from inconsistent race identification between the death certificate (source of data for numerator of death rates) and data from the Census Bureau (denominator); and from undercounts of some population groups in the census. The net effects of misclassification and under coverage result in death rates estimated to be overstated by 1 percent for the white population and 5 percent for the black population. (Rosenberg HM, Maurer JD, Sorlie PD, Johnson NJ, et al. Quality of death rates by race and Hispanic origin: A summary of current research. National Center for Health Statistics. Vital Health Stat 2 (128).

Source: National Center for Health Statistics (2001).

just the opposite (e.g., Libby et al., 1997), that is, that HMOs and managed care plans are better for African American health consumers because they are more inclined to promote health and to promote disease prevention through preventive services. The fact remains that regardless of the type of health insurance, African Americans experience differences in the level and type of health care they receive.

Third, some studies attempt to show that biological/genetic differences between Black and White persons could explain most of the disparities found in health and health care. According to Gornick (2000), when six major risk factors are studied—smoking, systolic blood pressure, cholesterol level, body-mass index, alcohol intake, and diabetes—only 31 percent of the excess mortality between Black and White adults could be explained; another 38 percent was explained by income differences. This analysis leaves 31 percent of the excess mortality unexplained.

A fourth explanation for the continued disparities in health and health care can be traced to race-based discrimination in health care. Given that integration in the provision of health services is a relatively recent event in the United States, it should come as no surprise that systematic discrimination still exists in some pockets of the health-care system. Some of the current level of racial

Table 39.4

No health care coverage among persons under 65 years of age, according to selected characteristics, United States, selected years, 1994–1999 (Data are based on household interviews of a sample of the civilian noninstitutionalized population)

Characteristic	1994[1]	1995	1996	1997[1]	1998	1999
Number in Millions						
TOTAL [2]	40.0	37.1	38.6	41.0	39.2	38.5
Percent of Population						
TOTAL, AGE ADJUSTED [2,3]	17.2	15.9	16.5	17.4	16.5	16.1
TOTAL, CRUDE [2]	17.5	16.1	16.6	17.5	16.6	16.1
Age						
UNDER 18 YEARS	15.0	13.4	13.2	14.0	12.7	11.9
UNDER 6 YEARS	13.4	11.8	11.7	12.5	11.5	11.0
6-17 YEARS	15.8	14.3	13.9	14.7	13.3	12.3
18-44 YEARS	21.7	20.4	21.1	22.4	21.4	21.0
18-24 YEARS	30.8	28.0	29.3	30.1	29.0	27.4
25-34 YEARS	21.9	21.1	22.4	23.8	22.2	22.1
35-44 YEARS	15.9	15.1	15.2	16.7	16.4	16.3
45-64 YEARS	12.0	10.9	12.1	12.4	12.2	12.2
45-54 YEARS	12.4	11.6	12.4	12.8	12.6	12.8
55-64 YEARS	11.2	9.9	11.6	11.8	11.4	11.4
Sex [3]						
MALE	18.5	17.2	17.8	18.5	17.5	17.2
FEMALE	16.1	14.6	15.2	16.2	15.5	15.0
Race [3,4]						
WHITE	16.6	15.3	15.8	16.3	15.2	14.7
BLACK	19.7	18.2	19.6	20.2	20.7	19.4

[1]The questionnaire changed compared with previous years.
[2]Includes all other races not shown separately and unknown poverty level.
[3]Estimates are age-adjusted to the year 2000 standard using three age groups: under 18 years, 18–44 years, and 45–64 years.
[4]The race groups' white and black sample sizes are too small to obtain reliable estimates.
Notes: Persons not covered by private insurance, Medicaid, Child Health Insurance Program (CHIP), public assistance (through 1996), state-sponsored or other government-sponsored health plans (starting in 1997), Medicare, or military plans are included.

Source: National Center for Health Statistics (2001).

disparities can be explained by personal discrimination on the part of providers; however, the vast majority of the race-based discrimination in health care takes place at the societal level (Williams & Rucker, 2000). According to Williams and Rucker (2000), societal discrimination has changed over time from the in-your-face Jim Crow racism to the more faint laissez-faire racism.

The various causes of racial disparities in health and health-care provide insights into the possible solutions or policy options to address this persistent issue. The more knowledge that can be brought to bear in the policy-making process, the more refined and informed the resulting public policy will be. The next section offers some insight into how health policy is developed and implemented.

THE CHARACTER OF HEALTH POLICY MAKING IN THE UNITED STATES

The Ethical Dilemma for the U.S. system: Egalitarian Distribution from a Libertarian System of Delivery

One challenge to eliminating disparities in access to, and quality of, health care is the ethical dilemma posed by the expectations placed upon the current health-care delivery system. Williams and Rucker (2000) argue that the current health-care inequalities go against the American egalitarian principles that dictate equal treatment of all health-care consumers. While this may be true, it does not reflect this society's commitment to individual liberties. The fact is that there is no single, overriding social value that is superior to all other values. Consumers may have rights, but providers have rights, too. We as a nation have not decided whether the rights of one group are subordinate to the rights of another.

The general question has been posited by health economists such as Uwe Reinhardt (1986) in his search for an enduring theory of justice. Reinhardt (1986) put forward the question, To what extent should the individual liberties of health-care providers be curtailed in the name of justice within the realm of health care? The answer to such a question would make it possible to rank alternative ways to distribute economic privileges such as health care.

The current U.S. health-care system is the only system in the Western industrialized nations that attempts to pursue an egalitarian distribution of health care from a libertarian system of delivery. Reinhardt (1986) reminds us that libertarian philosophers argue that individual liberty is the overriding social value to which all other values are subordinate (p. 7). Hence, in the libertarian credo health-care providers have the right to determine whom to serve and whom not to serve and what price should be charged for providing services.

As the opposite end of the extreme are the various theories of distributive justice championed by egalitarian philosophers. These philosophers argue that "equal respect for individuals" or "equality of opportunity" should serve as the overriding values of a just society and that individual liberty should be subordinate. This philosophical view requires that at the very minimum, all members of a society should have equal access to certain basic commodities such as health care.

The dilemma posed by the attempt to accommodate simultaneously both the egalitarian and the libertarian theories of justice is partially responsible for the failure to develop strategies to eradicate inequities in medical care. The ethical confusion generated by the extreme opposing views of justice prevents the development of policy on any level to address the racial disparity issue in health care. At some point America will have to decide whether it wants a health-care system that distributes health care as a business or one that distributes it via some other, more socially oriented mechanism.

Federalism

A second dimension of the public policy that contributes to the challenges of eliminating the race disparities in health is the distribution of authority with a federal system of government. The concept of federalism has evolved since the founding of the United States more than two centuries ago. In its infancy, federalism was a legal concept that defined the balance of power between the federal government and the states as outlined in the Constitution. This division initially stressed the independence of each level of government from the other, while integrating the notion that some functions, such as national defense, were the exclusive territory of central government, while other functions, such as education, police protection, and health care, were the responsibility of state and local governments.

As the concept of federalism has evolved, the responsibilities assigned to each level of government have shifted. Lee and Benjamin (1999) suggest that such shifts do not pose a serious problem for health policy provided two conditions are met: (1) regulatory boundaries and fiscal accountability are compatible, and (2) the various levels of government possess the administrative infrastructures, management techniques, and capabilities to assume the responsibilities assigned to them.

The prime example of the shared relationship between the federal government and the states in the realm of health policy is the Medicaid program. Medicaid is ostensibly the public program designed to address the health-care needs of the poor. As such, it does not directly address the issue of race disparities in health because it targets income and not race as its eligibility criterion. Beyond this particular issue is the dysfunctional outcome produced by the multiple, yet uncoordinated, federal-state programs and the corresponding impacts of the failure of one level of government to meet the conditions outlined by Lee and Benjamin (1999). They offer the example of the case where Medicaid cutbacks at the state level leave the federal government paralyzed in its attempts to shield the poor from the adverse effects on access to care. Such situations have led to the argument that what matters most in the structure of the relationship within federalism is not so much the distribution of power but the relationships among levels of government (Vladeck, 1979).

Pluralism

A third challenge to eliminating racial disparities is the interest group politics that influence the function of democratic governments. Political theorists argue that the number and diversity of interest groups prevent any one group from having undue influence on the political system. This view has been heavily criticized by well-recognized political scientists such as Bachrach (1967) and Schattscheider (1960). If the interest group model works as effectively as some political theorists argue, then there should be no racial disparities in health because the appropriate interest group (NAACP, Urban League, etc.) would have influenced both federal and state laws to effectively address this issue.

Instead, many have come to realize what Ginzberg (1977) has identified as the four power centers in the health-care industry that influence the environment of health care and the function of government: (1) physicians, (2) large insurance organizations, (3) hospitals, and (4) a highly diversified group of participants in the profit-making activities within the health-care arena.

It comes as no surprise that while the interests of big business tend to be well served by health policy in the United States, the interests of minority consumers are too often ignored. Medical politics is the term used often by Silver (1976a) and Marmor et al. (1976) to describe the imbalanced market, where some participants have unequal power, and those with the lion's share of power have the greatest investment in the effects of policy. As a result, cost containment has dominated the health-care policy debates for the last 40 years, while access issues have received less attention than they deserved.

Policy Implementation

The fourth challenge to eliminating racial disparities in health is policy implementation. It has been persuasively argued (e.g., Feder, 1977) that the nature of the health-care system is determined by the balance of power among political actors and also by the relationships of such interest groups to government actors. Public policy observers recognized that policy making travels through at least three stages: (1) agenda setting, the fluid process through which issues are debated in public and subsequently placed on the agenda for government action; (2) policy adoption, the process of compromise and trade-offs required of legislatures, executives, and bureaucracies to define broad outlines of policy from the alternatives available for consideration; and (3) policy implementation, the process by which agency administrators develop policy by addressing the issues required to carry out policy adopted by legislation (Estes, 1980; Sabatier & Mazamania, 1979).

Over the past 20 years there have been a few policies adopted by Congress to address the racial health disparities issue. The challenge with much of this legislation is not unlike that of most legislation: statutory ambiguity. Creative evolution is fostered in the implementation phase of the policy process when Congress fails to draft its legislation in a fashion that provides clear direction to the agencies charged with implementing a specific law.

The context of health policy implementation is influenced to a great extent by the technological changes in the provision of health care. It becomes more difficult to design specific statutes to address the health disparity issue when the practice of medicine changes at a rapid pace. For example, knowledge of which specific health-care procedures produce quality outcomes is in a constant state of flux. Therefore, a health-care law that precisely establishes a minimal level of access to a specific type of care would be destined for rapid obsolescence.

The end result is that regulatory agencies tend to have a great deal of discretion in implementing laws promogulated by the Congress, particularly when the bureaucracy faces an environment relatively free of interest groups in opposition to the program. To the extent that the interests of the minority are not represented by senior administrators within governmental structures, then we cannot expect that issues such as racial disparities in health will receive the attention they deserve at the policy implementation stage. For example, while it may be against the law to discriminate on the basis of race in the provision of health care, in the absence of regulatory enforcement, providers are likely to go unpunished for failing to provide equal access to health care.

Incrementalism

Incrementalism poses yet another challenge to eliminating health disparities. The nature of the public policy process in American government is such that many small steps are preferred to one large step. This process is perhaps best described by Lindblom (1959) as the incremental decision model. In its most basic form, this model posits that policy is made in small increments and that policy is rarely modified in significant ways. Policymakers prefer reform in incremental steps because the consequences of policy change are difficult to model, and such unpredictability makes for uncalculated risk in the political market.

The implication of the incremental process to policy development and adoption for the racial health disparities issue is that a complete solution should not be expected in a given policy term. Rather, one should expect that any change should emerge over time in a series of small steps. This approach is not without critics. Researchers such as Estes (1982) have examined the institutional and class basis of public policy. This research lends some support to the view that defects such as racial health disparities are rooted deeply in the structure of a class society and that the only appropriate solution is a radical transformation in the current health-care system, creating a national health service. Those who hold this view are not convinced that tinkering with the health-care system itself will achieve outcomes such as the elimination of health disparities.

Given a policy process characterized by limited government roles, federalism, pluralism, administrative bargaining, and incrementalism prospects remain relatively dim for a public policy solution to the racial health disparity problem. Given the current state of racial politics in the United States, a race-based policy option is completely beyond the consideration of policymakers.

REFORMS OF THE 1990S AND THEIR IMPACT ON ELIMINATING RACIAL DISPARITIES IN ACCESS TO HEALTH CARE

Over the past 25 years, there have been heightened national visibility of the inequities in the U.S. health-care system and a corresponding growth in public interest in addressing the issue of racial disparities in health care. The Congress and the executive branches of the federal government have initiated a wide range of policies and programs in an attempt to close the gap in health status of and access to, and the quality of, care for African Americans. Some states have also been quite proactive in their attempts to address this issue through legislation and systematic programs. This section explores some of the major federal health-care programs, policies, and practices enacted in the late 1990s to govern the racial disparities in health and health care in the United States.

Office of Management and Budget (OMB) Revised Standards (1997)

In order to eliminate racial disparities in health and health care, such disparities must first be identified. In 1997, the federal Office of Management and Budget (OMB) assumed a leadership role in the effort to collect better race/ethnicity data at the federal level when it published *Revisions to the Standards for the Classification of Federal Data on Race and Ethnicity* to address the need for more refined data on ethnicity than that mandated by OMB's 1977 Directive No. 15 (OMB, 1977, 1997). The 1997 standards established the following race categories:

- American Indian/Alaskan Native
- Asian
- Black/African American
- Native Hawaiian/Other Pacific Islander
- White

In addition to these categories, a minimum of two ethnic categories were established with the 1997 standards: (1) Hispanic or Latino; and (2) not Hispanic or Latino. By January 1, 2003, all federal agencies were required to integrate the new standards into all data collection efforts. The first major implementation of these new standards was the 2000 census, which was designed to conform to the 1997 standards. It is important to note that these standards are not applicable to states and private industry and that OMB does not mandate the collection of racial and ethnic data; it sets the standards by which data are collected and presented by federal agencies.

Initiative to Eliminate Racial and Ethnic Disparities in Health (1998)

During the second term of the Clinton administration, a commitment was made to eliminate disparities in six areas of health status by 2010 while continuing to pursue the goal to improve the overall health of every American. This commitment resulted in the federal Health and Human Services initiative, which provides a focus on infant mortality, cancer screening and management, cardiovascular disease, diabetes, HIV/AIDS, and immunization.

Consumer Bill of Rights and Responsibilities (1997)

In 1997, the Advisory Committee on Consumer Protection and Quality in Health Care was convened by President Clinton to advise him on changes occurring in the health-care system and to recommend measures to promote and assure health-care quality, value, and protection of consumers. The infamous Patients' Bill of Rights originated with this committee, although it was originally called a Consumer Bill of Rights and Responsibilities (CBRR). The CBRR prohibits racial discrimination in the delivery of health services and in the marketing and enrollment practices of health-care providers. Given the access to care concerns that African Americans had with the widespread implementation of managed care plans, these recommendations offered enhanced authority for monitoring nondiscrimination and ensuring compliance with federal civil rights laws. Acting on the specific recommendations of this Advisory Committee, President Clinton issued an executive memorandum in 1998 that required all federal agencies to ensure that all health plans under their respective purviews comply with CBRR.

Report of U.S. Commission on Civil Rights, "The Health Care Challenge: Acknowledging Disparity, Confronting Discrimination, and Ensuring Equality" (1999)

In 1999, the U.S. Commission on Civil Rights, using an ambitious rationale that equal access to quality care is a civil right, conducted a comprehensive study to address the issue of access to quality health care in Health and Human Services-sponsored programs. The report, "The Health Care Challenge: Acknowledging Disparity, Confronting Discrimination, and Ensuring Equality," provided a range of recommendations for eliminating racial disparities in health care and improvement of civil rights enforcement activities of HHS. A brief summary of this commission's targeted and specific recommendations follows.

HHS should develop a comprehensive minority health database, including information on health status, service utilization rates, and methods of financing. All operating divisions should be required to contribute to their individual functions (for example, the [Centers for Medicare and Medicaid] should provide information on Medicare and Medicaid use; the National Institutes of Health should provide disease-specific information; and the Food and Drug Administration should provide information on drug and treatment effectiveness) (U.S. Commission on Civil Rights, 1999)

Minority and Health Disparities Research and Education Act of 2000

The "Minority Health and Health Disparities and Education Act of 2000" was enacted by Congress, with overwhelming bipartisan support, to address racial disparities in health. This act allocated $153.5 million in fiscal year 2001 to achieve the following objectives:

- Expand research on factors contributing to health disparities.
- Increase public awareness and improve training for public health professionals.
- Create a new center at the National Institutes of Health (NIH) to address health disparities and establish a grant program to further biomedical and behavioral research, education, and training.
- Support minority health research at medical institutions.
- Establish a loan repayment program to encourage more members of minority or other health disparity populations to become biomedical research professionals.

Moreover, the act charges the National Academy of Sciences with conducting a comprehensive study to assess the extent of racial and ethnic differences in the quality of health care received by patients, not attributable to known factors such as access to care, ability to pay, or insurance coverage; evaluate potential sources of these disparities, including the role of bias, discrimination, and stereotyping at the provider, patient, institutional, and health system levels; and lastly, provide recommendations regarding interventions to eliminate health-care differences.

Department of Health and Human Services (HHS) Policies and Initiatives

The Department of Health and Human Services (HHS) has historically played a leadership role in developing policies and initiatives designed to expand access to health care and eliminate racial disparities in health. A brief overview of the most important of these policies and initiatives is in order because of the pivotal role in addressing health disparities.

HHS Title VI Regulations (1964)

The HHS regulations issued to implement Title VI of the Civil Rights Act of 1964 serves as an important tool to monitor the behavior of providers who receive federal financial assistance. Under these regulations all entities that apply for federal financial assistance shall, as a condition of participation, assure that they will operate in compliance with all requirements of Title VI.

These regulations require further that all recipients must keep records and submit compliance reports "in such form and containing such information" as the responsible HHS official determines is necessary to assess whether the recipient is complying with the regulations (45 C.F.R. section 80.6b). According to Smith (1998), these regulations were directly responsible for the integration of hospital and nursing homes in the United States.

Healthy People 2010 (2000)

A second major initiative of HHS is the comprehensive, nationwide health promotion and disease prevention agenda known as Healthy People initiative. In January 2000, the HHS secretary and surgeon general David Satcher, M.D., released the plan for Healthy People 2010. This initiative was developed in conjunction with over 350 national organizations and 250 state agencies. Together, this group developed Healthy People 2010, a plan with two overarching goals for achievement: "increase quality and years of healthy life" and "eliminate health disparities." Healthy People 2010 targets disparities by race and ethnicity, as well as by gender, education or income, disability, living in rural communities, and sexual orientation.

In response to President Clinton's "National Initiative to Eliminate Racial and Ethnic Disparities in Health (1998)," HHS developed an initiative to eliminate disparities in six areas of health access and outcomes by the year 2010. These areas were chosen because they affect multiple race and ethnic groups. Significant disparities have been identified, and reliable national data exist that permit tracking progress and results of efforts to eliminate disparities (U.S. Department of Health and Human Services, 2000). A major component of this effort is a program administered by the Centers for Disease Control and Prevention (CDC): Racial and Ethnic Approaches to Community Health 2010 (or REACH 2010). This program aims to help communities organize and mobilize resources to reduce disparities in target areas. Phase I grants support of the planning and development of demonstration programs that use a collaborative multiagency and community participation model to identify or develop appropriate data sources and develop intervention strategies and evaluation measures. In Phase II, the CDC intends to select from among the Phase I grantees to fund the implementation and evaluation of selected interventions in collaboration with local, state, and national partners, as well as disseminate and publish the results and lesson learned (Federal Register, 1999).

In response to the HHS initiative, CMS (formerly known as HCFA) is requiring each state Peer Review Organization (PRO) to target one of six national clinical conditions or access outcomes for elderly and disabled minority Medicare beneficiaries. They identified one of the PROs as a "Disadvantaged Area Support" PRO (DAPRO) and charged it with supporting the other PROs in collecting data, identifying populations, and designing and evaluating interventions.

By setting specific objectives, Healthy People 2010 provides benchmarks that can be used by providers, federal and state health entities, and their partners across the country to measure progress toward reducing the gap and ultimately eliminating health disparities.

The fact that a number of federal laws, policies, and practices governing racial disparities in health and health care were initiated over the past ten years is encouraging for an increasingly multicultural population; however, these initiatives are not always clear and consistent with the goal to eliminate racial disparities in health. As the efforts to improve the health care of African Americans increase in number, it becomes imperative to better understand the laws, policies, and practices designed to achieve the goal of eliminating racial disparities in health and health care.

CLOSING THE GAP

Civil Rights Enforcement

One of the most straightforward remedies to the racial health disparity issue is to renew the government's commitment to enforcing existing legal mandates and federal regulations that deal with discrimination in medicine. Smith (1998) reminds us that given the history of overt discrimination in medical care, it is clear that such mandates and regulations were ineffective until the institutional commitment and capacity to enforce them were created. Legal scholars such as Noah (1998) argue that existing statutes such as Title VI of the Civil Rights Act of 1964 offer promise but are not currently being enforced. Title VI prohibits health-care institutions that receive federal financial assistance from discriminating on the basis of race in providing goods or services. Given that Medicare and Medicaid are forms of federal financial assistance, this law and the corresponding regulations extend to nearly all hospitals, nursing homes, and other health-care facilities in the United States. According to Noah (1998), the courts have held that Title VI prohibits both intentional and disproportionate adverse impact, thereby making the documentation of adverse impact a powerful strategy for addressing and correcting discrimination in health care.

One would be remiss to avoid the unique role that judicial activism could bring to bear in resolving the challenges of the racial disparities in health. This is a form of public policy where the third arm of government, the judicial branch, has asserted itself in a position to address the problems of disadvantaged groups. Some examples include the Supreme Court's 1954 *Brown v. Topeka Board of Education* decision, which reversed the governmentally sanctioned "separate but equal" discrimination embodied in Jim Crow laws; and the 1989 *Richmond v. Croson* decision, where the Supreme Court struck down a municipal affirmative action system for construction contracts. Some of the more extreme forms of judicial activism include instances where lower courts have effectively taken over the day-to-day operations of schools, prisons, and hospitals in the name of racial representation.

To date, the courts have not asserted their power in the policy arena to address the racial health disparity issue. There have been relatively very discrimination cases pursued in the courts under Title VI of the Civil Act of 1964. Most of the cases heard by the courts have centered on the potential adverse impacts of hospital closures on communities of color, not on cases involving individual patients and providers. The lack of lawsuits in this arena most likely is the result of the exemption of individual providers from the antidiscrimination policy embodied in Title VI of the Civil Rights Act of 1964. This is clearly a case where the individual rights of physicians to choose patients in the interest of their business supersede the individual rights of citizens to be seen by the physician of their choice.

Discrimination in health care has been a constant for African Americans. The segregation/integration dichotomy has not offered the insight needed to eliminate disparities in health and health care. African Americans ultimately need better health and better access to health care when appropriate. Whether this care is provided by White physicians in integrated facilities or Black providers in segregated ones is irrelevant. To the extent that the courts can assume a more active role in addressing the issues involved in eliminating racial disparities in health and health care, their participation should be embraced.

Education and Training

A second remedy needed to eliminate racial disparities in health and health care is intensive educational campaigns about the problem. The medical community is the appropriate place to start, although the general public and other professional communities should be included in such efforts. As with any successful campaign or program, such an effort should began with research aimed at identifying the most effective ways to raise awareness of, and increase sensitivity to, the issues of race in the practice of medicine. For example, in the case of increasing the awareness of the benefits of the flu shot among elderly African American Medicare beneficiaries, Cahill, Tanamor, and Green (1999) found that involving church leadership in educational campaigns proved to be most effective. In the case of raising the awareness of race issues and sensitivity toward these issues, medical school curricula should clearly be targeted. Researchers such as Geiger (1996) have called for educating every physician to the "dilemmas associated with race and health care."

A second educational and training goal needed to make progress toward the elimination of racial disparities in health and health care is to increase the number of African American health professionals. Research has informed us that African American physicians are significantly more likely than other physicians to care for vulnerable patient populations such as African Americans (Komaromy et al., 1996). In their recent research findings, Libby et al. (1997) reported that in order to reach racial and ethnic population parity with the supply of physicians, the United States needs to triple the number of Native American medical residents and double the number of African American and Hispanic residents.

From a policy perspective it is important to mention that affirmative action programs in medical school admission processes have been successful in recruiting and retaining physicians from disadvantaged backgrounds. Nickens and Cohen (1996) have defended such affirmative action program on multiple grounds, including societal obligation to meet the health needs of all citizens. Other reports (Editorial, 1999) provide estimates that indicate that affirmative action is responsible for nearly 40 percent of all U.S.-trained physicians from disadvantaged backgrounds.

Improved Data for Monitoring Access to, and Quality of, Care

Williams and Rucker (2000) posit that "any concerted effort to address racial bias in the medical arena requires systematic and routine data of its occurrence." They cite differences among groups of Hispanics as a particular example of how socioeconomic status serves as an intervening variable when the influences of ethnicity are examined among Mexicans, mainland Puerto Ricans, and Cubans.

Given the widespread nature of discrimination in health care, it is clear that racial data are needed for every medical encounter. The collection of data on racial differences could also aid in the efforts to enforce civil rights laws. Such data could also assist medical facilities such as hospitals, nursing homes, and home health agencies in designing unique programs to address disparities at the provider level.

Public–Private Partnerships in Developing Report Cards and Monitoring the Behavior of Providers

Smith (1998) argues that as a result of structural changes in the organization of health care, there are new opportunities to monitor the way in which medical care is delivered. As a result, there has been a shift in power from individual providers to large health plans and major purchasers of care (Smith, 1998). These changes were coupled with a shift in the methods of payment from fee-for-service arrangements to managed care and risk-sharing agreements, thereby resulting in a greater need for external monitoring of provider behavior. As individual providers responded to these changes, physicians, hospitals, and other service providers began to standardize and integrate their clinical and financial information. Herein lies the opportunity for a new type of monitoring called "report cards," which could be used for enhanced civil rights monitoring of health-care delivery.

Smith (1998) indicates that a modification of the existing data systems with the OMB common racial classification scheme would facilitate report cards that could be used to monitor disparities in health plans, health-care institutions, and communities. Some examples include broadly accepted indicators of health and health-care delivery (such as breast cancer death rates and specific preventive measures) that have evolved from the efforts of private-public professional partnerships over several decades.

CONCLUSION

This chapter presents a positive trend in access to care for African Americans over the decade of the 1990s. The federal government is perhaps responsible for the lion's share of this improvement with the implementation of a broad range of health policies across a number of agencies, including the U.S. Department of Health and Human Services, the Civil Rights Division of the Department of Justice, and several innovative, proactive states such as Washington. In spite of these gains, racial disparities on the major indicators of health status and access to care persist. These disparities are greatest for African Americans who are very young, uninsured, low-income, and aged. The U.S. health-care system comprises fragmented, noncomprehensive programs, duplicative and confusing administrative structures, and uncoordinated multiple programs serving similar populations. These characteristics foster the development of independent interest groups that may impede the implementation of a comprehensive solution to the problem of racial disparities in health.

The federal government has responded to the persistent racial disparities in health and health care with a number of policies and initiatives ranging from programs that target specific segments of the African American population (such as Medicare and Medicaid beneficiaries) to increases in funding for research and education activities. While it is perhaps premature to assess the impact of many of these initiatives, there have been some notable gains reported from the National Center for Health Statistics. Keppel and colleagues (2002) reported that all racial and ethnic groups experienced improvements for 10 of 17 health status indicators developed as an objective of Healthy People 2000 (including prenatal care, infant mortality, teen births, death rates for heart disease, homicide, motor vehicle crashes, and work-related injuries; tuberculosis case rate, syphilis case rate, and poor air quality). These indicators provide a means to quantify and assess the progress on the Healthy People 2010 objective to eliminate disparities in health among population groups. The indicators reflect various aspects of health and include infant mortality, teen births, and prenatal care, as well as death rates from all causes, including heart disease, stroke, lung and breast cancer, suicide, and work-related injuries.

A great deal more needs to be done to eliminate racial disparities in health and health care. We need the courageous and moral leadership of both public and private actors. The U.S. health-care system is a complex arrangement of individuals and institutions from the private sector. It is time for private-sector actors to meet at the table with public-sector actors to work in partnership to achieve the goals of Healthy People 2010. Smith (1998) reminds that we have the technological capacity to address the racial disparities in health issues; now all we need is a commitment from both the public and private sectors to make the possible a reality.

REFERENCES

Aday, L. (2001). *At risk in America: The health and health care needs of vulnerable populations in the United States.* 2d ed. San Francisco: Jossey-Bass.

Bachrach, P. (1967). *The theory of democratic elitism: A critique.* Boston: Little, Brown.

Byrd, W.M., & Clayton, L.A. (2000). *An American health dilemma.* New York: Routledge.

Cahill, K., Tanamor, M., & Green, L. (November 1999). *Increasing beneficiary knowledge through improved communications: Research findings for the African American Medicare population.* Final Draft, Health Care Financing Administration.

Chappell, P.J. (2002, unpublished) Self-Assessed health status by state, race/ethnicity, sex and age, 1998–2000. Centers for Disease Control and Prevention, National Center for Health Statistics. Source: http://cdc. gov/nicipc.htm.

Editorial. (1999). Affirmative action. *Lancet 353(9146),* 1.

Estes, C.L. (1980). The aging enterprise. San Francisco: Jossey-Bass.

Estes, C.L. (1982). Austerity and aging in the United States: 1980 and beyond. *International Journal of Health Services, 12*, 733.

Feder, J.M. (1977). *The politics of federal hospital insurance.* Lexington, MA: Lexington Books.

Federal Register. (May 18, 1998). Medicaid program-Medicaid managed care. Vol. 63, No. 52-021, 045, 13111–13328. Office of the Federal Register, National Archives and Records Administration. Washington, DC: U.S. Government Printing Office.

Federal Register. (May 18, 1999). Racial and Ethnic Approaches to Community Health 2010; (REACH 2010) Demonstration Projects; Notice of Availability of Funds. Vol. 64, No. 95, 26977–26981. Office of the Federal Register, National Archives and Records Administration. Washington, DC: U.S. Government Printing Office.

Geiger, H.J. (1996). Race and health care—An American dilemma? *New England Journal of Medicine, 335(11)*, 815–816.

Ginzberg, D. (1978). Health reform: The outlook for the 1980s. *Inquiry, 15*, 311–326.

Ginzberg, E. (1977). Regionalization and health policy. Washington, DC: U.S. Government Printing Office.

Gornick, M.E. (2000). *Vulnerable populations and Medicare Services: Why do disparities exist?* New York: Century Foundation Press.

Heckler, M.M. (1985). Report of the secretary's task force on Black and minority health. Washington, DC: U.S. Department of Health and Human Services.

Heffler, S., Levit, K., Smith, C., Smith, S., Cowan, C., Lazenby, H., & Freeland, M. (2001) Health Spending growth up in 1999; faster expected in the future. *Health Affairs, March–April 20(2)*, 193–203.

Keppel, K.G., Percy, J.N., & Wagener, D.K. (January 2002). Trends in racial and ethnic-specific rates for health status indicators: United States, 1990–98. Health people statistical notes, no. 23. Hyattsville, MD: National Center for Health Statistics.

Kingdon, J.W. (1984). *Agendas, alternatives, and public policies.* Boston: Little, Brown.

Komaromy, M., et al. (1996). The role of Black and Hispanic physicians in providing health care for underserved populations. *Black and Hispanic Physicians and Underserved Populations 334(20)*, 1305–1310.

Lee, P., & Benjamin, A.E. (1999). Health policy and the politics of health care. In S.J. Williams & P.R. Torrrens (Eds.), Introduction to Health Services, 5th ed. Albany, NY: Delmar.

Levit, K., Smith, C., Cowan, C., Lazenby, H., & Martin A. (2002). Inflation spurs health spending in 2000. *Health Affairs, 21(2).*

Libby, D.L., Zhou, Z., & Kindig, D.A. (1997). Will minority physicians supply meet U.S. needs? *Health Affairs, (Millwood) 16(4)*, 205–214.

Lindblom, C.E. (1959). The science of "muddling through." *Public Administration Review, 10*, 79–88.

Lowi, T.J. (1979). *The end of liberalism: The second republic of the United States.* New York: Norton.

Marmor, T.R. (1973). *The politics of Medicare.* Chicago: Aldine.

Marmor, T.R., Whittman, D.A., & Heagy, T.C. (1976). The politics of medical inflation. *Journal of Health Politics, Policy and Law, 1*, 69–84.

Memorandum on Federal Agency Compliance with the Patient Bill of Rights. (February 20, 1998). http://www.gpo.gov/nara/pubpapas/srchpaps.html

Minority Health and Health Disparities Research and Education Act of 2000.

National Center for Health Statistics. (1998). Health, United States, 1998, with socioeconomic status and health chartbook. Hyattsville, MD.

National Center for Health Statistics. (2000). Health, United States, 2000, with socioeconomic status and health chartbook. Hyattsville, MD.

National Center for Health Statistics. (2001). Health, United States, 2001. Urban and Rural Health chartbook. Hyattsville, Maryland, DHHS Publication No (PHS) 01-1232.

National Center for Health Statistics (2002). Health, United States, 2002, with socioeconomic status and health chartbook. Hyattsville, Maryland.

National Center for Health Statistics (2003). Health, United States, 2003, with chartbook on trends in the health of Americans. Hyattsville, Maryland.

Nickens, H.W., & Cohen, J.J. (1996). On affirmative action [Policy Perspectives]. *Journal of the American Medical Association, 275(7)*, 572–574.

Noah, B.A. (1998). Racial disparities in the delivery of health care. *San Diego Law Review, 35*, 135–178.

Office of Management and Budget (OMB). (October 30, 1997) G2 Federal Register, pp. 58782–58786.

Office of Management and Budget (OMB). (May 12, 1977). Statistical Directive 15, Racial and ethnic standards for federal statistics and administrative reporting.

Reinhardt, U. (1986). Uncompensated hospital care. In F. Sloan, J. Blumstein, & J. Perrin (Eds.), *Uncompensated hospital care: Rights and responsibilities*, (pp. 1–15). Baltimore: Johns Hopkins University Press.

Rosenberg, H.M., Maurer, J.D., Sorlie, P.D., Johnson, N.J. et al. (1999). Quality of death rates by race and Hispanic origin: a summary of current research. National Center for Health Statistics. *Vital Health Statistics, 2(128)*, 1–13. Can also be accessed by http://www.cdc.gov/nchs/data/series/sr_02/sr02_128.pdf.

Sabatier, B., & Mazamania, D. (1979). Conditions of effective implantation. *Policy Analysis, 5*, 481–504.

Schattscheider, E.E. (1960). *The semisovereign people*. New York: Holt, Rinehart, & Winston.

The Secretary of Health and Human Services. (October 24, 1997). Policy statement of race and ethnicity in DHHS data collection activities.

Silver, G.A. (1976a). Medical politics, health policy, party health platforms, promise and performance. *International Journal of Health Services, 6*, 331–343.

Silver, G.A. (1976b). *A spy in the house of medicine*. Germantown, MD: Aspen.

Silver, G.A. (1978). *Preface: The uncertainties of federal child health policies*. Hyattsville, MD: National Center for Health Services Research.

Smith, D.B. (1998). Addressing racial inequities in health care: Civil rights monitoring and report cards. *Health Politics, Policy and Law, 23(1)*, 75–105.

U.S. Commission on Civil Rights. (September 1999). The health care challenge: Acknowledging disparity, confronting discrimination, and ensuring equality: Volume 1—"The Role of government and private health care programs and initiatives."

U.S. Department of Health and Human Services (2000). *Healthy People 2010, Conference Edition*. Vol. 1. Washington, D.C.: U.S. Government Printing Office.

U.S. Department of Justice. (August 16, 2000). Enforcement of Title VI of the Civil Rights Act of 1964: National origin discrimination against persons with limited English proficiency, Policy Guidance, 65 Federal Register 50123.

Vladeck, B.C. (1979). The design of failure: Health policy and the structure of federalism. *Journal of Health Politics, Policy and Law, 4*, 522–535.

Williams, D.R., & Rucker, T.D. (2000). Understanding and addressing racial disparities in health care. *Health Care Financing Review, 21(4)*, 75–90.

CHAPTER 40

African Americans and Access to Health Care: Trends in the Use of Health Services

LLEWELLYN J. CORNELIUS

HISTORICAL ISSUES OF ACCESS TO CARE FOR AFRICAN AMERICANS

While current interests focus on developing mechanisms to reduce disparities in access to medical care, historically, African Americans encounter a multitude of obstacles that either prevented or delayed them from obtaining medical care. Some of these factors still serve as significant barriers to obtaining medical care. This chapter focuses on disparities in the use of medical services by African Americans.

Using a Conceptual Model

The framework used to examine these disparities is the Andersen and Aday Behavioral Model of the Use of Services, first formulated by Ronald Andersen in 1968 (Andersen, 1968) and later expanded on by Ronald Andersen and Lu Ann Aday (Andersen et al., 1987; Aday et al., 1998) (see Figure 40.1). According to Andersen and Aday, several factors determine whether or not people are able to obtain medical care:

- **Predisposing factors**—age, gender, educational status, income, race ethnicity
- **Need factors**—their perceived needs for health services (as reflected by their perceived health status and/or disability days
- **Enabling factors**—the ability to finance health care through insurance and/or personal resources (income); having a regular place they can go to for medical care; the availability and convenience of services

The predisposing, need, and enabling factors interact with each other simultaneously to facilitate or hinder access to medical care. Under this model it is assumed that in a "just" health-care system, resources are allocated based on a person's "need" for medical care, rather than because of personal characteristics (predisposing) or other factors (enabling factors). This framework is ideal for looking at disparities among African Americans, because it seeks to reduce inequities based on race. Thus, information from the components of the Andersen/Aday model is used, wherever possible, to examine how African Americans are faring on issues of access to care.

Figure 40.1
Andersen and Aday access to medical care framework

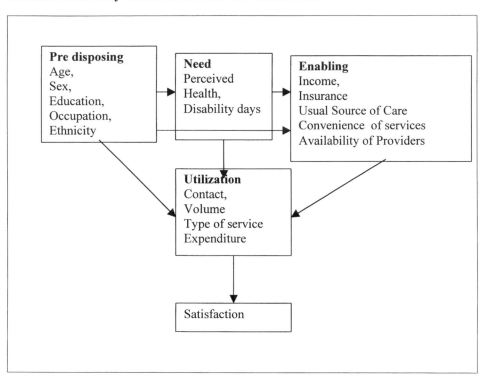

Source: Andersen et al. (1987).

Ability to Pay

While data on specific racial and ethnic groups were not reported before 1965, it is known that since 1932 non-Whites fared worse than Whites on measures of access to medical care (Committee on the Costs of Medical Care, 1933; Andersen et al., 1975; USDHHS, 1994, 1998, 2003). One of the reasons for disparities in the use of medical services is the inability to pay for medical services. Before the depression, the vast majority of Americans could not obtain health care, simply because the only mechanism that was available for paying to obtain medical care was the individual's personal resources. In 1933, the Committee on the Costs of Medical Care reported nearly half of the families who had incomes below $1,200 could not obtain medical care, while slightly less than 14 percent of the highest income group (those who earned $10,000 or more) could not obtain medical care in 1932. The committee also concluded that although African American families were not systematically studied, it could be safely assumed that they were receiving less medical care than were White Americans because of their lower incomes (Committee on the Cost of Medical Care, 1933).

Other data document the magnitude of poverty for African Americans during the depression. Jaynes and Williams (1989) report that in 1939, 93 percent of African Americans were poor, compared to 65 percent of White Americans (Jaynes & Williams, 1989). Based on these factors, it is clear that very few African Americans in the depression could afford to pay for medical care. While the overall percent of uninsured Americans began to decline following the introduction of employment-based health insurance in the 1930s (Starr, 1982), significant inroads in insurance coverage for African Americans did not occur in this area until the passage of the Medicare program (mainly for the elderly) and the Medicaid program (mainly for the poor on cash assistance programs) in 1965; both of these programs were amendments to the Social Security Act of 1935.

Discrimination

A second historical reason for the significant disparities between African Americans and other groups in access to medical care was the systematic discrimination and mistreatment of African Americans by health-care providers and institutions. Following the 1896 Supreme Court *Plessy v. Fergusson* ruling, which allowed for the creation of so-called separate but equal institutions for Whites and non-Whites, African Americans were systematically prohibited from using many hospitals and clinics. This systematic discrimination was further compounded by prevailing negative attitudes toward African Americans by the medical profession in the early twentieth century. Some physicians characterized the Negro as being physically inferior to Whites and thus not worthy of medical attention (Brandt, 1978). In fact, this negative attitude set the stage for the launching of the now infamous Tuskegee Experiment on the effects of untreated syphilis on the Negro male that began in 1932 (and the continuation of this experiment until 1972), where a cohort of Negro men were denied access to treatment for syphilis in spite of what was already known in 1932 about the long-term effects of untreated syphilis (Brandt, 1978). This study created a general suspicion/distrust of the health-care system that still exists today.

Following the Supreme Court ruling on *Brown v. Board of Education* of Topeka in 1954, which declared segregation in public schools unconstitutional, organizations such as the Medical Committee on Human Rights, the National Medical Association, and the Student National Medical Association attempted to address these discriminatory practices. These organizations intensified their efforts to desegregate health facilities, lobbying for better health insurance and for increasing the number of health professionals of color in the United States.

Increasing Health-Care Providers of Color

The efforts mentioned above led to the implementation of several programs both to increase the number of health providers of color and to serve a greater proportion of disadvantaged Americans—the Health Professions Educational Assistance (HPEA) Act of 1963 (which provided funds to support medical education), Neighborhood Health Centers, Community Mental Health Centers, and the National Service Corps (which attempted to encourage physicians to work in poor urban areas and in rural areas). These activities were designed to complement the commitment to the training of African American physicians provided by Meharry Medical College and Howard University, which graduated the majority of the African American physicians in the United States between 1920 and 1968.

In spite of the aforementioned lobbying efforts, these structural disparities in access to medical care persisted until the passage of several organizational and financing policies that were designed to increase the number of physicians serving indigent populations. Between the early 1930s and the passage of the Kerr-Mills program in 1960, America's commitment to providing health care to the poor was limited to a few states. This effort involved providing vendor payments to hospitals and physicians for services delivered to the aged, the blind, the disabled, and needy families, the provision of charity care at faith-based institutions, and the provision of uncompensated care at institutions built with federal funds from the Hill-Burton program (the Hospital Survey and Construction Act of 1947) (Stuart & Blair, 1971; Anderson, 1984). In 1960, the Social Security Act was amended to include a provision for providing matching funds to states for paying physicians and hospitals for delivering medical care to the aged who were poor (U.S. Department of Health, Education and Welfare, 1962).

THE WAR ON POVERTY AND THE ERA OF HEALTH-CARE COSTS CONTAINMENT (1965–PRESENT)

It was suggested before that the period preceding 1965 can best be classified as a period when African Americans encountered significant obstacles to obtaining health-care services due to discrimination, a lack of access to providers, and an inability to pay for medical services. The period following 1965 can best be characterized by a significant increase in the availability of insurance coverage, an elimination of blatant forms of discrimination, but a lingering smaller disparity between African Americans and other groups. An explanation of the latter point follows.

Medicare and Medicaid Programs

One of the most notable contributions to this reduction in disparities in access to care was the introduction of the Medicare and Medicaid programs to meet the needs of the elderly and medically indigent. However, because of the way that these programs were designed, each of these programs contained elements that contributed to gaps in insurance coverage for African Americans. The Medicaid program (Title XIX of the Social Security Act) represented an expansion of earlier public insurance programs for the aged, the blind, the disabled, and the medically needy (U.S. Department of Health, Education, and Welfare, 1975). The 1965 legislation tied the eligibility for Medicaid to enrollment in one of two cash assistance programs: Aid to Dependent Children (ADC) and Supplemental Security Income (SSI) (U.S. Department of Health, Education, and Welfare, 1977). These programs served portions of the poor who met eligibility requirements based on resources, assets, and other criteria.

In addition to providing coverage for the enrollees in these two programs, Medicaid had the option of extending coverage to other poor persons as well as to the "medically needy" whose family income was above the poverty line. States were given the option both to participate and to decide which services to provide over and above a set of minimally required services (U.S. Department of Health, Education, and Welfare, 1975). Although Medicaid was meant to improve access to medical care for the poor, Starr explains that when the Medicaid program began in 1965, it "omitted from coverage most two-parent families, and childless couples, widows, and other single persons under the age of sixty-five years, families with fathers working at low-paying jobs, and the medically needy in twenty-two states that did not provide coverage" (Starr, 1982, p. 374).

The Medicare program was a second policy that evolved from the pre-1965 Kerr-Mills program. The Medicare program provides health-care coverage for persons over 65 and a subset of persons with disabilities. However, Medicare contains lifetime caps on the use of medical services and limitations in coverage. Thus, one typically needs to supplement Medicare with either Medicaid or private insurance to cover needed health services.

Passage of Antidiscrimination Laws

In addition to the introduction of financing programs to increase the number of poor and indigent Americans with health coverage, a second significant contribution to the reduction of disparities in access to care was the passage of several antidiscrimination laws in the 1960s to eliminate blatant discrimination practices. In 1964 Title VI of the Civil Rights Act was passed. This act prohibited discrimination on the basis or race, color, or national origin to recipients of federal funds from the Department of Health, Education, and Welfare (USDHHS, 2002a). In addition, under

the Community Service Assurance under Title VI of the Public Health Service Act requires recipients of Hill-Burton funds to make services provided by the facility available to persons residing in the facility's service area without discrimination on the basis of race, color, national origin, creed, or any other ground unrelated to the individual's need for the service or the availability of the needed service in the facility. These requirements also apply to persons employed in the service area of the facility if it was funded under Title XVI of the Public Health Service Act. (USDHHS, 2002b)

These laws gave hospitals a powerful incentive to alter their practices, since the federal government could withhold funds to health-care institutions that engaged in discrimination against patients served by a health-care facility or by employees of that facility.

Changes in Reducing Disparities

As reflected by the data that follow, there was a significant reduction in disparities in access to care for African Americans following the introduction of the policies mentioned above (see Tables 40.1–40.6 and Figures 40.1–40.2). Data on the percent of African Americans and Whites who have a usual source of medical care to go to for their health needs shows that, while a greater percent of Whites and African Americans did not have a usual source of care in 1996 than in 1977, the differences between these two groups are small.

As seen in Table 40.1, in 1977, 19.7 percent of African Americans and 13.1 percent of Whites did not have a usual source of care. By 1996, 26.6 percent of African Americans and 23.4 percent of Whites did not have a usual source of care. By contrast, significant gaps remain between the percent of African Americans and Whites who usually go to an emergency room or a hospital outpatient clinic (Table 40.1). In 1977, 13.8 percent of African Americans and 4.3 percent of Whites usually went to a hospital outpatient dependent or emergency room for their care. By 1996, 21.8 percent of the African Americans and 11.3 percent of Whites usually went to a hospital outpatient department or emergency room for their care. What is significant about this pattern is that persons who regularly go to a hospital outpatient department or emergency room have lower continuity of care than persons who usually go to a physicians' office for their care (Fleming & Andersen, 1986). Thus, by relying on hospital outpatient departments and emergency rooms for their care, African Americans are less likely to see the same provider when they come into the health-care system.

As in the case of estimates of the percent of African Americans with a usual source of care, there was a narrowing of the gap between the percent of uninsured African Americans and Whites. This occurred as a result of an increase in the percent of uninsured Whites. In 1980, 19 percent of African Americans and 11.4 percent of Whites under 65 were uninsured (Table 40.2). By contrast, in 1999, 19 percent of African Americans and 15 percent of Whites under 65 were uninsured.

It should be noted that regardless of age, African Americans were at least three times as likely as Whites to have Medicaid coverage (Table 40.2). In 1980, 17.9 percent of African Americans and 3.9 percent of Whites under 65 had Medicaid coverage. At the same time 23.2 percent of the elderly African Americans and 6.6 percent of elderly Whites had Medicaid coverage. In 1999, 18.6 percent of African Americans and 7.0 percent of Whites under 65 had Medicaid, while 18.2 percent of elderly African Americans and 5.7 percent of elderly Whites had Medicaid. The significance of this finding is that physicians are less likely to accept Medicaid patients than Medicare or private insurance patients. In addition, physicians may be able to accept only a portion (a quota) of these patients without running the risk of bankrupting their medical practices, as a result of the differences in

Table 40.1
Usual source of care by race, 1977–1996

Characteristic	1977 African Americans	1977 Whites	1987 African Americans	1987 Whites	1996 African Americans	1996 Whites
Usual Source of Care						
No usual source	19.7	13.1	22.9	17.0	26.6	23.4
Physician's Office	45.9	70.3	53.6	74.2	68.5	65.3
Hospital outpatient Department/						
Emergency room	13.8	4.3	12.2	3.6	21.8	11.3
Health center and Other	10.7	4.2	11.2	5.0	0.0	0.0
Reasons for having no usual source of care						
Does not get sick	64.8	65.5	76.9	78.0	73.9	65.5
New to area	10.6	20.6	18.6	19.2	3.0	5.7
Source no longer available	8.6	13.6	11.2	11.2	1.8	3.4
Goes to different places	23.4	20.7	11.9	18.2	2.8	2.5

Sources: Kasper and Barrish (1982), Tables 1, 2, 6 and 7; Cornelius, & Cohen (1991), Tables 1, 2, 4 and 5; Weinick et al. (1997); U.S. Department of Health and Human Services (USDHHS), Agency for Health Care Research and Quality (2002); Available online: http://meps.ahrq.gov/Data_Pub/HC_FYData96.htm#hc012/66666666 (last accessed 07/08/02).

Table 40.2
Health insurance status by race and age, 1980–1999

Characteristic	1980 African Americans	1980 Whites	1989 African Americans	1989 Whites	1999 African Americans	1999 Whites
Under 65 Private						
Insurance	60.1	81.9	58.7	79.3	58.2	76.7
Medicaid	17.9	3.9	17.8	5.1	18.6	7.0
No insurance	19.0	11.4	21.4	16.1	19.4	15.0
65 and older Private						
Insurance	26.5	68.3	43.0	79.8	40.3	67.5
Medicaid	23.2	6.6	20.4	5.6	18.2	5.7
Medicare only	40.6	21.0	29.9	13.9	37.0	25.1

Sources: NCHS (1989), Tables 117–118; NCHS (1999), Tables 133, 134; NCHS (2002), Tables 128–131.

Figure 40.2
Percent of African Americans who saw a physician within the last year,
1964–1998

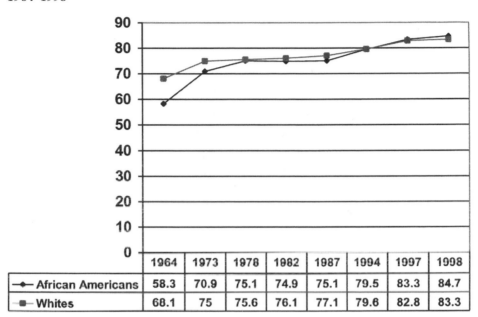

	1964	1973	1978	1982	1987	1994	1997	1998
African Americans	58.3	70.9	75.1	74.9	75.1	79.5	83.3	84.7
Whites	68.1	75	75.6	76.1	77.1	79.6	82.8	83.3

Sources: NCHS (1981), Table 32; NCHS (1989), Table 62; NCHS (1996), Table 77; NCHS (2001), Table 72.

reimbursement for providing care to patients with public insurance. Thus, persons with this type of health coverage may have to delay obtaining needed medical care.

In spite of remaining disparities that exist in aspects of the usual source of care and financing of health care, the gaps between the percent of African Americans and Whites who have seen a physician have all but been eliminated. In 1964, 58.3 percent of African Americans and 68.1 percent of Whites saw a physician at least once in the previous year. By 1998, 84.7 percent of African Americans and 83.3 percent of Whites saw a physician at least once per year (Figure 40.2). Similarly in 1987, 13 percent of African Americans and Whites were enrolled in a managed care plan, and by 1996, 58.3 percent of African Americans and 50.8 percent of Whites were enrolled in a managed care plan (Figure 40.3). While these patterns appear to be promising, greater access to providers does not necessarily mean an improvement in the health status of the population. In addition to seeing an increase in access to the system, one will need to see an improvement in the quality of care before concluding that equity of access to care has been achieved for African Americans.

While there was an increase in the percent of African Americans who gained entry into the system, there was a shift in where they went for care (Table 40.3). In 1975, 46.9 percent of all the ambulatory visits for African Americans and 40.6 percent of all the ambulatory visits for Whites were to generalists and family practitioners. This declined to about 25 percent for both African Americans and Whites in 1996. Likewise, in 1975, 6.1 percent of African Americans and 7.5 percent of Whites saw a general surgeon. This declined to 2.5 percent for both African Americans and Whites in 1996. This shift was offset by increases in the proportion of those seeing an internist, a pediatrician, or other physician.

Like overall data on the use of ambulatory services, data on the use of inpatient care (Table 40.4)

Figure 40.3
Percent of African Americans enrolled in managed care plans, 1987–1996

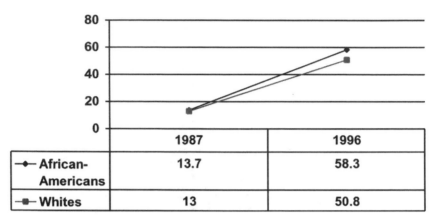

	1987	1996
← African-Americans	13.7	58.3
← Whites	13	50.8

Source: Weinick & Cohen (2000).

Table 40.3
Types of specialists seen for ambulatory visits by race, 1975–1996

Characteristic	1975 African Americans	1975 Whites	1985 African Americans	1985 Whites	1996 African Americans	1996 Whites
Access to specialty care General and family practice	46.9	40.6	35.4	30.0	24.6	25.2
Internal Medicine	9.9	11.1	10.4	11.8	20.2	13.1
Pediatrics	8.0	8.2	11.3	11.4	13.2	13.3
Obstetrics and Gynecology	11.9	11.9	9.9	8.7	11.5	8.6
General surgery	6.1	7.5	6.2	4.6	2.5	2.5
Ophthalmology	3.2	4.3	4.7	6.4	2.8	6.0
Orthopedic surgery	2.8	3.5	4.8	5.9	3.9	5.1
All others	11.0	16.5	17.2	22.3	21.3	26.2

Sources: NCHS (1999), Table 82; NCHS (2002), Table 85.

suggest that there is a shift in the use of inpatient services over time. Between 1964 and 1995 the number of hospitalized African Americans who were discharged increased from 84 to 108 per 1,000 African Americans, while it declined from 112 to 84.2 per 1,000 Whites. At the same time both the length of stay and the total number of days of care declined for these groups.

The data above suggest that some of the changes in disparities in access to care may be related to recent shifts in the organizations of care. The most notable shift in the organization of medical care followed the introduction of legislation, introduced during the 103d Congress (e.g., the Clinton Plan-H.R. 3600), to expand health insurance coverage to all Americans, while controlling the costs

Table 40.4
Selected hospitalization statistics by race, 1964–1995

Characteristic	1964 African Americans	1964 Whites	1990 African Americans	1990 Whites	1995 African Americans	1995 Whites
Discharges per 1,000 persons	84.0	112.4	112.0	89.5	108.0	84.2
Days of care per 1,000 persons	1062.9	961.4	875.9	580.9	730.9	458.5
Average length of stay	12.7	8.6	7.8	6.5	6.8	5.4

Source: USDHHS, NCHS (1999), Table 87.

of health care through community-based health cooperatives. While none of these universal health insurance proposals were enacted, one of the outcomes of this process was a dramatic increase in the number of managed care plans, sponsored by Medicare, Medicaid, and private insurance carriers. These plans included a variety of constraints and included limitations in the amount and type of medical services provided.

DISPARITIES IN ACCESS TO CARE FOR SELECTED PROCEDURES

Care Associated with Cancer, Heart Disease, Renal Disease, and Other Outcomes

In addition to seeing a shift in where care was provided to African Americans, there are also persistent disparities remaining in the receipt of specific types of medical care for African Americans. African American men are more likely than Whites to be overrepresented in each stage of prostate illness, from screening through surgical procedures and treatment for cancerous tumors (Robbins et al., 1999). African American men are less likely to get a digital rectal exam (DRE) or a prostate specific antigen (PSA) screening for prostate cancer (Myers, 1999; Myers et al., 1999). African American men with advanced stages of prostate cancer were less likely than other African Americans to know about screening practices (Conlisk et al., 1999). African Americans were more likely than Whites to have anterior as opposed to posterior tumors (Tiguert et al., 1999). Advanced prostate disease was more prevalent among African American men than White men (Powell et al., 1999). African American men were less likely to undergo radical prostatectomy (Klabunde et al., 1998).

Like prostate cancer screening, detection, and treatment, disparities also exist for African Americans in colon cancer treatment, treatment for heart disease and kidney disease, and prenatal care treatment. White males are more likely than others to have a colonoscopy (McMahon et al., 1999). While African American are more likely to have heart disease and kidney disease, they are less likely to undergo coronary artery bypass graft (CABG) surgery or renal dialysis for end-stage renal disease (ESRD) (Smedley et al., 2002; Furth et al., 2000). These disparities are also complicated by their lack of enrollment in clinical trials that focus on testing cutting-edge medical treatments. This issue is discussed in detail in another chapter.

Results of Multivariate Studies

In addition to the findings reported above, other researchers have found that disparities remain for African Americans, even after controlling for a multitude of factors. In a multivariate analysis of the use of medical care between 1977 and 1996, Weinick et al. (2000) report that even after one controlled for differences in health insurance, income, age, gender, marital status, education, region of the country, and residence within the United States, African Americans were more likely than Whites to lack a usual source of care. However, they also noted that a change in the insurance coverage or income for African Americans did result in a substantial reduction in the disparities found in the use of medical services or the availability of a usual source of care. In a second multivariate analysis, Furth and colleagues (2000) report that even after controlling for age, gender, socioeconomic status, geographic region, incident year of dialysis, and assigned cause of end-stage renal disease, African American patients were less likely than White patients to be activated on the kidney transplant waiting list. These findings suggest that determining whether African Americans really achieved equity of access to health care is complicated and requires a multifactorial analysis to control for the multiple barriers to medical care.

COMPARISONS BETWEEN AFRO-CARIBBEAN AMERICANS AND OTHER AFRICAN AMERICANS

While the data reviewed above focused on African Americans as a unitary group, there is research that highlights the importance of looking at access issues within racial and ethnic groups. In 1987 Schur and colleagues in the first analysis of access to care for Latino subpopulations (Mexican, Cuban, Puerto Rican, Central American and South American Latinos) concluded that Puerto Ricans were less likely to be uninsured than Mexican Americans or Cuban Americans (Schur et al., 1987). Recent analyses of these Latino populations continue to reinforce the differences found between Puerto Ricans, Cubans, and other Latinos and highlighted the importance of looking at issues of access to care within racial and ethnic populations (Berk et al., 1996). As such, data from the 1994 Commonwealth Fund Minority Health Survey are included here to see whether there are differences in access to care for African Americans who indicate that they were born in the Caribbean, as opposed to other African Americans.

While there were differences found between Afro-Caribbean Americans and other African Americans and between Whites on two of these indicators (insurance and having a limited choice in where to go for care), most of the differences found were between Afro-Caribbean Americans and Whites (on use of herbal medicine, barriers of access to specialty care, language differences, not being able to get an appointment, having paperwork to complete, transportation, being nervous or afraid, or encountering language barriers). For example, more than a third of the Afro-Caribbean Americans over 18 years of age were uninsured in 1994, compared to 24.1 percent of the other African Americans and 12.9 percent of the Whites (Table 40.5). Close to two-thirds (64.9 percent) of the Afro-Caribbean Americans indicated that they had limited choices in where they could go for care, compared to 51.7 percent of the other African Americans and 41.0 percent of Whites. These findings suggest that even if disparities between Whites and African Americans as a whole are reduced, barriers may continue to exist for Afro-Caribbean and African immigrants. Thus, when examining the disparities for African Americans, we need to be sensitive to the fact that, like Latinos, persons of African descent represent a mosaic of ethnic groups with different needs and thus require a mosaic of interventions (for example, we need data on Afro-Caribbean and African immigrants).

SUMMARY AND DISCUSSION

As indicated above, the progress in reducing disparities in access to care for African Americans is mixed. While most of the overall gaps in seeing a physician have been eliminated, gaps still appear in aspects of the treatment process, in the availability of health coverage, and in places where people

Table 40.5
Selected access to care characteristics by race, 1994

Characteristics	Afro-Caribbean American	Other African American	Whites
Health Insurance			
Private only	44.9	59.1	63.1
Any public insurance	19.1	16.7	24.0
Uninsured	36.0	24.1	12.9
Barriers to care			
Had a limited choice			
In where to go for care	64.9	51.7	41.0
Had to delay seeking care	35.1	34.8	32.8
Was refused care	0.7	3.6	1.7
Did not feel welcome by			
Health provider	23.8	30.5	21.3
No access to specialty care	34.2	14.6	9.0
Can't get appointment	19.1	12.7	8.9
Having to pay too much	45.3	36.1	37.0
Language differences	11.3*	4.3	3.8
Being nervous or afraid	19.8*	7.0	5.6
Having to wait too long	35.5	27.2	16.2
Transportation	10.0	8.1	4.5
Have paperwork to complete	21.9*	9.2	7.9
Measures of utilization			
Used herbal medicine	24.3*	16.0	12.8
Used home remedies	36.1	33.8	31.3
Made a visit to physician for preventive care	63.0	67.7	73.8
Made an ambulatory visit to a physician	89.9	89.5	87.2

Source: Lou Harris and Associates (1994).

*Standard error of a percent > 30 percent.

go for their care. This is true even after accounting for differences in health status, age, and other factors. Thus, while similar percentages of African Americans and Whites are gaining entry to the system, it is possible that there are gaps in the nature of the services they receive in ways that contribute to inequities in access to medical care.

It may be that the barriers that remain for access to desirable health care are subtle and exist within the continuum of the delivery of medical care. This point was first raised in the landmark 1985 Report of the Secretary's Taskforce on Black and Minority Health (USDHHS, 1985) and reinforced in the 2002 Institute of Medicine Report on Health Disparities (Smedley et al., 2002). These reports suggest that disparities in health are the result of a complex array of factors, including a lack of access to health-care providers, differences in health behaviors (e.g., diet, smoking, exercise), socioeconomic differences, and other environmental factors. This would further suggest that in order to reduce the disparities in the use of medical care for African Americans, we would need not only to think about the factors that contribute to barriers of access to medical care, as exemplified by the Andersen and Aday model, but also to examine other factors occurring in the continuum of the delivery of medical care (e.g., screening, detection, treatment and follow-up care).

Figure 40.4
Logic model for reducing health disparities through access to health care

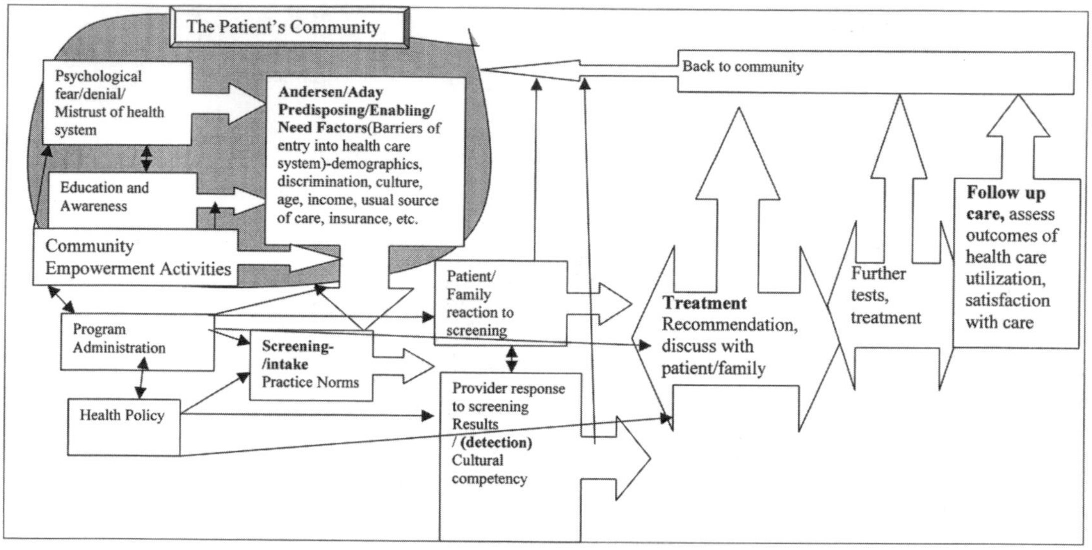

Source: As modified from Anderson et al. (1987), Figure 1.1.

Displayed in Figure 40.4 is a logic model that combines attempts to address these issues. This model evolves from the Ronald Andersen and Lu Ann Aday model described earlier (in Figure 40.1). The directions of the arrows suggest that reducing disparities is a complex process that is influenced by factors outside the provider and what the family encounters in the delivery of health care (e.g., the community, health policy, and program administration), as well as within the context of the provider, the patient, and his or her family. It also suggests that at each stage of the process, the patient and his or her family may leave the health-care system and return to his or her community. This can occur as a result of patients either being dissatisfied with the health system or finding a satisfactory resolution to their needs.

This model also suggests that policy and program management not only affect and influence the individual and his or her community, but also affect the delivery of health services. The complexity of the model suggests that examining equity in the use of medical care (i.e., the utilization of health care) is only part of what is needed to reduce disparities for African Americans. Interventions are needed both within the community, with providers, and across the health system in order to improve the delivery of medical care. The model also reaffirms the importance of using a multivariate approach for determining whether disparities in access to care have been achieved for African Americans. This approach also parallels the recommendations of the Institute of Medicine report that highlight the need to intervene on multiple levels, between the provider and the patient, in the financing of care, in the provision of language and interpreter services, and in the need to have patients participate in treatment decisions (Smedley et al., 2002).

RECOMMENDATIONS

Based on the approach taken in this chapter, it is believed that permanent reductions in disparities in access would occur when the following activities are satisfactorily addressed:

- The provision of universal comprehensive health insurance coverage is provided—to eliminate the lingering gaps in insurance coverage;
- The mobilization of all citizens to advocate for the development and passage of local, state, and federal legislation that addresses gaps in the organization and financing of medical care;
- The securing of access to providers that focuses on their need for the provision of screening, detection, treatment, and follow-up care;
- Ensuring that providers are given adequate patient time to focus on the continuum of care needed by patients;
- The provision of community-based health education efforts that emphasize the importance of timely medical interventions (preventive or otherwise);
- Ensuring that health-care providers master and demonstrate skills in the understanding and respecting of cultural differences, respecting and addressing the needs of different patient populations, and recognizing the right of patients and their families to play a significant role in the decisions made about their care;
- Ensuring that health-care institutions systematize the use of interpreters and translated documents and brochures to reach out to patients in their communities with multiethnic backgrounds;
- Ensuring that communities are empowered to influence the way that services are delivered to their residents; and
- Ensuring that providers find ways to address not just the needs of individual patients but other members of the family who may fall between the cracks.

It is believed that given the complexity of the health-care system, we will need to intervene on multiple levels to simultaneously address these complex and varied issues.

REFERENCES

Aday, L.A., Begley, C.E., Lairson, D.A., & Slater, C.H. (1998). *Evaluating the health care system: Effectiveness, efficiency, and equity, 2d ed.* Chicago: Health Administration Press

Anderson, O.W. (1984). Health Services in the United States: A growth enterprise for a hundred years. In T.J. Litman & L.S. Robins (Eds.), *Health, politics and policy* (pp. 67–79). New York: John Wiley & Sons.

Andersen, O.W. (1990). *Health services as a growth enterprise in the United States since 1875.* Ann Arbor, MI: Health Administration Press.

Andersen, R.M. (1968). *A behavioral model of families' use of health services.* Chicago: Center for Health Administration Studies, University of Chicago.

Andersen, R.M., Aday, L.A., Lyttle, C.S., Cornelius, L.J., & Chen, M.S. (1987). *Ambulatory care and insurance coverage in an era of constraint.* Chicago: Pluribus Press.

Andersen, R.M., Lion, L., & Andersen, O.W. (1975). *Two decades of health services: Social survey trends in use and expenditures.* Cambridge: Balinger.

Berk, M.L., Albers, L.A., & Schur, C.L. (1996). The growth in the U.S. Uninsured population: Trends in Hispanic subgroups. *American Journal of Public Health, 86,* 572–576.

Brandt, A.M. (1978). Racism and research: The case of the Tuskegee Syphilis Study. *Hastings Center Report, 8,* 21–9.

Committee on the Costs of Medical Care. (1933). *Medical care for the American people: The final report of the committee on the costs of medical care.* Chicago: University of Chicago Press.

Conlisk, E.A., Lengerivh, E.J., Demark-Wahnefried, W., Schildkraut, J.M., & Aldrich, T.E. (1999). Prostate cancer: Demographic and behavioral correlates of stage at diagnosis among Blacks and Whites in North Carolina. *Urology, 53,* 1194–1199.

Cornelius, L.J., Beauregard, K., & Cohen J. (1991). *Usual sources of medical care and their characteristics.* DHHS Pub No. (PHS) 91-0042. Rockville, MD: U.S. Department of Health and Human Services, Agency for Health Care Policy and Research.

Fleming, G.V., & Andersen, R.M. (1986). *The municipal health services program. Improving access, while controlling costs?* Chicago: Pluribus Press.

Furth, S.L., Garg, P.P., Neu, A.M., Hwang, W., Fivush, B.A., & Powe, N.R. (2000). Racial differences in access to the kidney transplantation waiting list for children and adolescents with end stage renal diseases. *Pediatrics, 106,* 756–761.

Jaynes, G.D., & Williams, R.M., Jr. (Eds.). (1989). *A common destiny: Blacks and American society.* Washington, DC: National Academy Press.

Kasper, J.A., & Barrish, G. (1982). *Usual sources of medical care and their characteristics. DHHS* Pub. No (PHS)-82-3324. Rockville, MD: U.S. Department of Health and Human Services, National Center for Health Services Research.

Klabunde, C.N., Potosky, A.L., Harlan, L.C., & Kramer, B.S. (1998). Trends and Black/White differences in treatment for nonmetastatic prostate cancer. *Medical Care, 36,* 1337–1348.

Lou Harris & Associates. (1994). *Health Care Services and Minority Groups: A Comparative Survey of Whites, African-Americans Hispanics and Asian Americans.* New York: Lou Harris & Associates.

McMahon, L.F., Wolfe, R.A., Huang, S., & Tedeschi, P. (1999). Race and gender variation in use of diagnostic colonic procedures in the Michigan Medicare Study. *Medical Care, 37,* 712–717.

Myers, R.E. (1999). African American men, prostate cancer early detection examination use. *Seminars in Oncology, 26,* 375–381.

Myers, R.E., Chodak, G.W., Wolf, T.A., Burgh, D.Y., McGrory, G.T., Marcus, S.M., Diehl, J.A., & Williams, M. (1999). Adherence by African American men to prostate cancer education and early detection. *Cancer, 86,* 1–2.

Powell, I.J., Banerjeem M., Sakr, W., Grignon, D.P., Jr, Novallo, M., & Pontes, E. (1999). Should African American men be tested for prostate carcinoma at an early age than White men? *Cancer, 85,* 472–477.

Robbins, A.S., Whittemore, A.S., & Van Den Eeden, S.K. (1999). Race, prostate cancer surival, and membership in a large health maintenance organization. *Journal of the National Cancer Institute, 91,* 801–803.

Schur, C.L., Bernstein, A.B., & Berk, M.L. (1987). The importance of distinguishing Hispanic subpopulation in the use of medical care. *Medical Care, 25,* 627–641.

Smedley, B.D., Stith, A.Y., & Nelson, A.R. (Eds.). (2002). *Unequal treatment: Confronting racial and ethnic disparities in health care.* Washington, DC: National Academy Press.

Starr, P. (1982). *The social transformation of American medicine.* New York: Basic Books.

Stuart, B.C., & Blair, L.A. (1971). *Health care and income: The distributional impacts of Medicaid and Medicare nationally and in the state of Michigan.* (2d ed.). Lansing: State of Michigan, Department of Social Services.

Tiguert, R., Gheiler, E.L., Tefilli, M.V., & Pontes, J.E. (1999). Racial differences and prognostic significance of tumor location in radical prostatectomy specimens. *Prostate, 37,* 230–235.

U.S. Department of Health and Human Services (USDHHS). (1985). *Report of the Secretary's Task Force on Black and Minority Health.* Washington, DC: U.S. Department of Health and Human Services.

U.S. Department of Health and Human Services (USDHHS), Agency for Health Care Research and Quality. (2002). *1996 Medical Expenditure Panel Survey file HC 12.* Retrieved July 8, 2002 from: http://meps.ahrq.gov/Data_Pub/HC_FYData96.htm#hc012/66666666

U.S. Department of Health and Human Services (USDHHS), National Center for Health Statistics (NCHS). (1981). *Health, United States, 1980.* Hyattsville, MD: U.S. Department of Health and Human Services, Public Health Service.

U.S. Department of Health and Human Services (USDHHS), National Center for Health Statistics (NCHS). (1989). *Health, United States, 1988.* Hyattsville, MD: U.S. Department of Health and Human Services, Public Health Service.

U.S. Department of Health and Human Services (USDHHS), National Center for Health Statistics (NCHS). (1994). *Health, United States, 1993.* Hyattsville, MD: U.S. Department of Health and Human Services, Public Health Service.

U.S. Department of Health and Human Services (USDHHS), National Center for Health Statistics (NCHS). (1995). *Health, United States, 1994.* Hyattsville, MD: U.S. Department of Health and Human Services, Public Health Service.

U.S. Department of Health and Human Services (USDHHS), National Center for Health Statistics (NCHS). (1996). *Health, United States, 1995*. Hyattsville, MD: U.S. Department of Health and Human Services, Public Health Service.

U.S. Department of Health and Human Services (USDHHS), National Center for Health Statistics (NCHS). (1998). *Health, United States, 1997*. Hyattsville, MD: U.S. Department of Health and Human Services, Public Health Service.

U.S. Department of Health and Human Services (USDHHS), National Center for Health Statistics (NCHS). (1999). *Health, United States, 1998*. Hyattsville, MD: U.S. Department of Health and Human Services, Public Health Service.

U.S. Department of Health and Human Services (USDHHS), National Center for Health Statistics (NCHS). (2001). *Health, United States, 2000*. Hyattsville, MD: U.S. Department of Health and Human Services, Public Health Service.

U.S. Department of Health and Human Services (USDHHS), National Center for Health Statistics (NCHS). (2002). *Health, United States, 2001*. Hyattsville, MD: U.S. Department of Health and Human Services, Public Health Service.

U.S. Department of Health and Human Services (USDHHS), National Center for Health Statistics (2003). Health, United States, 2003 with chartbook on trends in the health of Americans. Hyattsville, Maryland.

U.S. Department of Health and Human Service (USDHHS), Office for Civil Rights. (2002a). Part 80-Nondiscrimination under programs receiving federal assistance through the Department of Health, Education, and Welfare effectuation of Title VI of the Civil Rights Act of 1964. Retrieved May 26, 2002, from: http://www.hhs.gov/ocr/part80rg.html

U.S. Department of Health and Human Service (USDHHS), Office for Civil Rights. (2002b). Your rights under the community service assurance provision of the Hill Burton Act. Retrieved May 26, 2002, from: http://www.hhs.gov/ocr/hburton.html

U.S. Department of Health, Education, and Welfare. (1975). History and evolution of Medicaid. In A.D., Spiegel & S. Podair (Eds.), *Medicaid: Lessons for National Health Insurance*. Rockville, MD: Aspen Systems Corporation.

U.S. Department of Health, Education, and Welfare. (1962). Health Insurance for Aged Persons. Report submitted to the committee on ways and means, House of Representatives by the secretary of health, education and welfare, July 24, 1961. In U.S. Department of Health Education and Welfare (ed). Back ground on Medicare 1957–1962. Volume 12, 85th–87th Congress. Reports, studies and congressional considerations on health legislation. Washington, DC: Department of Health, Education and Welfare, Social Security Administration.

U.S. Department of Health, Education and Welfare, Health Care Financing Administration. (1977). *Data on the Medicaid Program: Eligibility, services, expenditures, fiscal years 1966–1977*. Washington, DC: U.S. Government Printing Office.

Weinick, R.M., & Cohen, J.W. (2000). Leveling the playing field: Managed care enrollment and hospital use, 1987–1996. *Health Affairs, 19*, 178–184.

Weinick, R.M., Zuvekas, S.H., & Cohen, J.W. (2000). Racial and ethnic differences in access to and use of health care services, 1977 to 1996. *Medical Care Research and Review, 57(Supplement)*, 36–54.

Weinick, R.M., Zuvekas, S.H., & Drilea, S.K. (1997). *Access to health care—sources and barriers: 1996*. MEPS Research Findings No. 3. AHCPR Publ. No. 98-0001. Rockville, MD: Agency for Health Care Policy and Research.

Zambrana, R.E., Dunkel-Schetter, C., & Collins, N.L. (1999). Mediators of ethnic-associated differences in infant birth weight. *Journal of Urban Health, 76*, 102–116.

Zegars, G.K., Pollack, A., & Pettaway, C.A. (1998). Prostate cancer in African American men: Outcome following radiation therapy with or without adjuvant androgen ablation. *International Journal of Radiation, Oncology, Biology and Physics, 42*, 517–523.

CHAPTER 41

African Americans in the Health-Care Workforce: Underrepresentation and Health Disparities

STERLING KING JR. AND
RICHARD JARVIS ENOCHS

INTRODUCTION

The length of days, the quality of one's life, liberty, and the pursuit of happiness depend in large measure on socioeconomic conditions of education, environment, and employment as well as on access to adequate health care. Whether health care is viewed as a right or a privilege, health is considered an important "good" in itself and is an important determinant of options and opportunities during the course of one's life. An extensive body of research has consistently revealed that African Americans have disproportionately higher rates of illness, disability, and death than their White counterparts (Smedley, Stith & Nelson, 2003; National Center for Health Statistics, 2002; Healthy People 2010, 2000; Mechanic, 2002; National Research Council, 1989; Report of the Secretary's Task Force on Black and Minority Health, 1985).

Health status is considered an indicator of a people's social position as well as its present and future well-being. Unhealthy conditions and childhood illnesses may hinder learning potential and create disadvantages that continue throughout the entire span of one's life. Inadequate prenatal care may lead to increased likelihood of premature birth, neurological damage, developmental impairment, or infant death.

According to the 1985 benchmark Report on Black and Minority Health, Blacks die in excess of 60,000 annually from preventable illnesses. The number of excess deaths is now estimated at over 91,000 (Hood, 2001). This disparity in mortality is attributed to the continuing disproportionate representation of Blacks in mortality rates associated with cancer, cardiovascular diseases, cirrhosis, diabetes, infant mortality, unintentional injuries, homicide, and recently, HIV/AIDS disease. In 1999, overall mortality was one-third higher for Blacks than for Whites (National Center for Health Statistics, 2002, p. 6). One of the overarching national goals noted in "Healthy People 2000" was to *reduce* health disparities among Americans (Healthy People 2000, 1990). Healthy People 2010 proposes a framework to *eliminate* health disparities as one of the two primary goals for the next decade (Satcher, 2000). The immense racial disparities in health that persist stem from several interacting factors and conditions (Ukawuilulu & Livingston, 1994; Abreu, 1999; Smedley, Stith & Nelson, 2003; Schneider et al., 2002; Meredith & Griffith-Forge, 2002; Deaton, 2002; Marmot, 2002).

Figure 41.1
Health-care workforce: Organizational overview

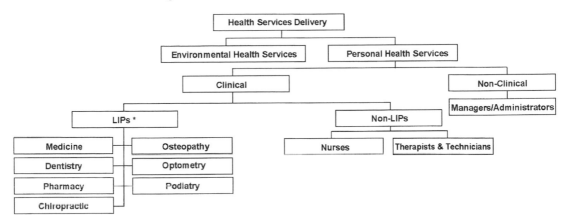

*LIPs—Licensed Independent Practitioners

The Focus of the Chapter

The main thrust of this chapter is to review and discuss issues related to the underrepresentation of Blacks among the front-line providers (FLPs) of health care and to consider strategies to increase their presence and participation in the health-care workforce. The basic premise is that there is a correlation between the underrepresentation of Blacks in the health professions and their over-representation in morbidity and mortality profiles. In essence, it is reasoned that if Blacks were present among front-line providers and other professions in proportion to their presence in the general population, their health disparities would be reduced and overall health status would significantly improve (Smedley, Stith & Nelson, 2003; Pogue et al., 2002; Komaromy et al., 1996; King & Bendel, 1995). The authors recognize that self-identifying as Black does not necessarily mean that an individual is an African American or a U.S. citizen.

This chapter provides a perspective on the dominant theme of underrepresentation of Blacks among front-line providers and related areas by (1) presenting background information on the health-care system and the essential categories of the health-care workforce that need to focus on health disparities; (2) discussing the underrepresentation of Blacks in the FLP professions in the health-care workforce; and (3) reviewing some challenges and opportunities confronting FLPs.

HEALTH-CARE DELIVERY SYSTEM

Health services delivery falls mainly into two categories: that which focuses on the delivery of environmental health services and that which focuses on the personal health services delivery system (see Figure 41.1). Workers are needed to support these two delivery strategies; however, the focus here is on those workers involved in personal health services delivery, especially FLPs (see Figure 41.2). FLPs are health-care professionals who are involved in the delivery of primary care. Traditionally, the term "primary care providers" referred almost exclusively to physicians in the specialty areas of family practice, pediatrics, internal medicine, and obstetrics-gynecology.

In this chapter, the term "front-line providers" offers a broader concept, involving those health professionals who have a first line of contact with consumers and patients seeking access to care.

Figure 41.2
Front-line providers (FLPs) of primary health care

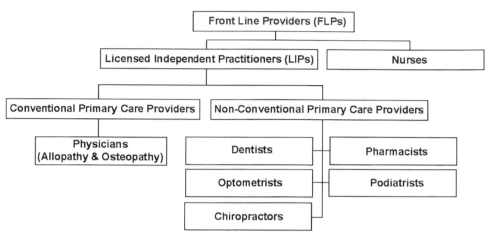

This includes licensed independent practitioners (LIPs) from the fields of medicine, osteopathy, dentistry, optometry, pharmacy, podiatry, and chiropractic (MODOPP-C). Nursing, by far the largest of the health professions, is also counted among the front-line providers, although not among the LIPs, as their scope of practice is largely dependent on physician partnership and protocol. Veterinarians are often included in the traditional health workforce model. However, they are excluded from this presentation because they are not involved in the delivery of personal health services. Conversely, chiropractors are often excluded from the traditional health workforce model but are included here due to their increasing presence in the delivery of personal health services.

Health services are labor-intensive. The large and diverse health-care workforce can be broadly divided into two segments: clinical and nonclinical professions. Clinicians, by their training and role definition, perform tasks directly related to personal health services. This category includes a wide range of caregivers from physicians, dentists, and nurses to therapists and skilled technicians, along with sundry aides and other allied health personnel who work in a variety of settings. The millions of nonclinical staff include managers, administrators, lawyers, information systems personnel, various clerks, and other nonhealth professionals who are a part of the health-care workforce. The nearly fourteen million persons who were employed in health-care settings and/or as health professionals in 1998 made up 10 percent of the nation's total labor force (Kovner & Salsberg, 2002).

Viewing Health Care Employment

There are two ways to view health-care employment, each of which may be correct depending on what one seeks to emphasize. The first is to focus on the vast majority of health personnel that work in health services settings such as hospitals, nursing homes, and ambulatory care facilities. The second view takes into account the nearly 17 percent of health personnel who are employed in organizational settings that the U.S. Census Bureau considers as not part of the health services delivery system. These include physicians who teach at medical schools, pharmacists who work for pharmaceutical companies, and nurses who work in school health offices (National Center for Health Statistics, 2002; Kovner & Salsberg, 2002).

Although some of the fastest growing occupations are concentrated in health-care services, many health-care career fields are suffering severe labor shortages (Pogue et al., 2002; Berliner & Ginzberg, 2002). Health-care services are fueled by the growth and needs of an aging population, which will continue to require more services, and the increased use of innovative medical technology for intensive diagnosis and treatment.

Despite advances in technology and changes in the social, economic, and political environment, the health-care worker ultimately determines the availability, adequacy, and cost of health services. Activities designed to improve health-care access, enhance quality, and control costs must take into account the production, supply, distribution, and use of the health-care workforce. Similarly, any change in organization, financing, technology, or evaluation will also impact the health-care workforce.

Historical Setting for the Twenty-First-Century Health-Care Workforce

The U.S. health-care system is in a period of transition and turbulence, and efforts to reform it are confronted with the issue of a shortage of health professionals. This is particularly true of nurses, pharmacists, and physicians in certain rural and underserved urban areas (Kimball & O'Neil, 2002; U.S. Department of Health and Human Services, 2002). Accurate data about the supply and functional distribution (geographic and specialty) are necessary to promote reform intended to achieve universal access, equity, cost containment, and quality of care (King & Bendel, 1995; Eisenberg, 2002).

It is noteworthy that such a seemingly simple issue as the number of physicians, nurses, and pharmacists in the United States has historically been debated. The questions arise in part because of the different sources of data and the different ways of counting and tracking health workers. Some figures on health-care employment report only health "sector" employment and exclude health professionals in other settings (National Center for Health Statistics, 2002). In 1988, questions were raised whether the number of pharmacists in the United States was accurately known. When there is an unpredicted "shortage" of certain health professionals, questions arise as whether there was an earlier overestimate of their number (U.S. Department of Health and Human Services, 2000).

Important Developments

Efforts to determine the number of physicians needed to deliver health services to the U.S. population and to establish health personnel policy date back to the 1910 Flexner Report. Based on his analyses, Abraham Flexner proposed an 80 percent reduction in the number of medical schools and an annual graduation rate of 3,500 students to meet the projected needs of the population for physician services over one or two generations (Ginzberg, 1989). Public policy issues and considerations related to the health workforce do not take place in a vacuum. Rather, they emerge from, and are to be understood within, the context of the greater socioeconomic fabric of society. This is especially true when the focus is on the Black community, given the racial history of our nation (Smith, 1999), because the history of an organization or a society leaves a residue that persists long after the reason that gave rise to it has passed.

War and its aftermath provide an important point of departure for understanding the context within which social, political, and economic development takes place within a society. After the Civil War and during the post-Reconstruction period, a number of "Negro" medical schools and hospitals were established. Eight medical schools for African Americans emerged between 1865 and 1910 (Howard University Medical School, Washington, D.C. [1868]; Meharry Medical College, Nashville, Tennessee [1876]; Leonard [Shaw] Medical School, Raleigh, North Carolina [1882–1915]; Louisville National Medical College, Louisville, Kentucky [1887–1911]; Flint Medical College, New Orleans, Louisiana [1889–1911]; Knoxville Medical College, Knoxville,

Tennessee [1895–1910]; the Medical Department of the University of West Tennessee [1900–1923]; and Chattanooga National Medical College, Chattanooga, Tennessee [ca. 1902]) (Smedley, Stith & Nelson, 2003, p. 105). By 1920 only Howard and Meharry remained viable (Smith, 1999). A number of post–World War II contextual elements are related to our present situation. President Harry S Truman's 1948 executive order to desegregate the U.S. armed forces created a significant spark for civil rights. The ending of the Korean War in 1953, under the leadership of a World War II hero (President Dwight D. Eisenhower), was followed by the May 17, 1954, U.S. Supreme Court decision in *Brown v. Board of Education*. The Civil Rights legislation of the 1960s and much of the historic health legislation flowed, in large measure, from the 1955 Montgomery Bus Boycott and the ensuing Civil Rights Movement. Following the 1963 March on Washington, the Office of Economic Opportunity (OEO) was established in 1964 and became the lead agency in the domestic "War on Poverty." The historic Eighty-ninth Congress, which adjourned in 1966, enacted a total of 15 pieces of legislation that had far-reaching impact on health services. The most publicized of these were Medicare and Medicaid, Titles XVIII and XIX of the 1965 amendments to the Social Security Act (Litman, 1997, p. 3).

In 1965 OEO funded medical schools, health departments, hospitals and community groups to develop and administer neighborhood health centers in underserved communities (Sardell, 1988). Since the mid-1960s, neighborhood health centers and community health centers under the U.S. Department of Health and Human Services (DHHS) have been instrumental in promoting and delivering health services in the Black community. The Community Health Center (CHC) Program is a federal grant program funded under Section 330 of the U.S. Public Health Service Act that provides primary and preventive health-care services in medically underserved areas throughout the United States and its territories.

The above-mentioned historical events are very important. These are among the many elements that framed the contextual environment within which to view the current landscape of the African American health-care workforce as a part of the larger health-care industry in our nation in the twenty-first century.

Health-Care Workforce: Overview

The human factor is the unique and indispensable element in every organization or social system, and health-care workers are the key variable in the health-care delivery system. The health-care workforce is at the front line of interaction between the multiple stakeholder interests in health-care delivery. Health professionals provide the operational backbone of the health-care delivery system and are in a good position to help the system address disparities in health. This chapter provides a synoptic view of selected groups in the health workforce and speaks to the role, professional presence, education, and training of African Americans in this milieu. The issue of health disparities between the minority and majority population in the United States, while it is complex and not well understood, has something to do with the adequacy of front-line providers.

HEALTH-CARE WORKER EDUCATION: SUPPLY VERSUS DEMAND

The U.S. educational system that produces health professionals has been unsuccessful in generating a representative supply of health professionals from the Black community. The idea posited here is that there is a relationship between the level and distribution of resources available for use by a given population or community and its health status. Communication and interpersonal dynamics within families and between families and clinicians may influence both the reporting of symptoms and the generation of diagnoses (Roberts, 2002; Van Ryn & Burke, 2000; Phillips et al., 2000; Abreu, 1999; Targonski et al., 1994).

The alignment of FLPs to patterns of utilization appears to have greater significance for service delivery to the Black community. This is not to suggest that more medical care per se equals better health (Wildavsky, 1976; Eisenberg, 2002). However, some indicators point to a relationship between resource availability, accessibility, the ability to control disease and injury at various stages of life, service utilization, and health status (McGinnis et al., 2002; Williams, 1998). When considering the adequacy of the supply of health professionals, the growth rate relative to population is an important supply issue. The need to recruit and train more physicians from Black and ethnic minority groups remains an imperative. Extensive research suggests that the diagnostic and treatment decisions of health-care providers, as well as their feelings toward the patients, are significantly influenced by the patients' race and ethnicity (Smedley, Stith & Nelson, 2003, p. 11; van Ryn & Burke, 2000; Schulman et al., 1999; Abreu, 1999; Komaromy et al., 1996).

Medical Schools, Enrollment, and Future FLPs

The traditional approach to the health workforce has focused on the physician. There are two types of physicians and two approaches to medical education: allopathic (M.D.) and osteopathic (D.O.). Allopathic medicine is based on the theory that successful therapy derives from creating a condition antagonistic or different from the condition being treated. Osteopathic medicine stresses a theory that the body is capable of making its own remedies given proper nutrition, environmental conditions, and normal structural relationships. It is distinguished from allopathic mainly in its greater focus on body mechanics and manipulative methods in diagnosis and therapy (Kovner & Salsberg, 2002, p. 82). Upon completion of their education and training, allopathic and osteopathic physicians are both considered medical physicians, have the same scope of practice, and are licensed by all states and the District of Columbia. For this reason, the education and training of medical doctors and doctors of osteopathy, though separate, are discussed below under the heading of medicine.

In 1980, there were 126 allopathic medical schools in the United States. The closing of the medical school at Oral Roberts University in 1989 reduced the number to 125. The recently established medical school at Florida State University, which was provisionally accredited in 2002, restores the number to 126. Of these, 75 (60 percent) are publicly sponsored medical schools. The others are privately operated, not-for-profit institutions. Four of these schools (3 percent) are located at historically Black colleges and universities (HBCUs). They are Howard University, Meharry Medical College, Charles R. Drew University of Medicine and Science, and Morehouse School of Medicine (Association of American Medical Colleges, 2002). First-year enrollments and graduations from the allopathic medical schools have been relatively stable over the past two decades.

As indicated in Table 41.1, in 1980 there were 16,930 first-year medical students enrolled. The total medical student population that year was 65,189, as shown in Table 41.2. This compares with a first-year enrollment of 16,856 in the year 2000 out of a student population total of 66,444. The Black, non-Hispanic first-year enrollment consisted of 3,708 in 1980–1981 (5.7 percent of the total) and 5,051 in 1999–2000 (7.6 percent). The number of allopathic medical graduates was 15,113 in 1980, of whom 712 (4.7 percent) were Black, non-Hispanic. There were 15,704 such graduates in the year 2000, of whom 1,111 (7.1 percent) were Black, non-Hispanic.

The role, size, composition, and distribution of physicians in the nation continue to be examined by health services researchers, and concern has been expressed about the increased number of medical specialists compared with primary care physicians. This concern arises in part because an increase in medical specialists has been associated with higher costs and decreased continuity of care (Whitcomb, 1995; Wennberg et al., 1993; Ginzberg, 1992). The period between 1965 and 1992 saw an increase in the rate of medical specialists from 56 per 100,000 to 123 per 100,000 population. During this same period the rate of primary care physicians increased from 59 per 100,000 to only 67 per 100,000 population (Melnick & Rouse, 2001, p. 238).

Table 41.1

First-year enrollment and graduates of health professions schools and number of schools, according to profession, United States, selected years, 1980–2000

(Data are based on reporting by health professions schools)

Profession	1980	1990	1996	1998	1999	2000
First-year enrollment						
Chiropractic[1]	--------	1,485	--------	--------	--------	--------
Dentistry	6,132	3,979	4,237	4,347	4,268	4,314
Medicine (Allopathic)	16,930	16,756	17,058	16,867	16,790	16,856
Medicine (Osteopathic)	1,426	1,844	2,274	2,692	2,745	2,848
Nursing:						
Licensed practical	56,316	52,969	--------	--------	--------	--------
Registered, total	105,952	108,580	119,205	--------	--------	--------
Baccalaureate	35,414	29,858	40,048	--------	--------	--------
Associate degree	53,633	68,634	72,930	--------	--------	--------
Diploma	16,905	10,088	6,227	--------	--------	--------
Optometry	1,202	1,258	1,438	--------	1,369	--------
Pharmacy	8,035	8,033	8,740	8,571	8,346	8,123
Podiatry	718	599	630	676	623	606
Public Health[2]	3,348	4,087	5,342	5,376	5,575	5,839
Graduates						
Chiropractic	2,049	1,661	--------	--------	--------	--------
Dentistry	5,256	4,233	3,810	4,041	4,095	--------
Medicine (Allopathic)	15,113	15,398	15,907	16,314	15,996	15,704
Medicine (Osteopathic)	1,059	1,529	1,932	2,096	2,169	2,304
Nursing:						
Licensed practical	41,892	35,417	--------	--------	--------	--------
Registered, total	75,523	66,088	94,757	--------	--------	--------
Baccalaureate	24,994	18,571	32,413	--------	--------	--------
Associate degree	36,034	42,318	56,641	--------	--------	--------
Diploma	14,495	5,199	5,703	--------	--------	--------
Optometry	1,073	1,115	1,210	1,237	--------	--------
Pharmacy	7,432	6,956	8,003	7,400	7,141	7,260
Podiatry	577	671	680	592	584	583
Public Health	3,326	3,549	5,064	5,308	5,568	5,879
Schools[3]						
Chiropractic	14	17	--------	--------	--------	--------
Dentistry	60	56	54	55	55	55
Medicine (Allopathic)	126	126	125	125	125	125
Medicine (Osteopathic)	14	15	17	19	19	19
Nursing:						
Licensed practical	1,299	1,154	--------	--------	--------	--------
Registered, total	1,385	1,470	1,508	--------	--------	--------
Baccalaureate	377	489	523	--------	--------	--------
Associate degree	697	829	876	--------	--------	--------
Diploma	311	152	109	--------	--------	--------
Optometry	16	17	17	17	17	17
Pharmacy	72	74	79	81	81	82
Podiatry	5	7	7	7	7	7
Public Health	21	25	28	28	28	28

-------Data not available.

[1]Chiropractic first-year enrollment data are partial data from eight reporting schools.

[2]Number of students entering Schools of Public Health for the first time.

[3]Some nursing schools offer more than one type of program. Numbers shown for nursing are number of nursing programs.

Source: Adapted from National Center for Health Statistics (2002), page 275, Table 104.

Table 41.2

Total enrollment of minorities in schools for selected health occupations, according to detailed race and Hispanic origin, United States, academic years 1980–1981, 1990–1991, and 1999–2000

(Data are based on reporting by health professions associations)

Occupation, detailed race, and Hispanic origin	1980-81	1990-91	1999-2000[1]	1980-81	1990-91	1999-2000[1]
Dentistry[2]	Number of students			Percent distribution of students		
All races	22,842	15,951	17,242	100.0	100.0	100.0
Black, non-Hispanic	1,022	940	808	4.5	5.9	4.7
White, non Hispanic[3]	20,208	11,185	11,106	88.5	70.1	64.4
Hispanic	519	1,254	912	2.3	7.9	5.3
American Indian	53	53	99	0.2	0.3	0.6
Asian	1,040	2,519	4,317	4.6	15.8	25.0
Medicine (Allopathic)						
All races[3]	65,189	65,163	66,444	100.0	100.0	100.0
Black, non-Hispanic	3,708	4,241	5,051	5.7	6.5	7.6
White, non Hispanic[3]	55,434	47,893	42,589	85.0	73.5	64.1
Hispanic	2,761	3,538	4,322	4.2	5.4	6.5
Mexican	951	1,109	1,746	1.5	1.7	2.6
Mainland Puerto Rican	329	457	482	0.5	0.7	0.7
Other Hispanic[4]	1,481	1,972	2,094	2.3	3.0	3.2
American Indian	221	277	574	0.3	0.4	0.9
Asian	1,924	8,436	12,950	3.0	12.9	19.5
Medicine (Osteopathic)						
All races[6]	4,940	6,792	10,388	100.0	100.0	100.0
Black, non-Hispanic	94	217	399	1.9	3.2	3.8
White, non Hispanic[7]	4,688	5,680	8,019	94.9	83.6	77.2
Hispanic	52	277	370	1.1	4.1	3.6
American Indian	19	36	65	0.4	0.5	0.6
Asian	87	582	1,535	1.8	8.6	14.8
Nursing, registered[2,5]						
All races	230,966	221,170	238,244	--------	100.0	100.0
Black, non-Hispanic	--------	23,094	23,611	--------	10.4	9.9
White, non Hispanic[3]	--------	183,102	193,061	--------	82.8	81.0
Hispanic	--------	6,580	9,227	--------	3.0	3.9
American Indian	--------	1,803	1,816	--------	0.8	0.8
Asian	--------	6,591	10,529	--------	3.0	4.4
Optometry[2,4]						
All races	4,540	4,650	5,313	100.0	100.0	100.0
Black, non-Hispanic	57	134	108	1.3	2.9	2.0
White, non Hispanic[3]	4,148	3,706	3,619	91.4	79.7	68.1
Hispanic	80	186	269	1.8	4.0	5.1
American Indian	12	21	30	0.3	0.5	0.6
Asian	243	603	1,287	5.4	13.0	24.2

See footnotes at end of table.

Table 41.2 (continued)

(Data are based on reporting by health professions associations)

Occupation, detailed race, and Hispanic origin	1980-81	1990-91	1999-2000[2]	1980-81	1990-91	1999-2000[2]
Pharmacy[7]	Number of students			Percent distribution of students		
All races	21,628	22,764	32,537	100.0	100.0	100.0
Black, non-Hispanic	945	1,301	2,697	4.4	5.7	8.3
White, non Hispanic[3]	19,153	18,325	22,184	88.6	80.5	68.2
Hispanic	459	945	1,086	2.1	4.2	3.3
American Indian	36	63	156	0.2	0.3	0.5
Asian	1,035	2,130	6,414	4.8	9.4	19.7
Podiatry						
All races	2,577	2,226	2,258	100.0	100.0	100.0
Black, non-Hispanic	110	237	192	4.3	10.6	8.5
White, non-Hispanic[3]	2,353	1,671	1,576	91.3	75.1	69.8
Hispanic	39	148	122	1.5	6.6	5.4
American Indian	6	7	10	0.2	0.3	0.4
Asian	69	163	358	2.7	7.3	15.9

-------Data not available.

[1]Data for osteopathic medicine, podiatry, and optometry are for 1971–1972. Data for pharmacy and registered nurses are for 1972–1973.

[2]Data for podiotry exclude New York College of Podiatric Medicine. Data for registered nurses are for 1996–1997 and optometry are for 1998–1999.

[3]Excludes Puerto Rican schools.

[4]Includes race and ethnicity unspecified.

[5]Includes Puerto Rican Commonwealth students.

[6]In 1990 the National League for Nursing developed a new system for analyzing minority data. In evaluating the former system, much underreporting was noted. Therefore, race-specific data before 1990 would not be comparable and are not shown. Additional changes in the minority data question were introduced for academic years 1992–1993 and 1993–1994 resulting in a discontinuity in the trend.

[7]Prior to 1992–1993 pharmacy total enrollment data are for students in the final 3 years of pharmacy education. Beginning in 1992–1993 pharmacy data are for all students.

Notes: Total enrollment data are collected at the beginning of the academic year. Data for chiropractic students and occupational, physical, and speech therapy students were not available for this table.

Source: Adapted from National Center for Health Statistics (2002), pp. 276–277, Table 105.

Overall, the rate of physicians, regardless of specialty, increased from 155.6 per 100,000 population in 1970 to 260 per 100,000 population in 1996. Between 1970 and 1996 the ratio of physicians to the population increased about 67 percent (Melnick & Rouse, 2001, p. 238). All 50 states and the District of Columbia require physicians to be licensed in order to practice.

The Association of American Medical Colleges identifies Blacks, Native Americans, Mexican Americans, and mainland Puerto Ricans as underrepresented minorities in relation to their representation in the general population (AAMC, 2002). A number of studies have documented that African American and other minority physicians are more likely to serve underserved populations, serve in underserved communities, and be more attuned to social and cultural differences of their race and ethnicity (Komaromy et al., 1996; King & Bendel, 1995; Pogue et al., 2002; Roberts, 2002). This can be a crucial factor in addressing disparities in health.

It has been long recognized that the medical school environment has a major effect on the professional characteristics that its students acquire. A school's applicant pool is a major determinant of the composition of its student body (Barzansky & Etzel, 2002). Medical school is the first formal step in the professional education of physicians. This usually requires four years of training following baccalaureate education. The first two years usually involve didactic classroom instruction, followed by two years that are primarily clinical instruction. Concerns have been expressed about the appropriateness and adequacy of the model and curriculum of traditional medical education. Questions and criticisms have been raised about the overemphasis on high-tech tertiary care and for not encouraging primary care, about an overemphasis on organ systems rather than the whole patient, for not preparing physicians to work in managed care environments or ambulatory care settings. The underrepresentation of Blacks and other minorities in the medical school population is a matter of continuing concern in reference to health disparities.

In response to these questions and concerns, there has been a reassessment of medical school curricula, and some schools have modified or are contemplating modification of the traditional curriculum. Examples include course work and instruction related to cultural competence, alternative or complementary medicine, and commencing clinical training earlier in the educational process.

Based on population data from the U.S. census, selected Association of American Medical Colleges data report a total of 433,255 physicians in 1980, of whom 13,243 or 3.1 percent were Black. In 1990, they report a total of 586,715 physicians, of whom 20,874 or 3.6 percent were Black (AAMC, 2002, p. 328).

Developments Producing FLPs

In the 1960s the prevailing public policy view was that the United States had a shortage of physicians (Fein, 1967; Haynes, 1969; National Advisory Commission on Health Manpower, 1967). This shortage was considered to exist in three dimensions (1) finite numbers, (2) geographic distribution, and (3) specialty distribution.

The issue of physician shortage was addressed in a threefold manner. First, in terms of finite numbers, the approach was to establish new medical schools and expand the capacity of existing medical schools. For example, in 1965 there were 88 allopathic medical schools in the United States. By 1975 the number had increased to 114, and by 1985 to 127 (Mick, 1999, p. 408). Two of the newly established medical schools are at a HBCU. Second, federal efforts to improve the supply and distribution of physicians have included the National Health Service Corps (NHSC), loan forgiveness, and extensive support for family practice programs to facilitate the training and deployment of front-line providers to medically underserved areas. Third, it was argued by some that the demand was not for physicians but for the services that physicians provided. Therefore, if other categories of health personnel could be appropriately trained and given the legal authority and scope of function to perform clinical tasks that were then limited to the physician, the physician shortage would correspondingly be reduced. This gave rise to two distinct, but related, categories of practitioners in the mid-1960s: the physician assistant (PA) and the nurse practitioner (NP). Both the PA and the NP have been significantly deployed in ambulatory care settings. In terms of professional alignment, the PA was viewed as an extension of medicine, and the NP was viewed as an extension of nursing.

FLPs-Physician Assistants

PAs are formally trained to provide preventive, diagnostic, and therapeutic services. Working under the direct supervision of physicians, their duties are determined by the supervising physician and by state law. They take medical histories, examine and treat patients, order and interpret laboratory tests and X-rays, and make diagnoses. In 47 states and the District of Columbia, PAs may prescribe medications. In many rural areas and medically underserved communities, PAs may be the principal care providers, where a physician may be present for only one or two days each week. Under such circumstances, the PA confers with the supervising physician and other medical personnel as needed and as required by state law. According to the American Academy of Physician Assistants, there were about 40,469 certified PAs in clinical practice in January 2000 (U.S. Department of Labor, 2002, p. 261). All PA programs must meet the same curriculum standards in order to be accredited by the Accreditation Review Commission on Education for the Physician Assistant (ARC-PA). In 2002 there were more than 130 PA programs accredited by ARC-PA (AAPA, 2003).

USMGs and IMGs

The physician workforce in the United States further comprises two groups: first, U.S. citizens who are trained in U.S. medical schools (USMGs) accredited by the Liaison Committee for Medical Education (LCME) or the American Osteopathic Association (AOA) and second, persons who attended medical school outside the United States, Puerto Rico, and Canada. These foreign-trained physicians are referred to as international medical graduates or IMGs. In order to enroll in accredited U.S. Graduate Medical Education (GME) programs, IMGs must be certified by the Educational Commission for Foreign Medical Graduates (ECFMG) IMGs have been involved in filling the gap to some extent, by practicing in specialties, geographic locations, and employment settings USMGs tend to avoid. The number of IMGs has increased steadily during the past three decades, but they have consistently represented approximately one-fourth of both the physician workforce and the GME population in the United States (Whelan et al., 2002). In 1970 there were 57,217 IMGs. The number increased to 97,726 by 1980; 131,764 by 1990 and to 196,961 by 2000.

FLPs—Osteopathy

Osteopathy developed after the Civil War under the leadership of Andrew Taylor Still, a former army physician. The first osteopathic school was opened in 1892. They have had a particular presence in the Midwest, where most of their schools have been located. The National Center for Health Statistics reports that in 1980, there were 427,122 *active* physicians in the United States or 189.8 per 100,000 population; 17,130 (4 percent) of these were doctors of osteopathy. The number for 1990 had increased to 567,610 (or 230 per 100,000 population) and included 27,994 (5 percent) osteopathic physicians. By the year 2000 the number of active physicians was 772,296 (or 277.8 per 100,000) and included 44,605 (6 percent) osteopathic physicians. Excluded from the count are physicians with unknown addresses and those who work less than 20 hours per week in diagnosis, treatment, and patient compliance (National Center for Health Statistics, 2002, p. 274).

In 1980, there were 14 osteopathic schools of medicine with a total first-year enrollment of 1,426. By the year 1990, the number of osteopathic medical schools had increased to 15 with a first-year enrollment of 1,750. The first-year enrollment had increased to 2,848 by the year 2000 in 19 schools. The number of Black, non-Hispanic students enrolled in these schools in 1980 was 94 or 1.1 percent; by the year 2000 that number had increased to 399 or 3.2 percent (see Table 41.2). In terms of graduates during the same period, the patterns in the aggregate are quite similar. In 1980 there were 1,059 osteopathic graduates. For the years 1990 and 2000 the number of osteopathic graduates was 1,529 and 2,304, respectively (see Table 41.1).

FLPs—Dentists

Dentists are among the front-line providers. Blacks are underrepresented in the dental profession, and the African American is underserved with respect to dental services (Butters & Winter, 2002; Cherry-Peppers et al., 1995). Dental services and oral health care are very important to the quality of life and are a significant factor in disease prevention. As stated in the Surgeon General's Report on Oral Health in America, "despite dramatic improvements in oral health," a disproportionate number of African Americans and individuals from other racial, ethnic, social, economic, and cultural populations do not have access to dental services and oral health care (U.S. Department of Health and Human Services, National Institutes of Health, NIH, 2000). Elderly African Americans have been found to be at a greater risk for poor dental health profiles. When compared with Whites, they were more likely to report lower rating of dental care, less frequent use, fewer teeth, and severe periodontal disease, creating nutritional vulnerability (Schoenberg & Gilbert, 1998). Among Native Americans, Type II diabetes has been found to be associated with significant increases in periodontal disease and tooth loss (Skrepcinski & Niendorff, 2000). Similarly, African American and other minority children have poorer oral health than White children, although the reasons for the disparities have been unclear. Increasing access to oral health care for African Americans and eliminating health disparities will require significant changes in the way dental services are currently provided (Bureau of Health Professions, 2002).

Based on data compiled by the Bureau of Health Professions, in the year 2000 there were 168,000 active dentists in the United States, excluding dentists in military service, U.S. Public Health Service, and Department of Veteran Affairs. This amounted to 60.4 per 100,000 population. In 1990 there were 147,500 active dentists or 59.5 per 100,000 population (National Center for Health Statistics, 2002, p. 274). Over 90 percent of all active dentists in the United States today are in private practice. About 79 percent of all dentists practice general dentistry; the remainder practice in one of the nine specialties. Based on American Dental Association data, in 1996, there were 166,425 professionally active dentists in the United States, of whom 4,659 or 2.8 percent were African American (Brown et al., 2000). Great disparities in oral health status continue, and the demand for dental services will persist.

Dental Education

Dental education programs in the United States are at the postbaccalaureate level and require a minimum of four academic years of basic dental education, leading to one of two equivalent degrees: doctor of dental surgery (D.D.S.) or doctor of dental medicine (D.M.D.). The Dental Admission Test (DAT) is required of all applicants for admission to the first-year class of U.S. dental schools. In 1980 there were 60 dental schools in the United States with a total enrollment of 22,842. By the year 2000 there were 55 dental schools in the United States with a total enrollment of 17,242. Of this number, 808 (4.7 percent) were African American. In 2001 there were approximately 8,000 applicants competing for 4,407 positions in the first-year class. The Commission on Dental Accreditation of the American Dental Association is the recognized accrediting agency for all dental and dental auxiliary education programs. All 50 states and the District of Columbia require evidence that a candidate has passed parts I and II of the National Board Dental Examinations, which are administered by the Joint Commission on National Dental Examinations.

Dental education programs are still largely segregated along racial lines. Blacks made up about 3 percent of the students in the predominantly White dental schools. In 2001, 32 of the 51 predominantly White dental schools had fewer than ten Black students in the aggregate; 6 had only one Black student (Journal of Blacks in Higher Education, 2002). Nearly 40 percent of all Black students are enrolled at two HBCUs. The dental school at Howard University was founded in 1881, and the Meharry Medical College-Dental School was established in 1886.

FLPs—Optometrists

Optometrists are trained and licensed to examine people's eyes, to diagnose vision problems and eye diseases, and to provide selective eye treatment. They administer drugs to patients to aid in diagnosing eye vision problems and, in some states, are licensed to prescribe a limited range of pharmaceuticals. They also diagnose disorders due to systemic diseases such as high blood pressure and diabetes and refer patients to other health-care practitioners as needed. Optometrists prescribe eyeglasses and contact lenses and provide vision therapy and low-vision rehabilitation. It is reported that more than half the people in the United States wear eyeglasses or contact lenses (U.S. Department of Labor, 2003). All states and the District of Columbia require that optometrists be licensed.

To be licensed, optometrists must earn a doctor of optometry degree (O.D.) from an accredited optometry school and pass both a written and a clinical state board examination. This requires four years of professional training preceded by at least three years of study at an accredited college or university. Many states permit applicants to substitute the examinations of the National Board of Examiners in Optometry, which is usually taken during the student's academic career, for part or all of the written examination. Licenses are renewed every one to three years, and continuing education credits are required for renewal. In 2000, there were 17 optometry schools in the United States accredited by the Accreditation Council on Optometric Education of the American Optometric Association. African Americans make up less than 3 percent of the optometric student population. For first-year enrollment in 1980, there were 57 (1.3 percent) Black, non-Hispanic students out of 4,540 first-year students. In 1990 there were 134 (2.9 percent) Black, non-Hispanic first-year students out of 4,650 students compared with 108 (2 percent) in 2000 out of 5,313 (NCHS, 2002).

There are about 29,000 active optometrists or 11.1 per 100,000 population (NCHS, 2002, p. 274). Optometrists are not to be confused with ophthalmologists, who are physicians with residency training in ophthalmology, although they provide some of the same services. As managed care expands and state government considers increasing the scope of practice of optometrists, there have been questions and conflict about the overlapping roles of optometrists and ophthalmologists.

Glaucoma and diabetic eye disease are the main causes of blindness in the United States and are five times more likely to occur in Blacks than in Whites.

FLPs—Pharmacists

Of the licensed independent practitioners in the United States, pharmacists represent the third largest health professional group with about 196,000 active members in 2000. However, the recent study (USDHHS, 2000) indicates that by the year 2010 there will be a shortage of pharmacists to fill health-care needs across the United States.

Most pharmacists are employed and practice in pharmacies or drugstores, hospitals and medical centers, other retail stores with pharmacies (grocery stores and mass merchandising stores), and other institutional settings such as long-term care facilities. Pharmaceutical manufacturers, managed care and health insurance plans, consulting groups, home health care, and universities employ smaller numbers of pharmacists. Pharmacists are trained in dispensing prescription medications and, under the recently developed concept of pharmaceutical care, provide a range of services critical to medication use and quality health care. These services include assuring the safety of medication use, reduction of medication errors, and in general providing drug therapy with a goal of assuring a beneficial outcome and an improved quality of life for patients. The Hepler and Strand (1990) model of pharmaceutical care also includes a role for pharmacists to monitor drug therapy and manage defined disease states, serve on clinical care teams with physicians, nurses, and allied health-care providers and on health services research teams that focus on outcomes, and be consultants in drug utilization programs.

In the 1990s, the pharmacy profession extended the educational requirements to a doctorate-level entry degree, requiring additional clinical training and expanded practice skills, thus preparing pharmacists to take on more complex clinical roles such as counseling patients, advising other health professionals on drug use issues, and participating in disease management programs.

Pharmacists have a major role in identifying improvements in the drug use and distribution process and other steps that can be taken to reduce the likelihood of medication errors (USDHHS, 2000). In those disease states where medication therapy is a prime intervention, medication compliance and the reduction of medication-related illnesses contribute to the reduction of related morbidity. The prevalence of hypertension in the African American community can be a target health problem for increased pharmacist attention to help provide cost-effective drug therapy for this segment of the population (Taylor, 2002). Inappropriate medication prescribing, drug interactions, and nonadherence to medication regimen can result in unintentional adverse outcomes (Johnson & Bootman, 1995; Bieszk et al., 2003).

In 2000, there were 82 schools and colleges of pharmacy in the United States, including one in Puerto Rico. According to a recent report by the American Association of Colleges of Pharmacy, the 81 U.S. schools and colleges of pharmacy employed a total of 3,806 full-time faculty during the 2002–2003 academic year, including 2,357 males and 1,449 females. This composite number included a total of 206 African Americans (5 percent), of whom 94 were male and 112 were female (AACP, 2002, p. 2). Of the 50 states plus the District of Columbia, 44 have at least one school of pharmacy. Howard University, Florida A&M, Texas Southern University, and Xavier University in New Orleans schools of pharmacy have enrolled and graduated predominantly African American students. In 1998, 232 African American students graduated nationally. These four schools combined graduated 163 students, slightly over 70 percent of the total number of African American students who graduated in the United States.

When compared to the national population in 2000, there have been some notable changes toward pharmacy graduates becoming more representative of the U.S. population at large since 1980. Specifically, the percentage of African American graduates in 1998, while greater than in 1980, was still only about half the population value (13 percent). In 1978, 2,000 Black pharmacists were in practice in the United States, and some 12,000 were needed to deliver care to the non-Black community (Robinson & King, 1978).

FLPs—Podiatrists

According to the American Association of Colleges of Podiatric Medicine (AACPM, 2001), podiatry, a branch of medicine, is all about diagnosing and treating ailments and deformities of the human foot and ankle—parts of the body that take a daily pounding. In 1980 there were 7,000 podiatrists in the United States for a ratio of 3.0 per 100,000 population. By the year 1995, 10,300 podiatrists in patient care were a ratio of 3.9 per 100,000 population in the United States (NCHS, 2002). About half of all podiatrists practice in five states: New York, Pennsylvania, Ohio, California, and Illinois, but they are licensed in all 50 states plus Puerto Rico and the District of Columbia.

Entrance requirements consist of the MCAT, the same examination taken by physicians, and may include the GRE (Xavier Premed, 2001). Seven colleges of podiatric medicine provide graduate professional education in a four-year curriculum. Five of these universities are freestanding, one within an academic health center and one within a university. In 1999–2000, the total population of 2,258 podiatry students in six of the seven colleges of podiatric medicine had 192 (8.5 percent) Black enrollees (NCHS, 2002).

Most podiatric medical school graduates pursue postgraduate education and training at over 300 hospitals and institutions. While there is no college of podiatric medicine that primarily targets the minority enrollee, there is a Council on Podiatric Medical Education–approved residency and externship program at Howard University Hospital in Washington, D.C. Xavier University of Louisiana, which addresses the need for minority podiatrists in its unique July 2001 Handout Number 11 from the Premedical Office program "Overview of Podiatry," indicates that as the populace of the United States has grown and aged, the need for podiatrists has increased tremendously and is predicted to continue to increase in the foreseeable future. The need for minority practitioners is particularly severe. Although appreciable numbers of the poor, minority, rural and inner city communities have foot ailments, less than 2.0 percent of the nation's podiatrists are members of minority groups. (Xavier Premed, 2001, p. 1)

National statistics from the Foot Health Foundation of America point to the fact that African Americans generally experience diabetic complications, such as amputation, at rates 1.5 to 2.5 percent higher than for Whites. In addition, about 20 percent of hospital admissions for diabetic patients are due to foot infections, which are also the most common predecessor to amputation (Foot Health Foundation of America, 2002).

Foot Problems and Diabetes.   According to the American College of Podiatric Medicine, African Americans are 1.7 times more likely to have diabetes than the general population, with 25 percent of African Americans between the ages of 65 and 74 diagnosed with the disease. The prevalence of diabetes in the African American population has fueled the need for podiatrists. Podiatrists represent a front-line professional in the foot health of diabetics. The federal Centers for Disease Control estimates that up to 85 percent of diabetic foot and leg amputations can be prevented with proper foot care (Foot Health Foundation, 2002; Balance, 2001).

Foot Health Foundation (an educational initiative of the American Podiatric Medical Association), reported that diabetes is the seventh leading cause of death (sixth leading cause of death by disease) in the United States (Foot Health Foundation, 2002). Diabetes is also the most common cause of end-stage renal disease (ESRD) in the United States (Balance, 2001, p. 1).

Approximately 2.3 million or 10.8 percent of all African Americans have diabetes. However, nearly one-third are unaware that they have the disease. African Americans are 1.7 times more likely to have diabetes than non-Hispanic Whites of similar age. One in four African American women over 55 years of age has diabetes. African Americans experience higher rates of amputation than Hispanic or White Americans with diabetes. They are 1.5 to 2.5 times more likely to suffer from lower limb amputations. After an amputation, the chance of another amputation within three to five years is as high as 50 percent. The five-year mortality rate after amputation ranges from 39 to 68 percent (Foot Health Foundation of America, 2003).

Foot disease is the most common complication of diabetes leading to hospitalization. In 1996, foot disease accounted for 6 percent of hospital discharges listing diabetes and lower-extremity ulcers, and in 1996, the average hospital stay was 13.7 days. The key to amputation prevention in diabetic patients is early recognition and regular foot screenings, at least annually, from a podiatric physician; podiatrists as a group have documented success in the prevention of amputation.

FLPs—Chiropractors

Chiropractic is a branch of the healing arts that emphasizes the relation between structure and function of the body. Doctors of chiropractic focus on treatment of the body's structural and neurological systems by manual manipulation of the spine or other body parts to restore proper alignment. Chiropractors consider a person as an integrated being, but special attention is given to spinal biomechanics and musculoskeletal, neurological, vascular, nutritional, emotional, and environmental relationships (American Chiropractic Association, 2002). Doctors of chiropractic do not use pharmaceuticals or surgical procedures. Sports and back injuries constitute an important part of chiropractic practice. Chiropractors use standard procedures and tests to diagnose conditions but make great use of X-ray of the skeletal system as a diagnostic tool. The word "chiropractic" comes from Greek words that mean "done by hand."

Daniel David Palmer, an Iowa merchant, founded the chiropractic method in 1895. Palmer established the first college of chiropractic in Davenport, Iowa. The Council on Chiropractic Education (CCE) and its Commission on Accreditation have accredited 15 of the 17 chiropractic schools in the United States. Chiropractic education consists of a minimum of two years of undergraduate education and four years of study at a chiropractic college where, upon graduation, a doctor of chiropractor (D.C.) degree is awarded. Doctors of chiropractic are licensed to practice in all 50 states and the District of Columbia. In 1995, there were 47,200 active chiropractors (National Center for Health Statistics, 2002).

FLPs—Nurses

Nurses work to promote health, prevent disease and help patients to cope with illness and injury, and to have a peaceful death. Nursing has many definitions. For the registered nurse, the common emphasis is the five-step nursing process. This process involves *assessment:* collecting and analyzing data about a patient; *diagnosis:* making a judgment on the cause, condition, and path of the illness; *planning:* creating a care plan with specific treatment goals; *implementation:* supervising or carrying out the treatment plan; and *evaluation:* continuous assessment of the plan. The state board of nursing in each state establishes its own legal definition and defines and interprets the authority and scope of practice of registered nurses. Nursing professionals and professional associations also provide definitional perspectives, which focus on the diagnosing and treatment of human responses.

There are multiple sources of data about the number of nurses and nurse education programs in the United States. In terms of numbers, nurses are by far the largest category of health professionals. The generic term "nurse" is applied to a variety of practitioners. The mix of registered nurses (R.N.s) ranges from nurse researchers with doctorate and master's degrees, to nurses (nurse practitioners and nurse midwives) at the four-year baccalaureate, postbaccalaureate, and two-year associate degree and diploma levels. According to data compiled by the Bureau of Health Professions, in 1980 there were 1,272,900 active registered nurses in the United States or 560.0 per 100,000 population. By 1999, the number had increased to 2,271,300 *active* registered nurses or 832.9 per 100,000 population (NCHS, 2002, p. 274). Despite these increases, some states report current and projected shortages of R.N.s, due largely to recent declines in nursing school enrollment and an aging R.N. workforce (Bureau of Labor Statistics, 2003; Berliner & Ginzberg, 2002; Kimball & O'Neil, 2002; USDHHS, 2002).

All states and the District of Columbia require that prospective registered nurses must graduate from an approved nursing program and pass a national licensing examination, the National Council Licensure Examination for RN (NCLEX-RN), developed by the National Council of State Boards of Nursing. Nurses may be licensed in more than one state, either by endorsement of a license issued by another state, by examination, or through a multistate reciprocity licensing agreement. Periodic license renewal is required by all states, and this may involve continuing education. In some states, certain categories of nurses may prescribe pharmaceutical products or deliver babies. In other states, they may not, since state laws govern the tasks that R.N.s may perform.

FLPs—Licensed Practical Nurses

The term "nurse" is also applied to licensed practical nurses (L.P.N.s), or licensed vocational nurses (L.V.N.s), as they are called in California and Texas. Working under the supervision of R.N.s or physicians, they provide basic bedside care for the sick, injured, convalescent, and disabled. They may perform a range of caregiving tasks such as take vital signs, prepare and administer medication, collect samples for testing, perform routine laboratory tests, apply and change wound dressing, and help patients with personal hygiene. After completing a state-approved practical nursing program,

L.P.N.s/L.V.N.s are required to pass a national examination and are licensed by each state. In 2000, approximately 1,100 state-approved programs provided practical nursing training. Most of these programs last about one year and include both classroom study and supervised clinical practice. Approximately 700,000 L.P.N.s were employed in 2000 (Bureau of Labor Statistics, 2003).

FLPs—Unlicensed Assistive Personnel

A variety of unlicensed assistive personnel (U.A.P.) are included among the other nursing personnel, such as nurses' aides and assistants, orderlies, and technicians who work under the supervision of R.N.s (or physicians). They perform simple tasks and comfort measures such as patient hygiene and linen change. Although they are not licensed by the states, nurses' aides who work in long-term care facilities that are reimbursed by Medicare and Medicaid are required by federal regulations to complete a specified educational program and pass a written and practical test. In addition, home health agencies that are Medicare-certified must hire certified home health aides. African Americans are generally disproportionately represented among U.A.P.s.

Nursing Education.   There are three major educational routes to registered nursing: associate degree in nursing (ADN), bachelor of science degree in nursing (BSN), and diploma programs administered in hospitals. ADN programs offered by junior and community colleges take two to three years; BSN programs, offered by colleges and universities, require four to five years; hospital-based diploma programs take two to three years. The American Nurses Association recommends that states require a baccalaureate degree to practice nursing. Many diploma-educated and ADN nurses later enroll in baccalaureate programs to prepare for a broader scope of nursing practice. A bachelor's degree is often required for administrative positions, and it is a prerequisite for admission to graduate nursing programs in research, teaching, consulting, or a clinical specialization.

In all states and the District of Columbia, registered nurses must graduate from an accredited school of nursing and pass a national licensing examination to obtain a nursing license. Both the American Association of Colleges of Nursing (AACN) and the National League for Nursing accredit nursing programs. The AACN accredits baccalaureate and graduate programs. The NLN accredits all nursing programs. Neither organization has complete data on the various programs. Of the 1,666 R.N. programs in 2000, over half (885) were at the ADN level, while 695 were BSN programs and 86 diploma programs.

Today, most Black nurses are trained at HBCUs. There are 23 such institutions that offer bachelor's programs and as a group trained 4,200 students in 2002. Of the 23 programs, 12 offer the master's degree. Yet, Blacks make up about 9 percent of all nurses in the United States in 2002 (Journal of Blacks in Higher Education, 2002).

Clinical practice, teaching, and nursing administration/management are three broad areas within which registered nurses with baccalaureate degree can earn master's degrees. The focus on a nursing content within these three broad areas may include maternal-child health, adult health, community health, or psychiatric-mental health. The generic category of advanced practice nurses with a clinical focus include nurse practitioner (N.P.), nurse midwife (N.M.W.), clinical nurse specialist (C.N.S.), and certified registered nurse anesthetist (C.R.N.A.). In 2000 there were approximately 196,275 (7.3 percent) advanced practice R.N.s, including about 88,186 nurse practitioners (Bureau of Labor Statistics, 2002, USDHHS, 2000).

Health Services Administrators

Skilled administrators are in great demand to manage the hospitals, primary and ambulatory care centers, community health centers, nursing homes, health departments, managed care organizations, mental health centers and hospitals, and integrated delivery systems. Hospitals and health service agencies are known to be among the most complex organizations in our society and the most challenging to manage. Health services administrators strategically plan, organize, coordinate, and provide directional leadership in health services organizations. Leaders in health services organizations face numerous challenges. Included among the challenges are changes in the financing and payment structures, greater accountability for quality while containing costs, uncertainties created by new policy initiatives, turbulence in the competitive environment, pressures to provide uncompensated care, separate requirements imposed by the public and private payers, and preserving the integrity of the organization through maintaining the highest ethical standards.

Historically, the top manager in most large health institutions was a physician or a nurse with little or no training for an administrative role. The recognized need for specially trained, nonclinical, health-oriented administrators stems from the complex nature of the health industry and the historical context within which the institutions and health professions operate (Raffel & Raffel, 1994). Leaders are needed who understand the sociology of medicine and the complex pattern of interactive relationships and constraints that govern the delivery of health services. This is especially true when the focus is on health disparities and the recognized need for cultural competence in providing health to medically underserved populations.

Education. Educational programs in health administration are located in a number of settings. These settings include schools of public health, medical schools, business schools, schools of allied health, schools of government or public administration, or a combination of the above. Academic training and degrees are offered at the baccalaureate, master's, and doctorate level. At the master's level the most common degrees are the master of health administration (M.H.A.) or master of health services administration (M.H.S.A.), master of public health (M.P.H.), master of business administration (M.B.A.), or master of public administration (M.P.A.) (Pew Health Professions Commission, 1995). The Accrediting Commission on Education for Health Services Administration (ACEHSA) accredits master's degree level programs. Postbaccalaureate programs usually last one to two years. The accrediting process does not apply to baccalaureate programs at this time.

The Association of University Programs in Health Administration (AUPHA) is a voluntary organization of over 120 graduate and baccalaureate programs in the United States and Canada that represents most of these programs (AUPHA, 2000). The 28 schools of public health, which are accredited by the Council of Education for Public Health (CEPH), continue to play an important role in training health services administrators. In the post–9/11 era, with new concerns about homeland security, bioterrorism, and the capacity of the health sector to respond to exigent situations, the training and orientation provided in schools of public health will likely take on even greater significance. In 1984, the graduate program in health services administration at the Howard University School of Business became the first master's degree program at an HBCU to receive ACEHSA accreditation and Full (Type A) membership in AUPHA. Although the graduate program at Howard is now inactive, the baccalaureate program in health administration in the Division of Allied Health remains active and is one of three such programs at an HBCU. The baccalaureate programs at Florida A&M University and Tennessee State University are both certified by AUPHA.

SOME CHALLENGES FACING TODAY'S HEALTH-CARE WORKFORCE

Health-care workers are the key variable in the health-care delivery system in that they are at the front line of interaction between the multiple stakeholder interests in health-care delivery. Multiple stakeholder interests include, but are not limited to, the public or recipients of health-care services, suppliers of health-care products, and the proper use and allocation of technology.

Despite advances in technology and changes in the social, economic, and political environment, the health-care worker ultimately determines the availability, adequacy, and cost of health services. Consequently, activities designed to improve health-care access, enhance quality and reduce racial disparities, and control costs must take into account the production, supply, distribution, and use of the health-care workforce. Similarly, any change in organization, financing, technology, or evaluation also impacts the health-care workforce.

The health-care system continues to change, at an ever-increasing rate and toward increasing degrees of complexity. These changes are reflected in the *who*: the number and complexion of the types of workers that will be needed; in the *what*: the nature of their practice and work; and the *where:* geographic, organizational, and technological settings. The historic roles for physicians, nurses, and other health-care workers are being altered and transformed. Managed care, competition, the patterned increase in corporatization, the development of integrated delivery systems, and advances in medicine and technologies are all impacting the health workforce. Health-care workers are reevaluating their role and their relationship to all components of the health-care delivery system.

Included among the forces and factors affecting the health workforce are the following:

- As turbulence in the global economy intensifies and competition increases, health-care organizations and facilities are governed more by concerns with costs, productivity, outcomes, and efficiency than in the past, resulting in a reevaluation of the number and types of workers needed and how they are best used.
- Hospitals, which employ the largest number of health-care workers, are under increasing pressure to reduce costs. Staff reduction and a redesign of operations are now commonplace.
- There are continuing concern about access and increased concern with outcomes and quality.
- HMOs and various managed care arrangements, along with other purchasers of care, are constraining the role of physicians and other licensed independent practitioners (LIPs), altering their autonomy.
- The substitution of lower-cost workers in many settings.
- Competence, skills that promote customer relations and patient satisfaction, computer literacy, and flexibility are items of concern for all settings.
- Cross-training of workers as a cost-saving measure. Nurses are asked to do nursing aide duties.

RECOMMENDATIONS

To address the concerns regarding the great disparities in health and the underrepresentation of Blacks in the health-care workforce discussed in this chapter (and elaborated on in other chapters) within the sociopolitical and economic contexts of American society will require innovative and long-term commitment of societal resources. A number of organizational policies and program efforts, at both the macro and micro level, have been undertaken in the past to help alleviate the problem, and some have reported varying degrees of success (Ukawuilulu & Livingston, 1994). While some of these policies and program efforts are ongoing, we offer the following recommendations.

- *Improvements in the Educational and Economic Status.* Improvements in the educational and economic status of Blacks must be at the heart of any successful strategy to bridge the gap and eliminate disparities. On the educational side, pipelines must be created and expanded at the early stages in order to facilitate recruitment and enhance retention of Blacks with an orientation to science and the health professions. This means, among other things, giving budgetary substance and programmatic meaning to the bold slogan "No Child Left Behind." The focus with funding must be on the entire spectrum, from Headstart to postbaccalaureate. Entrepreneurship and economic self-sufficiency must become an integral part of the pedagogy in order to achieve the necessary improvements in economic status. Throughout the spectrum of education, students must be reminded and the lesson must be taught that 'to do good' and 'to do well' are not mutually exclusive.
- *Cultural Competence.* Cultural competence is an important factor related to the issue of health disparities (Maxey, 2002). Such competence is best developed in a diverse and culturally sensitive environment. Culture refers to those nonbiological, humanly transmitted beliefs and traits that determine and influence how we *relate* to the social (to other people), political (to the government) and economic (to the resources) spheres

of life. Since these *traits* are not transmitted through the genes, educators and health professionals should be trained about the nature and importance of cultural competence.

- *A More Positive Ambience.* Health professional schools should provide a more positive ambience conducive to learning for minority students. This will be facilitated by the presence of a proportionate number of Black and minority faculty persons who will provide role models for the minority students.

- *An Afrocentric Curriculum.* Where appropriate, a scientifically based Afrocentric curriculum should be utilized throughout the educational spectrum. Such curricula would reflect the historic and contemporary contributions of Blacks to the fields of science, medicine, and the related health professions.

- *Recruitment and Retention.* Aggressive recruitment campaigns that are innovative, comprehensive, and long-term in nature must be undertaken. In addition to the students, the mobilization and participation must involve mentors, parents, and partners in the diverse educational and professional communities in both the public and private sectors. Retention is equally important and merits serious attention. This is especially true at the early stage of the pipeline, where the school dropout rate is unacceptably high for African American males.

CONCLUSION

Racial and cultural diversity are the hallmarks and core strengths of American democratic society. However, this cherished diversity is not reflected on a proportional basis, especially for Blacks, among front-line providers in the health-care workforce. The underrepresentation of Blacks in the health-care workforce is a problem of crisis proportion. The issue of health disparities and the underrepresentation of Blacks among FLPs, which urgently needs to be addressed, will require multiple and targeted strategies. Recognition of the problem and the enactment of policies aimed at establishing parity in the number of Blacks among FLPs will require enlightened leadership, an unwavering political will, and a steadfast commitment to the proposition that life, liberty, and the pursuit of happiness are among the endowments and rights granted to all people by their Creator. The frontal assault on affirmative action undertaken by powerful political interests threatens to undermine the good-faith initiatives and efforts by institutions and individuals in our society who seek to increase the population of participants in the workforce from the Black and other underrepresented minority communities. These public policy assaults send a perverse signal that racial parity is no longer a desirable goal for our society and that the status quo and the "good ol' days" are a preferred state. This appears to run counter to our societal objective, "to form a more perfect union, establish justice, insure domestic tranquility."

ACKNOWLEDGMENT

In Memoriam, January 25, 2003:

Coauthor, the late Dr. Richard Jarvis Enochs was a committed health-care administrator and a distinguished health services administration educator on the faculty of Tennessee State University for 18 years. In tribute to his legacy, an endowed chair is being established at Tennessee State University to honor his memory.

Best Regards to you and your family and thanks for your good work.
Sterling King, Jr.

REFERENCES

Abreu, J.M. (1999). Conscious and nonconscious African American stereotypes: Impact on first impressions and diagnostic ratings by therapists. *Journal of Consulting and Clinical Psychology, 67(3)*, 387–393.

American Academy of Physician Assistants, PA Education. http://www.aapa.org/edinfo.html. Accessed: 1/17/03.

American Association of Colleges of Pharmacy. (2002). 2002–03 Profile of Pharmacy, Institutional Research Report Series. Distribution of 2002–03 full-time pharmacy faculty by rank, gender and race/ethnicity. Table 3, Page 2.

American Association of Colleges of Podiatric Medicine, (2001). Podiatric Medicine (http://aacpm.org/default.asp) Accessed: 12/21/02.

American Association of Colleges of Podiatric Medicine. (2002). CPME 300, Approved Residencies in Podiatric Medicine, (March 2002) http://aacpm.org/residencies/index.asp. Accessed: 12/21/02.

American Chiropractic Association. (2002). What is chiropractic? http://www.amerchiro.org/media/whatis/education.shmtl. Accessed: 1/11/2003.

Association of American Medical Colleges (AAMC). (2002). *Minority Student Opportunities in United States Medical Schools*, 16th ed. Washington, DC: AAMC.

Association of University Programs in Health Administration (AUPHA). (2000). Health Services Administration Education 2001–2003 Directory of Programs. Washington, DC: AUPHA.

Balance: Perspectives in Diabetes Management. (Autumn 2001). Volume 2, Number 2, University of Massachusetts Medical School. New York: BioScience Communications.

Barzansky, B., & Etzel, S. (2002). Educational programs in U.S. medical schools, 2001–2002. *Journal of the American Medical Association, 288,* 1067–1072.

Berliner, H.S., & Ginzberg, E. (2002). Why this nursing shortage is different. *Journal of the American Medical Association, 288,* 2742–2744.

Bieszk, N., Patel, R., Heaberlin, A., Wlasuk, K., & Zarowitz, B. (2003). Detection of medication nonadherence through review of pharmacy claims data. *American Journal of Health-System Pharmacy, 60,* 360–366.

Brown, R.S., Schwartz, J.L., Coleman-Bennett, M., & Sanders, C. (2002). The Black and White of dental education in the United States: Enrollment and graduation trends. *Journal of the National Medical Association, 92 (11),* 536–543.

Bureau of Health Professions. (2002). Dental Initiative, Topic of Interest #3. Oral health disparities. U.S. Department of Health and Human Services.

Bureau of Labor Statistics (January 2003). *Occupational Outlook Handbook, 2002–2003 Edition.* Bulletin 2540. U.S. Department of Labor.

Butters, J.M., & Winter, P. (2002). Professional motivation and career plan differences between African American and Caucasian dental students: Implementation for improving workforce diversity. *Journal of the National Medical Association, 94,* 492–504.

Cherry-Peppers, G., Sinkford, J.C., Newman, E.S., Sanders, C.F., & Knight, R.S. (1995). Primary oral health care in Black Americans. *Journal of the National Medical Association, 87,* 136–140.

Deaton, A. (2002). Policy implications of the gradient of health and wealth. *Health Affairs, 21 (2),* 13–30.

Eisenberg, John. (2002). Physician utilization: The state of research about physicians' practice patterns. *Medical Care, 40,* 1016–1035.

Epstein, A.M., & Ayanian, J.Z. (2001). Racial disparities in medical care. *New England Journal of Medicine, 344,* 1471–1473.

Fein, R. (1967). The doctor shortage—An economic diagnosis. Washington, DC: Brookings Institution.

Foot Health Foundation of America (http://www.foothealthfdn.com/diabetes.htm). Accessed 12/21/2002.

Ginzberg, E. (1989). Physician supply in the year 2000. *Health Affairs (Millwood), 8,* 84–90.

Ginzberg, E. (1992). Physician supply policies and health reform. *Journal of the American Medical Association, 268,* 3135–3118.

Haynes, M.A. (1969). Distributions of Black physicians in the United States, 1967. *Journal of the American Medical Association, 210,* 93–95.

Healthy People 2000. (1990). National health promotion and disease objectives. DHHS Publication No. (PHS) 91-50213. Washington, DC: U.S. Government Printing Office.

Healthy People 2010. (2000). Vol. 1. U.S. Understanding and improving health. Department of Health and Human Services. Washington, DC: U.S. Government Printing Office.

Hepler, D.C., & Strand, L. (1990). Opportunities and responsibilities in pharmaceutical care. *American Journal of Hospital Pharmacy, 47(3)*, 533–43.

Hood, R.G. (2001, June). Fighting invisible barriers to equitable health care. *Journal of the National Medical Association, 93*, 197–200.

Johnson, J.A., & Bootman, J.L. (1995). Drug-related morbidity and mortality: A cost of illness model. *Archives of Internal Medicine, 155*, 1949–56.

Journal of Blacks in Higher Education. (2002). Taking the pulse of Blacks in academic nursing. http://www. jbhe.com/news_views/34_nursing.html. Accessed: 1/17/2003.

Kimball, B., & O'Neil, E. (2002). Health care's human crisis: The nursing shortage. Princeton, NJ: Robert Wood Johnson Foundation.

King, G., & Bendel, R. (1995). A statistical model estimating the number of African-American physicians in the United States. *Journal of the National Medical Association, 87*, 264–272.

Komaromy, M., et al. (1996). The role of Black and Hispanic physicians in providing health care for underserved populations. *New England Journal of Medicine, 334*, 1305–1310.

Kovner, C.T., & Salsberg, E.S. (2002). The health care workforce. In A.R. Kovner & S. Jonas (Ed.), *Health care delivery in the United States* (7th ed.). New York: Springer.

Levy, D.R. (1985). White doctors and Black patients: Influence of race on the doctor patient relationship. *Pediatrics, 75(4)*, 639–643.

Licensed Practical and Licensed Vocational Nurses. http://www.bls.gov/oco/ocos102.htm Accessed: 12/20/2002.

Litman, T.J. (1997). The relationship of government and politics to health and health care: A sociopolitical overview. In T.J. Litman & L.S. Robbins (pp. 3–45), *Health politics and policy*. Albany, NY: Delmar.

Marmot, M. (2002). The influence of income on health: Views of an epidemiologist. *Health Affairs, 21*, 31–46.

Maxey, R. (2002). NMA develops strategic plan against health disparities. *Journal of the National Medical Association, 94*, 288–289.

McGinnis, J.M., Williams-Russo, P., & Knickman, J.R. (2002). The case for more active policy attention to health promotion. *Health Affairs, 21*, 78–93.

Mechanic, D. (2002). Disadvantage, inequality, and social policy. *Health Affairs, 21(2)*, 48–59.

Melnick, D., & Rouse, B. (Eds.). (2001). *Portrait of health in the United States* 1st ed. Lanham, MD: BERNAN.

Meredith, L.S., & Griffith-Forge, N. (2002). The road to eliminating health disparities. *Medical Care, 40*, 729–731.

Mick, S.M. (1999). Health care professionals. In S.J. Williams & P.R. Torrens (Eds.), *Introduction to health services*, 5th ed. Albany, NY: Delmar.

Minority nursing statistics. http://www.minoritynurse.com/statistics.html. Accessed: 12/20/2002.

Mort, E.A., Edwards, J.N., Emmons, D.W., Covery, K., & Blumenthal, D. (1996). Physician response to patient insurance status in ambulatory care clinical decision-making: Implications for quality care. *Medical Care, 34*, 783–797.

National Advisory Commission on Health Manpower. Report to the President (1967). Washington, DC: U.S. Government Printing Office.

National Center for Health Statistics (NCHS). (2002, August). *Health, United States with Chartbook on Trends in the Health of Americans*. USDHHS Publication No. 1232, Hyattsville, MD.

National Research Council. (1989). A common destiny: Blacks and American society. Washington, DC: National Academy Press.

Pew Health Professions Commission. (1995). Critical challenges: Revitalizing the health professions for the twenty-first century. San Francisco: UCSF Center for the Health Professions.

Phillips, K.A., Mayer, M.L., & Aday, L.A. (2000). Barriers to care among racial/ethnic groups under managed care. *Health Affairs, 19*, 65–75.

Pogue, V.A., Norris, K.C., & Dillard, M.G. (2002). Kidney disease physician workforce: Where is the emerging pipeline? *Journal of the National Medical Association, 94 (Suppl.)*, 39S–44S.

Raffel, M.W., & Raffel, N.K. (1994). *The U.S. health system: Origins and functions*. Albany, NY: Delmar.

Report of the Secretary's Task Force on Black and Minority Health. (1985). Executive Summary, Vol. 1. USDHHS, Washington, DC: U.S. Government Printing Office.

Roberts, E.M. (2002). Racial and ethnic disparities in childhood asthma diagnosis: The role of clinical findings. *Journal of the National Medical Association, 94*, 215–223.

Robinson, I.C., & King, R.C. (1978, July). Black pharmacists in the U.S.: How their status is changing. *American Druggist Magazine, 178* (July), 13–16, 67.

Sardell, A. (1988). *The U.S and experiment in social medicine, the community health center program, 1965–1986*. Pittsburgh: University of Pittsburgh Press.

Satcher, D. (2000). Eliminating racial and ethnic disparities in health: The role of the ten leading health indicators. *Journal of the National Medical Association, 92*, 315–318.

Satcher, D. (2001). American women and health disparities. *Journal of the American Medical Women's Association, 56*, 132–134.

Schneider, E.C., Zaslavsky, A.M., & Epstein, A.M. (2002). Racial disparities in the quality of care for enrollees in managed care. *Journal of the American Medical Association, 28*, 1288–1294.

Schoenberg, N.E., & Gilbert, G.H. (1998). Dietary implications of oral health decrements among African-American and white older adults. *Ethnicity & Health, 3(1-2)*, 59–70.

Schulman, K.A., et al. (1999). The effect of race and sex on physicians' recommendations for cardiac catheterization. *New England of Medicine, 340*, 618–626.

Skrepcinski, F.B., & Niendorff, W.J. (2000). Peridontal disease in American Indians and Alaska Natives. *Journal of Public Health Dentistry, 60 (Suppl 1)*, 261–266.

Smedley, B.D., Stith, A.Y., & Nelson, A.R. (2003). Institute of Medicine. (2003). Unequal treatment: Confronting racial and ethnic disparities in health care. In B.D. Smedley, A.Y. Stith, & A.R. Nelson (Eds.), Washington DC: National Academies Press.

Smith, D.B. (1999). Health care divided: Race and healing a nation. Ann Arbor: University of Michigan Press.

Targonski, P.V., Persky, V.W., & Addington, O.P. (1994). Trends in asthma mortality among African Americans and Whites in Chicago through 1991. *American Journal of Public Health, 84*, 1830–1833.

Taylor, S.D. (2002). Using pharmaceutical care to improve medication compliance and health outcomes among minority elderly with hypertension (http://mcuaaar.iog.wayne.edu/pis/Stephanie.htm). Accessed 1/11/2003.

Ukawuilulu, J.O., & Livingston, I.L. (1994). Black health care providers and related professionals: Issues of underrepresentation and change. In I.L. Livingston (Ed.), *Handbook of Black American health: The mosaic of conditions, issues, policies and prospects*. Westport, CT: Greenwood.

U.S. Census Bureau, Statistical Abstract of the United States: 2001. (2001). (121st ed.). Washington, DC: U.S. Government Printing Office.

U.S. Department of Health and Human Services. (2000). *Report to the Congress, the pharmacist workforce: A study of the supply and demand for pharmacists*. Rockville, MD: Health Resource and Services Administration, Bureau of Health Professions.

U.S. Department of Health and Human Services. (2002). *Projected supply, demand and shortage of registered nurses: 2000–2020*. Rockville, MD: National Center for Health Workforce Analysis.

U.S. Department of Health and Human Services, National Institutes of Health. (2000). *Oral Health in America. A report of the Surgeon General*. Rockville, MD: National Institute of Dental and Craniofacial Research.

U.S. Department of Labor. Bureau of Labor Statistics. (2003, January). *Occupational Outlook Handbook* (2002–2003 ed.). Bulletin 2540.

van Ryn, M., & Burke, J. (2000). The effect of patient race and socio-economic status on physician's perceptions of patients. *Social Science and Medicine, 50*, 813–828.

Verdon, W. (February 9, 1999). What are the major causes of sight loss? *Optometry, 10*, http://www.spectacle.berkeley.edu/class/opt10/lec3.shtml. Accessed: 1/17/2003.

Wennberg, J., Goodman, N., Nease, R., & Keller, R. (1993). Finding equilibrium in U.S. physician supply. *Health Affairs, 12*, 89–104.

Whelan, G.P., Gary, N.E., Kostis, J., Boulet, J.R., & Hallock, J.A. (2002). The changing pool of international medical graduates seeking certification training in graduate medical education programs. *Journal of the American Medical Association, 288*, 1079–1094.

Whitcomb, M. (1995). A cross national comparison of generalist physician workforce data. *Journal of the American Medical Association, 274*, 692–695.

Wildavsky, A. (Winter 1977). Doing better and feeling worse: The political pathology of health policy. *Daedalus (Journal of the American Academy of Arts and Sciences), 106 (1)*, 105–123.

Williams, D.R. (1998, September). How income, race and other factors influence health. Author Series. Issue Number 4, Vol. 1. Robert Wood Johnson Foundation Investigator Awards in Health Policy Research. Washington, DC: Association for Health Services Research.

Xavier Premed: Overview of Podiatry. (2001). Information Handout #11 from the Premedical Office of Xavier University of Louisiana. http://www.xupremed.com/AInfoSeries/Info11.Pod.htm. Accessed: 12/21/02.

CHAPTER 42

Geographic Information Systems Perspective on Black American Health

JOSEPH R. OPPONG AND SARA M. GARCIA

INTRODUCTION

By providing a digital lens for exploring the dynamic connections between human populations, their health and well-being, and the changing physical and social environments, geographic information systems (GIS) are transforming traditional approaches to epidemiology. Where people live and the environments they experience throughout their lives impact their health. This is very true for the population of interest in this chapter—Black Americans. Thus, understanding the geography of ill health and disease depends critically on the ability to combine data from multiple social and environmental factors that affect human health. GIS provide the universal link that allows integration and analysis of these data needed for understanding disease distributions and are thus an invaluable tool for epidemiology and geographical analysis of disease. GIS, with its mapping capabilities, can be used to assess environmental risk factors, identify places and/or subpopulations (e.g., African Americans) that need surveillance and control programs, and present information to the public.

This chapter uses GIS to examine the health status of Black Americans in the United States. The goal is to demonstrate the utility of GIS applications in health and disease research while highlighting selected associated problems. This chapter presents the view that the utility of GIS for health research hinges critically on data quality and availability at different scales of resolution.

GEOGRAPHIC INFORMATION SYSTEMS AND HEALTH

Disease maps portray the geographical extent of disease visually and help to identify the spatial conditions that contribute to it. Maps show with a unique efficiency the distribution of phenomena in space and are effective visualization tools. All maps convey factual information, but beyond that, by communicating the nonrandom geographic distribution of disease clearly, disease maps usually stimulate the formation of causal hypothesis. Nevertheless, GIS are more than mere visualization of spatially referenced data or, as in the case of this chapter, disease mapping. GIS are systems for the collection, storage, integration, analysis, and display of spatially referenced data (Gatrell & Löytönnen, 1998).

Due to their ability to combine data from many sources by area unit (e.g., zip code, county, or census tract), GIS provide a tool for probing links between disease and the physical environment, while controlling for other factors such as lifestyle or race, for example, African Americans or other at-risk minority populations. They permit studies of geographic clustering of disease and associated spatial phenomena or variables. Given a set of individuals diagnosed with some disease together with some address reference, we can aggregate the cases into any fixed set of area units and define measures of relative risk, such as standardized morbidity or mortality ratios. Moreover, GIS permit exploration and modeling of disease risk around a point (e.g., a city, a nuclear reactor, or a mine) or along a line (e.g., a river or road) (Gatrell & Löytönen, 1998).

GIS are invaluable for health education. When displaying relative disease risk information using commonly understood geographic boundaries (e.g., zip codes or counties), GIS help to communicate its immediate significance to a public who might otherwise not comprehend their risk. Disseminating risk information this way usually generates greater participation in planning and policy. Thus, GIS offer a supportive environment for planning population-based public health programs, program evaluation, and community-based decision making.

Due to all these benefits, application of GIS in health research has burgeoned in recent years. Yasnoff and Sondik (1999) from the U.S. Centers for Disease Control and Prevention have proclaimed GIS a core technology for effective public health decisions. It is particularly suited for disease surveillance and monitoring. Some recent applications include vector-borne diseases (Glass et al., 1995), water-borne diseases (Clarke et al., 1991), environmental health (Barnes & Peck, 1994), modeling exposure to electromagnetic fields (Wartenberg et al., 1993), and quantifying lead hazards in a neighborhood (Wartenberg, 1992). Bishai et al. (1998) applied GIS to the analysis of tuberculosis (TB) transmission patterns in Baltimore. GIS analyses have also been used to predict host infection status for the Sin Nombre virus, which is carried by deer mice (Boone et al., 2000). The National Cancer Institute is supporting the use of GIS for investigations into the relationships between breast cancer and the environment on Long Island and to estimate exposures to environmental contamination (National Cancer Institute, 1999)

The Focus of the Chapter

This chapter uses GIS to examine the health status of Black Americans in the United States. It highlights disease conditions that contribute to, and reflect, racial disparities. We seek to answer the question whether states with a predominantly high Black population have health characteristics comparable to those of other states. For example, is the heart disease mortality rate higher in predominantly Black states such as Louisiana, Mississippi, Alabama, Georgia, and South Carolina than elsewhere? How does the White mortality rate in such states compare to the rates in other states? Is the Black rate higher than for Whites and other races? Is the risk of morbidity and mortality higher in a predominantly Black region than elsewhere? We address these questions using mortality data (rates per 100,000) for the following five selected health conditions—cardiovascular disease, malignant neoplasm, diabetes, end-stage renal disease (ESRD), and HIV-AIDS. These diseases were selected because of their disproportionate occurrence among Blacks. The goal is to demonstrate the utility of GIS applications in health and disease research and highlight some of the associated problems. This chapter argues that the utility of GIS for health research hinges critically on data quality and availability at different scales.

GIS are used in this study basically as a visualization tool to highlight racial health disparities, that is, between Blacks and Whites. Population data for these maps came from the U.S. 2000 census figures (http://www.census.gov/Press-Release/www/2001/tables/). Mortality data were gathered from the racial mortality tables provided by the National Center for Health Statistics (NCHS) using the Beyond 20/20 software. The maps were compiled using ArcGIS 8.1 from ESRI.

RATIONALE FOR CHOOSING SELECTED DISEASES

Several considerations influenced the selection of health problems for Black Americans included in this study. First, we examined the ten leading causes of death for all races in the country and selected four diseases from that list. Next, we compared the health status of Black Americans to Healthy People 2010 goals to see which diseases deserved the most attention. We then considered the determined level of health disparity between Blacks and Whites in the country. Finally, we contrasted morbidity and mortality among Black Americans to current national statistics for all races. This subjective prioritization led us to the following five diseases—cardiovascular disease, malignant neoplasm (cancer), diabetes, HIV-AIDS, and end-stage renal disease.

Our premise was that few biological differences exist between races/ethnicities that would make one racial/ethnic group more susceptible to disease than others. Yet, because race/ethnicity is a social construct with powerful social effects, cultural and socioeconomic correlates of race/ethnicity strongly affect health status and other quality of life indicators. Consequently, persistent racial differences in health probably reflect historic policies and practices based on inequalities in living conditions that produce pathogenic conditions for minority populations. For example, economic status impacts health differences even for people of the same race or ethnic group. Generally, those with higher household incomes have better health status than those with lower incomes. Thus, structural or other factors that keep one group of people poor will also produce higher rates of disease among them. A brief justification is presented for each of the five diseases included in this chapter.

Heart Disease

Cardiovascular disease is the leading cause of death nationally, accounting for 40.1 percent of all deaths in 1999 (American Heart Association, 2002). Minority and low-income populations suffer a disproportionate burden of death and disability from cardiovascular disease. Between 1987 and 1995, the age-adjusted death rate for coronary heart disease nationally declined by 20 percent, but for Blacks, the overall decrease was only 13 percent (Anderson, 2001). Disparities also exist in the prevalence of risk factors for cardiovascular disease. For example, racial and ethnic minorities have higher rates of hypertension, tend to develop it at an earlier age, and are less likely to undergo treatment to control their high blood pressure.

Cancer

Cancer is the second leading cause of death in the United States, accounting for more than 544,000 deaths each year (Anderson, 2001). About half of those who develop the disease die from it, but minority groups suffer disproportionately from cancer. Disparities exist in both mortality and incidence rates. For men and women combined, Blacks have a cancer death rate about 35 percent higher than that for Whites (171.6 vs. 127.0 per 100,000). In Black men, the death rate for cancer is about 50 percent higher than it is for White men (226.8 vs. 151.8 per 100,000) (Landis et al., 1999). Similarly, the death rate for lung cancer is about 27 percent higher for Blacks than for Whites (49.9 vs. 39.3 per 100,000). The prostate cancer mortality rate for Black men is more than twice that of White men (55.5 vs. 23.8 per 100,000).

Diabetes

Diabetes was the fifth leading cause of death for Black Americans in 1999 (Anderson, 2001), and the age-adjusted death rate due to diabetes among Black Americans is more than twice that for

Whites. On average, Black Americans are twice as likely to have diabetes as White Americans of similar age. Death rates for people with diabetes are 27 percent higher for Black Americans compared with Whites (National Diabetes Information Clearinghouse, 2002). Furthermore, Black Americans with diabetes are more likely to develop diabetes complications and experience greater disability from the complications than White Americans with diabetes.

HIV-AIDS

Representing only an estimated 12 percent of the total U.S. population, African Americans make up almost 38 percent of all AIDS cases reported in the United States. In 2000, more African Americans were reported with AIDS than any other racial/ethnic group. Nearly half (47 percent) of the 42,156 AIDS cases reported that year were Black Americans. Furthermore, almost two-thirds (63 percent) of all women reported with AIDS were African American (CDC, 1998b). Moreover, African American children accounted for almost two-thirds (65 percent) of all reported pediatric AIDS cases. The 2000 rate of reported AIDS cases among African Americans was 58.1 per 100,000 people, more than two times the rate for Hispanics and eight times the rate for Whites.

End-Stage Renal Disease

End-stage renal disease (ESRD), a serious condition in which the kidneys fail to rid the body of wastes, afflicts more than 50,000 people each year in the United States. ESRD is the final stage of a slow deterioration of the kidneys, a process known as nephropathy. Diabetes is the most common cause, producing about one-third of new cases (U.S. Renal Data System 1999). Another important cause is hypertension. African Americans and Native Americans develop diabetes, nephropathy, and ESRD at rates higher than average, but the reasons are not fully understood. In 1997, Black American constituted 29 percent of new ESRD patients as compared to 12.6 percent for the American population.

THE GEOGRAPHIC DISTRIBUTION OF BLACK POPULATION AND BLACK MORTALITY IN THE UNITED STATES

Based on the 2000 census, Blacks make up more than 25 percent of the population in southeastern states including Alabama, Georgia, Louisiana, Mississippi, and South Carolina (Figure 42.1). The District of Columbia, with 60 percent, has the highest concentration of Blacks in the country. Delaware has almost 28 percent. Besides Texas, with 11.5 percent, and California and Nevada, with 6.7 percent and 6.8 percent, respectively, the central, western and northern states have approximately 5 percent or less (Figure 42.1).

Blacks have a higher mortality rate and lower life expectancy than any racial group in the United States. In 2000, the age-adjusted death rate for Blacks in the United States was 30 percent higher than for White non-Hispanics (Minino & Smith, 2001). Life expectancy for the total population was a high 76.9 years, 74.1 years for males and 79.5 for females. For Whites it was 77.4 years for both sexes, 74.8 for males and 80 years for females. In contrast, for Blacks it was 71.8 for both sexes, 68.3 for males and 75.0 for females. Infant mortality rates reveal a similar pattern—6.9 per 1,000 live births for all groups, 5.7 for Whites, 5.6 for Hispanics, and 14.0 for Blacks. Clearly, Blacks have a lower health status. Of the states with age-adjusted death rates exceeding 1,000 per 100,000 population, about 80 percent (seven out of nine) had Black populations constituting 15 percent or higher of the total population. Thus, states with higher Black percentage of their total population

Figure 42.1
Percent Black population in the United States

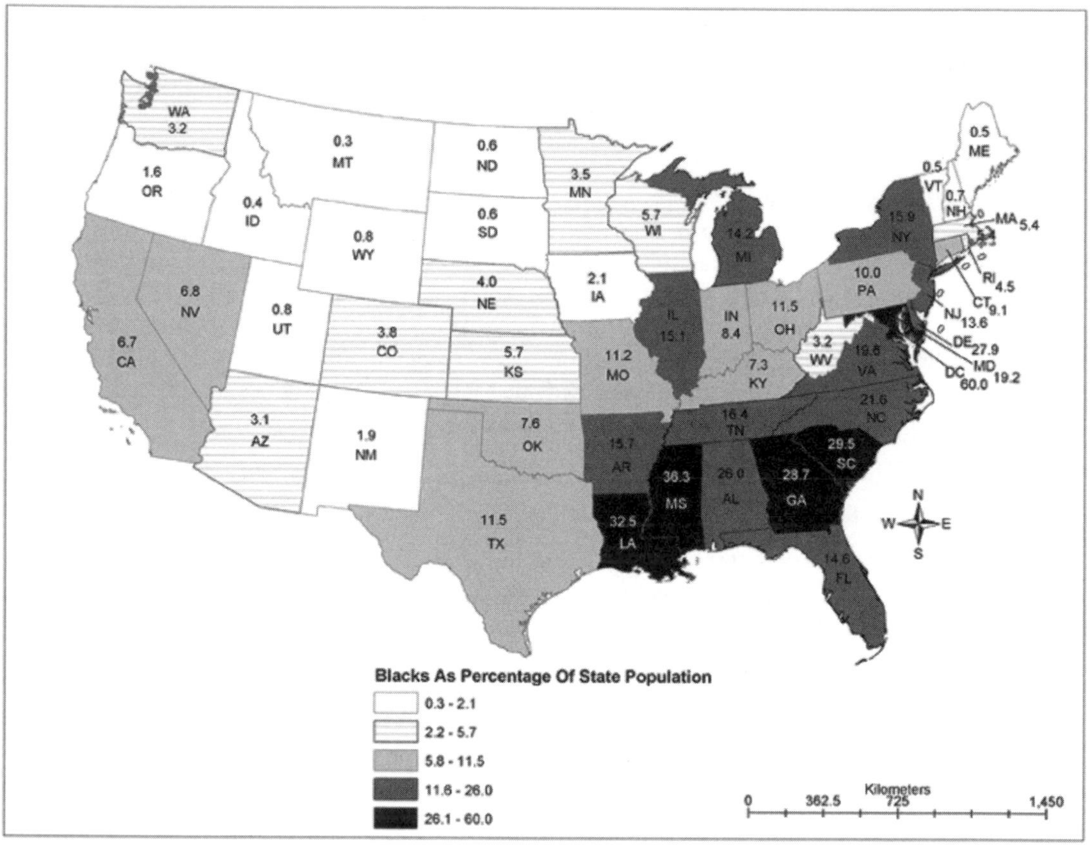

Blacks As Percentage Of State Population

- 0.3 - 2.1
- 2.2 - 5.7
- 5.8 - 11.5
- 11.6 - 26.0
- 26.1 - 60.0

Source: The population data used to create this map are from the census 2000.

have higher death rates (Table 42.1). How do mortality rates for different causes of death vary spatially for Blacks and Whites?

Major Cardiovascular Disease Mortality, 1996–1998

Heart disease was the leading cause of death in 2001. The age-adjusted death rate for major cardiovascular disease, including heart disease, hypertension, and stroke, was 338.8 per 100,000. Figure 42.2 shows the geography of major cardiovascular disease mortality in the United States between 1996 and 1998. The map contrasts racial age-adjusted mortality rates for Blacks and Whites. Each dark bar represents a state's Black mortality rate, while the light one represents its White mortality rate. A bar's height corresponds to the magnitude of the mortality rate as compared to the others.

Generally, cardiovascular disease mortality rates are high for both Blacks and Whites. However, the mortality rate for Blacks equals or exceeds the rate for Whites in every state except Maine, Montana, North Dakota, South Dakota, and Vermont. These states have very small (less than 1 percent) Black populations. As expected, high mortality rates dominate in states with high concentrations of Blacks. Moreover, heart disease mortality for Whites appears to be higher than usual in states with high Black concentration. For example, Louisiana, Mississippi, Georgia, and South Car-

Table 42.1
Percent Black population and age-adjusted death rates for high Black states

State	Percent Black	Age-adjusted death rate per 100,000 population
Alabama	26.0	1013.6
Arkansas	15.7	1002.1
District of Columbia	60.0	1036.2
Georgia	28.7	1004.2
Kentucky	7.3	1005.2
Louisiana	32.5	1020.4
Mississippi	36.3	1074.8
Tennessee	16.4	1021.2
West Virginia	3.2	1010.7

olina have White mortality rates that are almost as high as the Black rates and definitely higher than the predominantly White states.

Malignant Neoplasm Mortality, 1996–1998

Malignant neoplasm, or cancer, was the second leading cause of death in 2000. In 1998, 53 percent of all cancer-related deaths in the United States were associated with four sites: lung/bronchus, colon/rectum, prostate, and female breast, but cancer-related death does not affect racial/ethnic populations similarly. Blacks have higher cancer death rates (Howe et al., 2001). Data from 1998 indicated that death rates for lung and bronchial cancer were higher for Blacks than for other races/ethnicities. Female breast cancer death rates were highest for Blacks, followed by Whites. Similarly, Blacks had the highest death rate for colorectal cancer, followed by Whites, but death rates for prostate cancer were more than twice as high for Blacks as for Whites (Gargiullo et al., 2002).

Figure 42.3 shows the geography of malignant neoplasm mortality from all causes, 1996 to 1998. The pattern is similar to cardiovascular disease mortality. States with large Black populations have disproportionately high mortality rates. Even in states with large White populations, the Black mortality rate tends to be higher except in Nevada and New Hampshire.

Diabetes Mortality, 1996–1998

Diabetes was the sixth leading cause of death in 2000 for the country. Nationally, the death rate for Blacks was disproportionately high, 39.1 per 100,000 compared to 15.9 per 100,000 for Whites (CDC, 1999). Diabetes mortality rates for Blacks are almost double those for Whites in almost every state with a significant Black population (Figure 42.4). For example, Texas' Black diabetes mortality rate (42.9 per 100,000) is more than double that for Whites (16.5 per 100,000). This pattern is repeated across the county. Thus, diabetes deaths occur disproportionately among Blacks. Disparities in mortality rates such as these suggest that the health status of Blacks in the United States today remains inferior in every state.

HIV-AIDS Mortality, 1996–1998

Compared to Africa, HIV-AIDS has had a less severe effect in the United States. Nevertheless, the severity of its impact varies substantially between ethnic groups. Blacks have been affected more

Figure 42.2
Cardiovascular disease mortality rates (per 100,000) for Whites and Blacks

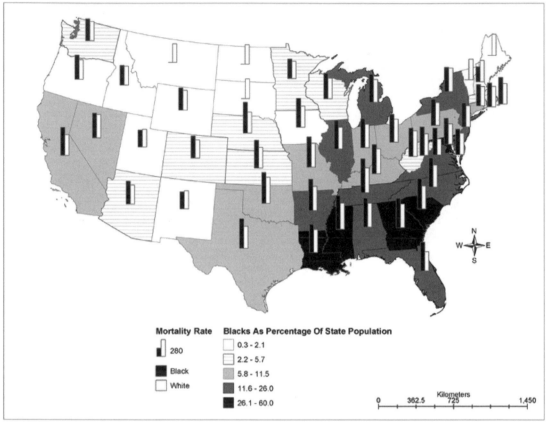

Source: All mortality data are from the National Center for Health Statistics (NCHS) Web site. The NCHS also provided the software needed to analyze the information downloaded from http://www.cdc.gov/NCHS during the early part of 2002.

severely than any other group. According to the 2000 Census, African Americans comprised 12.3 percent of the US population, but have accounted for 39 percent of the estimated AIDS cases diagnosed since the beginning of the epidemic (CDC, 2002). The AIDS diagnosis rate among African Americans was almost 11 times the rate among whites. For African American women it was even greater—23 times the diagnosed rate for White women. African American men had almost a 9 times greater rate of AIDS diagnosis than White men. Sixty-two percent of children born to HIV-infected mothers were African American. In 1999, AIDS became the fifth leading cause of death in the United States among people aged 25 to 44, and the leading cause of death for Black men in this age group. Among Black women in this age group, HIV ranked third.

HIV-AIDS mortality is on the decline in the United States. However, it seems that all across the country and even in states with small percentages of Black populations, Blacks experience the brunt of AIDS mortality. This is the most dramatic of the four maps presented in this chapter. It is easy to see the disproportionate mortality occurring in each state. Virginia and Florida's mortality rates are perhaps the most striking. The majority of HIV deaths in largely Black states occur among Blacks (Figure 42.5). Even in states where Blacks do not make up a large portion of the population, they lead in HIV mortality. States like Montana, Idaho, and Utah that have only 0.3 to 0.8 percent Black populations have larger Black mortality rates than White rates. In the northeastern tip of the

Figure 42.3
Malignant neoplasm mortality rates (per 100,000) for Whites and Blacks

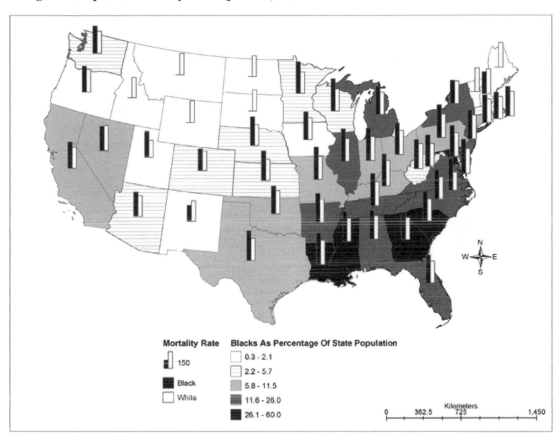

Source: All mortality data are from the National Center for Health Statistics (NCHS) Web site. The NCHS also provided the software needed to analyze the information downloaded from http://www.cdc.gov/NCHS during the early part of 2002.

United States, where few Blacks live, Maine, Vermont, and New Hampshire, the situation is the same. The Black HIV mortality rate is more than twice that in the White populations.

End-Stage Renal Disease

End-stage renal disease mortality appears to be concentrated in the southeastern portion of the United States (see Figures 42.6a and 42.6b, each of which presents a slightly different view of the ESRD problem). At 2,921.2 per 100,000 people, the District of Columbia has the largest mortality rate in the country. South Carolina (1,442.4), Alabama (1,554.8), Louisiana (1697.2), and Mississippi (1,699.3) follow closely behind. Note that all five states have large proportions of Black residents. The south-central and the northeastern states also have considerable mortality rates of ESRD. Most of these states also contain sizable Black populations.

Most striking, however, is that ESRD mortality seems to be minimal in those states with small Black populations. This is seen most dramatically in the northeastern and northwestern tips of the country. The areas least affected by ESRD mortality are also those with the smallest Black populations. For example, less than 1 percent of the population in Maine, Vermont, and New Hampshire is made up of Blacks. Maine, Vermont, and New Hampshire also have some of the lowest mortality rates for ESRD.

Figure 42.4
Diabetes mortality rates (per 100,000) for Whites and Blacks

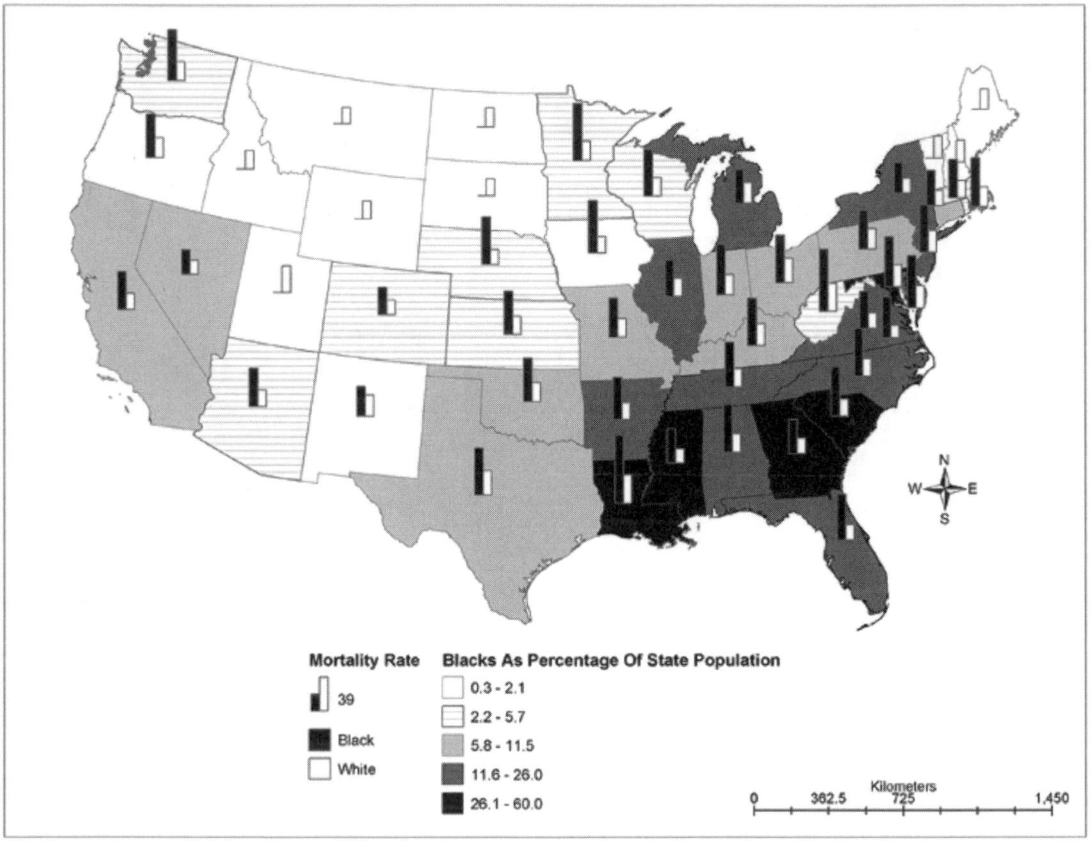

Source: All mortality data are from the National Center for Health Statistics (NCHS) Web site. The NCHS also provided the software needed to analyze the information downloaded from http://www.cdc.gov/NCHS during the early part of 2002.

Figure 42.6b presents a different perspective of ESRD mortality and the distribution of the Black population in the United States. The view from the northwestern tip of the nation clearly shows that the largest populations of Black Americans reside in the Southeast. Although some states in the Northwest have relatively little ESRD mortality, the eastern half of the United States is experiencing dramatically higher rates. Washington, D.C., the region with the highest concentration of Black Americans, also has the largest mortality rate for ESRD.

GIS AND BLACK AMERICAN HEALTH

The five disease maps presented portray the disparities in health status between Blacks and Whites in the United States quite compellingly. By showing the percent Black as a background for the mortality rates for Whites and Blacks, these maps permit easy comparison and comprehension of the relative differences between Whites and Blacks and their variation among the states. These maps show that regardless of location, Blacks generally have a lower health status. However, national maps and data comparing states conceal this. As noted before, GIS here are used mainly as a visualization tool. Their capacity for organizing large sets of data by location for analysis and mod-

Figure 42.5
HIV-AIDS mortality rates (per 100,000) for Whites and Blacks

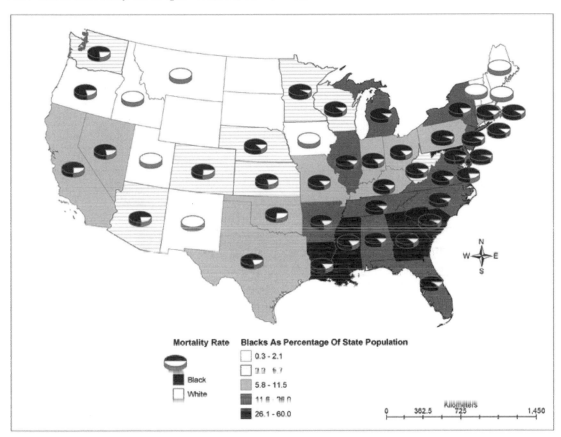

Source: All mortality data are from the National Center for Health Statistics (NCHS) Web site. The NCHS also provided the software needed to analyze the information downloaded from http://www.cdc.gov/NCHS during the early part of 2002.

eling has not been touched here. For example, it is possible to determine whether Blacks who live in areas with high levels of pollution have higher rates of morbidity and disease than those who do not. Similarly, we can verify whether Whites who live in similar environments have corresponding rates of morbidity and mortality as Blacks. Thus, GIS are invaluable as a visualization tool for displaying spatial disparities in health status. Given detailed data, for example, household-level data, GIS can be used to provide detailed insights into the relationship between household environment characteristics, genetic or cultural characteristics such as race and ethnicity, and exposure to disease. We illustrate this with county-level cancer mortality data (Figures 42.7–42.9).

Cancer in Texas

Cancer is the second leading cause of death in Texas, exceeded only by heart disease. In 2004, the American Cancer Society estimated that 84,530 new cases of cancer will be diagnosed in Texas, with 34,830 deaths (American Cancer Society, 2004). For all cancer sites combined and the leading cancer sites in Texas—colon, rectum, lung, and bronchus for both sexes, prostate cancer in males, and breast cancer in females—Black American males have significantly higher incidence and mor-

Figure 42.6
End-stage renal disease mortality rates (per 100,000) and percent Black population

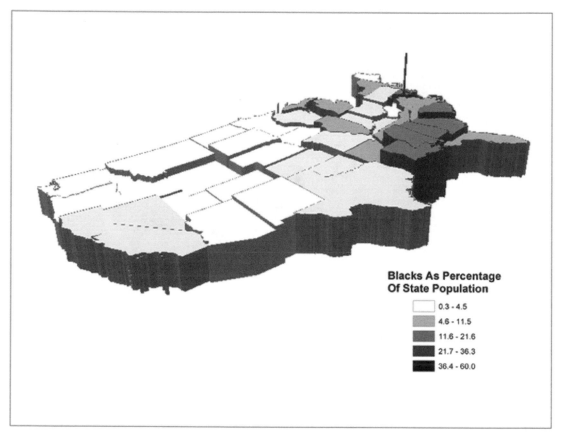

Blacks As Percentage
Of State Population

☐ 0.3 - 4.5
▨ 4.6 - 11.5
▨ 11.6 - 21.6
▨ 21.7 - 36.3
▨ 36.4 - 60.0

Note: State death rates are relative to each other. The larger the height of each state's boundary, the larger the mortality in that state.

Source: ESRD data are from the electronic version of the United States Renal Data System 2001 Annual Data Report (www. usrds.org/reference.htm).

tality rates than White non-Hispanic males. For example, while the difference in prostate cancer incidence between Blacks and Whites is only about 40 percent, the difference in mortality is a dramatic 140 percent (TDH, 2001). Similarly, while breast cancer incidence is lower in Black American females, mortality is significantly higher in Blacks. Having better access to diagnostic facilities, White females are more likely to be diagnosed and treated early for the disease, while Black women, lacking such access, are diagnosed with more stages of the disease.

Black Americans are disproportionately concentrated in the urban areas of the state and northeastern Texas (Figure 42.7). The Dallas Fort-Worth metroplex in north-central Texas, the Houston area in southeast Texas, and the I-35 corridor centering on Austin, the state capital, are particularly noteworthy. Few Blacks live in West Texas, the area dominated by Hispanics. Hispanics are found mostly in West and South Texas.

Total cancer mortality for all races, 1980–1998, age-adjusted to 1970, is presented in Figure 42.8. East Texas has significantly higher cancer mortality than West Texas. Consistently, areas with high concentrations of Blacks have high total cancer mortality (TDI, 2001). Thus, the relationship between percent Black population in a county and the cancer mortality rate appears quite startling. West

Figure 42.7
End-stage renal disease mortality rates (per 100,000) and percent Black population (northwest perspective)

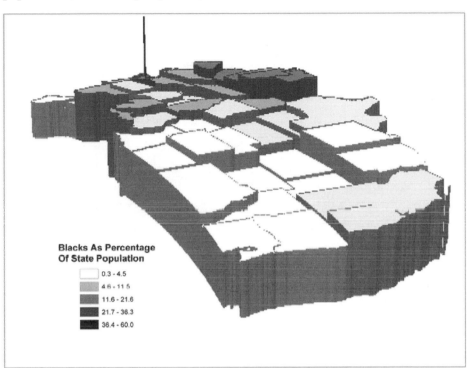

Note: State death rates are relative to each other. The larger the height of each state's boundary, the larger the mortality in that state.

Source: ESRD data are from the electronic version of the United States Renal Data System 2001 Annual Data Report (www.usrds.org/reference.htm).

Texas with few Blacks has low cancer mortality rates, while East Texas and urban areas of the state have higher rates (Figure 42.9). As the Texas Department of Health noted, the "geographic differences are found to be proportionate to the race/ethnic distribution of the population" (p. 22).

DATA PROBLEMS IN GIS AND HEALTH

The power of GIS to combine data from many sources, using many different scales, projections, and data models, is a major strength, but also a major weakness. Maffini et al. (1992) declare that data integration is a major problem because geographic data are not of equal quality. Integrating available data compiled for different purposes and frequently at different scales presents a new set of problems and increases the potential of error in the data (Chrisman, 1992).

Another problem is that these maps conceal spatial variation within the states and wrongly suggest that the rates of mortality are uniform throughout the state. Nothing is further from the truth. Moreover, an impression of sudden breaks, for example, from a high mortality area (state/county/zip code) to a low mortality one, remains. In reality, spatial variations are more gradual. The problem is with the level of aggregation of reported data, a problem that is frequently compounded by confidentiality of health data. The exciting news is that provided that clean data are available, GIS can be used no matter the spatial scale (state, county, zip code, or house address). However, since accuracy is scale-

Figure 42.8
Percent Black population in Texas counties, 1980–1998

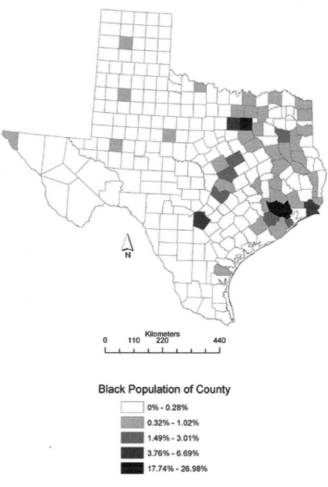

Black Population of County

	0% - 0.28%
	0.32% - 1.02%
	1.49% - 3.01%
	3.76% - 6.69%
	17.74% - 26.98%

Source: Population Counts are from the Texas Department of Health's Epigram Population and Mortality Data Analysis Software.

dependent, inherent errors and uncertainty in each data set compound data error in GIS (Fotheringham, 1992; Openshaw, 1992).

Frequently, however, inaccurate generalizations can result from such simple disease maps based
on ratios (morbidity rate, mortality rate, etc.). Where the denominator is small (e.g., total population
is low), an insignificantly small number of events (e.g., deaths) can produce astronomically huge
ratios and wrongly suggest a hot spot. Figure 42.8 illustrates this problem. Zapata County located
on the southwest border and Duval County to its northeast show extremely high mortality rates of
95,799 and 44,004 deaths per 100,000 people, respectively. Amazingly, these astoundingly high rates
are based on one death in each county. The reason for these rates is simply the small total population
of Blacks in these counties. For example, for the entire period, 1980–1998, Zapata County had a
total of 14 Blacks only.

Thus, great care should be exercised in disease mapping to ensure that the disease data being
mapped make sense. As Monmonier (1996) cautions, not only is it easy to lie with maps, but it is
essential. The cartographer's paradox is that to avoid hiding critical information in a fog of detail,

Figure 42.9
Malignant mortality rates (per 100,000) in Texas
counties, 1980–1998

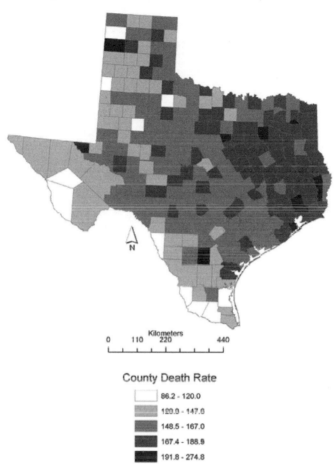

County Death Rate

	86.2 - 120.0
	120.0 - 147.0
	148.5 - 167.0
	167.4 - 188.9
	191.8 - 274.8

Source: Age-adjusted (1970 US Population) death rates are from the Texas
Department of Health's Epigram Population and Mortality Data Analysis
Software.

the map must offer a selective, incomplete view of reality. Such "lies" can range from "little white lies" (suppressing details selectively to help the user see what needs to be seen) to more serious distortions in which the visual image suggests conclusions that would not be supported by careful epidemiological analysis. Careful use of GIS will avoid such distortions.

Finally, while locational data for GIS are easy to obtain in the United States, health data are not. Public policies and legal guidelines regarding confidentiality and privacy of health-care information remain a patchwork of uncoordinated state and federal policies (Council on Competitiveness, 1996). While federal legislation provides some common restrictions on releasing federally held information on individuals, state regulations vary greatly and frequently preclude the release of information at anything other than the most general level (e.g., county level instead of address level). Using such data in a GIS produces what Jacquez (1998) called spatial uncertainty. Using area centroids instead of exact locations can produce misleading results (Jacquez, 1998).

Figure 42.10
Black malignant mortality rates (per 100,000) in Texas counties, 1980–1998

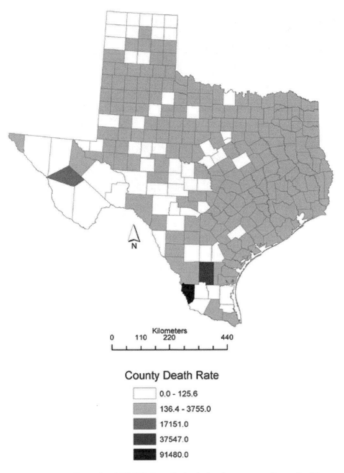

Source: Age-adjusted (1970 US Population) death rates are from the Texas Department of Health's Epigram Population and Mortality Data Analysis Software.

CONCLUSION

GIS are invaluable for graphically displaying spatial disparities in health status. Applied to Black American health, they confirm the existence of significant disparities in health status between Blacks and Whites. Areas with high concentrations of Blacks tend to have disproportionately high mortality rates from the five selected diseases examined in this study. Not only do the leading Black states have higher mortality, but also mortality rates for Whites in these states tend to be higher than in other states. Using GIS as a visualization tool, we have shown that unusually high mortality rates occur in the southeastern block of states that lie in close proximity to each other and have disproportionately high concentrations of Blacks. A simple report presenting the mortality rates from these causes, for example, in alphabetical order, would not reveal the underlying geographic relationships (proximity of high mortality states to each other) or the related variable of percent Black population.

In conclusion, fundamental epidemiological research tasks are accomplished easily using GIS, but data quality, lack of spatial detail, and spatial consistency between data sets impede their utility. Properly used, GIS can be a risk communication tool. They provide an effective method to take complex information and communicate it in an easy-to-understand format to the general public. However, improper usage can produce misleading generalizations and incorrect results.

REFERENCES

American Cancer Society. (2002). *Cancer facts and figures 2002*. Available at: <http://www.cancer.org/eprise/main/docroot/stt/stt_0>. Accessed December 2, 2002.

American Cancer Society. (2004). Cancer Facts and Figures, 2004 Estimates. http://www.cancer.org/docroot/STT/stt_0.asp.

American Heart Association. (2002). *2002 Heart and Stroke Statistical Update*. Available at: <http://www.americanheart.org/presenter.jhtml?identifier=3000090>. Accessed December 2, 2002.

Anderson, R.N. (2001). Deaths: Leading causes 1999. *National Vital Statistics Report, 49(11)*.

Barnes, S., & Peck A. (1994). Mapping the future of health care: GIS applications in health care analysis. *Geographic Information Systems, 4*, 31–33.

Bishai, W., et al. (1998). Molecular and geographic patterns of tuberculosis transmission after 15 years of directly observed therapy. *Journal of American Medical Association, 280*, 1679–1684.

Boone, J.D., et al. (2000). Remote sensing and geographic information systems: Charting sin Nombre virus infections in deer mice. *Emerging Infectious Diseases, 6(3)*, 248–258.

Centers for Disease Control and Prevention (CDC) (1998b). *HIV/AIDS Surveillance Report, 10(2)*.

Centers for Disease Control and Prevention (CDC). (1999). *Chronic diseases and their risk factors: The nation's leading causes of death*. Atlanta, GA: U.S. Department of Health and Human Services Centers for Disease Control and Prevention. http://www.cdc.gov/nccdphp/statbook/pdf/cdrf1999.pdf

Centers for Disease Control and Prevention (CDC). (2001). *HIV/AIDS Surveillance Report, 13(1)*, 1–41.

Centers for Disease Control and Prevention (CDC). (2002). HIV/AIDS Surveillance Report 2002. http://www.cdc.gov/hiv/stats/hasrl402.htm.

Chrisman, N.R. (1992). Modeling error in overlaid categorical maps. In M. Goodchild, & S. Gopal (Eds.), *The accuracy of spatial databases* (pp. 21–34). New York: Taylor & Francis.

Clarke, K.C., McLafferty, S.L., & Tempalski, B.J. (1996). On epidemiology and geographic information systems: A review and discussion of future directions. *Emerging Infectious Diseases, 2*, 85–92.

Clarke, K.C., Osleeb, J.R., Sherry, J.M., Meert, J.P., & Larsson, R.W. (1991). The use of remote sensing and Geographic Information Systems in UNICEF's dracunculiasis (Guinea worm) eradication effort. *Preventative Veterinary Medicine, 11*, 229–235.

Council on Competitiveness. (1996). Integration of health information systems: The highway to health—Part II. *Drug Benefit Trends, 8(12)*, 11–13, 17–18, 24–26, 28.

Cromley, E.K., & McLafferty, S.L. (2002). *GIS and public health*. New York: Guilford.

Cuthe, W.G., Tucker, R.K., Murphy, E.A., England, R., Stevenson, E., & Luckardt, J.C. (1992). Reassessment of lead exposure in New Jersey using GIS technology. *Environmental Research, 59*, 318–325.

Fotheringham, A.S. (1992). Scale-independent spatial analysis. In M. Goodchild, & S. Gopal (Eds.), *The accuracy of spatial databases*. New York: Taylor & Francis.

Gargiullo, P., Wingo, P.A., Coates, R.J., & Thompson, T.D. (2002). Recent trends in mortality rates for four major cancers, by sex and race/ethnicity—United States, 1990–1998. *Morbidity and Mortality Weekly Report, 51(03)*, 49–53.

Gatrell, A.C. & M. Löytönen (eds.) 1998. *GIS and Health*. Philadelphia: Taylor and Francis.

Glass, G.E., Schwartz, B.S., Morgan, J.M., III, Johnson, D.T., Noy, P.M., & Israel, E. (1995). Environmental risk factors for Lyme disease identified with geographic information systems. *American Journal of Public Health, 85*, 944–948.

Howe, H.L., et al. (2001). Annual report to the nation on the status of cancer (1973 through 1998), featuring cancers with recent increasing trends. *Journal of National Cancer Institute, 93*, 824–842.

Jacquez, G.M. (1998). GIS as an Enabling Technology. In A.C. Gatrell & M. Löytönen (Eds.), *GIS and health* (pp. 17–28). Philadelphia: Taylor & Francis.

Landis, S.H., Murray, T., Bolden, S., et al. (2000). Cancer statistics, 2000. *CA: A Cancer Journal for Clinicians, 50(1)*, 2398–2424.

Maffini, G., Arno, M., & Bitterlich, W. (1992). Observations and comments on the generation and treatment of error in digital GIS data. In M. Goodchild, & S. Gopal (Eds.), *The accuracy of spatial databases* (pp. 55–67). New York: Taylor & Francis.

Minino, A.M., & Smith, B.L. (2001). Deaths: Preliminary data for 2000. *National Vital Statistics Report, 49*, (12). Hyattsville, MD: National Center for Health Statistics.

Monmonier, M. (1996). *How to lie with maps*. 2d ed. Chicago: University of Chicago Press.

National Cancer Institute (NCI). (1999). Geographic Information Systems (GIS) for the Long Island Breast Cancer Study Project (LIBCSP). http://rcb.nci.nih.gov/RFP/85074/appendb.pdf

National Diabetes Information Clearinghouse. (2002). *Diabetes overview*. Bethesda, MD: NIH Publication No. 02-3873.

Openshaw, S. (1992). Learning to live with errors in spatial databases. In M. Goodchild and S. Gopal (Eds.), *The accuracy of spatial databases* (pp. 263–276). New York: Taylor & Francis.

Reikes, S.T. (2000). Trends in end-stage renal disease: Epidemiology, morbidity, and mortality. *Postgraduate Medicine 108(1)*. http://www.postgradmed.com/issues/2000/07_00/reikes.htm

Rosenberg, H.M., et al. (1999). Quality of death rates by race and Hispanic origin: A summary of current research. Hyattsville, MD: U.S. Department of Health and Human Services, CDC, National Center for Health Statistics, *Vital and Health Statistics* Series 2, No. 128.

Texas Department of Health (TDH). (2001). *Health disparities in Texas: An epidemiological review of priority health outcomes*. Austin: Texas Department of Health.

U.S. Renal Data System (USRDS). (1999). *Annual data report*. Bethesda, MD: National Institutes of Health, National Institute of Diabetes and Digestive and Kidney Diseases.

Wartenberg, D. (1992). Screening for lead exposure using a Geographic Information System. *Environmental Research, 59*, 310–317.

Wartenberg, D., Greenberg, M., & Lathrop, R. (1993). Identification and characterization of populations living near high-voltage transmission lines: A pilot study. *Environmental Health Perspective, 101*, 626–632.

Yasnoff, W.A., & Sondik, W.A. (1999). Geographic Information Systems (GIS) in public health practice in the new millennium. *Journal of Public Health Management and Practice, 5(4)*, ix–xii.

CHAPTER 43

The Human Genome: Implications for the Health of African Americans

GEORGIA M. DUNSTON AND
CHARMAINE D. M. ROYAL

INTRODUCTION

The ultimate goal of the Human Genome Project (HGP) is to map and sequence the three billion nucleotides in the human genome. The publication of a complete and accurate human genome reference sequence at the dawn of the twenty-first century is the new foundation for a scientific revolution in thinking on the biology of disease, human identity, and health promotion in the emerging era of genomic medicine.

This chapter focuses on the benefits of knowledge gained from the HGP and research on human genome variation for improving the health of African Americans. It begins with a background section on sequencing the human genome and connects the mapping and sequencing of the human genome with population differences in the structure of human genome sequence variation. This is followed by a section on eliminating health disparities, which relates knowledge gained on population-based differences in the structure of human genome sequence variation to gene mapping strategies for common complex diseases targeted in Healthy People 2010, a set of health objectives for the nation to achieve over the first decade of the new century. Thus, the HGP provides the foundation for anticipated benefits to the field of medicine in better understanding and eliminating race and ethnicity-based health disparities in common diseases of public health interest, such as diabetes, hypertension, and cancer.

Motivated by the search for disease-causing and disease-susceptibility genes, the genome revolution anticipates the development of genetic tests as new diagnostic tools, individualized drug treatments (pharmacogenomics), and new strategies for disease prevention. Because genes encode biology underlying disease susceptibility, as well as biology underlying superficial phenotypic characteristics used historically in race and ethnicity-based group classifications, knowledge gained from the HGP is relevant not only to the biology of disease but also to the biology of race. Thus, the HGP has ignited controversy on the relative role, function, and/or contribution of genes versus environmental factors in the biology and prevalence of common complex diseases and related strategies for eliminating race- and ethnicity-based health disparities.

This chapter highlights knowledge on DNA sequence variation in African Americans and their ancestral African populations instructive in understanding the evolution of human genome variation and instrumental in mapping disease-causing and disease-susceptibility genes. Attention is also given to probing complex social, legal, and ethical issues surrounding human genome discoveries and the implications as well as applications of this knowledge for eliminating health disparities in African Americans. Core scientific issues posed by the HGP, with particular emphases on the role and importance of community education and engagement in the genome revolution, are addressed in the section on existing and emerging paradigms and issues. This is followed by a section on new perspectives in genomic science, which includes information on the emergence of the National Human Genome Center (NHGC) at Howard University and significance of including African Americans and other populations of contemporary African ancestry in the mainstream of human genome research. This section includes recommendations for globalization of the NHGC research agenda through worldwide collaboration on Genomic Research in the African Diaspora (GRAD) Project. The chapter concludes with a section on the NHGC at Howard University and its interface with the HGP and the significance of the GRAD Project to the future of health care in America and the global community.

BACKGROUND

Sequencing the Human Genome

Many agree that the sequencing of the human genome is perhaps the most ambitious scientific undertaking of humankind for the benefit of humankind in the history of Western science. The HGP is an international cooperative research initiative to sequence and map the entire complex of human genes, now estimated to be 30,000–40,000 in number, collectively defined as the human genome (Lander et al., 2001). In the United States the HGP is coordinated by the National Human Genome Research Institute (NHGRI) at the National Institutes of Health (NIH) and the U.S. Department of Energy (DOE) (Cantor, 1990). The U.S. HGP began officially in 1990 as a 15-year international effort with a narrowly defined set of scientific goals, which included (1) mapping all the genes in human DNA; (2) determining the entire sequence of the three billion chemical bases that make up human DNA; (3) storing the information gained from sequencing the genome in electronic databases; (4) improving tools for computer-assisted database management, genomic analyses, and transfer of related technologies to the private sector; and (5) addressing the ethical, legal, and social issues (ELSI) arising from the HGP (U.S. Department of Energy, 1990).

Construction of Genetic and Physical Maps. The strategic plan for sequencing the human genome was partitioned into three stepwise periods for assessing progress toward the ultimate goal of producing an accurate and finished reference sequence of the human genome (Collins & Galas, 1993; Collins et al., 1998). The first five-year goals included the construction of comprehensive genome maps of increasingly higher resolution (i.e., >> DNA marker density). The initial goal of low-resolution genetic maps with sequence-tagged sites (STS) spaced 2–5 centimorgans (cM / ~ one million nucleotides) was reached one year ahead of schedule with the publication of a 1 cM genetic map in September 1994 (Murray et al., 1994). Comprehensive physical maps of higher resolution with STS approximately 100,000 nucleotides apart were completed three years later in October 1998 (Deloukas et al., 1998). Concurrent with progress in the construction of genetic and physical maps, new disease genes were rapidly discovered. Progress during the second five-year period was distinguished by a near doubling every two years in the number of mapped gene tags, from approximately 7,500 in 1994, to 15,000 in 1996, and 30,011 in 1998.

Genetic maps have been most successfully used to find high-penetrance genes responsible for rare Mendelian inherited disorders, like cystic fibrosis and muscular dystrophy (Collins, 1995). With improved technology and increasing numbers of markers, more refined genetic maps have become useful in mapping genes that interact with environmental factors in increasing susceptibility to common non-Mendelian inherited disorders, such as asthma, heart disease, diabetes, cancer, and psychiatric conditions (Collins & McKusick, 2001). It is generally recognized that all diseases have a genetic component. However, the relative contribution of genes versus environmental factors as determinants of disease varies. In some diseases like sickle-cell anemia (Kan et al., 1980) and Tay-Sachs disease (Lau & Neufeld, 1989), single genes play a major role in disease causation; in others like Type II diabetes, hypertension, and cancer, multiple genes and multiple environmental factors contribute to disease susceptibility (Collins, 1999), and still in others like HIV-AIDS, environmental factors play a major role in disease (Hill, 2001). As new genes are identified, cloned, and studied, the dissection of disease processes is better defined and understood at a molecular or mechanistic level. Over time, this is expected to lead to the development of new therapies, prevention strategies, and more accurate diagnosis of early steps in the disease process, before the manifestation of clinical disease.

Pilot projects to assess the feasibility of large-scale sequencing of the human genome were initiated in the second five-year period of the HGP. Progress during this time in reducing the effective cost of sequencing made it possible to begin the third and final period of large-scale sequencing of the human genome in 1998, with publication of a "working draft" of the human genome in 2001, followed in 2003 by publication of a finished human genome sequence, two years ahead of schedule (Venter et al., 2001; Lander et al., 2001; Collins et al., 2003). It is noteworthy that in the summary of principles agreed to at the First International Strategy Meeting on Human Genome Sequencing in Bermuda 1996, scientific leaders of the HGP agreed that all human genomic sequence information, generated by centers funded for large-scale human sequencing, should be freely available and in the public domain in order to encourage research and development and to maximize its benefit to society. The decision was made to deposit the sequence in public databases within 24 hours of its assembly, with no restrictions on its use or redistribution (retrieved 1/21/03 from http://www.genome.gov/page.cfm?pageID=10506376). This critical decision made the sequence immediately available to anyone with an Internet connection, ensuring that the knowledge would be available to the public and potentially of benefit to all.

The completion and publication of a "working draft" of the human genome in 2001 were facilitated by the recognition of ubiquitous single nucleotide polymorphisms (SNP), the most common DNA marker systems, providing the highest-resolution genome maps with STS occurring on average every 1,000 nucleotides across the genome (Sachidanandam et al., 2001). SNP variants do not occur at random but are correlated with near neighbor SNPs that are inherited together in blocks, called haplotypes (i.e., nonrandom array of linked markers). As part of the SNP Consortium Allele Frequency Projects, Gabriel et al. (2002) characterized haplotype patterns across 51 autosomal regions in samples from Africa, Europe, and Asia and showed that the human genome can be parsed objectively into haplotype blocks: sizable regions over which there is little evidence for historical recombination and within which only a few common haplotypes are observed. The boundaries of blocks and specific haplotypes were highly correlated across populations.

Construction of Haplotype Maps.   The most recent effort in the HGP "tool chest of resources" for mapping genes underlying susceptibility to common diseases is the construction of human haplotype maps, based on patterns of common SNP haplotypes in populations. Haplotype-based methods offer a powerful approach to disease gene mapping based on the association between causal mutations and the ancestral haplotypes on which they arose. In October 2002, the NHGRI launched the International Human Haplotype Map Project Consortium to construct comprehensive haplotype maps to facilitate comprehensive disease association studies (retrieved 1/24/03 from http://www.genome.gov/page.cfm? pageID=10005336). Since the structure of variation is not randomly distributed in the genome and profiles of SNP polymorphisms differ among populations, it is imperative that basic information on the types, frequencies, and distribution of SNP polymorphisms in all human populations is ascertained. While it is anticipated that a publicly available SNP map of 100,000 SNPs (one SNP per 30,000 nucleotides) is likely to be sufficient for studies in some relatively homogeneous populations, denser maps will be required for studies in large, heterogeneous populations, such as African Americans (Gabriel et al., 2002).

To facilitate SNP discovery and haplotype map construction in African Americans, it is critical that common public resources of DNA samples and cell lines become available as rapidly as possible. Also, to maximize SNP discovery and haplotype mapping for disease susceptibility genes in African Americans, a resource is needed that enriches for SNP polymorphisms and haplotype variation in diverse geographic areas of Africa. A strategic plan for collection of a population resource to facilitate haplotype construction in African Americans and other African diaspora populations has been developed by a team of investigators at the newly formed National Human Genome Center (NHGC) at Howard University (http://www.genomecenter.howard.edu). This plan was publicly announced and presented to the group of international biomedical scientists and minority health scientists invited to the Genomic Research in the African Diaspora (GRAD) Project Workshop I held at the Wye River Conference Center in Queenstown, Maryland, May 2002. Implementation of the GRAD Project is a core research initiative of the NHGC.

Eliminating Health Disparities

With the emergence of genomewide high resolution SNP haplotypes for mapping low penetrance genes, the resources of the HGP goals could be applied to mapping genes underlying susceptibility to common complex diseases of public health interests, thus directing high-resolution HGP resources toward addressing the national public health agenda on disease prevention, health promotion, and the elimination of race- and ethnicity-based health disparities. The visibility of the HGP along with the recognition of genomic variation among populations in SNP haplotypes has focused attention on the genetic contribution to complex diseases in general and in race- and ethnicity-based health disparities in particular. As an outgrowth of his "One America in the 21st Century: Initiative on Race," on February 21, 1998, in a radio address, President Clinton committed the nation to the ambitious goal of eliminating health disparities experienced by racial and ethnic minority populations by the end of 2010 (retrieved 9/16/02 from http://www.cnn.com/ALLPOLITICS/1998/02/21/clinton.radio). The elimination of race- and ethnicity-based health disparities by 2010 was incorporated in Healthy People 2010 (HP 2010), a set of health objectives for the nation to achieve over the first decade of the new century (http://www.healthypeople.gov/Document/tableofcontents.htm).

President Clinton also placed David Satcher, the 16th U.S. surgeon general and assistant secretary for health, in charge of the program to eliminate health disparities. During his four-year term from 1998 to 2002, Dr. Satcher played a historic role in focusing national attention on the need for high-quality science and research on eliminating race- and ethnicity-based health disparities as a public health issue (retrieved 1/30/03 from http://raceandhealth.hhs.gov/sidebars/report.html). Another landmark outgrowth of the Clinton administration's initiative on race was the National Academies' Institute of Medicine's report on "Unequal Treatment: Confronting Racial and Ethnic Disparities in Health Care" (2002). This report documents a large body of research underscoring the existence of health disparities; the disproportionate burden of disease among minority populations; and that minorities are more likely to receive lower-quality health care, regardless of income and insurance coverage. Another major political accomplishment of the Clinton administration in the arena of race- and ethnicity-based health disparities was the creation of the NIH National Center for Minority Health and Health Disparities (NCMHD). The NCMHD was established by the passage of the Minority Health and Health Disparities Research and Education Act of 2000, Public Law 106-525, and signed by the president of the United States on November 22, 2000 (http://lcweb2.loc.gov/law/usa/

us060525.pdf). The general purpose of the NCMHD is to conduct and support research, training, dissemination of information, and other programs with respect to minority health conditions and other populations with health disparities. Within NIH, the NCMHD serves as the focal point for planning and coordinating minority health and other health disparities research (http://www.ncmhd. nih.gov.).

The NIH defines health disparities as differences in the incidence, prevalence, mortality, and burden of diseases and other adverse health conditions that exist among specific population groups in the United States (retrieved 1/28/03 from http://healthdisparities.nih.gov/whatare.html). The NCMHD is charged with the responsibility of coordinating the development of a comprehensive health disparity research agenda that identifies and establishes priorities, budgets, and policy that govern the conduct and support of all NIH-sponsored minority health and other health disparities research and training activities. In an excerpt from his swearing in as the first director of the NCMHD, Dr. John Ruffin stated that "while the diversity of the American population is one of the nation's greatest assets, one of its greatest challenges is reducing the profound disparity in health status of America's racial and ethnic minorities . . . the NIH can play a vital role in addressing and easing health disparities involving cancer, diabetes, infant mortality, AIDS, cardiovascular illnesses, and many other diseases" (retrieved 2/3/03 from http://www.nih.gov/news/pr/jan2001/od-09.html). Likewise, human genome variation in the American population is one of the nation's greatest assets and in conjunction with high-resolution gene-mapping resources can be used to probe the biology of complex diseases and race- and ethnicity-based health disparities. This connects the research goals of the HGP with the public health goals of HP 2010.

The Case of African Americans and the Use of Appropriate Methodology

Now that the nation is challenged to close the gap in health disparities, a better understanding of population-based DNA sequence variation in common complex diseases is paramount in the rational design of DNA based strategies for diagnosis and treatment of human disease, as well as in the design of innovative genome-based technologies for health promotion and disease prevention. When comparing health outcomes of most common complex diseases by race and ethnicity, African Americans consistently have higher rates of disease, disability, and death than Caucasians (Clayton & Byrd, 2001). Historical documentation of disparities in the burden of death and illness experienced by African Americans, as compared with the U.S. majority White population as a whole, has existed since the government began tracking such statistics. These disparities persist and in some areas continue to grow. Table 43.1 shows examples of health disparities in the mortality rate of five common diseases of public health interest in Blacks and Whites for both males and females.

Population-based Strategies for Eliminating Health Disparities.   Since multiple genes and environmental factors are implicated in common complex diseases of public health interests, the prevention of these diseases relies on identifying risk factors and implementing intervention in high-risk groups. Advances in genome technology now make it possible to map all genes underlying susceptibility to common complex diseases and determine their function in disease susceptibility. Technology developments to detect genes have outpaced the current use of genetic test results in medical practice. Before such genetic tests can be used in patient management, their clinical validity must be established (Burke et al., 2002). Determining the clinical validity of genetic tests involves measuring the clinical sensitivity of the test, specificity, positive predictive value, and negative predictive value with respect to disease occurrence. Estimates of clinical measurements of genetic testing are based on epidemiologic studies, which are used to measure not only the clinical sensitivity and specificity but also the population attributable fraction of disease due to the disease-susceptibility genes (Yang et al., 2000). In addition to determining the clinical sensitivity of an increasing number

Table 43.1
Health disparities by age-adjusted death rates by race and sex

Diseases	MALE (Per/100,000)		FEMALE (Per/100,000)	
	White	Black	White	Black
Heart Disease	162	232	88	147
	144	208	104	129
Cancer				
Stroke	25	47	22	37
Diabetes Mellitus	14	29	11	29
Hypertension	2	8	2	7

Source: National Vital Statistics Report (2000).

of genetic tests spawned by the HGP, assessing gene–environment interaction in common complex diseases is an important public health research priority in the post–HGP era. Indeed, there is an increasing need for population-based epidemiologic studies to assess (1) prevalence of gene variants, (2) magnitude of disease risk associated with gene variants, and (3) magnitude of disease risk associated with gene–gene and gene–environment interactions (Khoury, 1999). As more genes and their numerous allelic variants are discovered, it becomes crucial to assess how modifiable epidemiological risk factors such as diet or drugs interact with genetic risk factors to influence disease risks. Stratifying risk for disease among individuals with risk factors according to genetic susceptibility at one or more loci will improve the predictive value for disease occurrence among biologically susceptible individuals and may thus help target preventive and therapeutic interventions (Zhao et al., 1997).

The Biology of Race.   The identification of numerous genetic markers differentially expressed among populations has stimulated debate regarding the validity of racial/ethic categories for biomedical and genetic research (Risch et al., 2002). The focus of the dialogue from the genetic perspective has been the relative merit of the concept of "race" or "ethnicity." Population clusters identified by genotype analysis seem to be more informative than those identified by race (Wilson et al., 2001). The advent of genomic medicine and individualized medicine raises questions about the utility of ethnic labels in assessing populations risks for complex disease (Schwartz, 2001). As medicine becomes increasingly more individualized, a more refined definition of human biology and racial identity will be forthcoming. Old concepts of race as genetically defined biological groups are challenged in the light of new knowledge from genomic science that indicates that approximately 85 percent of the variance due to genetic variation is within populations while 15 percent or less is due to differences between races (Lewontin, 1972; Latter, 1980; Barbujani et al., 1997; Stephens et al., 2001).

Risch and Merikangas (1996) have argued that the future of genetic studies of complex human disease may depend, to a large extent, on applications of new "association" type methods to family-based data. The emergence of the population-based incident case-control study and the nested case-control methods have also contributed to methodologic improvements in study design and methodologic inference (Khoury & Yang, 1998). Although the case-control study is one of the primary tools of epidemiology, questions have been raised about the appropriateness of its use in association studies of a candidate gene with occurrence of disease, because of the possible effect of population stratification (Ewens & Spielman, 1995).

Population stratification occurs when the population under study is assumed to be homogeneous with respect to allele frequencies but in fact comprises subpopulations that have different allele frequencies for the candidate gene. Given that the African American population is genetically heterogeneous because of its African ancestry and subsequent admixture with European and Native Americans, case-control studies with African Americans are highly susceptible to spurious associations (Parra et al., 2001; Pfaff et al., 2002). If subpopulations also have different risks of disease, as is often observed in health disparity studies, then subpopulation membership is a confounder, and an association between the candidate gene and disease may be incorrectly estimated without properly accounting for population stratification. Studies by Kittles et al. (2002) at the NHGC show the confounding effect of population stratification in case-control studies of CYP3A4-V, an A to G promoter variant associated with prostate cancer in African Americans. Population stratification among the African American samples was detected by genotyping ten unlinked genetic markers. Sharp differences in CYP3A4-V frequencies were observed between Nigerian and European American controls (0.87 and 0.10, respectively; P<0.0001). African Americans were intermediate (0.66). An association uncorrected for stratification was observed between CYP3A4-V and prostate cancer in African Americans (P = 0.007). A nominal association was also observed among European Americans (P = 0.02) but not Nigerians. The unlinked genetic marker test provided strong evidence of population stratification among African Americans. Because of the high level of stratification, the corrected P-value was not significant (P – 0.25). These results reveal the potential for confounding of association studies with African Americans and the need for study designs that take into account substructure caused by differences in ancestral proportions between cases and controls.

EXISTING AND EMERGING PARADIGMS AND ISSUES

This section underscores the importance of recognizing different perspectives on the efficacy of knowledge gained from the HGP and research on human variation. It addresses the difficulty in separating the biomedical aspects of the science of complex diseases and health disparities from the sociopolitical and social aspects. It is predicated on the realization that essentially all aspects of life— health, disease, behaviors, etc.—reflect the interaction of genes operating in an environment (Khoury et al., 2000). Neither genes alone nor the environment alone causes disease, since the latter requires the interaction of both. The nature and proportion of the contributions of the two determine what is observed and defined as disease.

The Interaction of Biology and the Environment

Genetics are not expressed in a vacuum and must be studied in the context of the relevant physical, chemical, and psychosocial environments (Khoury et al., 2000). A common tendency is to elevate the objective validity of the genetics without recognizing the regulating influence of environmental factors. A question often posed to investigators at the NHGC is, Why focus on the genetics of diseases in African Americans, if there is no biological basis for racial and ethnic group classifications? The common response to this question is that virtually all diseases and disorders result from interactions between genes and environment (Gelehrter et al., 1998; Khoury et al., 2000). Knowledge gained from the HGP and research on human variation clearly shows that the DNA sequence of each individual genome is unique and that biological relationship influences the degree of DNA sequence sharing/similarity among individuals. Since genes are always expressed in the context of an environment, shared environments/experiences (i.e., physical, chemical, psychosocial) of populations must be considered in dissecting out the determinants of disease.

The multiplicity of genetic and environmental variables interacting in disease must be better defined and understood for informed decision making on optimal strategies for eliminating race- and ethnicity-based health disparities. New and more comprehensive genetic epidemiology models of complex diseases are needed today, models that include the dynamic interaction of multiple genes in multiple environments and broaden perspectives based on static linear models of complex disease that implicate either genes or environment as separable and discrete determinants of disease. This is a challenging endeavor, but it is the mission of the NHGC—to explore the science and teach the knowledge about DNA sequence variation and its interaction with the environment in the causality, prevention, and treatment of diseases common in people of African ancestry.

Social factors are necessarily part of the environment and must be included in genetic epidemiology models. Most existing studies of gene–environment interactions define the environment narrowly in terms of physical factors such as air, food, and shelter. New studies must integrate measures of the social environment as a major part in gene–environment interactions. Few existing genetic epidemiology models factor in social or psychosocial environment. The latter must be included in contemporary gene–environment investigations of race- and ethnicity-based health disparities in common complex diseases.

Since gene expression in the complex diseases of interest is significantly influenced by the environment in a broad sense, major attention must be given to the identification of environmental factors that can be more quickly and easily manipulated than genes. This is particularly true for African Americans, for whom psychosocial determinants of health may be more apparent and provide a more effective strategy for health promotion and disease prevention. Thus, systematic, concerted efforts must be made to engage African Americans in genetic epidemiology research that combines the strengths of powerful gene mapping strategies with equally powerful instruments for assessing psychosocial factors interacting with genes as a basis for effective health care.

If the environment significantly influences the expression of underlying genetic systems that are part of the cell's operating machinery, then the environment may be perceived as a stimulus for awareness of internal operations. Since disease is an expression of gene–environment interactions, disease is associated with a subset of internal biological systems as well as a subset of external environmental factors. Moreover, it must be recognized that disease itself is a social variable (Winkleby et al., 1990; Pincus et al., 1998).

It is conceivable that what may be considered a disease in one group may not be viewed as such in another group. Since variation is an enduring characteristic of life, questions may be asked about the function or role of variation in health and disease. It may be argued that the influence of the environment is greater in societies where biological homogeneity is dominant, while the opposite is true in those where diversity is dominant. Genomic research in African Americans provides opportunities to relate patterns in environmental triggers with patterns in biological responses. The latter appears to be an important step in human growth and development toward conscious control of internal operating systems. That common complex diseases are present in varying degrees in all populations suggests that disease susceptibility is a vulnerability of the architecture or programming of the species, not any particular subset or group of individuals. In other words, given the appropriate stimulus, the biological response would be similar and predictable. Persistence of the same stimuli reinforces the associated response and increases its chance of being recognized.

Variation in the external environment together with variation in the internal response increases the capacity to distinguish parts of an inseparable whole, thus making it known (conscious awareness). It is intriguing to reframe the context for genomic research that greater understanding of the psychosocial environmental determinants of disease may uncover. Such a context would underscore the value of genomic research in minority populations as instructive for growth toward a future of "individualized medicine" characterized by conscious control of internal systems as opposed to the fear of manipulation and exploitation of unique genomic circuitry.

African American Involvement in Genomic Research

Participation in genomic research designed to empower individuals to take greater control of their own biological response would be far more compelling for African Americans than expectations based on current socioeconomic and political systems. Genomic variation in groups, all groups, can be characterized and used as the foundation for defining healthy versus diseased psychosocial constructs. Genomic research on gene–environment interactions that also incorporate measures of the psychosocial environment offers benefits that apply not only to the study group but more broadly to humankind as a whole. The design of such research will not be easy, but neither was the task of sequencing the 3 billion nucleotides in the human genome. The greatest value of the latter will be determined by the ingenuity and resolve that are now given to devising a comprehensive strategy to "map and sequence environmental stimuli" that are reducible to a common biological language.

Because of the history of African Americans in America, this group perhaps like no other U.S. minority population is enriched for the identification of major psychosocial factors associated with the expression of race- and ethnicity-based health disparities. Thus, genomic research in African Americans can be a model for engagement of minority populations in human genome research.

Implications of Research Involvement.   The engagement of African Americans in human genome research has several ethical, legal, and social implications, which must receive ample consideration by researchers seeking to involve this population in such studies. In formulating hypotheses and conceptualizing study designs, it is essential that the ultimate goal be improvement in the health and well-being of the community. As previously stated, African Americans suffer disproportionately from several of the most common complex diseases. The ethical principles of beneficence and justice would demand, therefore, that biomedical research in African Americans focus primarily on elucidating the genetic and environmental components of these diseases, thus facilitating early detection, effective treatment, and, ultimately, prevention. The increasing interest in, and misrepresentation of, information on genetic factors purported to influence intelligence, crime, and other sociobehavioral traits have (justifiably) generated suspicion and fear that genetics research has become just another tool for perpetuating racism and lending credence to the notion that African Americans are inferior (Dula, 1994; King, 1997). This oversimplification of the determinants of such complex traits consistently leads to the generation of spurious explanations for disparities (real or perceived) and the ills of society, ignoring the more serious moral, political, and social contributors (Blakey, 1999).

Population genetics studies should be aimed at identifying gene-based differences and similarities within and among populations, with the hope of gaining a better understanding of their biomedical significance and a greater appreciation for the diversity that contributes to the uniqueness of our species. In view of the stigma already associated with the so-called minority status, any disvalued trait associated with African Americans or other non-White groups will likely be amplified (King, 1992; Nickens, 1996). In an effort to minimize this, researchers should endeavor to ensure that their presentation and publication of results do not foster stigmatization and discrimination and also be willing to counteract misrepresentation or misinterpretation of their findings.

Another factor that could potentially minimize harm to the population is the involvement of African Americans in all aspects of the research process (Blakey, 1997; Jackson, 1997; Armstrong et al., 1999). Though this may not guarantee protection from harm, it increases the likelihood that the research agenda will correlate with priorities of the community and facilitates increased sensitivity to African American history and culture, which is essential in the recruitment of study participants. Indeed, the impact of the U.S. Public Health Service Syphilis Study on the participation of African Americans in biomedical research cannot be overstated (Cox, 1998; Bonner & Miles, 1997; Shavers-Hornaday et al., 1997; Talone, 1998). It must be noted, however, that the general mistrust within the Black community dates back to the 1800s, when brutal "experiments" were conducted on enslaved Africans (Blakey, 1987; Dula, 1994; Gamble, 1993). This history of medical experimentation, as an outgrowth of institutional and societal racism, has created the need for genetic and other biomedical researchers to expend extra effort in gaining the trust of the African American community in order to procure their participation in studies. An example of a model for genetics research in the African American community is the African American Hereditary Prostate Cancer (AAHPC) Study (Powell et al., 2001; Royal et al., 2000).

The AAHPC Study Network was established in 1997 to examine the genetics of hereditary prostate cancer (HPC) in African Americans. It is a research collaboration involving investigators at Howard University (Coordinating Center); the National Human Genome Research Institute, NIH; and six Collaborative Recruitment Centers across the United States. The network comprises a multidisciplinary group of urologists, radiation oncologists, molecular biologists, geneticists, nurses, epidemiologists, data managers, statistical geneticists, and other professionals, the majority of whom are African American, creating a unique opportunity for the involvement of African Americans in human genetics research, both as researchers and as participants.

Solicitation for participation in genetics research requires adequate education/engagement about the research goals, as well as their relevance and anticipated value to the African American community. This is one of the first steps in attempting to obtain informed consent, arguably the tenet of biomedical ethics that is most difficult to implement in biomedical research, particularly genetics research. The paradigm shift in informed consent for genetic studies, from a focus on minimal physical risks to the often more detrimental psychosocial risks, many of which may still be unknown, indeed makes "informed consent" in genetics somewhat of a misnomer. As such, researchers must endeavor to disclose known benefits (without overpromising), risks (physical and psychosocial), and limitations to potential participants and ensure volunteerism.

The protection of privacy and confidentiality, which includes the securing of samples obtained and information generated from the research, is another vital element in the research process. The general principles governing privacy of individual and familial information generated from genetics research have been well articulated (OPRR, 1993; Rothenberg, 1995, Botkin, 2001; Clayton et al., 1995; Harper, 1993; Weiss et al., 1997). However, recently there have been much concern and discussion surrounding the storage and use of anonymous samples that may be linked to groups identifiable by common ancestry (Beskow et al., 2001; Foster et al., 1998; NBAC, 1999; Wadman, 1998). The subsequent use (or misuse) of the samples and data generated from genetics studies is a concern that is frequently raised by individuals, families, or communities solicited for participation in human genome research or engaged in discussion about the research (Botkin, 2001; Clayton et al., 1995; Harper, 1993; Weiss et al., 1997). African Americans are often more sensitive to this issue, because of inherent fears about the intents of research given the history of African Americans being manipulated and exploited by those with authority in the U.S. social system (Roberson, 1994; King, 1997; Armstrong et al., 1999; Freimuth et al., 2001). Since the research focus of investigators at the NHGC is on African Americans and other people of African ancestry, special attention is given to addressing this overriding concern relevant to the engagement of Africans Americans in the mainstream of human genome research.

Issues Related to Clinical Application.   Given that genetic tests are usually developed soon after genes have been isolated, an examination of the implications of genetic testing/screening in African Americans is undoubtedly relevant to this discussion. Genetic discrimination in insurance and employment are presently two of the most pressing concerns in this arena (Hudson et al., 1995; Rothenberg et al., 1997). Persons who utilize genetic testing are at increased risk of being denied employment, promotions, and/or health insurance; having insurance premiums increased; losing health insurance and/or employment; and/or having genetic information disclosed to third parties. In addition, fear of genetic discrimination could create other public health problems by resulting in reluctance of individuals and groups to participate in genetics research, share genetic information with health-care providers or family members, and utilize available preventive and treatment services (Hudson et al., 1995).

The occurrence of widespread discrimination against African Americans with sickle-cell trait in the 1970s has undoubtedly set the tone for the current spectrum of concerns regarding genetic testing/ screening in this population (Bowman, 1992; Murray, 1997). One of the leading contributors to the sickle-cell fiasco was the pervasion of inaccurate information. Misinformation and misperceptions concerning the natural history and symptomatology of the disease, distinction between disease and trait, interpretation of test results, prevalence of disease, and the value of testing were widespread among health-care providers and the general public, as well as state and federal agencies. The current rapid advances in genetic mapping and sequencing technology will likewise culminate in a period of incomplete knowledge, creating even more opportunities for the propagation of misinformation and its adverse effects, especially for the more challenging, complex disorders, many of which are most prevalent in African Americans.

A significant body of literature indicates that due to various financial, structural, and cultural factors, African Americans have diminished access to, and utilization of, health-care services, in general (Nickens, 1996; Russell & Jewell, 1992; Schensul & Guest, 1994; Smedley et al., 2002; Andrulis, 1998). These barriers are potentially even more restrictive in terms of genetic services. The ability to pay for genetic services may be influenced not only by possible genetic discrimination but by a more fundamental variable—possession of health insurance. Approximately 25 percent of African Americans lack health insurance, and many who do have insurance are likely to be insured through the Medicaid program, which provides very limited coverage (Nickens, 1996; Smedley et al., 2002).

Structural barriers include inconvenient locations and the significant underrepresentation of African Americans among providers of genetic services. Genetic services are more often available at tertiary care institutions, which may be inaccessible to communities that are likely to have transportation limitations, such as those in remote locations. In addition, due to inadequate outreach by many institutions, there is a general lack of awareness, within these diverse and remote communities, of genetic risks, benefits, and available services. With the increasing infiltration of genetics into primary health care, it is conceivable (and certainly desirable) that proximity to tertiary-care institutions may eventually become a less significant factor in this regard.

The delivery of culturally relevant and nondiscriminatory genetic services to African Americans could potentially be hampered by the fact that African Americans represent approximately only 1.1 percent of the U.S.-based American Society of Human Genetics membership, which includes medical geneticists, genetic counselors, cytogeneticists, and so on (Mittman, 1998). Even though an increase in the number of African Americans providing genetic services may not, by itself, guarantee the provision of culturally appropriate and equitable health care, it will undoubtedly ease cross-cultural communication and contribute to empowerment of the community (King, 1992).

Aspects of African American culture that seem relevant to the utilization of genetic services are spirituality and the concept of time (Hughes et al., 1996). Spirituality, as an integral facet of African American culture, provides for many the basis for reliance on faith in God and the power of prayer in all aspects of life (Pinderhughes, 1982; Russell & Jewell, 1992). Consequently, some may abstain from utilizing genetic services for fear of intervening in divine destiny and because of the belief that God is in absolute control.

With regard to time orientation, Nobles (1991) noted that African philosophy emphasizes a focus on the past and present, rather than the future. The African American's treatment of time as a possible outgrowth of this philosophy is illustrated by Akbar (1991) in his statement, "The Black Psychology time focus is on the recent past of the African American experience and the present conditions of oppression and its multifarious manifestations. The future is not considered as relevant." Consequently, the predictive and probabilistic nature of genetics may limit uptake of certain genetic services by some African Americans. Finally, another very plausible, possibly overriding determinant of the uptake of genetic services by African Americans is the inherent mistrust and suspicion of the entire health-care system. There is indeed a need for appropriately designed empirical studies to further explore these perspectives.

As mentioned earlier, it appears that if certain genetic diseases are found to occur more frequently among people of color, group members are at increased risk for stigmatization and discrimination. Another, even more disturbing, outcome is that because of the connection to a non-White group, these diseases might receive lower priority in terms of research for treatment and prevention (King, 1992; Nickens, 1996). Nickens (1996) pointed out that despite the differences in disease frequency between cystic fibrosis and sickle-cell disease (CF:1/2500; SCD:1/600) and the fact that in the United States there are 50 percent more individuals with sickle-cell disease than cystic fibrosis, sickle-cell research was allocated about $18 million by the NIH in fiscal year 1992, while for the same year, cystic fibrosis research at the NIH was budgeted for $46 million. Consequently, some African Americans have attributed the nearly half-century hiatus between identification of the cause of sickle-cell disease and effective therapeutic options (hydroxyurea and bone marrow transplantation) to this apparent inequitable allocation of resources. Considering that sickle-cell disease is a single gene disorder and was the first human disease to be understood at the molecular level, many remain skeptical about the "promise" of the Human Genome Project and other human genome research to alleviate suffering from the more complex diseases common in African Americans.

NEW PERSPECTIVES IN GENOMIC SCIENCE

The Uniqueness of the Human Genome in Human Biology and Identity

With the completion of the human genome sequence comes a new knowledge base for biomedical science and humankind, a knowledge base that is as old as the origins of humankind and as new as the most recent gene discovery. This knowledge base connects all living systems and has the capacity to transform our most basic concepts of life and human identity. Knowledge gained from the HGP is unique in its capacity for science to liberate society from incomplete constructs of biology and human identity based on a very limited and incomplete picture of the human genome. This section underscores the scientific and social imperatives for African American participation in the HGP at all levels of investigation, interpretation, and communication at this critical junction in the evolution of DNA sequence-based biology and genomic medicine. The sequencing of the human genome is applicable not only to biomedical science in the identification of genes of clinical relevance but also to more fundamental questions such as, What does the sequence of the human genome reveal about the interdependent relationship of human biology, self-identity, and health?

The HGP provides the foundation for innovative approaches to studying the natural history of genes underlying biology and their distribution in human populations as well as the relationship of the latter to health disparities. New paradigms (i.e., statistical models) for decoding sequence variation and new bioinformatics tools are required to manage and decipher the tidal wave of data generated from population-based genomic studies of complex diseases. Most large-scale, population-based studies conducted by leading research groups in the United States and abroad have not included large numbers of African Americans. The engagement of African Americans and their African ancestral populations in the mainstream of HGP will require building collaborative research networks between African Americans and African biomedical scientists.

The National Human Genome Center (NHGC) at Howard University

The major goal of the NHGC is to bring multicultural resources and perspectives to the HGP in efforts to explore the science of, and teach the knowledge about, DNA sequence variation and its

Figure 43.1
The National Human Genome Center Organizational Chart

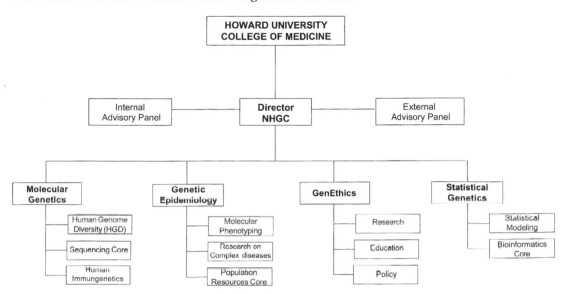

interaction with the environment in the diagnosis, treatment, and prevention of diseases common in African Americans and other African diaspora populations. Population-based differences in human genome sequence variation are "natural resources" for probing the characterization of complex diseases associated with racial health disparities.

The NHGC is organized in four core research areas: (1) Molecular Genetics with state-of-the-art resources for high throughput genotyping is focused on candidate gene analysis and characterizing genomic variation in African Americans and other people of African descent. Dr. Rick Kittloo, a molecular evolutionary biologist, is codirector of Molecular Genetics and leads population-based studies of prostate cancer genetics; (2) Genetic Epidemiology encompasses the continuum from gene discovery to risk characterization and evaluation of genetic tests and services. Dr. Charles Rotimi is director of Genetic Epidemiology and principal investigator of the international Africa America diabetes mellitus (AADM) genetic study of Type II diabetes; (3) Statistical Genetics and Bioinformatics focuses on the development of new mathematical models, software, and methodologies for analyzing complex genetic epidemiologic data. As director of this research area, Dr. George Bonney provides leadership in the rapidly evolving arena of computational biology; and (4) GenEthics, led by Dr. Charmaine Royal, focuses on the ethical, legal, and social implications (ELSI) of knowledge gained from the HGP and research on human variation with particular attention to issues surrounding community engagement and participation in human genome research. See Figure 43.1, which illustrates the interrelationship of these four components at the NHGC.

The Contributions of the NHGC-HU in Reducing Racial Health Disparities

The NHGC is directly involved in the inclusion of African Americans at all levels of investigations in the identification of genes underlying susceptibility to common complex diseases in African Americans and people of African descent. Research in progress led by NHGC investigators includes studies on the genetics of prostate and breast cancer, hypertension, obesity, diabetes, human pigmentation, and asthma. Studies are also conducted on research methodology, molecular and cell biology, informed consent, and other ethical issues related to individual and community participation in human genome research. Population studies include the systematic collection and storage of detailed epidemiologic, family, and medical history information along with blood samples. The NHGC is unique in its epidemiological database and inventory of DNA and cell resources for analyzing the genetic and molecular basis of common, complex disease.

As active research scientists, NHGC investigators serve as mentors in preparing a new generation of biomedical research scientists for twenty-first-century genomic medicine. As an academic research center located in a predominantly African American community, the NHGC is particularly interested in the issues and challenges of engaging African Americans in human genome studies and is keenly aware of the need to expand the benefits of human genome research to the African American and other medically underrepresented minority communities. Thus, in addition to the important functions of research and education, the success of the NHGC is determined by its capacity to inform, engage, and empower its constituent communities to instructively use knowledge gained from human genome research to prevent disease, promote health, and eliminate health disparities.

Research Activities.   Research at the NHGC is focused on characterizing the structure of human genome variation in African Americans and other African diaspora populations and relating this structure to population-based differences in disease susceptibility, sensitivity to drugs, the influence of environmental factors, and organ transplantation. Deciphering the "language of biology" structured in DNA sequence variation is a new frontier for genomic medicine, public health, comparative genomics, and human evolutionary biology.

Genetic differences between the majority U.S. White population and U.S. minority Black populations cannot be equated with pathology in the absence of appropriately designed studies. Toward this end, a major objective of the NHGC is to ascertain well-defined and systematically characterized reference resources for Genomic Research in the African diaspora (GRAD). Using a comprehensive study design based on the biological, environmental, and biocultural evolution of the African diaspora, a major goal of the GRAD Project is the determination of "candidate genotypes and phenotypes" for complex diseases of public health interests in race- and ethnicity-based health disparities. The specific objectives of the GRAD Project are (1) identification of genomic polymorphisms in ancestral populations of African Americans; (2) molecular phenotyping of genotypically defined biological specimens; (3) establishment of complementary epidemiological databases; and (4) development of statistical genetic models for analyses of population admixture and family studies. Among the research resources expected from the GRAD Project are:

• A database of genetic variants, allele frequencies, haplotypes, haplotype frequencies, and possibly, selected blinded phenotypes found within the populations of African descent;

• A curated repository of genomic DNA from cell lines of sampled African/African diaspora populations;

• Tools (e.g., microarrays or their equivalent) for use in studies of biomedical, biocultural, or historical aspects of African and African-derived populations;

• Sources of analytic, molecular, bioethical, bioinformatic, historical, anthropological, and other expertise concerning African-derived populations, as a resource to aid investigators in studies of these populations and communities;

• Investigator training opportunities; and

• Community engagement, policy development, and public education approaches.

The GRAD Project is designed to engage community participation in using science as a tool for decision making in disease prevention, health promotion, and the elimination of health disparities. Advances in genomic science must be accountable to the community, and rewards for participation in research must accrue to all stakeholders. As stated by Bruce Alberts, president of the National Academy of Sciences and chair of the National Research Council, "in the coming century, scientists will be judged not only for how well they generate new knowledge, but also for how well they help solve local and global problems" (Alberts, 2000). Thus, the GRAD Project provides research resources and infrastructure that enable Howard University in particular—and the research community in general—to conduct urgently needed state-of-the-art science into health issues that greatly affect the well-being of African Americans and other persons of African descent.

The research activities of the NHGC are geared toward the long-term objectives of developing a comprehensive center for information, expertise, and reference resources on human genome variation and tools to characterize human genome variation in support of investigator-driven research at Howard University and elsewhere. The special mission of the NHGC in the American scientific society and academic community is to advocate for, facilitate, and become major participants in the development of a new paradigm for genomic research that will result in discoveries applicable to the health and well-being of all society, with special emphasis on communities of African descent in the United States and around the world.

CONCLUSIONS

Knowledge gained from the HGP and research on human variation is forcing a paradigm shift in biology, a shift that is not just an incremental change or transition in thinking about the causes of disease in human populations but rather a transformation in thought about human biology in relationship to disease in populations. The new perspectives in genomic science integrate human biology, identity, and health. It recognizes how an individual or a group defines itself as a function of culture and environment that can influence biological function and disease susceptibility. The fine structure of human genome variation revealed by the HGP provides a comprehensive perspective of humankind's biological heritage and a new foundation for self-discovery and a better understanding of how the diversity of molecules in complex biological systems work cooperatively in unity to express life and maintain health.

REFERENCES

Akbar, N. (1991). The evolution of human psychology for African Americans. In R.L. Jones (Ed.), *Black psychology*, 3d ed. Berkeley, CA: Cobb and Henry, pp. 99–123.

Alberts, B. (2000, February 4). Science must help set the global agenda. *HMS Beagle*, Issue 84.

Andrulis, Dennis. (1998). Access to care is the centerpiece in the elimination of socioeconomic disparities in health. *Annals of Internal Medicine, 129*, 412–416.

Armstrong, T., Crum, L., Rieger, R., Bennett, T., & Edwards, L. (1999). Attitudes of African Americans toward participation in medical research. *Journal of Applied Social Psychology, 29(3)*, 552–574.

Barbujani, G., Magagni, A., Minch, E., & Cavalli-Sforza, L.L. (1997). An apportionment of human DNA diversity. *Proc Natl Acad Sci USA, 94*, 4516–4519.

Beskow, L., Burke, W., Merz, J., Barr, P., Terry, S., Penchaszadeh, V., Gostin, L., Gwinn, M., & Khoury, M. (2001). Informed consent for population-based research involving genetics. *Journal of the American Medical Association, 286*, 2315–2321.

Blakey, M.L. (1987). Skull doctors: Intrinsic social and political bias in American physical anthropology, with special reference to the work of Ales Hrdlicka. *Critique of Anthropology, 7*, 7–35.

Blakey, M.L. (1997). Past is present: Comments on "In the Realm of Politics: Prospects for Public Participation in African-American Plantation Archaeology." *Historical Archaeology, 31(3)*, 140–145.

Blakey, M.L. (1999). Beyond European enlightenment: Toward a critical and humanistic human biology. In A.H. Goodman & T.L. Leatherman (Eds.), *Building a new biocultural synthesis: Political-economic perspectives on human biology*. Ann Arbor: University of Michigan Press, pp. 379–405.

Bonner, G.J., & Miles, T.P. (1997). Participation of African Americans in clinical research. *Neuroepidemiology, 16*, 281–284.

Botkin, J.R. (2001). Protecting the Privacy of family members in survey and pedigree research. *Journal of the American Medical Association, 285(2)*, 207–211.

Bowman, J.E. (1992). The plight of poor African Americans: Public policy on sickle hemoglobins and AIDS. In H.E. Flack & E.D. Pellegrino (Eds.), *African American perspectives on biomedical ethics*. Washington, DC: Georgetown University Press, pp. 173–187.

Burke, W., et al. (2002). Genetic test evaluation: Information needs of clinicians, policy makers, and the public. *American Journal of Epidemiology, 156(4)*, 311–318.

Cantor, C.R. (1990). Orchestrating the Human Genome Project. *Science, 6, 248(4951)*, 49–51.

Clayton, E.W., et al. (1995). Informed consent for genetic research on stored tissue samples. *Journal of the American Medical Association, 274(22)*, 1786–1792.

Clayton, L.A., Byrd, W.M. (2001). Race: A major health status and outcome variable 1980–1999. *Journal of the National Medical Association, 93(3 Suppl)*, 35S–54S.

Collins, F.S. (1995). Positional cloning moves from perditional to traditional. *National Genetics, 9*, 347–350.

Collins, F.S. (1999). Shattuck lecture—medical and societal consequences of the Human Genome Project. *New England Journal of Medicine, 341(1)*, 28–37.

Collins, F.S., & Galas, D. (1993). A new five-year plan for the U.S. Human Genome Project. *Science, 262*, 43–46.

Collins, F.S., Green, E.D., Guttmacher, A.E., & Guyer, M.S. (2003). A vision for the future of genomics research. *Nature, 422*, 835–847.

Collins, F.S., & McKusick, V.A. (2001). Implications of the Human Genome Project for Medical Science. *Journal of the American Medical Association, 285(5)*, 540–544.

Collins, F.S., Patrinos, A., Jordan, E., Chakravarti, A., Gesteland, R., & Walters, L.R. (1998). New goals for the U.S. Human Genome Project: 1998–2003. *Science, 282*, 682–689.

Cox, J.D. (1998). Paternalism, informed consent and Tuskegee. *International Journal of Radiation Oncology Biology Physics, 40(1)*, 1–2.

Deloukas, P., et al. (1998). A physical map of 30,000 human genes. *Science, 23, 282(5389)*, 744–746.

Dula, A. (1994). African American suspicion of the healthcare system is justified: What do we do about it? *Cambridge Quarterly of Healthcare Ethics, 3*, 347–357.

Ewens, W.J., & Spielman, R.S. (1995). The transmission/disequilibrium test: History, subdivision, and admixture. *American Journal Human Genetics, 57(2)*, 455–464.

Foster, M.W., Bernsten, D., & Carter, T.H. (1998). A model agreement for genetics research in socially identifiable populations. *American Journal of Human Genetics, 63*, 696–702.

Freimuth, V.S., et al. (2001). African Americans' views on research and the Tuskegee Syphilis Study. *Social Science and Medicine, 52*, 797–808.

Gabriel, S.B., et al. (2002). The structure of haplotype blocks in the human genome. *Science, 296, (5576)*: 2225–2229.

Gamble, V. (1993). A legacy of distrust: African Americans and medical research. *American Journal of Preventive Medicine, 9(6 Suppl)*, 35–38.

Gelehrter, T., Collins, F., & Ginsberg, D. (1998). *Principles of medical genetics*. 2d ed. Baltimore: Williams & Wilkins.

Harper, P.S. (1993). Research samples from families with genetic diseases: A proposed code of conduct. *British Medical Journal, 306(6889)*, 1391–1394.

Hill, A.V. (2001). The genomics and genetics of human infectious disease susceptibility. *Annu Rev Genomics Hum Genet, 2*, 373–400.

Hudson, K.L., Rothenberg, K.H., Andrews, L.B., Kahn, M.J.E., & Collins, F.S. (1995). Genetic discrimination and health insurance: Annual Urgent Need for Reform. *Science, 270*, 391–393.

Hughes, C., Lerman, C., & Lustbader, E. (1996). Ethnic differences in risk perception among women at increased risk for breast cancer. *Breast Cancer Research and Treatment, 40*, 25–35.

Jackson, F.L. (1997). Concerns and priorities in genetic studies: Insights from recent African American biohistory. *Seton Hall Law Review, 27(3)*, 951–970.

Kan, Y.W., Trecartin, R.F., & Dozy, A.M. (1980). Prenatal diagnosis of hemoglobinopathies. *Annual New York Academy of Science, 344*, 141–150.

Khoury, M.J. (1999). Human genome epidemiology: Translating advances in human genetics into population-based data for medicine and public health. *Genetic Medicine, 1(3)*, 71–73.

Khoury, M., Burke, W., & Thomson, E. (Eds.). (2000). Genetics and public health in the 21st century. Using genetic information to improve health and prevent disease. New York: Oxford; 2000, pp. 3–23.

Khoury, M., & Yang, Q. (1998). The future of genetic studies of complex human diseases: An epidemiologic perspective. *Epidemiology, 9(3)*, 350–354.

King, P.A. (1992). The past as prologue: Race, class, and gene discrimination. In G.J. Annas & S. Elias (Eds.), *Gene mapping: Using law and ethics as guides.* Oxford: Oxford University Press, pp. 94–111.

King, P.A. (1997). The dilemma of difference. In E. Smith & W. Sapp (Eds.), *Plain talk about the Human Genome Project: A Tuskegee University conference on its promise and perils . . . and matters of race* (pp. 75–81). Tuskegee, AL: Tuskegee University Publications Office.

Kittles, R.A., et al. (2002). CYP3A4-V and prostate cancer in African Americans: Causal or confounding association because of population strafication? *Hum Genet. 110(6)*, 553–560.

Lander, E.S., et al. (2001). The Genome International Sequencing Consortium. Initial sequencing and analysis of the human genome. *Nature, 409*, 860–921.

Latter, B.D.H. (1980). Genetic differences within and between populations of the major human subgroups. *American Nat, 116*, 220–237.

Lau, M.M., & Neufeld, E.F. (1989). A frameshift mutation in a patient with Tay-Sachs disease causes premature termination and defective intracellular transport of the alpha-subunit of beta-hexosaminidase. *Journal Biological Chemistry, 15, 264(35)*, 21376–21380.

Lewontin, R.C. (1972). The apportionment of human diversity. *Evol Biology, 6*, 381–398.

Mittman, I.S. (1998). Genetic education to diverse communities employing a community empowerment model. *Community Genetics, 1(3)*, 160–165.

Murray, J.C., et al. (1994). A comprehensive human linkage map with centimorgan density. Cooperative Human Linkage Center (CHLC). *Science, 265(5181)*, 2049–2054.

Murray, R.F., Jr. (1997). The ethics of predictive genetic screening: Are the benefits worth the risks? In E. Smith & W. Sapp (Eds.), *Plain talk about the Human Genome Project: A Tuskegee University conference on its promise and perils . . . and matters of race* (pp. 139–150). Tuskegee, AL: Tuskegee University Publications Office.

National Bioethics Advisory Commission (NBAC). (1999). Research involving human biological materials: Ethical issues and policy guidance. Available at Web address: http://bioethics.gov/pubs.html

National Center for Human Genome Research. (1990). *Understanding our genetic inheritance. The U.S. Human Genome Project: The first five years.* FY 1991–1995. Springfield, VA: National Technical Information Service.

National Vital Statistics Report. (2000). Age-adjusted death rates by race and sex, United States, 1998. *National Vital Statistics Report, 48(11)*, 63–64.

Nickens, H. (1996). Health Services for Minority Populations. In T.H. Murray, M.A. Rothstein, & R.F. Murray Jr. (Eds.), *The Human Genome Project and the future of health care.* Bloomington: Indiana University Press, pp. 58–78.

Nobles, W.W. (1991). African philosophy: Foundations for Black psychology. In R.L. Jones (Ed.), *Black psychology*, 3d ed. Berkeley, CA: Cobb & Henry, pp. 47–63.

Office of Protection from Research Risks (OPRR), Department of Health and Human Services. (1993). Human Genetics research. In *Protecting Human Research Subjects—Institutional Review Board Guidebook*, Chapter H. Bethesda, MD: National Institutes of Health.

Parra, E.J., et al. (2001). Ancestral proportions and admixture dynamics in geographically defined African Americans living in South Carolina. *American Journal of Physical Anthropology, 114(1)*, 18–29.

Pfaff, C.L., Kittles, R.A., & Shriver, M.D. (2002). Adjusting for population structure in admixed populations. *Genetic Epidemiology, 22(2)*, 196–201.

Pincus, T., Esther, R., De.Waly, D., & Callahan, L. (1998). Social conditions and self-management are more powerful determinants of health than access to care. *Annals of Internal Medicine 129*, 406–411.

Pinderhughes, E.B. (1982). Family functioning of Afro-Americans. *Social Work, 27*, 91–96.

Powell, I., et al. (2001). African American Hereditary Prostate Cancer Study: A model for genetic research. *Journal of the National Medical Association, 93(4)*, 120–123.

Risch, N., Burchard, E., Ziv, E., & Tang, H. (2002). Categorization of humans in biomedical research: Genes, race and disease. *Genome Biology, 3(7)*, comment 2007.

Risch, N., & Merikangas, K. (1996). The future of genetic studies of complex human diseases. *Science, 273(5281)*, 1516–1517.

Roberson, N.L. (1994). Clinical trial participation. Viewpoints from racial/ethnic groups. *Cancer Supplement, 74(9)*, 2687–2691.

Rothenberg, K. (1995). Genetic information and health insurance: State legislative approaches. *Journal of Law, Medicine & Ethics, 23*, 312–319.

Rothenberg, K., Fuller, B., Rothstein, M., Duster, T., Kahn, M., Cunningham, R., Fine, B., Hudson, K., King, M-C., Murphy, P., Swergold, G., & Collins, F. (1997). Genetic information and the workplace: Legislative approaches and policy challenges. *Science, 275*, 1755–1757.

Royal, C., et al. (2000). Recruitment experience in the first phase of the African American Hereditary Prostate Cancer (AAHPC) Study. *Annals of Epidemiology, 10(8)*, 68–77.

Russell, K., & Jewell, N. (1992). Cultural impact of health-care access: Challenges for improving the health of African Americans. *Journal of Community Health Nursing, 9(3)*, 161–169.

Sachidanandam, R., et al. (2001). The International SNP Map Working Group. A map of human genome sequence variation containing 1.42 million single nucleotide polymorphisms. *Nature, 409(6822)*, 928–933.

Schensul, J.J., & Guest, B.H. (1994). Ethics, ethnicity, and health care reform. In A. Dula & S. Goering (Eds.), *It just ain't fair: The ethics of health care for African Americans*. Westport, CT: Praeger, pp. 24–40.

Schwartz, R.S. (2001). Racial profiling in medical research. *New England Journal of Medicine, 344*, 1392–1393.

Shavers-Hornaday, V.L., Lynch, C.F., Burmeister, L.F., & Torner, J.C. (1997). Why are African Americans under-represented in medical research studies? Impediments to participation. *Ethnicity and Health, 2(1/2)*, 31–45.

Smedley, B., Stith, A., & Nelson, A. (Ed.). (2002). *Unequal treatment: Confronting racial and ethnic disparities in health care*. Washington, DC: National Academies Press.

Stephens, J.C., Schneider, J.A., Tanguay, D.A., Choi, J., Acharya, T., Stanley, S.E., Jiang, R., et al. (2001). Haplotype variation and linkage equilibrium in 313 human genes. *Science, 293(5529)*, 489–93.

Talone, P. (1998). Establishing trust after Tuskegee. International Journal of Radiation Oncology Biology Physics, 40(1), 3–4.

U.S. Department of Energy. (1990). Office of Health and Environmental Research. Human Genome Program; and National Institutes of Health (United States). National Center for Human Genome Research. (1990). Understanding Our Genetic Inheritance. *The U.S. Human Genome Project: The first five years*. FY 1991–1995. Springfield, VA: National Technical Information Service.

Venter, J.C., et al. (2001). The sequence of the human genome. *Science, 291*(5507), 1304–1351.

Wadman, M. (1998). "Group debate" urged for gene studies. *Nature, 391*, 314.

Weiss, K.M., et al. (1997). Proposed model ethical protocol for collecting DNA samples. *Houston Law Review, 33(5)*, 1431–1474.

Wilson, J.F., et al. (2001). Population genetic structure of variable drug response. *National Genetics, 29*, 265–269.

Winkleby, M.A., Fortmann, S.P., & Barrett, D.C. (1990). Social class disparities in risk factors for disease eight-year prevalence patterns by level of education. *Preventive Medicine, 19*, 1–12.

Yang, Q., Khoury, M.J., Coughlin, S.S., Sun, F., & Flanders, W.D. (2000). On the use of population-based registries in the clinical validation of genetic tests for disease susceptibility. *Genetics in Medicine, 2(3)*, 186–192.

Zhao, L.P., Hsu, L., & Davidov, O. (1997). Population-based family study designs: An interdisciplinary research framework for genetic epidemiology. *Genetics Epidemiology, 14*, 365–388.

Web Sites

http://www.cnn.com/ALLPOLITICS/1998/02/21/clinton.radio
http://www.genomecenter.howard.edu
http://www.genome.gov/page.cfm?pageID=10005336
http://www.genome.gov/page.cfm?pageID=10506376
http://www.healthdisparities.nih.gov/whatare.html
http://www.healthypeople.gov/Document/tableofcontents.htm
http://lcweb2.loc.gov/law/usa/us060525.pdf
http://www.ncmhd.nih.gov.
http://www.nih.gov/news/pr/jan2001/od-09.html
http://www.raceandhealth.hhs.gov/sidebars/report.html

CHAPTER 44

Ethnic Disparities in Transplantation: A Strategic Plan for Their Elimination

CLIVE O. CALLENDER, PATRICE V. MILES,
MARGRUETTA B. HALL, AND
SHERILYN GORDON

INTRODUCTION

A difference, in order to be a difference, must really make a difference. Ethnic disparities are differences between Caucasians and African Americans (Blacks) in health that are very real. Statistical and epidemiological analysis of the following health issues clearly identify the Caucasian and African American health disparities: cancer, diabetes, neonatal mortality, obesity, hypertension, kidney failure, and transplantation. These are examples of some of the many health disparities that exist between African Americans and Caucasians.

My career began as a kidney transplant fellow in 1971 at the University of Minnesota after returning from Africa (Nigeria). Between 1971 and 1973, I became aware of the transplant disparity, and I was taught the art and science of transplant, its technology and the fundamental immunology, by Dr. John S. Najarian and Dr. Richard L. Simmons. I shall never forget a "pearls" that Dr. Simmons shared with me in 1972 and that remains true more than 30 years later: "One of the greatest risk factors for kidney transplantation was being Black." The fact that there are many transplant disparities is now obvious. The question that persists is, What is the extent of the transplant disparity between Blacks and Caucasians, and why does it persist today? Furthermore, what can we do to eliminate this disparity? This chapter represents an effort to answer these questions and discuss the key issues surrounding these transplantation disparities. Furthermore, we recommend steps to be taken to help find the answers, which will finally contribute to the elimination of these disparities.

Enumeration of Key Issues Surrounding Transplantation

There are many issues surrounding transplantation. However, based on the personal experience of the lead author (Dr. Callender), as well as a review of the literature in the field, 12 salient issues are discussed:

1. Race and science. The importance of the complete replacement of the term "race" in science by the word "ethnicity."

Figure 44.1
Kaplan-Meier three-year graft survival by ethnic group for cadaveric kidney transplants, 1988–1998

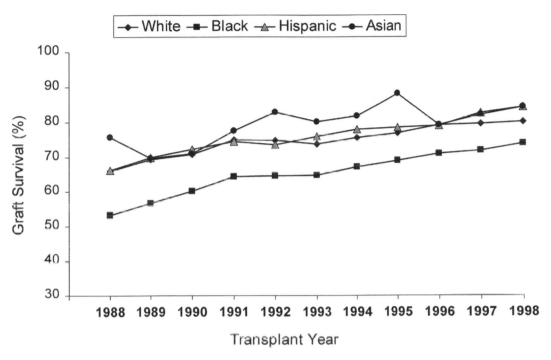

Source: United Network for Organ Sharing (2002). The Organ Procurement and Transplantation Network. Richmond, VA. Retrieved October 31, 2002.

2. The fate of kidneys transplanted into Blacks. African Americans after kidney transplantation have 10–20 percent poorer graft survival rates than all other ethnic groups (at two to five years after kidney transplantation). This fact is true in the living related donor (LRD), living unrelated donor (LURD), and cadaver donor (CD) transplant situations (see Figure 44.1).

3. The fate of donated African American kidneys. Kidneys of African Americans have statistically significantly inferior graft survival rates regardless of which ethnic group they are transplanted into, including African Americans.

4. Waiting times for Blacks in transplantation. Blacks wait twice as long as Whites for kidney transplants.

5. Prevalence and incidence rates for kidney failure in Blacks. The incidence and prevalence rates of end-stage renal disease (ESRD) for Blacks is disproportionate because of their increased susceptibility to hypertension (HTN) and diabetes, which is two to four times that of Caucasians.

6. Delayed Black patient referral rates for transplantation. Blacks are referred later for kidney transplantation, are wait-listed later, and are transplanted later than Caucasians regardless of financial status.

7. The green screen. Green stands for lack of dollars or medical insurance.

8. Dialysis survival rates for Blacks. Survival rates on dialysis for Blacks are the best of all ethnic groups.

9. Compliance rate for Blacks. Blacks are no more noncompliant than any other ethnic group (many previous communications have incorrectly stated this fact).

10. The effects of institutionalized racism—deep-rooted conscious or subconscious classifications of ethnic groups into superior and inferior classes.

11. Inequitable allocation schema. Inequitable allocation because of racial discrimination as a consequence of Human Leukocyte Antigens (HLA) emphasis.

12. Unique posttransplantation drug responses in Blacks. Blacks after transplantation are afflicted with diabetes when placed on prograf twice the rate of Caucasians.

DISCUSSION OF THE KEY SELECTED ISSUES

Race and Science

"Race" is a term that has been used to designate one racial group as superior to another (Callender, 1997; Freeman, 1998a). This was first used negatively by Shockley and others in the 1950s and by others more recently to suggest that Blacks are inferior to Whites (Callender et al., 2002a). Since the designation of race is a sociopolitical construct, it has absolutely no place in science. Scientists such as anthropologists and geneticists and immunogeneticists, as well as others, have long been aware that we are all members of one race, the Homosapiens species. This was further demonstrated conclusively by the human genome mapping completed in 2001.

Callender et al. (2002a) also notes that at the Fourth International Samuel Kountz Symposium in Washington, D.C., in 1997, the consensus was that the term "race" should be replaced by ethnicity and not be used in science any longer to denote African Americans or Blacks as it is denigrating and inappropriate (Callender, 1997; Freeman, 1998a, 1998b; Odocha, 2000). While this position is initially disturbing and often offensive to many Whites, the time has come to effectively address this issue. It is important to be reminded that humankind's (the Homo sapiens species) birthplace is in Africa (Jackson, 1989; Hurley, 1989; Johnson, 1989).

The Fate of Kidneys Transplanted into Blacks

Data accumulated over the past 20 years have identified that Blacks are the ethnic group that, in spite of many immunosuppressive improvements, continue to have statistically poorer three-year kidney transplant graft survival rates than all other ethnic groups, whether LD (living donor) related or unrelated, or CD (cadaver donor) (Young & Gaston, 2000).

The kidney transplant graft survival discrepancy has existed some 30 years after it was first identified. Many hypotheses have been offered and disproved for example, too few Black donors (Callender, 1989), HLA-mismatch, inequitable allocation (Callender et al., 1998; Gaston et al., 1993; Milford et al., 1987; Greenstein et al., 1989) noncompliance (Schweizer et al., 1990), and the green screen (Young & Gaston, 2000; Opelz et al., 1989; Callender, 1998).

The three hypotheses that remain and should be the focus of future research, are the high statistical correlation of (1) hypertension (HTN) (Cosio et al., 1995; Cosio et al., 1997); (2) immune hyper-responsiveness (Kerman et al., 1991); and (3) the unstudied role of institutionalized racism as a contributor (Callender, 1995). The recent observation that hypertension in Blacks is highly correlated (Gaston et al., 1993; Cosio et al., 1995; Cosio et al., 1997) with poor graft survival in Blacks is consistent with the observation that 90 percent of Blacks are hyperimmune responders (Kerman et al., 1991) and that when this group's inordinately poorer graft survival is eliminated, graft survival in the remaining 10 percent of Blacks is equal to that of Caucasian graft survival rates. The questionable role of institutionalized racism (Callender, 1995; Callender et al., 2002a) in the poorer graft survival of kidney transplantation in African Americans (Blacks) has never been studied and is discussed later in this chapter.

The Fate of Donated Kidneys from African Americans

Every study that has looked at the graft survival of African American-donated kidneys has confirmed what Opelz et al. (1977) first identified, that kidney donations from African Americans have statistically significantly inferior graft survival rates regardless of which ethnic group they are transplanted into. When this observation was initially published, it was my opinion that the problem was an inadequate African American kidney donor pool, (Callender, 1989; Callender et al., 1998; Callender, 1999; Callender et al., 1998). However, when we had larger numbers of African American kidney donors, we would find that this was a statistical quirk or anomaly. Also at that time, African American recipients of African American-donated kidneys represented only 3 percent. Now more than 26 percent of African American kidney recipients receive African American kidneys, and the number of African American donor kidneys studied now exceeds nearly 14,000 (Callender et al., 2002a). These data present a clear picture of why more research is needed.

In the past, theories as to anatomical and physiological ethnic differences in the number and quality of the glomeruli of African American kidneys have not provided us with the answers we seek (Friedman, 1987; Kasiske et al., 1991; Koyama et al., 1994). An infusion of additional research funds is necessary to help us resolve this enigma and possibly find the connections to whatever gives African Americans their predilection to HTN, diabetes, (Callender, 1989; Friedman, 1987), and their immunologic hyperresponsiveness.

In 1978–1982, we began our Black donor education efforts (Callender et al., 1982). Successful Black donor education efforts from 1982 to 1988 (Callender, 1989; Hall et al., 1991), and from 1986 to 1992 (Callender et al., 1991; Callender, 1991; Callender, 1994) helped to substantially increase the numbers of Blacks signing donor cards and the transplant awareness of Blacks. The Black donor program also played a major role in increasing the number of African American organ donors per million (ODM) from 8 ODM in the 1980s to more than 34.7 ODM in 1996 (see Tables 44.1 and 44.2) and 40.8 ODM in 2001. The community grassroots methodology utilized in these successful efforts, combined with a mass media campaign in the African American population, led to the conceptualization of the National Minority Organ Tissue Transplant Education Program (MOTTEP) in 1991 (Callender, 1994; Callender et al., 1995; Callender et al., 2001; Callender et al., 2002b).

With National MOTTEP, the previously applied methodology was expanded to all minority populations, including African Americans (Blacks), Latinos (Hispanics), American Indians, Alaskan Natives, Asians, and Pacific Islanders. Although conceptualized in 1991, National MOTTEP received official contract funding in 1993 (thanks to the support of former congressman Louis Stokes and funding from the Office of Research on Minority Health (ORMH), 1993–1995). Since 1995, National MOTTEP has been receiving grant funding from the ORMH, which is now the National Center on Minority Health and Health Disparities, and the National Institute of Diabetes and Digestive and Kidney Diseases (NIDDK) totaling $10 million when combined with the initial contract funding. When the efforts began in the 1980s, minority donations were at 16 percent of the total donations compared to 27.2 percent of total donations in 2001.

Waiting Times for Blacks in Transplantation

Blacks wait nearly twice as long (see Figure 44.2) as Caucasians for kidney transplants. The report of the Office of Inspector General and the reports of Ayanian et al. (1999) and Epstein et al. (2000) notwithstanding in 1989, African Americans waited nearly two years (21 months) while Caucasians waited one year (12 months). In 1996, African Americans waited nearly four years (43 months), while their Caucasian counterparts waited less than two years (22 months) for kidney transplants. Recent studies by Ayanian, Epstein, and others demonstrate that this is just the tip of the iceberg

Table 44.1
Number of cadaveric donors recovered during 1998–2001

Year of Donation	Donor Ethnicity							
	White		Black		Hispanic		Asian	
	# of Donors	% of Total	# of Donors	% of Total	# of Donors	% of Total	# of Donors	% of Total
1988	3,401	6.1	359	4.5	264	4.0	29	2.6
1989	3,284	5.9	346	4.4	301	4.6	54	4.8
1990	3,701	6.7	439	5.6	302	4.6	41	3.6
1991	3,625	6.5	467	5.9	356	5.4	47	4.1
1992	3,561	6.4	513	6.5	348	5.3	70	6.2
1993	3,799	6.9	555	7.0	432	6.6	57	5.0
1994	3,974	7.2	584	7.4	422	6.4	92	8.1
1995	4,143	7.5	611	7.7	486	7.4	82	7.2
1996	4,160	7.5	652	8.3	486	7.4	88	7.8
1997	4,136	7.5	652	8.3	552	8.4	102	9.0
1998	4,412	8.0	656	8.3	600	9.1	100	8.8
1999	4,366	7.9	640	8.1	633	9.7	111	9.8
2000	4,464	8.1	692	8.8	641	9.8	120	10.6
2001	4,427	8.0	737	9.3	735	11.2	141	12.4
Total	55,453	100.0	7,903	100.0	6,558	100.0	1,134	100.0

Source: United Network for Organ Sharing (2002). The Organ Procurement and Transplantation Network. Richmond, VA. Retrieved October 31, 2002.

when it comes to access to renal transplantation for African Americans and other minorities and women (Callender et al., 2002a).

The work of Schulman et al. (1999) and others (Wolfe et al., 2000; Gaston et al., 1993; Scott et al., 2002; Alexander & Seghal, 1998) indicates that African Americans and other minorities are victims of institutionalized racism due to their ethnicity. Additionally, because of their ethnicity, they have unequal and inferior access not only to transplants and the transplant waiting list but to health care in general. This chapter addresses the fact that many of these barriers to equal access can be overcome by physician and patient empowerment and education programs directed to both minority and majority groups. This should be part of a national strategy aimed at educating these groups and is exemplified by the MOTTEP Phase III demonstration project.

Prevalence and Incidence Rates for Kidney Failure in Blacks

The inordinately high prevalence and incidence of end-stage renal disease (ESRD) in African Americans are attributed to their predilection to hypertension and diabetes mellitus, which occurs two to four times as often as in Whites. This predilection leads to many unanswered questions relative to why these diseases have such a predilection for the African American and Hispanic/Latino populations. In spite of the many hypotheses related to the ingestion of inordinate amounts of lead, sugar, and salt and obesity, no definitive cause for this disproportionate incidence of hypertension

Table 44.2
Number of cadaveric and living donors, population size (in thousands), and organ donors per million (ODM), population by ethnicity

Year of Donation	Ethnicity											
	White			Black			Hispanic			Asian		
	# of Donors	Population	O.D.M.	# of Donors	Population	O.D.M.	# of Donors	Population	O.D.M.	# of Donors	Population	O.D.M.
1990	5,301	188,596	28.1	659	29,404	22.4	518	22,571	22.9	73	7,090	10.3
1991	5,408	189,634	28.5	757	29,855	25.4	610	23,391	26.1	96	7,439	12.9
1992	5,412	190,726	28.4	835	30,346	27.5	636	24,283	26.2	119	7,817	15.2
1993	5,844	191,697	30.5	957	30,795	31.1	734	25,222	31.1	116	8,184	14.2
1994	6,141	192,538	31.9	1,013	31,210	32.5	733	26,160	28.0	179	8,511	21.0
1995	6,615	193,328	34.2	1,047	31,590	33.1	855	27,107	31.5	158	8,846	17.9
1996	6,735	194,037	34.7	1,112	31,951	34.8	916	28,099	32.6	160	9,186	17.4
1997	6,935	194,746	35.6	1,172	32,339	36.2	1,043	29,182	35.7	189	9,537	19.8
1998	7,532	195,414	38.5	1,208	32,713	36.9	1,115	30,252	36.9	215	9,863	21.8
1999	7,694	196,049	39.2	1,284	33,092	38.8	1,153	31,337	36.2	220	10,186	21.6
2000	8,438	196,929	42.8	1,373	33,619	40.8	1,319	32,832	40.2	278	10,620	26.2
Total	72,055	2,123,694	33.9	11,417	346,922	32.9	9,562	300,436	32.2	1,803	97,279	18.5

Source: United Network for Organ Sharing (2002). The Organ Procurement and Transplantation Network. Richmond, VA. Retrieved October 31, 2002.

Figure 44.2

Kaplan-Meier median waiting time for cadaveric kidney transplants by ethnic group, for registrations added during 1988–1998

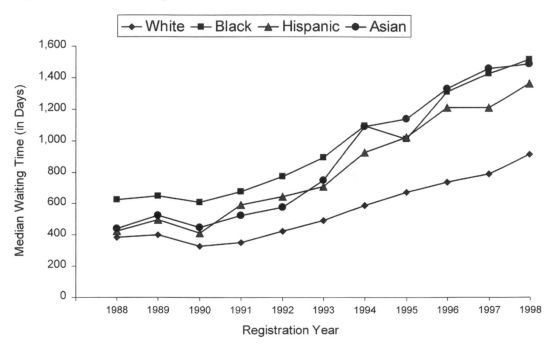

Source: United Network for Organ Sharing (2002). The Organ Procurement and Transplantation Network. Richmond, VA. Retrieved October 31, 2002.

(HTN) and Type II diabetes mellitus in African Americans has been identified. The fact that it occurs is indisputable; however, why it occurs remains a puzzle and a focal point for further research efforts.

Delayed Black Patient Referral Rates for Transplantation

When it comes to transplantation, major factors such as Blacks being referred later for kidney transplantation, being wait-listed later, and being transplanted later than Caucasians regardless of financial status were thought to be socioeconomically related. Recent studies make it clear that the presence or absence of finances or health insurance is not (Schulman et al., 1999; Williams, 1999) the reason. Recently, the Institute of Medicine (IOM) "Unequal Treatment" (Smedley et al., 2000) documents that when African Americans have the fiscal resources and the health insurance, they are still placed at the end of the queue, (i.e., referred later for transplants and transplanted later than Whites who have health insurance and/or cash). These studies suggest the patient's ethncity or gender sadly determines whether or not the patient will be referred to a kidney specialist or for transplant evaluation. This lengthens, therefore, the waiting time for kidney transplantation. The biases of the health-care providers (the physicians) determine whether the patient will be referred early or late or not referred at all. When a patient is told he or she has kidney failure, the denial that occurs is predictable and the responsibility for helping that patient deal appropriately with his or her illness at that time requires support, patience, education, and family support. This is expected to be facilitated equitably by the health-care provider (physician) (Callender et al., 2002a).

The release of the IOM report (Smedley et al., 2002) confirms that physician biases, which are ethnically related, determine the direction and speed of patient care. When ESRD is added to the equation, the delay appears to increase the posttransplant mortality of African Americans (Epstein et al., 2000) and decreases the transplant patient's graft survival rates (Kasiske et al., 1998). Once again, this unequal treatment of the African American renal patient requires special attention and the reeducation of the physician and the African American community. According to Distant (Santana, 2002), sometimes physicians will refer only patients who the physicians think will benefit most from transplants, and sometimes, they may not think that an African American will benefit as much as a White male. He further indicates that White males have the highest transplant and referral rates, followed by White females and Black males. African American women have the lowest rates. Distant (Santana, 2002) also attributes this to attitudes and beliefs on the part of the physician and the need for attitude changes on the part of health-care providers toward minorities.

The Green Screen

In order to be included on the national transplant waiting list, patients must meet medical, psychological, and financial requirements. Callender (1996) coined the term "green screen," meaning that if an individual does not have the financial resources (insurance or lack of insurance coverage for certain medical procedures, Medicare or Medicaid, or cash, the "green"), one will not even get on the waiting list and, therefore, will not receive a transplant. The bottom line is that a physician will not refer such a patient for transplantation because of a lack of resources, and many hospitals cannot afford to incur such costs. The green screen was used to describe a rationale for the observation that African Americans, who died from end-stage liver disease (ESLD) two to three times more often than Whites with ESLD, were identified on liver transplant waiting lists far less than expected. For example, Blacks represent 12 percent of the population, but they make up 35 percent of the patients on the kidney transplant waiting lists. On liver transplant waiting lists, Blacks were noted to make up approximately 10 percent of the patients waiting. It was clear to me that this grossly underrepresented the ESLD incidence of African Americans with liver disease and that these findings required an investigation.

Since the incidence of ESLD and mortality rate from ESLD in African Americans is two to three times those of the Caucasian population, a closer look at the liver transplant referral practices suggested to me that the reasons were socioeconomic. Therefore, I suspected and, thereafter, identified the absence of health insurance or money (greenbacks) as the most likely cause. The scenario depicted in the *John Q* movie was present nearly everywhere I looked in the late 1980s and 1990s, and it became crystal-clear to me that this green screen, when applied, eliminated the socioeconomically deprived from transplant waiting lists. For ESLD, or heart failure patients, this led to an early (premature) demise.

The green screen is unbiased and, whether the person is Black or White, is irrelevant. If there is no green (health insurance or cash), the patient is not eligible for the transplant. Since one-third of poor people are Black, this often meant the persons whom the green screen was likely to affect were African Americans. Therefore, this helped explain why Blacks were underrepresented on liver and cardiac transplant waiting lists. The validity of this hypothesis was present in 1996 and is still present today. This fact is evident in extrarenal transplantation and leads to increased mortality rates in minorities, one-third of whom are poor.

Does there exist a green screen in kidney transplantation? Yes, but to a lesser degree. One difference is that if one does not get a kidney transplant, his or her life can be sustained on dialysis (the artificial kidney). Second, 90 percent of members of the population are likely to have health insurance of one kind or another. Among the 5–10 percent that are uninsured or underinsured is where the green screen can be found. The fact is that some transplant centers will not refer a patient for transplantation if there is no ability to pay for the required medication after transplantation, which would result in a rejection of the transplanted kidney. The exact number of how many kidney (ESRD) patients are affected by this green screen effect is less well known.

Better Dialysis Survival Rates for Blacks and Their Implications

A surprising data item to many is that Black survival rates on dialysis are the best of all ethnic groups (Ayanian et al., 1999; Epstein et al., 2000). The fact that African American ESRD patients survive longer on dialysis than all other ethnic groups, have poorer graft survival rates after transplantation, and wait longer for transplantation than all other ethnic groups is paradoxical, but nonetheless a fact (Kasiske et al., 1998; Alexander & Seghal, 2001; Wolfe et al., 2000; Ojo et al., 2001; Callender et al., 2002a).

My hypothesis is that this is associated with the observation that 90 percent of Black ESRD patients remain on dialysis (10 percent of Black ESRD are on transplant waiting lists) while 80 percent of white ESRD patients remain on dialysis (while 20 percent of White ESRD patients are on transplant waiting lists). I believe, therefore, that the healthier White patients are transplanted, while the healthier Black patients remain on dialysis, and this is one explanation for the observation that the Blacks who remain on dialysis fare better than Whites on dialysis. This hypothesis remains to be tested and confirmed by data analysis (Callender et al., 2002a). This is very undesirable, however, as the healthier Black patients should also be referred for transplantation. A determined and concentrated effort must be made to recruit Black patients for transplantation before dialysis and earlier after being on dialysis—this is an undesirable disparity that must not be looked on with favor until the percentage of Blacks transplanted is equal to the percentage of Caucasians transplanted and the better dialysis survival rate in Blacks persists.

Compliance Rates for Blacks

In the past, poorer African American kidney graft survival rates were attributed to African American noncompliance (Rovelli et al., 1989; DeLone et al., 1989). However, recent data by Greenstein and Siegel (1998) document that there is no difference in noncompliance between African Americans and other ethnic groups. In addition, these data revealed that no statistically significant data differences existed when compared and contrasted with Caucasians and confirm that kidney graft failures in African Americans are therefore not caused by noncompliance. In fact, kidney graft survival rates for African Americans are poorer even before they leave the hospital after the transplant. It is crucial to identify other factors contributing to these statistically significant poorer graft survival rates (Opelz et al., 1989; Sumrani et al., 1989; Dunn et al., 1989; Rodey et al., 1989).

The Effects of Institutionalized Racism

As previously mentioned, we are all of the same race (species)—Homo sapiens. While each ethnic group may differ from another, this is not a contributing factor for racism. It is our differences that makes this species durable. Therefore, it is the *concept* that these differences render one ethnic group superior to another that is the malignant side (face) of racism. This race concept (superior vs. inferior), is a sociopolitical construct (Callender, 1997; Freeman, 1998b; Odocha, 2000) and is destructive (Callender et al., 2002a). The federal government and OMB are equally guilty in perpetrating this farce as they continue to categorize human beings into different races when only one race exists. All human beings should be categorized according to ethnicities and cultures and even languages, but never as different races. This remains an issue that needs to be met head-on and properly dealt with whenever this attempt to categorize us as different races is presented (Callender et al., 2002a).

Racism is a very destructive phenomenon that can be traced back to slavery. During the period of slavery, 1609 to 1865, those of African descent were enslaved in America and owned by Whites and others. After slavery was abolished, there was a need for some to categorize White Americans from this subclass of Americans. This began the era of gross (overt) racism when former slaves were dealt with severely and horribly by decapitation, castration, and murder for behavior characterized by former slave owners as improper. This era, from 1865 to the 1960s, was replaced by the theories supported by Shockly and others that Blacks were inferior by virtue of lower IQs, and so on (Callender et al., 2002a). This ushered in the era of covert racism (Callender, 1997; Freeman, 1998; Odocha, 2000), characterized by more tolerant and more restrained treatment of the former slaves (Negroes) when their behavior was deemed unacceptable. This covert racism remains and is associated with the same superior/inferior construct, which relegates those of African descent to be considered inferior human beings. This so-called unconscious or subconscious racism—institutionalized racism (IR)—is found in many Whites, Blacks, and others who are racist to the core, while being largely unaware of their racist practices (behaviors) (Schulman et al., 1999; Williams, 1999; Smedley et al., 2002; Callender et al., 2002a. Freeman, 1998b).

In many instances, Blacks are treated as invisible; for example, information is of value only if a White person validates it; if a Black stands in line, a White person invariably will step in front of him or her as though he or she is invisible. The book entitled, *The Invisible Man* written by Ralph Ellison in the 1960s, brilliantly captures this illustration. This also reflects the way Blacks and women are treated differently in the medical field (i.e., the women because of their sexual differences, and the African Americans or Blacks because of their complexions). These practices are widespread and flagrantly practiced by many Americans, Whites and others, without an awareness of their behavior. Institutionalized racism may well be one of the major reasons that African Americans traverse more rapidly from the cradle to the grave than other Americans.

The role of institutionalized racism in transplantation for Blacks is reflected in the superior–inferior mentality and accounts for the referral rates and disproportionate waiting times for Blacks and other minorities due to the fact that Whites are given preferential treatment for waiting lists. The unequal treatment that the IOM speaks of represents institutionalized racism at its most malignant, and because these behaviors are often subconsciously carried out, they require special strategies for their eradication.

On a larger scale, institutionalized racism may be one of the most important factors why African Americans have disproportionately poorer health when compared to Caucasians. It is not the genotype or genome, but rather the racist environment that African Americans live in (are forced to tolerate) from day to day that makes a difference. No less important is the brainwashing of Blacks for 400 years, which has led victimized Blacks to think that White is right and fostered Blacks' self-hate (which may be an unrecognized, very potent source of illness and disease in Blacks). The need for a national strategy to organize our minority communities first and then the majority communities is essential to overcoming this malignant entity. National MOTTEP has identified this as its Phase III endeavor (focus).

Inequitable Allocation Schema

Another factor contributing to longer waiting times involves human leukocyte antigen (HLA) matching. HLA matching is used to identify good matches for kidney transplants. Distant (Santana, 2002) points out that African Americans tend to have HLA genotypes different from those of other ethnic groups. Since the 1980s (Gaston et al., 1993; Zachary, 1993; Gaston, 1993), the racial discriminatory use of HLA has been pointed out in several articles indicating that the allocation of organs by the Organ Procurement and Transplantation Network (OPTN) is racially discriminatory favoring Whites (Caucasians) over African Americans. However, this allocation schema practiced by the United Network for Organ Sharing (UNOS) was not modified until 1995, and many believe remains suboptimal as of this writing.

While the HLA antigens in Whites have been defined since the 1980s, this has not been the case with the African American population. It is interesting to note that it is the allocation schema based upon the well-defined HLA antigens in Whites that was the basis for the sharing of organs in this country. This occurred with an apparent total disregard for the negative impact this had upon the African American population. Points and organs were awarded to those patients with the best HLA antigen matches. This practice was clearly discriminatory to African Americans and favored North American Whites. This was articulated, and attempts to further define and overcome these HLA ethnic differences were attempted, by Milford et al. (1987) and others. Gaston et al. (1993) have articulated the illegality of these practices. These data were presented at the first and second International Samuel L. Kountz Symposia in 1985 and 1989, respectively, in an attempt to minimize or eliminate these discriminatory practices, but to no avail. In spite of efforts by Dr. Starzl and others (personal communication, July 2000), the national organ allocation system proceeded to award points for organ allocation schema based upon HLA antigen matching until 1995, when these practices were altered, and points were awarded only for HLA-B and DR matches. It is hoped that in the twenty-first century, this practice of awarding points for HLA-B matches will be eliminated altogether (Callender et al., 2002b).

Unique Posttransplantation Drug Responses in Blacks

Blacks after kidney transplantation are afflicted with diabetes when placed on tacrolimus (prograf) twice the rate of Caucasians. African American and Latino (Hispanic) populations have two times (twice) the rate of posttransplant diabetes mellitus (PTDM) after receiving prograf (tacrolimus) (Neylan et al., 1997; Neylan et al., 1998; Johnson et al., 2000). This complication is modified by reducing the dose of prograf but remains as a permanent problem requiring insulin therapy in African Americans. This is problematic because of the African American graft survival rates and the high incidence of acute rejection episodes in the African American kidney transplant population. When this regimen is combined with MMF (Mycophenalate Mofetil) (Cellcept), however, rejection episodes can be reduced from the previous rate in excess of 40 percent to less than 10 percent (Neylan et al., 1997; Neylan et al., 1998; Johnson et al., 2000). While the reasons for this ethnic association remain a mystery, more importantly, it is a microcosm of the uniquely different performance of African Americans when it comes to transplantation and kidney failure (Kjellstrand, 1988). The elucidation of this observation may help us unravel the other enigmas surrounding African American ethnicity and transplantation. African American pharmacokinetic differences in the P450 cytochrome oxidose system are well known and have an impact on the absorption of cyclosporine as well as prograf and the immunosuppressibility of the African American immune system (Nagashima et al., 2001).

RECOMMENDATIONS: THE NEW PARADIGMS NECESSARY TO ELIMINATE ETHNIC TRANSPLANT DISPARITIES

More than 30 years after completing my transplant fellowship at the University of Minnesota, the unique transplant disparity between African Americans and other ethnic groups remains as baffling today as it was in 1972. This disparity mandates interdisciplinary research of the highest magnitude and will ultimately be of benefit to all ethnic groups. The following recommendations for change are needed in order to help eliminate these ethnic health disparities in the field of transplantation.

1. An appropriation of at least an additional $200 million to the National Center on Minority Health and Health Disparities within the National Institutes of Health will promote the cross-fertilization of great scientific minds in an area that needs it desperately, in order to eliminate the disparities previously mentioned. This will allow national extramural programs to unify their research methodologies to address the elimination of each of the areas of Caucasian–African American health disparity.

The areas are:

a. The fate of the Black kidney after donation.

b. The poorer graft survival rate of the African American transplant recipient.

c. African American longer transplant waiting times.

d. African American delayed referral to kidney and transplantation specialists.

e. The incidence of ESRD in African Americans being two to four times that of Caucasians because of predilection to hypertension and diabetes.

f. Better African American survival rates on dialysis since this is the treatment of choice. Is this a good thing? No, it would be better to have more African American kidney transplants with better transplant graft survival rates.

g. Why the association of posttransplant diabetes mellitus (PTDM) after prograf (tacrolimus) therapy and why the poorer absorption from the gastrointestinal (GI) tract of cyclosporine, prograf (tacrolimus) and the relative intolerance of mycophenolate mofetil, all suggestive of significantly different ethnic pharmacokinetics.

h. Continue the study of African American noncompliance rates.

2. The elimination of the term "race" and its replacement by the term "ethnicity" in the science and health arena and by the federal government (the Office of Management and Budget [OMB] and the Census Bureau).

3. The development of a strategic plan with goals, objectives, and implementation dates utilizing a community-organized effort to eliminate institutionalized racism by grassroots efforts aimed to educate the majority community and empower minority communities.

4. The elimination of all inequitable allocation schema using HLA as the basis for organ allocation by UNOS—this will require eliminating the awarding of points for HLA-A and B locus matches in the allocation schema.

5. The identification of ways to totally eliminate the green screen as an obstacle to transplantation by the use of luxury taxes (e.g., alcohol, cigarette, or state or federal income tax assessments), or other national remedies including National Health Insurance. The United States is the richest country in the world and still does not have health care as a right for all Americans.

6. The involvement of the minority community in the prevention of these maladies by changing lifestyles cannot be overemphasized.

7. The development of an organized educated minority community effort to aggressively attack institutionalized racism.

8. The education of the majority community and their enlistment in the job of reducing and eliminating institutionalized racism must follow item #7.

CONCLUSION

We have identified that disparities exist between African Americans and other ethnic groups in transplantation. However, these disparities can be eliminated with a comprehensive strategic plan that makes the eradication of these disparities a priority. This disparity can be addressed with adequate funding of at least $200 million appropriated to the center that specifically addresses minority health issues—the National Center on Minority Health and Health Disparities within the National Institutes of Health. Only a national, comprehensive, coordinated, strategic plan will allow us to eliminate these transplantation disparities between Caucasians and African Americans.

Another way to eliminate disparities within the transplant field is to ensure that appropriate funding is provided for the continuation of national initiatives, such as the National Minority Organ Tissue Transplant Education Program (MOTTEP), which has as its mission to reduce the rate and number of ethnic minority Americans needing organ and tissue transplants. This is crucial due to the disproportionate rate of diabetes, hypertension, substance abuse, and other health issues within minority populations.

National MOTTEP utilizes a grassroots methodology and empowers the community to become active participants in the campaign to educate its local communities by implementing creative activities, such as MOTTEP-sponsored teams at sporting events, parades, school programs, and barbershop and beauty salon campaigns, to promote the program's mission. Community volunteers are recruited to be at the table during the planning and implementation stages of the program. Community involvement, education, and empowerment are key elements in spreading the message. As a result of National MOTTEP's efforts, the number of organ donors within the African American community has increased by 13 percent nationally. However, it is important to note that due to the number of individuals awaiting transplant, especially kidneys, there is a critical need for more minority donors.

Prevention and intervention strategies are key to solving the donor shortage in the field of transplantation. While simultaneously promoting the need for more minority donors, National MOTTEP's health promotion campaign provides screenings and information to the community such as:

- Learning how to read nutritional labels;
- Reducing daily fat intake;
- Cutting back on sugar;
- Eating more fruits and vegetables;
- Baking, broiling, or boiling meats; and
- Drinking more water on a daily basis.

Phase I of National MOTTEP was directed toward increasing organ/tissue donations, and Phase II, which began in 1995, addresses preventing the need for transplantation in the first place. Phase III will be directed toward aggressively attacking institutionalized racism through community education using the same coordination, collaboration, and implementation methods used in Phase I and Phase II. Community education and empowerment must be a major part of this national strategy in order to effect change and eliminate health disparities.

ACKNOWLEDGMENT

Tables and Figures provided by Yulin Cheng, BS and Wida Cherikh, PhD

REFERENCES

Alexander, G.C., & Seghal, A.R. (1998). Barriers to cadaveric renal transplantation among Blacks, women, and the poor. *Journal of the American Medical Association, 280*, 13, 1–5.

Alexander, G.C., & Seghal, A.R. (2001). Why hemodialysis patients fail to complete the transplantation process. *American Journal of Kidney Disease, 37*, 2, 321–328.

Ayanian, J.Z., et al. (1999). The effect of patients' preferences on racial differences in access to renal transplantation. *New England Journal of Medicine, 341*, 22, 1661–1669.

Callender, C.O. (1987, April). Organ donation in the Black population: Where do we go from here? *Transplantation Proceedings, 19*, 2, Suppl 2, 36–40.

Callender, C.O. (1989). The results of transplantation in Blacks are just the tip of the iceberg. *Transplantation Proceedings, 21*, 3, 3407–3410.

Callender, C.O. (1991, July 8–10). Organ and tissue donation in African Americans: A national stratagem. *Proceedings of the surgeon general's workshop on increasing organ donation. Background papers.* Washington, DC: U.S., Department of Health and Human Services, pp. 145–162.

Callender, C.O. (1994). ESRD and transplantation in minorities: A proposed national transplant strategy based on community education and empowerment. *Contemporary Dialysis & Nephrology, 15*, 8, 23–25.

Callender, C.O. (1995). Kidney transplant allocation in America: An African American transplant surgeon's perspective. *Current Opinions in Clinical Transplant, 11*, 356–357.

Callender, C.O. (1996). Liver allocation and organ donation in 1996: One Black transplant surgeon's perspective. Presented to Secretary Shalala: Forum on liver allocation and organ donation. (Testimony).

Callender, C.O. (1997). Summation. *Transplantation Proceedings, 29*, 3779 3780.

Callender, C.O. (1998, June 18). Putting patients first: Resolving allocation of transplant organs. Support for HHS regulations with OPTN partnership and minority inclusion. Presented to Joint Hearing of the House Commerce Committee Subcomittee on Health and Environment and the Senate Labor and Human Resources Committee. *Testimony.*

Callender, C.O. (1999). Ethnicity and matching for organ and tissue donation and transplantation. *Minority Health Today*, November-December, 1: 6–9.

Callender, C.O., Bayton, J.A., Yeager, C.L., & Clark, J.E. (1982). Attitudes among blacks toward donating kidneys for transplantation: A pilot project. *Journal of the National Medical Association, 74*, 8, 6–8.

Callender, C.O., Bey, A.S., Miles, P.V., & Yeager, C.L. (1995). A national minority organ/tissue transplant education program: The first step in the evolution of a national minority strategy and minority transplant equity in the USA. *Transplantation Proceedings, 27*, 1, 1441–1443.

Callender, C.O., Hall, M.B., & Branch, D. (2001, July). An assessment of the effectiveness of the MOTTEP model for increasing donation rates and preventing the need for transplantation—adult findings: Program years 1998 and 1999. *Seminars in Nephrology*, 419–428.

Callender, C.O., Hall, L.E., Yeager, C.L., & Barber, J.B., Jr. (1991). Organ donation and Blacks: A critical frontier. *New England Journal of Medicine, 325*, 6, 442–444.

Callender, C.O., & Miles, P.V. (1998). The organ donor shortage: We are the solution—A Black transplant surgeon's perspective. Retrieved January 3, 1998, from http:\\www.blackhealthnet.com.

Callender, C., Miles, P., Hall, M., & Gordon, S. (2002a). Blacks and Whites and kidney transplantation: A disparity! But why and why won't it go away? *Transplantation Reviews, 16*, 3, 163–176.

Callender, C., Miles, P., & Hall, M. (2002b). National MOTTEP: Educating to prevent the need for transplantation. *Ethnicity and Disease, 12*, 1, S1-34 - S1-37.

Callender, C.O., Miles, P.V., & Yeager, C.L. (1998). Organ transplantation in cardiovascular and related disease: Educating yourself and your patients. *Urban Cardiology, the ABC Digest, 5*, 1, 8–17.

Cosio, F.G., et al. (1995). Racial differences in renal allograft survival: The role of systemic hypertension. *Kidney International, 47*: 1136–1141.

Cosio, F.G., et al. (1997). Relationships between arterial hypertension and renal allograft survival in African American patients. *American Journal of Kidney Disease, 29*: 419–427.

DeLone P., et al. (1989). Noncompliance in renal transplant recipients: Methods for recognition and intervention. *Transplantation Proceedings, 21*, 6, 3892–3984.

Dunn, J., et al. (1989). Impact of race on the outcome of renal transplantation under cyclosporine-prednisone. *Transplantation Proceedings, 21*, 6, 3946–3948.

Epstein, A.M., et al. (2000). Racial disparities in access to renal transplantation: Clinically appropriate or due to under use or overuse? *New England Journal of Medicine, 343*, 21, 1537–1544.

Freeman, H.P. (1998a). The meaning of race in science—considerations for cancer research. Communication President's Cancer Panel Meeting, April 9, 1997. *American Cancer Society*, G1-G7.

Freeman, H.P. (1998b). The meaning of race in science-considerations for cancer research. *Cancer, 82*: 219–225.

Friedman, E.A. (1987). Race and diabetic nephropathy. *Transplantation Proceedings, 19*, 2, Suppl 2, 77–81.

Gaston, R.S. (1993, September 13). System for allocating donor kidneys works against Blacks: Emphasis on antigen match puts efficiency ahead of equity. *American Medical Association* (News Release), 2–3.

Gaston, R.S., et al. (1993). Racial equity in renal transplantation: The disparate impact of HLA-based allocation. *Journal of the American Medical Association, 270*, 1352–1355.

Greenstein, S.M., Schechner, R., Senitzer, D., Louis, P., & Veith, F.J. (1989). Does kidney distribution based upon HLA matching discriminate against Blacks? *Transplantation Proceedings, 21*, 6, 3874–3875.

Greenstein, S., & Siegal, B. (1998). Compliance and noncompliance in patients with a functioning renal transplant: A multicenter study. *Transplantation, 66*, 1718–1726.

Hall, L., et al. (1991). Organ donation and Blacks: The next frontier. *Transplantation Proceedings, 23*, 5, 2500–2504.

Hurley, C.K. (1989). HLA: A legacy of human evolution. *Transplantation Proceedings, 21*, 6, 3876–3877.

Jackson, F.L.C. (1989). HLA diversity within the context of general human heterogeneity: Anthropological perspectives. *Transplantation Proceedings, 21(6)*, 3869–3871.

Johnson, A.H. (1989). The Black population in the United States. *Transplantation Proceedings, 21*, 6, 3880.

Johnson, C., et al. (2000). Randomized trial of tacrolimus (prograf) in combination with azathioprine or mycophenolate mofetil versus cyclosporine (Neoral) with mycophenolate mofetil after cadaveric kidney transplantation. *Transplantation, 69*, 1–8.

Kasiske, B.L., et al. (1991). The effect of race on access and outcome in transplantation. *New England Journal of Medicine, 324*, 6, 302–307.

Kasiske, B.L., et al. (1998). Race and socioeconomic factors influencing early placement on the kidney transplant waiting list. *Journal of American Society of Nephrology, 9*, 2142–2147.

Kerman, R.H., et al. (1991). Possible contribution of pretransplant immune responder status to renal allograft survival differences of Black versus White recipients. *Transplantation, 51*: 338–342.

Kjellstrand, C.M. (1988). Age, sex, and race inequality in renal transplantation. *Archives of Internal Medicine, 148*, 6, 1305–1309.

Koyama, H., Cecka, J.M., & Terasaki, P.I. (1994). Kidney transplants in Black recipients: HLA matching and other factors affecting long-term graft survival. *Transplantation, 57*, 7, 1064–1068.

Milford, E.L., Ratner, L., & Yunis, E. (1987). Will transplant immunogenetics lead to better graft survival in Blacks? Racial variability in the accuracy of tissue typing for organ donation: The fourth American workshop. *Transplantation Proceedings, 19*, 2, Suppl 2, 36–40.

Nagashima, N., Watanabe, T., Nakamura, M., Shalabi, A., & Burdick, J. (2001). Decreased effect of immunosuppression on immunocompetence in African Americans after kidney and liver transplantation. *Clinical Transplantation, 15*, 111–115.

Neylan, J.F., et al. (1997). Immunosuppressive therapy in high-risk transplant patients: Dose-dependent efficacy of mycohenolate mofetil in African-American renal allograft recipients. *Transplantation, 1997*, 64, 1277–1282.

Neylan, J.F., et al. (1998). Racial differences in renal transplantation after immunosuppression with tacrolimus versus cyclosporin. *Transplantation, 65*, 515–523.

Odocha, O. (2000). Race and racialism in scientific research. *Journal of the National Medical Association, 92*, 96–98.

Ojo, A.O., et al. (2001). Survival in recipients of marginal cadaveric donor kidneys compared with other recipients and wait-listed transplant candidates. *Journal of American Society of Nephrology, 12*, 289–297.

Opelz, G., Mickey, M.R., & Terasaki, P.I. (1977). Influence of race on kidney transplant survival. *Transplantation Proceedings, 9*, 1, 137–142.

Opelz, G., Pfarr, E., Engelmann, A., & Keppel, E. (1989). The collaborative transplant study—kidney graft survival rates in Black cyclosporine-treated recipients. *Transplantation Proceedings, 21*, 6, 3918–3920.

Rodey, G., Parker, M., Neylan, J., Lowance, D., O'Brien, D., & Whelchel, J. (1989). Antibodies to public class 1 epitopes in the American Black population. *Transplantation Proceedings, 21*, 6, 3878–3879.

Rovelli, M., et al. (1989). Noncompliance in renal transplant recipients: Evaluation by socioeconomic groups. *Transplantation Proceedings, 21*, 6, 3979–3981.

Santana, S. (2002). Minorities and organ transplants: Long waits and low referral rates. *Association of American Medical Colleges Reporter, 11*, 8, 8–9.

Schulman, K.A., et al. (1999). The effect of race and sex on physicians' recommendations for cardiac catheterization. *New England Journal of Medicine, 340*, 618–626.

Schweizer, R.T., et al. (1990). Noncompliance in organ transplant recipients. *Transplantation, 49*, 374–377.

Scott Collins, K., et al. (2002). Diverse communities, common concerns: Assessing health care quality for minority Americans. Findings from the commonwealth fund 2001 health care quality survey. Retreived March 30, 2002, http://www.cmf.org.

Smedley, B.D., Stith, A.Y., & Nelson, A.R. (2002). *Unequal treatment: Confronting racial and ethnic disparities in health care*. Institute of Medicine, National Academy Press, Washington, DC.

Sumrani, N.B., Hong, J.H., Hanson, P., & Butt, K.M.H. (1989). Renal transplantation in Blacks: Impact of immunosuppressive regimens. *Transplantation Proceedings, 21(6)*, 3943–3945.

United Network for Organ Sharing. (2002). The Organ Procurement and Transplantation Network. Richmond, VA. Retrieved October 31, 2002.

Williams, D.R. (1999). Race, socioeconomic status, and health: The added effects of racism and discrimination. *Annals of the New York Academy of Sciences, 896*, 173–188.

Wolfe, R.A., et al. (2000). Differences in access to cadaveric renal transplantation in the United States. *American Journal of Kidney Disease, 36*, 5, 1025–1033.

Young C.J., & Gaston, R.S. (2000). Renal transplantation in Black Americans. *New England Journal of Medicine, 343*, 21, 1545–1552.

Zachary, A.A. (1993). Is there racial bias in transplantation? *Journal of the National Medical Association, 85*, 11, 821–824.

CHAPTER 45

Transforming Structural Barriers to Improve the Health of African Americans

COLLINS O. AIRHIHENBUWA, J. DEWITT WEBSTER, AND TITILAYO OLADOSU

INTRODUCTION

Eliminating health disparities between African Americans and other U.S. minorities and the White U.S. population is a key goal of Healthy People 2010. It is well documented that African Americans have poorer health and excess premature deaths compared to White Americans. It is also known that most of these deaths are preventable (USDHHS, 2000). The main argument presented in this chapter is that bridging the disparity gap requires elimination of institutional barriers that consign the health of African Americans to a lower status when compared to Whites. The emphasis on institutional and structural barriers also means that notions of empowerment that focus on the individual's control of his or her environment will be examined for their limitations in developing context-based interventions.

Health promotion interventions tend to focus on individual empowerment, largely because empowerment tends to focus on individual control (or lack of control). However, a shift in public health and health promotion to focus on institutional and structural impediments to positive health behavior has been more recent. Even though the actual call for such a shift is not new, the actualization of the shift is more recent and still in progress. Increasingly, a multidisciplinary coalition of health educators, sociologists, health economists, psychologists, and professionals from other disciplines is addressing the complex forces that marginalize the health of African Americans. Moreover, evidence of the role of institutional racism and structural discrimination as causes for the lower health status of African Americans has gained increasing centrality in public health objectives.

According to a congressionally mandated report from the National Academy of Sciences Institute of Medicine, "minorities tend to receive a lower quality of healthcare than non-minorities, when access-related factors, such as patient's insurance status and income are controlled" (Smedley et al., 2002, p. 1). In addition, "minorities may experience other barriers to healthcare, even when insured at the same level as Whites, including barriers of language, geography, and cultural familiarity. Further, financial and institutional arrangements of health systems, as well as the legal, regulatory, and policy environment in which they operate, may have disparate and negative effects on minorities' ability to attain quality care" (p. 1). The report further highlights existing disparities between U.S. racial/ethnic minorities and Whites, indicating that African Americans and other minorities are less likely to be given appropriate care and medication for life-threatening conditions associated with cardiac diseases, cancer, and HIV/AIDS, to name three. The report's findings conclude that the marginal health status of African Americans and other minorities is due to several factors, including (a) bias, prejudice, and stereotyping on the part of health-care providers; (b) uncertainty about a patient's condition, which can lead to diagnosis based on the person's identity and status (i.e., age, gender, socioeconomic status, race, ethnicity); (c) variations in health plans, with poorer health insurance coverage for minorities and insurance company caps on coverage for treatment; (d) a shortage and/or absence of physicians (particularly minority physicians) in minority communities, and (e) a mistrust of health-care providers due to experiences with discrimination in hospitals in particular and society in general (Smedley et al., 2002).

In this chapter we address contextual issues and strategies to help eliminate these structurally and institutionally related health disparities associated with African Americans. Specifically we (a) describe structural and institutional forces that create and maintain the disparities between the health status of African Americans and that of Whites, (b) discuss the context of the issues and strategies for health disparities using the five contextual domains of the UNAIDS/Penn State Communications Framework for HIV/AIDS (UNAIDS, 1999), and (c) recommend a contextual approach to public health and health education/promotion interventions to eliminate the institutional and structural barriers to improving the health of African Americans.

DISPARITIES IN HEALTH STATUS BETWEEN AFRICAN AMERICANS AND WHITES

Approximately 12 percent of the U.S. population (33.9 million people) is African American. The African American population is increasing in diversity with immigrants from many African and Caribbean countries. Over half of the nation's African American population (53 percent) lives in the South; 37 percent reside in the Northeast and Midwest combined; 10 percent live in the West. In 1997, nearly one fourth of all African Americans earned more than $50,000 a year. Yet, as a whole, when compared to other racial and ethnic groups living in the United States, African Americans continue to be relatively poor. For example, in 1999, about 22 percent of African American families lived in poverty, compared to 13 percent for the United States as a whole and 8 percent for non-Hispanic White Americans (USDHHS, 2001).

Disparities in the health status of the African American and White populations persist. African Americans of both sexes and in all age groups are more likely than Whites to be ill or to die prematurely. Although there was an increase in life expectancy for African Americans (males and females) from 69.1 years in 1990 to 71.8 years in 2000, life expectancy is still 5.6 years less than for Whites (77.4 years) and 5.1 years less than the overall life expectancy for all races (76.9 years) (CDC, 2002). The age-specific excess deaths for Blacks compared with Whites in 1991 (over ten years ago) ranged from 64 percent for persons aged 15–25 to 11 percent for persons 65 years and older (Fingerhut & Makuc, 1992). Today, more than 80 percent of excess deaths continue to be attributed to minorities and the poor, and these deaths are associated with diseases with "preventable or controllable factors" (O'Malley et al., 1999).

Infant mortality in 1999 among African Americans was 2.5 times higher than that of Whites, up from 2.4 in 1998. This increase follows a widening trend that has continued over the last two decades (CDC, 2002). For example, in 1989, the infant mortality rate for Whites was 8.2 per thousand live births compared to 17.7 for Blacks (Health Trends, 1992). The gap is even wider (8.1 for Whites and 18.6 for Blacks) when the mother's race is used to classify infant mortality rate. The percent of low-birth-weight babies among Black mothers is almost three times that of Whites. The 1989 rate of 13.3 percent (compared to 5.7 percent for Whites) has been increasing annually from the 12.7 percent in 1980 (USDHHS, 1991). While the recent report from the Centers for Disease Control and

Prevention (2002) shows a national decrease in the infant mortality rate of 3 percent from 1998 to 1999, African American mothers still have the highest infant mortality rate (14.1 compared to 5.8 for White mothers). Furthermore, between 1995 and 1999, the percent change in infant mortality rate was 7.9 percent for White mothers compared to 4.1 percent for Black mothers, and there is only a slight decrease in the percent of low-birth-weight babies among Black mothers between 1989 and 1999 (13.3 percent compared to 13.2 percent) (CDC, 2002). Effective use of preventive services can significantly improve the health status of women and children.

In addition to the higher infant death rates among African Americans, as compared to Whites, the death rates from other conditions are also higher. For example, death rates from heart disease are 40 percent higher for African Americans than for Whites. Additionally, cancer deaths are 30 percent higher for African Americans, with prostate cancer deaths for African American men double the rate of White men. Similarly, although African Americans have mammograms at nearly the same rate as White women, they still have higher breast cancer death rates. Finally, African Americans are seven times more likely to die from HIV/AIDS and six times more likely to be victims of homicide than Whites (USDHHS, 2000). Although overall suicide rates for non-Hispanic Whites are almost twice those of African Americans, suicide rates for young Black men are equivalent to those of young White men. In addition, the suicide rate for 10- to 14-year-old African Americans increased at nearly twice the rate for non-Hispanic Whites in the same age group (233 percent vs. 120 percent) (USDHHS, 2001).

The mental health problems of persons in high-need populations are especially likely to occur jointly with substance abuse problems, as well as with HIV infection or AIDS (Amaro et al., 2001). Detection, treatment, and rehabilitation become particularly challenging in the presence of multiple and significant impediments to well-being. African Americans are more likely to be incorrectly diagnosed than White Americans. They are more likely to be diagnosed as suffering from schizophrenia and less likely to be diagnosed as suffering from an affective disorder. The pattern is long-standing but cannot yet be fully explained.

THE CONTEXT OF HEALTH DISPARITIES

One of the two primary goals of Healthy People 2010 is to eliminate health disparities in the United States, including differences that occur by gender, race or ethnicity, education or income, disability, geographic location, or sexual orientation. To address the elimination of health disparities, we discuss the contexts of the marginal health status of African Americans within the domains of policy, socioeconomic status, culture, gender, and spirituality. These are the five domains of the UNAIDS/Penn State communications framework for HIV/AIDS published in 1999.

Domain I: Government and Policy

The focus here is the role of policy and law in supporting or hindering health interventions to improve health. Historically, the reductions in federal financing programs slowed the decentralization of health-care resources through block grants and attenuated the increasing accessibility of minorities and the disadvantaged to health-care services. For example, the Health Education-Risk Reduction (HERR) Grants Program was cut by 25 percent as a consequence of the 1980s block grant policy (Kreuter, 1992). More recently, it was shown that the federal dollars expended for HIV/AIDS prevention and treatment among African Americans was proportionally less than the amount for Whites. This disparity was particularly disturbing given that African Americans have a disproportionately higher prevalence of HIV/AIDS (Friday et al., 2001).

One government policy designed to address health disparities is the Racial and Ethnic Approaches to Community Health (REACH 2010). REACH is a CDC initiative that resulted from President Bill Clinton's Initiative on Race. It was inaugurated in June 1997 with the goal to eliminate racial and ethnic disparities in health among U.S. minority populations, which parallels one of the Healthy People 2010 goals. REACH 2010 addresses six priority areas: infant mortality; breast and cervical cancer screening and management; cardiovascular disease; diabetes; HIV/AIDS; and child and adult immunizations. REACH 2010 is a two-phased demonstration project supporting 36 community coalitions to design, implement, and evaluate a five-year, community-driven intervention to eliminate health disparities (CDC, 2001).

Generally, the projects are specific to particular minority populations. For example, Nashville REACH 2010 Coalition conducted focus groups of African American women to understand why the death rates for CVD and diabetes were 78 percent–134 percent higher among Nashville's African American women than among the majority population in Nashville (CDC, 2001). "Reach Out," a Chicago initiative, draws on church leadership in African American and Hispanic communities. Using church members, focus groups of low-income women were conducted during the planning phase of "Reach Out" to determine breast and cervical cancer screening behaviors. The results prompted initiation of three pilot educational forums in churches to mobilize women to be screened for breast and cervical cancer (CDC, 2001).

A second government policy established to eliminate health disparities is the creation of geographic residences known as the empowerment zones (EZ) and enterprise communities (EC). Over the last few decades, inner cities have experienced many severe problems such as concentrated poverty, increasing crime, an exodus of jobs, declining schools, middle-class flight, and a deteriorating tax base. At the same time, many rural areas experienced a decline in the agricultural base to their economies, decreasing populations, and increasing poverty rates. Through the EZ/EC initiative, an urban or rural economically distressed area develops a comprehensive strategy to promote economic opportunity and community revitalization. The Community Empowerment Program was enacted into law by the U.S. Congress in August 1993 and initiated through competitive grants in January 1994. A high rate of poverty was an eligibility requirement for communities to apply. EZs were created in 1994 to focus federal resources on some of the nation's most destitute areas. The ten-year program provides communities and local governments with federal resources to implement new development plans.

The program is framed under four key principles: (a) economic opportunity—jobs, entrepreneurial initiatives, small business expansions, job training, and so on; (b) Sustainable community development—safe streets, accessible human services, vital civic spirit, and lifelong learning; (c) community-based partnerships—between residents, political and government leadership, community groups, health and social service groups, religious organizations, the private and nonprofit sector, centers of learning and other community institutions; and (d) strategic vision for change—strategic map for revitalization that builds on community assets and coordinates responses to community needs (USHUD, 2002).

These two government-initiated efforts are cited as examples to underscore the increasing recognition that marginal health status is more a function of complex social and political factors rather than individual decision making alone. While a comprehensive evaluation of these programs will be useful in understanding effective contextual strategies to eliminate disparities, the relative socioeconomic disadvantage of minorities remains an undeniable factor contributing to low health status.

Domain II: Socioeconomic Status

The focus here is the collective or individual assets and liabilities that may promote or prevent positive health behavior. Inequalities in income (i.e., SES) and education are clearly linked to U.S.

Figure 45.1
Relationship between education and median household income among adults aged 25 years and older, by gender, United States, 1996

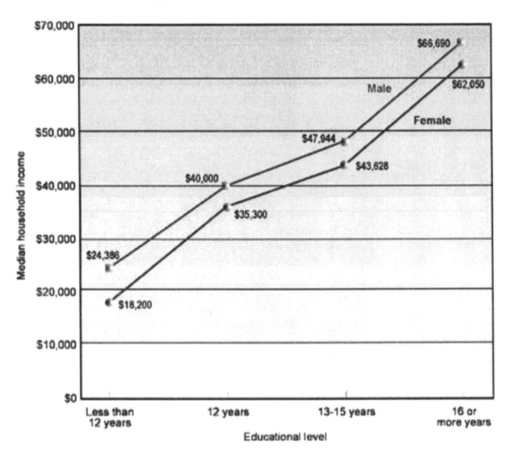

Relationship Between Education and Income

Source: U.S. Department of Commerce (1997).

health disparities. According to the U.S. Department of Health and Human Services (2000), "income and education are intrinsically related and often serve as proxy measures for each other" (p. 13) (see Figure 45.1). Generally, population groups with the highest poverty rates and least amount of education experience the most negative health outcomes. Specific disparities in morbidity and mortality rates are associated with heart disease, diabetes, obesity, elevated blood lead level, and low birth weight. In contrast, "higher incomes permit increased access to medical care, enabling people to afford better housing in safer neighborhoods, and provide opportunities to engage in health-promoting behaviors" (USDHHS, 2000).

Income inequality between Blacks and Whites in the United States "stalled in the mid-1970s and widened in the early 1980s" (Williams, 2002, p. 593) and then decreased slightly in the 1990s (Couch & Daly, 2002). Still, distinct demographic differences continue to exist by race, ethnicity, household composition, and geographic locations in relation to poverty (see Figure 45.2). For example, nearly

Figure 45.2
Percentage of persons below the poverty level by race and ethnicity and type of household, United States, 1996

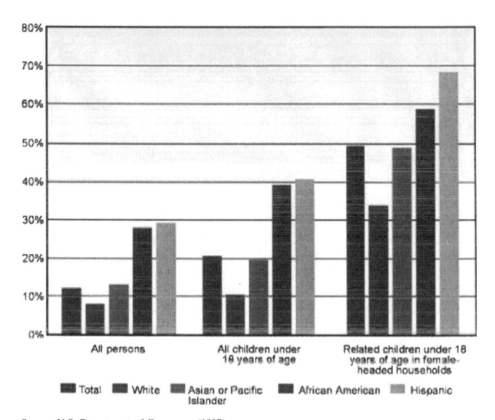

Source: U.S. Department of Commerce (1997).

40 percent of Black children and 40 percent of Hispanic children under age 18 live below the poverty level compared to 10 percent of White children. In addition, more striking is children below age 18 living in female-headed households, where nearly 70 percent of Hispanic children and nearly 60 percent of Black children live in poverty. Nearly 33 percent of White children below age 18 live in female-headed households (USDHHS, 2000).

Life expectancy is also linked inextricably to income level. For example, 65-year-old White men from high-income families outlive low-income men by 3 years. Similarly, limited activity due to chronic disease affects individuals from the lowest-income families three times more than individuals in the highest-income bracket (USDHHS, 2000).

Over the past several decades the average education level in the United States has steadily increased. As with income level, education level translates into more years of life. Moreover, a child's welfare and survival are linked directly to his or her mother's level of education attainment. For example, higher levels of education may (1) increase the likelihood of obtaining or understanding health-related information needed to develop health-promoting behaviors and beliefs in prevention

Figure 45.3
**Percentage of adults aged 25 to 64 years by educational level and race and
ethnicity, United States, 1996**

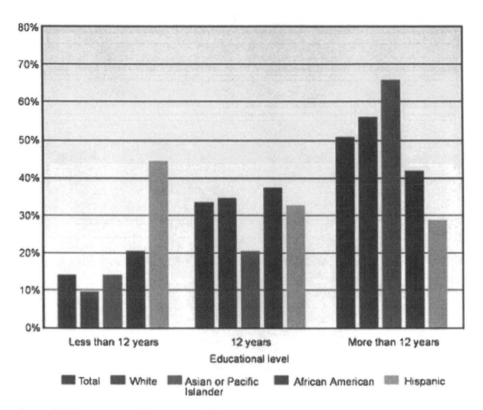

Educational Attainment

Source: U.S. Department of Commerce (1997).

and (2) delay the onset of beginning a family, thus ensuring a higher state of readiness for the mother
to support her children.

Among people aged 25 to 64 years in the United States, the overall death rate for those with less
than 12 years of education is more than twice that for people with 13 or more years of education.
Furthermore, the infant mortality rate is almost double for infants of mothers with less than 12 years
of education as compared with those with an educational level of 13 or more years. But again,
educational attainment differs by race and ethnicity (see Figure 45.3). For example, in 1996 less
than 10 percent of Whites between 25 and 64 years had less than 12 years of schooling, compared
with more than 20 percent of Blacks and 44 percent of Hispanics. Furthermore, during the same
year, only 41 percent of Blacks and even fewer Hispanics (28 percent) had obtained more than 12
years of education. These figures are in contrast to Whites (55 percent) and Asians (65 percent) (US
DHHS, 2000). Surprisingly, children of Black women with 13 or more years of school still have a
higher infant mortality rate than White women (Williams, 2002), suggesting that education alone is
not the sole contributor to health disparities in the United States.

Poor health is the result of low socioeconomic status rather than a population's racial or ethnic identity. Though low economic status is linked with poor health status, evidence abounds that other factors, such as structural discrimination and institutional racism (Williams & Collins, 1995), total assets, housing, prior socioeconomic status, and social mobility (Kumanyika & Golden, 1991; King & Williams, 1995; Williams & Collins, 1995) disproportionately affect African Americans in low-income groups. These factors ultimately contribute to poor health status. Therefore, focusing only on individual income fails to address the social context and environment in which a disproportionate number of African Americans find themselves (Auslander et al., 1992; House & Williams, 2000) or the differential experiences between Blacks and Whites. Additionally, reports abound comparing a White and a Black middle-class person of the same income, occupation, and education and finding that they have separate experiences where the Black faces discrimination in housing and in interactions with employees in service professions.

Eliminating socioeconomic disparities would not necessarily address cultural differences. Differences in culture such as diet and exercise may be positive or negative but must be seriously examined within a group's context.

Domain III: Culture

As articulated in the PEN-3 model, positive, existential, or negative characteristics promote or hinder prevention and care practices. Culture is central to planning, implementing, and evaluating health promotion intervention among African Americans. For more information on the PEN-3 model, see Airhihenbuwa (1995).

There are current debates as to whether race should be discontinued as an identifier for different groups (Oppenheimer, 2001). This debate results from the realization that race is a social construction. Current information about the biologic and genetic characteristics of African Americans, Hispanics, American Indians, Alaska Natives, Asians, Native Hawaiians, and Pacific Islanders does not explain the health disparities experienced by these groups compared with the White, non-Hispanic population in the United States. These disparities are believed to be the result of the complex interaction among environmental factors and cultural differences in addition to genetic variation. Although race is a social construction, its appropriation in definition of power and consignment of minorities to lower status suggests that we should continue to use it to define the context of disparity.

Using race to define disparities, however, does not suggest that race is useful in defining solutions to the problems created by disparity. Culture and ethnicity allow us to develop effective strategies for eliminating disparities. Thus, understanding the contexts of race, ethnicity, and culture is important, for different purposes for eliminating disparity. Stated differently, race remains a useful identifier for defining the problem, but the solution lies more in employing culturally based understanding and intervention. For example, racism may help to explain the inability of African Americans to purchase wholesome food at reasonable prices. Culture helps to construct the contexts of how food can be transformed into positive consumption patterns for improved health.

African Americans have made great strides in education, income, and other indicators of social well-being. Their improvement in social standing is marked, attesting to the resilience and adaptive traditions of African American communities in the face of slavery, racism, and discrimination. Thus, resiliency has become a positive aspect of the African Americans' ability to survive and thrive under oppressive conditions. Contributions have come from diverse African American communities, including immigrants from Africa, the Caribbean, and elsewhere. Nevertheless, significant problems remain.

Adaptive traditions have sustained African Americans through long periods of hardship imposed by the larger society. Their resilience is an important resource from which much can be learned. African American communities must be engaged, their culture supported and built upon, and their trust gained in attempts to prevent disease and provide health. Mutual benefit will accrue to African Americans and to the society at large from a concerted effort to address the mental health needs of African Americans. Whether for mental, social, or physical health, differences exist between males and females.

As the majority of Black clients receive care from White professionals, cultural differences are often encountered. Many Blacks are suspicious of White health-care institutions because of past abuse of Blacks for medical experimentation and demonstration (Savitt, 1982; Jones, 1982; Pernick, 1985).

Racism has separated Blacks and Whites to the extent that White health-care professionals are unaware of the Black experience (i.e., suffering, discrimination) and the effect it has on Black people. This ignorance may prevent White professionals from fully or better understanding both the cultural appropriateness of their clients' behaviors and the adaptive qualities of such behaviors. White professionals may, therefore, discount the value of, or incorrectly label the behavior of, a Black client as abnormal. Conversely, ignorance of the Black lifestyle may also contribute to the health-care workers' tendency to attribute certain behaviors to racial differences when such behavior should be ascribed to personal malfunctioning and/or psychopathology.

Domain IV: Gender Relations

The focus here is the status of women in relation to men in society and community and the influence on sexual negotiation. Whereas some differences in health between men and women are the result of biological differences, others are more complicated and require greater attention and scientific exploration. Some health differences are obviously gender-specific, such as cervical cancer in women and prostate cancer in men.

Overall, men have a life expectancy that is six years less than that of women and have higher death rates for each of the ten leading causes of death. For example, men are two times more likely than women to die from unintentional injuries and four times more likely than women to die from firearm-related injuries. Although overall death rates for women currently may be lower than for men, women have shown increased death rates over the past decade in areas where men have experienced improvements (e.g., lung cancer). Women also are at greater risk for Alzheimer's disease than men and are twice as likely as men to be affected by major depression.

In addressing the social embeddedness of health among African American women, Williams (2002) presented the following findings:

1. White women's life expectancy is 5.2 years more than Black women's.

2. The female Black–White mortality ratio declined from 1.7 in 1950 to 1.5 in 1998.

3. White females are more likely to survive cancer than Black females.

4. African American males and females are more likely to die of diabetes than their White counterparts.

5. African American women have close to twice the rates of hypertension as White women.

The issue of gender for African American women has the added burden of racism. Thus, it is not possible to address issues of women's health without addressing racism. To focus on gender without addressing race suggests that African American women should "choose between racial issues and women's issues and therefore polarizes the debate" (Kumanyika et al., 2001, p. 9). An example of such polarization offered by the authors is the case of lupus erythematiosus, which disproportionately affects African American women, and osteoporosis, which disproportionately affects White women. The priority of research attention on the latter over the former is the politics of race.

Given all the negative health indicators confirming lower health status of African Americans, one institutional strategy that continues to be effective in promoting and improving the health of African Americans has been religion and spirituality.

Domain V: Spirituality

This involves the role of spiritual/religious values in promoting or hindering the translation of prevention messages into positive health actions. The important role of spirituality has been documented for health overall and for mental health in particular. The faith communities have, and will continue to share, a vast area of common interest, objective, and vision relative to improving overall health of the public (Evans, 1995). Spiritual establishments have been involved in health and well-being for decades, providing structures and mechanisms for promoting and nurturing positive health outcomes. In fact, researchers reviewing over two hundred empirical studies dating back to the nineteenth century found positive relations between spirituality and positive health outcomes (Larson et al., 1992; Bergin, 1983). For African Americans, spirituality is considered to be one of the most resilient cultural factors, contributing to a positive relationship between spirituality and positive psychological adjustment (Armstrong, 1996) and desirable health outcomes.

In light of the spirituality/health outcome linkage, there is increasing evidence of the involvement of church ministers in implementing effective church-based programs. A recent study looking at this link addresses the minister's role. Through semistructured interviews, a survey assessed the pastor-level factors that affect the successful recruitment and implementation of community-based health programs in Black churches. It was found that the commitment to holism (the spiritual, mental, emotional, physical, social person) and community serves as both enhancers of, and barriers to, some pastors' participation in health programs. While several pastors of Black churches recognized that health was important precisely because a lack of it could affect their spiritual goals, the overwhelming amount of commitment and responsibilities that their jobs entailed are possible barriers to their participation. "Although Black pastors appreciate being included in and benefiting from health research, minorities' history of being underserved and exploited can lead to suspiciousness and reluctance to participate" (Markens et al., 2002, p. 805). Therefore, it is suggested that "those interested in developing church-based health programs in Black communities must be attuned to how the same factors (commitment to holism and community) can both facilitate and hinder a program's development" (p. 805).

The framework presented above offers an opportunity to plan, implement, and evaluate health promotion programs in the community.

HEALTH CARE AND THE NEED FOR PROFESSIONALS

Structural discrimination and institutional racism are also synergistically responsible, in large part, for the persistent disparity of services available and accessible to Blacks, as opposed to Whites. This has been demonstrated in the way the policies and practices of the White medical community negatively impact the health of Blacks (Charatz-Litt, 1992), as well as the history of racism as an established characteristic of the health-care delivery system (Muller, 1985). These discriminatory practices are often exacerbated by limited resources (time and money), which further limit access to health care.

Accessibility, availability, acceptability, and affordability remain important criteria by which quality of health care is measured. In the discussion that follows, each criterion is discussed within the African American experience.

Accessibility

The underrepresentation of Black professionals in the health-care delivery system has complicated the problem of accessibility. Although Blacks constitute 12.3 percent (12.9 percent report Black alone or in combination with one or more other races) of the U.S. population and 13.6 percent of the population aged 20–29 (U.S. Census Bureau, 2002), they received only 7 percent of the medical degrees in 2001 (Barzansky & Etzel, 2001). Of the total number of graduates from schools of public health in 1999/2000 academic year, 9.8 percent were African American (Helsing, 2002). This figure increased from 2.5 in 1981/1982, which is a significant improvement, even though it still falls short of the population representation of African Americans. African Americans account for only 2 percent of psychiatrists, 2 percent of psychologists, and 4 percent of social workers in the United States. Moreover, African Americans may use alternative therapies more often than do Whites. Given these tremendous concerns, it is evident that health promotion interventions should focus on root causes of illnesses rather than solely on individual behavior change.

Availability

Even when services are available, they may not be as accessible to Blacks as to Whites, as the Black family is often faced with different barriers that complicate accessibility to health services. Some of these barriers include physicians' refusal to attend to patients who are indigent (Davidson, 1982) and patients who are Black (Charatz-Litt, 1992). The Institute of Medicine report also listed bias, prejudice, and stereotyping on the part of health-care providers (possibly unconscious) and negative racial attitudes and stereotypes that might be increased due to time pressure involved in seeing patients. Other findings include uncertainty about a patient's condition because symptoms are not clear-cut. This might lead to the provider relying on previous training that places greater expectations on the patient's condition based on age, gender, SES, race, and ethnicity. Finally, real or perceived discrimination in hospitals and society in general has led many minorities to mistrust health-care providers (Smedley et al., 2002).

In addition to racial discrimination, other barriers include limited accessibility to medical facilities, long waiting time at the office, inconvenient office hours, and absence of privacy within public and private clinics and emergency rooms (Davidson, 1982). For example, Forrest and Starfield (1998) point out that long travel time to clinics, long office waits, and no after-hour services reduce chances of initial contact with a primary care physician for acute health problems. They further report that these issues decrease the likelihood of a patient returning for scheduled follow-up appointments. When Blacks expressed a preference in their health-care providers, it was a desire to be attended to by Black health-care providers (Protor & Rosen, 1981) and comfort in the knowledge of Black counselors' presence on the counseling staff (Miles & McDavis, 1982).

Acceptability

Even if health-care recipients are not treated by Black personnel, the knowledge of the presence of Black staff in a particular health-care facility helps to alleviate some of the apprehension that Black clients may have about the service they will receive (Airhihenbuwa, 1989). Seemingly, the presence of Black faculty in health education and other public health academic departments should directly or indirectly enhance the recruitment and, more importantly, the retention of Blacks in these programs (Airhihenbuwa et al., 1989).

A recent U.S. Department of Health and Human Services-initiated study indicated that minorities are less likely than Whites to be given appropriate cardiac medications or to undergo bypass surgery.

They are also less likely than Whites to be placed on kidney dialysis or to receive kidney transplants. Disparities also exist in cancer diagnostic tests and treatment as well as HIV medications, which can delay progression to AIDS. Conversely, research suggests that minorities are more likely than Whites to receive more drastic, less desirable procedures such as lower limb amputations associated with diabetes (Smedley et al., 2002). An increase in the number of Black health professionals could definitely improve accessibility and, subsequently, the quality of health-care delivery to Black clients.

Affordability

Investigators have documented the continual disproportionate decrease in income levels among Blacks compared with Whites (Horton & Smith, 1990; Auslander et al., 1992). By 1995, the median wealth (net wealth) of White households was almost seven times that of African American households ($49,030 compared with $7,073). Also, White households in the lowest quintile of income had a net worth of $9,720, while African American households' net worth was $1,500. Furthermore, African Americans in the highest income quintile had a net worth of $40,866 compared to $123,781 for Whites (Williams, 2002). On the measure of wealth, the net worth of those on the lower quintile shows an average of $10,000 for Whites and $100 for Blacks (House & Williams, 2000). It is now evident that because of racism, SES indicators have different meanings across racial/ethnic groups, thus rendering the statistical control for SES meaningless (Kaufman et al., 1997; House & Williams, 2000). Moreover, wealth (assets over liability) is believed to be a better measure of socioeconomic differences, and a key source of wealth for the average American family is home ownership. In this light "fewer than half of Black households own their homes, compared with more than 70 percent of White households" (Williams, 2002, p. 592).

The public mental health safety net of hospitals, community health centers, and local health departments is vital to many African Americans, especially to those in high-need populations. In contrast, nearly one in four African Americans is uninsured, compared to 16 percent of the total U.S. population. Also, rates of employer-based health coverage are just over 50 percent for employed African Americans, compared to over 70 percent for employed non-Hispanic Whites. Medicaid covers nearly 21 percent of African Americans. Overall, only one-third of Americans with a mental illness or a mental health problem get care. Yet, the percentage of African Americans receiving needed care is only half that of non-Hispanic Whites. One study reported that nearly 60 percent of older African American adults were not receiving needed services (USDHHS, 2001). In addition, African Americans are more likely to use emergency services or to seek treatment from a primary care provider than from a mental health specialist.

Opportunity costs, or the synergy of time and money required to access available health services, is a major barrier for economically disadvantaged health consumers (Airhihenbuwa, 1992). Because their daily activities are not always quantifiable in dollars, their time is often valued less by health-care professionals.

EMPOWERMENT AND THE DISCOURSE ON GROUP DECISION MAKING

Empowerment is defined as "a process of helping people to assert control over the factors which affect their health" (Gibson, 1991, p. 369). In this definition, the individual is expected to change the environment, even though most programs do not examine the forces that shape individual behaviors. The complex and multidimensional empowerment model combines ideas from social reform, behavior change, social action, social support, and life-stage theories, perceptions of self-efficacy, and organizational and community-development theories (Kieffer, 1984). This multidisciplinary model is borrowed from Freire's discourse on raising critical consciousness. Although Freire is commonly credited with the empowerment model, he never used the word "empowerment" (Airhihenbuwa, 1999).

Since empowerment has meant that individuals are supposed to be empowered by interventionists to change repressive forces in their environment, two critical issues become evident: (1) can a disempowered person overcome repressive forces without an interventionist, and (2) what does it mean to empower an individual in a context where both the leadership and the followers believe that the leader should be entrusted with all key decisions as with ministers in church? These two questions reflect some issues with notions of empowerment as appropriated in the African American communities, leading some to wonder whether the empowerment model actually disempowers people in the African American communities. In fact, the notion of empowerment within the African American tradition has always been a central feature of the African American scholar. For example, George Washington Carver is best known for his creation of 325 products from peanuts, more than 100 products from sweet potatoes, and hundreds more from a dozen other plants native to the South. However, in addition to these creations, he pioneered the concept of "moveable schools" (schools without walls) by bringing practical agricultural knowledge to farmers, thereby promoting health, good nutrition, and self-sufficiency (empowerment) (Iowa State University, 2000, p. 2).

The objective changes resulting from empowerment are variable, because they reflect the diverse needs of individuals, groups, organizations, and communities and the contexts where empowerment occurs. They may comprise groups of empowered institutions and individuals or single groups of people living in, for example, housing units.

Techniques used to facilitate the transition from powerlessness to power have embraced consciousness-raising, training members in social competence, encouraging and accepting the client's definition of the problem, identifying and building upon existing strengths, analyzing how powerlessness is affecting the situation, identifying and using sources of power in the client's situation, teaching specific skills, mobilizing resources, and looking out for the welfare of the clients (Gutierrez, 1990). However, as was addressed in the UNAIDS framework, recognizing the domains of contextual influence is key to transforming social context. Raising consciousness and developing skills focus on learning to identify the contextual influences of behavior. For example, learning about good eating practices is important. It is equally important to recognize the availability of low-cost, unhealthy foods compared to healthy foods in a neighborhood. The relatively high cost of purchasing the same food items in a poor neighborhood compared to the price in an affluent neighborhood is another contextual constraint on good eating practice. Indeed, the "Wal-Martization" of small businesses has been visited upon African American communities for decades by other chain stores before the recent realization of this phenomenon in the White community.

The importance of root causes has meant that the language of public health is also going through transformation. For instance, the notion of community diagnosis is being replaced with community assessment (Airhihenbuwa et al., in press) with the realization that diagnosis preconditions the interventionists to look for problems while ignoring a community's assets. In an article focusing on community assets mapping, Parks and Straker (1996) cite several statements from community residents and community advocates that criticize the emphasis on problems. One community advocate stated that "although we have our problems, there are lots of good and positive things about our community" (p. 321). Another community member wanted to know when researchers were going to stop focusing on "the negative things in our neighborhood (and) . . . start seeing what's right here" (p. 321). Interventionists can begin community assessment efforts by, for example, promoting the African American rich tradition of eating green vegetables.

The goal of health promotion and education and of public health should, therefore, be directed toward achieving social justice and human rights in relation to the health status of all Americans. In the conclusion that follows, an examination is made of some of the reasons that health disparities between ethnic and racial groups continue to persist.

CONCLUSION

There continue to be persistent disparities between the health of African Americans and that of Whites. A new approach to eliminating disparity should focus on addressing factors in the physical and social environment that creates disparity. Health issues can be triangulated into those that are positive and should be encouraged for increased positive identity, those unique but indifferent to health that should be left untouched, and those that are negative and should be changed as articulated in the PEN-3 model (for more on a model for health promotion in the African American community that addresses these issues, see Airhihenbuwa, 1995, 1999).

Health promotion programs have been effective in helping communities to eliminate their contextual risks of disease, such as cancer, cardiovascular problems, and hypertension. Thus, targeting individuals for most health reduction efforts, without considering the effect of the various environments, may be counterproductive, because few have control over most environmental factors that influence them. The sociopolitical and environmental forces that influence health behavior must be transformed within the context of the culture (Airhihenbuwa, 1995). Finally, to promote preventive activities, African American and White health professionals need to become advocates for the people for whom the options of choice are rapidly decreasing. They need to focus on environmental and social issues that rob people of hope and dignity and contribute to poverty and crime. Contextual forces remain the primary impediment to eliminating disparities to improve the health of African Americans.

REFERENCES

Airhihenbuwa, C.O. (1989). Health education for African Americans: A neglected task. *Health Education, 20,* 9–14.

Airhihenbuwa, C.O. (1992). Health promotion and disease prevention strategies for African-Americans. In R.L. Braithwaite & S.E. Taylor (Eds.), *Health issues in the Black community* (pp. 267–280). San Francisco: Jossey-Bass.

Airhihenbuwa, C.O. (1995). *Health and culture: Beyond the Western paradigm.* Thousand Oaks, CA: Sage.

Airhihenbuwa, C.O. (1999). Of culture and multiverse: Renouncing "the universal truth" in health. *Journal of Health Education, 30,* 267–273.

Airhihenbuwa, C.O., Jack, L., Jr., & Webster, J.D. (in press). Community capacity and health intervention research in communities of color. In B. Beech, V. Setlwo, & M.F. Roohani (Eds.), *Race and research in focus: Perspectives on minority participation in health studies.* Washington, DC: American Public Health Association Press.

Airhihenbuwa, C.O., Olsen, L.K., St. Pierre, R.W., & Wang, M.Q. (1989). Race and gender: An analysis of the granting of doctoral degrees in health education programs. *Health Education, 20,* 4–7.

Amaro, H., Raj, A., Vega, R.R., Mangione, T., & Perez, L.N. (2001). Racial/ethnic disparities in the HIV and substance abuse epidemics: Communities responding to the need. *Public Health Reports 116,* 434–448.

Armstrong, T.D. (1996). Exploring spirituality: The development of the Armstrong measure of spirituality. In R.L. Jones (Ed.), *Handbook of test and measurements for Black populations* (pp. 105–115). Hampton, VA: Cobb & Henry.

Auslander, W.F., Haire-Joshu, D., Houston, C.A., & Fisher, E.B. (1992). Community organization to reduce the risk of non-insulin-dependent diabetes among low-income African-American women. *Ethnicity and Disease, 2,* 176–184.

Barzansky, B., & Etzel, S. (2001). Educational programs in U.S. medical schools, 2000–2001. *Journal of the American Medical Association, 286,* 1049–1055.

Becker, M.H. (1986). The tyranny of health promotion. *Public Health Review, 14,* 15–25.

Bergin, A.E. (1983). Religiosity and mental health: A critical reevaluation and meta-analysis. *Professional Psychology: Research and Practice, 14,* 170–184.

Centers for Disease Control and Prevention (CDC). (2002). National Center for Health Statistics. Retrived from the World Wide Web: www.cdc.gov/nchs.

Centers for Disease Control and Prevention (CDC). (2001, August). National Center for Chronic Disease and Health Promotion. REACH 2010.

Charatz-Litt, C. (1992). A chronicle of racism: The effects of the White medical community on Black health. *Journal of the National Medical Association, 84,* 717–725.

Collison, M.N.K. (September 30, 1992). Network of Black students hopes to create a new generation of civil rights leaders. *Chronicle of Higher Education,* A28–A2S.

Couch, K., & Daly, M.C. (2002). Black–White wage inequality in the 1990's: A decade of progress. *Economic Inquiry, 40,* 31–41.

Davidson, J.M. (1982). Physician participation in Medicaid: Background and issues. *Journal of Health Politics and Policy Law, 6,* 703.

Edelman, M.R. (1989). Black children in America. In J. Dewart (Ed.), *The state of Black America 1989* (pp. 63–76). New York: National Urban League.

Evans, C. (1995). Presidential address. Public health: Vision and reality. *American Journal of Public Health, 86,* 476–479.

Fingerhut, L.A., & Makuc, D.M. (1992). News from NCHS. *American Journal Public Health, 82,* 1168–1170.

Forrest, C.B., & Starfield, B. (1998). Entry into primary care and continuity: The effects of access. *American Journal of Public Health, 88,* 1330–1336.

Friday, J.C., Lillie-Blanton, M., & Kates, J. (Eds.). (2001, April). Mobilizing the fight: HIV/AIDS in the African American Community. *Minority Health Today.* Washington, DC: Kaiser Family Foundation.

Gibson, C.H. (1991). A concept analysis of empowerment. *Journal of Advanced Nursing, 16,* 354–361.

Gutierrez, L.M. (1990). Working with women of color: An empowerment perspective. *Social Work, 35,* 149–153.

Health Trends. (1992). New vital statistics confirm worsening of Black health. *Ethnicity and Disease, 2,* 192–193.

Helsing, K. (2002). Association of Schools of Public Health Annual Data Report. Washington, DC: Association of Schools of Public Health.

Horton, E.P., & Smith, J.C. (Eds.). (1990). *Statistical record of Black Americans.* Detroit: Gale Research.

House, J.S., & Williams, D.R. (2000). Paper Contribution B: Understanding and reducing socioeconomic and racial/ethnic disparities in health. In B.D. Smedley & S.L. Syme (Eds.), *Promoting health: Intervention strategies from social and behavioral research* (pp. 81–124). Washington, DC: National Academy Press.

Iowa State University. (2000). The legacy of George Washington Carver. Retrieved November 28, 2002, from Iowa State University, Special Collections Department, e-Library.Web site: http://www.lib.iastate.edu/spcl/gwc/bio.html.

Jones, J. (1982). *Bad blood: The Tuskegee Syphilis Experiment—a tragedy of race and medicine.* New York: Free Press.

Kaufman, J.S., Cooper, R.S., & McGee, D.L. (1997). Socioeconomic status and health in Blacks and Whites: The problem of residual confounding and the resiliency of race. *Epidemiology, 8,* 621–628.

Kieffer, C.H. (1984). Citizen empowerment: A developmental perspective. In J. Rappaport, C. Swift, & R. Hess (Eds.), *Studies in empowerment: Steps toward understanding and action* (pp. 9–36). New York: Haworth Press.

King, G., & Williams, D.R. (1995). Race and health: A multidimensional approach to African-American health. In B.C. Amick, S. Levine, A.R. Tarlov, & D.C. Walsh (Eds.), *Society and health* (pp. 93–130). New York: Oxford University Press.

Kreuter, M.W. (1992). PATCH: Its origin, basic concepts and links to contemporary public health policy. *Journal of Health Education, 23,* 135–139.

Kumanyika, S.K., & Golden, P.M. (1991). Cross-sectional differences in health status in U.S. racial/ethnic minority groups: Potential influence of temporal changes, disease, and lifestyle transitions. *Ethnicity and Disease, 1,* 50–59.

Kumanyika, S.K., Morssink, C.B., & Nestle, M. (2001). Minority women and advocacy for women's health. *American Journal of Public Health, 91,* 1383–1388.

Lamarine, R.J. (1989). First do no harm. *Health Education, 20,* 22–24.

Larson, D.B., Sherill, K.A., Lyons, J.S., Craige, F.C., Thielman, S.B., Greenwold, M.A., & Larson, S.S. (1992). Associations between dimensions of religious commitment and mental health reported in the American Journal of Psychiatry and the Archives of General Psychiatry: 1978–1989. *American Journal of Psychiatry*, 149, 557–559.

Markens, S., Fox, S.A., Taub, B., & Gilbert, M.L. (2002). Role of Black churches in health promotion programs: Lessons from the Los Angeles mammography promotion in churches program. *American Journal of Public Health, 92*, 805–810.

Miles, G.B., & McDavis, R.J. (1982). Effects of four orientation approaches on disadvantaged Black freshmen students' attitudes toward the counseling center. *Journal of College Student Personnel, 23*, 413–418.

Muller, C. (1985). A window of the past: The position of the client in twentieth century public health thought and practice. *American Journal of Public Health, 75*, 470–476.

O'Malley, A.S., Kerner, J., Johnson, A.E., & Mandelblatt, J. (1999). Acculturation and breast cancer screening among Hispanic women in New York City. *American Journal of Public Health, 89*, 219–227.

Oppenheimer, G.M. (2001). Race, ethnicity, and the search for a new population taxonomy. *American Journal of Public Health, 91*, 1049–1055.

Parks, C.P., & Straker, H.O. (1996). Community assets mapping: Community health assessment with a different twist. *Journal of Health Education, 27*, 321–323.

Pernick, M.S. (1985). *A calculus of suffering.* New York: Columbia University Press.

Protor, E., & Rosen, A. (1981). Expectations and preferences for counselor's race and their relation to intermediate treatment outcomes. *Journal of Counseling Psychology, 28*, 40–46.

Put AIDS funds where needed. (1999, September 30). *Los Angeles Times*, p. 10.

Savitt, T.L. (1982). The use of Blacks for medical experimentation and demonstration in the old South. *Journal of Southern History, 48*, 331–335.

Smedley, B.D., Stith, A.Y., & Nelson, A.R. (Eds.) (2002). *Unequal treatment: Confronting racial and ethnic disparities in health care.* Washington, DC: National Academy Press.

Terborg, J.R. (1986). Health promotion at the worksite. In K.H. Rowland & G.R. Ferris, *Research in Personal and Human Resource Management*, vol. 4. Greenwich, CT: JAI.

UNAIDS/Penn State. (1999). Communications Framework for HIV/AIDS: A New Direction. UNAIDS/Penn State Project. Edited by C.O., Airhihenbuwa, B. Makinwa, M. Frith, & R. Obregon. Geneva, Switzerland: UNAIDS.

U.S. Department of Commerce, Bureau of the Census. (1997). *Current population survey.* Washington, DC: U.S. Government Printing Office.

U.S. Department of Health and Human Services (USDHHS). (1991). *Health United States and Prevention Profile.* Public Health Service, Centers for Disease Control, National Center for Health Statistics Pub. No. (PHS) 1-1232. Hyattsville, MD.

U.S. Department of Health and Human Services (USDHHS). (2000). *Healthy People 2010: Understanding & improving health.* 2d ed. Washington, DC: Goverment Printing Office.

U.S. Department of Health and Human Services (USDHHS). (2001). Mental health: Culture, race, and ethnicity—a supplement to mental health: A report of the surgeon general. Rockville, MD: USDHHS, Substance Abuse and Mental Health Services Administration.

U.S. Department of Housing and Urban Development (USHUD). (2002, June 7). HUD's Initiative for renewal communities, urban empowerment zones and urban enterprise communities. Retrieved June 12, 2002, from the World Wide Web: http://www.hud.gov/offices/cpd/ezec/index.cfm.

Williams, D.R. (2002). Racial/ethnic variations in women's health: The social embeddedness of health. *American Journal of Public Health, 92*, 588–597.

Williams, D.R., & Collins, C. (1995). U.S. socioeconomic and racial differences in health: Patterns and explanations. *Annual Review of Sociology, 21*, 349–386.

CHAPTER 46

Issues Surrounding the Involvement of African Americans in Clinical Trials and Other Research

OSCAR E. STREETER JR., ALOYSIUS B. CUYJET, KEITH NORRIS, AND KEVIN HYLTON

INTRODUCTION

Research is "the creator of old knowledge, and the creation of new knowledge. It is progress, but we need to make sure the progress is appropriate for the patients we treat, and we don't do something prematurely. That is why we perform clinical trials" (Leffall, 1998). Historically, the idea of comparative observations in medicine is part of the scientific revolution of the 1600s, part of the "experimental philosophy" movement of the upper and middle classes in Europe (Meldrum, 2000). However, arguably, the first documented comparative intervention trial was that of the British naval surgeon James Lind's 12 scurvy patients' response to the use of oranges and lemons (Lind, 1753). The 12 sailors with scurvy were treated in pairs with cider, elixir vitriol, vinegar, seawater, two oranges with a lemon, and nutmeg. If this experiment was performed today, the two sailors on citrus that improved within a week would have been judged as having 100 percent cure rate, p = 0.09. However, using today's statistical method of confidence intervals, it would be considered "suggestive but consistent with no (0%) effect," and would be deemed an underpowered study, with a larger trial needed to confirm the positive citrus intervention results to a no-treatment arm (Pirozzo & Glasziou, 1999). Despite its lack of power, the results eliminated scurvy in the English navy and led to the slur for a British person of Limey (originally a sailor).

Unfortunately, during the twentieth century, clinical trial research suffered from major lapses in ethical conduct, leading to distrust by society at large of clinical research. First were the murders and tortures in human experimentation conducted by Nazi doctors in the concentration camps (the so-called Doctors' Trial) (Shuster, 1997). These men were tried in Nuremberg, Germany, by the International Military Tribunal, made up of judges from the four Allied powers (the United States, Britain, France, and the former Soviet Union). The Doctors' Trial began on December 9, 1946, and ended on July 19, 1947. Of 23 defendants, 16 were found guilty; 7 were sentenced to hanging, the remainder to prison terms of life imprisonment to 25, 15, and 10 years; and there were seven acquittals. The chief prosecutor, Telford Taylor, and the International Military Tribunal viewed the proceedings as a murder trial, or "crimes against humanity." Testifying for the prosecution were three physicians, Leo Alexander, Werner Leibbrand, and Andrew Ivy, who outlined in their testimony the initial principles of ethical research conduct that would be formulated into the Nuremberg Code. The ten principles of the Nuremberg Code are:

1. The voluntary consent of the human subject is absolutely essential.

2. The experiment should be such as to yield fruitful results for the good of society, unprocurable by other methods or means of study, and not random and unnecessary in nature.

3. The experiment should be so designed and based on the results of animal experimentation and knowledge of the natural history of the disease or other problem under study that the anticipated results will justify the performance of the experiment.

4. The experiment should be conducted as to avoid all unnecessary physical and mental suffering and injury.

5. No experiment should be conducted where there is an a priori reason to believe that death or disabling injury will occur; except, perhaps, in those experiments where the experimental physicians also serve as subjects.

6. The degree of risk to be taken should never exceed that determined by the humanitarian importance of the problem to be solved by the experiment.

7. Proper preparations should be made and adequate facilities provided to protect the experimental subject against even remote possibilities of injury, disability, or death.

8. Only scientifically qualified persons should conduct the experiment. The highest degree of skill and care should be required through all stages of the experiment of those who conduct or engage in the experiment.

9. During the course of the experiment the human subject should be at liberty to bring the experiment to an end if he has reached the physical or mental state where continuation of the experiment seems to him to be impossible.

10. During the course of the experiment the scientist in charge must be prepared to terminate the experiment at any stage, if he has probable cause to believe, in the exercise of good faith, superior skill, and careful judgment required of him, that a continuation of the experiment is likely to result in injury, disability, or death to the experimental subject.

THE STUDY OF UNTREATED SYPHILIS IN THE NEGRO MALE

The study that has continued to be cited by African Americans not to participate in clinical trials is the Tuskegee Syphilis Study, which really should be referred to as the "U.S. Public Health Service Study of Untreated Syphilis in the Negro Male" (Brawley, 1998). Dr. Otis W. Brawley, while director of the Office of Special Populations Research at the National Cancer Institute, reviewed the original documents gathered during the U.S. Senate hearings and investigation in 1972 and the book *Bad Blood* by James Jones (Jones, 1981) for his review. Dr. Brawley's review was first presented at the Kellogg Executive Conference Center on the campus of Tuskegee University in February 1997, where he spoke at the conference "Overcoming 'Bad Blood' in Cancer Clinical Trials: Tuskegee Trial Revisited," organized by Oscar Streeter Jr., M.D., and Mack Roach III, M.D., on behalf of the Radiation Therapy Oncology Group (RTOG). It had the participation from nearly all of the cooperative groups, the National Cancer Institute, the Office of Women's Research, and the Office for the Protection of Human Subjects of the National Institutes of Health. It was convened for the express purpose of understanding how to increase minority involvement in cancer clinical trials and the barriers to participation (Cox, 1998). Starting in the 1980s, the National Cancer Institute actively encouraged starting with the Office of Special Populations (now the Center to Reduce Cancer Health Disparities) minority enrollment in cancer clinical trials, because the expanding body of data was showing that Black cancer patients treated in formal clinical trials have the same outcome as Whites cancer patients receiving the same treatments (Bach et al., 2002; Curran et al., 1993; Graham et al.,

1992; Roach, Alexander et al., 1992; Roach et al., 1997; Roach, Krall, et al., 1992; Streeter et al., 1999).

Epstein and Ayanian (2001) analyzed longitudinal data and noted that there is little evidence that measures of health care and outcomes have changed substantially over the past 30 years, especially as evidenced by the abbreviated life expectancy of African Americans as compared to White Americans. Among the reasons cited as possible explanations for the persistent racial disparities were that much of the evidence is based on administrative data and thus may not reflect unmeasured differences in clinical, cultural, or socioeconomic factors. Second, they suggest that some clinicians may believe that Whites are more likely than Blacks to prefer more aggressive treatments or interventions. Third, few studies have rigorously evaluated differences in clinical outcomes that may directly be related to differences in the use of therapies or interventions.

Because clinical trials form the scientific basis of modern medical practice and for evidence-based medicine, we suggest that part of this discrepancy may also reflect inadequate representation of African Americans and other minorities in prior clinical trials. Hence, if those populations have not been adequately represented in the study sample, the optimal therapy may be incompletely or inadequately defined. The underrepresentation of African Americans, women, and other minorities in clinical trials is exceedingly important, because the trials establish standards of care and lead to product approval and indications. If a particular clinical trial's population pool is does not have appropriate numbers of particular minority groups or underserved populations, this may leave the following questions unanswered: (1) is the product safe? (2) is the product effective? (3) is the dose correct? and (4) is this the best therapy for me?

Dans et al. for the Evidence-based Medicine Working Group (1998) recently addressed the applicability of randomized clinical trials to actual practice and raised important questions that the practitioner must be able to answer before recommending a specific therapy or intervention for a particular patient. These questions included biological, social, and economic issues as well as epidemiological considerations. For some disease processes there are clear pathophysiologic differences that result in different treatment responses. For example, Black hypertensive patients are generally more responsive to diuretics than some other classes of antihypertensive- ACE inhibitors. However, some recent trials suggest that target organ protection may occur independently of blood pressure-lowering effects, especially with angiotensin receptor blockers or angiotensin converting enzyme inhibitors. Thus, it is unknown whether benefit (target organ protection) may be derived in populations reported to be less responsive to a specific class of drugs despite the absence of an equivalent pharmacological response (blood pressure lowering). Another area of concern is driven by patient differences that may alter treatment response; these include differences in drug metabolism or environmental factors that may affect therapeutic/toxic ratios. Regarding social and economic issues, there may be important differences in both patient and provider compliance that may alter treatment response, safety, and efficacy.

Others have observed that even in trials that have included minorities, the number enrolled is often inadequate for subset analysis. Halpern et al. (2002) recently argued that underpowered trials could be justified only in two situations: first, for rare diseases where the capacity to enroll adequate numbers may be limited and second, where the results of a small trial may be combined with similar trials in a prospective meta-analysis. The conduct of otherwise underpowered trials should be considered unethical.

There are no precise data on minority representation in clinical trials. Most estimate that minority representation averages less than 5 percent in pivotal trials supporting drug safety and efficacy. Svensson (1989) raised major questions regarding this issue when he reviewed the representation of African Americans in 50 published clinical trials of new drugs. He found that the proportion of Black subjects was less than their proportion in the general population and that investigators did not consider racial differences as a potential source of variability. He concluded that insufficient data existed to accurately assess either the efficacy or safety of new drugs in African Americans. Additional concerns involved the exclusion of women from many major trials and the recognition that there were differences in responses of women to certain drugs. This led to the 1994 National Institutes of Health (NIH) Guidelines on the Inclusion of Women and Minorities in Clinical Trials. These guidelines specified that race/ethnicity was to be analyzed but no specific requirements regarding the degree of representation were defined.

The Food and Drug Administration Modernization Act of 1997 required the FDA and NIH to consult on the inclusion of women and minorities in clinical trials and provided for the establishment of a NIH Clinical Trials data bank. However, it is not clear how these guidelines have been implemented or how closely they are being followed. Thus, 14 years after Svensson's expressed concerns, King (2002) in a recent editorial titled "Racial Disparities in Clinical Trials" begins, "The rational use of a new drug or treatment should be based on the results of controlled clinical trials that are well designed, avoid bias, and include subjects representing the full range of patients who are likely to receive the treatment once it is marketed. In addition to age, sex, diet, underlying disease, and the concomitant use of other medications, race and genetic factors may play pivotal parts in the variability of subjects' responses to a medication. Regrettably, minority groups are underrepresented in most clinical trials."

To better quantify the representation of women, Blacks, and the very old (aged 80 or more), Hall (1999) recently reviewed 28 studies that are frequently cited in references or whose conclusions are utilized to support evidence-based medicine. Twenty-three of the 28 studies enrolled a majority of males; Blacks and the elderly, with the exception of isolated systolic hypertension in the latter, were greatly underrepresented. As Hall notes in his discussion, adequate representation of women, Blacks, or very old patients is one issue, but having adequate numbers to power the studies for statistical comparison is a separate issue.

The reasons for minorities being underrepresented in clinical trials are multifactorial and complex. Harris et al. (1996) analyzed their difficulties enrolling an African American cohort for the African American Antiplatelet Stroke Prevention Study (AAASPS). They identified four major barriers: a general lack of awareness of clinical trials, an inherent sense of mistrust of the medical system in general and trials in particular, economic factors, and communication gaps. Powell et al. (2001) detailed a number of barriers to minority participation in clinical trials. These include less access to health care, lack of physician recommendation, distrust of medical research, patient compliance issues, cultural beliefs, negative experiences with the health-care system, educational and literacy status, and transportation and time costs. Similarly, barriers exist for minority physicians and include lack of information about, and experience with, clinical trials, provider compliance issues, complex forms and procedures required for participation, and start-up costs.

This chapter reviews the evidence of African Americans treated in modern clinical trials in the areas of heart disease, cancer, kidney disease, and HIV/AIDS.

HEART DISEASE CLINICAL TRIALS

In 1985, *The Report of the Secretary's Task Force on Black and Minority Health* (USDHHS, 1985) was released. The report confirmed what was long suspected, that there were significant disparities in health-care outcomes between Whites and minority groups within the population of the United States. It further confirmed that cardiovascular diseases, as for Whites, were the leading cause of morbidity and mortality in Blacks and that the morbidity and mortality rates were higher for Black Americans as compared to White Americans.

Today, cardiovascular diseases remain the leading cause of death in the United States, and the age-adjusted death rates for African American men and women are higher when compared, respec-

Figure 46.1
Years of potential life lost to total heart disease before age 75 by race and gender

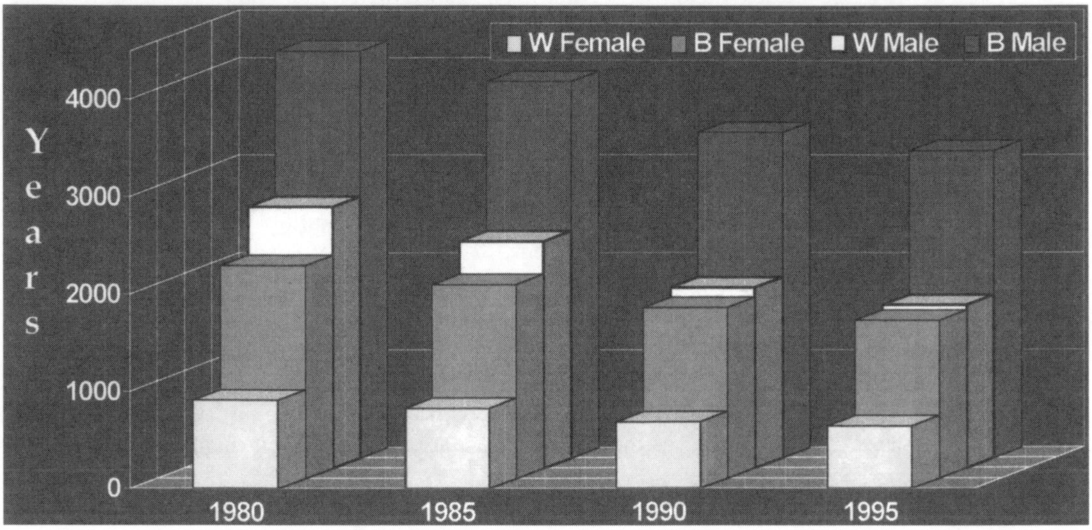

Source: Clark et al. (2001).

tively, to Whites men and women and when compared to other population groups. Although the death rates have declined over time for all groups, the disparity in outcomes persists. In 1990 and 1998, the age-adjusted death rates per 100,000 population for heart disease for Whites were, respectively, 145.3 and 123.6 and for Blacks, 211.8 and 188.0. Thus, the rates declined by 15 percent for White non-Hispanics but only by 11 percent for Black non-Hispanics (Keppel et al., 2002).

Clark et al. (2001) recently reviewed the current status of coronary heart disease (CHD) in African Americans and noted that they have the highest overall CHD mortality rate and the highest out-of-hospital coronary death rate of any ethnic group in the United States. Because the onset of CHD occurs at an earlier age among U.S. Blacks, the disparity in health-care outcomes is even greater when translated into years of potential life lost (see Figure 46.1). They considered possible reasons to account for the disproportionate coronary heart disease. These included a high prevalence with clustering of CHD risk factors, excess cardiovascular risk associated with diabetes mellitus, increased target organ damage and prevalence of hypertension, heterogeneity of acute coronary syndromes, delays in identification of high-risk individuals, and limited access or delays in accessing care.

The vast number of cardiovascular clinical trials suggests the potential magnitude of the problem. Cheng (1999) listed 2,250 acronyms for cardiology trials between 1990 and 1996. Another 1,000 acronyms were added between 1996 and 1999. The *Cardiovascular Trials Review, Sixth Edition* summarizes 682 trials that have had a major impact on cardiology evidence-based clinical practice. The review includes both pharmacological- and device-based studies (Kloner & Birnbaum, 2001). Schindler (2001) also compiled a database of clinical trials in cardiology and lists a total of 1,687 trials between 1992 and 2001.

Current trials cover the entire spectrum of cardiovascular disease and include:

1. Acute Myocardial Infarction
   a. Thrombolytic Therapy
   b. Interventional Therapy: Early versus Late

    c. Anticoagulation and Antiplatelet Therapies
    d. Remodeling after Myocardial Injury
2. Acute Coronary Syndromes and Non ST Elevation Myocardial Infarctions
3. Stable Angina and Silent Ischemia
4. Interventional Cardiology
    a. Percutaneous Transluminal Coronary Angioplasty versus Medical Therapy
    b. Percutaneous Transluminal Coronary Angioplasty with Stenting versus Coronary Artery Bypass Grafting
    c. Medical Therapy and Brachytherapy to Prevent Restenosis
    d. Other Therapies—Laser
5. Heart Failure
6. Dysrhythmia
7. Atherosclerosis
8. Hypertension
9. Dyslipidemia
10. Atrial Fibrillation and Anticoagulation
11. Venous Thromboembolism
12. Valvular Heart Disease
13. Cardiomyopathy

Because the number of trials and the areas covered are beyond the scope of this chapter, we focus on three areas because of their direct impact on cardiovascular morbidity and mortality: coronary heart disease, heart failure, and lipid disorders.

CORONARY HEART DISEASE

Prevalence

While ischemic heart disease is the leading cause of death in the U.S. population, there is a persistent perception that coronary heart disease is relatively uncommon among Black Americans. This notion, in part, stems from the Coronary Artery Surgery Study (CASS), where Black men and women evaluated for chest pain had a higher percentage of normal coronary arteries on coronary angiography as compared to White men and women. However, it needs to be emphasized that of the 24,900 study patients, only 573, or 2.3 percent, were Black Americans (Maynard et al., 1986). Despite the paucity of minority representation, the data from CASS are frequently referenced to support this perception. These data reinforced the notion that coronary heart disease was less prevalent among Black Americans derived from the Evans County (McDonough et al., 1965) and Charleston Heart Studies (Keil et al., 1984). Although the two studies observed a lower prevalence of CHD among Black men as compared to White men, the prevalence of CHD was the same for Black women and White women.

Keil et al. (1993), reporting 30-year follow-up data from the Charleston Heart Study, indicated that the coronary disease death rate was somewhat lower for Black men than White men but higher among Black women as compared with White women. The Multiple Risk Factor Intervention Trial (Multiple Risk Factor Intervention Trial Research Group, 1982) included 7.2 percent Black men among the 12,866 men assigned to either special intervention (SI) or usual care (UC), but race/ethnicity was not considered as a variable in the baseline-defined subgroups as the study was intended to define differences among smokers, those who are hypertensive, and one's lipid status.

Interventions

Reperfusion, whether achieved by primary angioplasty with or without stenting or by the administration of thrombolytic (clot-dissolving) drugs, is the gold standard for the management of acute myocardial infarction (AMI) with ST segment elevation (STE). Ford and Cooper (1995) reviewed the available evidence from a number of data sets and concluded that Black Americans were about half as likely as White Americans to receive interventional therapy for coronary heart disease. Even after adjusting for a number of variables, including age, sex, socioeconomic status, disease severity, and comorbid conditions, large differences persisted. They did note a direct correlation between the cost of the intervention and the magnitude of the disparity. Chen et al. (2001) more recently reviewed racial differences in the utilization of coronary angiography after acute myocardial infarction to ascertain what role, if any, the race of the treating physician played. They again documented that Black patients had lower rates of cardiac catheterization than White patients, regardless of the attending physician's race. Their study was based on administrative data, and, as the authors note, they were unable to determine whether coronary angiography was underused, appropriately used, or overused in either Black or White patients.

Data analyzed from the National Hospital Discharge Survey (Gillum et al., 1997) indicated that while the rates of coronary artery bypass grafting (CABG), cardiac catheterization, and percutaneous transluminal coronary angioplasty (PTCA) increased between 1980 and 1993, large racial disparities persist in the utilization of CABG and PTCA. Scott and the NHLBI PTCA Registry Investigators (Scott et al., 1994) reviewed the National Heart, Lung, and Blood Institute 1985–1986 Percutaneous Transluminal Coronary Angioplasty Registry. The enrolled patients included 1,939 Whites (90.8 percent) and 76 Blacks (3.6 percent). Black patients were more likely to have multivessel disease, and complete revascularization was achieved in 26 percent of Black patients as compared with 44 percent of White patients. The authors also reported on five-year follow-up data, and despite the presence of more cardiovascular risk factors, symptoms and multivessel disease among Black patients, there was no significant difference in mortality, CABG, or repeat PTCA as compared with White patients. However, the sample of Black patients in the registry is small, mirroring the problem of enrollment of minority patients in randomized trials.

Prior to the ascendancy of interventional techniques in the management of acute myocardial infarction (AMI), thrombolytic therapy was the mainstay and remains as the initial intervention in the management of AMI when intervention is not available. However, the major trials evaluating the efficacy of reperfusion therapies in acute ST elevation myocardial infarction, including thrombolytic therapy and percutaneous transluminal coronary angioplasty with and without stenting, do not have adequate minority representation. These trials constitute the major landmark studies and include GISSI (Grupo Italiano per lo Studio della Streptochinasi nell'Infarto Miocardico), TIMI (Thrombolysis in Myocardial Infarction), TAMI (Thrombolysis and Angioplasty in Myocardial Infarction), GUSTO (Global Utilization of Steptokinase and Tissue Plasminogen Activator for Occluded Coronary Arteries), PAMI (Primary Angioplasty in Myocardial Infarction), and ISIS (International Study of Infarct Survival). Collectively, these studies represent a sample of over 220,000 patients with either suspected or confirmed myocardial infarction treated with a variety of thrombolytic (clot-dissolving) therapies, interventions including primary angioplasty with or without stenting and other miscellaneous interventions.

Taylor et al. (1993), for the TIMI Investigation, analyzed race and prognosis in the Thrombolysis in Myocardial Infarction Phase II Trial. Of the 2,885 patients, only 174 (6.03 percent) were Blacks. The analysis confirmed the high prevalence of recognized cardiovascular risk factors among minority patients with AMI and also noted a statistically significant greater decrease in fibrinogen levels in response to thrombolytic therapy in Black patients as compared to Whites and Latinos. More importantly, thrombolytic therapy with appropriate supplemental measures was associated with comparable one-year mortality in White, Black, and Latino patients. It is difficult to interpret these findings in the context of the small sample size relative to randomized clinical trial experience and the documented underutilization of reperfusion therapies in Black patients with AMI.

More recently, data from the National Registry of Myocardial Infarction 2 were analyzed (Taylor et al., 1998). The registry included 236,166 Whites and 17,141 Blacks and is intended to examine current treatment and in-hospital mortality for Black patients in the reperfusion era. Black patients with acute myocardial infarction (AMI) were less likely to receive thrombolytic therapy, coronary angiography, other catheter-based interventions, or coronary artery bypass surgery than Whites with AMI. Despite these statistically significant differences, there were no significant differences in hospital mortality between the two groups, begging the question of defining optimal therapy since there is a higher mortality for Blacks' post–hospital discharge for AMI. Sheifer et al. (2000) also reviewed published data documenting race and gender differences in the treatment of coronary heart disease. Their analysis concluded that racial differences were driven by socioeconomic factors, process-of-care variables, and patient preferences. Gender differences tended to be influenced by clinical factors. Importantly, they also note that "our understanding is limited by deficiencies in currently available datasets."

Scott and the National Heart Lung and Blood Institute PTCA Registry Investigators (Scott et al., 1994) report that there may be no significant differences in angioplasty outcomes in Black Americans as compared to Whites. Similar findings were more recently reported by Mastoor et al. (2000). However, these reports do not address the central issue of minority representation in randomized prospective trials, and without appropriate representation in these trials, it is impossible to determine the risk/benefit ratio and the impact on outcomes among Black patients with coronary heart disease.

HEART FAILURE

Nearly five million Americans have the syndrome of heart failure (HF), occurring with equal frequency among males and females. Approximately 550,000 new cases are diagnosed annually, and the incidence is 10 per 1,000 among individuals greater than 65 years of age. HF results in one million hospital discharges annually and constitutes Medicare's single largest expense. Most ominously, the five-year mortality rate is as high as 50 percent.

The American College of Cardiology/American Heart Association Task Force on Practice Guidelines recently revised the "Guidelines for the Evaluation and Management of Chronic Heart Failure in the Adult: Executive Summary" (American College of Cardiology/American Heart Association, 2001). The guidelines specifically note under the section characterized as "Special Subpopulations," "Many subgroups are underrepresented in most trials, and some present unique problems. These include women and men, racial minorities, and elderly patients." The "Heart Failure" section of the most recent edition of the *Clinical Evidence Concise* (Barton, 2002) categorically states, "Systematic reviews have found strong evidence that adding a beta-blocker to an angiotensin converting enzyme inhibitor significantly decreases mortality and admission to hospital. Subgroup analysis in Black people found no significant effect on mortality." Barton's summary fails to point out that this conclusion is based on a subgroup analysis derived from a single study utlizing buncindolol as the beta-blocker (Eichhorn et al., 2001) and, therefore, should not be generalized to all Black patients with heart failure.

Heiat et al. (2002) recently reviewed 59 Heart Failure Randomized Clinical Trials that included 50 or more participants and were published in English between 1985 and 1999. Twelve studies (20 percent), which included 51 percent of the total population studied, provided data on racial/ethnic distribution. Only 15 percent of participants were categorized as non-Whites and, as noted by Heiat et al., none of the trials specifically targeted women or minority populations. They found that patients enrolled in the trials were younger, more frequently male, more likely to have low ejection fractions, and most commonly Whites. They also did not find a significant change in representation in the study populations from the late 1980s through the more recently published trials. Lastly, they concluded that the published trials have focused on a relatively narrow segment of the heart failure population and that the consequences of underrepresenting minorities, women, and elderly are unknown. They recommended that future trials should adequately represent the demographics of population with the syndrome of heart failure.

The recently published Valsartan Heart Failure Trial (Val-HeFT) (Cohn et al., 2000) included 344 Blacks (African American and South African) among the 5,010 patients, who were randomized. However, as the authors note, the sample size was small, and subgroup analysis failed to reveal a significant reduction in the combined end-point of mortality and morbidity (relative risk, 1.11; 95 percent confidence interval, 0.77 to 1.61). The discussion of the baseline demographics of Val-HeFT concludes that the average patient is a 63-year-old White male with NYHA Class II Heart Failure (HF) and antecedent coronary heart disease. The 344 Black patients enrolled in Val-HeFT were younger and had more severe HF with hypertension as the underlying cause. There were more Black patients in the lowest ejection fraction quartile than in any of the other three quartiles.

The potential problems with inadequate minority representation are well illustrated by the controversy generated by Exner et al. (2001) when they reported a lesser response to angiotensin-converting enzyme inhibitor therapy in Black as compared to White patients with left ventricular dysfunction. They reanalyzed their data from the Studies of Left Ventricular Dysfunction (SOLVD) prevention and treatment trials using a matched-cohort design and concluded that enalapril therapy was not associated with a significant reduction in the risk of hospitalization for heart failure among Black patients. The conclusion was heavily criticized, and the authors noted in their introduction, "A critical impediment to the analysis of racial differences in therapeutic response is the underrepresentation of Black patients in trials of therapy for heart failure." Thus, it is unclear whether the underutilization of angiotensin-converting enzyme inhibitors in the management of heart failure as reported by Luzier and DiTusa (1999) is, in part, a consequence of underrepresentation of all population subgroups in randomized clinical trials.

Conversely, Yancy et al. for the U.S. Carvedilol Heart Failure Study Group (2001) reported a benefit of similar magnitude in both Black and non-Black patients in a prospective cohort that included 19.8 percent Black patients (217 of 1,094). In summary, the current evidence for optimal management of heart failure is primarily based on clinical trial data that, with a few exceptions, do not include adequate representation of Blacks, women, and other population subgroups. Hence, optimal therapy for these groups may be incompletely or inadequately defined.

LIPID DISORDERS

Substantial literature supports lipid-lowering interventions for both primary and secondary prevention of cardiovascular events, but, as with other areas, minorities have not been adequately represented in the clinical trials. LaRossa (1995), reviewing the early trials of cholesterol reduction, noted that several issues were not addressed. Among these were the effect of reductions in triglycerides, increases in high-density lipoprotein, and the effects in women and individuals aged greater than 60 years. The question of differences among various population subgroups was not referenced. Even much of the epidemiological data that has established the range of serum cholesterol values in the population developing coronary heart disease is based on findings from the Framingham study, which represents a relatively homogeneous population sample (Kannel, 1995).

LaRossa et al. (1999) recently reported a meta-analysis of randomized clinical trials to assess the effect of statins on risk of coronary heart disease. Their analysis included a total cohort of 30,817 and included two primary prevention and three secondary prevention trials. The Air Force/Texas Coronary Atherosclerosis Prevention Study (AFCAPS/TexCAPS) consisted of a total cohort of 6,605 enrollees, of whom 3 percent were Black and 7 percent were Hispanic. In absolute numbers, there were 101 Black patients in the placebo limb and 105 in the intervention arm. The paucity of minority representation is somewhat surprising given that 3,337 of the total cohort of 6,605 were recruited from Lackland Air Force Base in San Antonio. Women represented 15 percent of the study cohort (Downs et al., 1998).

The West of Scotland Coronary Prevention Study (WOSCOPS) (Shepherd et al., 1995) included only White, middle-aged males. Of the secondary prevention trials, the Scandinavian Simvastin Survival Study (4S) (Scandinavian Simvastin Survival Study Group, 1994) enrolled subjects of primarily Nordic extraction; and the Long-term Intervention with Pravastatin in Ischemic Disease trial (LIPID) (Simes et al., 2002) enrolled subjects from 67 centers in Australia and 20 in New Zealand. The ethnic/racial breakdown of the 9,014 patient cohorts is not reported. Lastly, the CARE (Cholesterol and Recurrent Events) (Sacks et al., 1996) study's cohort is segregated as 92 percent and 93 percent Whites and 8 percent and 7 percent as other races in the placebo and treatment arms, respectively.

LaRossa et al. concluded that interventions with statins and the attendant reduction in LDL-Cholesterol decrease the risk of coronary heart disease and all-cause mortality. They also conclude that the risk reduction was similar for men and women as well as for both elderly (≥ 65 years of age) and middle-aged persons. However, they further note that currently available data do not allow them to draw any conclusions about these effects on total mortality "in these age and sex groups beyond those that are already published." The benefits of LDL-Cholesterol lowering from statin therapy "appear to be universal, not defined by sex or age." We would argue that lipid phenotype may be influenced by race/ethnicity and may represent a potentially important variable influencing outcomes. This factor has not been addressed in trials published to date. While Prisant et al. (1996) and Jacobson et al. (1995) have demonstrated the safety of statins in Black Americans, it again begs the question if statin therapy will have the same effect in reducing cardiovascular morbidity and mortality.

It is anticipated that the recently completed Antihypertensive Lipid Lowering Heart Attack Trial (ALLHAT) may be able to provide trial-based results on which to base statin therapy in Black Americans. Of the 10,362 patients randomized in the lipid arm of the trial, 38 percent were Black (n = 3938) and 49 percent were women (n = 5,077).

RECOMMENDATIONS AND CONCLUSIONS

Epidemiology

Cardiovascular diseases are the leading cause of morbidity and mortality in the U.S. population, and the age-adjusted death rates are highest for Black men and women. Because much of the epidemiological data is based on the Framingham Study, which does not include a substantial minority population, perhaps the first important question to address is, Why do Black Americans have a significantly higher morbidity and mortality from cardiovascular diseases as compared to White Americans?

It is hoped that answers to this above mentioned question will be provided by the Jackson Heart Study (JHS) (Crook & Taylor, 2002). As detailed by Taylor (2001), there are four primary goals of the JHS. These are (1) to establish a large-scale, single-site prospective epidemiological study of cardiovascular disease in Black Americans; (2) to identify risk factors for the development and progression of CVD in Black Americans; (3) to build research opportunities at minority institutions and expand minority investigator participation; and (4) to attract minorities to careers in public health and epidemiology. Based on modified projected estimates, the study expects to enroll 5,500 Black men and women from the tri-county area around Jackson, Mississippi, who will be followed prospectively to determine the role of cardiovascular risk factor clustering in the development of atherosclerotic disease. At the time of this writing, 90 percent, or approximately 5,000, of the projected target of participants have been successfully recruited (Personal communication January 27, 2004, between A. Cuyjet with H. Taylor). The JHS will also seek to assess the impact of sociocultural factors in the development of cardiovascular disease and to examine the role of environmental and familial factors. Lastly, JHS will look for novel risk factors that may account for the increased cardiovascular morbidity and mortality in this population. The study participants will be followed for three years and, when completed, the JHS will be the largest epidemiologic investigation of cardiovascular disease among Black Americans. It is hoped that the findings from this study will provide the basis for future clinical trials to assess the efficacy of interventions for primary and secondary prevention.

Interventions

Multiple randomized clinical trials that form the basis for evidence-based medicine have demonstrated the efficacy and safety of thrombolytic therapy, percutaneous transluminal angioplasty, and antiplatelet interventions in the management of acute myocardial infarction and acute coronary syndromes; the reduced morbidity and mortality with appropriate treatment in the management of heart failure; and the safety and efficacy of statin therapy for primary and secondary prevention of coronary heart disease. None of these data sets, in aggregate, include adequate representation of Black Americans or other population subgroups, and, therefore, conclusions and recommendations derived from these studies and applied to other groups represent an extrapolation of the study conclusions. It is unknown whether or how this impacts disparities with respect to outcomes. Repeating prospective randomized trials to include the appropriate population subgroups cannot be ethically done for interventions of proven benefit. Therefore, the information may be inferentially derived from prospective case-control studies, equivalency trials, or registry databases. However, we clearly need to increase participation and enrollment of all underrepresented groups in future clinical trials and for trials conducted in the United States, especially enrollment of Black Americans.

We also need to increase minority representation as researchers and trialists, and we need important epidemiological data to understand the root causes for the increased cardiovascular burden among Black Americans. Hopefully the Jackson Heart Study (JHS) will provide these answers. As detailed by Taylor (2001), there are four primary goals of the JHS. These are (1) to establish a large-scale, single-site prospective epidemiological study of cardiovascular disease in Black Americans; (2) to identify risk factors for the development and progression of CVD in Black Americans; (3) to build research opportunities at minority institutions and expand minority investigator participation; and (4) to attract minorities to careers in public health and epidemiology.

Health Disparities Research

Since trials of proven benefit cannot be ethically repeated with placebo limbs, Baquet et al. (2002) have proposed a model for formally conducting health disparities research. The components of the model include:

1. Surveillance, which includes selection of a specific disparity by race/ethnicity, geographic location, age or socioeconomic status and disease category and selection of a desired outcome with a comparison population.
2. Explanatory Research, which includes incidence and mortality disparities, evaluation of behavioral and cultural factors, access to health services, geographic influences, prognostic factors, genetic/biological factors, and the impact of race versus social class as factors.
3. Intervention Research, Development, and Evaluation, which includes the development and evaluation of the intervention designed to reduce or eliminate the disparity.

4. Translation/Application of Research Results, which includes the application of results to the defined population and evaluation of the intervention application.

Adoption of a formal research model to address current disparities and allocation of adequate resources to conduct the appropriate studies should begin to focus on, and sustain attention on, the issue of health-care disparities as well as provide answers that lead to effective interventions based on the evidence. Further, federal guidelines should rigorously mandate inclusion criteria for future prospective clinical trials to ensure that they are adequately powered to provide conclusive evidence for all appropriate population subgroups.

Health-care Policy

Fiscella et al. (2000) propose that disparities in health care should be considered a quality issue and may be addressed through organizational quality improvement. They argue that health care alone cannot eliminate disparities that are attributable to socioeconomic, cultural, and educational factors and that it is difficult to isolate disparities due to racial/ethnic causes from those due to socioeconomic causes.

The National Conference on Cardiovascular Disease Prevention (Cooper et al., 2000), recognizing the striking differences in cardiovascular death rates by race/ethnicity, socioeconomic status, and geography, recommended a comprehensive, population-wide approach with attention to all population subgroups that emphasizes primary risk factor prevention and risk factor detection and management.

Lastly, the results of recently completed or soon to be completed clinical trials, such as ALLHAT and AASK, that directly impact recommendations to clinical practice in Black Americans and other minority or population subgroups, should be applied as quickly as possible, perhaps utilizing the quality improvement model as an impetus.

CANCER CLINICAL TRIALS

Childhood Cancer Survival Is Not Race-Dependent

One of the initial speakers at the "Overcoming 'Bad Blood' in Cancer Clinical Trials: Tuskegee Trial Revisited" Conference, held on the campus of Tuskegee University in Alabama on February 23–25, 1997, was Dr. W. Archie Bleyer. Bleyer, at that time, was professor and head of pediatric oncology at the M.D. Anderson Cancer Center. He was also group chairman of the Children's Cancer Group (CCG). He pointed out the fact that nationally, 75 percent of children at that time were on clinical trials, with survivorship in this group steadily advancing over the last 20 years. However, adolescent patients between the ages of 15 and 19 with cancer were not usually on clinical trials, where only 5 percent of all adults with cancer were on clinical trials (Bleyer, 1997). Dr. Bleyer also pointed out that children, the majority of whom were African American children with cancer and who did not live in a rural setting, had the benefit of participating in clinical trials.

A 30-year review was performed of 5,305 children and adolescents younger than 21 years of age treated for a newly diagnosed cancer, other than brain tumors, at St. Jude Children's Research Hospital. It was found that there was less than 2 percent lost to follow-up (Pui et al., 1995). In the "early" treatment era, African American children did significantly poorer in this population studied than White children for all forms of cancer combined ($p < .001$), with ten-year Kaplan-Meier estimates of 37 percent, +/− 3 percent for African American children versus 50 percent, +/− 1 percent for White children. This difference largely reflected the poorer prognosis of African American children with the most common childhood cancer, acute lymphoblastic leukemia (ALL). After 1968, practically all children at St. Jude were treated on clinical trials, and in the "recent" treatment era, there are no significant differences in treatment outcome by race for specific disease categories for all forms of cancer combined. The ten-year survival rates were 67 percent, $+/-$ 6 percent for African American children and 66 percent, $+/-$ 3 percent for White children, a significant improvement for African American children.

The Perpetuating Myth that African Americans Don't Participate in Clinical Trials

The Radiation Therapy Oncology Group (RTOG), a multi-institutional cooperative organization funded by the National Cancer Institute and involving clinical trials that involve radiation therapy alone or in conjunction with surgery and/or chemotherapeutic drugs, decided to assess the degree to which the sociodemographic characteristics of patients enrolled in RTOG clinical trials were representative of the general population (Chamberlain et al., 1998). Sociodemographic data were collected on 4,016 patients entered in 33 open RTOG studies between July 1991 and June 1994. The data were analyzed using—unique at that time for a cooperative clinical trials group—a Demographic Data Form (A5 Form) developed by members of the Special Population Committee of the RTOG. This Demographic Data Form (A5 Form) included educational attainment, age, gender, and race. For comparison, the authors obtained similar data from the U.S. Department of Census 1990 data sample. Also compared were the RTOG data with Surveillance Epidemiology and End Results (SEER) data for patients who received radiation therapy to determine how RTOG patients compared with cancer patients in general and with patients with cancers at sites typically treated with radiotherapy. The results were quite revealing. Despite the public perception that African Americans do not volunteer for clinical trials, the results were contrary to this perception. In fact, in every age group of African American men and at nearly every level of educational attainment, the proportion of RTOG trial participants mirrored the proportion in the census data.

Of the 4,016 patients entered into 33 RTOG cancer trials, 3,375 patients had newly diagnosed cancer; of these, 170 (5.0 percent) did not complete the questionnaire, in and of itself an extraordinarily high completion rate. The data included adequate numbers of Whites, 2,426 (87.7 percent) and African American patients, 339 (12.3 percent), for a total of 2,765 patients for analysis in this study. Other racial groups had insufficient numbers to make comparisons, 170 (5.3 percent) were Hispanic, and 73 (2.3 percent) were of other ethnicities, where four in this group did not answer the questions.

More than a third (36.5 percent) of the patients had attended college or technical school, and another third (32.8 percent) had graduated from high school only. Only 18 patients (0.5 percent) reported never attending any school. More than 99 percent of the individuals surveyed answered questions regarding their race and marital status. Questions related to education and birth date were also usually answered, a 93 percent compliance, unheard of in any other study of such large numbers.

For every age group and at each level of educational attainment, the proportions of White RTOG patients were comparable to the proportions in the census and SEER data. The proportion of African American male subjects 65 years old or older was comparable with the census data in the age and educational categories. Significant differences were noted only in the youngest category of African American men, where the RTOG accrues more in the lower educational categories and fewer with college experience for the time period analyzed (June 1991 through June 1994). In the age group 20–54 years, 45.3 percent of the African American male RTOG participants did not complete high school in comparison with 18.9 percent in the U.S. census ($p = 0.0001$). Similar, but not statistically significant, comparisons were observed in the 55–64-year group ($p = 0.09$).

As with men, RTOG trials accrued a considerably larger proportion of younger, less educated African American women than the census reported. In the 20–54-year-old group, 52.3 percent of the African American female trial participants had attained less than 12th grade education compared with 17.5 percent in the census ($p = 0.0001$). For other age groups, the results for African American women parallel with the data sample from the 1990 census data sample. What also surprised Chamberlain et al., using SEER for comparison was that the RTOG enrolled proportionately more African American men to trials when all cancer sites were combined, for prostate and head and neck cancer trials in particular. In head and neck trials, the RTOG enrolled nearly twice as many African American men as would be predicted by SEER data. In lung cancer clinical trials, RTOG underrepresented African American men significantly (7.9 percent of RTOG trials, N = 178 vs. 17.6 percent of the SEER data, $p = .041$); however there was no difference in brain cancer trials (3.0 percent of RTOG trials, N = 325 vs. 3.0 percent of the SEER data, $p = 0.93$). There were no racial differences in RTOG accrual and SEER incidence data for women on trials in brain, lung, and head and neck cancer. However, the trials accrued nearly twice the proportion of African American women in cervical cancer trials and in all sites combined, compared to the SEER data. It must be noted that most of the RTOG member institutions at that time were mainly located in medium-sized to large urban areas, where most African Americans live. A significant overrepresentation of less-educated African Americans in the youngest age category were trial participants. This is counter to the expectation that better-educated patients are more likely to enroll in trials.

African American Women in Breast Cancer Clinical Trials

Looking at the most representative trial that compared Black and White females with breast cancer receiving comparable doses of Adriamycin-based therapy, now a standard in chemotherapy, was the Cancer and Leukemia Group B Trial 8541 (CALGB 8541) analysis of Black and White females by Roach et al. (1997). Univariate analysis (Cox Regression Model) comparing Blacks and Whites shows a risk ratio of overall survival in favor of Whites of 1.35 (95 percent CI, 1.01-1.80, $p = 0.04$), but a disease-free survival (DFS) RR of 1.24 (95 percent CI, 0.97–1.58, $p = 1.24$).

African American Men on Prostate Cancer Clinical Trials

In five randomized clinical trials (RCT) evaluating prostate cancer treatment that had more than ten Blacks in each arm, Streeter and Roach (1999) reviewed those studies (Crawford et al., 1990; Kennealey et al., 1996; Roach, Krall et al., 1992; Smith et al., 1996; Vogelzang et al., 1995). The outcomes in these randomized trials, with comparable care, was either equal outcomes for African American patients in four studies when corrected for severity of disease, to do better in one study, or to do worse in two early studies in the pre-PSA screening era, when Blacks had higher acid phosphatase levels.

Esophageal Cancer Outcomes for African Americans Receiving Chemoradiation

In reported retrospective nonrandomized trials of esophageal carcinoma, African Americans have a reported lower survival from esophageal cancer than Whites. None of these studies accounted for the extent of disease or the methods and quality of treatment. Streeter et al. (1999) reviewed the data that included only patients treated on the chemoradiation arm of the RTOG-8501 esophageal carcinoma trial, which has become the standard of care for nonresected esophageal cancer (Al-Sarraf et al., 1997; Herskovic et al., 1992). The purpose was to see if there were any differences in overall survival between African American and White patients receiving the same standard of care (Streeter et al., 1999).

In the combined modality arm of RTOG-8501, there were 119 patients, 37 African Americans and 82 Whites, who met the treatment criteria for receiving the "standard of care" of 5000 cGy and four courses of Cisplatin (75 mg/m^2) and Fluorouracil (1,000 mg/m^2 for four days). The results showed that despite African American patients having larger tumors at presentation, higher incidence of weight loss of ten pounds or more, and more difficulty swallowing at time of study entry, race did not appear to be a statistically significant factor for overall survival in a Cox regression model analysis. For Whites the Kaplan-Meier median overall survival was 17 months, and for Blacks it was 14.1 months (unadjusted $p = 0.2757$). This finding was consistent with a growing body of literature that race alone does not determine survival when the extent of disease is accounted for and all patients receive the same standard of care, which is afforded to patients that participate in cancer clinical trials (Dignam et al., 1997; Pui et al., 1995; Roach, Alexander et al., 1992; Roach et al., 1997; Roach, Krall et al., 1992).

African Americans and White Americans Fare Equally on Clinical Trials

Peter Bach et al. in a review of MEDLINE English-language abstracts from 1966 through January 2000 reported an overall survival for Black and White patients treated similarly for cancer. Studies were included that had at least 10 Blacks and Whites using actuarial measures; presented outcomes within stage, adjusted for stage, or based on cohorts with balanced stage distributions; and specified that Blacks and Whites in the study received similar treatment. This reduced the number from 891 initial citations to 89 unique cohorts in 54 articles that met their stringent inclusion criteria. Data synthesis resulted in 189,877 White and 32,004 Black patients with 14 different cancers. Compared with Whites, Blacks had an overall excess risk of death (Hazard Ratio [HR], 1.16; 95 percent confidence interval [CI], 1.12-1.20). However, after correction for deaths due to other causes, the cancer-specific HR was reduced to 1.07 (95 percent CI, 1.02–1.13). Of the 14 cancers, Blacks were at a significantly higher risk of cancer-specific death only for cancer of the breast, uterus, or bladder. The conclusion of the authors was that there were only modest cancer-specific survival differences for Blacks and Whites treated for similar-stage cancer. The most important part of this analysis was that differences in cancer biology between racial groups are unlikely to be responsible for a substantial portion of the survival discrepancy (Bach et al., 2002).

RESEARCH AND CLINICAL TRIALS FOR CHRONIC KIDNEY DISEASE INVOLVING AFRICAN AMERICANS

Introduction

Since the initial Medicare funding in 1972 for the End-Stage Renal Disease (ESRD) Program, there has been a rapid and continuous rise in the number of patients receiving dialysis and/or transplantation for the treatment of ESRD (U.S. Renal Data System, 2002). As early as 1977 a report by Easterling (1977) and subsequently others (Ferguson et al., 1987; Jones & Agodoa, 1993; Martins et al., 2002; Norris & Agodoa, 2002; Norris & Owen, 1995; Rostand et al., 1982) noted significant racial differences in the incidence of ESRD. The greatest disparity continues to be for African Americans, who suffer from the highest rate of ESRD in the country (995 cases/million), a fourfold greater incidence as compared to Whites (254 cases/million) (U.S. Renal Data System, 2002).

A recent analysis of the third National Health and Nutrition Examination Survey (NHANES 3)

Table 46.1
National Kidney Foundation—Kidney disease outcomes quality initiative (NKF-F/DOQI) classification of chronic kidney disease

Stage	Description	GFR (mL/min/1.73m^2)
1	Kidney damage with normal or ↑ GFR	>90
2	Mild ↓ GFR	60-89
3	Moderate ↓ GFR	30-59
4	Severe ↓ GFR	15-29
5	Kidney failure	<15 or dialysis

Source: National Kidney Foundation (NKF) (2002).

suggested that as many as ten million Americans have chronic kidney disease (CKD), with the prevalence being greatest among African Americans (Jones et al., 1998). Moreover, CKD is one of 28 focus areas highlighted in *Healthy People 2010*, the nation's blueprint to increase quality and years of healthy life and eliminate health disparities (U.S. Department of Health and Human Services, 2000). The national recognition of CKD as a critical area of racial/ethnic disparity in health status highlights the magnitude and clinical importance of this issue as a critical area of not only individual but public health concern.

Etiology

The disproportionately high rates of ESRD among African Americans are linked to a similar disparity in the prevalence of CKD, which, like ESRD, is driven primarily by diabetes and hypertension (Coresh et al., 2001; Jones et al., 1998; Klag et al., 1997; Nzerue et al., 2002). CKD was recently stratified into five stages to better assist in the early identification and clinical management of afflicted patients (see Table 46.1). A summary of many of the contributing factors underlying the high rates of CKD and ESRD within the African American community is listed in Table 46.2.

Treatment, Prevention, and/or Intervention of CKD

Not unlike many other areas of health care, even when African Americans are afflicted at disproportionately high rates, many of the renal clinical trials contain relatively few African American participants. Indeed, the landmark trial by Lewis and colleagues, which demonstrated the efficacy of angiotensin converting enzyme inhibitors (ACEI) in reducing the progression of CKD in 409 participants with Type I diabetes, included only 15 African Americans (Lewis et al., 1993). This was critical since ACEI were felt to be of limited value in African Americans due to reports of lesser antihypertensive efficacy (Lewis et al., 1993; Materson & Reda, 1994; Materson et al., 1994), and thus the study provided no new data to suggest ACEI might be an effective treatment for African Americans with diabetic nephropathy and hypertension.

A subanalysis of the Modification of Diet in Renal Disease Study suggested that a lower mean

Table 46.2
Key contributing factors to increased risk for kidney disease among African Americans

High prevalence of Diabetes	High prevalence of Hypertension
Sub-optimal quality of and access to medical care	Excess exposure to environmental nephrotoxins such as heavy metals
Cultural beliefs/attitudes that delay presentation to a health care provider and adherence to recommendations	Potential genetic predisposition to developing chronic kidney disease and /or receptor polymorphisms affecting response to therapy
Dietary habits such as high sodium and fat intake	Excessive use of illicit or prescribed drugs

Sources: Chuahirun & Wesson (2002); Coresh et al. (2001); Freedman et al. (1999); Jones et al. (1998); Klag et al. (1997); Norris et al. (2001); Nzerue & Hewan-Lowe (2000); Perneger et al. (1994); Winston et al. (1998).

arterial pressure might be necessary for optimal renal protection in African Americans or any patient with proteinuria (more than 1 gram/day), but only 53 of the 548 enrollees were African American (Hebert et al., 1997). The African American Study of Kidney Disease and Hypertension (AASK) is the largest prospective CKD study to focus on, and successfully recruit, African American participants (Whelton et al., 1996). AASK examined the effects of two levels of blood pressure (usual, ~135–140/85–90 and strict ≤ 120/80 mmHg blood pressure control) and three classes of initial antihypertensive therapy (ACEI, beta blocker [BB] or calcium channel blocker [CCB]) on the progression of hypertensive renal disease and clinical outcomes (Agodoa et al., 2001). The AASK results suggest that blood pressure can be controlled in African Americans with CKD (Wright, Agodoa et al., 2002), and outcomes were improved when achieving either the usual and low blood pressure goal when ACEI, BB, or CCB was used as initial therapy with diuretics and other agents added as needed to reach target levels (Bakris et al., 2000; Wright, Bakris et al., 2002). Importantly, secondary clinical outcomes including the development of ESRD, doubling of serum creatinine, or death were lower in the ACEI group in comparison to the beta blocker and dihydropyridine calcium channel blocker, suggesting that ACEI inhibitors should be used as initial antihypertensive therapy in African Americans with hypertensive nephrosclerosis, contrary to previous suggestions (Agodoa et al., 2001; Wright, Bakris et al., 2002).

Cardiovascular and renal protective effects in subjects with CKD via inhibition of the renin-angiotensin system were also supported by the Microalbuminuria, Cardiovascular, and Renal Outcomes (MICRO-HOPE) substudy of the Heart Outcomes Prevention Evaluation (HOPE) Study Investigators (2002). More recently, another class of drugs that block the renin-angiotensin system, the angiontensin receptor blockers (ARBs), has been reported in three large multicenter clinical trials to delay the progression of diabetic nephropathy (Brenner et al., 2001; Lewis et al., 2001; Parving et al., 2001). While the study had only 16 non-Whites of 590 total participants (Parving et al., 2001), the "Renoprotective effect of the angiotensin-receptor antagonist Irbesartan in patients with nephropathy due to type 2 diabetes" study had 228 Blacks of 1,715 total participants (Lewis et al., 2001) and the "Effects of Losartan on renal and cardiovascular outcomes in patients with type 2 diabetes and nephropathy" study (Brenner et al., 2001) had 230 Blacks of 1,513 total participants. Although these numbers are not sufficient for generating independent analyses, the inclusion of nearly15 percent Black participants in the latter two studies strongly suggests that the positive outcomes extended to Blacks, as well as non-Blacks.

The emerging data from prospective randomized trials suggests that interruption of the renin-angiotensin system as initial therapy for treating hypertensive and diabetic nephropathy, the two leading causes of ESRD in African Americans, confers additional protection beyond blood pressure control, with a goal of achieving blood pressure levels below 140/90 mmHg and possibly below 120–130/75–80 mmHg in patients with heavy proteinuria and/or diabetes (Bakris et al., 2000). Importantly, these recommendations hold true for African Americans.

RECOMMENDATIONS AND FUTURE PROSPECTS

The well-documented racial/ethnic clustering of CKD and ESRD provides a solid background for the critical need to develop effective public health strategies, including community-based education and screening and ensuring adequate resources to support cost-effective early treatment of CKD. These strategies must focus on the CKD risk factors outlined in Table 46.2, with a major emphasis on the two leading risk factors, diabetes and hypertension (Crook & Taylor, 2002). Developing linguistically and culturally sensitive/appropriate educational messages and the inclusion of "at-risk" communities as partners in developing effective outreach programs are critical strategies for success. It is estimated that early treatment of CKD could reduce national health-care costs for ESRD by as much as $60 billion over the next ten years (Trivedi et al., 2002), not including the reduction in personal affliction/suffering, lost wages, and family/community impact.

Summary

African Americans continue to suffer from disproportionately high rates of both CKD and ESRD. Diabetes and hypertension account for over 70 percent of U.S. patients entering the ESRD program. The development and implementation of prevention strategies and early interventions must remain the cornerstone of addressing the CKD. Hopefully, these actions will attenuate the progressive rise in CKD and ESRD with their attendant costs in individual/community burden and rising health-care expenditures and ultimately contribute to achieving the national health goals outlined by former surgeon general David Satcher to increase quality and years of healthy life and to eliminate health disparities.

CLINICAL TRIALS FOR AIDS

History of HIV/AIDS Clinical Trial

When AIDS first emerged in the United States as a public health problem, there was no drug to combat the underlying immune deficiency, and very little treatments existed to address its associated opportunistic diseases. However, over the past 20 years, HIV/AIDS clinical trials have resulted in the development of drugs to fight both HIV infection and its concomitant diseases. At the forefront of these efforts is the National Institute of Allergy and Infectious Diseases (NIAID).

NIAID's AIDS research agenda includes funding research programs that increase basic knowledge of the pathogenesis, natural history, and transmission of HIV disease and to support research that promotes progress in its detection, treatment, and prevention. These programs include the Adult AIDS Clinical Trials Group (AACTG), the Pediatric AIDS Clinical Trials Group (PACTG), the Terry Beirn Community Programs for Clinical Research on AIDS (CPCRA), the HIV Vaccine Trials Network (HVTN), and the HIV Prevention Trials Network (HPTN). The clinical and organizational components of these programs are funded through cooperative agreements. These programs collectively are the largest AIDS treatment and prevention initiative in the United States (National Institute of Allergy and Infectious Diseases, 2002).

The Adult AIDS Clinical Trials Group (AACTG) is the largest HIV clinical trials organization in the world. It is a nationwide multicenter clinical trial network that investigates therapeutic interventions for HIV infection, AIDS, and complications of HIV-associated immune deficiency in adults. AACTG plays a major role in setting standards of care for HIV infection and opportunistic diseases related to HIV/AIDS in the United States and the developed world. The AACTG has been pivotal in providing the data necessary for the approval of therapeutic agents, as well as the treatment and prevention strategies, for many opportunistic infections and malignancies. The AACTG is an expansion of NIAID's first major program to evaluate potential treatments for people with AIDS, which began in the summer of 1986.

In 1996, the original AIDS Clinical Trials Group branched into two separate programs, the Adult AIDS Clinical Trials Group and the Pediatric AIDS Clinical Trials Group (PACTG). The PACTG is a national multicenter clinical trials network that conducts studies designed to evaluate treatments for HIV-infected children and adolescents and for developing new approaches for the interruption of mother-to-infant HIV transmission. The PACTG is a joint effort of the National Institute of Allergy and Infectious Diseases (NIAID) and the National Institute for Child Health and Human Development (NICHD). It includes the Community Programs for Clinical Research on AIDS (CPCRA), the AIDS Vaccine Evaluation Group (AVEG), the Division of AIDS Treatment Research Initiative (DATRI), and the pharmaceutical industry-sponsored studies for IIIV-infected adults (NIAID, 2001).

The Community Programs for Clinical Research of AIDS (CPCRA) is a network of community-based health centers and clinics that conduct research through a national network of community-based clinical units in areas of the country hardest hit by the HIV epidemic. CPCRA's research agenda centers around a core of antiretroviral treatment trials that are augmented with substudies and other trials focused on issues of current interest. The CPCRA was established in 1989 to expand research opportunities to communities of color, to women, and to others affected by HIV (NIAID, 2001). NIAID also supports clinical research on vaccine and nonvaccine strategies to prevent HIV infection through HVTN and the HPTN, respectively. The HVTN and HPTN opened in 2000 and have enrolled thousands of study participants.

The HVTN is a global network of clinical sites that evaluate preventive HIV vaccine in all phases of clinical trials. HIVNET's goals are to conduct domestic and international multicenter trials to evaluate promising vaccines and other interventions to prevent sexual, perinatal, and parenteral transmission of HIV. The domestic HIVNET sites have implemented the Vaccine Preparedness Study (VPS) to determine HIV seroincidence, the relative risk of HIV seroconversion with counseling, and the willingness of individuals to enroll in HIV vaccine efficacy trials (NIAID, 2001).

AFRICAN AMERICAN PARTICIPATION IN AIDS CLINICAL TRIALS

Since 1986, more than 50,000 volunteers have enrolled in AACTG studies. In 1996, 35 percent of the patients enrolled in AACTG trials were African American, 25 percent were Hispanic/Latino, and 1.5 percent were other minorities (NIAID, 2001). In 2001, 52 percent of persons enrolled in AACTG studies were Whites, 26 percent African American, 19 percent Hispanic, and 3 percent

Asian/Pacific Islander or Native American (NIAID, 2002). For the PACTG studies, more than 18,000 children, adolescents, and pregnant women have been enrolled since 1987.

Unlike the AACTG studies, there has been greater enrollment of African Americans in PACTG studies. In 1996, approximately 52 percent of the patients enrolled in the PACTG studies were African American, 29.7 percent were Hispanic/Latino, and less than 1 percent were other minorities (NIAID, 2001). In 2001, 47 percent of the patients enrolled in PACTG were African American, 25 percent were Hispanic, and 1 percent Asian/Pacific Islander or Native American (NIAID, 2002). CPCRA 16 enrolling units and 160 collaborating sites have enrolled more than 25,000 HIV-infected individuals in clinical trials. In 2001, 4,244 people participated in CPCRA studies. Of those, 49 percent were African American, 13 percent were Hispanic, and 1 percent were Native American or Asian/Pacific Islander. In 2001, HVTN and HPTN studies enrolled 383 and 9,517 people, respectively. Of those in the HVTN, 21 percent were African American, 3 percent were Hispanic, and 1 percent Native American or Asian/Pacific Islander. In the HPTN, 57 percent of participants were African American, 7 percent Hispanic, and about 3 percent Native American or Asian/Pacific Islander. The VPS has enrolled participants at high risk for HIV infection, including gay men, IDUs, and women at heterosexual risk. Two of these cohorts, IDUs and women, involve predominantly minorities (NIAID, 2002).

Differences in Clinical Trial Outcomes

It is difficult to discern whether or not there are differences in clinical outcomes for African Americans enrolled in AIDS clinical trials. Historically, most AIDS clinical trials have not reported racial and/or ethnic differences in outcomes among study participants. In initial studies of the efficacy of zidovudine (AZT) on patients with AIDS, very few studies reported on racial ethnic differences of study participants. In those instances that race and ethnicity were reported (Diaz et al., 1995; Fischl et al., 1990; Jacobson et al., 1996; Lagakos et al., 1991; Volberding et al., 1990), the number of African Americans who were enrolled in these studies was so small that statistical analysis to explain differences between treatment arms was not possible (El-Sadr & Capps, 1992).

In recent years there has been an increase in the number of African Americans enrolled in clinical trials as indicated by the AACTG, PACTG, and the CPCRA. However, because data from most of the privately funded trials, unpublished studies, and expanded-access program access are unavailable (Gifford et al., 2002), it is still largely unknown whether or not differences in therapeutic outcomes in AIDS clinical trials can be attributed to racial and ethnic differences.

The central issue for African Americans in relation to AIDS clinical trials is access. Although African Americans are disproportionately impacted by HIV/AIDS, they are underrepresented in AIDS research (El-Sadr & Capps, 1992; Gifford et al., 2002; King, 2002; Mabunda-Temple, 1998; Sengupta et al., 2000; Stone et al., 1997). Historically, enrollment of African Americans in AIDS clinical trials have been less than the national prevalence rate for African Americans diagnosed with AIDS (Sengupta et al., 2000). Despite efforts to improve minority enrollment from the onset of AIDS into clinical trials, underenrollment of African Americans continues.

The lack of participation in AIDS clinical trials creates a host of challenges in explaining whether or not there are differences in clinical outcomes that can be attributed to race and/or ethnicity. The reasons for the underrepresentation of African Americans in AIDS clinical trials are similar to those of other clinical trials where there is underenrollment of African Americans. The factors include, but are not limited to, distrust of the medical institution, physician's attitude, patient's knowledge of clinical trials, and structural factors such as poverty and access to medical care (Corbie-Smith et al., 1999; Gifford et al., 2002; Sengupta et al., 2000; Shavers-Homaday et al., 1997; Stone et al., 1997). These issues are seldom considered by sponsors of clinical trials (El-Sadr & Capps, 1992).

SUMMARY OF HIV/AIDS CLINICAL TRIALS

It is incumbent for both potential patients and researchers to both participate and reach out to the underserved and minority groups for participation in clinical trials in all areas of disease research. More than technical (a surgery technique, radiation technique, a monitoring device), pharmaceutical advances require testing on a diverse group of ethnic populations not only for validation of widespread efficacy but for safety. We do know, especially in cancer, heart disease, hypertension, and renal disease, research leads to improved quality-of-life interventions for African American patients. We must continue to participate and support research in these areas that lead to early mortality in significant portions of our society. More importantly, in HIV/AIDS research, we must articulate to the population that is HIV positive the history of research in this area, how it had led to extended life for so many, and that further research will continue this positive past.

Implications

There are several implications for the underrepresentation of African Americans in AIDS clinical trials. Most notable is that because African Americans are underenrolled, they will not benefit from the therapeutic drugs and vaccines that are emerging (Mabunda-Temple, 1998). Individuals in clinical trials generally benefit from their participation, even though the effectiveness of experimental treatments has not been demonstrated. Moreover, patients with little social resources benefit from participating in these clinical trials because they may also receive medical care and other resources. Prospective patients also benefit when participation in research is inclusive enough that results may be generalized to the patient who ultimately will use the drugs (Gifford et al., 2002). Race and genetic factors may play a central role in the variability of patients' response to a medication. However, given the paucity of data on the effectiveness of new drugs in members of minority group, this is still, for the most part, unknown (King, 2002).

REFERENCES

Agodoa, L.Y., et al. (2001). Effect of ramipril versus amlodipine on renal outcomes in hypertensive nephrosclerosis—A randomized controlled trial. *Journal of the American Medical Association, 285,* 2719–2728.

Al-Sarraf, M., et al. (1997). Progress report of combined chemoradiotherapy versus radiotherapy alone in patients with esophageal cancer: An intergroup study. *Journal of Clinical Oncology, 15,* 277–284.

American College of Cardiology/American Heart Association. (2001). Guidelines for the evaluation and management of chronic heart failure in the adult: Executive summary. *Journal of the American College of Cardiology, 38,* 2101–2113.

Bach, P.B., Schrag, D., Brawley, O.W., Galaznik, A., Yakren, S., & Begg, C.B. (2002). Survival of Blacks and Whites after a cancer diagnosis. *Journal of the American Medical Association, 287(16),* 2106–2113.

Bakris, G.L., et al. (2000). Preseving renal function in adults with hypertension and diabetes: A consensus approach. *American Journal of Kidney Disease, 36,* 646–661.

Baquet, C.R., Hammond, C., Commiskey, P., Brooks, S., & Mullins, C.D. (2002). Health disparities research—a model for conducting research on cancer disparities: Characterization and reduction. *Journal of the Association for Academic Minority Physicians, 13,* 33–40.

Barton, S. (2002). Heart failure: What are the effects of treatments? *Clinical Evidence Concise, 7,* 9–11.

Bleyer, W.A. (1997, February 24). Adolescents in National Cancer Trials. Paper presented at the Overcoming "Bad Blood" in Cancer Clinical Trials, Tuskegee Revisited, Tuskegee, AL.

Brawley, O.W. (1998). The study of untreated syphilis in the Negro male. *International Journal of Radiation Oncology Biology Physics, 40(1),* 5–8.

Brenner, B.M., et al. (2001). Effects of losartan on renal and cardiovascular outcomes in patients with type 2 diabetes and nephropathy. *New England Journal of Medicine, 345(12),* 861–869.

Chamberlain, R.M., et al. (1998). Sociodemographic analysis of patients in Radiation Therapy Oncology Group clinical trials. *International Journal of Radiation Oncology Biology Physics, 40(1)*, 9–15.

Chen, J., Rathore, S.S., Radford, M.J., Wang, Y., & Krumholz, H.M. (2001). Racial differences in the use of cardiac catherization after acute myocardial infarction. *New England Journal of Medicine, 344*, 1443–1449.

Cheng, T.O. (1999). Acronyms of clinical trials in cardiology—1998. *American Heart Journal, 137*, 726–765.

Chuahirun, T., & Wesson, D.E. (2002). Cigarette smoking predicts faster progression of type 2 established diabetic nephropathy despite ACE inhibition. *American Journal of Kidney Disease, 39(2)*, 376–382.

Clark, L.T., et al. (2001). Coronary heart disease in African Americans. *Heart Disease, 3*, 97–108.

Cohn, J.N., Tognoni, G., Glazer, R., & Spormann, D. (2000). Baseline demographics of the Valsartan Heart Failure Trial. *European Journal of Heart Failure, 2*, 439–446.

Cooper, R., et al. (2000). Trends and disparities in coronary heart disease, stroke, and other cardiovascular diseases in the United States—findings of the national conference on cardiovascular disease prevention. *Circulation, 102*, 3137–3147.

Corbie-Smith, G., Thomas, S.B., Williams, M.V., & Moody-Ayers, S. (1999). Attitudes and beliefs of African Americans toward participation in medical research. *Journal of General Internal Medicine, 14(9)*, 537–546.

Coresh, J., et al. (2001). Prevalence of high blood pressure and elevated serum creatinine level in the United States: Findings from the Third National Health and Nutrition Examination Survery (1988–1994). *Archives of Internal Medicine, 161*, 1207–1216.

Cox, J.D. (1998). Paternalism, informed consent and Tuskegee. *International Journal of Radiation Oncology Biology Physics, 40(1)*, 1–2.

Crawford, E.D., et al. (1990). Leuprolide with and without Flutamide in advanced prostate cancer. *Cancer, 66*, 1039–1044.

Crook, E.D., & Taylor, H. (2002). Traditional and non-traditional risk factors for cardiovascular and renal disease in African Americans: A project of the Jackson Heart Study Investigators. *American Journal of the Medical Sciences, 324(3)*, 115.

Curran, W.J., et al. (1993). Recursive partitioning analysis of prognostic factors in three Radiation Therapy Oncology Group malignant glioma trials. *J. National Cancer Institute, 85*, 704–710.

Dans, A.L., Dans, L.F., Guyatt, G.H., & Richardson, S. (1998). Users' guides to the medical literature: XIV. How to decide on the applicability of clinical trial results to your patient. Evidence-Based Medicine Working Group. *Journal of the American Medical Association, 279*, 545–9.

Diaz, T., et al. (1995). Differences in participation in experimental drug trials among persons with AIDS. *Journal of Acquired Immune Deficiency Syndromes, 10(5)*, 562–568.

Dignam, J.J., Redmond, C., Fisher, B., Costantino, J., & Edwards, B. (1997). Prognosis among African-American women and lymph node negative breast carcinoma: Findings from two randomized clinical trials of the National Surgical Adjuvant Breast and Bowel Project (NSABP). *Cancer, 80*, 80–90.

Downs, J.R., et al. (1998). Primary prevention of acute coronary events with lovastatin in men and women with average cholesterol levels. *Journal of the American Medical Association, 279*, 1615–1622.

Easterling, R.E. (1977). Racial factors in the incidence and causation of end stage renal disease. *Transactions of the American Society for Artificial Internal Organs, 23*, 28–32.

Eichhorn, E.J., Domanski, M.J., Krause-Steinrauf, H., Bristow, M.R., & Lavori, P. (2001). A trial of the beta-blocker bucindolol in patients with advanced heart failure. *New England Journal of Medicine, 344*, 1659–1667.

El-Sadr, W., & Capps, L. (1992). The challenge of minority recruitment in clinical trials for AIDS. *Journal of the American Medical Association, 267*, 954–957.

Epstein, A.M., & Ayanian, J.Z. (2001). Racial disparities in medical care. *New England Journal of Medicine, 344*, 1471–1473.

Exner, D.V., Dries, D.L., Domanski, M.J., & Cohn, J.N. (2001). Lesser response to angiotensin-converting-enzyme inhibitor therapy in Black as compared with White patients with left ventricular dysfunction. *New England Journal of Medicine, 344*, 1351–1357.

Ferguson, R., Grim, C.E., & Opgenorth, J. (1987). The epidemiology of end-stage renal disease: The six year South Central Los Angeles experience, 1980–1985. *American Journal of Public Health, 77*, 864–874.

Fiscella, K., Franks, P., Gold, M.R., & Clancy, C.M. (2000). Inequality in quality-addressing socioeconomic, racial, and ethnic disparities in health care. *Journal of the American Medical Association, 283*, 2579–2584.

Fischl, M.A., et al. (1990). The safety and efficacy of zidovudine (AZT) in the treatment of subjects with mildly symptomatic human immunodeficiency virus type 1 (HIV) infection: A double-blind, placebo-controlled trial. *Annals of Internal Medicine, 112(18)*, 1373–1382.

Ford, E.S., & Cooper, R.S. (1995). Racial/ethnic differences in health care utilization of cardiovascular procedures: A review of the evidence. *HSR: Health Services Research, 30*, 238–251.

Freedman, B.I., Soucie, M.J., Stone, S.M., & Pegram, S. (1999). Familial clustering of end-stage renal disease in Blacks with HIV-associated nephropathy. *American Journal of Kidney Disease, 34(2)*, 254–258.

Gifford, A.L., et al. (2002). Participation in research and access to experimental treatments by HIV-infected patients. *New England Journal of Medicine, 345(18)*, 1373–1582.

Gillum, R.F., Gillum, B.S., & Francis, C.K. (1997). Coronary revascularization and cardiac catheterization in the United States: Trends in racial differences. *Journal of the American College of Cardiology, 29*, 1557–1562.

Graham, M.V., et al. (1992). Comparison of prognostic factors and survival for non-small cell lung cancer. *Journal of the National Cancer Institute, 84*, 1731–1735.

Hall, W.D. (1999). Representation of Blacks, women, and the very elderly (Aged≥80) in 28 major randomized clinical trials. *Ethnicity & Disease, 9*, 333–340.

Halpern, S.D., Karlawish, J.H.T., & Berlin, J.A. (2002). The continuing unethical conduct of underpowered clinical trials. *Journal of the Medical Association, 288*, 358–362.

Harris, Y., Gorelick, P.B., Samuels, P., & Bempong, I. (1996). Why African Americans may not be participating in clinical trials. *Journal of the National Medical Association, 88*, 630–634.

Heart Outcomes Prevention Evaluation (HOPE) Study Investigators. (2002). Effects of ramipril on cardiovascular and microvascular outcomes in people with diabetes mellitus: Results of the HOPE study and MICRO-HOPE substudy. *Lancet, 355*, 253–259.

Hebert, L.A., et al. (1997). Effects of blood pressure control on progressive renal disease in Blacks and Whites. *Hypertension, 30*, 428–435.

Heiat, A., Gross, C.P., & Krumholz, H.M. (2002). Representation of the elderly, women, and minorities in heart failure clinical trials. *Archives of Internal Medicine, 162*, 1682–1688.

Herskovic, A., et al. (1992). Combined chemotherapy and radiotherapy compared with radiotherapy alone in patients with cancer of the esophagus. *New England Journal of Medicine, 326(24)*, 1593–1598.

Jacobson, M.A., Gundacker, H., Hughes, M., Fischl, M.A., & Volberdine, P. (1996). Zidovudine side effects as reported by Black, Hispanic, and White/non-Hispanic patients with early HIV disease combined analysis of two multi-center placebo controlled trials. *Journal of Acquired Immune Deficiency Syndrome and Human Retrovirology, 11*, 45–52.

Jacobson, T.A., et al. (1995). Efficacy and safety of pravastatin in African Americans with primary hypercholesterolemia. *Archives of Internal Medicine, 155*, 1901–1906.

Jones, C.A., & Agodoa, L. (1993). Kidney disease and hypertension in Blacks: Scope of the problem. *American Journal of Kidney Disease, 21(4* [suppl]), 6–9.

Jones, C.A., et al. (1998). Serum creatinine levels in the U.S. population; Third National Health and Nutrition Examination Survey. *American Journal of Kidney Disease, 32(6)*, 992–999.

Jones, J. (1981). *Bad blood: The Tuskegee Syphilis Experiment*. New York: Free Press.

Kannel, W.B. (1995). Range of serum cholesterol values in the population developing coronary artery disease. *American Journal of Cardiology, 76*, 69C–77C.

Keil, J.E., Loadholt, C.B., Weinrich, M.C., Sandifer, S.H., & Boyle, E.J. (1984). Incidence of coronary heart disease in Blacks in Charleston, South Carolina. *American Heart Journal, 108 (Part 2)*, 779–786.

Keil, J.E., Sutherland, S.E., Knapp, R.G., Lackland, D.T., Gazes, P.G., & Tyroler, H.A. (1993). Mortality rates and risk factors for coronary disease in Black as compared with White men and women. *New England Journal of Medicine, 329*, 73–78.

Kennealey, G.T., et al. (1996). Analysis of time to treatment failure by extent of disease and race in a randomized, multicenter trial comparing Casodex (Bicalutamide) (C) with Eulexin (Flutamide) (E), each combined with Luteinizing Hormone Releasing Hormone. *Proceedings of the American Society of Clinical Oncologists, 15*, 251.

Keppel, K.G., Pearcy, J.N., & Wagener, D.K. (2002). Trends in racial and ethnic-specific rates for health status indicators: United States, 1990–98. Department of Health and Human Services. Centers for Disease Control and Prevention National Center for Health Statistics. *Healthy People 2000: Statistical Notes, 23*, 1–16.

King, T.E. (2002). Racial disparities in clinical trials. *New England Journal of Medicine, 346*, 1400–1402.

Klag, M.J., Stamler, J., Brancati, F.L., Neaton, J.D., Randall, B.L., & Whelton, P.K. (1997). End-stage renal disease in African-American and White men: 16-year MRFIT findings. *Journal of the American Medical Association, 277(16)*, 1293–1298.

Kloner, R.A., & Birnbaum, Y. (2001). *Cardiovascular Trials Review.* 6th ed. Darien, Connecticut: Le Jacq Communications.

Lagakos, S.W., Fischl, M.A., Stein, D.S., Lim, L., & Volderbing, P. (1991). Effects of zidovudine therapy in minority and other subpopulations with early HIV infection. *Journal of the American Medical Association, 266(19)*, 2709–2712.

LaRossa, J.C. (1995). Unresolved issues in early trials of cholesterol lowering. *American Journal of Cardiology, 76*, 5C–9C.

LaRossa, J.C., Ile, J., & Vupputuri, S. (1999). Effect of statins on risk of coronary disease—A meta-analysis of randomized controlled trials. *Journal of the American Medical Association, 282*, 2340–2346.

Leffall, L., Jr. (1998, November 12–14). Keynote address. Paper presented at the Cancer Prevention and Control through Community Leadership: A Challenge for the Year 2000, Atlanta, GA.

Lewis, E.J., Hunsicker, L.G., Bain, R.P., Rhode, R.D., (1993). The effect of angiotensin-converting-enzyme inhibition on diabetic nephropathy. *New England Journal of Medicine, 329*, 1456–1462.

Lewis, E.J., et al. (2001). Renoprotective effect of the angiotensin-receptor antagonist irbesartan in patients with nephropathy due to type 2 diabetes. *New England Journal of Medicine, 345(12)*, 851–860.

Lind, J. (1753). *A treatise of the scurvy.* Edinburgh: Sands, Murray, & Cochran.

Luzier, A.B., & DiTusa, L. (1999). Underutilization of ACE Inhibitors in heart failure. *Pharmacotherapy, 19(11)*, 1296–1307.

Mahunda Temple, G. (1998). Recruitment of African Americans in AIDS clinical trials: Some recommended strategies. *Journal of the Association of Black Nursing Faculty, 9(3)*, 61–64.

Martins, D., Tareen, N., & Norris, K.C. (2002). The epidemiology of chronic renal disease in African Americans. *American Journal of Medical Sciences, 323(2)*, 65–71.

Mastoor, M., Iqbal, U., Pinnow, E., & Lindsay, J. (2000). Ethnicity does not affect outcomes of coronary angioplasty. *Clinical Cardiology, 23*, 379–382.

Materson, B.J., & Reda, D.J. (1994). Correction: Single-drug therapy for hypertension in men. *New England Journal of Medicine, 330*, 1689.

Materson, B.J., et al. (1994). Single-drug therapy for hypertension in men. A comparison of six antihypertensive agents with placebo. *New England Journal of Medicine, 328(13)*, 914–921.

Maynard, C., Fisher, L.D., Passamani, E.R., & Pullum, T. (1986). Blacks in the coronary artery surgery study: Risk factors and coronary artery disease. *Circulation, 74*, 64–71.

McDonough, J.R., Hames, C.G., Stulb, S.C., & Garrison, G.E. (1965). Coronary heart disease among Negroes and Whites in Evans County, Georgia. *Journal of Chronic Diseases, 18*, 433–468.

Meldrum, M.L. (2000). A brief history of the randomized controlled trial. In C.J. Allegra & B.S. Kramer (Eds.), *Understanding clinical trials, 14(4)*, pp. 745–760. Philadelphia: W.B. Saunders.

Multiple Risk Factor Intervention Trial Research Group. (1982). Multiple Risk Factor Intervention Trial: Risk factor changes and mortality results. *Journal of the American Medical Association, 248*, 1465–1477.

National Institute of Allergy and Infectious Diseases (NIAD). (2001). *Minority health initiatives: Acquired immunodeficiency syndrome.* Retrieved December 2002, from http://www.niaid.nih.gov/facts/mwhhp3.htm

National Institute of Allergy and Infectious Diseases (NIAD). (2002). *HIV infection in minority populations—Fact sheet.* Retrieved December 2002, from http://www.niaid.nih.gov/factsheets/minor.htm

National Kidney Foundation (NKF) Kidney Disease Outcome Quality Initiative (K/DOQI) Advisory Board.

(2002). K/DOQI clinical practice guidelines for chronic kidney disease: Evaluation, classification, and stratification. Kidney Disease Outcome Quality Initiative. *American Journal of Kidney Diseases, 39(suppl 2),* S1–246.

Norris, K.C., & Agodoa, L.Y. (2002). Race and kidney disease: The scope of the problem. *Journal of the National Medical Association, 94(8),* 39S–44S.

Norris, K.C., & Owen, W.F. (1995). The dilemma of hypertension in the ESRD African American community. *Neprhology News & Issues, 9(3),* 14–16.

Norris, K.C., et al. (2001). Cocaine use, hypertension and end-stage renal disease. *American Journal of Kidney Disease, 38(3),* 523–528.

Nzerue, C.M., Demissachew, H., & Tucker, J.K. (2002). Race and kidney disease: Role of social and environmental factors [Review]. *Journal of National Medical Association, 94(suppl 8),* 28S–38S.

Nzerue, C.M., & Hewan-Lowe, R.L.J., Jr. (2000). Cocaine and the kidney: A synthesis of pathophysiologic and clinical perspectives. *American Journal of Kidney Disease, 35,* 783–795.

Parving, H.H., Lehnert, H., Brochner-Mortensen, J., Gomis, R., Andersen, S., & Arner, P. (2001). The effect of irbesartan on the development of diabetic nephropathy in patients with type 2 diabetes. *New England Journal of Medicine, 345(12),* 870–878.

Perneger, T.V., Whelton, P.K., & Klag, M.J. (1994). Risk of kidney failure associated with the use of acetaminophen, aspirin and non-sterioidal anti-inflammatory drugs. *New England Journal of Medicine, 331,* 1675–1679.

Pirozzo, S., & Glasziou, P. (1999). *Can we prove hypotheses?* Retrieved December 7, 2002, from http://www.sph.uq.edu.au/PPH/1stYear/Hypothesis/sld008.htm.

Powell, J.H., Cuyjet, A.B., & Phillips, E.H. (March 23, 2001). I.M.P.A.C.T. Project—Increase Minority Participation and Awareness of Clinical Trials. Paper presented at the National Medical Association Clinical Investigator Training Workshop. Nassau, Bahamas.

Prisant, L.M., et al. (1996). Efficacy and tolerability of lovastatin in 459 African Americans with hypercholesterolemia. *American Journal of Cardiology, 78,* 420–424.

Pui, C.H., Boyett, J.M., Hancock, M.L., Pratt, C.B., Meyer, W.H., & Crist, W.M. (1995). Outcome of treatment for childhood cancer in Black as compared with White children: The St. Jude Children's Research Hospital Experience, 1962 through 1992. *Journal of the American Medical Association, 273(8),* 633–637.

Roach, M., III, Alexander, M., & Coleman, J.L. (1992). The prognostic significance of race and survival from laryngeal carcinoma. *Journal of the National Medical Association, 84(8),* 668–674.

Roach, M., III, et al. (1997). Race and survival from breast cancer: Based on Cancer and Leukemia Group B trial 8541. *Cancer Journal from Scientific American, 3(2),* 107–112.

Roach, M., III, Krall, J., et al. (1992). The prognostic significance of race and survival from prostate cancer based on patients irradiated on Radiation Therapy Oncology Group protocols (1976–1985). *International Journal of Radiation Oncology Biology Physics, 24(3),* 441–449.

Rostand, S.G., Kirk, K.A., Rutsky, E.A., & Pate, B.A. (1982). Racial differences in the incidence of treatment for end-stage renal disease. *New England Journal of Medicine, 306,* 1276–1279.

Sacks, F.M., et al. (1996). The effect of pravastatin on coronary events after myocardial infarction in patients with average cholesterol levels. Cholesterol and Recurrent Trial investigators. *New England Journal of Medicine, 335(14),* 1001–1009.

Scandinavian Simvastin Survival Study Group. (1994). Randomized trial of cholesterol lowering in 4,444 patients with coronary heart disease: The Scandinavian Simvastatin Survival Study (4S). *Lancet, 344(8934),* 1383–1389.

Scott, N.A., Kelsey, S.F., Detre, K., Cowley, M., & King, S.B., III. (1994). Percutaneous transluminal coronary angioplasty in African-American patients (the National Heart, Lung, and Blood Instiue 1985–1986 Percutaneous Transluminal Coronary Angioplasty Registry). *American Journal of Cardiology, 73(16),* 1141–1146.

Sempos, C.T., Bild, D.E., & Manolio, T.A. (1999). Overview of the Jackson Heart Study: A study of cardiovascular disease in African American men and women [Jackson Heart Symposium: Cardiovascular Disease in African Americans]. *American Journal of the Medical Sciences, 317(3),* 142–146.

Sengupta, S., Strauss, R.P., DeVellis, R., Quinn, S.C., DeVellis, B., & Ware, B.W. (2000). Factors affecting African American participation in AIDS research. *Journal of Acquired Immune Deficiency Syndrome Human Retrovirology '97, 24*, 275–284.

Shavers-Homaday, V.L., Lynch, C.F., Burmeister, L.F., & Torner, J.C. (1997). Why are African Americans under-represented in medical research studies? *Ethnic Health, 2*(1–2), 31–54.

Sheifer, S.E., Escarce, J.J., & Schulman, K. (2000). Race and sex differences in the management of coronary artery disease. *American Heart Journal, 139*, 848–857.

Shepherd, J., et al. (1995). Prevention of coronary heart disease with Pravastatin in men with hypercholesterolemia. *New England Journal of Medicine, 333*(20), 1301–1307.

Shuster, E. (1997). Fifty years later: The significance of the Nuremberg Code [Special Article]. *New England Journal of Medicine, 337*(20), 1436–1440.

Shindler, O. (2001). Clinical Trials in Carilology. Retrieved June 28, 2002 from http://www2.umdnj.edu/~shindler/trials/trails_c.html

Simes, R.J., et al. (2002). Relationship between lipid levels and clinical outcomes in the Long-term Intervention with Pravastatin in Ischemic Disease (LIPID) Trial: To what extent is the reduction in coronary events with pravastatin explained by on-study lipid levels? *Circulation, 105*(10), 1162–1169.

Smith, D.C., Trump, D.L., Vogelzang, N.J., Redman, B.G., Flaherty, L.E., & Pienta, K.J. (1996). The effect of African American race on response and survival in Phase II trials of patients with hormone refractory prostate cancer. *Proceedings of ASCO, 15(Supplement)*, 242.

Stone, V.E., Mauch, M.Y., Steger, K., Janas, S.F., & Craven, D.E. (1997). Race, gender, drug use, and participation in AIDS clinical trials: Lessons from a municipal hosptial cohort. *Journal of General Internal Medicine, 12(3)*, 150–157.

Streeter, O.E., Jr., et al. (1999). Does race influence survival for esophageal cancer patients treated on the radiation and chemotherapy arm of RTOG #85-01? *International Journal of Radiation Oncology Biology Physics, 44*(5), 1047–1052.

Streeter, O.E., Jr., & Roach, M., III. (1999). Racial differences in the incidence, behavior, and management of tumors of the genitourinary tract. In Z. Petrovich, L. Baert, & L.W. Brady (Eds.), *Carcinoma of the kidney and testis, and rare urologic malignancies* (pp. 431–445). Berlin: Springer-Verlag.

Svensson, C.K. (1989). Representation of American Blacks in clinical trials of new drugs. *Journal of the American Medical Association, 261*, 263–265.

Taylor, H.A. (2001). Capacity building for research in minority health. *American Journal of the Medical Sciences, 322*(5), 257–258.

Taylor, H.A., Canto, J.G., Sanderson, B., Rogers, W.J., & Hilbe, J. (1998). Management and outcomes for Black patients with acute myocardial infarction in the reperfusion era. *American Journal of Cardiology, 82*, 1019–1023.

Taylor, H.A., et al. (1993). Race and prognosis after myocardial infarction. Results of the thrombolysis in myocardial infarction (TIMI) phase II trial. *Circulation, 88(4 Pt 1)*, 1484–1494.

Trivedi, H.S., et al. (2002). Slowing the progression of chronic renal failure: Economic benefits and patient's perspectives. *American Journal of Kidney Disease, 39*(4), 721–729.

U.S. Department of Health and Human Services. (1985). Report of the Secretary's Task Force on Black and Minority Health, Volumes I and II. Washington, D.C.: United States Government Printing Office.

U.S. Department of Health and Human Services. (2000). *Healthy People 2010* (conference Edition). 2 vols.

U.S. Renal Data System. (2002). *USRDS 2002 Annual Data Report: Atlas of End-Stage Renal Disease in the United States.* Bethesda, MD: National Institutes of Health, National Institute of Diabetes and Digestive and Kidney Diseases.

Vogelzang, N.J., et al. (1995). Goserelin versus orchiectomy in the treatment of advanced prostate cancer: Final results of a randomized trial. Zoladex Prostate Study Group. *Urology, 46*(2), 220–226.

Volberding, P., et al. (1990). Zidovudine in asymptomatic human immunodeficiency virus infection. A controlled trial in persons with fewer than 500 CD4-positive cells per cubic millimeter. The AIDS Clinical Trials Group of the National Institute of Allergy and Infectious Diseases. *New England Journal of Medicine, 322*, 941–949.

Whelton, P.K., et al. (1996). Recruitment experience in the African American Study of Kidney Disease and Hypertension (AASK) Pilot Study. *Contol Clin Trials, 17(suppl 4)*, 17S–33S.

Winston, J.S., Burns, G.C., & Klotman, P.E. (1998). The human immunodeficiency virus (HIV) epidemic and HIV-associated nephropathy. *Seminars in Nephrology, 18(4)*, 373–377.

Wright, J.T., Jr., et al. (2002). Successful blood pressure control in the African American Study of Kidney Disease and Hypertension. *Archives of Internal Medicine, 162(14)*, 1636–1643.

Wright, J.T., Jr., et al. (2002). Effect of blood pressure lowering and antihypertensive drug class on progression of hypertensive kidney disease: Results from the AASK Trial. *Journal of the American Medical Association 288(19)*, 2421–2431.

Yancy, C.W., et al. (2001). Race and the response to adrenergic blockade with carvedilol in patients with chronic heart failure. *New England Journal of Medicine, 344(18)*, 1358–1365.

CHAPTER 47

Eliminating Racial and Ethnic Disparities in Health: A Framework for Action

IVOR LENSWORTH LIVINGSTON AND
J. JACQUES CARTER

> Today changes must come fast; and we must adjust our mental habits, so that we can accept comfortably the idea of stopping one thing and beginning another overnight. . . . We must assume that there is probably a better way to do almost everything. We must stop assuming that a thing which has never been done before probably cannot be done at all.
>
> —Donald M. Nelson

INTRODUCTION

It has been approximately a decade since we wrote the summary chapter in the first edition of this book. Since that time, many things have changed, some for the better and some for the worse. One thing is certain: we have gotten older and, hopefully, wiser since the publication of the first edition in 1994. Unfortunately, what has gotten worse, with rare exceptions, is the overall health of the racial and ethnic minority populations in the United States. This scenario is especially true for African Americans, which is the group of primary interest for the book.

The 1990 census estimated that African Americans or blacks (as they will subsequently be called) constituted 12.3 percent of the United States population, thereby being the Nation's largest minority group. . . . Blacks as a group are disproportionately poor and experience a greater incidence of morbidity and mortality from chronic diseases and other health conditions compared with their White counterparts. As the nation approaches the 21st century, it is troubling that the moral, social, legislative and economic consciences of America have not been sufficiently touched to eradicate these racial and health injustices. (Livingston & Carter, 1994, p. 399)

One of the things that have changed is an increase in the African American population. As of April 1, 2000, the U.S. population stood at 281.4 million. Of this total, 36.4 million, or 12.9 percent were reported to be Black, or African American. This number includes 34.7 million people, or 12.3 percent, who reported only Black, in addition to 1.8 million people, or 0.6 percent, who reported Black as well as one of the other races (McKinnon, 2001[1]). However, this figure may be lower than the actual number, because African Americans are overrepresented among the people who are hard to reach through the census (e.g., homeless and incarcerated). Census takers often miss young to middle-aged African American males because they are overrepresented in these vulnerable populations (Williams & Jackson, 2000).

The Census Bureau projects that by the year 2035 there will be more than 50 million African American individuals in the United States, comprising 14.3 percent of the population. The African American population is represented throughout the country, with the greatest concentrations in the Southeast and mid-Atlantic regions, especially Louisiana, Mississippi, Alabama, Georgia, South Carolina, and Maryland (U.S. Census Bureau, 2000). One indicator that the relative health status of African Americans and other minority groups has gotten progressively worse is the clarion call to urgently address racial and ethnic disparities. This call has come from the federal, state, and local governments. It also includes academic, private, and community-based organizations (CBOs), often working in collaborative efforts.

The vulnerability of African Americans to adverse health may be mediated by several environmental factors and experiences (e.g., homelessness, poverty, access to desirable health care; health policy). Such experiences influence behavioral choices (drug abuse, oral health), affect availability of services (e.g., influenza vaccinations for the Black elderly, [Østbye et al., 2003]), and may directly impact physiologic function or status (e.g., cancer, heart disease) (Hogan et al., 2001). These topics have been addressed in the previous chapters of this volume. These chapters appear under five headings and are summarized and placed in Figure 47.1.

The Focus of the Chapter

While a reiteration is made in this concluding chapter of the racial and ethnic disparities in health and related experiences, the intent is to provide information and discuss directions to reduce existing racial disparities in health. Given that individual health and health care are complex and dynamic processes involving simultaneous inputs and outputs from various (macro-level and micro-level) areas and given that a paucity of conceptual models exist explaining these processes, two complementary models (i.e., one structural, the other functional and action-oriented) are introduced as a framework for action. In essence, this chapter offers collective and integrative insights, as well as a conceptual framework for action, that can be utilized in a sustaining manner for future efforts directed at eliminating racial and ethnic disparities in health, especially for African Americans, as well as for other foreign-born Blacks who for now fall under this "umbrella" label.

WHY THE URGENT NEED TO ELIMINATE RACIAL AND ETHNIC HEALTH DISPARITIES?

An Overview

Similar to the view expressed in the federal government publication *Healthy People 2010*, the view taken in this chapter is that racial and ethnic health disparities are a result of the complex interaction among genetic variations, environmental factors, and specific health behaviors. This complex series of interactions is addressed later in the chapter with the introduction of certain designated models. Why the overwhelming need and urgency to eliminate racial and ethnic health disparities, especially for African Americans? Although evidence in support of the answer to this question is presented throughout this chapter, the following quotation succinctly and pointedly addresses the issue:

Even though the Nation's infant mortality rate is down, the infant death rate among African Americans is still more than double that of Whites. Heart disease death rates are more than 40 percent higher for African Amer-

Figure 47.1
The complex arrangement of selected conditions that have the potential to influence racial and ethnic health disparities

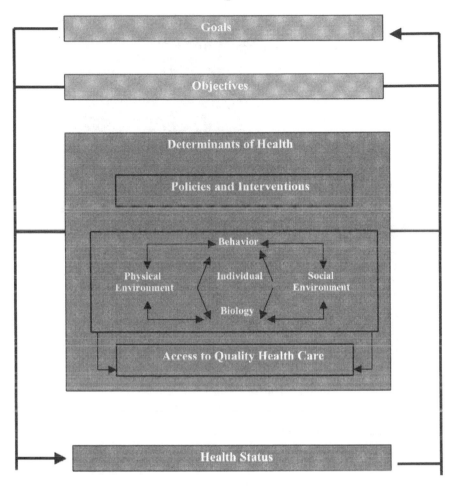

Source: USDHHS (2000).

icans than for Whites. The death rate for all cancers is 30 percent higher for all African Americans than for Whites; for prostate cancer, it is more than double that for Whites. African American women have a higher death rate from breast cancer despite having a mammography screening rate that is nearly the same as the rate for White women. The death rate from HIV/AIDS for African Americans is more than seven times that for Whites; the rate of homicide is six times that for Whites. (USDHHS, 2000, p. 12)

From a public health perspective, racial and ethnic disparities in health threaten to diminish efforts to improve the nation's overall health and productivity. The United States is becoming increasingly diverse. While White Americans currently constitute approximately 71 percent of the population, by the year 2050 nearly one in two Americans will be a person of color (U.S. Bureau of the Census, 2000).

The Costs to Society.   Another way to look at the price of health disparities is to examine its economic costs to society. It has been said (Smedley et al., 2002) that:

from an economic standpoint, the costs of inadequate care may have significant implications for overall health-care expenditures. Poorly managed chronic conditions or missed diagnosis can result in avoidable, higher sub-sequent healthcare costs. For example, inadequately treated and managed diabetes can result in far more expensive complications, such as kidney disorder requiring dialysis or transplantation. To the extent that mi-nority beneficiaries of publicly funded health programs are less likely to receive high quality care, these ben-eficiaries—as well as taxpayers that support public healthcare programs—may face higher healthcare costs. (Smedley et al., 2002, p. 31)

This higher burden of disease and mortality among minorities has profound implications for all Americans, simply because it results in a less healthy nation and higher costs for rehabilitative or tertiary care (Smedley et al., 2002). Overall, these minority groups experience a disproportionate burden of chronic and infectious illnesses. For these reasons the federal Healthy People 2010 initia-tive has established an overarching goal of eliminating health disparities, noting that "the health of the individual is almost inseparable from the health of the larger community, and . . . the health of every community in every State and territory determines the overall health status of the Nation" (USDHHS, 2000, p. 15). That is why the vision for Healthy People 2010 is "Healthy People in Healthy Communities." Healthy People 2010 is designed to achieve two overarching goals: (a) in-crease quality and years of life and (b) eliminate health disparities (USDHHS, 2000).

Life Expectancy of African Americans

The best overall index of health is life expectancy (LE), and for Black Americans it underscores their deplorable health crisis. White females and White males have rates of 80.0 years and 74.9 years, respectively; Black females and Black males have rates of 74.9 and 68.2 years, respectively. It is also important to note that while LE rates are increasing for Whites, they have recently been decreasing for Blacks (Minino et al., 2002). According to the Centers for Disease Control (McGinnis, 1990), Blacks experience in excess of 60,000 excess deaths each year by not having at least similar life expectancy and mortality rates of Whites.

The Heterogeneity of the Black U.S. Population

Although the terms "African American" and "Blacks" have been used interchangeably in this chapter, in some respects the former implies the existence of a homogeneous group. While the latter is sometimes seen as less desirable because of its possible negative connotations, by its generic label it is the umbrella term under which a variety of non-American Blacks and foreign-born or immigrant Blacks can be identified (Livingston, 1994). An examination of contemporary Black Americans shows that they are a heterogeneous group which consists of those born in the United States and immigrants from the Caribbean (French-speaking, like Haiti; English-speaking, like Jamaica), South America, and Africa. Each group differs in terms of heritage, language, culture, health beliefs, and health practices (Watts, 2003). In the past, the majority of foreign-born Blacks immigrated from the Caribbean. In recent years the numbers of immigrants from Africa have been increasing (USINS, 2002). By 2000, 2.2 million Blacks in the United States (6.3 percent) were born outside the United States and another 1.4 million Blacks (3.9 percent) had at least one parent who was foreign-born (Kington & Lucas, 2003; USDHHS, 2001). The need to disaggregate racial and ethnic data or information that is collected on or about African Americans is important, given the heterogeneity of the Black population in the United States. Foreign-born Blacks may have different health experiences. By disaggregating the "Black health data," a different picture may emerge concerning racial and ethnic disparities in the United States.

In the area of socioeconomic status (SES), which is usually correlated with improved health, foreign-born Blacks have a reported advantage. This advantage remained even when SES was controlled (Singh & Siahpush, 2002). In the case of low-birth-weight (LBW) infants (a noted risk factor for infant mortality), it was reported that the rate of LBW in infants of African-born women (3.6 percent) was closer to the rate in infants of U.S.-born White women (2.4 percent), whereas the rate in infants of U.S.-born Black women remained high (7.5 percent) (David & Collins, 1997). Having made this distinction concerning the heterogeneity of the Black U.S. population, space limitations and the focus of the chapter will not permit further comments on this issue. However, when subsequent reference is made to African Americans, the assumption is that this reference consists of both U.S.-born Blacks as well as foreign-born Blacks.

RACIAL DISPARITIES IN HEALTH AND RELATED CONDITIONS: AN OVERVIEW

Because the previous chapters adequately presented a comprehensive view of important areas where African Americans suffer disproportionate disparities in health compared to their White counterparts, a brief overview is presented to further underscore the urgent need to address these issues.

Summary Statements Underscoring Health Disparities

The existence of significant racial and ethnic disparities in health care has been widely reported and documented in various government reports, including Healthy People 2010 (USDHHS, 2000), "A Public Health Action Plan to Prevent Heart Disease and Stroke" (USDHHS, 2003), and Health, United States, 2003 (Fried et al., 2003). Most striking are the differences between the incidence, prevalence, and mortality of many diseases affecting African Americans when compared to the U.S. population as a whole. Although life expectancy and overall health for most Americans have improved tremendously over the past two decades, there continue to be major disparities in the burden of disease/illness and death experienced by African Americans in this country.

The three leading causes of death in the United States in 2003 were heart disease, cancer, and stroke. In each of these categories, the African American death rate was significantly greater than the White rate (Fried et al., 2003). In fact, when one looks at the ten leading causes of mortality in this country, the African American rate exceeds the White rate in every category except chronic obstructive lung disease, suicide, and Alzheimer's disease. The ten leading causes of death in the United States in 2003 for African Americans were heart disease, cancer, stroke, unintentional injuries, diabetes, homicide, HIV/AIDS, chronic lower respiratory disease, kidney disease, and influenza and pneumonia (NCHS; Fried et al., 2003).

Recent reports have suggested that whereas heart disease is decreasing among Whites, it may be increasing among African American men (Hames & Greenlund, 1996).

Understanding Racial and Ethnic Health Disparities: Using the E-I-I Framework

To the best of these authors' knowledge, apart from the federal government's Healthy People 2010 initiative, there is a relative void in the literature regarding what approaches to take in the battle against eliminating health disparities. What is clear, however, is that whatever approach is taken has to be multifaceted and interdisciplinary. Only with such approaches can the "war" on eliminating racial and ethnic disparities be successfully waged. This being the case, classic public health views suggest that the major determinants of a population's health status and the primary explanations of disparities among population groups are to be found in the *social, physical,* and *economic environ-*

Figure 47.2
An interactionist view of health: The E-I-I Model

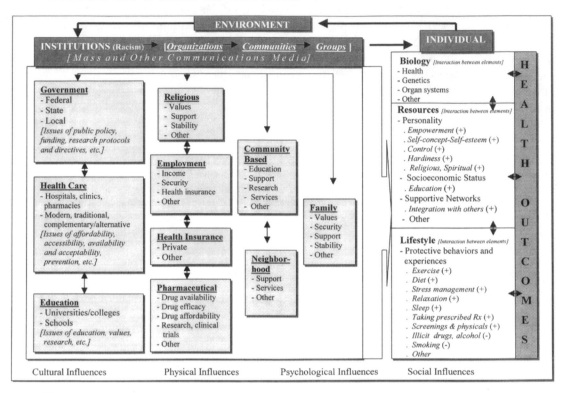

Note: ◆▶ = Reciprocal relationships; (+) = Desirable; (−) = Undesirable

Source: Livingston (2004).

ments (see Figures 47.2 and 47.3). These environments are, in turn, determined by the *larger society's norms, values, political economy*, and *social stratification* (King, 1996).

There are as many conditions that determine health as there are conditions that cause health disparities. Therefore, to more successfully address and, eventually, eliminate racial and ethnic health disparities require an in-depth understanding of the multifaceted array of interacting conditions contributing to their development (Livingston & Carter, 1994; USDHHS, 2000). In attempting to address this complex array of conditions, as was mentioned before, two complementary models are introduced as a guiding framework.

The first model, which is more structural in its composition, is called the *Environment-Institution-Individual (or E-I-I) Model* (see Figure 47.2). The second model (see Figure 47.3) is called the *Action Model for Reducing Racial and Ethnic Health Disparities* (or *AMFRREHD*). The AMFRREHD, which complements the E-I-I model and is derived from it, is a more process-oriented model that illustrates the interacting pattern of a variety of conditions (i.e., at the macro level and micro level). These conditions contribute both individually and collectively to racial and ethnic health disparities. These models identify the salient conditions that contribute to racial and ethnic health disparities. In so doing, they provide insights, as well as "action-oriented" strategies as to where public health officials and others can successfully intervene to ultimately eliminate health disparities.

Figure 47.3
Action model for reducing racial and ethnic health disparities (AMFRREHD)

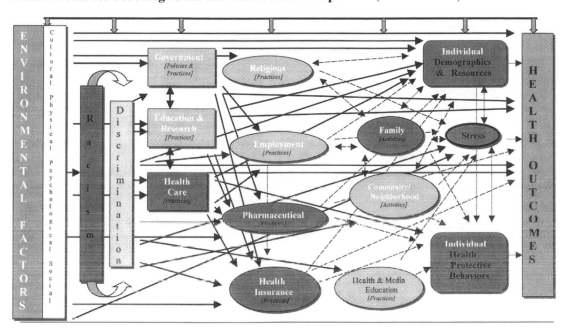

Source: Livingston (2004).

*Selected array of interrelated factors contributing to racial and ethnic health disparities

Note: ▬▬▶ = Macro-level relationships; ---▶ = Meso-level relationships, ••••▶ = Micro-level relationships; ◀▬▶ = Main reciprocal relationships; ➤ = Darker color structures and conditions selectively emphasized in the chapter.

The E-I-I Model

The E-I-I model of health (which was formerly referred to as the E-I-O model in the earlier edition of this book; see Livingston & Carter, 1994), was partly derived from the Health Field Concept or HFC (for greater details, see Laframbosie, 1973; Lalonde, 1974; Livingston & Carter, 1994).

The Health Field Concept.   The HFC was originally used to formulate strategies for improving the health of Canadians. The utility of HFC in addressing emergent public health concerns of contemporary society has been expressed in the past (Terris, 1984). In the context of improving the health of Blacks in the United States, the HFC has also been suggested as a basis to develop effective health promotion and disease prevention programs (see Thomas, 1992).

The General Organization of the E-I-I Model.   The E-I-I model (see Figure 47.2) has three main components: (1) *environment [E]*, (2) *institution [I]*, and (3) *Individual [I]*. In the E-I-I model, the individual subsumes *biology, resources,* and *lifestyle.* What is emphasized in the E-I-I model is that although the three domains of the model have reciprocal relationships, activities basically begin with the overarching influences of the *environment*, which in turn influences a variety of *institutions* (including organizations, communities, and groups), and these collective influences impact on the *individual.* Here at the individual level, racial and ethnic disparities are manifested. However, to fully understand these health outcomes, one has to fully appreciate the interactive contributions first with the predisposing influence of the environment and, next, the various institutional contributions that are made. The way in which behavior is viewed in the model as being affected by and affecting multiple levels of influence (McLeroy et al., 1988). Additionally, there is the possibility of various reciprocal relationships between individuals and their environments, which has been addressed in the past (Stokøls 1992).

As seen in Figure 47.2, the desirable qualities African Americans [I] must have for good health include their biological makeup (e.g., their physical health); resources (e.g., positive personality qualities, such as self-concept; education; and a supportive network of friends and family); and positive lifestyle qualities (e.g., exercising, eating appropriately, and having regular screenings and physical examinations). The desirable qualities that are supported in the literature have a (+) next to them. Conversely, the undesirable ones (e.g., smoking) have a (−) next to them. The E-I-I model demonstrates the functional importance among the three components, where the dominant environment [E], with its various *macro-level* sources of influence (e.g., cultural, physical, psychological, and social), subsumes both institutions [I], as well as individuals [I]. As the dominant source of influence, the environment subsumes major institutions in society that are subsequently influential themselves (e.g., government, health care, and education). As seen in Figure 47.2 (and later in Figure 47.3), institutions, in turn, subsume *meso-level* structures as organizations (e.g., religious, employment, health insurance, and pharmaceuticals); communities (e.g., community-based organizations and neighborhood support organizations); and groups (e.g., the family). Lastly, although the macro-level structures remain influential, the meso-level structures in turn have an impact on the *micro-level* conditions and individuals.

Comparison with the Healthy People 2010 Model

There are some similarities between the E-I-I model and the conceptual model suggested in Healthy People 2010 (see Figure 47.4; USDHHS, 2000). For this model, determinants of health are influenced by prior goals and objectives. Determinants of health, which is at the core of the model, consist on the periphery of the model of "policies and interventions" and "access to quality care." These conditions, in turn, subsume and have reciprocal relationships with the interacting "physical" and "social environments." Whereas the E-I-I model has biology, resources, and lifestyle under the individual component, this model has similar inclusions of biology and behavior.

Given that the E-I-I model implies that the initial intent of any effort will first have goals to achieve, followed by objective means of achieving the goals, the Healthy People 2010 model has these factors built in to the model. As seen in Figure 47.4, all arrows eventually lead to the overall health status of individuals. In a similar manner the E-I-I model (see Figure 47.2), as well as the action-oriented, derived model (see Figure 47.3), are assessed in terms of the health outcomes of individuals. Given that the AMFRREHD (see Figure 47.3) provides more specific information pertaining to the three main components of the E-I-I model, as well as the suggested relationships between structures and conditions at the macro level, meso level and micro level, it is the preferred framework to use as a guide for any comprehensive actions aimed at eliminating racial and ethnic health disparities.

ELIMINATING RACIAL AND ETHNIC HEALTH DISPARITIES: THE AMFRREHD

As previously mentioned, the E-I-I model provides useful information about the important inter-relationships between its three main components: the environment, institutions, and individuals. What AMFRREHD illustrates, especially in a more functional and action-oriented manner, are the various direct (or main) paths (indicated in bold lines) and indirect paths between the representative macro-level, meso-level and micro-level structures derived from the E-I-I model. Whereas the E-I-I model provided the proximity of various structures and conditions with a suggested subset of characteristics

Figure 47.4
Healthy people in healthy communities: A systematic approach to health improvement

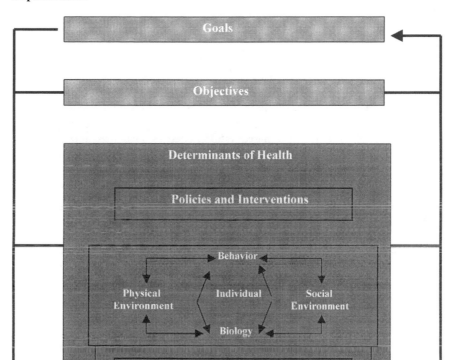

Source: USDHHS (2000).

for each, the AMFRREHD places these structures, as well as some additions (e.g., racism at the macro level and stress at the micro level), in a functional and researchable manner, hence, the latter's "action-oriented" nature. Because the AMFRREHD was derived from the E-I-I model, the proximity placement of all structures is consistent with the three dominant parameters of the E-I-I model.

The published literature suggests many factors that individually and collectively contribute to racial and ethnic health disparities. Such factors include (1) access to, distribution of, and availability of health-care services (Fiscella et al., 2000); (2) stress (Rowley & Tosteson, 1993; Livingston et al., 2003); (3) genetics (Goldenberg et al., 2000); (4) the environment (Bryant & Mohai, 1999); (5) economic status and socioeconomic status (Fiscella & Franks, 1997); and (6) behavior (Lantz et al., 1998).

The Environment: A Mosaic of Areas for Improvement

The *Oxford English Dictionary* defines environment as "the conditions under which any person lives." As the "umbrella" domain in the E-I-I model, the environment is external to the individual, yet it influences health in many ways through a mosaic of subdomains (e.g., social, cultural, psychological, and physiological domains).

Racism and Discrimination.   As seen from Figure 47.3, racism and, subsequently, discrimination are major contributing factors to the current racial and ethnic health disparities. "Racism and discrimination are umbrella terms referring to beliefs, attitudes and practices that denigrate individuals or groups because of phenotypic characteristics (e.g., skin color and facial features) or ethnic group affiliation" (USDHHS, 2001, p. 38). Although these conditions reside at the macro level, any successful efforts at reducing disparities will have to address ways of improving on the fundamentally racist nature of American society, which, in turn, can be traced to stress and ill health of African Americans (Livingston, 1985; Clark, et al., 1999).

While the AMFRREHD indicates that not all of the relationships implied between the three levels (i.e., macro, meso, and micro) are necessarily affected by the socially derived, institutionally racist, and discriminatory practices of the wider U.S. society, the dominant position is that an understanding of the racism–health connection is fundamental to any sustained success at eliminating racial and ethnic health disparities. This position has support in the recent literature on minority health (e.g., Clark et al., 1999; Watts, 2003; Krieger, 2003). Again, based on the importance of racism and discrimination in the model, as indicated by their direct and indirect connections to all macro-level institutional (e.g., government, education, health care), meso-level institutional (e.g., religion, employment pharmaceutical), and micro-level conditions (e.g., individual resources, health protective behaviors, health), it is viewed as perhaps the most important environmental factor that must be addressed.

Despite improvements over the last several decades, research continues to document racial discrimination in housing rentals and sales (Yinger, 1995) and in hiring practices (Kirschenman & Neckerman, 1991). On a much broader scale, racism and discrimination have even been documented in the administration of medical care. For example, there have been fewer diagnostic and treatment procedures for African Americans versus Whites (Shiefer et al., 2000). It has been said that racism and discrimination adversely affect physical and mental health and place minorities at risk for mental disorders such as depression and anxiety (USDHHS, 2001).

Poverty as an Impediment to Health.   While the experiences of poverty are primarily at the micro level, the contributing conditions (as seen in Figure 47.3) are at macro and meso levels. As a social environmental condition, the poverty level for African Americans in 1999 stood at 24 percent versus 8 percent for Whites. Expressed another way, the per capita income for racial and ethnic groups (African Americans = \$14,397; Hispanic Americans = \$11,621; Asian Americans = \$21,134) is much lower than that for Whites (\$24,109) (U.S. Census Bureau, 1999).

While the national poverty rate for U.S. children is nearly 20 percent, almost 37 percent of African Americans 18 years and younger live in poor families (U.S. Census Bureau, 1999). African Americans move in and out of poverty, but their periods of poverty tend to last longer, making them more likely than Whites to suffer from long-term poverty (O'Hare, 1996). In the case of older African Americans, they are almost three times as likely as Whites to be poor. The poverty rate among single African American women living alone or with nonrelatives is very high (Ruiz, 1995). Because of longer life expectancies, older African American women (75.0) are far more numerous than older African American men (68.3) (Minino & Smith, 2001).

It has been known for some time that people living in poverty, whatever their race or ethnicity, have the poorest overall health (see reviews by Krieger, 1993; Yen & Syme, 1999). Because of the relationship between poverty and ill health, fundamental institutional changes are needed to improve the socioeconomic status of a vast majority of those African Americans who are poor. The existing realities of institutional racism and the accompanying legacy of poverty all underscore the need for collective action and change in the status quo. Advocates of the status quo remaining the same have been relatively successful in restricting the economic advancements of Blacks in America. It is the lack of such economic and other related advances by Blacks that has substantially contributed to the vast racial disparities in health that currently exist (Livingston & Carter, 1994).

Some legislative enactments have had a positive impact on African American behavior and poverty experiences. These included, for example, the Civil Rights Act of 1964; Medicaid and Medicare legislation of 1965; and Title VI of the Civil Rights Act, which prohibited racial discrimination in any institution receiving federal funds. All these legislations combined to create a "Civil Rights Era" in health care for Blacks (Sidel & Sidel, 1984; Shea & Fullilove, 1985). The passage of Medicare (Title XVIII) and Medicaid (Title XIX) legislation was intended to open the health system to Blacks, the handicapped, the indigent, and the elderly poor (Cobb, 1981). Irrespective of these legislative and policy accomplishments, Blacks remain disproportionately poor and unhealthy (Livingston & Carter, 1994).

As a summary statement, it can be said that low-income people have death rates that are twice the rates for people with incomes above the poverty level (USDHHS, 2001). Poverty reduces a person's opportunities for long life by increasing the chances of infant death, chronic disease, and traumatic death (USDHHS, 2000).

No single indicator of health status makes the connection between poverty and poor health more clear than does infant mortality. It has been said (Smedley, Stith, & Nelson, 2002) that poor preg- nancy outcomes including prematurity, low birth weight, birth defects, and infant death are associated with low income, low educational level, and low occupational status along with other indicators of social and economic disadvantage. Therefore, the fact that Black babies are twice as likely as White babies to die before their first birthday indicates that the poverty–health relationship for Blacks is especially significant and in need of urgent improvement.

Since Blacks are disproportionately poor, race (i.e., being Black) is mistakenly viewed as a proxy for poverty or low SES. Therefore, given the relationship between low SES or poverty and health outcomes for Blacks, it is evident that for any meaningful improvement to occur, major interventions are needed at the macro levels and meso levels of American society. If successful, these interventions should produce greater equality in living standards and general economic well-being for African Americans as a group.

Infrastructure Decline and Environmental Hazards.   From a structural point of view, major in- terventions are needed from federal, state, and local governments to address (e.g., through revitalization projects) the decaying infrastructure of inner cities. Help is needed (e.g., through more effective govern- mental regulation and community "grassroots" actions) to reduce the number of environmental hazards that currently exist and are increasing (see connecting arrows in Figures 47.2 and 47.3).

More than 57 percent of Blacks live in central cities, and this is viewed as the highest concentration of any racial and ethnic group (Bullard, 1992). Urban decay includes (1) densely congested neigh- borhoods; (2) unsanitary and dilapidated housing; (3) crime- and drug-infested neighborhoods; (4) inadequate and/or unwilling police presence; (5) high unemployment; and (6) ill-staffed and deteri- orating schools.

Poverty in America has become increasingly concentrated in urban areas. In essence, poor neigh- borhoods have few resources and suffer from considerable distress. They also have the disadvantage of high rates of unemployment, homelessness, substance abuse, and crime. In terms of crime, irre- spective of who is committing it, these actions disproportionately affect racial minorities. For African Americans, the rate of victimization for crimes of violence is higher than for any other ethnic or racial group (Maguire & Pastore, 1999). Exposure to community violence, as a victim or a witness, leaves immediate and sometimes long-term effects on mental health, especially for youth (Miller et al., 1999). More than 40 percent of inner-city young people have seen someone shot or stabbed (Schwab-Stone et al., 1999).

The quotation that follows is an example of what is happening at an increasingly alarming rate in poor, Black, inner-city communities across America. This particular experience, entitled "NW Housing Complex a Tangle of Drugs, Despair," is associated with an urban housing complex in northwest Washington, D.C. called Sursum Corda (which is Latin for "lift up your hearts," a name given initially to the development by the Catholic Church and its planners).

The urban village is now an infamous housing complex of North capital Street. It is a place where a nun lived for nine years until the risks became too great, where visiting federal prosecutors were shot at, where some residents help drug dealers out of fear and where 14-year-old Jahkema Princess Hansen was fatally shot January 23 after apparently witnessing a murder. For police, Sursum Corda is one of the most daunting of the 100 or so open-air drug markets in the city. (Kovaleski & Fahrenthold, 2004, p. A1, Column 1)

Pollution and Environmental Hazards.   From a more physical point of view, decay of inner cities also means exposures to pollution and environmental hazards (Greenberg, 2000). According to the Institute of Medicine (1999), despite significant improvements in environmental protection over the past several decades, millions of people who live in the United States continue to live in unsafe and unhealthy environments.

Modernization has brought with it different types of pollution and environmental hazards. Pollutants include, for example, exhaust fumes from motor vehicles, natural and artificial chemicals in emissions from factories, and chemical fertilizers, herbicides, and pesticides that are manufactured and used in agriculture and other industrial wastes (Doll, 1992). A major environmental hazard affecting Blacks is lead poisoning.

Data from the Third National Health and Nutrition Examination Survey (NHANES III) (Pirkle et al., 1994) found African American children to be lead-poisoned at more than twice the rate of non-Hispanic White children. The incidence of Black children with blood levels more than 15 ug/dL of blood is 55 percent. It is important to note that lead toxicity begins at blood levels as low as 10 to 15 ug/dL (Walker et al., 1992). The failure of organizations (e.g., health care, government, research and/or others) to successfully intervene in this area has had serious consequences for Black children. Examples of possible health consequences from Black children ingesting lead, especially over a protracted period, include mental problems, hyperactivity, and possible maladjusted behaviors leading to violent crimes (Needleman, 1990).

Toxic pollution/hazards have a negative impact on Blacks and other minorities and need to be improved through the collective interaction of Black community residents as well as by the federal government. There is a disproportionate number of uncontrolled toxic waste sites located in Black and Hispanic communities (Commission for Racial Injustice, 1987). Also, large commercial hazardous waste landfills and disposal facilities are more likely to be found in rural communities in the southern Black Belt (General Accounting Office, 1983).

With Blacks disproportionately represented in the inner-city and poor communities of America, they are more at risk to experience severe health dysfunctions. Greater organizational involvement is needed to intervene in, and to address, issues pertaining to environmental racism and environmental equity (see Mohai & Bryant, 1992, 1998; Bryant, 2001; Mohai & Kershner, 2002).

INSTITUTIONS: INPUT, INTERVENTION, AND IMPROVEMENT

Nothing Exists in a Vacuum

In a significant measure what we (i.e., Americans) have is not a health care system but a disease care system. We have created a medical-care complex that is pretty darn good at diagnosing disease, managing disease, and sometimes curing disease—but not nearly so good at preventing disease. And sometimes it is only too good at creating disease. (David, 1993, pp. 31–32)

In attempting to illustrate the impact institutions have on individuals and their ultimate health outcomes, the AMFRREHD (seen in Figure 47.3) illustrates the dominant a priori role racism plays in affecting the policy and practices of these institutions. One of the reasons why racism is viewed in this chapter as environmentally derived and sustained is that if these major institutions (e.g., government, education, health care) existed in another environment (i.e., another country), their resultant policies and practices may have been different. In other words, it is the "American" experiences, which are institutionally racist (Livingston, 1985; Turner & Skidmore, 1999), that have, over time, permeated the daily fabric of social and organizational life, hence the connecting lines (seen in Figure 47.3) between the racist and discriminatory environment and institutions at the *macro level* (e.g., government, education and research, health care), *meso level* (e.g., religions, employment, mass media community, family), and micro level (e.g., individual resources, stress, health protective behaviors and health outcomes).

The Health-Care Institution

While the position taken in this chapter, as illustrated by the complex array of relational arrows in the AMFRREHD in Figure 47.3, is that racism ultimately impacts the health of Black Americans, for some the issue is still debatable, controversial, and complex (Krieger, 2003; The Health Care Challenge, 1999).

Because of space limitations, a brief discussion is presented around the health-care institution as both a representative and influential macro-level institution that has had a profound impact on existing racial and ethnic health disparities.

Health Care: A Right or a Privilege?   According to Cockerham (1992), because health care is more "of an opportunity rather than a commodity, it should be available as a right to all Americans, regardless of living conditions or financial status" (p. 262). However, historical lessons learned from the United Kingdom suggest that if increased access to health care is not accompanied by fundamental changes in the institutional structure of society (e.g., reducing poverty), the health of poor people does not dramatically improve (Wilkinson, 1986).

Access to Health Care is Only Part of the Problem.   It is frequently assumed that simply improving access to medical care will eliminate racial disparities in health. While access to health care plays a very important role in racial health disparities, it is tied to a variety of other conditions such as discrimination and cultural barriers (The Health Care Challenge, 1999). This fact notwithstanding, access to health care plays a very important role, it is estimated that medical care accounts for about 10 percent of the variation in health status (Anderson et al., 1995). Lack of health insurance is a barrier to seeking health care. Nearly one-fourth of African Americans are uninsured, a percentage 1.5 times greater than the White rate (Brown et al., 2000). In the United States, health insurance is typically provided as an employment benefit (see Figure 47.3). Because African Americans are often employed in marginal jobs, the rate of employer-based coverage among employed African Americans is substantially lower than the rate among employed Whites (53 percent vs. 73 percent; Hall, 1999).

According to a congressionally mandated report from the National Academy of Sciences Institute of Medicine, "minorities tend to receive a lower quality of healthcare than non-minorities, when access-related factors, such as the patient's insurance status and income are controlled" (Smedley et al., 2002, p. 1). In addition, "minorities may experience other barriers to healthcare, even when insured at the same level as Whites, including barriers of language, geography, and cultural familiarity."

The report's findings conclude that the marginal health status of African Americans and other minorities is due to several factors, including (a) bias, prejudice, and stereotyping on the part of health-care providers; (b) uncertainty about patient's condition, which can lead to diagnosis based on the person's identity and status (i.e., age, gender, socioeconomic status, race, ethnicity); (c) variations in health plans, with poorer health insurance coverage for minorities and insurance company caps on coverage for treatment; (d) a shortage and/or absence of physicians (particularly minority physicians) in minority communities; and (e) a mistrust of health-care providers due to experiences with discrimination in hospitals in particular and society in general (Smedley et al., 2002).

Any comprehensive organizational effort aimed at improving utilization of health services by Blacks has to address the accompanying interrelated issues of affordability, availability, and acceptability of health care (see health-care institutions in the E-I-I model in Figure 47.2). These three conditions of affordability, availability, and acceptability, along with accessibility mentioned above, are referred to as the four "As" of health care utilization (Livingston & Carter, 1994).

Affordability of Health Care.   Insurance coverage affects whether or not a person (i.e., Black) gains access to care and the manner in which that care is delivered. "Most basically, individuals completely lacking health insurance may delay or forgo care that has the potential to dramatically improve their health and functioning and even prevent premature death" (U.S. Congress, Office of Technology Assessment, 1992, p. 43).

Studies have reported that the uninsured have a higher relative probability of in-hospital death than the insured. Of specific importance, however, is the report that the probability of in-hospital death was greater for Blacks than for Whites (Johnson, 1991). Data analyzed from the 1996 Medical Expenditure Panel Survey (MEPS) found that African Americans and Latinos, regardless of insurance coverage, were almost twice as likely as Whites to receive care from a hospital-based provider. Those who were uninsured were also more likely to rely on hospitals for care (Lillie-Blanton et al., 2001).

Availability of Health Care.   Historically, many White physicians would not accept Blacks as patients. This fact, coupled with the dearth of Black physicians, has contributed to many Blacks who have no identified physician and/or no regular source of care except hospital clinics or emergency rooms (McDavid, 1990). This being the case, the supply of African American clinicians is important. Reports reveal that African American physicians are five times more likely than White physicians to treat African American patients (Komaromy et al., 1996). Also, African American patients rate their physicians' styles of interaction as more participatory when they see African American physicians (Cooper-Patrick et al., 1999).

Acceptability of Health Care.   Organizational intervention is needed to improve the perception Blacks have of medical care and the quality of services rendered to them as a group. While several factors may contribute to how acceptable the health-care services are to Blacks, a salient issue has been racial compatibility between provider and patient (Rosenthal & Kosciulek, 1996; Wilson, 2002). This being the case, how Blacks utilize health-care services may be significantly improved if there is a visible representation of Black (and other minority) health-care providers in these health-care facilities.

Racial Disparities in Medical Treatment.   To further underscore the antecedent importance of racism in the AMFRREHD (see Figure 47.3), a rich literature attests to the persistence and prevalence of racist beliefs and discriminatory behaviors in contemporary American society (Steinhorn & Diggs-Brown, 1999). In 1990, the American Medical Association (AMA) took formal note of the racial differences in health care (Krieger, 2003). While the AMA emphasized the probable roles of SES and sociocultural factors and noted the limitations of many studies, it acknowledged "that disparities in treatment decisions may reflect the existence of subconscious bias. . . . The health care system, like all other elements of society, has not fully eradicated this [racial] prejudice" (Geiger, 2001, p. 217).

Coronary artery disease (CAD) and acute myocardial infarction (AMI) are the most intensively and elaborately studied topics associated with racial and ethnic differences in care. The primary reason for this focus on CAD and AMI is that CAD is the leading cause of death among all Americans. Recent trends have suggested that whereas CAD is decreasing among White men, it may be increasing among African American men (Hames & Greenlund, 1996). It is reported that African Americans are significantly less likely to receive appropriate cardiac procedures or therapies (Canto et al., 2000). For example, they are less likely to be catheterized, and if they are catheterized, African Americans are frequently 20 percent to 50 percent less likely to undergo a revascularization procedure. They are less likely than Whites to receive beta blockers, thrombolytic drugs, or aspirin (Geiger, 2001). Similar practices exist in other disease areas. For example, discriminatory practices involving end-stage renal disease (ESRD) has been reported in the past (Livingston & Ackah, 1992).

Research: The Underutilization of African Americans. Blacks and Hispanics are less likely to participate in surveys and clinical studies; therefore, there is little information about risk groups within these minority populations (Anderson et al., 1987). Apart from the need to know the race-specific efficacy of new pharmaceutical drugs/therapy, there are other compelling reasons that Blacks should, in the future, be included more in clinical studies and related research. Two such factors are (a) that Blacks often receive care at academic hospitals located in central cities and (b) that Blacks are disproportionately impacted by certain diseases/diagnoses (McDavid, 1990). In a recent analysis of 28 clinical and related studies, it was reported that 23 of these studies had enrolled a majority of males. Blacks, females, and the elderly were substantially underrepresented (Hall, 1999).

Schooling and Employment. As seen in Figure 47.3, there is a connection between racism, employment, the family, and African Americans' socioeconomic (SES) background. In 1980 approximately 50 percent of all African Americans older than 25 had completed high school. By the year 2000, the numbers increased to 78.5 percent. At the college level, African Americans have had increases in those who have earned a college degree (Leslie, 1995). However, more education has not always amounted to more economic payoff for African Americans. It has been reported that White high school graduates earn only slightly less than African Americans who have attended (but not completed) college (Schaefer, 2004). Black employment rates are consistently more than twice the White rates, and the teenage unemployment rate may reach as high as 40 percent in some cities (Lindsey & Beach, 2004).

Pharmaceuticals. The relatively new field known as ethnopsychopharmacology investigates ethnic variations that affect medication dosing and other aspects of pharmacology. Most of the research in this field has focused on gene polymorphisms (DNA variations) affecting drug metabolizing enzymes (USDHHS, 2001). A faster rate of metabolism leaves less drug in the circulation, whereas a slower rate allows more drug to be recirculated to other parts of the body. For example, African Americans and Asians are, on average, more likely than Whites to be slow metabolizers of several medications for psychosis and depression (Lin et al., 1997). Clinicians who are not aware of these differences may inadvertently prescribe doses too high for minority patients by giving them the dose normally prescribed for Whites.

Health Insurance. Both access to, and affordability of, health care are tied to African Americans having the needed health insurance. In U.S. society health insurance is usually tied to one's place of employment. Given that a vast number of African Americans are unemployed, this reality has important implications for health disparities (USDHHS, 2001).

As a summary statement, it was said that based on the analyses of many different types of covered services, three distinct patterns were observed: (1) Black beneficiaries used fewer preventive and health promotion services (e.g., influenza immunization and mammography); (2) underwent fewer diagnostic tests (see Figure 47.2 under lifestyle health protective behaviors) (e.g., colonoscopy, fewer common surgical procedures such as coronary artery bypass graft); and (3) underwent more types of procedures associated with poor management of chronic disease, such as partial or complete lower limb amputations (as a result of diabetes) (Gornick, 2003). Other nonelective surgeries resulting from poor management included bilateral orchiectomy (removal of both testes, usually in the treatment of cancer); excisional debridement (removal of tissues, usually associated with the treatment of ulcers); and arteriovenostomy (used with renal dialysis) (Gornick et al., 1996).

The Black Family.   While the Black family has been a "tower of strength" for its members over the years, a greater burden of negative life experiences and stress is more likely to impact low-income families. These families are the ones most likely to have challenges associated with single-parent households, coresident issues, and financial stress (Conger et al., 2002). In 2000, the median family income for African Americans ($31,778) was just 62 percent of that for non-Hispanic Whites. Approximately 23 percent of African Americans and about two-thirds of those living in single-parent families live below the poverty level (Lindsey & Beach, 2004).

Community/Neighborhood.   African Americans who are poor are usually found in communities that offer them various challenges (e.g., financial, mental, physical, environmental) on a daily basis. Depending on the nature of these challenges, as well as their resources (see Filter Resource Capability System in Livingston, 1994), they are likely to be affected, for example, with stress and/or death. It has been said (Jenkins & Bell, 1997), that Blacks are more likely to be the victims of serious violent crimes in their communities. Many times non-Whites who themselves may not be victims of crimes know of someone who was a victim (Breslau, 1998).

The link between violence and psychiatric symptoms and illness has been established (Fitzpatrick & Boldizar, 1993; Schwab-Stone et al., 1999). It has been reported (Fitzpatrick & Boldizar, 1993) that over one-fourth of African American youth who had been exposed to violence had symptoms severe enough to warrant a diagnosis of posttraumatic stress disorder (PTSD).

THE INDIVIDUAL: IMPROVEMENTS THROUGH PREVENTION, RESPONSIBILITY, AND EMPOWERMENT

It has been said, "Man as a rule finds it easier to rely on healers than to attempt the more difficult task of living wisely" (David, 1993, p. 32). Whether it is the E-I-I model (see Figure 47.2) or the AMFRREHD (see Figure 47.3), the individual component is very important because it is the activity at this micro level that is finally responsible for the manifestations of different rates of morbidity and mortality that demonstrate the need to eliminate racial and ethnic health disparities. As a matter of fact, from a design perspective (see Baron & Kenny, 1986), the block of conditions (i.e., biology, demographics, resources, stress and health protective behaviors) associated with the individual can be viewed as mediating variables between the dominant predictor variables (i.e., the environment—racism, and the various levels of institutions—health care through the family) and the criterion variable (i.e., health outcomes). At this stage of the model, because all these conditions pertain to the individual, prevention is advocated as the most appropriate strategy to eliminate racial and ethnic health disparities. Following the parameters in the AMFRREHD, a brief overview is presented about African Americans' demographics and resources, stress, and their health protective behaviors, all in the context of their individual and collective impact on selected health outcomes.

Demographics

One of the most striking demographic characteristics in minority health statistics continues to be the difference between African Americans and Whites. For example, the age and gender-adjusted death rate for all causes is 60 percent higher in African Americans as a group compared with their White counterparts (USDHHS, 1995). The health status gap between African Americans and Whites has, for the most part, not narrowed in the last 50 years. This race–health gap is even wider for some health outcome indicators, such as infant mortality (Carmichael & Iyasu, 1998).

Biology and Resources

From a genetic point of view, African Americans may have a predisposition for certain diseases (e.g., sickle-cell anemia). However, in the case of other diseases that disproportionately afflict the Black community (e.g., hypertension, diabetes), it has been argued in the past that some of them can be prevented if African Americans have the needed "resources" (e.g., the requisite stress management skills—see Livingston, 1986/1987, 1988, 1991, 1992, 1993, 1994; Livingston & Carter, 1994) and/or engage in the needed health protective behaviors (see Figure 47.3).

It is important to nurture and cultivate the various resources that African Americans possess, which in turn can serve to moderate the stresses they experience by living in an institutionally racist U.S. society. For example, through mutual affiliation, loyalty, and resourcefulness, African Americans have developed adaptive beliefs, traditions, and practices. Results from surveys indicate that 85 percent of African Americans have described themselves as "fairly religious" or "very religious" (Taylor & Chatters, 1991), and prayer is among their most common coping resources. Social support, through religious participation, have been reported to be important predictors of health outcomes (Livingston et al., 1991).

As seen in Figure 47.2, empowerment is a desirable resource quality to have because it is positively related to health outcomes. According to Henry (2001), empowered individuals are more likely to take proactive steps in terms of personal health, while disempowered individuals are more likely to take a fatalistic approach.

Since empowerment has meant that individuals are supposed to be empowered by interventionists to change repressive forces in their environment, two critical issues become evident: (1) can a disempowered person overcome his or her repressive forces without an interventionist and (2) what does it mean to empower an individual in a context where both the leadership and the followers believe that the leader should be entrusted with all key decisions as with ministers in church? These two questions reflect some issues with notions of empowerment as appropriated in the African American communities, leading some to wonder whether the empowerment model actually disempowers people in the African American communities. In fact, the notion of empowerment within the African American tradition has always been a central feature of the African American scholar.

Stress

While African Americans may experience stress from several sources, racism has been reported to be a very important correlate with stress (Clark et al., 1999). African Americans who are distressed (or stressed) or have a mental illness may present their symptoms according to certain idioms of distress. African American symptom expression can differ from what most clinicians are trained to expect and, therefore, may lead to diagnostic and treatment planning problems (USDHHS, 2001). From a prevention point of view, stress has been reported to be associated with a variety of health outcomes that are very germane to the African American population (e.g., adverse pregnancy outcomes, or APO; heart disease; diabetes; suicide).

African Americans experience a disproportionate incidence of morbidity and mortality from coronary heart disease (CHD) compared to their White counterparts (Jones et al., 2002). SES is inversely related to CHD and often remains predictive independent of other risk factors. Persons with atherosclerosis and increased reactivity to laboratory-induced mental stress demonstrate a generalized exaggerated response to everyday life stresses (Fredrikson et al., 1990) and are at greater risk for myocardial ischemia and CHD events (Brian et al., 1997).

African Americans have higher rates of diabetes and suffer disproportionately due to complications of the disease compared with White Americans (USDHHS, 2000; Livingston, 1993). The number of persons with diabetes in the African American, Hispanic, and Native American communities is 1–5 times greater than in White communities (Flegal et al., 1991). Deaths from diabetes are 2 times higher for African Americans than White Americans, and diabetes-related renal failure is 2.5 times higher in the African American population than in the Hispanic population (Clark, 1998).

While various factors are associated with the etiology of diabetes, stress is increasingly recognized as both a possible antecedent and consequent associated with diabetes. It has been said that for people who have diabetes, the fight-or-flight (stress) response (see a discussion in Livingston, 1992) does not work well. Because insulin is not always able to allow the extra energy into cells (which is a by-product of the stress reaction), glucose piles up into the blood resulting in a lack of glycemic control (Peyrot & McMurry, 1992). Blood glucose (BG) elevations secondary to stress hormone release have been an accepted component of the stress response.

It has been reported that the stressors faced by middle-class African Americans may account for the pattern of suicide risk. For both African Americans and Whites, rates of suicide are much higher for males than females (McLoyd & Lozoff, 2001). While SES is inversely related to the suicide rates for Whites, it is positively related to the suicide rates for African American males (Lester, 1998). Middle-class status is often recent, tenuous, and marginal for African Americans (Anderson, 1999). African Americans are less likely than Whites of similar income to translate their higher economic status into desirable housing and neighborhood conditions (Alba et al., 2000). This being the case, it is not surprising that a recent study found that while suburban residence was associated with lower mortality risk for Whites, it was predictive of markedly elevated mortality risks for African American men (House et al., 2000).

Health Protective Behaviors

These behaviors are crucial for the health outcomes that African Americans are likely to exhibit (see Figure 47.3). From a prevention point of view, because these activities occur at the micro level, they are under the direct control of African Americans. However, as indicated in Figure 47.3, stress can be an influence on these positive (+) activities, either positively (i.e., enhancing them) or negatively (i.e., inhibiting them). Additionally, health education and/or the media can have an influence on these activities as well (see Livingston, 1986/1987, 1993, Livingston et al., 2003).

As cardiovascular disease (CVD), which includes coronary heart disease, is the number one killer of all Americans, a summary statement is made about the variety of risk factors associated with CVD. It should also be said that most of these CVD risk factors are associated with other diseases (e.g., diabetes) that disproportionately affect African Americans. Most, if not all, of these risk factors, can be reduced through appropriate health protective behaviors. These risk factors include elevated blood pressure, cigarette smoking, hypercholesterolimia, excess body weight, sedentary lifestyle, and diabetes. The clustering (comorbidity) of CVD risk factors in African Americans plays a very important role in excess mortality from CHD observed in African Americans.

SOME CLOSING VIEWS ON ELIMINATING RACIAL AND ETHNIC HEALTH DISPARITIES: WHERE DO WE GO FROM HERE?

The models (see Figures 47.2 and 47.3) presented in this chapter, as well as the discussion that ensued, underscore the fact that health disparities are a result of a complex set of interrelated factors. The E-I-I model and the AMFRREHD clearly demonstrate that health outcomes, which are manifested at the micro or individual level [I], are not independent of conditions at the larger, macro-environmental level [E], macro-institutional [I], and smaller meso-level institutions (organizations, communities, and groups). It has been said (Hogan et al., 2001):

Health care factors probably play an important role in creating and sustaining health disparities, but these factors exist downstream from the non-health-care forces that create disease in the first place. All of these factors likely act together to create racial and ethnic disparities, and they should be measured and addressed more holistically. (p. 136)

Focusing on CVD Risk Factors

Given that cardiovascular diseases remain the number one killer of all Americans, including Black and African Americans, it is pragmatic to focus preventive efforts at controlling and/or prevention CVD and its associated risk factors in the Black community (NCHS, 2003). These deaths, disabilities, and social and economic costs are expected to increase due to the aging of the so-called baby boomers. As for the health disparities, they are thought to be the result of the complex interactions among genetic variations, environmental factors, and specific health behaviors (Office of Minority Health, 2003). Stated differently, these disparities are likely related to a greater prevalence of risk factors for CVD, including hypertension, diabetes, hyperlipidemia, obesity, smoking, and sedentary lifestyles. Some of these may have a genetic predisposition among African Americans. This is not to downplay the impact that discrimination, cultural barriers, and lack of access to health care might have on poorer health outcomes for African Americans (U.S. Commission on Civil Rights, 1999). Lowering the mortality rate for CVD in African Americans must involve "embracing prevention as the first step" (USDHHS, 2003). We must find ways to decrease those risk factors that have been closely associated with this deadly condition. Distinct from age, family history, or genetic determinants are modifiable risk factors such as high blood pressure, cigarette smoking, and high-fat diets.

The Need to Emphasize Prevention

Any public health programs that are developed to improve overall morbidity and mortality of the noted conditions among African Americans must first be directed at prevention. That is, we should increase the funding for programs directed at reducing and eliminating modifiable risk factors that impact these mortality figures. Although the public health policies should be developed at the federal level (see Figures 47.2 and 47.3) since this is a national problem, such programs must be implemented at the state and local level if they are to be effective. Above all, these programs should be field-tested if need be, and they must be culturally specific and sensitive to the unique needs of at-risk, inner-city African Americans (Resnicow & Braithwaite, 2001).

Fostering Innovative Programs and Collaborative Efforts

Success in eliminating racial and ethnic health disparities will not be achieved by government agencies acting alone (see the interconnections between various institutions in Figure 47.2). There must be collaborations and innovative partnerships between governmental bodies, community agencies, health-care organizations, insurance companies, and professional bodies at the local, state, and national levels. While there is consensus on these race and ethnic-related health disparities, there is a relative absence on how to intervene to reduce these disparities using a conceptual framework. This being the case, the E-I-I model (see Figure 47.2) and the more action-oriented AMFRREHD (see Figure 47.3) are suggested as guiding frameworks to follow.

Increased Support For the Unique Contributions of Historically Black Colleges and Universities (HBCUs): Funding and Focused Research

In order to accomplish the goal of eliminating health disparities among African Americans, a new paradigm is required. The recent Institute of Medicine report on Racial and Health Disparities provided two major recommendations to move toward the new paradigm. The recommendations were to (1) increase intervention and demonstration research projects focused on minority communities and (2) include minority institutions and researchers in implementing research in minority communities.

Implementation of this paradigmatic shift began in 1996 at the Centers for Medicare and Medicaid Services (CMS), formerly the Health Care Financing Administration, with the Historically Black Colleges and Universities (HBCU) Health Services Research Grant program. Using President Bush's executive order focusing on HBCUs (13256), CMS has allocated funding for HBCUs to conduct research focusing on the reduction of health disparities among African Americans. To date, and as a result of CMS funding to several HBCUs, various major topical areas that are most germane to the health of the Black community have been funded. Some such funded projects include empirical research on hypertension, diabetes, prostate cancer, depression, and long-term care and housing for the elderly (Personal communication with Dr. Richard Bragg, Minority Coordinator, Health Services Research, CMS, October 2003).

This model recognizes the tremendous potential of HBCU investigators to reduce health disparities. In the past, HBCU researchers have not had a major role in research aimed at reducing health disparities. Majority institutions have been the recipients of federal dollars to reduce health disparities, and yet disparities continue. HBCUs may be the "missing link" in the battle to overcome health disparities. HBCU investigators are crucial to the conduct of research that will impact the health care and health behavior of African Americans. These investigators have the unique expertise, knowledge, and sensitivity that are necessary to address the pressing health-care and health financing issues of African Americans. HBCU researchers have demonstrated their ability to involve African Americans described as "hard to reach" in research studies. They have long-standing linkages with the African American community that result in recognition of HBCU researchers as authentic voices within the community.

HBCU researchers recognized their role in reducing health disparities and subsequently formed a partnership with CMS in 1996 to develop the HBCU Research Network for Health Services and Health Disparities. The network promotes health services research by and for African Americans to address the health needs of African Americans and disseminate information about health disparities. CMS partners with the network to conduct research conferences and seminars that highlight research conducted by network members related to health disparities.

Implementation of this model requires a paradigmatic shift and "out of the box" thinking, because historically, there have been major disparities in the allocation of research dollars between majority institutions and HBCUs. In addition to direct allocation of funds to HBCUs to conduct research with African Americans, specific recommendations and strategies for a research agenda to decrease health disparities among African Americans include (1) establishing partnerships with community-based organizations, faith-based organizations, health providers, health associations, HHS agencies, and majority institutions, (2) increasing the number of HBCU researchers capable of conducting health services research, (3) increasing the infrastructure of HBCUs to conduct health services research, (4) increasing the funding for CMSs HBCU research program, and (5) developing intervention projects within each of the six areas in the President's Initiative and the areas of asthma, obesity, oral health, mental health, and cultural competence (see Figures 47.2 and 47.3 for the interconnection between government and educational institutions, such as HBCUs).

The Need for Individual Empowerment

While institutions will continue to play an important role in African American health, as discussed in this chapter and as illustrated in the E-I-I model (see Figure 47.2) and the AMFRREHD (see Figure 47.3), African Americans have to become more responsible for their health and empowered to engage in protective lifestyle behaviors. Also, greater long-lasting health achievements will come to African Americans only when they understand, believe, and practice disease prevention behaviors.

Good health cannot be purchased. Therefore, the notion that we can spend to receive health is an oversimplification. There is little that medicine (i.e., institutions) can do about, for example, advance cases of cirrhosis of the liver resulting from alcoholism, lung carcinoma due to smoking, and fatal wounds resulting from homicide. In short, for African Americans, these conditions should, if possible, be prevented before they enter the medical "pipeline," hence the need for primary prevention accompanied by individual actions.

CONCLUSION

Elimination of health disparities among African Americans will require a major commitment of time and resources. According to a fact sheet published by the Department of Health and Human Services, the elimination of health disparities will require a national effort including the public and private sectors, individuals, and communities working together. It is anticipated that the initial cost in time and resources will be offset by improvements in the health status of African Americans and subsequent reductions in costs due to a decrease in the incidence of preventable diseases and disorders.

The above-mentioned realities notwithstanding, the road ahead to improving the health status of Blacks, although difficult, is not insurmountable. Sustained success, however, will require action that leads to bold, innovative, comprehensive, and culturally sensitive directives by politicians, health-care personnel, and researchers. However, based on both the E-I-I model (Figure 47.2) and the derived AMFRREHD (Figure 47.3), conceptual and guiding frameworks are presented that can be added to the armamentarium of needed approaches and tools to successfully eliminate racial and ethnic health disparities.

Given the relative difficulty in changing the policies and practices of macro-level social institutions and given the preference for prevention over intervention, a great deal of effort must be spent on educating at-risk African Americans about the value of consistently engaging in needed health protective activities, as well as increasing their "resource capabilities" discussed in the chapter. Health promotion can be used on a larger basis, and health education can be used on a more individual level to disseminate the needed health information. The bottom line is that African Americans have to fully appreciate that they have perhaps the most important role to play in improving their health status. That is, they must become more responsible and empowered to adopt "healthy" lifestyle behaviors. However, for some African Americans to become inculcated with these "alien" views, they must abandon existing values and beliefs that have been practiced over the years. Hence, for these individuals, sustainable change involving a new, but more health-oriented, value system, will occur only through organizational initiatives bordering on cognitive restructuring with the accompanying resocialization involving the new ways of behaving.

The consequences of inaction and/or failure to improve the health of African Americans living in America will have disastrous moral, political, and social consequences. If allowed to occur, these ensuing consequences will be unprecedented in the history of this nation.

NOTE

1. This report discusses data for 50 states and the District of Columbia, but not Puerto Rico. The Census 2000 Redistricting Data (Public Law 94–171). Summary File was released on a state-by-state basis in March 2001.

REFERENCES

Alba, R.D., Logan, J.R., & Stults, B.J. (2000). How segregated are middle-class African Americans? *Social Problems, 47*, 543–558.

American Cancer Society. (2003). Cancer Facts and Figures (p. 2).

Anderson, E. (1999). The social situation of the Black executive: Black and White identities in the corporate world. In M. Lamont (Ed.), *The cultural territories of race: Black and White boundries* (pp. 3–29). Chicago: University of Chicago Press.

Anderson, N.B., Bastida, E., Kramer, B.J., Williams, D.R., & Wong, M. (1995). Panel II: Macrosocial and environmental influences on minority health. *Health Psychology, 14(7)*, 601–612.

Anderson, R., Mullner, R.M., & Cornelius, L.J. (1987). Black–White differences in health status: Methods or substance? *Milbank Quarterly, 65*, 72–99.

Baron, R.M., & Kenny, D.A. (1986). The moderator-mediator variable distinction in social psychological research: Conceptual, strategic, and statistical considerations. *Journal of Personality and Social Psychology, 51*, 1173–1182.

Breslau, N., Kessler, R.C., Howard, D.C., Schultz, L.R., Davis, G.C., & Andreski, M.A. (1998). Trauma and posttraumatic stress disorder in the community. *Archives of General Psychiatry, 55*, 626–632.

Brian, G.K., Becker, L.C., Blumenthal, R.S., et al. (1997). Exaggerated reactivity to mental stress is associated with exercise-induced myocardial ischemia in an asymptomatic high-risk population. *Circulation, 96*, 4246–4253.

Brown, E.R., Ojeda, V.D., Wyn, R., & Levan, R. (2000). *Racial and ethnic disparities in access to health insurance and health care.* Los Angeles: UCLA Center for Health Policy Research and the Henry J. Kaiser Family Foundation.

Bryant, B. (2001). Key research & policy issues facing environmental justice. In C. Hartman (Ed.), *Challenges to Equality, Poverty and Race In America* (pp. 228–231). New York: M.E. Sharpe.

Bryant, B., & Mohai, P. (1999). *Race and the incidence of environmental hazards.* Boulder, CO: Westview Press.

Bullard, R.D. (1992). Urban infrastructure: Social, environmental, and health risks to African Americans. In B.J. Tidwell (Ed.), *The state of Black America.* New York: Urban League.

Canto, J.G., et al. (2000). Relation of race and sex to the use of reperfusion therapy in Medicare beneficiaries with acute myocardial infarction. *New England Journal of Medicine, 342*, 1094–1100.

Carmichael, S.L., & Iyasu, S. (1998). Changes in the Black-White infant mortality gap from 1983 to 1991 in the United States. *American Journal of Preventive Medicine, 15*, 220–227.

Clark, C. (1998). How should we respond to the worldwide diabetes epidemic? *Diabetes Care, 21*, 475–476.

Clark, R., Anderson, N.B., Clark, V.R., & Williams, D.R. (1999). Racism as a stressor for African Americans— A biopsychosocial model. *American Psychologist, 54(10)*, 806–816.

Cobb, W.M. (1981). The Black American in medicine. *Journal of the National Medical Association, 78*, 1185–1244.

Cockerham, W.C. (1992). *Medical sociology* (5th ed.). Englewood Cliffs, NJ: Prentice-Hall.

Commission for Racial Justice. (1987). Waste and race in the United States: A national report on the racial and socioeconomic characteristics of communities with hazardous waste sites. New York: United Church of Christ.

Conger, R.D., Wallace, L.E., Sun, Y., Simmons, R.L., McLoyd, V.C., & Brody, G.H. (2002). Economic pressure in African American families: A replication and extension of the family stress model. *Developmental Psychology, 38(2)*, 179–193.

Cooper-Patrick, L., Gallo, J.J., Powe, N.R., Steinwachs, D.M., Eaton, W.W., & Ford, D.E. (1999). Mental health service utilization by African Americans and Whites: The Baltimore Epidemiologic Catchment Area Follow-up. *Medical Care, 37*, 1034–1045.

David, R. (1993). The demand side of the health care crisis. *Harvard Magazine, 95*, 31–32.

David, R.J., & Collins, J.W. (1997). Differing birthweight among infants of U.S.-born Blacks, African-born Blacks, and U.S.-born Whites. *New England Journal of Medicine, 337*, 1209–1214.

Doll, R. (1992). Health and environment in the 1990s. *American Journal of Public Health, 82*, 933–943.

Fiscella, K., & Franks, P. (1997). Poverty or income inequality as predictor of mortality: Longitudinal cohort study. *British Medical Journal, 314(7096)*, 1724–1727.

Fiscella, K., & Franks, P., Gold, M.R., & Clancy, C.M. (2000). Inequality in quality: Addressing socioeconomic, racial, and ethnic disparities in health-care. *Journal of the American Medical Association, 283(19)*, 2579–2584.

Fitzpatrick, K.M., & Boldizar, J.P. (1993). The prevalence and consequence to exposure to violence among African American youth. *Journal of the American Academy of Child and Adolescent Psychiatry, 32*, 424–430.

Flegal, K., et al. (1991). Prevalence of diabetes in Mexican Americans, Cubans and Puerto Ricans from the Hispanic and Nutrition Examination Survey, 1982–1984. *Diabetes Care, 14*, 628–638.

Fredrikson, M., Tuomisto, M., & Melin, B. (1990). Blood pressure in healthy men and women under laboratory and naturalistic conditions. *Journal of Psychosomatic Research, 34*, 675–686.

Fried, V., Prager, K., MacKay, A., & Xia, H. (2003) Health, United States, 2003. Chartbook on Trends in the Health of Americans. Hyattsville, Maryland: National Center for Health Statistics. Available: http://www.cdc.gov/nchs/data/hus/hus03.pdf (Retrieved January 25, 2004).

Geiger, H.J. (2001). Racial and ethnic disparities in diagnosis and treatment: A review of the evidence and a consideration of causes. In B.D. Smedley, A.Y. Smith, & A.R. Nelson (Eds.), *Unequal treatment—Confronting racial and ethnic disparities in health care* (pp. 216–247). Washington, DC: National Academies Press.

General Accounting Office. (1983). Siting of hazardous waste landfills and their correlation with racial and economic status of surrounding communities. Washington, DC: General Accounting Office.

Goldenberg, R.L., Hauth, J.C., & Andrews, W.W. (2000). Intrauterine infection and preterm delivery. *New England Journal of Medicine, 342(20)*, 1500–1507.

Gornick, M. (2000). *Vulnerable populations and Medicare services: Why do disparities exist?* New York: Century Foundation Press.

Gornick, M.E. (2003). A decade of research on disparities in Medicare utilization: Lessons for the health and health care of vulnerable men. *American Journal of Public Health, 93(5)*, 753–759.

Gornick, M.E., et al. (1996). Effects of race and income on mortality and use of services among Medicare beneficiaries. *New England Journal of Medicine, 335*, 791–799.

Greenberg, D. (2000). Reconstructing race and protest—Environmental justice in New York City. *Environmental History, 5(2)*, 223–250.

Hall, W.D. (1999). Representation of Blacks, women, and the very elderly. *Ethnicity and Disease, 9*, 333–340.

Hames, C.G., & Greenlund, K.L. (1996). Ethnicity and cardiovascular disease: The Evans County heart study. *American Journal of the Medical Sciences, 311*, 130–134.

The Health Care Challenge (September, 1999). Acknowledging disparity, confronting discrimination, and ensuring equality. United States Commission on Civil Rights.

Henry, P. (2001). An examination of the pathways through which social class impacts health outcomes. *Academy of Marketing review, [Online], 01 (03)*. Available at: http://www.amsrev/theory/henry03-01.html

Hogan, V.K., Njoroge, T., Durant, T.M., & Ferre, C.D. (2001). Eliminating disparities in perinatal outcomes—Lessons learned. *Maternal and Child Health Journal, 5(2)*, 135–140.

House, J.S., et al. (2000). Excess mortality among urban residents: How much, for whom, and why? *American Journal of Public Health, 90*, 1898–1904.

Institute of Medicine. (1999). *Toward environmental justice: Research, education and health policy needs.* Washington, DC: National Academy Press, p. 2.

Jenkins, E.J., & Bell, C.C. (1997). Exposure and response to community violence among children and adolescents. In J. Osofsky (Ed.), *Children in violent society* (pp. 9–31). New York: Guilford Press.

Johnson, C. (1991). Challenge for the minority physician: Gaining quality health care for the underserved. *Journal of the National Medical Association, 83*, 563–568.

Jones D.W., Chambless, L.E., Folsom, A.R., Heiss, G., et al. (2002). Risk factors for coronary heart disease in African Americans: The Atherosclerosis Risk in Communities Study, 1987–1997. *Archives of Internal Medicine, 162*, 2565–2572.

King, G. (1996). Institutional racism and the medical/health complex: A conceptual analysis. *Ethnicity and Disease, 6*, 30–46.

Kirschenman, J., & Neckerman, K.M. (1991). "We'd love to hire them, but . . .": The meaning of race for employers. In C. Jencks & P.E. Patterson (Eds.), *The urban underclass* (pp. 203–234). Washington, DC: Brookings Institution.

Kobasa, S.C. (1979). Stressful life events, personality, and health: An inquiry into hardiness. *Journal of Personality and Social Psychology, 37*, 1–11.

Komaromy, M., Grumbach, K., Drake, M., Vrazizan, K., & Lurie, N. (1996). The role of Black and Hispanic physicians in providing health care for the underserved populations. *New England Journal of Medicine, 334*, 305–310.

Krieger, N. (1993). Epidemiologic theory and societal patterns of disease. *Epidemiology, 4*, 276–278.

Krieger, N. (2003). Does racism harm health? Did child abuse exist before 1962? On explicit questions, critical science, and current controversies: An ecosocial perspective. *American Journal of Public Health, 93(2)*, 194–199.

Kovaleski, S.F., & Fahrenthold, D.A. (2004). NW housing complex a tangle of drugs, despair. *The Washington Post, (Sunday)*, A1, Column 1.

Laframboise, H.L. (1973). Health policy: Breaking the problem down in more manageable segments. *Canadian Medical Association Journal, 108*, 388–393.

Lalonde, M. (1974). *A new perspective on the health of Canadians*. Ottawa: Canadian Department of Health and Welfare.

Lantz, P.M. (1996). Socioeconomic factors, health behaviors and mortality. *Journal of the American Medical Association, 279*, 1703–1708.

Lantz, P.M., House, J.S., Lepkowski, J.M., Williams, D.R., Mero, R.P., & Chen, J. (1998). Socioeconomic factors, health behaviors, and mortality: Results from a nationally representative prospective study of US adults. *Journal of the American Medical Association, 279(21)*, 1703–8.

Leslie, C. (November 6, 1995). "You can't high-jump if the bar is set too low." *Newsweek*, 82–83.

Lester, D. (1998). *Suicide in African Americans*. Commack, NY: Nova Science.

Lillie-Blanton, M., Martinez, R.M., & Salganicoff, A. (2001). Site of medical care: Do racial and ethnic differences persist? *Yale Journal of Health Policy, Law and Ethnics, 1(1)*, 1–17.

Lin, K.M., Cheung, F., Smith, M., & Poland, R.E. (1997). The use of psychotropic medications in working with Asian patients. In E. Lee (Ed.), *Working with Asian Americans: A guide for clinicians* (pp. 388–399). New York: Guilford.

Lindsey, L.L., & Beach, S. (2004). *Sociology* (3d Ed.). Upper Saddle River, NJ: Pearson Prentice-Hall.

Livingston, I.L. (1985). Alcohol consumption and hypertension: A review with suggested implications. *Journal of the National Medical Association, 77*, 129–135.

Livingston, I.L. (1986/1987). Blacks, lifestyle and hypertension: The importance of health education. *Humboldt Journal of Social Relations, 14*, 195–213.

Livingston, I.L. (1988). Stress and health dysfunctions: The importance of health education. *Stress and Medicine, 4(3)*, 155–161.

Livingston, I.L. (1990). Perceived control, knowledge and fear of AIDS among college students: An exploratory study. *Journal of Health and Social Policy, 2*, 47–65.

Livingston, I.L. (1991). Stress, hypertension and renal disease in Black Americans: A review with implications. *National Journal of Sociology, 5(2)*, 143–181.

Livingston, I.L. (1992). *The ABC's of stress management—taking control of your life*. Salt Lake City, UT: Northwest.

Livingston, I.L. (1993). Renal disease and Black Americans: Selected Issues. *Social Science and Medicine, 37(5)*, 613–621.

Livingston, I.L. (1994). Social status, stress, and health: Black Americans at risk. In I.L. Livingston (Ed.), *Handbook of Black American health: The mosaic of conditions, issues, policies and prospects* (pp. 236–252). Westport, CT: Greenwood Publishing.

Livingston, I.L., & Ackah, S. (1992). Hypertension, end-stage renal disease and rehabilitation: A look at Black Americans. *The Western Journal of Black Studies, 16*, 103–112.

Livingston, I.L., & Carter, J.J. (1994). Improving the health of the Black community: Outlook for the future. In I.L. Livingston (Ed.), *Handbook of Black American health: The mosaic of conditions, issues, policies and prospects* (pp. 398–417). Westport, CT: Greenwood.

Livingston, I.L., Levine, D.M., & Moore, R. (1991). Social integration and Black intraracial blood pressure variation. *Ethnicity and Disease, 1(2)*, 135–149.

Livingston, I.L., & Marshall, R. (1991). Cardiac reactivity and elevated blood pressure levels among young African Americans: The importance of stress. In D.J. Jones (Ed.), *Prescriptions and policies: The social well-being of African Americans in the 1990s* (pp. 77–91). New Brunswick, NJ: Transactions.

Livingston, I.L., Otado, J., & Warren, C. (2003). Stress, adverse pregnancy outcomes and African American females: Assessing the implications using a conceptual model. *Journal of the National Medical Association, 95(11)*, 1103–1109.

Lucas, J.W., Barr-Anderson, D.J., & Kington, R.S., (2003). The health status, health insurance, and health care utilization patterns of immigrant Black men. *American Journal of Public Health, 93*, 1740–1747.

Maguire, K., & Pastore, E. (Eds.). (1999). *Sourcebook of criminal justice statistics*. Washington, DC: U.S. Government Printing Office.

McCarty D.J. et al. (1995). Incidence of systemic lupus erythematosus. Race and gender differences. *Arthritis and Rheumatism, 38(9)*, 1260–1270.

McCord, C., & Freeman, H.P. (1990). Excess mortality in Harlem. *New England Journal of Medicine, 322*, 173–177.

McDavid, L.M. (September, 1990). An overlooked resource: The Black patient (pp. 67–70). Conference Proceedings: Primary care research: An agenda for the 1990s. The Agency for Health Care Primary Research (AHCPR).

McGinnis, J.M. (1990). Prevention in 1989: The state of the nation. *American Journal of Preventive Medicine, 6(1)*, 1–5.

McLoyd, V.C., & Lozoff, B. (2001). Racial and ethnic trends in children's and adolescents' behavior and development. In N.J. Smelser, W.J. Wilson, & F. Mitchell (Eds.), *America becoming: Racial trends and their consequences*. Washington, DC: National Academy Press.

McKinnon, J. (2001). The Black population: 2000. Census 2000 Brief. U.S. Census Bureau. U.S. Department of Commerce, Economics and Statistics Administration.

McLeroy, K.R., Bibeau, D., Stecklor, A., & Glanz, K. (1988). An ecological perspective on health promotion programs. *Health Education* Quarterly, *15*, 251–377.

Miller, L.S., Wasserman, G.A., Neugebauer, R., Gorman-Smith, D., & Kamboukos, D. (1999). Witnessed community violence and antisocial behavior in high-risk, urban boys. *Journal of Clinical Child Psychology, 28*, 2–11.

Minino, A.M., Arias, E., Kochanek, K.D., Murphy, S.L., & Smith, B.L. (2002). Deaths: Final data for 2000. *National Vital Statistics Reports, 50(15)*, Hyattsville, MD.

Minino, A.M., & Smith, B.L. (2001). Deaths: Preliminary data for 2000. National Center for Health Statistics, *National Vital Statistics Reports, 49(12)*.

Mohai, P., & Bryant, B. (1992). Race, poverty, and the environment. *EPA Journal, 18*, 6–8

Mohai, P., & Bryant, B. (1998). Is there a "race" effect on concern for environmental quality? *Public Opinion Quarterly, 62*, 475–505.

Mohai, P., & Kershner, D. (2002). Race and environmental voting in the U.S. Congress. *Social Science Quarterly, 83(1)*, 167–189.

National Center for Health Statistics (NCHS). (2002). Health, United States, 2002: With chartbook on trends in the health of Americans. Hyattsville, MD: U.S. Government Printing Office.

National Center for Health Statistics (NCHS). (2003). Health, United States, 2003: With Chartbook on Trends in the Health of Americans. Hyattsville, Maryland: U.S. Government Printing Office.

Needleman, H. (November 9, 1990). The quite epidemic: Low dose toxicity in children. Paper presented at the Charles A. Dana Award Presentations for Pioneering in Health and Higher Education, New York.

Niaura, R., Stoney, C.M., & Herbert, P.N. (1992). Lipids in psychological research: The last decade. *Biological Psychology, 34*, 1–43.

Office of Minority Health. (2003a). Disease burden & risk factors. Fact Sheet. Center for Disease Control and Prevention.

Office of Minority Health. (2003b). Eliminate disparities in cardiovascular disease. Fact Sheet. Center for Disease Control and Prevention.

O'Hare, W.P. (1996). A new look at poverty in America. *Population Bulletin, 51*, 1–48.

Østbye, T., Taylor, D.H., Lee, A.M., Greenberg, G., & van Scoyoc, L. (2003, December). Racial differences in influenza vaccination among older Americans 1996–2000: longitudinal analysis of the Health and Retirement Study (HRS) and the Asset and Health Dynamics Among the Oldest Old (AHEAD) survey. *BioMedical Public Health 2003, 3*, 41.

Peyrot, M.F., & McMurry, J.F. (1992). Stress buffering and glycemic control: The role of coping styles. *Diabetes Care, 15(7)*, 842–846.

Pirkle, J.L., et al. (1994). The decline in blood levels in the United States: The National Health and Nutrition Examination Survey (NHANES III). *Journal of the American Medical Association, 272*, 284–291.

Resnicow, K., & Braithwaite, R.L. (2001). Cultural sensitivity in public health. In R.L. Braithwaite & S.E. Taylor (Eds.), *Health issues in the Black community* (2d) (pp. 516–542). San Francisco, California: Jossey-Bass Publishers.

Rosenthal, D.A., & Kosciulek, J.F. (1996). Clinical judgment and bias due to client race and ethnicity: An overview with implications for rehabilitation counselors. *Journal of Applied Rehabilitation Counseling, 27(3)*, 30–36.

Rowley, D.L., & Tosteson, H. (1993). Preterm delivery among African American women: A research strategy. *American Journal of Preventive Medicine, 9(6 Suppl)*, 1–123.

Ruiz, D.S. (1995). A demographic and epidemiologic profile of the African American elderly. In D.K. Padgett (Ed.), *Handbook of ethnicity, aging and mental health*. Westport, CT: Greenwood Press.

Schaefer, R.T. (2004). *Racial and ethnic groups* (9th ed.). Upper Saddle River, NJ: Prentice-Hall.

Schwab-Stone, M., Chen, C., Greenberger, E., Silver, D., Lichtman, J., & Voyce, C. (1999). No safe haven II: The effects of violence exposure on urban youth. *Journal of the American Academy of Child and Adolescent Psychiatry, 38*, 359–367.

Shea, S., & Fullilove, M.T. (1985). Entry of Black and other minority students in U.S. medical schools: Historical perspectives and recent trends. *New England Journal of Medicine, 313*, 933–940.

Shiefer, S.E., Escarce, J.J., & Schulman, K.A. (2000). Race and sex differences in the management of coronary artery disease. *American Heart Journal, 139*, 848–857.

Sidel, V.W., & Sidel, R. (Eds.). (1984). *Reforming medicine: Lessons of the last quarter century*. New York: Pantheon Books.

Singh, G.L., & Siahpush, M. (2002). Ethnic-immigrant differentials in health behaviors, morbidity and cause-specific mortality in the United States. *Human Biology, 74(1)*, 83–109.

Smedley, B.D., Stith, A.Y., & Nelson, A.R. (Eds.). (2002). *Unequal treatment: Confronting racial and ethnic disparities in health care*. Washington, DC: National Academy Press.

Steinhorn, L., & Diggs-Brown, B. (1999). *By the color of our skin: The illusion of integration and the reality of race*. New York: Dutton.

Stokøls, D. (1992). Establishing and maintaining healthy environments: Toward a social ecology of health promotion. *American Psychologist 47*, 6–22.

Taylor, R.J., & Chatters, L.M. (1991). Religious life. In J.S. Jackson (Ed.), *Life in Black America*. Newbury Park, CA: Sage.

Terris, M. (1984). Newer perspectives on the health of Canadians: Beyond the Lalonde report. *Journal of Health Policy, 5*, 327–337.

Thomas, S.B. (1992). Health status of the Black community in the 21st century: A futuristic perspective for health education. *Journal of Health Education, 23*, 7–13.

Turner, M.A., & Skidmore, F. (Eds.). (1999). *Mortage lending discrimination: A review of existing evidence*. Washington, DC: Urban Institute.

U.S. Census Bureau. (1999). *Statistical abstract of the United States. The National Data Book*. Washington, DC: Author.

U.S. Census Bureau (2000a). Brief: Overview of race and Hispanic origin. Washington, DC: Author.

U.S. Census Bureau. (2000b). Retrieved on March 15, 2001 from, http://www.census.gov.

U.S. Commission on Civil Rights. (September 1999). The health care challenge: Acknowledging disparity, confronting discrimination, and ensuring equality.

U.S. Congress, Office of Technology Assessment. (1992). *Does health insurance make a difference?—Background paper, OTA-BP-H-99*. Washington, DC: U.S. Government Printing Office.

U.S. Department of Health and Human Services (USDHHS). (1985). *Report of the Secretary's Task Force on Black and Minority Health*. Washington, DC: U.S. Government Printing Office.

U.S. Department of Health and Human Services (USDHHS). (1995). *Health in the United States, 1994*. DHHS Publication No. PHHS, 95–1232.

U.S. Department of Health and Human Services (USDHHS). (2000). *Healthy people 2010: Understanding and improving health* (2d ed.). Washington, DC: U.S. Government Printing Office.

U.S. Department of Health and Human Services (USDHHS). (2001). *Mental health: Culture, race, and ethnicity—A supplement to mental health: A report of the surgeon general.* Rockville, MD: USDHHS, Public Health Service, Office of the Surgeon General.

U.S. Department of Health and Human Services (USDHHS). (2003). *A public health action plan to prevent heart disease and stroke.* Atlanta, GA: U.S. Department of Health and Human Services, Center for Disease Control and Prevention.

U.S. Immigration and Naturalization Service (USINS). (2002). *Statistical yearbook of the Immigration and Naturalization Service.* Washington, DC: U.S. Government Printing Office.

Walker, B., Goodwin, N.J., & Warren, R.C. (1992). Violence: A challenge to the public health community. *Journal of the National Medical Association, 84*, 490–496.

Watts, R.J. (January 31, 2003). Race Consciousness and the health of African Americans. *Online Journal of Issues in Nursing, 8(1)*, Manuscript 3. Available: http://nursingworld.org/ojin/topic20/tpc20_3.htm (Retrieved January 31, 2004).

Wilkinson, R.G. (1986). *Class and health.* London: Travistock.

Williams, D.R., & Jackson, J.S. (2000). Race/ethnicity and the 2000 census: Recommendations for African American and other Black populations in the United States. *American Journal of Public Health, 90*, 1728–1730.

Wilson, K.B. (2002). Explanation of vocational rehabilitation acceptance and ethnicity: A national investigation. *Rehabilitation Bulletin, 45(3)*, 168–176.

Yen, I.H., & Syme, S.L. (1999). The social environment and health: A discussion of the epidemiologic literature. *Annual Review of Public Health, 20*, 287–308.

Yinger, J. (1995). *Closed doors, opportunities lost: The continuing costs of housing discrimination.* New York: Russell Sage Foundation.

Index

802; affordability, 803; availability, 802; background, 801

Structural barriers, health improvements and the context of health disparities: domain I–government and policy, 794–795; domain II–socioeconomic status (SES), 795–799; domain III–culture, 799–800; domain IV–gender relations, 800–801; domain V–spirituality, 801

Structural barriers and health improvements overview: accomplishments and future needs, 805; background, 792–793; context of health disparities, 794–801; empowerment and group-decision making, 36, 151, 349, 394, 621, 788, 795, 803, 851, 854; health-care and the need for professionals, 801–803

Stuart, B.C., 703

Student National Medical Association, 703

Substance use/abuse: African American nursing students, 443; alcohol use, 347–348; background and epidemiology, 344, 390, 645; Carter Center, 560; co-morbidity, 202, 483; Drug Abuse Warning Network (DAWN), 340–341; health indicator, 427–428; injection users, 242; mental health and distress, 373, 619, 643, 645–646; National Household Survey on Drug Use and Health (NHSDUH, formerly NHSDA), 329–330; prevention and intervention, 269, 271, 308, 609; prisons, 646–648; reducing disparities, 788; socioeconomic status (SES), 390–400, 845; STDs and HIV, 247–248, 644, 794; violence, 456. See also Drug use/abuse

Sudden cardiac death (SCD): definition, rates and epidemiology, 4–10; racial differences, 22–23, 226–228. See also Coronary heart disease (CHD)

Suicide and self-directed violence: adolescent and teenagers, 223; black male, 223, 226; discrimination, mental health and stress, 220, 230, 562, 851–852; epidemiology, definition and description of the problem, 291, 300–301; forticide, 225; interpersonal violence, 229–230; methods, 304; morbidity, 305–306; prisons, 844, 647, 649; prevention, racial variations, and recommendations, 306–309, 562, 698, 794, 839; protective factors, 306; rates, 303; sociodemographic variation, 301–304; socioeconomic status (SES), 219–220; suicidal ideation, 300, 464

Sullivan, Louis W., 520–521

Supplemental Security Income (SSI), 704

Supreme Court, 649, 696, 703, 720

Surveillance Epidemiology and End Results (SEER), 97, 596, 820

Suspicion, 140, 152, 159, 200, 329, 454, 703, 765, 768

Svensson, C.K., 810–811

Swartz, O.J., 559, 561

Swift, E.K., 567, 687

sympatho-adrenomedullary (SAS), 476, 488

Symptomatic myocardial ischemia, 32–33

Systemic diseases, 162, 187, 728

Systemic lupus erythematosus (SLE), 72, 166, 400

Systolic blood pressure, 10, 27, 57–58, 60, 218, 395, 414, 682. See also Hypertension

Tareen, N., 71

Task Force on Black and Minority Health, 80, 556, 716, 811

Teacher professional development, 620–621

Teachers, 620, 622, 679

Telfair, J., 129–130, 136–137, 138, 140–141

Texas border counties, 603

Third National Health and Nutrition Examination Survey (NHANES III), 26, 58, 65, 428, 433, 820, 846

Thrombolysis in Myocardial Infarction, 814

Thrombolytic therapy or treatment, 34–35, 44, 812, 814–815, 818

Thyroid gland, 166

Tissue necrosis factor alfa, 85

Tissue plasminogen activator, 44, 48, 814

Title VI of the Civil Rights Law of 1964, 662

Tobacco: alcohol use/abuse, 506, 596; allergens, 122; CHD, 26, 36; CVD, 26, 36; future issues to address, 586; health indicator, 427; Healthy People 2010 objectives and health indicators, 427; inner-city children and secondary smoke, 166; lung cancer, 228; multiple myeloma, 172; nutrition and cancer, 172, 191, 195, 228; occupational allergens, 122; periodontal disease oral cancer, 188, 191; poverty and low birthweight babies, 361; pregnancy, 464; prevention, 195; racial and gender differences in cancer, 420; racial and health disparities, 586, 593; risk factor for pregnancy outcomes, 464; SES and asthma, 172; SIDs, 363. See also Cigarette smoking

Tosteson, H., 843

Total cholesterol, 6, 26, 412

Toxic Waste and Race in the United States, 654

Toxic waste facilities, 653, 655, 659–660. See also Toxic waste sites

Toxic waste production and disposal, 653–654

Toxic waste sites, 654–655, 658, 846

Transaction, 130, 138, 391, 393–394

Transactional stress and coping model, 138

Transplantation: African American kidney donor pool, 779; African American recipients of African American donated kidneys, 779; Black donor education, 779; compliance rates for Blacks, 784; di-

About the Editor and Contributors

IVOR LENSWORTH LIVINGSTON Ph.D, M.P.H., C.H.E.S., is a tenured, graduate Professor of Medical Sociology and Social Epidemiology in the Department of Sociology and Anthropology and an Adjunct Professor, Department of Community Health and Family Practice, School of Medicine, Howard University. He obtained his Ph.D. in Medical Sociology from Howard University, his Master's of Public Health (MPH) from the Harvard School of Public Health, and his Post Doctoral Certificate in Cardiovascular Epidemiology from the Johns Hopkins School of Hygiene and Public Health (now called the Johns Hopkins Bloomberg School of Public Health). He is also a nationally certified health education (stress) specialist (CHES). He is an affiliated member of the Resource Persons Network, Office of Minority Health Resource Center, U.S. Department of Health and Human Services. He advises organizations on a variety of issues, including HIV/AIDS, hypertension, mental health, time management, and stress. He is also a Technical Advisory Board Member of the District of Columbia Community Health Assessment Initiative (DC CHAI) for the Latino Health Care Collaborative (LHCC). He frequently reviews manuscripts for various journals (e.g., *Journal of the National Medical Association, American Journal of Epidemiology*) and proposals for various organizations (e.g., Centers for Medicare and Medicaid Services, National Institute of Drug Abuse). As President of the consulting firm StressHealth Institute International, he conducts stress management seminars and workshops in the United States, as well as overseas. His main research interests include the social epidemiology of cardiovascular and immunological diseases in African Americans and people of color in the Caribbean and other parts of the developing world. Dr. Livingston is the author of *The ABCs of Stress Management*, coauthor of *Understanding Stress Using Pointed Illustrations*, and the editor of the first edition of the *Handbook of Black American Health: The Mosaic of Conditions, Issues, Policies and Prospects*. Based on his research on stress, he has appeared on various radio and television programs. His recent publications on topics that deal with Alcohol Consumption, HIV/AIDS, Hypertension, Cardiac Reactivity, End-stage Renal Disease, Stress Management, Health Education and Promotion, and Violence have been published in a variety of scholarly journals. Some of these journals include *Ethnicity and Disease, Health Promotion International, Health and Social Policy, Humboldt Journal of Social Relations, Journal of Black Studies, Journal of the National Medical Association, National Journal of Sociology, Pediatric AIDS and HIV Infection, Social Science and Medicine, The Urban League Review, Humanity and Society, The Western Journal of Black*

Studies, International Third World Studies and Review, The West Indian Medical Journal, and *Stress and Medicine*.

YAW ACKAH, Ph.D., is a Professor in the Department of Sociology/Criminal Justice at Delaware State University. He received an M.A. in Urban Studies and Criminal Justice; and a Ph.D. in Social Control and Deviance/Medical Sociology, both from Howard University. He is currently the Coordinator of the Criminal Justice Program in the Sociology Department at Delaware State University.

LAWRENCE Y.C. AGODOA, M.D., F.A.C.P., was appointed Director of the Clinical Affairs Program in the Division of Kidney, Urologic, and Hematologic Diseases at the National Institute of Diabetes, Digestive and Kidney Diseases of the National Institutes of Health (NIH) in 1987. Presently, he is Adjunct Professor of Medicine at the Uniformed Services University of the Health Sciences, F. Edward Hebert School of Medicine, and Program Director at the National Institutes of Health. His current duties include Director, Office of Minority Health Research Coordination at the National Institute of Diabetes and Digestive and Kidney Diseases (NIDDK), NIH, Program Scientist and Coordinator of the African American Study of Kidney Disease and Hypertension (AASK) Cohort Study, Director of the End-Stage Renal Disease Program, and Co-Project Officer of the U.S. Renal Data System (USRDS) at the NIDDK.

COLLINS O. AIRHIHENBUWA, Ph.D., M.P.H,. is a Professor in the Department of Biobehavioral Health, Pennsylvania State University. He is internationally known for his research on culture and health behavior. He is the author of a cultural model (PEN-3) for health behavior with a focus on people of African descent.

CHINUA AKUKWE, M.D., M.P.H., is an Adjunct Professor of Preventive and Community Health and an Adjunct Professor of Global Health at the George Washington University (GWU) School of Public Health and Health Services in Washington, D.C. He is a member of the GWU Medical Center Committee on Faculty Support and Professional Development; a member of the American College of Epidemiology; and a Fellow of the Royal Society of Medicine, London; and he is on the Editorial Board of the *American Journal of Public Health*. Dr. Akukwe's major areas of interest are maternal and child health services, minority health issues, and the HIV/AIDS epidemic in Africa.

SHAFFDEEN A. AMUWO, Ph.D., M.P.H., is an Associate Dean, Community, Government and Alumni Affairs, and an Assistant Professor, Community Health Sciences, University of Illinois at Chicago, School of Public Health. His areas of expertise involve the training of minorities in health professions; development and evaluation of K–20 pipelines for potential biomedical and public health research scientists; elimination of health disparities; public health aspects of family violence (victimization of dependents, child abuse/neglect); international health/immigrant health; cultural competence; and community participatory research.

ROSS E. ANDERSEN, Ph.D., is an Associate Professor of Medicine at the Johns Hopkins University School of Medicine, Division of Gerontology and Geriatric Medicine, and Associate Director for Fellowship Training. He is a Fellow of the American College of Sports Medicine and author of multiple peer review articles on physical activity and obesity.

JAMES C. ANTHONY, Ph.D., is Professor at the Johns Hopkins University (JHU), Bloomberg School of Public Health in the Departments of Mental Health and Epidemiology and at the JHU School of Medicine in the Department of Psychiatry & Behavioral Sciences. In addition, he is Director of the NIDA Drug Dependence Epidemiology Training Program in the Department of

Mental Health. His research interests are in the area of psychiatric epidemiology in general and drug dependence epidemiology in particular.

TONYA D. ARMSTRONG, Ph.D., is a Licensed Psychologist at the Alase Center for Enrichment in Durham, North Carolina. Dr. Armstrong is also a candidate for the master's degree in Theological Studies at Duke Divinity School. Her current research interests lie at the intersection of psychology and spirituality, particularly the psychospiritual development of children and adolescents. Furthermore, Dr. Armstrong is interested in identifying and implementing practical means by which church communities can offer long-term, preventive, and holistic care.

ERIC J. BAILEY, Ph.D., M.P.H., is currently a Medical Anthropologist and a Health Scientist Administrator in the National Center on Minority Health and Health Disparities at the National Institutes of Health. He was also an Associate Professor at Indiana University, Indianapolis, and an Assistant Professor of Anthropology at the University of Houston. Dr. Bailey recently published *African American Alternative Medicine: Using Alternative Medicine to Prevent and Control Chronic Diseases* (Praeger, 2002). His book examines African American alternative medical therapies from a clinical and cultural relativistic perspective. Dr. Bailey has broad-based research experience in several chronic diseases including hypertension, diabetes, prenatal care, cancer, alternative medicine, and HIV/AIDS and has published research findings and lectured for the past 20 years on issues related to medical anthropology

KI MOON BANG, Ph.D., M.P.H., is a Senior Epidemiologist at the National Institute for Occupational Safety and Health, Centers for Disease Control and Prevention in Morgantown, West Virginia. He is an Adjunct Professor in the Department of Community Medicine, West Virginia University School of Medicine. He is also an affiliated member of the Resource Persons Network, Office of Minority Health Resource Center, U.S. Department of Health and Human Services. He has published numerous articles and books on the issues of respiratory health and cancer. His research interests include asthma, chronic obstructive pulmonary diseases, tuberculosis, cancer, and pneumoconiosis.

DEBORAH BLOCKER, D.Sc., M.P.H., R.D., is an Assistant Professor in Nutrition and Food Science in the Urban Public Health Program at Hunter College, CUNY. From 2002 to 2004, she was awarded a postdoctoral fellowship in Cancer Prevention and Control at the Lineberger Comprehensive Cancer Center, University of North Carolina at Chapel Hill. Dr. Blocker earned an undergraduate degree in nutritional science from Cornell University, a master's degree in public health from the University of California at Berkeley, and a master's degree in maternal and child health and aging and doctoral degree in nutrition from Harvard School of Public Health. Her research interests are cancer prevention, minority diet, and health. She has conducted several research projects focusing on minority health and nutritional status.

A. WADE BOYKIN, Ph.D., is a Professor and Director of the Developmental Psychology Graduate Program in the Department of Psychology at Howard University. Since 1994, he has served as Codirector of CRESPAR, the Center for Research on the Education of Students Placed at Risk, a U.S. Department of Education-funded national research and development center jointly operating out of Howard University and Johns Hopkins University.

CHRISTINE M. BRANCHE, Ph.D., is the Director, Division of Unintentional Injury Prevention, National Center for Injury Prevention and Control at the Centers for Disease Control and Prevention (CDC) in Atlanta, Georgia. She has done extensive work in the area of injury prevention in drowning, water recreation, sports and recreation, falls among the elderly, and fire-related injury prevention. She has authored several scientific publications, many of which uncover new problems in injury control. Once at the CDC, Dr. Branche has received numerous awards for her work.

ROBERT M. BROWN III, Ph.D., is a Senior Policy Analyst in the District of Columbia's Department of Health. Dr. Brown is a medical sociologist and focuses on issues in health, illness, and the promotion of health protective behaviors, with a particular interest in the challenges and realities faced by underserved and disadvantaged groups. He speaks on topics that include effective coping in the face of adversity; family and community violence; reinvesting in, and strengthening, families; and embracing health protective behaviors as a way of life. Dr. Brown has bee a featured guest on the *Audrey Chapman Radio Show* (96.3 WHUR, Howard University): *Living in Uncertain Times—April 5th, 2003* and on the NAACP Radio Report with Neil Duke (88.9 WEAA, Morgan State University): *The Health Implications of Social Challenges.*

SAMUEL L. BROWN, Ph.D., M.B.A., is currently an Assistant Professor in the School of Public Administration at the University of Nebraska at Omaha. He teaches graduate courses in both the Public Administration and Public Health programs, including courses in Nonprofit Management, Nonprofit Financial Management, Health Care Finance, and Health Administration/Management. He has published in the *Health Care Finance Review*, *Psychiatric Services*, and the *Journal of Health Care for the Poor and Under-served* and has an article that will appear in and the *Journal of Health and Human Services*. Dr. Brown has an active research agenda that combines health services research with topics in the nonprofit sector. His health services research interests span the spectrum of cost, quality, and access issues for underserved populations.

CLIVE O. CALLENDER, M.D., is the LaSalle D. Leffall Jr. Professor of Surgery at Howard University College of Medicine. In 1973, he helped develop the first minority-directed dialysis and transplant center and histocompatibility and immunogenetic laboratory in this country. His work in minority organ/tissue donation education has been chronicled in the *New England Journal of Medicine*. In 1991, he conceptualized the National Minority Organ Tissue Transplant Education Program (MOTTEP), the first national program of its kind targeting African Americans, Hispanics, Asians, Pacific Islanders, American Indians, and Alaska Natives. National MOTTEP's community-based efforts have reached more than six million persons around the world. As the senior African American transplant surgeon, Dr. Callender has authored more than 100 scientific publications.

J. JACQUES CARTER, M.D., M.P.H., currently serves as a full-time attending physician at the Beth Israel Deaconess Medical Center in Boston and is an Assistant Professor of Medicine, at Harvard Medical School. Since completing his training, Dr. Carter has held a number of clinical and administrative positions, including medical directorships of several local and national health care organizations. A former director of one of the major clinical clerkships, he now serves as a teacher, adviser, and mentor for Harvard medical students. His biography has been included in *Who's Who in Medicine and Healthcare* and *Who's Who in America.*

EARLE C. CHAMBERS, M.P.H., is a doctoral student at the University of Pittsburgh, Graduate School of Public Health in the Department of Epidemiology. He received his master's of public health in 1999 from the University of Illinois at Chicago, School of Public Health. During his graduate work he has collaborated on projects designed to address issues of health disparities in diabetes risk. He is currently the principal investigator on a study that examines the effect of psychosocial stress on hyperinsulinemia, insulin resistance, and the metabolic syndrome in low- and normal-birth-weight African Caribbean adolescents.

HOWARD D. CHILCOAT, Sc.D., is Associate Professor at the Johns Hopkins Bloomberg School of Public Health in the Department of Public Health. Dr. Chilcoat is a psychiatric epidemiologist and biostatistician who has focused on the epidemiology of drug use and related disorders. Specifically, he is interested in understanding factors that influence the transition between stages of drug use. His research has extended to other psychiatric disorders, including posttraumatic stress disorder, as well as youth violence.

MITCHELL L. COHEN, M.D., is Director, Division of Bacterial and Mycotic Diseases, National Center for Infectious Diseases, CDC. He received his undergraduate and medical degrees from Duke University. His postgraduate training was in internal medicine at the University of Texas Southwestern Medical School, and his Infectious Disease Fellowship was completed at the University of Washington in Seattle. Since 1976, he has held positions in the Enteric Diseases Branch; Hospital Infections Program; and Office of the Director in the Division of Bacterial and Mycotic Diseases. His research interests include the epidemiology of antimicrobial resistance, food-borne diseases, and the application of molecular biology techniques to answer epidemiologic questions. He has been editor and reviewer for a number of scientific journals. He is a Fellow in the American College of Physicians, the Infectious Diseases Society of America, and the American Academy of Microbiology. Dr. Cohen has been a member of several advisory committees, including the Recombinant DNA Advisory Committee, National Institutes of Health, and the National Advisory Committee on Microbiological Criteria for Foods.

JAMES W. COLLINS JR., M.D., M.P.H., is the Medical Director, Neonatal Intensive Care Unit and an Associate Director of Pediatric Residency at the Children's Memorial Hospital in Chicago. Dr. Collins is also an Associate Professor of Pediatrics at Northwestern University, Chicago. Dr. Collins' research interest focused in perinatal epidemiology. "Differing Intergenerational Birth Weights among the Descendants of U.S.-born and Foreign-born Whites and African-Americans in Illinois" was recently published in the *American Journal of Epidemiology* (2002). He is a member of the Secretary Advisory Committee on Infant Mortality. Recently, he was awarded a Jonas Salk leadership award in research from the March of Dimes.

LLEWELLYN J. CORNELIUS, Ph.D., is currently an Associate Professor at the University of Maryland, School of Social Work. He received his doctorate from the University of Chicago, School of Social Services Administration, and has extensive research experience in examining access to medical delivery and the outcome of care for African Americans and Latinos. He is experienced in using SAS, SPSS, STATA and SUDAAN to analyze complex survey data. His recent accomplishments include being the recipient of the University of Chicago's 1996 Elizabeth Butler young alumni award for his contributions to health-care research on African Americans and Latinos and being inducted into the Honor Society of Phi Kappa Phi.

CARLOS J. CRESPO, Ph.D., is an Associate Professor in the Department of Social and Preventive Medicine of the University at Buffalo, State University of New York. Previous work experience includes working for the Centers for Disease Control and Prevention and in the Office of Prevention, Education and Control of the National Heart, Lung, and Blood Institute at NIH. His main area of research involves the epidemiology of physical activity in the prevention of chronic diseases and research on minority health issues. He has an extensive record of publications in the areas of exercise, minority health, obesity, and nutrition. He is also a contributing author to more than ten government publications, including the *Surgeon General's Report on Physical Activity and Health* and the *Sixth Report of the Committee on Detection, Evaluation and Treatment of Hypertension*. He is a past President of the Mid-Atlantic Chapter of the American College of Sports Medicine and currently serves on the Board of Directors of the American Council for Exercise.

ALEXANDER E. CROSBY, M.D., M.P.H., currently works as a medical epidemiologist in the Division of Violence Prevention in the National Center for Injury Prevention and Control of the Centers for Disease Control and Prevention in Atlanta, Georgia. His work involves descriptive and analytic research and community technical assistance in prevention of self-directed violence, interpersonal violence among adolescents, firearm-related injuries, and assaultive violence among minorities. He completed two residencies, the first in family practice and the second in general preventive medicine and public health. Dr. Crosby received his B.A. in chemistry from Fisk University in Nashville, his M.D. from Howard University College of Medicine in Washington, D.C., and his M.P.H. in Health Policy and Management from Emory University School of Public Health in Atlanta, Georgia.

MARTHA R. CROWTHER, Ph.D., M.P.H., is an Assistant Professor, Department of Psychology, the University of Alabama and Faculty Scholar, Center for Mental Health and Aging, the University of Alabama. Dr. Crowther's interests are focused on clinical geropsychology. Her primary research interest examines the nature, impact, and consequences of custodial grandparenting as well as designing effective interventions to reduce stress in this population. Additionally, she has explored the relation between spirituality and mental health across the life span and cultural diversity in research and clinical training.

ALOYSIUS B. CUYJET, M.D., M.P.H., F.A.C.C., is an Assistant Professor of Medicine and Director of Critical Care Medicine, University of Medicine and Dentistry–New Jersey Medical School. He was previously Chief of Medicine, United Healthcare System in Newark, New Jersey, until that facility closed. Research interests include hypertensive heart disease and health-care delivery in urban environments.

ANN M. DELLINGER, Ph.D., M.P.H., is an epidemiologist and Team Leader, Motor Vehicle Injury Prevention Team, Division of Unintentional Injury Prevention, National Center for Injury Prevention and Control, Centers for Disease Control and Prevention. Dr. Dellinger received her B.S. from the University of San Diego, her M.P.H. from San Diego State University, and her Ph.D. in epidemiology from the University of California at Los Angeles. Her topics of interest include older adult transportation, child passenger safety, unintentional injury, epidemiologic methods, and behavior and public health. Her recent publications are in the areas of fatal crashes among older drivers and driving cessation among older drivers.

GEORGIA M. DUNSTON, Ph.D., is Professor and Chair of Microbiology, Howard University College of Medicine, and Founding Director of the newly formed National Human Genome Center (NHGC) at Howard University. She earned a Ph.D. in Human Genetics from the University of Michigan Ann Arbor and conducted postdoctoral work in Tumor Immunology at the National Cancer Institute, NIH. Dr. Dunston's research focuses on the biomedical significance of population-based DNA sequence variation. Her research on human genome variation in disease susceptibility has been the vanguard of current efforts at Howard University to build national and international research collaborations focusing on the genetics of diseases common in African Americans and other Africa diaspora populations. Dr. Dunston is program director of the coordinating center for the Africa America Diabetes Mellitus Study, an international collaboration to map genes for Type II diabetes in ancestral populations of African Americans, and the coordinating center for the African American Hereditary Prostate Cancer Study Network, a national cooperative formed to map and characterize genes for prostate cancer in African Americans. The NHGC is instrumental in bringing multicultural perspectives and resources to an understanding of knowledge gained from the Human Genome Project and research on human genome variation. Dr. Dunston has served on the National Advisory

Council for the National Institute of Environmental Health Sciences; the Genetic Basis of Disease Review Committee, National Institute of General Medical Sciences, NIH; and the National Research Council Committee on Human Genome Diversity. She is recognized extensively for her accomplishments as a scientist, scholar, and role model.

CAPTAIN MARK S. EBERHARDT, Ph.D., is a Commissioned Officer in the U.S. Public Health Service; holds the rank of Director, Research Scientist; and is assigned to the National Center for Health Statistics, Centers for Disease Control and Prevention in Hyattsville, Maryland. Captain Eberhardt published CDC's first national chartbook on urbanization and health, entitled *Urban and Rural Health Chartbook, Health, United States 2001*. Other research interests include the epidemiology of diabetes and chronic diseases. He was a corecipient of the 2001 Modan Memorial Award from the American Diabetes Association and has held adjunct appointments with Emory University and the Medical University of South Carolina.

ANGELA T. ECHIVERRI, B.S., is a Research Associate in the Center for Natural Medicine and Prevention and the Research Center on Ethnicity, Health, and Behavior at the Charles R. Drew University of Medicine and Science. She earned her B.S. with a double major in psychobiology and Latin American studies from the University of California, Los Angeles. Her interests are in ethnic disparities in access to quality health-care resources and services.

RICHARD A. ENGLISH, Ph.D., is Professor and Dean of the School of Social Work at Howard University. He and Dr. F. Ross-Sheriff developed the Displaced Populations Program for M.S.W. students at the School of Social Work. The program emphasis includes the homeless, refugees, immigrants, and disaster victims. He has conducted research on homeless families, human service organizations, and African American families.

RICHARD JARVIS ENOCHS, Dr. P.H., M.P.H., M.S.W. (in memoriam—January 25, 2003), was an Associate Professor and Director of Health Care Administration and Planning, a joint program of Tennessee State University and Meharry Medical College. He also served as Interim Director (1996–1998) of the master's of science in public health program at Meharry Medical College. He was a former Executive Director of the Delta Health Center in Mound Bayou, Mississippi. He served in the Commissioned Corps of the U.S. Public Health Service.

ROBERT G. FABIAN, Ph.D., is a Research Associate, School of Public Health, University of Illinois at Chicago. His areas of research interests are in environmental and health economics. He has done consulting work for such agencies as USEPA and the Illinois Institute for Environmental Quality. He is a coauthor on environmental and health-economics articles in a variety of journals. He is also coauthor of books for Ballinger and Blackstone Books and the University of Chicago Press.

CAROLYN FORD, Pharm. D., is Chairperson of the Department of Pharmacy Practice at Hampton University School of Pharmacy. Most recently, she became the Coprincipal Investigator of Hampton University's Project for Health Disparities Reduction, which is funded by the National Center on Minority Health and Health Disparities. Dr. Ford has served as the Downlink Coordinator for the Healthy People 2000 Progress Review for Black Americans videoconference. The National Pharmaceutical Association invited her to present "Health Disparities: Implications for the Pharmacists" at their annual meeting in 2000. She is also a member of several community-based organizations that focus on eliminating health disparities. She is actively involved with the Minority Health Coalition of South Hampton Roads and the Minority Health Research Consortium of Hampton Roads.

IVIS T. FORRESTER-ANDERSON, Ph.D., R.D., is Professor and the Director of the Didactic Program in Dietetics at Morgan State University in Baltimore. She is involved in research that has focused on interventions to narrow health disparities associated with the minority population. Over the past five years she has been involved in research addressing prostate cancer and other diet-related chronic diseases such as cardiovascular diseases, hypertension, and diabetes. She is a member of various professional organizations including the American Dietetic Association, International Board of Lactation Consultants, American Association of Family and Consumer Sciences, and the Institute of Food Technologists. Dr. Forrester-Anderson has been an active member of the National HBCU Health Care Services Research Network and has served as the Secretary/Treasurer.

SHEILA A. FOSTER, J.D., is a Professor of Law at Fordham University. She is the author of numerous publications on environmental justice in top law journals, including the *California Law Review*, *Harvard Environmental Law Review*, and the *Ecology Law Quarterly*. In addition, Professor Foster has provided legal support and assistance to a number of grassroots environmental justice groups in New York, New Jersey, and Pennsylvania. She is also on the Environmental Law Committee of the New York Bar Association.

GARY H. FRIDAY, M.D., M.P.H., is Associate Professor of Clinical Neurology at the Thomas Jefferson University and Medical Director, Main Line Health Stroke Program. His research interest is in stroke.

YVONNE W. FRY, M.D., is Chief of the Maternal and Child Health Team, National Center for Primary Care, and Assistant Professor of Clinical Pediatrics, Department of Pediatrics, Morehouse School of Medicine. She also serves as Director of Clinical Services for the Georgia Association for Primary Care.

KRISTI R. FULTZ-BUTTS, M.P.H., has had professional training conducting analysis on Youth Risk Behavior Surveillance data, as well as coauthoring the 2001 *Revised Group B Streptococcal Disease Prevention Guidelines* and now as an epidemiologist conducting analysis on Behavioral Risk Factor Surveillance System data, all of which was done at the Centers for Disease Control and Prevention in Atlanta, Georgia. Her research interests include epidemiology of diabetes and cancer and the effects of food consumption on chronic diseases.

SARA M. GARCIA, B.S., is currently working on a M.S. in applied geography at the University of North Texas in Denton while an intern in Geographic Information Systems at the city of Garland in Texas. Her research interest focuses on applying Geographic Information Systems to disease problems. Her master's thesis is on HIV-AIDS in Texas.

BRIAN K. GIBBS, Ph.D., M.P.A., OTR/L, is an Instructor in Public Health Practice and Director of the Program to Eliminate Health Disparities in the Division of Public Health Practice, Harvard School of Public Health. Since 1990, he has participated in research and evaluation activities in minority health, health disparities, and adolescent violence prevention. He is the project director for Cherishing Our Hearts and Souls, a coalition established to educate communities, providers, and policymakers about the intersections of racism and health. Dr. Gibbs is a former Program Chair and Associate Professor of Occupational Therapy within the School of Allied Health Sciences, Florida Agricultural & Mechanical University. He has 17 years of clinical practice and management experience in the field of occupational therapy.

JULIE GILCHRIST, M.D., is a pediatrician and medical epidemiologist in the National Center for Injury Prevention and Control, Centers for Disease Control and Prevention. She graduated from Rice

University with degrees in human physiology and sports medicine before attending the U.T. Southwestern Medical School at Dallas (Texas). She completed a pediatrics residency at the University of Pennsylvania's Children's Hospital of Philadelphia and an epidemiology fellowship at CDC. In her current work, she is responsible for research and programs in drowning prevention and water safety promotion, and sports and recreation-related injury prevention. She facilitated the development of CDC's research agenda for prevention of injuries in sports, recreation, and exercise and has been recognized for her efforts to establish a sports injury prevention program at CDC.

RICHARD F. GILLUM, M.D., is a medical officer with an area of expertise in cardiovascular epidemiology at the National Center for Health Statistics. He has been recognized for his various scholarly contributions, especially in the area of the epidemiology of cardiovascular diseases.

JOAN L. GLUCH, R.D.H., Ph.D., is Director of Community Health and Adjunct Associate Professor in the Department of Community Oral Health at the University of Pennsylvania School of Dental Medicine. She provides the management and leadership for the academic service learning courses in community health and focuses her research activities on health promotion demonstration projects in the community. Dr. Gluch is the principal investigator for the School of Dental Medicine's Minority Oral Health Outreach Initiative Program, PennSmiles, that combines education, screening, and referral programs with mobile dental care with schoolchildren in West Philadelphia. She also is the project director of the Health Outreach Program with HIV/AIDS clients in collaboration with the Oral Medicine Department's Center for Medically Complex Patients.

SHERILYN GORDON, M.D., who is a Clinical Instructor and Transplantation Fellow at the Dumont-UCLA Transplant Center in Los Angeles, graduated magna cum laude from Howard University with a degree in microbiology. She subsequently received her medical degree at Washington University in St. Louis, Missouri, then returned to Howard University for surgical training. Her interest in transplantation was sparked by the active transplant program there and prompted her to conduct three years of transplantation research at the University of Pittsburgh during her residency.

TERESA GRANT, L.P.C., L.C.A.D.C., is currently a doctoral student at Howard University in the Counseling Psychology Department and is licensed in substance abuse and counseling in the state of Maryland and the District of Columbia. She has six years of experience working with dual-diagnosed clients in urban populations. Her current research interests are in the forensics-mental health-substance-abuse population.

B. LEE GREEN, Ph.D., M.Ed., is Associate Professor, Texas A&M University, College of Education, Department of Health and Kinesiology with research interests in cancer prevention and control, community health, and health disparities.

MARGRUETTA B. HALL, Ph.D., M.Sc., is the Senior Principal of MBH Limited: Evaluation Research Services.

FREDERICK D. HARPER, Ph.D., is Professor of Counseling at Howard University. He is former editor of the *Journal of Multicultural Counseling and Development* and the *International Journal for the Advancement of Counseling.* Dr. Harper has presented 110 conference papers and authored or edited more than 100 publications, including 12 books and monographs and numerous publications on alcohol and other drugs. His most recent book is *Culture and Counseling: New Approaches* (2003).

LA MAR HASBROUCK, M.D., M.P.H., F.A.C.P., is a medical officer with the National Injury Center, Atlanta, Georgia. In addition, he is an Assistant Professor of Clinical Medicine at Emory University. He was the lead CDC scientist for the development and release of the U.S. Surgeon General's Report on Youth Violence (2001). He has provided international public health service in Harare, Zimbabwe, Kingston, Jamaica, Bangladesh, and Brazil. He holds a B.A. degree, in ethnic studies and an M.P.H. in behavioral sciences from the University of California-Berkeley. He holds an M.D. degree from the joint medical program of the Charles R. Drew University of Medicine and Science and UCLA School of Medicine. He joined the CDC in 1998 as a member of the select corps of "Disease Detectives," the Epidemic Intelligence Service.

AKIMA R. HOWARD, Pharm.D., is the Director of Drug Information and an Assistant Professor in the Department of Pharmacy Practice at Hampton University School of Pharmacy. She received her bachelor of science degree and doctor of pharmacy degree from Florida Agricultural and Mechanical University in 1995 and 1997, respectively. In 1998, she completed a pharmacy practice residency with Florida A&M University's Miami campus. She completed an ASHP-accredited specialized residency in Drug Information Practice at the Medical University of South Carolina in Charleston, South Carolina, in 1999. She is licensed by exam in South Carolina and Virginia and is a member of several national pharmaceutical associations. Dr. Howard also has over seven years of experience as a pharmacist. Dr. Howard's teaching responsibilities include, but are not limited to, developing the didactic and experiential drug information component of the pharmacy curriculum. In her role as a drug information specialist, she teaches students the skills of drug information retrieval, literature evaluation, and effective medical information communication.

ALTAF HUSAIN, M.S.W., is a doctoral candidate at the Howard University School of Social Work. His area of specializing is displaced populations with an emphasis on Muslim immigrant and refugee families. His dissertation focuses on the resettlement and adaptation of Somali refugee adolescents to the United States. He holds an M.S.W. from Case Western Reserve University's Mandel School of Social Sciences. His diverse experience includes lecturing at the International Islamic University in Malaysia and working with Vietnamese refugees in a UNHCR camp in Kuala Lumpur, Malaysia, and serving on a site visit team to monitor their repatriation back to Vietnam.

KEVIN HYLTON, Ph.D., is a Research Scientist in the Center for Community Prevention and Treatment Research at the MayaTech Corporation. In this role he manages and directs evaluations of HIV/AIDS program. He currently coordinates the evaluation activities of the Centers for Disease Control and Prevention's (CDC) Minority AIDS Initiative Programs. Prior to joining MayaTech, he served as a Research Scientist for a CDC's HIV/AIDS Prevention Research Synthesis Project. Dr. Hylton has a Ph.D. in medical sociology from Howard University. He is an American Sociological Association Minority Fellow and a Fogarty Minority International Research Fellow.

ROBERT J. JAGERS, Ph.D., is the Associate Director for Research at Howard University Center for Research on the Education of Students Placed at Risk (CRESPAR). He is also Principal Investigator on the Contextual Enhancements to Promote Children's Developmental Competencies Project, funded by the Office of Educational Research and Improvement of the U.S. Department of Education. This project reflects Dr. Jagers' interest in basic and applied research supporting the development, implementation, and evaluation of culturally appropriate wellness promotion programs for inner-city African American children and adolescents. Dr. Jagers received his Ph.D. in developmental psychology from Howard University in Washington, D.C. He worked as a research associate at the

University of Chicago prior to joining the faculty at the University of Illinois at Chicago, where he was an associate professor of African American studies and psychology.

EDGAR JACKSON KENTON III, M.D., is Professor of clinical neurology at Thomas Jefferson University. Since 1972 he has developed the Division of Neurology at the Lankenau Hospital in Wynnewood, Pennsylvania, and currently serves as Chief of Cerebrovascular Diseases of the Main Line Health Systems Hospitals. He is current President of the American Board of Psychiatry and Neurology and President of the Pennsylvania/Delaware Affiliate of the American Heart Association. He is the immediate past Chairman of the Medical Advisory Committee of the American Stroke Association, a Division of the American Heart Association, and past President of the American Heart Association of Southeastern Pennsylvania. He has served on the National Board of the American Heart Association and the Association of Black Cardiologists and presently serves on the board and chairs the Practice Committee of the American Academy of Neurology. He publishes and presents extensively at regional, national, and international meetings on stroke and access to health care for minorities.

STERLING KING JR., Dr. P.H., M.P.H., is an Associate Professor of Management at the Howard University School of Business. For more than a decade during his earlier tenure at Howard, Dr. King served as Department Chair and Director of the Graduate Program in Health Services Administration. His research interests include the health workforce and ethical considerations in health services delivery.

SHAFFIRAN LIVINGSTON, B.S.N., R.N., C.M.T., is vice president of the StressHealth Institute International, which is a stress management consulting organization conducting stress management seminars in the United States and overseas. She is also a critical care registered nurse, as well as a nationally certified massage therapist. She is the coauthor of *Understanding Stress Using Pointed Illustrations*.

RON C. MANUEL, Ph.D., is an Associate Professor of Sociology in the Department of Sociology and Anthropology at Howard University in Washington, D.C. His research interests include the study of the interplay of social structural arrangements with indicators of the social psychology of health behaviors and outcomes—particularly in aging and minority populations.

HAROLD MARGOLIS, M.D., has held positions in the Arctic Investigations Program; Hepatitis Branch, Division of Viral and Rickettsial Diseases; Office of the Director, Division of Viral Hepatitis; and Office of the Director, Centers for Disease Control and Prevention. His research interests include the epidemiology of infections with hepatitis viruses, control of vaccine preventable diseases, evaluation of community-based disease prevention, vaccine development and evaluation, and development of molecular epidemiologic methods. He is a Fellow in the American Academy of Pediatrics and the Infectious Diseases Society of America.

DAVID MARTINS, M.D., is an Assistant Professor of medicine and Associate Director of the Clinical Research Center at the Charles R. Drew University of Medicine and Science. He is a board-certified internist and an American Society of Hypertension certified specialist in clinical hypertension. He is the recipient of an NIH young investigator award to the genetics of hypertension in African Americans. He is a coinvestigator at Drew University for the NIH-funded African American Study of Kidney Disease and Hypertension and the principal investigator of a community-based health center site of the NIH-funded Antihypertensive and Lipid Lowering Treatment to Prevent Heart Attack (ALLHAT) Trial.

TROYE MCCARTHY, M.A., is a doctoral student of political science at Howard University. Her areas of concentration in political science are public administration/public policy and American government. She received her master's degree in public administration from George Mason University, and a B.A. in sociology from Hampton University. Her primary research interest is in the analysis of welfare reform policies and the outcomes of welfare reform legislation on program participants. In addition to this area of research, she focuses on minority health and health-care policy analysis.

MARIAN MCDONALD, Dr.P.H., M.P.H., M.A., is Associate Director for Minority and Women's Health for the National Center for Infectious Diseases, CDC. She received her Dr.P.H. and M.P.H from U.C. Berkeley's School of Public Health. Before coming to CDC, she was a Professor at Tulane's School of Public Health & Tropical Medicine. Dr. McDonald has worked in minority health and women's health for three decades. She founded a number of Latino health programs in New Orleans and worked as consultant to the National Center for Farmworker Health. She is nationally known in the field of cultural competence in public health and the recruitment and retention of a bilingual health workforce. Awards include a Harmony Award finalist for promoting multicultural unity and Delta Omega, the National Public Health Honor Society.

HUGH M. MCLEAN, Ph.D., joined the faculty of the School of Pharmacy at Hampton University in January 1999. He became Chairman of the Department of Pharmaceutical Sciences in 2001. He currently teaches Medicinal Chemistry I and II, in addition to serving as the Program Director for the Minority Biomedical Research Support (MBRS) Grant and the Minority Institutions Drug Abuse Research Program (MIDARP) Grant at Hampton University. His research interests include drug development, particularly novel anti-inflammatory steroids, substance abuse, and stress-related diseases. Dr. McLean has approximately ten years of teaching experience at the college level. In addition, he has worked in the chemical/pharmaceutical industry for a total of approximately nine years in a variety of positions.

JOHN I. MCNEIL, M.D., is an Assistant Professor at Howard University, where he serves as the Chief of the Division of Infectious Diseases. His interest has been in HIV/AIDS capacity building and training to health-care organizations and providers. He serves as the Principal Investigator of the National Minority AIDS Education and Training Center and a Co-Principal Investigator of the Pennsylvania Mid-Atlantic AIDS Education and Training Center.

PATRICE V. MILES is the Director of Corporate and Community Relations for the National Minority Organ Tissue Transplant Education Program (MOTTEP). She has ten years' experience in the area of community health education, which includes community-based outreach, program administration, and marketing and promotion. Ms. Miles' accomplishments include assisting in National MOTTEP's expansion efforts from 3 cities to 16 cities nationally, creating successful health promotion campaigns, and assisting more than 35 cities in the development and strategic planning of health promotion and disease prevention programs. Between 1993 and 1995, she produced and cohosted *A Focus on Health*, a two-hour weekly radio talk show in Washington, D.C. She is the author or coauthor of more than 15 publications relating to organ and tissue donation and transplantation.

KIMBERLY N. MONTGOMERY, M.Ed., is a second-year doctoral student, counseling psychology, Howard University. Her research interests include psychological counseling of Black collegiate and professional athletes (career, academic, socioemotional), and child and family counseling (family violence). She specializes in sports counseling and child and family counseling and is treasurer of the Association of Black Psychologists, D.C. Chapter, August 2002–present.

HECTOR F. MYERS, Ph.D., is Professor of Psychology at UCLA and Director of the Research Center on Ethnicity, Health & Behavior and the Center for Natural Medicine and Prevention at the Charles R. Drew University of Science & Medicine. He has published more than 100 articles, book chapters and abstracts, has received consistent NIH funding for his research, and has received distinguished teaching and mentoring awards from UCLA and from major scientific and professional societies for his mentoring of minority students. Dr. Myers has been actively involved in research on psychosocial and biobehavioral factors that contribute to racial/ethnic disparities in health.

MARGUERITE E. NEITA, Ph.D., M.T. (ASCAP), is an Associate Professor in the Department of Clinical Laboratory Science, the College of Pharmacy, Nursing and Allied Health Sciences, at Howard University. As a laboratory scientist, she has had extensive experience in London, England, and in Jamaica, W.I. She currently teaches Clinical Immunology to undergraduate students at Howard University. Her interests include the cause and prevention of diseases among minority populations in the United States and the developing countries of the world.

KEITH NORRIS, M.D., is the Associate Dean for Research and the Director of the Clinical Research Center at the Charles R. Drew University of Medicine and Science. He is a member of the National Kidney Foundation Kidney Disease Outcomes Quality Initiative national advisory board. He is a board-certified nephrologist and an American Society of Hypertension-certified specialist in clinical hypertension. He is the editor in chief of the journal *Ethnicity and Disease* and has over 100 scholarly publications and over 90 research abstracts. He is active in community education around broad issues impacting minority health and is the principal investigator at Drew University for the NIH-funded African American Study of Kidney Disease and Hypertension.

BRANDI N. ODOM, B.S., is a Research Associate in the Center for Natural Medicine and Prevention and the Research Center on Ethnicity, Health, and Behavior at the Charles Drew University of Medicine and Science. She earned her B.S. with a major in psychobiology from the University of California, Los Angeles. Her interests are in disparities in access to quality dental and other health care among African Americans.

TITILAYO OLADOSU, M.S., is a doctoral student, Department of Biobehavioral Health, Pennsylvania State University. She works as an HIV/AIDS peer educator/counselor with the Office of Health Education and Promotion, Pennsylvania State University. Her area of interest includes the design, planning, implementation, and evaluation of culturally appropriate community-based health promotion strategies to address nutrition therapy for HIV/AIDS patients among Africans and African Americans.

LATEEF A. OLOPOENIA, M.D., is an Adjunct Professor of Medicine in the Physician Assistant Program, Howard University. He is an infectious disease specialist by training, with research interests in cardiovascular and infectious diseases. Currently, he is the President of the Global Council on Water Related Diseases.

SARAH J. OLSON, M.S., CHES, is the Assistant to the Director for Partnership and Education, Division of Unintentional Injury Prevention, National Center for Injury Prevention and Control, Centers for Disease Control and Prevention. She received an M.S. degree in biology from Tulane University and is a certified health education specialist. She was the State Director, Public Health Promotion Division, Texas Department of Health, before serving as the Director of Health Education and Disease Management for a large HMO. Ms. Olson joined CDC to lead the Home and Recreation

Injury Prevention Team, directing unintentional injury research and programs. She has worked extensively in unintentional injury, especially fires and older adult fall prevention.

JOSEPH R. OPPONG, Ph.D., is an Associate Professor of Geography at the University of North Texas, Denton. He holds a B.A. in geography from the University of Ghana and M.A. and Ph.D. from the University of Alberta, Edmonton, Canada. His research centers on medical geography, particularly the application of spatial analysis and GIS techniques to health issues. He has published extensively on AIDS in Africa and health-care delivery. His latest book titled *HIV-AIDS in Africa: Beyond Epidemiology* is in press. Dr. Oppong was the Chair of the Africa Specialty Group of the Association of American Geographers from 1999 to 2002. He is currently the Permanent Member and U.S. Representative to the International Geographical Union (IGU) Commission on Health and the Environment (CHE).

JANE A. OTADO, Ph.D., is currently the Research Subject Advocate (RSA) for the General Clinical Research Center (GCRC), College of Medicine at Howard University in Washington, D.C. Previously, she worked as a Research Associate within the Department of Medicine, Howard University Hospital, Washington, D.C. Her major areas of interest are maternal, infant and child health, minority aging and health, HIV/AIDS, social determinants of health, disparities in health, and utilization of health-care services. Her current research interests include perceived barriers to care among children with chronic health conditions; stress and adverse pregnancy outcomes; social support and prenatal care utilization; and migration patterns among southern Black mothers and birth outcomes. Dr. Otado is a member of National Center for Children in Poverty and a member of the Association of Teachers of Preventive Medicine.

JOAN C. PAYNE, Ph.D., is Professor of Communication Disorders and a nationally and internationally recognized scholar on adult neurogenic language disorders. A member of the Academy of Aphasia, she has presented her research in Africa, South America, South Africa, the Caribbean, and throughout the United States. She is the author of the evaluation instrument for older adults, the Communication Profile: A Functional Assessment, and the text *Adult Neurogenic Language Disorders: Assessment and Treatment: A Comprehensive Ethnobiological Approach*. Currently, she is Principal Investigator for the project "The Relationship between Proinflammatory Cytokines and Neurobehavioral Outcomes in Stroke Patients," an interdisciplinary project funded through the Howard University Mordecai Wyatt Johnson Award Program. Dr. Payne is also Principal Investigator for the project "Functional Neuroimaging Studies of Speech Motor Control and Language Processing," a collaborative research contract between Howard University and the National Institutes of Health's National Institute on Deafness and Other Communication Disorders. Her ongoing research is part of the Howard University Center for the Study of Stroke in African Americans.

ROBERT W. PINNER, M.D., is Director, Office of Surveillance, National Center for Infectious Diseases, CDC. He is Clinical Assistant Professor, Division of Infectious Diseases, Department of Medicine, Emory University School of Medicine, Atlanta, Georgia. He has board certification in internal medicine and infectious diseases. His numerous awards include the Secretary's Awards for Distinguished Service, 1998, DHHS. He provides leadership and consultation for many national and international activities, informatics, and surveillance. He has served as temporary adviser to the World Health Organization on meningitis, encephalitis, and epidemiologic surveillance initiatives. He is coeditor of emerging infections section in the *Annals of Emergency Medicine* and in the *Infection Control and Hospital Epidemiology*. He is a member of the American Society for Microbiology;

Council of State and Territorial Epidemiologists; and the Infectious Diseases Society of America. His scientific interests are public health surveillance, especially for infectious diseases; trends in infectious diseases mortality; and the epidemiology of several bacterial and fungal diseases. He is author or coauthor of 45 publications.

DEBORAH PROTHROW-STITH, M.D., is Associate Dean for Faculty Development, Professor of Public Health Practice, and Director of the Division of Public Health Practice at the Harvard School of Public Health. Her current areas of research include the recent increase in violent behavior by girls and reducing racial and ethnic disparities in health. She developed and wrote the first violence prevention curriculum for schools and communities, entitled *Violence Curriculum for Adolescents*, and cowrote *Deadly Consequences*, the first book to present the public health perspective on violence to a mass audience. Dr. Prothrow-Stith is also the Principal Investigator for the Harvard Center for Public Health Preparedness, established under a CDC grant to prepare the public health workforce of Massachusetts and Maine to respond to incidents of bioterrorism.

MAURICE F. RABB, M.D., is an internationally known retinal specialist and serves as Professor of Ophthalmology at the University of Illinois, and he is Chairman of the Department of Ophthalmology at Mercy Hospital. He graduated from the University of Louisville School of Medicine, and his postgraduate medical training includes an ophthalmology residency at the University of Illinois. He has received several major awards, including an honorary doctor of science degree from the University of Louisville. He has held numerous federal government appointments, serving on the Ophthalmic Advisory Committee of the FDA, and the National Advisory Council of the National Eye Institute. He is a past President of the Chicago Ophthalmological Society and served as Interim Vice Chancellor at the University of Illinois from 1984 to 1987. As a retinal specialist, Dr. Rabb spearheaded the use of fluorescein angiography in the treatment of retinal eye disease. He has coauthored and edited five medical textbooks and over 60 scientific articles and has lectured throughout the United States and internationally.

MARIA CRISTINA RANGEL, M.D., Ph.D., is an Epidemiologist at the Epidemiology and Surveillance Division of the National Immunization Program at the Centers for Disease Control and Prevention (CDC). Dr. Rangel's research interest is the epidemiology of adult vaccine-preventable diseases, particularly the determinants of racial/ethnic disparities in influenza vaccination.

LE ROY E. REESE, Ph.D., is Team Leader for the Effectiveness and Evaluation Research Team in the Division of Violence Prevention at the Centers for Disease Control and Prevention. He joined the CDC after spending several years as a Professor of Psychology and Black Studies at Chicago State University, where he codirected a prevention research team conducting school and community-based prevention research in Chicago. Dr. Reese completed his training specializing in child and family psychology with research foci that address the prevention of health-compromising behavior among children and their families residing in underresourced communities and the promotion of wellness and broad-based social and behavioral competences. Specifically, he is interested in the role of culture in promoting the physical and psychological health and adjustment of ethnic minority communities in the United States.

REBECCA REVIERE, Ph.D., is an Associate Professor in the Department of Sociology and Anthropology and director of the Graduate Certificate Program of Women's Studies at Howard University in Washington, D.C. She teaches courses in Social Psychology, Medical Sociology, Death and Dying, and the Sociology of Mental Health. Her research interests include health care for women in prison, gender and race differences around mortality issues, and end-of-life caregiving.

FARIYAL ROSS-SHERIFF, Ph.D., is a Graduate Professor and the Director of the Ph.D. Degree Program in Social Work at Howard University. Her area of specialization is in displaced populations. These populations include two major groups: (1) international refugees, immigrants, and undocumented migrants, and (2) within the United States her focus is on the homeless and disaster victims. Within displaced populations Dr. Ross-Sheriff's work emphasizes women, children, and the elderly. With Dr. R.A. English, she has developed the M.S.W. specialization in Social Work with Displaced Populations. She has taught in this specialization area for 15 years.

DIANE L. ROWLEY, M.D., M.P.H., is Director of the Research Center on Health Disparities, Public Health Sciences Institute, Morehouse College. The center focuses on studies of social and cultural influences on racial and ethnic health disparities.

KAKOLI ROY, Ph.D., is an Economist at the Epidemiology Program Office, Centers for Disease Control and Prevention (CDC). Her current research in public health include explaining trends in infectious disease epidemiology with particular focus on assessing the impact of socioeconomic factors on disease burden, economic analyses of treatment strategies at a time of increasing antibiotic resistance, and economics of quarantine to control a smallpox outbreak. Dr. Roy received her Ph.D. in economics from the University of Cincinnati. Before joining CDC in 2000, she held a faculty position at the University of Bonn, Germany. Her research also includes work on the economics of volunteering, impact of minimum wage increases on employment distribution, and political economy of immigration policy and social protection.

CHARMAINE D.M. ROYAL, Ph.D., is Assistant Professor in the Department of Pediatrics (Division of Medical Genetics) and Principal Investigator in the GenEthics Unit of the National Human Genome Center, Howard University College of Medicine. Her areas of interest include research on the ethical, legal, and social implications (ELSI) of human genetics/genome research for African Americans and other people of color; establishment of genetics education programs for both the professional and public sectors of these communities; and development of domestic and international polices related to human genetics/genome research and genetic services.

YOLANDA ANN SLAUGHTER, D.D.S., M.P.H., is Assistant Professor and Course Director for Geriatric Dentistry at the University of Pennsylvania School of Dental Medicine. She completed a fellowship in geriatric medicine at the University of Connecticut Travelers Center on Aging and earned her M.P.H. degree in epidemiology at the University of Michigan. She is the first dentist to receive a Brookdale National Fellowship for aging research. Dr. Slaughter's research explores the oral health beliefs and oral health behaviors among African American elders with the goal of developing community-based, ethnically relevant health promotion programs.

DAVID A. SLEET, Ph.D., F.A.A.H.B., is the Associate Director for Science, Division of Unintentional Injury Prevention, National Center for Injury Prevention and Control, Centers for Disease Prevention and Control. He taught and helped establish the Graduate School of Public Health at San Diego State University. He authored a statewide injury control plan in Perth, Australia, and conducted the first study in Finland on the potential safety benefits of airbags. Dr. Sleet has contributed more than 150 articles, book chapters, and reports on injury prevention, health promotion, and preventive medicine. He is on the adjunct faculty at Curtin University (Australia) and on the teaching faculty in the School of Public Health at Emory University, Atlanta, Georgia.

JACQUELINE MARIE SMITH, Ph.D., is an Associate Professor at Howard University. She has served on technical panels for national studies on foster care and African American Catholics, as a policy analyst for the Office of the Assistant Secretary of Policy, Planning and Evaluation at HHS, and a visiting scholar at Chapin Hall at the University of Chicago. Her recent publications include "Foster Care Children with Disabilities" in the *Journal of Health and Social Policy* and "The Demography of African American Families at the End of the 20th Century," which will appear in *Child Welfare Revisited: An Africentric Perspective.*

OSCAR E. STREETER JR., M.D., is an Associate Professor of Clinical Radiation Oncology at the Keck School of Medicine at the University of Southern California, where he has been a faculty member since 1990. He has served several administrative duties in the past, as Chief of Service for Radiation Oncology at the Los Angeles County—USC Medical Center, and until 2000, Chief of Service for Radiation Oncology at the USC/Norris Comprehensive Cancer Center. He also is a certified acupuncturist, in a joint practice with Dr. Paulette Saddler, his wife in Pasadena, California, as well as at USC/Norris.

CAROLYN A. STROMAN, Ph.D., is an Associate Professor in the Howard University Department of Communication and Culture, where she teaches health communication courses. Her research interests center around the cognitive and psychological effects of exposure to health information. Her recent research has examined African American college students' processing of HIV and drug prevention messages, and the role of culturally relevant health communications in health promotion in African Americans.

JOSEPH TELFAIR, Dr. P.H., M.S.W.-M.P.H., is an Associate Professor of Maternal and Child Health, School of Public Health, University of Alabama at Birmingham and School of Social Work, University of Alabama. His expertise and areas of publication include community-based and culturally competent research and evaluation, health practice issues of women, teens and children with chronic conditions (and their families), issues of access to, and utilization of, health care for the poor, people of color/persons in rural areas, and systems-level program consultation and evaluation. Based on his expertise and scholarly work, Dr. Telfair serves on the NIH/NHLBI SCD Advisory Committee, SCD Association of America's Medical and Research Advisory Committee, and the DHHS Office of Minority Health Project Advisory Committee on Cultural Competency Curricular Modules.

REYNOLD LEWIS TROWERS, M.D., F.A.C.E.P., is an Assistant Clinical Professor of Medicine, College of Physicians and Surgeons, Columbia University and the Director, Department of Emergency Medicine at Harlem Hospital Center. He is the Paramedic Medical Director at the Harlem EMS station and Emergency Preparedness Coordinator for Harlem Hospital. He holds faculty positions at Columbia University and the City University of New York, Sophie Davis Medical Schools. Research interests include asthma, domestic violence, cancer screening in the emergency setting, and health information systems.

EUGENE S. TULL, Dr. P.H., M.T., is an Assistant Professor of Epidemiology at the University of Pittsburgh, Graduate School of Public Health. He has served as Principal Investigator of several large epidemiological studies that have assessed risk factors for the development of Type I and Type II diabetes in Caribbean populations. He is currently the Principal Investigator and Director of the

University of Pittsburgh Minority International Research Training (MIRT) Program, which provides research training in epidemiological methods for African American and other minority students. Dr. Tull has directed several recent research projects through the MIRT Program that have provided important data linking psychosocial factors such as spirituality and internalized racism to diabetes and other metabolic abnormalities in Black populations.

JAY K. VARMA, M.D., joined CDC as an Epidemic Intelligence Service officer in 2001. His research interests include laboratory-based public health surveillance and the epidemiology of antimicrobial resistance. In addition to scientific manuscripts, he has authored or coauthored several essays and one book.

DONALD R. WARE, M.D., M.P.H., is the Physician and Grand Medical Director of the Conference of Grand Masters and Grand Chapters of Prince Hall Masons. These primarily African American organizations have approximately 500,000 current dues-paying members. He is a cardiologist in private practice. He served as the Medical Officer of the National High Blood Pressure Education Program of the National Institutes of Health from 1976 to 1980. Dr. Ware was responsible for the first White House Conference on High Blood Pressure in Black Americans and later was one of the first Macy Senior Fellows in Health Policy at Harvard University's Schools of Medicine, Public Health and the John F. Kennedy School of Government.

JACQUELINE A. WATSON, D.O., M.B.A., is a family practice physician by training and has an M.B.A. with a concentration in health management and policy. She is the Founder, President, and CEO of Health Concepts International, (HCI), a health-care management and consulting firm located in Washington, D.C., that specializes in providing health promotion and disease prevention strategies and solutions, particularly for racial/ethnic, women and underserved populations. Dr. Watson is the Chair of the Health and Wellness Committee (HWC) of the District of Columbia Chamber of Commerce and is a past Chair of the Public Health and Welfare Committee for the District of Columbia Commission on African and Caribbean Affairs.

J. DeWITT WEBSTER, M.P.H., is a doctoral candidate in the Department of Biobehavioral Health at Pennsylvania State University. His research interests include sociocultural factors affecting health outcomes, such as HIV/AIDS, in the United States and other countries. His professional experience includes training of public health professionals in a variety of domestic and international settings and teaching university-level health promotion courses.

CYNTHIA G. WHITNEY, M.D., M.P.H., has worked at CDC since 1993, taking part in the Epidemic Intelligence Service and Preventive Medicine Residency training programs and serving as a Staff Epidemiologist in the Respiratory Diseases Branch since 1997. Her postgraduate medical training was in internal medicine at the University of Minnesota and in preventive medicine through the Centers for Disease Control and Prevention (CDC). She directs the Pneumococcal Epidemiology Program for the Respiratory Diseases Branch and is Clinical Assistant Professor of Medicine at the Emory University School of Medicine, where her clinical duties include care of patients with HIV and AIDS. Her primary research interests include the epidemiology of pneumococcal disease, drug resistance, and prevention using vaccines. Other interests include the epidemiology of streptococcal diseases and perinatal infections.

DAVID R. WILLIAMS, Ph.D., M.P.H., is Harold W. Cruse Collegiate Professor of Sociology, Senior Research Scientist at the Institute of Social Research, and Faculty Associate in the Center for Afro-

American and African Studies at the University of Michigan. His research has focused on social influences on health, and he is currently interested in the trends and determinants of socioeconomic and racial differences in mental and physical health. He is the author of more than one hundred scholarly papers in scientific journals and edited collections, and his research has appeared in leading journals in sociology, psychology, medicine, public health and epidemiology. He is a member of the editorial board of 5 scientific journals and has served as a reviewer for more than 40 others. In 1995, he received an Investigator Award in Health Policy Research from the Robert Wood Johnson Foundation, and in 2001, he was elected as a member of the Institute of Medicine of the National Academy of Sciences. Currently, he is a member of the Board of Directors for the Academy for Health Services Research and Policy, the Robert Wood Johnson Foundation's National Advisory Committee on Changes in Health Care Financing, and was a member of the Institute of Medicine Committee on Understanding and Eliminating Racial and Ethnic Disparities in Health Care and also serves on its Panel on Race, Ethnicity and Health in Later Life.

KIM M. WILLIAMS, M.S.W., Ph.D., is an Association of Teachers of Preventive Medicine fellow in STD/HIV prevention at the Rollins School of Public Health at Emory University. Her research interests include the examination of contextual and cultural factors influencing risk for HIV/STDs, barriers to HIV/STD health services and developing tailored multilevel interventions for racial and ethnic minority communities.

LEIGH A. WILLIS, M.A., is a Ph.D./M.P.H. candidate in medical sociology and the Department of Health Behavior in the School of Public Health at the University of Alabama, Birmingham. His African American health interests are mental health, sexual risk, and violence prevention. He recently published an article entitled, "Ready to Die: A Postmodern Explanation of the Increase of African-American Adolescent Male Suicide" in *Social Science and Medicine*. He currently serves on the Alabama Suicide Prevention Task Force.

COLWICK M. WILSON, Ph.D., is an Associate Professor in the Department of Counseling and Family Sciences at Loma Linda University. His areas of research include racial differences in mental health status, religion and health, and immigration status and health.

VERNETTA D. YOUNG, Ph.D., is currently an Associate Professor of Administration of Justice in the Department of Sociology and Anthropology at Howard University. Her research has focused on race, gender, and crime. She has published articles on the role that race and gender have played on the history of juvenile institutions, the patterns of criminal behavior (including drug use), and the incarceration and victimization of women. Her research interests also extend to the inclusion of works by African Americans in the field of criminology/criminal justice.